Environmental Governance in Europe

Environmental Governance in Europe

An Ever Closer Ecological Union?

ALBERT WEALE,
GEOFFREY PRIDHAM,
MICHELLE CINI,
DIMITRIOS KONSTADAKOPULOS,
MARTIN PORTER,
and
BRENDAN FLYNN

OXFORD
UNIVERSITY PRESS

OXFORD
UNIVERSITY PRESS

Great Clarendon Street, Oxford OX2 6DP
Oxford University Press is a department of the University of Oxford.
It furthers the University's objective of excellence in research, scholarship,
and education by publishing worldwide in

Oxford New York

Athens Auckland Bangkok Bogotá Buenos Aires Calcutta
Cape Town Chennai Dares Salaam Delhi Florence Hong Kong Istanbul
Karachi Kuala Lumpur Madrid Melbourne Mexico City Mumbai
Nairobi Paris São Paulo Singapore Taipei Tokyo Toronto Warsaw

and associated companies in Berlin Ibadan

Oxford is a resistered trade mark of Oxford University Press
in the UK and certain other countries

Published in the United States
by Oxford University Press Inc, New York

British Library Cataloguing in Publication Data

Data available

Library of Congress Cataloging in Publication Data
Environmental governance in Europe : an ever closer ecological union? / Albert Weale . . .
[et al.].
p.   cm.
Includes bibliographical references and index.
1. Environmental policy—Europe.   2. Environmental protection—Europe.   I. Weale,
Albert.
GE190.E85 E55 2000   363.7′056′094—dc21   00–037485
ISBN 0–19–829708–4

1 3 5 7 9 10 8 6 4 2

Typeset by Graphicraft Limited, Hong Kong
Printed in Great Britain
on acid-free paper by
Biddles Ltd
Guildford, Surrey

Acknowledgements

This work reports research funded under the Single European Market Programme of the UK's Economic and Social Research Council (ESRC). The first director of the ESRC's research programme, David Mayes, was helpful in facilitating contacts with other research groups in Europe interested in environmental policy, especially through the COST A7 programme. We have drawn on the fruits of that collaboration here, and we are grateful to David Mayes for making it possible. To Iain Begg who took over as programme director we are especially grateful for the support and enthusiasm he showed towards our work, particularly the opportunities he offered for dissemination and publication.

Any study of different national systems of policy, which is in part what we attempt here, has to depend upon knowledgeable informants. We were fortunate in having a series of formal research partners who provided advice, comment and research materials, and we should like to offer our thanks to them. They include: Maarten Hajer in the Netherlands; Louis Lemkow in Spain; Armando Montanari in Italy; Susannah Verney in Greece; and Gerd Wagner in Germany.

A number of other scholars or policy-makers were regular sources of advice and information. They include: Mikael Skou Andersen, Carmen Casal, Michael Faure, Martin Jänicke, Dimitra Katohianou, Jürgen Lefebvre, Rudolf Lewanski, David Lewis, Duncan Liefferink, Timothy O'Riordan, Evangelos Raftopoulos, George Tsekouras, Hermann Vollenburgh, and Helmut Weidner.

We also wish to thank all those public officials, environmental activists, and decision-makers who gave up their time to be interviewed. They are too numerous to mention here and, for reasons of confidentiality, they cannot always be named in the text, but we are extremely grateful to them for all the insights they have provided.

This has been a large and complicated project. Although the ESRC was the primary source of funding, other support and assistance have also proved important. Albert Weale would like to thank the Department of Government at the University of Essex for general research support relevant to the project and Carol Ward in particular for work on party manifestos. He would also like to thank Andrea Williams for invaluable research assistance in the collection of data and the conduct of interviews.

The readers of the draft manuscript for Oxford University Press provided perceptive comments, as well as welcome encouragement. We owe a special debt to Andrew Jordan, who read and commented on the manuscript thoroughly and saved us from a number of errors. We hope all those who read the draft see an improvement in this version.

Finally, we thank Dominic Byatt and Amanda Watkins at Oxford University Press for their help and support throughout.

Contents

List of Figures   xi
List of Tables   xii
List of Boxes   xiii
List of Abbreviations   xiv
A Note on Terminology   xvi

Introduction   1

   The Institutionalization of Environmental Policy   2
   Principal Questions   6
   Plan of Work   10

I: Environmental Governance in the European Union   13

Introduction to Part I   15

   Theories of European Integration   15
   Plan of Part I   25

1 The Single Market and the Environment: From Issue Linkage to
   Political Choice   29

   The Single Market and Barriers to Trade   32
   Environmental Protection and Economic Competitiveness   34
   Market Failure and Single Market Success   37
   The Issue of Waste Management   38
   Political Choice and the Single Market   40
   Conclusions   48

2 Programmes, Principles, and Policies   53

   Policy Content: The Action Programmes   56
   Policy Content: General Principles   62
   The Justification of Policy: Ecological Modernization   75

3 Actors and Institutions in Environmental Governance   86

   The Main Institutional Actors   87
   Other Institutions   104
   Conclusions   107

4 Patterns of Environmental Governance in the European Union   113

   Setting the Agenda: Problems, Issues, and Science   114
   Policy Formulation and Standard-Setting   117
   Decision-Making and Inter-Institutional Relations   123
   Conclusion   130

II: Comparative Environmental Governance   135

Introduction to Part II   137

   Causes of Convergence and Divergence   139
   Comparing Theories of Convergence and Divergence   146

5 National Policies on the Environment: Evolution, Principles,
   and Style   150

   Cross-National Policy Evolution and Patterns   150
   Policy Principles and Policy Styles   155
   Conclusions: Convergence and Divergence in Cross-National Perspective 183

6 The Institutionalization of Environmental Policy   192

   Administrative Concentration and Environmental Policy: Towards Secular
   Convergence?   194
   Environmental Administration in the Six States   202
   Conclusions   227

7 Domestic Politics and Society-Related Variables   235

   Public Opinion   237
   Political Parties   246
   Environmental Organizations   256
   Economic Interests   268
   Conclusions: Domestic Politics and Environmental Issue Dynamics   281

8 National Systems and Multi-Level Governance: Convergence
   through Compliance?   295

   Implementation, Compliance, and EU Environmental Governance   296
   National Problems of Implementation   303
   Understanding Implementation in a System of Multi-Level Governance 322
   Conclusions   329

9 Convergent and Divergent Trends in European Environmental Policy 338

   Comparative Trends   342

III: Case Studies in the Policy Process 351

Introduction to Part III 353

10 Water Quality and European Environmental Governance 356

The Early Water Directives 356
The Urban Waste-Water Treatment Directive 360
Has There Been a Europeanization of National Water Policy? 363
Conclusions 375

11 Air Pollution Control and Multi-Level Governance 384

The Large Combustion Plant Directive 386
Directives on Car Exhaust Emissions 397
Conclusions 407

12 Packaging and Packaging Waste 410

The Packaging and Packaging Waste Directive 412
From National Diversity in Approaching the 'Packaging Waste'
Problem . . . 416
. . . to the Impact of the German Packaging Ordinance 419
The Waste Management Hierarchy and the Single Market 421
Institutional Discussions 424
EU Policy Style 426
Conclusions 427
Appendix 427

IV: Models of Environmental Governance 435

Introduction to Part IV 437

13 Understanding European Environmental Governance 441

The Origins of EU Environmental Governance 441
The Functioning of Environmental Governance: Multi-Level Features 446
The Functioning of Environmental Governance: Horizontal Complexity 453
An Incomplete System 457
Conclusions 462

14 North and South in the European Union: From Diffusion to
Learning? 468

Is There a North–South Dichotomy? 470
Push and Pull in International Diffusion 475
From Diffusion to Learning? 481

15   Competing Models of European Environmental Governance   488

     Pathologies of the Status Quo   490
     A Constitutional Convention on Environmental Governance   492

Bibliography   499
Name Index   521
Subject Index   523

Figures

7.1   Percentage of respondents who identified the 'environment' as
     the most important problem facing member states, 1974 and 1993   239
7.2   Trends in environmentalism in party manifestos: six countries   248–9
11.1 Total emissions of sulphur oxides in member states,
     1980–1990   389
11.2 Total emissions of nitrogen oxides in member states,
     1980–1990   390

Tables

1.1	Environmental rule-making competences, 1967–1997	41
2.1	Principles of EU environmental policy	63
3.1	Environment commissioners and their terms of office	87
3.2	Support for more stringent environmental standards in the Council of Ministers, 1980–1995	96
II.1	Summary of main models of convergence and divergence	146
6.1	Relation of environment functions to ministries	195
6.2	Administrative concentration in six countries, 1982–1992	196
8.1	Transposition of environmental directives into national law, by country and year	300
8.2	Article 169 (Warning) letters, 1988–1992	301
8.3	Reasoned opinions, 1988–1992	302
8.4	References to the ECJ and judgments, 1988–1992	303
11.1	Positions taken on the setting of emission and fuel oil limits	406
12.1	DG XI estimates of quantities of packaging waste, the quantity of recycled packaging waste, and the percentage recycled, 1990	417

Boxes

Box 2.1   Illustrative examples of EU environmental policy measures   54–5
Box 6.1   Division of responsibility between central and subnational
           authorities   201

List of Abbreviations

ALARA	As Low as Reasonably Achievable
ANPA	Italian National Agency for Environmental Protection
BATNEEC	Best Available Technique not Entailing Excessive Cost
BPEO	Best Practicable Environmental Option
BPM	Best Practicable Means
BTM	Best Technical Means
CAP	Common Agricultural Policy
CDU	Christian Democratic Union (Germany)
CEGB	Central Electricity Generating Board (UK)
CFCs	Chlorofluorocarbons
CFI	Court of First Instance
CIEMAT	Centre for Energy, Environment and Technology Research (Specialist Agency of Spanish Environment Ministry)
CIMA	Spanish Inter-Misterial Committee on the Environment
CITES	Convention on International Trade in Endangered Species
COREPER	Committee of Permanent Representatives
CSU	Christian Social Union
DG	Directorate-General
DG XI	Directorate-General for Environment, Consumer Protection and Nuclear Safety (during period of study)
DoE	Department of the Environment (UK)
DSD	Duales System Deutschland (German Waste Management Scheme)
ECJ	European Court of Justice
EEA	European Environment Agency
EEB	European Environment Bureau
EIA	Environmental Impact Assessment
EMEP	European Monitoring and Evaluation Programme (Air Pollution Monitoring Programme)
EP	European Parliament
ESC	Economic and Social Committee (of EU)
ECSC	European Coal and Steel Community
ETBA	Greek Bank for Industrial Development
HMIP	Her Majesty's Inspectorate of Pollution
IMP	Indicative Multi-Year Programme
IPC	Integrated Pollution Control
IPCC	Intergovernmental Panel on Climate Change

IPPC	Integrated Pollution Prevention and Control
LCA	Life Cycle Analysis
LIFE	L'Instrument Financier pour l'Environnement (EU Programme for Financing Environmental Improvements)
LTRAP	Long-Range Transboundary Air Pollution Convention
MEDSPA	EU Programme for Financing Environmental Improvements (now incorporated into LIFE)
MEP	Member European Parliament
MOPT	Spanish Ministry of Public Works
MOPTMA	Spanish Ministry of Public Works, Transport and the Environment
MOPU	Spanish Ministry of Public Works and Urban Affairs
NEPP	National Environmental Policy Plan
NGO	Non-Governmental Organization
NRA	National Rivers Authority
PASOK	Greek Socialist Party
PCB	Polychlorobiphenyl
PERPA	Athens Environmental Pollution Control Project
PSOE	Spanish Socialist Workers' Party
QMV	Qualified Majority Voting
RCEP	Royal Commission on Environmental Pollution (UK Government Advisory Body)
RIVM	Rijks Instituut voor Volksgezondheid en Milieuhygiene (Dutch Government Research Institute and Advisory Body)
RWE	Rheinisch Westfalische Elektrizitätswerke (German Electricity Supply Company)
SEA	Single European Act
SEM	Single European Market
SGMA	General Secretariat of Spanish Environment Ministry
SMEs	Small and Medium Sized Enterprises
SMN	Stichting Milieu en Natuur (Dutch Non-Governmental Organisation)
SPA	Special Protection Area (Designated under EU Bird Protection Directive)
TENs	Trans-European Networks (EU infrastructure projects)
TEU	Treaty on European Union
UBA	Umweltweltbundesamt (German Environment Agency)
UCD	Union of Democratic Centre (Spanish Political Party)
UNECE	United Nations Economic Commission for Europe
UNEP	United Nations Environment Programme
VROM	Departement van Volkshuisvesting, Ruimtelijke Ordening en Milieuhygiene (Dutch Environment Ministry)
YPEHODE	Greek Ministry of Environment and Public Works

A Note on Terminology

Anyone who writes on more than twenty years of policy development in the European Union is faced with a problem of terminology. The original trio of treaty institutions (the European Coal and Steel Community, EURATOM, and the European Economic Community) became known as the European Communities, and then as the European Community. The European Community, together with the intergovernmental arrangements in home, foreign, and defence policies, became known as the European Union. Should one, writing today, reflect these changes in terminology, using the name correct at the time of the policy to which one is referring, or should one choose one name to cover all periods?

After some discussion, we decided on the latter course, and have chosen to designate the European level of policy-making as the European Union throughout. This decision is liable to offend both legal and historical purists. Environmental policy is strictly part of Community institutions, and it does seem odd to write about the formulation of environmental policy in the European Union in 1972. However, the alternative often involves some circumlocution, and also risks giving a greater sense of institutional discontinuity than we feel is warranted by the story we have to tell. So 'European Union' throughout it is.

We have sought to treat member states of the European Union in the order in which they are treated in official publications: Germany, Spain, Greece, Italy, the Netherlands and the UK.

Introduction

In the years since 1972, the European Union (EU) has created a system of environmental governance. With a wide range of legislative measures, extending from pollution control in water and air through policies on solid waste management, the control of genetically modified organisms, and the protection of the wildlife and countryside, to requirements for environmental administration, management, reporting, and audit, the EU's environmental policy is broad in scope, extensive in detail, and often stringent in effect.

To say this is already to say much. However, the significance of environmental governance in the EU goes beyond matters of legislation, important though they may be. It extends to the ways in which decision-making on environmental policy has become institutionalized within Europe, both at the level of the EU itself and in the practices of its member states. A system of environmental governance implies more than simply the existence of internationally agreed environmental measures or policies: it also implies that there are institutionalized arrangements for formulating, developing, and implementing policy. Such institutionalization involves the existence of both policy principles and a set of rules, conventions, norms and practices within which organizational actors function.

To say that there is a system of European environmental governance is also to say that member states have ceded some of their sovereignty in a field of vital policy importance to their citizens, such that a new, if non-monopolistic, locus of political authority has emerged to govern the European environment. A system of environmental governance thus means not only that there is now an institutionalized system of rule-making at work, but also that the rules for making rules—the rules that distribute political authority—have also come into being. This is not to say that the newly emerging political authority has simply supplanted the authority of the nation state: it is to say, at the very least, that it has come to complement it.

In this work we seek to understand this new system of environmental governance. We argue that it is multi-level, horizontally complex, evolving, and incomplete. The bulk of the book is taken up with the development of this characterization. However, before embarking on an understanding of how the European system of environmental governance came to take the form that it did, we need first to identify, if only in outline, the basic features of the phenomenon we are seeking to explain.

So in the remainder of this chapter we set out the primary features of the policies, institutions, and rule-making authority that we are seeking to understand.

THE INSTITUTIONALIZATION OF
ENVIRONMENTAL POLICY

In his comprehensive compendium of EU environmental policy measures, Nigel Haigh lists approximately 580 pieces of environmentally related legislation passed in the EU between 1959 and 1997.[1] Many of these individual pieces of legislation are amendments or revisions to existing measures. However, at the end of the 1990s approximately three hundred measures are operative. Most of them take the form of directives which member states are required to implement. Their range is striking. They cover all major categories of environmental protection and pollution control. Thus, there are directives on air pollution that specify ambient air quality standards for a range of pollutants, provide for national emission limits for sulphur dioxide and nitrogen oxides, and specify the maximum emission limit values for vehicles, as well as providing for the exchange of information among member states on air quality. Water pollution directives specify standards for bathing and drinking waters, as well as discharge standards for all but the smallest community or local authority in the Union. The same water pollution directives identify substances that should not be discharged to water and regulate nitrate pollution from farming activity. Directives in the area of waste management detail recycling targets for each member state, establish controls for the shipment or disposal of hazardous wastes, and seek to encourage cleaner technologies and greater producer responsibility.

If we move from the standards for pollutants to processes for the setting of standards, we find that here too there are significant EU policies. There are directives on integrated pollution control, environmental impact assessments, environmental management and auditing systems for firms, public access to environmental information, and the reporting of data by governments. The EU is also an important actor in international environmental policy, coordinating the position of member states and having formal responsibilities for negotiation and agreement on international treaties. For example, it has played an important role in international negotiations on global warming policy, and has been seen by some observers as moving to the point where it is a leader in supporting stringent standards of control on greenhouse gas emissions.[2]

We can put the significance of some of these measures into perspective by considering in outline the historical development of EU environmental policy. Environmental protection found no place in the Treaty of Rome. Prior to 1972, the year of the first formal commitment by the EU to environmental policy, there were only limited policy measures concerned with environmental protection. These included safety standards for radiation, both for workers in industry and for the public at large; controls on the testing of new chemicals, touching on safety requirements for an industrial sector whose marketing was international; and restrictions on vehicle noise. There were also early measures to protect the countryside in less favoured areas.[3] Thus, the extensive growth in environmental measures took place over a period of less than thirty years. Moreover, the growth did not take place in a continuous, smooth fashion, but reflected modulations in the broader international politics of the environment, moving sometimes at a rapid pace and sometimes more slowly.

The upsurge of interest in environmental protection that hit the developed world in the late 1960s and early 1970s had its effects on EU policy. In particular, the United Nations Conference on the Human Environment in Stockholm in 1972 crystallized the growing concern among policy-makers with the problems of environmental protection.[4] Although most environmental policy initiatives in the late 1960s and early 1970s in the developed world could be seen as the nationalization of environmental policy,[5] the developments at the level of the European Union—including measures to control noise and exhaust emissions from vehicles in 1970, standards on solvents in paints in 1973, and standards for the quality of surface drinking waters in 1975—were harbingers of more significant policies to come at the European level.

The oil-price-induced recession of the mid-1970s slowed down the pace of environmental policy developments both in member states and in the EU, but momentum was regained during the 1980s, when new problems, including those associated with acidification, eutrophication, the depletion of the ozone layer, and global climate change, began to appear on the policy-making agenda.[6] Under the influence of certain member states, the European Union began developing measures to tackle these new problems. Germany, in particular, underwent a 'conversion' on environmental issues in 1982, most notably on the issue of acidification, on which it had previously taken a sceptical view. As a result, issues like the control of acidifying emissions, standards for nitrate pollution in water, plans for a carbon/energy tax, and controls over waste disposal, as well as measures to protect habitat and species, were the subject of much discussion, deliberation, and decision between 1983 and 1992.

The recession of the early 1990s slowed down political interest in environmental measures and the pace of policy developments, just as occurred after the recession of the early 1970s. But by the latter half of the 1990s the EU was implementing increasingly stringent controls on water and air pollution as well as seeking to play a leadership role in international forums concerned with climate change.

Behind the legislative developments, a complex set of institutional processes emerged. A council of environment ministers, composed of the environment ministers from the member states, meets at least twice a year, and since 1989 usually twice per presidency.[7] Informal councils, which are held as forums for general discussion, are also the norm. Cases brought on matters of environmental law have been subject to numerous rulings and judgments in the European Court of Justice (ECJ). The Environment Committee of the European Parliament (EP) is one of the most high-profile and powerful of the EP committees. The Commission's Directorate-General responsible for the majority of environmental legislation and policy is Directorate-General XI (DG XI) and it oversees a network of active committees. Moreover, interest groups, both environmental and industrial, have become adept at lobbying the European institutions on environmental issues and in some cases have been endowed with an insider status which suggests that they too are part and parcel of the now institutionalized system of European environmental governance. Environmental issues now regularly spill over into industrial policy, transport policy, regional policy, agricultural policy, and tax policy, and actors responsible for policy-making in these issue-areas increasingly have to take environmental considerations into account when drafting legislation. Indeed, it has been argued that, with the requirement in the Single European Act that environmental protection should be a component of other EU policies, environmental policy came to be accorded unique status so that it has come to constitute a front-ranking objective of the EU.[8]

One obvious and visible sign of the growing European importance of environmental policy is the growth of organizational resources, notably but not exclusively related to DG XI. In 1987, for example, the full-time permanent professional staff in DG XI numbered between 50 and 60; by the mid- to later 1990s their number had grown to between 450 and 500. This growth was accompanied by a move to new and improved offices. It is true that a significant portion of this growth occurred in temporary rather than permanent staff, and to this extent the interpretation has to be qualified. Still, the growth is striking. Administrative capacity in relation to European environmental protection has also been increased by the establishment of the European Environmental Agency. Although the long-running dispute about the location of various important institutions, including the European Monetary Institute, held up the establishment of the agency, it is now housed in Copenhagen and staff have been appointed and programmes developed. While its formal remit is concerned primarily with the collection and standardization of data, one could argue that it has the potential to be a powerful force for the Europeanization of environmental policy, not least given the concerns that are often expressed about poor implementation of international agreements being disguised by the practice of countries collecting the data on their own performances.[9]

EU environmental policy thus has been developed in substance and institutionalized in process, both in terms of the emergence and growth of the structures of environmental governance at EU level, and in terms of the rules and processes underpinning its operation. Moreover, the evolution of the policy has had an effect on the pattern of rule-making authority with the Union. To understand this point, it is useful to introduce the distinction between primary and secondary rules.[10]

Primary rules define the policies that are decided, whether these are rules about air pollution standards, water emission limit values, or the designation of sites of biological and ecological importance. *Secondary rules*, by contrast, are rules about rules; they define how the primary rules are made and how they may be changed, and they concern such matters as whether a measure is to be taken by qualified majority voting or unanimity in the Council of Ministers, whether a matter falls within the co-decision procedures for the European Parliament, or indeed whether a rule can be made at all.

Early policy developments were not based on formal secondary rules empowering environmental policies, because environmental responsibilities did not find a place within the Treaty of Rome. So the earliest developments took place under a convention, agreed by heads of state, that its significance for European citizens was important enough to warrant action at the European level. Subsequently, secondary rules evolved or were agreed as the significance of environmental matters increased, and most of the secondary rules were generally formulated during the process of treaty change. Such treaty changes have been crucial to the evolution of environment policy and to the emergence of the existing system of environmental governance in the EU.

In 1987 the Single European Act formally incorporated an environmental competence into the Treaty of Rome, allowing environmental measures to be adopted by unanimous agreement. It also allowed for qualified majority voting in the Council of Ministers on environmental matters related to the completion of the single market, in a procedure (the 'cooperation procedure') that empowered the European Parliament. The Treaty on European Union (the Maastricht Treaty) which came into effect in November 1993 extended qualified majority voting to most environmental matters and introduced the co-decision procedure, giving the Parliament even greater scope to influence policy outcomes. The Treaty of Amsterdam makes the co-decision procedure the norm, and introduced the idea of sustainable development as a principle of EU policy.

Taken together, we can see that, not only is legislative and policy development extensive in the field of European environmental policy, but this development has also been accompanied by the institutionalization of environmental protection in the decision-making processes of the EU. The years since 1972 have seen not only an expansion of primary rules in the field of environmental policy, but also a transformation of a whole series of secondary rules. It is only by examining the nature of the rules, and in particular the co-evolution of primary and secondary rules, that we may come to understand the defining characteristics of European environmental governance. In other words, we must not focus our attention solely on the specifics of environmental policy and environmental practice, but must also seek to explore the institutional context within which that policy has evolved and according to which the practice of European environmental policy-making occurs.

PRINCIPAL QUESTIONS

In seeking to examine this evolving system of environmental governance, the contours of which we have just sketched, we argue that it is multi-level, horizontally complex, evolving, and incomplete. What does this mean?

To say that there is a system of governance is to say that there is a set of rules, conventions, norms, and practices in the making of international environmental policy in Europe that goes beyond international diplomacy (treaty making) and cooperation (regime formation). Such international processes of decision-making are therefore institutionalized in a system of 'government without statehood'.[11] It is this notion of government without statehood that we seek to capture by the term 'governance'. Environmental governance is just such a form of government in the field of environmental policy.

When we say that the system of governance is multi-level, we mean that important decisions are made at different tiers of authority—the EU, the national, and the subnational—and that we cannot understand what happens at any one level without also understanding what happens at these other levels. Moreover, the assumption is that this interrelationship of different tiers of political authority is not a phase through which the European system has to pass on its way to some more centralized and coherent structure of decision-making. National state executives and supranational institutions, distinctive national systems of policy-making and international mechanisms for problem solving coexist and will continue to play an important role in environmental policy-making.[12]

The horizontal complexity of the governance structure is also important. There are many actors involved in the making of decisions at any one level, and, even if we confine ourselves to the European level, we need to take into account not only a wide range of actors but also the institutional balance of power and authority between them. The dynamics of decision-making between the Commission, the Council, and the Parliament is itself complex, and extends into a system of policy networks in which interest groups, non-governmental organizations, scientists, and the media are all involved.

Finally, the EU system of environmental governance is both evolving and incomplete. It is evolving in the sense that not only does policy develop, but it develops in ways that, surprisingly often, raise fundamental questions about the balance of authority within the EU. There are therefore regular disputes, not only about the rules for environmental policy but also about the secondary rules, the rules for making rules. Also, because it is evolving rapidly, the system is incomplete, with important choices to be made in the future about its scope and effectiveness.

The growth of European environmental policy in this institutionalized form presents a set of intellectual puzzles that demand resolution. These puzzles fall into three broad categories: those concerned with the origins of this system of governance, those concerned with its functioning, and those concerned with its political significance.

In *origin*, as we shall see, European environmental policy developed in close association with the single market, often serving to facilitate and enhance its evolution. Yet, paradoxically, environmental protection has always had a rather ambiguous relationship with the single market. To what extent, then, have single market measures created their own integrative dynamic? How did the single market process give rise to a series of problems the resolution of which might involve the modification and restriction of the single market itself? What were the factors that led to the establishment of a European-level environment policy? What were the processes at work, and how far can they be related to more general theories of European integration? In other words, our interest lies in the relationship between the single market and environmental policy and the conditions under which a system of environmental governance came to be established within the European Union. We are interested in why European environmental policy evolved in the way that it did and how this evolution has given a distinctive shape and character to the European system of environmental governance.

Issues arising from the origins of the system also relate to our second set of puzzles about the *functioning* of the system, and in particular the way in which policy-making is institutionalized. By 'institutionalization', we mean the operation of the set of rules, conventions, norms, and practices that define environmental governance. Institutions, in this sense, are more broadly defined than organizations, which are patterns of institutional relationships that have material embodiment— budgets, offices and personnel.[13]

How, then, does this system of governance operate? What inputs does it receive? What are its standard operating procedures? How is it structured? If there is now a genuinely European set of rules with their own logic and autonomy, which do not simply compete with national environmental policies but form a political jurisdiction of their own, what is the character of this pattern of governance and what is its underlying logic? How are rules enacted and developed within the institutions that have been produced? In particular, how far are there routine and well developed ways of dealing with environmental problems that rest upon the participation of a set of actors at the European level, and how do such processes relate to national-level decision-making?

Here we encounter an apparent paradox. Environmental protection is a valence issue, that is to say an issue on which key political actors typically, in public at least, take a favourable stance committing themselves to positive measures. Few people are willing to say openly that they oppose environmental protection. Yet measures for environmental protection are simultaneously a subject of political contestation among European policy elites. Often the contestation arises because national politicians are unhappy with EU environmental policy, wanting it either to do more or to do less. As Majone has pointed out, the paradoxical element in this is that the member states, which complain about European regulation, are strongly represented at every stage of decision-making and their approval is required for most Commission proposals before they become law.[14] By contrast with the transfer of authority from subnational units to the nation state, which took place with much environmental administration in the 1970s, the development of EU environmental policy is necessarily constrained by the political power of its constituent members in a way in which expansion at the nation state level was never constrained.

Yet this contrast, in turn, poses a series of questions about environmental policy in Europe. How far is the political contestation between member states and the EU over environmental policy rooted in the domestic political circumstances of the member states and the incentives such circumstances offer to key decision-makers? Is it possible to imagine common patterns of concern and policy development across European countries, and if not, to what extent do distinct and incompatible national policy styles and patterns still predominate? Is there a logic of environmental policy that is driving countries to adopt similar policy strategies, or is the best way to understand environmental policy developments in terms of the historic legacies of national policy systems? The answers to these questions have obvious implications for the system of European environmental governance, since convergence would in principle make it easier to superimpose a European tier of governance on top of national systems. Of course, lack of convergence would not of itself preclude European-level governance; indeed, it could be said that the old catch-phrase about 'unity in diversity' implied the continued persistence of different national policy strategies. But lack of convergence would certainly give rise to the need to find new forms of environmental governance not yet in evidence at the level of the nation state, and would reinforce the multi-level features of any such system of governance.

What then of the *political significance* of EU environmental governance, and in particular its significance for the process of European integration? As we have noted, the making of EU environmental policy often involves not just decisions about the rules to be implemented, but also decisions about the rules for the making of the rules. In logical terms, the distinction between primary and secondary rules is clear. In political terms, however, matters are more complex and the distinction rests less on logical niceties and more on the form of political interaction that each type of rule is associated with. Probably the easiest means of seeing the political significance of the distinction is to note that, when making primary rules, more is typically taken for granted by actors within an institutional process. Thus, when fixing limits for emissions of gases from stationary or mobile sources, policy-makers seldom have to confront basic questions about the role and purpose of the institution of which they are a part. The problem comes to them as a routine problem within an existing institutional arrangement, the secondary rules of which they accept as defining their roles. (Of course, to say that an issue is routine in this sense is not to say that it is uncontroversial or easy to resolve.) With decision-making about secondary rules, however, broader questions about the balance of political authority are raised. A decision to expand the scope of EU institutions in the field of environmental policy carries extensive implications. One has only to think of the possible use of tax instruments to achieve environmental objectives to see this point. Whatever their objective merits as instruments of environmental policy, the greater use of taxes decided at EU level to control pollution would inevitably pose important questions about the overall shape of EU authority *vis à vis* the member states. In this sense, secondary rule creation is far from routine.

In distinguishing in this way between the politics of primary rules and the politics of secondary rules, we do not mean to presuppose any particular view about the relationship between the two. One way in which a change in secondary rules may occur is through a conscious and deliberate political decision, as happened in the case of environmental policy through the Single European Act and the Maastricht Treaty. However, there may be a sense in which these decisive moments simply recognize what has already taken place by means of the cumulative effect of incremental adjustments in the processes of primary rule-making. If environmental policy grows and evolves within the European Union as a result of the steady accretion over time of primary rule-making, then this is one way in which the secondary rules are changed. Institutionalization may take place by accretion and evolution, as well as by choice at a single moment of institutional decision. Indeed, in many significant respects, this is what happened in the case of environmental policy.

Why, then, make the analytic distinction between primary and secondary rules when in fact there may be no easy demarcation point? The answer to this question goes right to the heart of the unique character of the EU as a set of political institutions involving government without statehood. Those institutions are built upon the Monnet method of integration, a form of 'integration by stealth'.[15] According to this method, it is unproductive to raise constitutional questions about the institutional balance of political authority within the EU before the ground has been well prepared by the existence of functioning policy-making procedures of a technical kind. In such an approach, the distinction between primary and secondary rules is collapsed. But, of course, in order to appreciate the significance of this as the efficient secret of the Monnet method, we need to understand that primary and secondary rule-making are not only distinguishable in principle, but are habitually kept distinct in most political systems. By contrast, in the case of the EU's system of environmental governance, they are brought together.

The Monnet method has shaped the process of rule creation in the past, but can it continue in this form in the future? There are those who raise questions about the extent to which the Monnet method of integration has run its course. Is it any longer acceptable to pursue integration by stealth, particularly in a field like environmental policy, which has important implications for the legitimacy of governments in relation to their citizens? Does environmental policy reveal the limits of the Monnet method? We can turn to these questions about the political significance of EU environmental policy only at the end of our work, after we have looked at the origins and functioning of the system with which we are concerned.

PLAN OF WORK

This book is divided into four parts. In Part I we are concerned to analyse the European level of environmental policy and policy-making. Here we consider questions about the origins of the EU's system of environmental governance and also look at its functioning, the way it works in practice. We argue that there is a spillover logic at work, through an issue dynamic that links the creation of the single market to the development of environmental policy. However, environmental governance in Europe has gone beyond this single market rationale, and involves important questions about the institutional balance of the EU and the structures, processes, and principles that characterize environmental policy-making. Environmental policy can also be linked to important questions to do with the rights and entitlements of citizens within the new Europe that the single market helped to create.

A central aspect of the EU's system of environmental governance is its multi-level character. We argue in Part I that, among other things, this means both that member states have a privileged place within the horizontally complex processes of decision-making at the European level, and that developments at the European level need to be understood against the background of the domestic politics of member states. Part II then turns to the comparative politics and policy of the environment in six countries in the EU: Germany, Spain, Greece, Italy, the Netherlands, and the UK.[16] We seek to show how the domestic politics of these six member states affect their policy stances and general policy positions on matters of environmental policy in the EU. We also look at the extent to which their policy-making has been modified under the impact of the EU's system of environmental governance. Although only a sample of countries, they do represent a broad cross-section, ranging from the poorest to the richest and from founder members to entrants in the 1980s. Developments across these systems therefore represent a particularly robust test of the extent to which there are convergent trends in environmental policy within the countries of the EU. Although European integration and a system of European environmental governance do not absolutely require such convergence in order to function successfully, the extent of divergence, and therefore the extent of differences in policy preferences, will clearly have implications for the way in which we should conceive European trends and possibilities in the future.

In order to illustrate the European system of environmental governance in detail, we turn in Part III to a series of case studies of specific policy sectors. These are meant to show how environmental problems are handled, or not handled, by the horizontally complex multi-level system that we have been concerned to analyse in Parts I and II. Only by seeing how issues are processed at both the level of the nation state and the European level can we see how the European system of complex multi-level governance works.

Finally, in Part IV we look at the political significance of EU environmental policy, and we aim to draw conclusions from the analysis that has gone before. Here we seek to evaluate how well the decision-making and standard-setting capacity of the European system of environmental governance is performing. We ask how far environmental policy has become Europeanized, and we also consider whether the often noted contrast between northern and southern European countries is supported by the empirical evidence. We conclude by posing the question of whether the processes that have led to the formation of the European system of environmental governance so far are likely to prove a reliable guide for future reform. Has the Monnet method really run its course, or will the logic of integration that it has established be of significance for the future?

It is important for our theme that trends and developments are looked at over time. Although we focus on policy-making during the 1980s and the first half of the 1990s, we often need to look at the earlier history of environmental policy developments. Certainly, in seeking to understand the role and position of the member states, we frequently need to identify their styles and approach in a longer historical context, since much that is of interest to the theme of multi-level governance concerns the extent to which EU environmental policy has put pressure on member state governments to modify and reform their national environmental policy legacy, even when that legacy is long-standing and part of their national style of regulation.

Conversely, our claim that the EU's system of environmental governance is incomplete and evolving poses a problem: where do we end our story? Since it is central to our analysis that the final chapters of environmental policy development have still to be written, this is not a trivial problem. Although our analysis takes the period of the late 1980s and the first half of the 1990s as its main point of reference, we sometimes need to consider more recent trends. In general, we do not discuss developments after 1997, except where later information helps us interpret more accurately what went before. The year 1997 not only marks negotiations on the Treaty of Amsterdam, but also is the period when the political dynamics in Europe changed as a new generation of political leaders, particularly in Germany and the UK, began to come to the fore. So this work should be read largely as an account of the politics of environmental policy in the period between 1972, the date of the Stockholm conference, and 1997, the date at which the governments agreed the Treaty of Amsterdam. These twenty-five years must have been pretty action-packed to have included such significant changes as have taken place.

NOTES TO INTRODUCTION

1. N. Haigh, *Manual of Environmental Policy* (London: Cartermill International, 1992 and updated), appendix 1.
2. A. M. Sbragia and C. Damro, 'The Changing Role of the European Union in International Environmental Politics: Institution Building and the Politics of Climate Change', *Environment and Planning* C, 17:1 (1999), pp. 53–68.

3. See the list in Haigh, *Manual*, App. 1, and L. Krämer, *EC Treaty and Environmental Law* (London: Sweet & Maxwell, 1995), p. 1.

4. A. Jordan, 'Editorial Introduction: The Construction of the Multilevel Environmental Governance System', *Environment and Planning* C, 17:1 (1999), p. 3; R. Wurzel, 'Environmental Policy' in J. Lodge (ed.), *The European Community and the Challenge of the Future* (London: Pinter, 1993, 2nd edn), p. 180. For more general trends in the early 1970s, see A. Weale, *The New Politics of Pollution* (Manchester and New York: Manchester University Press, 1992), ch. 1.

5. Weale, *New Politics of Pollution*, pp. 186–7.

6. 'Acidification' is the process by which the air, soil, and waters become more acidic, leading to ecological damage, usually as a result of enhanced atmospheric concentrations of sulphur dioxide, nitrogen oxides, and ammonia. 'Eutrophication' is the over-enrichment of waters by nutrients, often as a result of run-off from agriculture using fertilizers. The depletion of the ozone layer refers to the thinning of the layer of stratospheric ozone that protects the earth from ultraviolet radiation. 'Global climate change' is the general term related to changes in the earth's climate pattern, and in particular the projected tendency for average global temperatures to rise over the next 50 years, as a result of emissions into the atmosphere from the burning of fossil fuels.

7. R. K. W. Wurzel, 'The Role of the EU Presidency in the Environmental Field: Does it Make a Difference which Member State Runs the Presidency?' *Journal of European Public Policy* 3:2 (1996), p. 274.

8. See L. Krämer, *Focus on European Environmental Law* (London: Sweet and Maxwell, 1992), p. 10.

9. House of Lords Select Committee on the European Communities (Sub-Committee F), *Implementation and Enforcement of Environmental Legislation*, Session 1991–92, Ninth Report, i. 84 (London: HMSO, 1992).

10. H. L. A. Hart, *The Concept of Law* (Oxford: Clarendon Press, 1961), ch. 5.

11. W. Wallace, 'Government without Statehood', in H. Wallace and W. Wallace (eds.), *Policy-Making in the European Union* (Oxford: Oxford University Press, 1996), pp. 445–6.

12. Compare G. Marks *et al.*, *Governance in the European Union* (London: Sage, 1996), p. *vii*.

13. Compare the approach of O. R. Young, *International Cooperation: Building Regimes for Natural Resources and the Environment* (Ithaca, NY: Cornell University Press, 1989), p. 5.

14. G. Majone, *Regulating Europe* (London and New York: Routledge, 1996), p. 61.

15. For the use of the term 'integration by stealth', see J. Hayward, 'Has European Unification by Stealth a Future?' in J. Hayward (ed.), *Élitism, Populism, and European Politics* (Oxford: Clarendon Press, 1996), pp. 252–7.

16. We have tried throughout to refer to these countries and to discuss them in the order in which they appear in publications of the EU itself.

Part I

Environmental Governance in the European Union

Introduction to Part I

In the Introduction we claimed that the European Union had developed a multi-level and horizontally complex system of environmental governance that was none the less evolving and incomplete. We identified three aspects of this system: the first was the development of environmental policies; the second was the expansion of institutions for making policies; the third was the effect of these first two developments on the structure of political authority within the European Union, that is to say on the rules for making rules.

To say that there is a system of governance, however, is no more than to point to a political fact. If we are properly to understand this system, we need to identify its underlying logic and to locate its place within the more general processes of European integration. To what extent, for example, is it a manifestation of more widespread trends, and how does it relate to other processes at work in the development of the European Union? Although every policy sector has its own logic, it cannot be detached from the political processes in which it is embedded, and understanding the character and workings of those processes is relevant to understanding how a particular policy area develops.

Environmental policy in this sense brings us to the heart of debates about theories of European integration and governance. Such theories seek to identify the main characteristics of the process of integration and the principal features of the institutional forms that European governance can take. These theories are concerned with such questions as how best to interpret the quickening pace of European integration in the 1980s and the extent to which it fitted into a process of integration more generally, as well as the extent to which the growth of the European Union has undermined the traditional preserves and authority of the nation state. In this chapter we review some of the principal propositions in these competing theories as a way of setting the general framework for our studies.

THEORIES OF EUROPEAN INTEGRATION

Within the theoretical literature, two views taken from International Relations have been overridingly dominant: work in the tradition of functionalism, now standardly identified as neo-functionalism; and work in the tradition of realism, now standardly identified as neo-realism.[1] Both perspectives are best regarded as clusters of pro-positions, each stating a particular orientation to the understanding of European integration, though there are many people who might adhere to some but not to all of the respective claims. Here we set out the key elements of the characteristic arguments of each side, in somewhat schematic form.

One central proposition for neo-functionalists is that functions or issue areas provide the usual foci for the process of integration, at least as far as the EU is concerned.[2] The idea is that the solution to problems in one area is bound to affect developments in other areas through processes of issue linkage and spillover. In a context in which states are not the exclusive or even predominant actors in the international system, these processes of issue linkage and spillover can bind diverse actors together in institutional forms the full extent of which no one agent can envisage. Thus, the outcomes of international developments are not predictable in advance.

The origins of this way of thinking go back to Mitrany's early formulation of the functionalist position in the 1940s, though subsequent developments have departed from his views.[3] Mitrany wished to replace the territorially based authority of the state with a system of international functional authority based on expertise rather than power. Monnet took up this perspective, arguing that it was only through functional integration, most obviously in areas like the production of iron and steel, that any breach could be made in the authority of the nation states. Since these early formulations, however, it has become common in neo-functionalist literature to stress the extent to which there is no hard and fast distinction between technical matters and political decisions.[4] The spillover from one issue area to another that neo-functionalists posit is only part of a more general process in which technical spillover in policy sectors provokes spillover from the making of policy to the making of institutions. In order to deal with the problems that the logic of decision-making throws up, states find that they need to transfer their authority to international bodies, and in the case of the EU this is aided by the existence of powerful supranational actors anxious to expand their own authority and scope of decision-making. It follows that the European Commission and the Court of Justice act to a significant degree independently of the member states and may initiate, strengthen, or complement processes that make for an increased transfer of authority.

Typically this transfer is not intended. Indeed, neo-functionalists stress the extent to which states find themselves enmeshed in processes the significance of which they did not fully realize at the time at which they embarked upon them. Thus, important constitutional change may emerge not as the result of an explicit and conscious bargain entered into by state actors, but by virtue of the fact that national executives are caught up in 'a web of unintended consequences spun by their own previous commitments'.[5] Moreover, non-state actors may help push the process along, themselves shifting their own expectations, activities, and loyalties from the national to the international level.

In the 1980s the attraction of this approach, which had been in the theoretical doldrums for some time, increased with the creation of the single market and the subsequent move towards economic and monetary union.[6] In this instance there seemed to be an almost textbook example of spillover. The single market itself created new questions and problems, and its full working out seemed to call for greater collective control of the levers of economic policy at the European level.[7] Moreover, no one could deny that monetary policy was at the heart of the traditional functions of the state. If the single market led to monetary union, even if this had not been appreciated by leading actors at the time of the Single European Act, who could gainsay the role of the functional logic?

If for neo-functionalists the increasing pace of European integration in the 1980s reflected an underlying logic of cooperation implicit in world economic changes of the previous twenty years, for neo-realists it continued to represent an intergovernmentalist bargain among leaders of nation states about the best way to secure national interests. For neo-realists European integration depends upon a convergence of preferences among the key actors in the international system, namely the nation states. Such states form alliances for self-interested reasons determined out of rational calculation. Often the formation of these alliances is closely related to the prevention of war, but sometimes it may simply be a way of dealing with interdependencies that arise from the operation of international trade.

In accounting for the emergence and working of the EU, the basic neo-realist claim is thus that 'the EU can be analysed as a successful intergovernmental regime designed to manage economic interdependence through negotiated policy coordination'.[8] Such interdependence arises from increasing transboundary flows of goods, services, factors of production, and pollutants. In this way there is a clear acknowledgement of spillovers in some sense within the neo-realist position. But the realist insists that political action to deal with such spillovers has to be taken by nation states in the light of their own calculations of their circumstances and interests. Interdependence through increased transboundary flows of various kinds certainly creates incentives for international policy coordination, but the form of interstate bargain that emerges stems from the way national governments define their own interests. The neo-realist is thus committed explicitly to a two-stage view of international regime formation. As Moravcsik puts it, 'international conflict and cooperation can be modelled as a process that takes place in two successive stages: governments first define a set of interests, then bargain among themselves in an effort to realize those interests'.[9] This does not imply that the preferences of governments remain static during the course of negotiation, since during negotiation participants can learn more about one another and the possibilities for cooperative solutions. It does imply, however, that the test of negotiated bargains is to be found in conformity with the range of acceptable solutions that domestic processes of policy formation define. Domestic interest aggregation places limits on the international agreements into which governments can enter.

The implication of this approach is that an international body like the EU will remain intact only so long as it can promise advantages to national policy-makers that they cannot obtain in other, less compromising, ways. Indeed, neo-realists claim that, far from undermining the state, the creation of international institutions like the EU can strengthen national executives.[10] For example, if it is difficult for governments to maintain their own agricultural industry because the costs of support are high, it may well be to their advantage to enter into international arrangements in which some of these costs are shared by other countries. Similarly, if national executives confront powerful interests in their own society, they may well find it advantageous to pray in aid of the power of an international body like the EU.

At the basis of this account of European integration is the traditional realist assumption that states are an irreducible unit of political organization, the actions of which are shaped by a concept of the national interest. States do not act irrationally, and it would be the height of irrationality from this perspective for states to enter into agreements that led to their own abolition. It follows that there are limits to which we can explain state action by an appeal to uncertainty. Rational action will always guard against those uncertainties most likely to lead to the destruction of the rational agent. It therefore also follows that there are limits to integration, and to the transfer of political authority that such integration eventually requires. Authority is lent, not transferred, by the nation state, and there are some sectors of policy, especially the high politics of defence and foreign policy, where the writ of integration will never run.

It seems, then, as though for every plausible neo-functionalist proposition there is an equally plausible neo-realist counter-proposition. If neo-functionalists stress the logic of policy, and eventually political, spillover, neo-realists echo Hoffmann's assertion of the 'logic of diversity' and the limits of functional integration.[11] If neo-functionalists stress the extent of unintended consequences, neo-realists point to policy outcomes that embody the power and preferences of the member states. If neo-functionalists stress the extent to which authority has been transferred, neo-realists explain the extent to which it would have been rational to have delegated it. If neo-functionalists identify the internationalization of civil society, neo-realists stress the continued importance of domestic political forums. And so on. For those who are not partisans of either side, the controversy is often more notable for its intensity than for its illumination. Yet it is not without point. We miss something about the logic of any policy sector if we do not relate it to broader questions about European integration. We may agree that there are international rules, institutions, and patterns of authority, but may not properly understand their working until we also see their relation to larger processes. However, for a number of reasons, this is not to say that we can simply take sides in the dispute between neo-functionalists and neo-realists.

Firstly, the two sides of the debate, though they are set up as rival claims about the character of the process of European integration, are not cast as hypotheses that can easily be tested by reference to available empirical evidence. One reason for this is that some of the notions that are central to the claims of each cannot be operationalized in any straightforward way. Consider, for example, the question about the extent to which authority has been transferred from the nation state to the European Union. We can certainly observe the European Union making decisions, some of which appear to be imposed against the will of member states, most obviously through the qualified majority voting procedure. But is this really a straightforward transfer of decision-making authority? States may be prepared to trade losses in one area for gains in another. States may be playing 'nested games', where the position that they take in the EU is embedded in a context in which they know that they will get something else that they want.[12] And in any case, the claim that has to be decisive between neo-functionalists and neo-realists is that authority is not only transferred but is transferred in some *fundamental* way. However, the extent to which the transfer is fundamental is not a simple matter of empirical observation.

Another reason why the debate cannot be regarded as amenable to straightforward empirical test is that some of the claims of each side are themselves modified or reinterpreted during the course of the debate, even when they might appear to be core propositions. Consider, for example, the question of whether technical spillover automatically leads to political spillover. Critics of neo-functionalism often assume that this is one of the claims that they are contesting, and they highlight the deterministic assumptions that appear to be built into this way of reasoning. However, the reply this elicits from neo-functionalists is that determinism or automaticity was never built into their assumptions, and that politicization of issues was always expected.[13]

The dilemmas associated with comparative evaluation are compounded by the fact that much of the argument turns not on whether a certain process is at work, but on the *extent* to which it is at work. Thus, neo-realists like Moravcsik can concede that there are unintended effects in EU policy decisions, but claim that they are important only at the margins.[14] In other words, the issue between the two camps is often one of degree. Moreover, in so far as neo-realists make claims about the likelihood of intergovernmental bargains collapsing in hard times, as the regime of international free trade collapsed in the 1930s, they are implicitly appealing to a subjunctive conditional statement (what would happen if . . . ?) of which we have no experience.

However, there is another more important reason why the theories cannot be evaluated simply as rivals. Both can be regarded as extrapolations from historical aspects of the process of European integration. In that sense, they may be complementary, at least in certain respects. Neo-functionalism owes much to the historical influence of the Monnet method of integration, the original basis upon which the Union was founded; neo-realism owes much to the intergovernmental processes that have proved significant at certain junctures of the Union's history. If we see the competing theories as attempts to characterize the whole integration process in terms of specific historical and institutional features, we can see how both neo-functionalism and neo-realism can with some plausibility claim to offer an account of that process.

As is well known, Monnet's own view was that European integration required a piecemeal, pragmatic approach, rather than the implementation of a previously conceived grand design, and it was this belief that lay behind the stress on putting technical issues first. In his own memoirs, he stressed that the starting-point for European integration had to be limited achievements, leading to *de facto* 'solidarity' from which a federation would grow. This notion of 'solidarity' appeared, for Monnet, to be defined in terms of the existence of common interests, created for example in the 'pooling' of coal and steel resources. He wrote that the European Coal and Steel Community (ECSC) provided for a breach in national sovereignty that was 'narrow enough to secure consent, but deep enough to open the way towards the unity that is essential to peace'.[15] On this view, European integration had to be achieved by small, incremental steps in policy sectors where issues of national sovereignty were not likely to be raised, rather than in the high politics of defence and foreign policy.[16] Indeed, this was the main feature of Monnet's method that marked it out from contemporaneous attempts at European federalism.

The Monnet approach also depended on the idea of issue linkage. In other words, integration not only focused on technical matters, but also involved an issue dynamic drawing broader considerations into the decision-making process, perhaps without anyone ever seeing that they are involved. Just as Monnet himself stressed the potential for industry and agriculture to provide the basis for the common interests that the pooling of sovereignty in certain spheres would enable, so he saw, even in specific areas of policy, the solution to specific problems as raising general concerns, most notably the need for better communications if prosperity was to be achieved. It is this aspect of Monnet's thought that provides the foundation for neo-functionalism.

Moreover, unification by stealth led to government by appointed officials chosen for their technical competence rather than for their political representativeness. Both Monnet and Hallstein stressed the importance of making the High Authority of the ECSC independent of elected representatives in contrast to those, like Dirk Spierenburg, who wished for greater political control.[17] European integration also followed the Monnet method in that it can be seen as an open-ended process, not the implementation of a constitutional blueprint. The bicycle metaphor is the one that is frequently used in this context: European unification is like riding a bicycle—you need to keep going forward in order not to fall off. The Monnet method thus rests upon the steady accumulation of powers at the supranational level, and not on a once-and-for-all constitutional bargain among contracting parties.

Putting these points together, we can see that there is a sense in which neo-functionalism will have to be an element in the characterization of the integration process, since it captures some of the assumptions that were programmed into that process by one of its leading designers. The Monnet method was never implemented in a pure form, however. In the negotiations setting up the ECSC, it was the smaller nations that insisted on the injection of political control through a council of ministers. Since the pattern adopted for the ECSC was to form the basis of the institutional arrangements of the EU, the division of decision-making authority between the Commission and the Council of Ministers that derived from this original institutional bargain meant that the structure of European governance was superimposed on the political institutions of the member states. At various other stages, including de Gaulle's insistence that the process of functional integration be limited by the reassertion of the authority of the nation states in 1965 and the decision to move away from the Luxembourg compromise to the system of qualified majority voting in the Council of Ministers in the Single European Act, the conscious decisions of member states have been crucial.

It is this aspect of the process that lends credence to intergovernmentalist claims that the European Union does not transcend the interests of member states, but merely provides them with a convenient institutional vehicle for achieving their own purposes. Moreover, to the extent to which theories of integration look at achievements, rather than aspirations, the persisting role of national interests cannot be ignored in any theoretical construction.

For these reasons, instead of regarding neo-functionalism and neo-realism as well formed empirical theories to be tested against the evidence, we prefer to see them as general conceptual maps, against which we can plot our course. They alert us to potentially important features of the landscape and pose important questions of navigation. Neither form of cartography is likely to prove definitive, however, although we shall try to identify points at which their rival claims can be assessed or evaluated.

Partly in view of the apparently interminable nature of the debate between neo-functionalists and neo-realists, some scholars have accepted that there are lessons to be learnt from both perspectives. Both Pollack and Pierson, for example, seek to offer a theory of European integration by taking on board certain neo-functionalist assumptions and adapting intergovernmentalism accordingly.[18] Stone Sweet and Sandholtz seek to construct what they claim is a theory to rival Moravcsik's liberal intergovernmentalism, which they see as little more than a theory of intergovernmental bargaining.[19] Their theory of supranational governance rests on an explanation of the transition from national to intergovernmental to supranational governance, which they argue derives from a social demand for European rules. In this account, rule creation provokes a process of institutionalization which facilitates and promotes further integration in a manner reminiscent of the spillover dynamic, and this is able to account for variation in integration between different issue areas. Stone Sweet and Sandholtz thus seem able to suggest an underlying dynamic for primary rule creation, an explanation that would complement, rather than undermine, neo-realist accounts of intergovernmental bargains which focus on different sorts of decision.

Other scholars, however, have sought to go beyond a synthesis of the approaches from International Relations to advocate different approaches, especially those drawn from the literature on Comparative Politics.[20] One important move here is to distinguish the domain of different sorts of theories, a move that has been made, among others, by John Peterson.[21] Peterson distinguishes the 'super-systemic' level of European politics, where decisions are made about major changes to the structure of European institutions from the systemic and sub-systemic levels where priority-setting decisions are made about alternative courses of action or numerous 'technical' decisions are made about the setting of standards. His claim is that, whereas theories of European integration drawn from International Relations may be appropriately applied at the super-systemic level, other sorts of theories, drawn from Comparative Politics, and in particular from the literature on comparative public policy, are more appropriately applied at the other levels.

Distinguishing the domain of theories in this way would seem to map well on to the distinction that we have made between primary and secondary rule creation in the field of environmental policy. If we consider secondary rule creation, then we are confronted by the following sorts of question: How is the emergence of environmental policy to be explained? What relationship does it have to the issues raised by the single market? How are the rules institutionalized, and why do they take the form that they do? How important are issue-driven features of the European environmental policy process by comparison with the policy preferences of national policy-makers acting at the European level?

These questions are essentially about the rules (in the broadest sense) under which decisions are taken, and it looks as though any explanation will have to make essential reference either to functional linkages or to convergent national preferences, or to some mixture of the two. Yet theories drawn from the literature of International Relations may be less suitable to understanding the processes of primary rule creation that are so important in shaping the decisions that are made in particular policy areas. Taking decisions *under* a set of rules is typically different from taking decisions *about* a set of rules, even when the cumulative effects of primary rule creation can lead to a change in the overall structure of the secondary rules. Primary rule-making is typically a more routine process than secondary rule-making, involving different actors and procedures in circumstances where the issues are relatively well defined, even if they are difficult to solve. Hence it may well be that highly general theories of EU integration are less well adapted to understanding how decisions are made in particular cases of problem-solving.

The theoretical framework in terms of which scholars are seeking to understand the functioning of primary rule creation in this sense draws upon institutionalist theories of politics.[22] Institutionalism itself is not so much a well defined body of propositions as a general approach that draws attention to certain important features of the decision-making process.[23] In particular, we suggest, it sees governance as resting on the interaction of four elements: rules that allocate decision-making competence to different bodies; conventions that govern the interpretation of these rules in cases of doubt or in circumstances in which the rules are silent; norms that constrain and define the range of acceptable preferences on the part of actors;

and practices that summarize behavioural regularities, to which normative expectations become attached, most notably in connection with the functional representation of interests in policy networks. Taking this framework of secondary rules as given, neo-institutionalists then seek to explain policy outputs in terms of the preferences of actors within the system who are seeking to achieve their ends within that framework.

It will be helpful to provide some illustrations. Theorists of the policy process within the literature of Comparative Politics claim that 'institutions matter'. As Weaver and Rockman parse this claim, it amounts to the proposition

that political institutions shape the processes through which decisions are made and implemented and that these in turn influence government capabilities. Features such as the extent to which decision-making is centralized, the degree to which decisions are subject to multiple vetoes, and the extent to which elites are stable and share common values and objectives may affect specific capabilities.[24]

In other words, the institutionalist says that we should forget about the political status of the EU as an international organization—that is, whether it is basically an intergovernmental or a supranational body—and treat it simply as a decision-making system. As such, it will share certain features with any other decision-making system. For example, if there are multiple points of veto, we should expect it to be difficult to change existing policies, and we might anticipate special interests to be disproportionately advantaged. Thus, just as presidential political systems, viewed in a comparative context, are slower to develop certain policy strategies than parliamentary systems, so the EU might be expected to display certain patterns of decision-making given its institutional arrangements.[25] Any such general tendency of a decision-making system, therefore, we might expect to find replicated in the case of the EU.

To this general approach it is possible to add one further element. This is the claim that policy is made under conditions of bounded rationality.[26] Institutions perform a number of functions, but one aspect of their working is particularly important, namely the extent to which they help decision-makers economize on information.[27] Since human beings are always only boundedly rational, they need to be able to rely on existing worked out rules in order to make decisions. Thus, policy-makers take as their starting-point existing accomplishments and activities. Within the framework of the EU, this assumption is in fact formally institutionalized in the notion of the *acquis communautaire*, that body of practice and principles that has already been decided upon and agreed to. In this sense, policy-making and development with the EU is always likely to be 'path-dependent': it will always be a development of what has gone before.

How might such an institutionalist approach fare in relation to neo-functionalism and neo-realism? That institutions matter is an assertion that has been made time and time again in the literature on the European integration process. It is made by intergovernmentalists, who emphasize the centrality of national governments in the integration process and who tend to focus on the EU as a coordinating mechanism between governments; but it has also been made by neo-functionalists, who are more likely to place emphasis on the role of the central European institutions as engines of the integration process.

In this context, Cram usefully distinguishes between three models applicable to the European institutions.[28] First, the European institutions may be considered as passive structures, 'providing . . . norms, values and procedures, alterable only with unanimous consent'. As she points out, this 'is quite consistent with the intergovernmentalist perspective, which focuses predominantly on the structural leadership exerted by national governments in international negotiations'.[29] In this model, the European institutions have no independent existence. They are little more than governmental tools, used to improve the efficiency of intergovernmental relations, disseminate policy ideas or information, and monitor cooperation. They provide a framework within which international or regional agreements may be negotiated.

The second model envisages the European institutions as playing a more active role: European institutions are not only responsive to national preferences, but also have a role to play in shaping shared beliefs and values and in coordinating expectations.[30] Indeed, with such an approach, institutions are able to influence goals and stimulate policy changes. From this perspective, European institutions would not only act as the framework within which national preferences are played out, but would contribute to the construction of that framework and those preferences. In so doing, they define for national actors the limits of acceptable and unacceptable intergovernmental practice.

The third model enhances even further the role of the European institutions. Here such institutions are seen as independent and purposive actors within the European policy process. In this model institutions are policy actors in their own right, able to develop their own agendas, strategies, and goals and able to alter European policy in a much more direct fashion than is allowed for by the two earlier models. The extent to which one allows for the autonomy of European institutions and their capacity for policy influence depends on normative assumptions about the nature of the European Union and the integration process. But there is also a clearly empirical question to be addressed, as Cram notes:

The most interesting debate on the significance of EU institutions is not . . . whether they have a role to play. Rather, the interesting question is whether the role played by EU institutions is simply that ascribed to them by the national governments of the EU member state, and strictly limited by these member states, or whether the EU institutions have developed a role for themselves which extends beyond that delegated to them by the member states.[31]

According to this argument, both neo-functionalists and neo-realists can accept the claim of those writers who stress the contribution of Comparative Politics analysis that institutions matter, but they interpret its significance in different ways. Ultimately, the only way in which we can assess which approach or, better, which combination of approaches, provides the more accurate map is by examining the processes that have historically been at work, which is what we seek to do in the case of environmental policy.

PLAN OF PART I

In this first part of this book, we pursue the analysis of EU environmental policy in the light of these general issues. We begin by being interested in the relationship between the *single market* and *environment policy* as a way of seeing the extent to which there is issue linkage and spillover at work. As we shall see, in setting out the issues arising from the creation of environmental standards, broader questions about the political legitimacy of the European integration process are raised. In exploring the issue dynamic underpinning the European environmental agenda, national differences and the potential for both conflict and accommodation are identified. Yet, without accepting fully the existence of any neo-functionalist logic, issue linkage and spillover can be seen as ways of accounting for the emergence of European environmental rule creation, even though a political decision was needed to sanction the development.

The problems posed by the creation of the single market naturally lead on to a consideration of the *policies* that have been developed to deal with environmental problems. However, we must look not simply at the evolution of a set of policies, but also the legitimating discourse that underpins and justifies policy. As a result, we are interested in the extent to which the European institutions have succeeded in encapsulating a set of distinct environmental *policy principles*. One way, though certainly not the only way, of examining those principles is through analysis of the publicly available policy frameworks issued by the Commission in successive action programmes. These frameworks not only reflect the priorities in the Treaty and in its revisions, they also anticipate and influence constitutional change on the environment front. For our purposes, they act as windows on to the principles that underpin European environment policy.

Secondary rule creation takes the form of the institutionalization of environmental policy-making, and in this context the analysis of the principal *institutional actors* is also important. Not only do institutions serve as arenas in which political, economic and societal actors operate, they also actively shape rules, norms, and conventions. Indeed, in some cases institutions even operate as purposive actors in their own right. However, while we might be tempted to define the European Commission, the European Parliament, and the European Court of Justice as agents of supranationalism, the story to be told about these institutions is in fact far more complex, since these institutions have long been subject to national pressures. For example, the 'infiltration' of the Commission by national officials is now well documented.[32] Similarly, while the Council of Ministers and the European Council might quite easily be categorized as intergovernmental organizations, these institutions have in fact well-established European credentials. If anything, the extension of qualified majority voting applied to environmental legislation helps to blur the edges of intergovernmentalism.

Patterns of governance need also to figure in our account of European environment policy. At the European level, this takes the form of an assessment of the processes by which legislation is passed. It is the European institutions that have formal responsibility for the making of policy, even if we recognize that policy is not made in a supranational vacuum, and that the source of policy rests as much with networks of national, international, regional, and transnational actors as it does with the European institutions. We acknowledge therefore the importance of policy networks and policy communities which cut across traditionally defined levels of analysis. Whereas the multi-level metaphor might suggest an emphasis on government as the source of governance, there is also the horizontal complexity, derived from the separation of powers in the EU's own decision-making procedures as well as the participation of interested parties in EU policy networks.

However, much of the focus of this study still rests on the interaction between levels of governance. We are therefore keen to bring in the *national dimension* at this point, by highlighting the distinctive role of the Council of Ministers. The member states are the lynchpins or cornerstones of the multi-level relationship, as they remain in the majority of cases (despite increasing powers exercised by the European Parliament) the final arbiters of environmental policy. As such, the Council acts as the most obvious, though clearly not the only, bridge between the European and the national levels. While this does not preclude any of the more direct relationships that are now commonplace, involving for example regional and local authorities, it would be misleading to play down the Council's inescapably pre-eminent role in European environmental governance.

To anticipate: our conclusions are that the European level matters, but that the extent to which it matters is impossible to judge by looking at solely European institutions, principles, and patterns. What becomes crucial, then, if we are to understand the nature of European environmental governance, is the interaction of the European, national and subnational levels, and the comparative politics and policies of the member states.

NOTES TO PART I INTRODUCTION

1. For a good recent summary of these debates, see L. Cram, 'Integration Theory and the Study of the European Policy Process', in J. J. Richardson (ed.), *European Union: Power and Policy-Making* (London and New York: Routledge, 1996), pp. 40–58. See also S. George, 'The European Union: Approaches from International Relations' in H. Kassim and A. Menon (eds.), *The European Union and National Industrial Policy*

(London: Routledge, 1996), pp. 11–25. We follow the convention of using the capitalized 'International Relations' for the discipline of study and 'international relations' for the subject matter, as well as following a similar convention for Comparative Politics.

For the functionalist tradition, see: E. B. Haas, *The Uniting of Europe: Political, Social and Economic Forces, 1950–1957* (Stanford, Calif.: Stanford University Press, 1986, 2nd edn); L. N. Lindberg, *The Political Dynamics of European Economic Integration* (London: Oxford University Press, 1963); D. Mitrany, *The Functional Theory of Politics* (London: Martin Robertson, 1975); and P. C. Schmitter, 'Examining the Present Euro-Polity with the Help of Past Theories', in G. Marks, F. W. Scharpf, P. C. Schmitter, and W. Streeck, *Governance in the European Union* (London: Sage, 1996), pp. 1–14. There is an interesting discussion of the distinctions between Mitrany's and subsequent functionalisms in P. Taylor, *Limits of European Integration* (London and Canberra: Croom Helm, 1983), ch. 1.

For the intergovernmentalist tradition, see: G. Garrett, 'International Cooperation and Institutional Choice: The European Community's Internal Market', *International Organization*, 46:2 (1992), pp. 533–60; S. Hoffmann, 'Obstinate or Obsolete? The Fate of the Nation-State and the Case of Western Europe', *Daedalus*, 95:3 (1966), pp. 862–916; A. Moravcsik, 'Negotiating the Single European Act', in R. O. Keohane and S. Hoffmann (eds.), *The New European Community* (Boulder, Colo., San Francisco and Oxford: Westview Press, 1991), pp. 41–84; A. Moravcsik, 'Preferences and Power in the European Community: A Liberal Intergovernmentalist Approach', *Journal of Common Market Studies*, 31:4 (1993), pp. 473–524; and Taylor, *Limits of European Integration*.

An interesting attempt to go beyond the dichotomy is in W. Sandholtz and J. Zysman, '1992: Recasting the European Bargain', *World Politics*, 42:1 (1989), pp. 95–128.

For a discussion of the applicability of these theories to environmental policy, see A. Jordan, ' "Overcoming the Divide" between Comparative Politics and International Relations Approaches to the EC: What Role for "Post-Decisional Politics"?' *West European Politics*, 20:4 (1997), pp. 43–70, and A. R. Zito, 'Task Expansion: A Theoretical Overview', *Environment and Planning* C, 17:1 (1999), pp. 19–35.

2. Schmitter, 'Examining the Present Euro-Polity with the Help of Past Theories', p. 5.
3. Cram, 'Integration Theory and the Study of the European Policy Process', pp. 41–3.
4. A point well made in Cram, 'Integration Theory', p. 43.
5. The phrase of a neo-realist that nicely captures one aspect of the neo-functionalist viewpoint; see Moravcsik, 'Preferences and Power in the EC', p. 475.
6. See E. J. Kirchner, *Decision-Making in the European Community* (Manchester and New York: Manchester University Press, 1992), p. 25.
7. Compare D. R. Cameron, 'The 1992 Initiative: Causes and Consequences', in A. M. Sbragia (ed.), *Euro-Politics: Institutions and Policymaking in the 'New' European Community* (Washington: Brookings Institution, 1992), pp. 23–74, and S. Hix, 'Approaches to the Study of the EC', *West European Politics*, 17:1, (1994), p. 4.
8. Moravcsik, 'Preferences and Power in the European Community', p. 474.
9. Ibid. 481.
10. See e.g. A. Milward *et al.*, *The European Rescue of the Nation State* (London: Routledge, 1992).
11. Hoffmann, 'Obstinate or Obsolete?'
12. G. Tsebelis, *Nested Games* (Berkeley: University of California Press, 1990).
13. Schmitter, 'Examining the Present Euro-Polity', p. 7.

14. Moravcsik, 'Preferences and Power in the European Community', p. 473.
15. J. Monnet, *Memoirs*, trans. R. Mayne, with forward by Roy Jenkins (London: Collins, 1978), p. 296.
16. Compare S. Mazey, 'The Development of the European Idea: From Sectoral Integration to Political Union', in J. J. Richardson (ed.), *European Union: Power and Policy-Making* (London and New York: Routledge, 1996), p. 29.
17. F. Laursen, 'The Role of the Commission', in S. S. Andersen and K. A. Eliassen (eds.), *The European Union: How Democratic Is It?* (London: Sage, 1996), pp. 119–41.
18. M. Pollack, 'The New Institutionalism and EC Governance', *Governance*, 9:4 (1996), pp. 429–58; P. Pierson, 'The Path to European Integration: An Historical Institutionalist Account', *Comparative Political Studies*, 29:2 (1996), pp. 123–63.
19. A. Stone Sweet and W. Sandholtz, 'European Integration and Supranational Governance', *Journal of European Public Policy*, 4:2 (1997), pp. 297–317. See also W. Sandholtz and A. Stone Sweet (eds.), *European Integration and Supranational Governance* (Oxford: Oxford University Press, 1998).
20. S. J. Bulmer, 'The Governance of the European Union: A New Institutionalist Approach', *Journal of Public Policy*, 13:4 (1994), pp. 351–80; Hix, 'Approaches to the Study of the EC'; J. Peterson, 'Decision-Making in the European Union: Towards a Framework for Analysis', *Journal of European Public Policy*, 2:1 (1995), pp. 69–93.
21. Peterson, 'Decision-making in the European Union'.
22. Bulmer, 'The Governance of the European Union'.
23. For useful accounts of institutionalism, see: B. Rothstein 'Political Institutions: An Overview', in R. E. Goodin and H.-D. Klingemann (eds.), *A New Handbook of Political Science* (Oxford: Oxford University Press, 1996), pp. 133–66; P. A. Hall and R. C. R. Taylor, 'Political Science and the Three New Institutionalisms', *Political Studies*, 44:5 (1996), pp. 936–57; J. Kato, 'Institutional Rationality in Politics: Three Varieties of Neo-Institutionalists', *British Journal of Political Science*, 26:4 (1996), pp. 553–82.
24. R. K. Weaver and B. A. Rockman, 'Assessing the Effects of Institutions', in R. K. Weaver and B. A. Rockman (eds.), *Do Institutions Matter? Government Capabilities in the United States and Abroad* (Washington: Brookings Institution, 1993), p. 7.
25. For this sort of analysis in the general case, see G. Tsebelis, 'Decision Making in Political Systems: Veto Players in Presidentialism, Parliamentarianism, Multicameralism and Multipartism', *British Journal of Political Science*, 25:3 (1995), pp. 289–325.
26. See e.g. H. Simon, *Reason in Human Affairs* (Oxford: Basil Blackwell, 1983).
27. D. C. North, *Institutions, Institutional Change and Ecnomic Performance* (Cambridge: Cambridge University Press, 1990), esp. ch. 4.
28. L. Cram, *Policy-Making in the EU: Conceptual Lenses and the Integration Process* (London: Routledge, 1997), 170–3.
29. Ibid. 171.
30. G. Garrett and B. Weingast, 'Ideas, Interests and Institutions: Constructing the European Community's Internal Market', in J. Goldstein and R. Keohane (eds.), *Ideas and Foreign Policy: Beliefs, Institutions and Political Change* (London: Cornell University Press, 1993), pp. 173–206.
31. Cram, *Policy-Making in the EU*, p. 173.
32. N. Nugent, *The Government and Politics of the European Community* (London: Macmillan, 1991, 2nd edn), pp. 65–6.

1

The Single Market and the Environment: From Issue Linkage to Political Choice

Many of the arguments about the processes of European integration that we reviewed in the previous chapter turn on the issue of spillover. In this chapter we look at the origins of EU environmental policy in terms of this concept. We consider in particular the relationship between the single market and environmental policy, on the assumption that the creation of the single market has been the most important device for increasing European integration.

How, then, does environmental protection relate to the single market? What is the relationship between market integration and the environment? How does it come about that economy and ecology are so intertwined? In seeking answers to these questions, we examine the nature and character of the issues raised by the single market programme as it affects environmental protection, and we consider the implications for market integration of the demand for greater environmental protection. That there is clearly a close relationship between the evolving European single market and the protection of the European environment is something that we seek to show, but the crucial question is how far this relationship develops from technical spillover to political spillover.

One can argue that the place of environmental policy in the process of European integration would have been ensured simply by virtue of the character of modern pollution problems. Many of the most important pollution problems of the 1980s and 1990s—acidification, stratospheric ozone depletion, and climate change—inevitably have a transboundary character, so that it may not be surprising to see the EU develop the capacity to deal with such problems. Indeed, it has been argued that the EU had developed as an international resource regime to deal with such problems by 1992.[1]

Despite the general appeal of regime analysis, however, it is difficult to identify the evolution of EU environmental policy with a simple logic of regime development, as that has customarily been employed in the field of the environment.[2] Firstly, the form and manner in which EU environmental policy evolved was conditioned by the use, implicit in the Monnet method, of economic means to achieve political ends. This has meant that the EU has not been concerned exclusively with cross-boundary pollution flows, but has also had to deal with the consequences for the single market of environmental regulation. Thus, EU involvement in environmental policy was not problem- or issue-specific in the way that is typical of international resource regimes like the International Whaling Commission, the International Arctic Committee, or the Rhine Commission, but rather it entailed issues of market regulation in a broad sense. Secondly, a number of the environmental issues at the forefront of EU policy do not always have a cross-boundary character. Indeed, the EU has provided a set of political institutions in which political actors could pursue issues that were more often concerned more with local public goods, like urban air quality or the quality of bathing waters, than international public goods. Thirdly, the EU has not played as significant a part in some European cross-boundary pollution problems as the designation 'international resource regime' suggests, since other bodies, significantly the United Nations Economic Commission for Europe, have played at least as strong a role.

Thus, rather than a simple story of environmental interdependencies calling forth an international regime, we need to understand the complex character of the issues that have come to dominate European environmental policy. What we describe in this chapter, therefore, is an *issue dynamic*, the basis of the possibility of technical spillover. What we mean by this can be simply explained. Once certain issues get on to a political agenda, they raise a set of questions that have to be answered by policy-makers. But the answers that policy-makers come up with to the original questions then give rise to further questions, and political actors find that they are confronted with problems and issues the significance of which they may have only dimly appreciated at first, or perhaps not appreciated at all.

Since the liberalization of trade is the chosen instrument of European integration, the character of the issue dynamic borrows much of its logic from the issues that are raised by the implications of free trade for the environment. But this relationship is complex. As Brack has argued, there are certain respects in which free trade can be good for the environment and certain respects in which it can be bad.[3] Free trade can be good for the environment because it facilitates specialization according to comparative advantage and thus promotes the efficient use of resources. As well as providing higher levels of resources for environmental investment, free trade is associated with transparent pricing, which works against environmentally damaging subsidies. Free trade also opens economies to the use of new technologies that can improve the potential for clean production and product diversification, taking pressures off unsustainable extractive industries. On the other hand, free trade promotes growth, which in turn increases pollution. Higher income does not always lead to higher expenditure on pollution control technology. Trade liberalization can imply agreements that undermine the effects of environmental standards, and countries with strict pollution controls can find they come under competition from countries with laxer standards.[4]

In the case of the European single market and environmental policy, much of this issue dynamic was played out. In order to advance the process of European integration, the single market programme was chosen as the most important instrument. The creation of the single market required policy-makers to pay attention to environmental issues because measures of environmental protection, either in the form of administrative regulation or by means of economic instruments, often threatened the functioning of the market. However, since any set of markets can give rise to market failures, including pollution externalities, the creation of the single market also had implications for policies of environmental protection. Hence, just as policies of environmental protection inevitably had implications for the single market, so the creation of the single market had implications for policies of environmental protection.

The issue dynamic does not stop there, however. The single market is a political creation. The institutional changes necessary to bring it about, most importantly but not exclusively changes in decision procedures, themselves raise large questions about the identity and purposes of the European Union. For instance, if the creation of the single market required the abandonment of unanimity in favour of majority voting in the Council of Ministers, the question might also be raised as to whether a policy like environmental protection should not also be pursued more vigorously on a supranational basis. And this question in turn meant that policy-makers were forced to ask larger questions about the political purposes that the creation of the single market was supposed to serve.

Among these questions, the following have become prominent. Can policies for environmental protection help achieve the goal of greater global competitiveness that some at least saw as integral to the creation of the single market? Should not environmental protection be part—perhaps even the central part—of the European 'social space' that some thought was necessary for the market to function? If European citizenship now exists, does that mean that there is a core level of environmental protection to which all citizens, wherever they live, are entitled? Should the European environment be construed as the responsibility of nation states cooperating to their mutual advantage, or should it instead be seen as a common European inheritance?

The issue dynamic involved in the relationship between the single market and the environment thus unravels in ways unforeseen and unintended by those taking political decisions. The single market and measures for environmental protection interact in complex ways, and the apparently self-contained questions about making each compatible with the other give way to larger questions about the role of the European Union in promoting its citizens' quality and form of life. Yet to say that an issue dynamic is at work is not to say that political actors will respond in predictable ways to the development of that dynamic, unless the logic of functionalism completely supersedes the logic of intergovernmentalism. Limitations of the operation of the issue dynamic will be an important indicator of the extent to which the integration process is actor-driven rather than functionally driven.

In this chapter, as in the book as a whole, we focus on the issues that arise in the setting of environmental standards for pollution control. We take this focus because we think that such issues bring out clearly the political dynamics that are involved. It is the contestation over standards that brings out the complex elements in the relation of environmental policy to European integration. We consider the development of the issue dynamic according to the outline logic we have sketched. That is, we begin with the self-contained, relatively technical questions about the single market and measures of environmental protection, showing how the pursuit of answers to the problems raised leads on to higher-order questions about the institutional and political basis of the single market, as tacit assumptions and operating procedures are brought out into the open. Our journey takes us from the fear of eco-protectionism to fundamental institutional reform in the European Union.

THE SINGLE MARKET AND BARRIERS TO TRADE

Because environmental protection was not mentioned in the Treaty of Rome, the early impetus to the development of policies was given by the perceived need to prevent countries erecting barriers to trade under the guise of measures for environmental protection. Eco-protectionism, as it has come to be called, would be the enemy of the development of the single market, as well as of the promotion of international free trade more generally.

The main way in which environmental measures can create barriers to trade is in terms of product standards, so it is not surprising that it was in the development of some forms of product regulation at the European level that the issue of environmental standards and their relation to market competition first emerged. Product standards are one of the many different kinds of standard that are applied for the purposes of environmental protection.[5] Such standards can be seen as having two distinct functions: the elimination or reduction of potentially damaging effects of a product on the environment, and the application of certain common commercial and technical requirements to all products of a particular type. These requirements are crucial in determining the extent to which a product can be traded between different markets. One early example of the issues involved is provided by the 1970 directive relating to the permissible sound levels and exhaust systems of motor vehicles, including cars, lorries, and buses.[6] The annex to the directive laid down maximum decibel emission values, and under the directive no country could exclude from its domestic markets vehicles that satisfied those standards. In effect, the measure was thus premissed on a principle of mutual recognition, subject to minimum harmonized standards being met.

Such measures clearly had an essential market rationale. One of the ways in which this can be seen is that the standards set were optional only for domestic producers. This meant that countries were not required to impose these emission limit values on all manufacturers of vehicles, but merely that they could not exclude such vehicles from their domestic markets if the vehicles did meet those standards. It would thus have been quite compatible with the directive to have continuing or increasing nuisance from noise in countries in Europe, since foreign vehicles might meet the harmonized standards, but the harmonized standards might be lower than domestic ones for the same vehicles, or domestically produced vehicles might not even meet the harmonized standards, so long as the manufacturers were not interested in exporting to other European countries. Similar directives relating to the noise emitted from farm vehicles or the composition of surfactants in detergents also provide examples of environmental directives adopted for common market reasons in the same mode.[7]

All these measures were adopted under Article 100 of the Treaty of Rome, dealing with the completion of the single market, and, as we shall see later, even after the passing of the Single European Act, there was still pressure to take environmental measures under Article 100a of the Treaty, dealing with single market measures, rather than under the environment provisions of Article 130r.

In the case of vehicles, there was a clear attempt at the European level to remove the barriers to trade that might flow from measures adopted to protect the environment. To understand the political dynamics of issues when there are such barriers, we can take the example of the Danish bottles law, which was first implemented in 1981. Under this legislation, soft drinks and beer could be marketed in Denmark only in approved containers for which a collection and refilling system existed to ensure a high percentage of reuse.[8] Containers had to be approved by the Danish National Environmental Protection Agency, and this agency could refuse approval if a suitable container of similar size had already been approved, or if it was believed that the planned collect-and-refill system would not encourage a high enough return rate. A subsequent amended order,[9] which was introduced in 1984 because of the European Commission's objections to the earlier order, allowed for non-approved containers to be used for up to 3,000 hl of product per producer per year. This derogation did not apply to metal containers. For foreign producers, the amended order also allowed the use of non-approved containers for a period while demand for the product was tested, as long as a deposit-and-return system was to be established.

The potential of this measure to create barriers to trade was identified in the Cecchini report, which noted that, 'if the requirement to use refillable bottles were dropped, beer exporters into Denmark could avoid the down-time in their bottling plants that is necessary to switch to refillable bottles'.[10] The Danish legislation was thought to be so serious in its implications for free trade that it was referred to the European Court of Justice by the Commission.[11] Although the Court decided that not all the measures used were disproportionate to the goal being sought, in our context the legal merits of the case are less interesting than the perceptions of the issues among policy-makers, particularly those favouring the development of the single market. These perceptions were that there was a contradiction between the goal of a single market and the priority that any one member state might want to give to the goal of environmental protection. Here we see clearly how the issues of the single market and environmental protection can be intertwined. If certain sorts of environmental measures are taken in a country, then it may be possible for foreign manufacturers to complain that their products are being discriminated against.

The development of the single market required as its precondition a new attitude to the setting of market rules, including a move away from the insistence that rules be harmonized in the European market and towards an acceptance of the principle of mutual recognition. Efforts in the 1970s to harmonize technical standards on a product-by-product basis had been driven by the same concerns as had inspired the creation of a common market. After the completion of the customs union and the removal of tariff barriers within the European Union, member states were able to undermine the spirit of the free trade by establishing or reinforcing non-tariff barriers, often in the form of technical standards. While technical harmonization at EU level was a response to such market-fragmenting practices by national authorities, it was never effective. The bureaucratic and time-consuming process of standard-setting item by item brought the EU into disrepute, and it became clear that technical harmonization alone would provide an inadequate foundation for the revitalized single market project.[12]

Acceptance of the principle of mutual recognition was thus part of a new approach to the proliferation of non-tariff barriers. While technical harmonization continued to be an option for European policy-makers, it was limited to 'essential requirements' (mainly health and safety matters) and standard-setting generally became the preserve of bodies situated outside the Commission. For all other forms of standard-setting, namely those considered 'non-essential', the principle of mutual recognition was to apply. This principle was first established in the European Court of Justice's *Cassis de Dijon* ruling in 1979[13] and has been confirmed in subsequent rulings and judgments of the Court. It asserted that a product lawfully manufactured and marketed in one member state should be able to move freely throughout the European Union. In practice, this has come to mean that those trading within the EU need not submit to certification procedures beyond those required in the product's country of origin,[14] and that, as long as minimum health and safety standards are met, the product has access to all markets within the European Union. Since environmental standards are an integral part of the market rules, the issues of mutual recognition and of environmental protection became entangled. The new approach to rule-making that underlay the creation of the single market also had significant implications for the relationship between environmental protection and the single market.

ENVIRONMENTAL PROTECTION AND
ECONOMIC COMPETITIVENESS

The interrelationship of environmental protection and barriers to trade arises most obviously in the case of products, because it is products that can travel across borders. However, many measures of environmental protection, and certainly many of the measures developed since the beginning of European policy in this field, are concerned with process control, for example in the specification of emission limit values for air pollution from manufacturing processes, or in the control of pollutants discharged to water from waste water treatment plants and other sources. Indeed, taken to its logical limits, environmental policy can involve a form of process control in which the entire complex of economic and environmental activities related to fulfilling a particular need are analysed, evaluated, and reordered.[15] It might seem at first sight as though there is less interrelationship between the single market and such process controls than there is between the single market and product controls. Yet, though the relationship may be attenuated, it is still there.

The principal issue has turned on the question of how far national environmental measures of process control disturb the 'level playing field' of competition on which, it is argued, the single market rests. Environmental pollution controls imposed on plants and processes will often raise the costs of production to those operating the plant; and, if the controls are uniform for a whole sector of manufacturing, they may have the potential to put that sector at a competitive disadvantage with comparable sectors in other countries.

The effect is well illustrated in the consequences of Germany's adoption of tighter pollution control standards under its own legislation in 1983. Although this was a purely domestic measure, taken under German legislation, its implementation established a political impetus to apply an equivalent measure to other European countries. (For a fuller discussion, see Chapter 11.) Although the pressure arose partly out of a perception of the international character of air pollution, particularly as associated with the problem of acidification, there was also a strong concern by German industry about the increased costs that it faced from a rise in price for domestically generated electricity.[16]

The significance of the issue of the level playing field has at various times been politically controversial. For example, it was common among UK policy-makers in the 1970s to argue that the greater assimilative capacity of the UK's natural environment, with its relatively short, fast flowing rivers and favourable westerly winds, should be treated as a natural advantage, just like other natural advantages.[17] Nigel Haigh has summarized the argument clearly:

Since Italian lemon growers take advantage of the sun that geography brings them, and grow lemons rather than engage in some other activity for that very reason, and since German industrialists benefit from proximity to continental markets as a result of geography, so also it is argued that Britain should quite properly profit from the ability to locate industries on estuaries or the coast where acute pollution problems are less likely to arise and where the sea water can assimilate or destroy the pollutants.[18]

Needless to say, this once often heard British position is not universally shared within Europe, but it does illustrate how identifying the relationships between environmental protection and the single market is as much a matter of political perception and interpretation as it is of the patterns of cause and effect operative in the market and the environment.

Concerns about competitiveness have led some to voice apprehension about the effect of environmental regulation on competition. For example, on some occasions the Commission has called for a vigilant competition policy and argued that:

whenever possible [integration of competitiveness and the environment requires a strategy that] should be built around solutions based on the competitive functioning of markets. This implies in particular emphasis on market-related instruments of environment policy.[19]

Yet this emphasis upon competition in the context of environmental policy also raises problems that have to be dealt with. It has implications for the issue of cooperation between companies that may need to be analysed with respect to the competition rules. For example, when member states legislate in the field of packaging waste with the aim of increasing the recycling or reuse of materials, cooperation between companies is often the only way by which they can meet these norms and run collection and retrieval systems privately. Thus, the German waste management system allows participating companies who pay a fee to place a 'green dot' on their products, showing that the packaging will normally be sorted out and can be recycled. This has been the object of a number of complaints which raise several important issues. In particular, concern has focused on the question of whether it is necessary that there be only one system, which gives rise to risk of monopoly power, and might be used as a barrier to entry against new competition, particularly from outside Germany.[20]

However, although the idea of the level playing field is important, there is also another aspect to the idea of economic competitiveness. So far we have presented the thinking about the single market in purely liberal terms, as though the concern were merely to remove barriers to trade. Yet there is a question begged in this analysis: to what extent is the single market truly a liberal project? To be sure, the creation of the single market and the emergent consequences of economic and monetary union can be thought of as effective instruments of political integration. This does not mean, however, that the liberal credentials of the single market programme are uncontested or have a uniform interpretation. It is clear that the support that Delors received from EU leaders for the pursuit of the single market programme stemmed from a variety of motives, not all of which were compatible with one another.[21] On the one side were those, like the UK government, who favoured the project because they saw it as creating a free trade area in Europe. On the other side were those who saw the single market as the necessary condition under which Europe could take on collectively the economic contest with the USA and Japan. The latter group were more productivist and corporatist in ideology than liberal. In other words, the single market encapsulated the struggle that Albert referred to as 'capitalism against capitalism'.[22]

In this context, the role of environmental policy in providing the basis for an interventionist strategy to promote economic competitiveness was important for certain member states. As we shall see in the next chapter, there was emerging in a number of European countries during the 1980s an ideology of ecological modernization, one of the central propositions of which was the claim that there was not always a zero-sum relationship between economic competitiveness and environmental protection. High standards of environmental protection were seen as the means by which Europe could become globally competitive against US and Japanese products. From this more corporatist perspective, there was a clear positive link between the issue of environmental standards and competitiveness that involved legislating for higher standards in order to establish a first-mover advantage in global markets.

MARKET FAILURE AND SINGLE MARKET SUCCESS

From the economic point of view, environmental pollution is an externality, that is to say a case where parties engaged in a trade do not bear the full costs of the transaction themselves but displace some of the costs on to third parties. The classic example of an externality was given by Pigou in the instance of the smoking chimney which pollutes the area in its vicinity: neither the owners of the factory nor those who buy its products need have the responsibility to pay for the extra cleaning of their homes and clothes that the nearby residents incur.[23] Externalities are an example of market failure, understanding that term in the strict sense to mean a case where the competitive equilibrium of the market does not lead to a so-called Pareto-efficient allocation of resources, itself defined as a state of affairs in which one person cannot be made better off without making someone else worse off.[24] The common prescription in such circumstances is for the political authorities to adopt a policy that will internalize all the costs of production to the parties engaged in the trade, thus eliminating the externalities and raising the economic welfare of the community.

To the extent that there were already externalities within the economies of Europe, the creation of a single market was likely to make them worse. The success of the single market programme was premissed on the assumption that it would raise the total volume of goods and services traded in Europe. But if, in the production and consumption of those goods and services, externalities are created, then it will follow that they too will increase, unless compensating measures are taken. The *success* of the single market could therefore result in a *failure* of environmental policy. The significance of this point was stressed by Haigh and Baldock in 1989:

What is clear is that if the predictions of the Cecchini report are even half true, then there will be a significant increase in economic growth of an unreconstructed kind which is bound to have an impact on the environment.[25]

Hence one of the ways in which environment and the single market were related was that the economic benefits associated with the single market could be offset by the growth in uncompensated externalities that the increase in the volume of goods and services traded would bring.

The political imperative behind the single market programme meant that it was bound to have high priority in the Commission and the Council in particular, and therefore no attention to the problem of environmental externalities was paid in the planning of 1992, or in the consultancy work that accompanied it.[26] However, a Task Force was established in 1989 to look into the environmental consequences of the single market, and it identified two main categories of impact.[27] The first contained those static impacts that were a result of the removal of barriers, while the second consisted of those dynamic impacts that resulted from the economic and industrial growth expected as a result of the barriers falling.

In the first group were problems such as how trade in animals, plants, and wastes could be effectively regulated without border controls. According to the Task Force, the solution to these types of problem lay in trust building within the EU, so that point-of-origin checks and enforcement procedures were mutually recognized. The second group concerned the more obvious effects, those that were expected as a result of dynamic growth stemming from the creation of the single market, per-haps most obviously the expected growth in road and air transport, putting more pressure on the environment. According to the Task Force, these effects would be especially critical in southern Europe, where infrastructure development would have to be extensive. The southern, less developed, periphery would also be more vulnerable to the rise in tourism, which could lead to increased economic and social tension in addition to overloaded sewerage systems, noise, air pollution, and destruc-tion of habitats, all of which are examples of external effects.

The Task Force acknowledged that its work on the economic side was com-pleted in a very short space of time and with limited resources, so that its results could be regarded only as estimates. Moreover, since the issues were complex and the interactions often unpredictable, consideration of the environmental impacts of the predicted growth was, and remains for the medium term, largely speculat-ive. None the less, even with these qualifications, it was clear according to the Task Force that the environmentally harmful effects of the single market could be serious. Once again, the intertwined logic of the single market and environmental policy was apparent.

THE ISSUE OF WASTE MANAGEMENT

Perhaps the clearest example in which we can observe the complex interrelation-ships between the single market and environmental protection is the case of waste management. Here are revealed the possibly antagonistic logics of market alloca-tion and sound environmental practice.

From the point of view of market economics, if waste is treated as a tradable commodity like any other, then it is subject to the same laws of efficiency. In general, economic efficiency is best served when use is made of the international division of labour, so that different countries, and different regions within countries, specialize in productive activities according to their comparative advantage. By this logic, it is most unlikely that countries or regions will find it economically advantageous to treat all their own domestically produced waste, and conversely some countries or regions will find it advantageous to treat or dispose of the waste of others. Moreover, in some cases of waste treatment, for example the disposal or treatment of especially hazardous waste such as PCBs, there may be strong scale economy arguments favouring treatment in one country for processors that take waste from a number of countries. As the waste management industry becomes more capital-intensive, in response to a rise in environmental standards, disposal plants need a larger and more reliable stream of material. The treatment of hazardous waste is particularly expensive for some member states, for example Spain and Greece, and needs sophisticated technology. As a result, the tendency for waste, especially hazardous waste, to be exported is particularly marked.[28]

If the principle of economics is to extend the market, the principle of waste treatment according to best practice, as it has so far evolved in European discussions, is to contract the market, in line with the so-called proximity principle. The proximity principle states that waste is best treated and disposed of as close to the source of its creation as possible. The underlying logic of this principle is based both on ideas of producer liability and on the problems of asymmetries of information that typically pervade the waste management business. If producers are made liable for the disposal of their own waste, then, so the argument goes, they will have an incentive to produce less of it in the first place and they will also have an incentive to ensure that its control is properly managed. Moreover, despite regulatory safeguards, it is clear that, when the production and the disposal of waste are too far separated, the producers have an incentive to mis-state the character and hazards associated with the waste, in effect taking advantage of asymmetries of information in order to reduce costs. These concerns can easily intermingle with a more basic sense among the population of a country that they should not be treating the waste produced by others, especially if those others are wealthier.

Some of these concerns surfaced in the legal controversy over the Wallonian waste decree heard by the European Court of Justice.[29] This case concerned the Commission and the Belgian region of Wallonia, which had passed a decree banning hazardous waste imports, particularly from France and Germany, into the region. The Commission had argued that waste was to be treated as a good, and therefore was subject to the freedom of movement regulations under Article 30 of the Treaty of Rome. Furthermore, existing EU legislation allowed only for the banning of particular shipments, not for a blanket ban. Although the Court agreed with the Commission that the ban was illegal under existing rules, it did comment that, as free trade requirements could be overridden sometimes by the environmental imperative (as in its Danish bottles ruling), waste should be disposed of as close to source as possible. It was also interesting that the Court chose not to agree with Advocate General Jacobs, who argued that the decree offended Article 36 because it distinguished between domestic and imported goods. In rejecting this stance, the Court further stressed the importance of keeping waste transport to a minimum.

This example illustrates the general point that the logic of the single market and the logic of good environmental practice can often conflict with one another. Moreover, this has implications for the dynamics of policy-making within Europe, since perceptions of how to handle the potential conflict of goals and perceptions, what weight to give to the competing considerations, and how to put administrative systems in place to control waste management will vary among the political actors concerned, be they Community institutions like the Commission or the Parliament, or national governments bargaining within the Council of Ministers.

POLITICAL CHOICE AND THE SINGLE MARKET

In looking at the issue dynamic between the single market and environmental policy, we have in effect been looking at the sources of political demand for primary rules. However, it is clear that the growth of rules for the regulation of products, as well for as other goods and services, could not have taken place without a change in the secondary rules for making primary rules. The system of *de facto* unanimity was simply too prone to the exercise of veto power by key players to secure the requisite change. Hence, in addition to the logic of issue spillover, we also need to look at the character of the political choices to which the issue linkage gave rise.

Since the emergence of environmental policy in the 1970s, the formal pattern of institutional authority has been changed three times: by the Single European Act, by the Maastricht Treaty, and by the Treaty of Amsterdam. Table 1.1 summarises the principal features of rule-making at each stage.

Before the Single European Act

The absence of environmental provisions in the Treaty did nothing to prevent legislation on environmental matters when the issue eventually became salient. But it did mean that the European institutions had to rely on rather unsatisfactory treaty bases when drafting that legislation: on Article 100, covering the single market; Article 36, allowing trade restrictions on the grounds of public health or the protection of humans, animals, or plants; and, after 1972, on the catch-all Article 235, which allowed the Commission to draft proposals as a way of achieving the broad objectives laid out in the Treaty. Between 1958 and 1972, these provisions allowed for the construction of the body of legislation that would later usher in a more coherent policy.

The ability to legislate in this way rested largely on a rather generous reading of Article 2 of the Treaty. But there were other hidden environmental measures

TABLE 1.1 *Environmental rule-making competences, 1967–1997*

	Pre-SEA[a] (1967–87)	SEA[a] (1987)–Maastricht (1993)	Maastricht (1993)–Amsterdam (1997)	Amsterdam
Legal basis	None: policy usually made under Articles 100, 235 Occasional use of Article 213 and Article 30 (Euratom)	Articles 130s and 100a Occasional use also of Article 42–43 for CAP related measures, and Article 118a	No major change; some use of Article 130d use of Articles 84(2), 228(3), 75, 113, 32, (Euratom)	No major change, although Article 100a(3) has been modified to extend the obligation to pursue a high standard of protection to the EP and ESC
Council voting	Unanimity	Article 100a: QMV[b]; Article 130s; general principle of unanimity reaffirmed with possibility of QMV allowed for subject to unanimous Council approval	QMV extended to Article 130s in general, but subject to broad and crucial exemptions (fiscal provisions, town and country planning, land use, management of water resources, energy related matters)	No extension of QMV; unanimity exemptions still apply
European Parliament powers	Consultation procedure, conciliation procedure (for acts with financial implications)	Council need only consult Parliament, and this was the case even where the Council decided to reach a decision on a proposal based on Article 130s by QMV. However, the cooperation procedure applied to any majority decisions taken under Article 100a	Cooperation procedure to be employed whenever QMV under Article 130s is used in principle; new co-decision principle to be used in relation to general action programme	Cooperation procedure generally abolished (except for EMU) and co-decision replaces this where it is currently used in Article 130s

[a] Single European Act.
[b] Qualified majority voting.

in the treaty, under the EURATOM Treaty, and within the Common Agricultural Policy (CAP) for example, though these were often incidental.[30] In all, nine directives and one regulation were adopted on this basis. These covered matters such as the regeneration and incineration of used oil; the classification, labelling, and packaging of dangerous substances; the noise levels and exhaust systems of motor vehicles; and countryside protection.[31]

However, it would be an exaggeration to claim that disparate legislative acts of this sort together comprised anything resembling a coherent policy.[32] As we have already seen, the creation of a customs union and the need for harmonization of laws was a priority in the newly created European Union. Removing trade distortions justified action that had implications for environmental protection. What is more, the pace of legislation at this stage in the policy's early evolution was determined exclusively by the member state governments on an *ad hoc* basis. The absence of an institutionalized framework on which to base European-level rules allowed for the dominant role of member states in what little environment policy there was. This amounted to little more than sporadic and unsystematized intergovernmental cooperation. Agendas and priorities were established on the basis of one-off preferences of national governments, as a consequence of specific concerns about progress towards the creation of a common market. The supranational institutions could do little more than react encouragingly to these intergovernmental proposals agreed on the basis of a lowest-common-demominator unanimity in the Council.

By the end of the 1980s, there were approximately 200 pieces of environmental legislation, many of them the product of compromises between differing national perspectives on environmental protection.[33] Uncertainty over the legality of much of the policy was dominated by discussion of whether or not the Commission and Council had acted *ultra vires* in this field, with legal opinion divided on the matter. The absence of a formal framework and of formal powers was a serious drawback to the construction of a coherent, effective, and institutionalized policy. It was not until the late 1980s that a further transformation of the policy was to begin.

Although evidence of any significant supranational activism is hard to find amid the pragmatism of the early years, the rule-shaping capacity of the European Commission is notable at this stage in the developing European environment policy. Although national sources of policy are still crucial, the capacity of the Commission (though perhaps not of the other European institutions) to develop symbolic policies creating a framework of principles, conventions, and informal rules is clear, as is shown for example in the successive action programmes discussed in the next chapter.

From the Single European Act to Maastricht

The White Paper on the completion of the internal market, the project that had originally been the rationale behind the Treaty of Rome, was to become the keystone of European integration in the 1980s.[34] It was based on the argument that a

Europe without barriers to trade would be a leaner, more efficient, and more competitive Europe, capable of holding its own against competition from industries in the USA, Japan, and the newly developing countries of the Far East. A combination of global, European, and indeed domestic developments created an atmosphere within which such dramatic economic and political change could take place. In concrete terms, this led to an ultimate agreement on a series of amendments to the founding treaty, now known as the Single European Act.

The Single European Act summed up the goal of creating a single market in terms of four essential freedoms: 'The internal market shall comprise an area without internal frontiers in which the free movement of goods, persons, services and capital is ensured in accordance with the provisions of this Treaty.'[35] Its aim was to provide a framework of decision-making within which a body of legislation could be proposed and agreed: legislation that would lead to the removal of physical, technical, and fiscal barriers to trade between the member states of the EU.

However, the White Paper on the completion of the internal market that formed the basis of much of the rationale for the Single Act failed to deal with the environmental issue. In spite of this, the Single European Act was heralded as a landmark in the development of a coherent European environment policy. Hildebrand points to three identifiable consequences of the treaty revisions: the direct impact of the soon-to-be-created single market upon the European environment; the effect of the new environmental provisions of the Single European Act; and the impact procedurally and substantively of new voting procedures to be used in EU decision-making.[36]

As we noted earlier, the Single European Act arose from a process that was politically ambiguous. The remarkable conjunction of political forces that combined in the early 1980s to provide the political preconditions for the passing of the Act represented different views about what European integration would bring.[37] Thus, countries like Britain wanted the enlargement of a free trade area that would be an extension abroad of the government's liberalization programme at home; the Mitterrand government in France was looking for a framework in which policies of economic renewal could be pursued without incurring the problems that redistributive Keynesianism had produced in the period 1981–2;[38] the Germans wished to further European integration for security and economic reasons; the less developed countries could see greater access to the structural funds of the EU; and so on. The single market programme in effect grew out of an elite consensus about the economic priorities to be pursued in Europe in the 1980s.

However, the Single European Act was also the device that introduced environmental responsibilities formally into EU policy-making. How did this come about? At one level, it would have been impossible to avoid, given the interrelationships set out in this chapter. There is an issue dynamic between the single market and environmental protection, and some way was needed to cope with the role of environmental standards in the scheme of mutual recognition. However, this problem could have been dealt with simply by an amendment to Article 100. With the introduction of Articles 100a and 100b, there was increased scope for the harmonization of European laws, including laws on environmental matters. These allowed for qualified majority voting when draft legislation reached the Council. The problem of externalities could have been dealt with through the recognition, built into Article 100, that the protection afforded to the environment be at a 'high level'.

In fact, the transformation of the secondary rules went further than this. The provisions of the Single European Act relating to the environment are contained within Title VII of the Treaty 'Environment', Articles 130r–130t. Article 130r laid down the aims and principles of the EU's environment policy. It dealt with the division of competences between the member states and the EU, and called for cooperation with third countries and international organizations on environmental matters. It also spelt out the four criteria to be considered before an environment policy is adopted: the availability of scientific and technical data; environmental conditions among the regions of the Community; the potential costs and benefits of the environmental action to be taken; and the economic and social development of the Community as a whole and its effect on the balanced development of the European regions. Article 130t allowed states to introduce stricter protective measures as long as they did not clash with other provisions in the treaty.

The implications of the new treaty provisions were far-reaching. Their breadth meant that almost any environmental measure could fall under the EU's competence. In a sense, however, the treaty provisions in the Single European Act only served to formalize a policy that existed beforehand. As spelt out in the Action Programmes, policy principles such as integration, polluter pays, rectification at source, and prevention were anything but novel.[39] In this sense the Commission's policy was translated into the formal treaty framework. However, the Single European Act did introduce for the first time the subsidiarity principle (in Article 130r(4)), which stated that the EU should take action only if the desired result could 'be attained better at Community level than at the level of the individual member states'.

How did it come about that Article 130 was inserted in the form that it was in the Single European Act? To some extent, the introduction of the article was only a recognition of what had been happening since 1972 anyway, rather as Molière's Monsieur Jourdain recognized that he had been speaking prose all his life. However, it is difficult to account for the introduction of the competence without invoking at a central point the preferences of the member states. Not only was the environmental competence valued in itself, by member states like the Netherlands and Denmark, but others such as Germany were anxious to protect the 'level playing field' by ensuring that their industries did not bear costs from which their competitors were free. These states were to insist that the amendments to the treaty include a reference to a high level of environmental protection to allay their fears about the effects of the single market.[40]

This demand for a recognition of environmental protection would meet an obvious objection from the southern member states, however, since a high level of environmental protection would stand in the way of their economic development, adding to their costs of production and potentially erecting barriers to trade for their products. In the intergovernmental conference, Ireland and Greece wanted to balance environmental obligations against the needs of economic development, and Greece, Ireland, and Portugal linked their support for the single market, with its implied high standard of environmental protection, to the issue of the cohesion funds.[41]

How then can we explain the Single European Act in the light of these conflicting preferences? It is clear that, in addition to the neo-functionalist logic we have invoked so far, we also need to appeal to an intergovernmentalist explanation that highlights the preferences of member states, and the advantages to some of them of sharing costs with others. To understand the bargain, we need to examine the preferences of both sides. The northern countries wanted the single market with a high standard of environmental protection, but without structural funds for the south. The southern countries wanted the structural funds, but without the single market and the high level of environmental protection. Neither side could achieve their first preference, but the option of the single market with the structural funds and a high level of environmental protection was the second-best outcome for both. In other words, the basic logic was that of a classic log-roll: each side could move away from an unsatisfactory status quo by conceding on the dimension of a complex set of issues that were least important to it.[42] No doubt the motives were more complex than this story suggests, but it makes a great deal of sense of what might otherwise seem obscure.

Within this general context, national governments were keen to see the Single Act provisions reflect their own concerns and priorities. Thus, the insistence on including the criteria of scientific and technical data, as well the recognition of regional conditions, in Article 130r(3) was due to the desire of the British government to safeguard what it saw as the essence of its own approach to environmental action.[43] It has also been suggested that, as far as the UK was concerned, it saw the introduction of environmental competences into Article 130 as a way of containing the issue of environmental protection, little realizing that in subsequent years the pressures on the EU to strengthen its environmental policy would become severe, often to the disadvantage of the UK itself.

It has also been asserted in some accounts that this requirement was insisted upon by the UK to ensure that, as the Commission fleshed out its new powers under Article 130, it would do so mindful of the member states' need for discretion.[44] If this were so, it would suggest that the 'web of unintended consequences' was firmly sown around UK decision-makers, and that rational self-interested preferences by government executives were not a powerful force—at least not in this one case. Although one cannot dismiss this possibility out of hand, we have found no independent evidence for it. Indeed, at the time when the Single European Act was passed there was much discussion in the UK environmental policy network about the significance of the potential clash between Articles 100a and 130r, so there was obviously some awareness of the open-ended nature of the commitment. What is more, there is some evidence both that the German *Länder* favoured putting the principle of subsidiarity on the EU agenda and that at various times Jacques Delors himself thought it could be used as an argument to limit the uncontrolled growth of EU environmental competences.[45]

The main institutional effect of the Single European Act on environmental policy was related to the new procedures for inter-institutional relations, provisions that were also to have a significant impact on substantive policy. The introduction of the cooperation procedure provided a new channel of EU decision-making which allowed the European Parliament a second reading of draft EU legislation. Ultimately this was intended to give the Parliament more of a say over legislative outcomes, though within clearly defined limits. It also, albeit indirectly, was intended to give European publics a greater influence over environmental policy formulation.

Under the Single European Act, the cooperation procedure applied only when a vote was to be taken by a qualified majority in the Council of Ministers. This is why Article 100a was so crucial. Article 100a relates to decisions affecting the completion of the internal market, but it could also be used for environmental purposes where relevant. However, under the new Environment title Articles 100, 235 (the basis of pre-1985 environmental legislation), and 130s, all required unanimity within the Council. The treaty provision (or legal base) selected for use by the Commission would determine not only the role to be played by the European Parliament, but also the extent to which the legislation required the unanimous or qualified majority support of member state governments. Hence the Single European Act changes created the possibility of a number of procedural wrangles, which were bound to affect relations between the European institutions and national governments, and which were particularly important in the case of the European Parliament and the Council of Ministers.

As we shall see subsequently, European institutions came gradually, and largely on the basis of the Single European Act provisions, to play an increasingly purposive environmental role within the policy process. Yet the capacity of Commission, Court, and Parliament to act independently was as much a source of inter-institutional rivalry as the supranational bodies vied with each other for power and influence over environmental policy-making. This was no doubt exacerbated by specific procedural rules created in the Single European Act. While the purposiveness of the European institutions might potentially be a force for institutionalized stability within the emerging system of environmental governance, it was at this point more of a source of confusion and insecurity.

The Maastricht Treaty and After

After 1987, environmental action by national governments, the European Commission, and the international community coalesced at the European level to create a new momentum for a more innovative and activist approach to environmental policy. Among the EU governments, this momentum in support of further reform of environmental decision-making grew as the prospect of yet another treaty change approached. While environmental questions were at first excluded from discussion at the 1991 intergovernmental conference on political union, which culminated in the Maastricht summit in December of that year, this did not deter those seeking to campaign for greater environmental clarity and effectiveness, though there were of course the inevitable differences of opinion among the member states.

Although the final version of the Treaty on European Union (TEU) did not satisfy those who had sought to place environmental matters at the heart of the new Union, the environmental provisions of the TEU did effectively 'green' the EU Treaty. Not only did the Preamble of the TEU now talk about the promotion of 'economic and social progress for their peoples within the context of the accomplishment of the internal market and of reinforced cohesion and environmental protection', but it also amended the pivotal Article 2. Previously, this had stated that one of the key goals of the Treaty was the promotion of 'continuous and balanced expansion'. After Maastricht, it was to refer to the need for 'a harmonious and balanced development of economic activities, sustainable and non-inflationary growth respecting the environment'. Further, Article 3(k) now stated, symbolically, that the Community was to include a 'policy in the sphere of the environment', confirming that the environment had become a fully fledged European policy.[46] Previously, the Single European Act had referred only to 'action by the Community relating to the environment'. Title XVI of the TEU dealt specifically with the environment, in Articles 130r–130t. The new treaty changes also set up a Cohesion Fund, which was to contribute to the environmental costs of the four poorest EU states.

As with the Single European Act, however, the most important political change at Maastricht was that affecting the passing of legislation. While the new co-decision procedure was to be used for the agreement of the Action Programmes, the cooperation procedure was to be the norm for the large majority environmental policy decisions. Both procedures involve the use of majority voting in the Council. There were, all the same, a few exceptions to this majority rule. These involve legislation on fiscal matters; on environmental issues with limited transnational implications (such as town and country planning); some aspects of water pollution policy; and policies likely to affect national energy policies. In spite of these excluded areas, the TEU in effect confirmed the use of qualified majority voting in the Council for most environmental legislation.[47] In so doing, it went a considerable way towards countering the earlier criticism levelled at the Single European Act that the Treaty's ambivalence over voting procedures and treaty bases was unnecessarily confrontational and confusing.

It also made it clear that the European Parliament was to play an even more important role in environmental decision-making than it had done in the past. The new co-decision procedure introduced under Article 189b allowed for the possibility of three different readings by the Council and Parliament, ending in cases of dispute with the intervention of a Conciliation Committee. Indeed, this has proven the worth of the environment policy as a test-case for other European policies, as in the first year of co-decision half of all procedures fell in the environment sphere. Such institutional changes, while they do not of themselves determine policy outcomes, play a significant role in shaping the balance among EU-level institutions.

Since Maastricht, the European Court of Justice (ECJ) has also had the capacity to fine national governments for failing to comply with its judgments. This is likely to have a significant impact on non-compliance rates.[48] The role of the ECJ was enhanced further over this period as a result of the increasing awareness and willingness of environmental groups to use the appeal process to embarrass member state governments over non-compliance with environmental legislation.

With the Treaty of Amsterdam, the most significant procedural change is the replacement of the cooperation procedure by the co-decision procedure, a change that strengthens the role of the European Parliament in the making of policy. This in turn can be expected further to strengthen the tendencies towards horizontal complexity that are discussed in Part III. The treaty also incorporates the principle of sustainable development, with the requirement that it be integrated with other policies. How far this will grow into more than a rhetorical commitment, only time will tell.

CONCLUSIONS

What general conclusions can be drawn about the origins of environmental policy from the analysis presented so far? At the beginning of the chapter we set out the idea of an issue dynamic, an unravelling set of questions which successively posed new problems for policy-makers. There are, we suggest, four points to be stressed about the character of this issue dynamic.

Firstly, the logic of issue linkage clearly applies to the case of the single market and environmental policy. The creation of the single market inevitably raises questions about environmental protection. At first these problems relate principally to the effects of environmental protection measures on the workings of the single market. However, as the single market acquires greater momentum in its development, so questions are raised, as they were in the Task Force report, on the consequences of the single market for the EU's environmental policy. Although these questions are not exclusively those of standards, inevitably they concern the issue of standards in large part. This is partly because it is the setting of standards that initially poses the prospect of there being environmental protection barriers to trade, partly because the balance between economic growth and environmental protection focuses on the stringency of environmental standards that should be imposed on products and manufacturing processes, and partly because the attempt to reconceptualize the problem of European economic competitiveness in terms of the ideology of ecological modernization carries the implication that high environmental standards are an essential precondition for improved economic performance.

Secondly, issue linkage was not of itself sufficient to shape the form and character of EU environmental policy. The preferences of member states, determined by the changing patterns of their own domestic policy processes, were important in determining the extent to which the authority to make environmental rules was to be transferred to the European level. More particularly, a transfer of some degree became impossible to resist once a large member state like Germany became convinced of the importance of legislating on a European level, if only to avoid competitive disadvantage in one of its own industries. Conversely, the UK was able to attenuate the force of the transfer by its insistence that policy-making be subject to criteria that it favoured.

Thirdly, the unfolding of the issue dynamic touches on some of the central topics in the politics of European integration. The challenge to the prevailing assumptions of how integration is best promoted through a single market is potentially profound. Once environmental considerations are brought to bear on the performance of the single market, questions are raised about whether an increase in the total volume of goods and services that are traded in the single market provides the best index to the economic and social welfare of the citizens of Europe. Moreover, given that changes in political procedures were necessary in order to achieve the implementation of the single market, it becomes impossible to isolate questions about the relationship between the single market and environmental protection from broader questions about the legitimacy of EU decision-making procedures.[49] No one can pretend that such controversies do not go to the heart of the processes of European integration.

Fourthly, and finally, it is clear that these controversies over environment and the single market raise broader political questions about the extent to which there is consensus about the character of the issues involved. So far we have only hinted at the differences in priorities and preferences of the national governments that have to bargain with one another, through the Council of Ministers, about environmental standards and their implications for the single market. Yet it is clear that these differences are often profound, and touch not simply on the stringency of standards to be imposed on polluting activities, but also on the place of environmental policy within the development of European integration. There are competing national policy styles, preferences, and priorities that are important in shaping European environmental policy, played out in unstable institutional processes. It is to the exploration of the consequences of these differences that the rest of our book will be devoted.

NOTES TO CHAPTER 1

1. P. M. Hildebrand, 'The European Community's Environmental Policy, 1957 to "1992": From Incidental Measures to an International Regime?' *Environmental Politics*, 1:4 (1992), pp. 13–44.
2. For useful general treatments, see O. R. Young, *International Cooperation: Building Regimes for Natural Resources and the Environment* (Ithaca, NY: Cornell University Press, 1989) and *International Governance: Protecting the Earth in a Stateless Society* (Ithaca, NY, and London: Cornell University Press, 1994).
3. D. Brack, 'Balancing Trade and the Environment', *International Affairs*, 71:3 (1995), pp. 497–514. More generally, see D. Vogel, *Trading Up* (Cambridge, Mass., and London: Harvard University Press, 1995).
4. Ibid. 498–501.
5. Other standards include source standards (such as process or emission standards), environmental standards (such as environmental quality standards), and target standards (such as biological or exposure standards). See B. Verhoeve and G. Bennett, 'Products and the Environment: An International Overview of Recent Developments', *European Environmental Law Review*, 31:3 (1994), p. 75. See, more generally, N. Haigh, *Manual of Environmental Policy: The EC and Britain* (London: Cartermill International, 1992 *et seq.*), ch. 3; A. Ogus, 'Standard Setting for Environmental Protection: Principles and Processes', in M. Faure, J. Vervaele, and A. Weale (eds.), *Environmental Standards in the European Union in an Interdisciplinary Framework* (Antwerp: MAKLU, 1994), pp. 25–37; and Royal Commission on Environmental Pollution, *Twenty-First Report: Setting Environmental Standards*, Cm. 4053 (London: The Stationery Office, 1998), pp. 3–5.
6. 70/157/EEC. This and its successors are discussed in Haigh, *Manual of Environmental Policy*, ch. 10.2.
7. For discussion, see Haigh, *Manual*, ch. 10.4 on 74/151/EEC for farm vehicles, and ch. 7.7 on 73/404/EEC for detergents.
8. Law no. 297, 08.06.78, and Order no. 397, 02.07.81.
9. Order 95, 16.03.84.
10. Commission of the European Communities, *Research on 'The Costs of Non-Europe' Executive Summaries: Groupe MAC, Technical Barriers in the EC* (Luxembourg: Commission of the European Communities, 1988), p. 22.
11. *Commission* v. *Denmark*, Case 302/86.
12. For an interesting discussion of the implications of this approach, see S. Woodcock, 'Competition among the Rules in the European Union', in D. G. Mayes (ed.), *The Evolution of the Single European Market* (Cheltenham, Glos.: Edward Elgar, 1997), pp. 66–86.
13. *Rewe-Zentrale AG* v. *Bundesmonopolverwaltung für Branntwein ('Cassis de Dijon')*, Case C-120/78.
14. M. Wise and R. Gibb, *Single Market to Social Europe* (Harlow: Longman, 1993), p. 77.
15. See Verhoeve and Bennett, 'Products and the Environment'. It is also worth noting that, to the extent to which consumers have preferences among products based on the way in which they were produced, as they do for example with wood from tropical rain forests, the distinction between product and process regulation is elided.

16. S. Boehmer-Christiansen and J. Skea, *Acid Politics* (London and New York: Belhaven, 1991), p. 203.
17. See the quotations in J. Golub, *British Integration into the EEC: A Case Study of European Environmental Policy*, D.Phil. thesis (Oxford University, 1994), pp. 131–3.
18. Haigh, *Manual*, p. 3.11.
19. Council Resolution of 3 December 1992 on Administrative Simplification for Enterprises, especially Small and Medium-Sized Enterprises, *Official Journal of the European Communities*, C 331/03 (16 December 1992).
20. Commission of the European Community, *XXIIIrd Competition Report*, COM(94) 161 Final, point 168. For further discussion, see Ch. 12 below.
21. G. Garrett, 'International Cooperation and Institutional Choice: The European Community's Internal Market', *International Organization*, 46:2 (1992), pp. 533–60. For a good journalistic treatment of these mixed motives, see C. Grant, *Delors: Inside the House that Jacques Built* (London: Nicholas Brealey, 1994), ch. 5.
22. M. Albert, *Capitalism against Capitalism*, trans. P. Haviland (London: Whurr, 1993).
23. A. C. Pigou, *The Economics of Welfare* (London: Macmillan, 1952, 4th edn), p. 184.
24. For a discussion of these ideas, see any good microeconomics text, e.g. D. M. Kreps, *A Course in Microeconomic Theory* (New York: Harvester Wheatsheaf, 1990), ch. 6.
25. N. Haigh and D. Baldock, *Environmental Policy and 1992* (London: Institute for European Environmental Policy, 1989), p. 45.
26. See A. Weale and A. Williams, 'Between Economy and Ecology? The Single Market and the Integration of Environmental Policy', *Environmental Politics*, 1:4 (1992), pp. 45–64.
27. Task Force on the Environment and the Internal Market, '1992: The Environmental Dimension', mimeo, 1989.
28. *The Economist*, 'A Survey of Waste and the Environment', 29 May 1993, p. 23.
29. *Commission v. Belgium*, Case C-2/90.
30. J. Lodge, 'Environment: Towards a Clean Blue–Green EC', in J. Lodge (ed.), *The European Community and the Challenge of the Future* (London: Pinter, 1989), p. 320.
31. See Hildebrand, 'The European Community's Environmental Policy', p. 19, who follows E. Rehbinder and R. Stewart, *Environmental Protection Policy* (Berlin and New York: Walter de Gruyter, 1985), pp. 16–17.
32. Hildebrand, 'The European Community's Environmental Policy', p. 19.
33. N. Haigh, 'A Green Agenda for the IGC: The Future of EU Environment Policy', paper for UACES conference, London, 29 March 1996.
34. Commission of the European Communities, *Completing the Internal Market*, COM(85) 310 final (Luxembourg: Commission of the European Communities, 1985).
35. Single European Act, *Official Journal of the European Communities*, L 169 (26 June 1987).
36. Hildebrand, 'The European Community's Environmental Policy', p. 34.
37. See e.g. Garrett, 'International Cooperation and Institutional Choice'.
38. P. A. Hall, *Governing the Economy* (Cambridge: Polity Press, 1986), pp. 195–98.
39. See the next chapter.
40. R. Corbett, 'The 1985 Intergovernmental Conference and the Single European Act', in R. Pryce (ed.), *The Dynamics of European Union* (London: Croom Helm, 1987), p. 246.
41. Ibid. 245, 249.

42. This formalizes a suggestion put in an interview with a high-ranking Commission official in Brussels.

43. R. Wurzel, 'Environmental Policy', in J. Lodge (ed.), *The European Community and the Challenge of the Future* (London: Pinter Press, 1993, 2nd edn), pp. 182–3, citing L. Krämer, *EEC Treaty and Environmental Protection* (London: Sweet & Maxwell, 1990), p. 67, and D. Vandermeersch, 'The Single European Act and the Environmental Policy of the European Economic Community', *European Law Review*, 12:6 (1987), p. 420.

44. J. Golub, 'Sovereignty and Subsidiarity in EU Environmental Policy', *Political Studies*, 44:4 (1996), pp. 688–91.

45. The former point is noted by Golub, 'Sovereignty and Subsidiarity', p. 689, citing J. Steiner, 'Subsidiarity under the Maastricht Treaty', in D. O'Keefe and P. Twomey (eds.), *Legal Issues of the Maastricht Treaty* (London: Chancery, 1994), p. 51. For Delors' position, see Grant, *Delors*, pp. 107–9 and 214.

46. Hildebrand, 'The European Community's Environmental Policy', p. 37.

47. Ibid.

48. J. D. Liefferink, *The Making of European Environmental Policy* (Manchester: Manchester University Press, 1996), p. 8.

49. On the general question of political legitimacy and the single market programme, see A. Weale, 'The Single Market, European Integration and Political Legitimacy', in D. G. Mayes (ed.), *The Evolution of the Single European Market* (Cheltenham, Glos.: Edward Elgar, 1997), pp. 199–225. See also Ch. 15 below for our own conclusions on these points.

2

Programmes, Principles, and Policies

In the previous chapter we argued that there was an issue dynamic linking the single market programme, as the major force for the renewal of European integration, with environmental policy. In this sense, issue linkage and consequent spillover have been characteristic of the development of EU environmental policy. However, in addition to the logic of spillover, we also saw that a series of intergovernmental bargains was necessary, both to give formal place to environmental policy in treaty reforms and to define the substantive scope and concerns that were to fall to the responsibility of the EU. These intergovernmental bargains were in one sense simply a formal recognition of the institutionalization of environmental policy that had taken place since 1972. However, they can still be regarded as an important element in their own right, part of the process by which environmental policy measures acquired a range and scope going beyond anything that could be conceivably related solely to the single market.

Institutionalization implies some degree of autonomy. To say that a policy field is institutionalized is to say that policy decisions are made according to the rules, conventions, norms, and practices that define the institution in which policy is made. Yet origins are still important. The issue dynamic deriving from integration through the single market led to a piecemeal and pragmatic development of environmental policy measures. To some extent this was compounded by the opportunistic policy style of the Commission, which meant that policy-making followed the logic of favourable openings in the ebb and flow of events, as well as the segmented and technical nature of much early policy, which meant that developments were often not coordinated. We can observe this in the heterogeneous nature of the policies that have been adopted, a cross-section of which are summarized in Box 2.1.

Despite the varied nature of these policies, we shall argue in this chapter that there has always been an attempt to articulate a principled content and rationale for EU environmental policy. The established policies are thus more than a series of discrete measures: they also constitute a policy field in which there has been an increasingly sophisticated attempt to develop a policy paradigm. EU institutions are not simply organizations and their associated rules for making decisions; they have also become developers of policy principles. They not only make decisions; they also seek to provide a rationale for the decisions that they make in terms of an understanding about what these policy problems are and how best they are to

Box 2.1 Illustrative Examples of EU Environmental Policy Measures (by date order of earliest measure)

Vehicle Emissions (70/220). This was a series of directives, beginning in 1970, aimed at controlling the emission of pollutants from vehicles, especially carbon monoxide, nitrogen oxides, and particulates.

Bathing Waters (76/160). The purpose of this directive is to raise the quality of bathing waters over time through the control of sewage. The directive sets maximum permissible concentrations of 19 pollutants found in bathing waters.

Titanium Dioxide Emissions (78/176). The directive aims to control the emission of titanium dioxide into water. It seeks to ensure that all member states have an adequate authorization scheme in place.

Environmental Impact Assessment (85/337). This directive requires the carrying out of an environmental impact assessment according to certain minimum standards before a large development project (e.g. road-building) can take place. It provides a list of projects for which environmental impact assessment is mandatory, although it does not impose constraints on the final decision.

Control of Emissions from Large Stationary Sources (88/609). This directive seeks to limit acidifying emissions, especially sulphur dioxide and nitrogen oxides, from stationary sources (e.g. power stations). Member states were required to draw up national emission reduction plans and to impose emission limit values on all plant above a certain size coming into operation from July 1987.

Genetically Modified Organisms (90/62). This directive aims to create a system of reporting and notification of technical information regarding the release of genetically modified organisms into the environment. The reporting procedures are required to meet certain standards, for example a maximum period of time within which the competent authorities have to be informed of the technical details.

Urban Waste Water (91/271). The purpose of this directive is to control the pollution of freshwaters, estuarine, and coastal waters. The directive seeks to achieve this aim by requiring all centres of population over 2,000 persons to have adequate sewerage systems by 2000 or 2005, depending on size.

Packaging Waste (94/62). This directive seeks to reduce the volume of packaging waste while harmonizing certain aspects of national waste management strategies and reducing barriers to trade. It requires member states to establish return, collection, and recovery systems, with targets for the recovery of waste for purposes other than disposal.

Protection of the Ozone Layer (3093/94). This regulation implements for EU countries the Montreal Protocol of the Vienna Convention, by placing restrictions on the production and distribution of CFCs and other substances that deplete stratospheric ozone.

Air Quality (96/62). This directive builds upon and consolidates earlier directives on air quality in respect of specific substances, e.g. lead. It provides a framework within which certain standards can be achieved for the control of air pollution. The directive also establishes a framework for the reporting of information on air quality.

be tackled. The EU policy paradigm, we shall argue, is one that policy-makers have sought to develop over time, so that we can observe an increasing elaboration of its constituent themes.

The intellectual dimension of policy, and in particular the need to understand policy paradigms, has been stressed in much work on the policy process of national systems.[1] A particularly important feature of this work is the suggestion that policies cluster around a core set of intellectual commitments that help define the character of the problems they are responsible for and provide paradigmatic solutions to those problems.[2] In this chapter we look at the extent to which a distinctive intellectual core understanding about the place of environmental policy in Europe has been developed alongside the expansion of policy functions and competences. Since we are looking at the development of policy principles, our account is concerned in part with the evolution of policy from its origins and in part with the way in which policy is currently conceived.

It is useful to draw a distinction between the *content* of policy on the one hand and the *rationale* or *justification* of policy on the other. Policy content is defined not only by specific policy measures, but also by the principles that the specific measures are thought to embody. Yet explicating content in terms of general principles is still different from providing a justification for adopting those principles, a distinction that we can illustrate with a simple example. If we say, as the EU does, that policy should aim at a high level of environmental protection in the making of its rules, then that principle in part defines the content of policy. Providing a justification or rationale for such a principle is a different matter, however; indeed, there may be a variety of reasons why policy-makers might choose to adopt such a stance, ranging from the belief that a high standard of protection bestows a competitive economic advantage on the system in which the high standards are implemented, through the view that quality-of-life considerations are needed to moderate a simple emphasis upon unrestricted economic growth, to a belief that a high standard of environmental protection presages a necessary fundamental restructuring of society. Policy content thus stands to rationale as conclusion stands to premiss.

In terms of rationale, we shall argue that there developed among EU policy-makers by the 1980s an elaborate account of the role of environmental policy in a modern society which played an important part in providing them with a legitimating discourse. We term this discourse 'ecological modernization'.[3] However, this is not to say that the discourse of ecological modernization was fully accepted within the institutional framework of European policy-making. Indeed, its ambiguities may well have reflected the complex political context within which environmental policy was being developed. Moreover, there is also an important question as to how far this discourse was politically effective, a problem that we raise at the end of the chapter.

In order to situate this discourse, it will be useful to look first at original conceptualizations of environmental policy in the EU.

POLICY CONTENT: THE ACTION PROGRAMMES

If we take a cross-section of EU policy measures, they appear to be diverse, and to reflect in both content and scope the circumstances in which they developed, most notably the policy-making style referred to above. We can see this if we look at the sample of measures identified in Box 2.1. It would be difficult to find a clear set of intellectual principles to explain why the EU is regulating not only international public goods, such as the protection of the environment from acidification or reductions in the emissions of greenhouse gases, but also local public goods, such as urban air quality or the quality of bathing waters. Moreover, the basis of standard-setting for a particular piece of legislation often depends on the particular national champion that originally advanced the measure. In large degree, it is impossible to escape the fact that there is an opportunistic and contingent character to the measures that have been adopted.

However, this is not to say that the content of policy is defined purely by the individual measures. In addition to those individual measures, the EU has always sought to define more general stances and conceptions of policy to provide a framework within which particular measures could find a place. One way of looking at the development of this general policy view is through an analysis of the Action Programmes. Though not legally binding, the Action Programmes are political declarations, reflecting the conceptualization of policy behind the practice of EU environmental policy.

The origin of the Action Programmes can be traced back to the earliest stages of EU environmental policy. The Paris summit, which was held on 19–20 October 1972, is now considered a landmark date in the emergence of a European-level environment policy. It began a process of change that would formalize and eventually institutionalize environmental policy at a supranational level. The declaration issued at the end of the summit called upon the EU institutions to develop an Action Programme on the environment by the end of July 1973. On 31 December 1972 ministers responsible for the environment met in Bonn, and the results of that meeting, together with documents from the member states and opinions from the Commission, the European Parliament, the Economic and Social Committee, and employers' and employees' organizations, formed the basis of the First Environmental Action Programme.[4] This was submitted by the Commission to the Council in April 1973 and was agreed in the November of that year. For the first time, it was stated by the Commission that economic growth was not an end in itself, and that reducing disparities in living conditions between the member states should be a primary EU objective. Although the Action Programme remained in legislative limbo, it did at least provide a framework within which environmental legislation could be drafted and agreed, setting out as it did the principles upon which laws might be based.[5]

Behind the earliest initiatives, it is possible to detect the influence of various political pressures, in particular those from the general public and from the international community, influencing national governments from all sides.[6] Industrial actors also saw the advantages of equalizing the environmental burden by creating a level playing field for the EU firms. Thus, we can see that, although political and social movements seeking improved quality-of-life measures, and policies of environmental protection and industrial pressures seeking a common regulatory framework, might be aiming at different ends, the measures they were forced to invoke were similar. Each saw in the construction of a European environment policy a way of achieving their own objectives. This was clear from the early legislative measures, such as the directive on vehicle emissions, or the common classification, packaging, and labelling of dangerous substances.

Behind the individual policy measures, however, larger issues of principle were broached. The declaration issued at the end of the Paris summit stated that economic expansion was not an end in itself: that the focus was on quality-of-life issues and living standards, rather than on environmental protection in its own right.[7] This emphasis on quality-of-life objectives was echoed in the Council's declaration on the First Action Programme of 22 November 1973, although the Council did bring in environmental protection as a factor:

[T]he task of the European Economic Community is to promote throughout the Community a harmonious development of economic activities and a continued and balanced expansion, which cannot now be imagined in the absence of an effective campaign to combat pollution and nuisances or of an improvement in the quality of life and the protection of the environment.[8]

The sentiments found in the Action Programme and in the Council declaration followed the same line as had the treaty in setting down the improvement of living and working conditions and the harmonious development of the EU economies as important goals. The sound management of resources was another of its main objectives.[9] So, rather than highlighting ecological issues or problems pure and simple, the Action Programmes were designed to initiate projects that would be of benefit to the peoples of the EU and its environment. Initially, these were broken down into three categories:

1. action to reduce or prevent pollution;
2. action to improve the environment and living conditions;
3. action in international organizations relating to the environment.[10]

Much of the First Action Programme was concerned, therefore, with setting out the requirements that would enable these objectives to be met. Such requirements were related mainly to perceived gaps in scientific knowledge and methodologies. The measures suggested were thus concerned primarily with the harmonization of activities and standards across the EU.

Since the First Action Programme was adopted in 1973, there have been four further programmes. The second, basically a continuation of the first, covered the years 1977–82. The Third Action Programme was in force from 1983 to 1987, with the Fourth and Fifth covering the post-Single European Act period up to the end of the century. All five Action Programmes provided important indications of policy orientation and suggested more specific measures to be pursued. They also reflected the spirit of the times, illustrating the gradual increase in concern over environmental issues, and the broadening scope of political activity in environmental matters. Through the window of the Action Programmes, it is possible to chart the development of European thinking on environmental matters.

The Second Action Programme (1977–82) continued to emphasize the need for complementary research and for educating citizens so that individuals will become aware of their responsibilities towards the environment.[11] It was clear that better coordination would be required to avoid duplication of effort across the EU and to speed up assessments of policy alternatives; and that the polluter-pays principle, highlighted in the programme, would need to be defined and explained in order for it to be used effectively as a policy instrument. It was also acknowledged that, to have a comprehensive environmental regime, the EU would need to continue its activities in international organizations.[12]

Specific measures taken to reduce pollution and nuisances over these early years included the priority investigation of the effect of lead, organic halogens, and hydrocarbons.[13] The Second Action Programme included plans to look at the problems of synergisms between pollutants and natural factors such a meteorology.[14] It was also recognized that the setting of standards was important, but that some substances would require further investigation before standards could be set for them. Named substances for which standards should be set as a priority included mercury, cadmium, organic chlorines and toxic chemicals, and micro-organisms in drinking water, as these were believed to be detrimental to human health.[15] There was also to be increased surveillance to aid the detection of law-breaking, as well as to improve ecosystemic understanding; and it was stated that quality objectives would henceforth be set with regard to local conditions.[16] Fresh surface waters and sea water were to be the first areas to be covered by quality objectives. This involved discussion of water uses, the establishment of a common methodology, the collation of data, and the determination of the level of decision making and action.[17]

The Second Action Programme listed the directives resulting from these investigations and pointed out the need to continue the work begun in 1973.[18] In looking at specific products and their pollution problems, work was initiated on vehicle noise and air pollution.[19] The Second Action Programme went on to extend this, giving slightly more space to problems caused by noise pollution.[20] Sectoral action was intended with a view to investigating technical measures which reduce pollution and improve the implementation of European legislation.[21] The priority sectors were identified as the paper and pulp industries, the titanium dioxide industry, and the iron and steel industry. Further studies were to be undertaken in the chemicals industry, the leather industry, and the wool industry. A third stage of investigation included other chemical industries, the food industry, the metallurgical industries, and the textile industries.[22] At the time, there was also concern about thermal, atmospheric, and water pollution caused by the energy-generating sector;[23] the long-term threat of marine pollution;[24] the protection of the Rhine Basin;[25] waste disposal;[26] and radioactive wastes.[27] The Second Action Programme continued work on these measures, introducing some specifics, such as eutrophication and pesticides, which required special investigation.[28]

By the time the Third Action Programme (1982–7) was agreed, the Council was careful to establish a list of priority areas. This was linked to a broadening of objectives as compared with the first two Action Programmes. The Third Action Programme thus had 13 areas of priority: integration; environmental impact assessments; reduction at source (especially of air pollution); reduction of marine pollution; reduction of soil pollution; the Mediterranean; noise; transfrontier pollution; hazardous chemicals; waste management; clean technology; environmentally sensitive areas; and cooperation with the developing world.[29] While there were obvious continuities, with projects like education and the reduction of marine pollution taken directly from the first two Action Programmes, other areas, such as soil pollution and the Mediterranean, were prioritized for the first time. The Action Programme also sought to develop further arguments along economic and competition lines in favour of strict environmental standards, for example to keep European cars competitive on the Japanese and US markets.[30] In retrospect, this can be seen as an anticipation of the central theme of ecological modernization.[31]

However, in spite of policy aims that were often far-reaching, the continued use of unanimous voting within the Council constrained action. In practice, the need to justify environmental policy in terms that were consistent with economic imperatives meant that lowest-common-denominator solutions were often the unsurprising consequence of policy debates around this time. None the less, substantive policy over this 15-year period covered a wide range of media, issues, and problems. The period was marked by increasing involvement of the EU in the international sphere, with European participation in, for example, the Washington Convention on Trade in Endangered Species (CITES) and the Bonn Convention on the Conservation of Migratory Species.[32] Legislation regulating air, water, noise pollution, waste disposal, the prevention of accidents, safety requirements for chemicals, wildlife, and habitat, as well as legislation introducing environmental impact assessments, was approved by the Council, though perhaps one of the most important priorities during this phase of European environment policy involved attempts to improve European water quality.

Since the ratification and implementation of the Single European Act (SEA), the policy of the late 1980s and early 1990s began to differ from that of the 1970s and early 1980s. Yet there are inevitably strands of continuity running through the last two decades. However, 'it would be too simplistic to regard it as a mere continuation of previous policy developments'.[33] The Fourth Action Programme, covering the years 1987–92, was produced not only to ensure continuity between the pre- and post-SEA eras, but also to confirm the new approach within the new treaty. In providing a legal base affording environment a high level of protection, the SEA allowed the Fourth Action Programme to use rather more ambitious language in expressing its goals, as the treaty allowed

that action taken by the Community relating to the environment shall be based on the principles that preventative action should be taken, that environmental damage should as a priority be rectified at source, and that the polluter should pay.[34]

Nineteen priorities were highlighted,[35] including some slight changes from those included in the Third Action Programme. These were: the development of strict environmental standards; integration; environmental impact assessments; the implementation of the polluter-pays principle; at source reduction of pollution; multimedia analysis of pollution; noise pollution; hazardous chemicals; biotechnology; nuclear installations; waste management; clean technology; transboundary pollution; environmentally sensitive areas; the Mediterranean; erosion and water management; cost effectiveness of action; participation in international organizations; and cooperation with developing countries. Alongside these areas of priority, emphasis was placed on the need to ensure the effective implementation of policy and to integrate environmental concerns into other EU policies, especially in planning policy, and on the potential benefits to be attained through strict environmental protection. This last point was a hint of the extent to which the justification of policy was beginning to be couched in terms of ecological modernization.

Monitoring and research subsequently became more important, exemplified by the July 1988 Task Force on the Greenhouse Effect[36] and by a preoccupation with environmental impact assessment. Attention continued to be placed on the control of pollution and more especially on the control of potentially dangerous noxious substances such as nitric oxide and sulphur dioxide emissions. Funds from the European Regional Development Fund were provided to assist in environmental projects for the first time, and the European Investment Bank contributed loans to that end. Conservation became a high priority, and popular awareness of environmental issues was further enhanced after a number of environmental disasters, Chernobyl being perhaps the most dramatic.[37]

Over this period a wide range of directives were issued—on ecosystem research, afforestation, protection of wildlife, biotechnology, animal experiments, water protection, the dumping of wastes, and sewage sludge in farming. Many of these directives sought to adopt a more preventive or anticipatory approach. This was highlighted in the principles that were set out in the Fourth Action Programme, which defined:

[the] challenge to make a definitive move away from reacting to environmental problems after they have arisen towards a general preventive approach based on the achievement of high standards in all environmental sectors, achieved through devoting a small part of the

EU's huge scientific technological and industrial resources and potential towards developing and bringing into use the equipment, technologies, management and administrative practices needed to achieve such standards; and at the same time to find means of deriving economic and employment gains from such a move.[38]

This effectively sums up the entire mood of EU environmental policy in the period after the Single European Act.

While the initial rationale behind EU environmental policy was concern about market distortions caused by national environmental regulations, and the original reasons for protecting the environment were related to the quality of life for the peoples of the EU, the Fifth Environmental Action Programme was emphatically titled *Towards Sustainability* and was explicitly global in its approach.[39] In many important ways, the Fifth Environmental Action Programme represented a departure for European environmental policy-making. Originally resulting from a political commitment made in the Dublin Declaration, it drew on the Dutch National Environmental Policy Plan and on Swedish, French, and Canadian environment plans, all of which in turn found their roots in the Brundtland report.[40]

The Fifth Action Programme was to differ from previous Programmes in that it revolved around themes, such as that of 'shared responsibility' and 'partnership', rather than around environmental problems, one important respect in which it followed the approach pioneered in the 1989 Dutch National Environmental Policy Plan. It sought to sketch new institutional structures and to introduce a bottom-up approach to environmental action, focusing on specific actors rather than on European regulatory mechanisms.[41] In addition to selecting target groups for specific action and creating new consultative forums, the 1992 Action Programme explicitly committed the member states of the EU to making their activities sustainable.

The first four Action Programmes cover the shift from thinking about environmental deterioration only in terms of its impact on people to embracing a commitment to protect the environment for its own sake. The Fifth Action Programme takes this gradual shift into a rather different gear; the explicit acceptance of the need to pursue sustainable development reflects the realization that environmental damage has long-lasting and far-reaching effects. Environmental policy is bound to be ineffective if it is piecemeal and uncoordinated. The Fifth Action Programme represents an attempt to cope with both the holistic character of environmental problems and the economically driven integration of Europe. Here again, it was influenced by the thinking of the Dutch Environmental Policy Plan, in which the focus was on moving away in policy terms from controlling pollution as an effect to dealing with the underlying causes of pollution.

Effective implementation was central, according to this programme. Procedurally, the focus on administrative subsidiarity, on improved dialogue not only between the European institutions but also between different levels of government, and on clearer relations with environmental lobbies meant that attention would be shifted, as it was elsewhere in European affairs, from initiation and decision-making to the consolidation and management of policies already in existence. Five target sectors were listed: industry, energy, transport, agriculture, and tourism. In these areas it was expected that the EU would have a special role. The programme sought, within this framework, to establish long-term priorities and policy objectives, and to set performance targets, something that had been seen as a step forward from previous Action Programmes.[42] In identifying these target sectors, the Fifth Action Programme was representative of what many saw as a changed style of environmental policy in the EU in the 1990s, compared with the 1980s, involving less emphasis on the passing of legislative measures and more on securing the cooperation of key actors. One official in our interviews quoted a Dutch proverb in this context: You catch more birds with sugar than with salt.

So far we have looked at general thinking on environmental policy and at its development as seen in successive Action Programmes. However, it is clear that, within this general thinking, attention has been paid to specific policy principles, and in the next section we look at some of the most important.

POLICY CONTENT: GENERAL PRINCIPLES

Through the Action Programmes and in other ways, policy-makers within the European Union have sought to provide a set of principles to guide developments and to justify measures that are taken. Together, these principles constitute the core of EU policy discourse. It would be a mistake to suppose that the new discourse emerged in a fully developed form, or even that there was always a conscious awareness that a transformation was taking place. But the institutionalization of EU environmental policy governance has to be understood, in part at least, in terms of the emergence of this new discourse; and in the remainder of this section we shall summarize, in a somewhat formal way, what we see as its main elements.

EU environmental policy documents, treaties, and legislation are characterized by the use of various principles. In order to reduce these to manageable dimensions, we can group them into four broad categories: (i) principles concerned with sound environmental management, in which category we include principles like that of prevention and action at source; (ii) principles concerned with the level at which environmental standards should be set, including a commitment to the prudent use of natural resources and to a high level of environmental protection in the setting of standards as well as the principle of precaution; (iii) principles concerned with the basis of task assignment in a system of multi-level governance, which include the principle of locating functions at the appropriate level or the principle of subsidiarity; and (iv) principles concerned with the integration of environmental considerations with other sectors of public policy, including the polluter-pays principle, the principle of integration, and the principle of sustainable development. Table 2.1 lists these principles and indicates in which action

TABLE 2.1 *Principles of EU environmental policy*

Principle	Action Programme	Single European Act	Maastricht
Environmental management			
Prevention	First	Yes	Yes
Action at source	First	Yes	Yes
Integrated pollution control	Fourth	No	No
Level of standard			
Prudent use	First	Yes	Yes
High standard	No	Yes	Yes
Precaution	No	No	Yes
Task assignement			
Appropriate level	First	No	No
Subsidiarity	No	Yes	Yes
External integration			
Polluter pays	First	Yes	Yes
Integration	Fourth	Yes	Yes
Sustainable development	Fifth	No	No

plan the principle was first discussed and whether or not it is recognized in the Single European Act or the Treaty on European Union.

A number of points should be made about this list. In the first place, the categorization of principles is in some measure at least an analytical convenience, rather than a hard and fast reflection of a clear difference of scope. For example, the polluter–pays principle can be regarded as much as a principle of sound environmental management as a principle of policy integration. Secondly, the list is by no means exhaustive. It omits certain principles that are regularly referred to in policy documents, including both the principle that states should seek to avoid cross-border harm, which was one of the principles of the First Action Programme, and the principle that policies should embody current scientific knowledge, which was also mentioned in the First Action Programme and which found a place in the Maastricht Treaty. Despite these limitations, the list does serve to emphasize how much EU environmental policy has sought to make explicit the policy principles upon which specific measures are taken. In what follows, we look at each of these categories of principle in turn.

Principles of Sound Environmental Management

An important principle under this heading is that of prevention, i.e. that action should be taken to prevent environmental problems from occurring rather than to control the effects of pollution once it has taken place. This principle is often defended on the grounds that prevention is cheaper than cure, and that designing processes and products so that their pollution outputs are minimized involves less cost than end-of-pipe solutions. The examples of directives that may be said to conform to this principle can be found in the area of chemicals regulation, where there are requirements for the potentially toxic effects of chemicals to be identified before they are marketed, so that restrictions can be placed on their use, and the so-called 'Seveso' directive on major accident activities of production, where manufacturers are required to prevent certain hazards arising.[43] The principle of prevention has also been important since the 1970s in the development of waste management strategies, where an emphasis has been placed on preventing waste arising in the first place; and, as Krämer points out, the principle also has an obvious logic in justifying the search for clean technologies.[44]

A related principle is that of taking action to rectify pollution at source. Such a principle seems logically consistent with an emphasis upon preventive action. Like the principle of prevention, it has been an important component in waste management policy, and it was invoked in the case of the Wallonian waste ban, where the European Court of Justice held that a restriction on the free movement of goods was in principle permissible, on the grounds that it was legitimate for Belgian regional authorities to require that waste be disposed of as close to its source of origin as possible. However, action at source raises a number of distinct issues, not least in its relationship to other principles of environmental policy. For example, it would appear to be a more stringent principle than that of the polluter pays, since the latter would allow pollution provided there was adequate compensation for its victims, whereas the principle of rectification at source would imply that the polluter ought to deal with the problem rather than merely compensate victims from its effects. It should also be clear that the principle cannot easily be applied to non-point sources of pollution.

The same principle also leads into what some have seen as one of the fundamental issues in the politics of standard-setting in the European Union, namely the debate between proponents of uniform emission limits and proponents of environmental quality standards. This contest is often presented as one between 'continental' styles of regulation on the one side and the UK's more pragmatic approach on the other. The principle of action at source would seem to suggest a bias in favour of uniform emission limits. However, in the way in which the issue has developed, the EU has been prepared to accept that both source emission controls and environmental quality standards have a legitimate place in pollution control. In any case, the characterization of the relative positions of the UK and other countries is overly simple: the UK, for example, has been prepared to regulate emissions as part of its air pollution control strategy since the nineteenth century.[45]

Within the general context of sound principles of environmental management, an important theme has been that of integrated pollution control, which involves looking at pollution in the round. Although not a policy principle in the strict sense, integrated pollution control does indicate a general approach to policy. The Third Action Programme explicitly introduced the theme of cross-media pollution control, in a form that was a substance-related focus on such issues as cadmium and asbestos control, but the notion received more prominence in the Fourth Action Programme. The idea of integrated pollution control is itself complex,[46] and the call for greater integration covered a number of logically distinct themes, ranging at a minimum from the proposal for a 'one-stop shop' for environmental regulation, through the claim that different media of pollution (air, water, land) should be regulated according to similar standards and similar criteria, to the notion that there should be a harmonization of environmental legislation and policy principles that had developed piecemeal and *ad hoc* over time. Despite these complexities, it was common for opinion among European policy-makers to be united on the need for greater integration, as was reflected both in successive Action Programmes and in policy developments in member states.[47]

The UK was primarily responsible for introducing this theme on to the policy agenda.[48] It reflected much of the policy thinking that had been going on in the UK since 1974 about the potential ineffectiveness of pollution control measures when they were applied solely to specific receiving media, and worries that the 'solution' to, say, an air pollution problem would merely involve the displacement of the problem to, say, water. The principle of integrated pollution control lay dormant in the UK's policy discourse, until it emerged at both the national and the European level in the 1980s. It is hardly surprising, therefore, that the appearance of the principle of cross-media control was welcomed by British officials when giving evidence on the draft Fourth Action Programme, in the following words:

for example, the sort of multi-media analysis referred to . . . is something which we support, and we have called on the Commission to produce new proposals relating to lead, specifically to lead in paint.[49]

The concern with cross-media pollution control was eventually to find expression in the Integrated Pollution Prevention and Control (IPPC) directive (96/61/EC), in which an attempt was made to provide a regime in which pollution could be controlled whichever medium it was discharged into.

Although it is possible to identify principles as concerned with the definition of sound environmental management, this is not to say that the meaning and implications of these principles are uncontroversial. As we have seen in the case of the principle of action at source, there can be a tension with other principles, such as the polluter-pays principle. More importantly, perhaps, the implementation of certain principles or approaches implies certain administrative and institutional preconditions. Effective preventive action, for example, requires an anticipatory capacity in the regulatory system which it might be difficult for poorer southern countries to supply and finance. Similarly, integrated pollution control requires that street-level bureaucrats be given some discretion as to how they administer the implementation of standards, a degree of discretion that may be at odds with some more legalistic traditions in member states. Hence, in talking about principles of technical competence, we are not referring exclusively to technical issues.

This broader political context becomes more important as we move to the consideration of other types of principle.

Principles of Standard-Setting

A principle found in the First Action Programme and repeated in subsequent versions concerns the prudent use of natural resources. The First Action Programme defines the principle by saying that the exploitation of natural resources that cause damage to the ecological balance must be avoided. In effect, this principle gives environmental protection independent value, a value that may need to be protected against other demands, for example those associated with the benefits of short-term economic exploitation of resources. In some ways, we can see implicit in this principle an anticipation of the idea in the Brundtland Report that environmental assets were to be used wisely in the context of a concern for intergenerational equity.[50] Both the Single European Act and the Maastricht Treaty gloss this requirement in terms of the need for the objectives of environmental policy to ensure 'a prudent and rational utilization of resources'.[51]

In this context, it is useful to consider the principle that was established in Article 100a(4) of the Single European Act, namely that, in considering rules for the single market, the Commission should take as its base 'a high level of protection' for the environment. It is clear from this provision that the formal incorporation of an environmental competence into EU decision-making in the 1980s was concerned with more than simply the harmonization of standards in such a way that free trade would be facilitated. The requirement for a high level of protection would be redundant if the harmonization of standards was all that was of concern, since such harmonization could clearly be achieved at a low standard within the framework of mutual recognition. Hence the requirement of a high standard suggests, as did the principle of the prudent use of natural resources, an implicit acceptance of the independent value to be attached to protecting the environment.

Clearly, however, the important question is exactly how high the standard should be, particularly as many environmental regulations show diminishing marginal returns, with the value of higher standards declining rapidly past a certain range. This issue became important once there was a demand in the 1980s for tighter standards, when the scientific basis for those standards was unclear. It was in this territory that the disputes over the principle of precaution took place.[52] To understand the significance of the precautionary principle, we need to understand the policy context in which the problem of precautionary action in the face of scientific uncertainty arose.

During the early part of the 1980s, there emerged among many policy-makers a perception that new problems of pollution had to be dealt with, and that new approaches were needed to cope with these new problems. The issue that came to symbolize this problem was acidification.[53] Unlike previous examples of pollution, the science of acidification was poorly understood and gave rise to contested hypotheses about cause-and-effect relationships. Moreover, everyone agreed that if acidification did have significant effects they were long-range, cumulative, and difficult to remedy once they had occurred. This in turn led policy-makers in the EU to stress the importance of precaution in the development of policies, and in particular to stress that positive action could not always wait for a complete understanding of the pollution problem at hand without risking the neglect of problems until the environmental damage had been done.

This precautionary approach had its origins in Germany, where the principle had been formally incorporated in legislation since 1974, though it was only developed and elaborated in policy discourse in the 1980s.[54] Within the German context, one element of the principle of precaution was to stress the advantages of prevention over remedial action in environmental policy. However, this was far from being the whole of the story. Precaution meant not merely being unwilling to run certain risks; it also meant treating some issues of emissions control as environmental risks, even when there was insufficient evidence to justify the claim that a particular type of emission was an environmental hazard.

The approach to which this gave rise should be distinguished from the principle, discussed earlier, that it is better to prevent pollution than to clear it up afterwards. As Konrad von Moltke has pointed out, the principle of prevention was implicit in the Second Action Programme, with its assertion that the best environmental policy consists in preventing pollution at source rather than subsequently trying to counteract its effects, and in many ways it is simply one of the commonplaces of modern environmental policy.[55] Precaution meant, among other things, dealing with uncertainties in environmental policy on the basis of an approach that tipped the burden of proof in favour of stringent environmental regulation where no clear-cut decision could be made.

The direct influence of the German discussion on EU policy thinking was commented upon by Nigel Haigh at the time of the Fourth Action Programme:

one large Member State, the Federal Republic of Germany, underwent a conversion of Saul in 1982 as a result of the death of its forests and invented this concept of the Vorsorge principle, which one sees reflected in the Fourth Action Programme. The insistence on tight standards is a reflection of this consciousness in Germany, and what has happened recently at Chernobyl and on the Rhine [the chemical spill from Sandoz] has only helped to reinforce that. That is going to be a major pressure over the coming years.[56]

Given this background, it is not surprising to see the emphasis on the requirement for a high standard of environmental protection in the Single European Act.

The principle of precaution itself was formally introduced into EU policy-making by the Maastricht Treaty. However, its significance in the process of policy-making is unclear, since it looks more like a general injunction to policy-makers than a principle that can be given clear policy content, let along strict legal force.[57] Indeed, when analysts have sought to identify a core meaning in the principle, it has proved remarkably difficult.[58] Moreover, application of the principle always has to be seen in the light of competing considerations, most notably those of scientific justification, cost, and the extent to which the policy measure in question is proportionate to the end being sought. The influence of the principle of precaution is therefore likely to be seen most clearly in those cases where weight is given to considerations of environmental protection despite countervailing considerations. It is, however, difficult to find measures that can unambiguously be cited as instances of a precautionary approach.

Principles of Task Assignment

Within a system of multi-level governance, actors need to find some basis upon which they can agree the division of powers and authority among themselves. This is especially important in a system like the EU, given the extent of the pooling of sovereignty it involves. The problem of task assignment is not solved by noting that the EU is a political system in which authority is shared among actors rather than parcelled out in discrete units, since even the limits of shared authority still need to be defined.

The First Action Programme adumbrated the principle of the 'appropriate level' for the assignment of functions. According to this principle, in each category of pollution it is necessary to establish the level of action (local, regional, national, Community, and international) best suited to deal with the pollution in question and the environmental zone to be protected. This principle resembles the standard economist's notion of task assignment, namely that the scale of political authority to set rules for the control of pollution should be at a level sufficient to internalize the relevant externality.[59] It is, in essence, a principle of functional effectiveness. Authority for setting rules related to pollution should be set at a level that is best suited to dealing with the problem at hand.

Within this principle of the appropriate level, there is implicit a recognition that different environmental regions may have their own special problems which need to be dealt with in a specific way. This aspect of environmental rule-setting was made explicit in both the Single European Act and the Maastricht Treaty. The Single European Act contained the requirement that EU policy should take account of the variety of regional needs, and this was made more explicit in the Maastricht Treaty, in the specification of both the principle that the diversity of situations should be recognized and the principle that environmental policy should take account of environmental conditions in Europe.

However, if the Single European Act and the Maastricht Treaty were to make explicit one aspect of the principle of appropriateness, there was another respect in which they were to change one of its fundamental presuppositions. Any principle that presupposes functional effectiveness as the basic criterion for the allocation of political authority will not attach any special importance to any one particular level of authority. The Single European Act, however, introduced a version of the principle of subsidiarity in to the assignment of environmental competences, with the requirement that the EU could take measures only when the objectives related to the protection of the environment could be attained better by EU action than by the member states.[60] In effect, this requirement introduces a bias towards the local, by imposing the test of showing that competence should be moved up from the member state level to the EU level because shared objectives are better achieved in that way.

The Maastricht Treaty consolidated this emphasis on preserving the powers of the member states by making a fuller statement of the principle of subsidiarity in the preamble to the Treaty. According to the relevant clause of the Treaty,

In areas that do not fall within its exclusive competence, the Community shall take action, in accordance with the principle of subsidiarity, only if and in so far as the objectives of the proposed action cannot be sufficiently achieved by the Member States and can therefore, by reason of the scale or effects of the proposed action, be better achieved by the Community.[61]

Following the first Danish referendum on the Maastricht Treaty in June 1992, the British government secured an EU review of environmental legislation, in an attempt to see whether some responsibilities could be repatriated.[62] The argument was that the principle of subsidiarity, according to which functions should be carried out at the lowest feasible level, implied that the regulation of bathing water quality, for example, should be a matter for member states and not for the EU. However, the review did not issue in a change of responsibility. The application of the principle of subsidiarity was not used to reassign competences for particular issues of policy.[63] Rather, it was interpreted as an opportunity to assert the importance of 'soft law' approaches to environmental regulation. In place of the formal directives and regulations that had characterized environmental policy during the 1980s, greater stress would be placed on voluntary agreements, negotiated rule making, and other non-legal forms of environmental policy control. Significantly, not a single piece of legislation has been repealed, and reform of the drinking and bathing waters directives has taken a great deal of time.

Principles of Policy Integration

Pollution typically has its source in a variety of otherwise legitimate activities, in particular transport, agriculture, and industry.[64] From this observation, the conclusion is often drawn that environmental protection cannot be the responsibility solely of a separate branch of environmental policy and administration, but that it has to be integrated into a wide range of public policies if harmful effects from those policies are to be anticipated and counteracted. Within the countries of the EU, this theme of integration had been most vigorously pursued by the Netherlands in its National Environmental Policy Plan of 1989,[65] from which the EU's Fifth Action Programme drew so much of its inspiration with its proposals for collaborative working relations between DG XI and other sections of the

Commission's administration, and the formalizing of contacts with interested parties outside the Commission through consultation groups. The principle of policy integration was formally recognized in the Single European Act, in which environmental protection requirements were made 'a component of the Community's other policies'.[66] This requirement was strengthened in the Maastricht Treaty by the formulation that environmental 'protection requirements must be integrated into the definition and implementation of other Community policies'.[67]

Although the Fifth Action Programme was the clearest attempt to examine what the policy implications of this principle might be, the importance of integration goes back to some of the earliest formulations of EU environmental policy. Thus, the First Action Programme declared that 'the activities of the Communities in different sectors in which they operate agriculture policy, social policy, regional policy, industrial policy, energy policy, etc. must take account of concern for the protection and improvement of the environment'.[68] The theme was also mentioned in a more general way when the projects to be undertaken under the auspices of the Action Programmes were introduced. As such, the EU's role in improving the standard of living of its citizens and their environment was believed to be 'inseparable from the organization and promotion of human progress' and needed to 'be integrated in devising and implementing common policies'.[69] References to the need for the environmental aspect of development to be taken into account early on in the planning process are identifiable.

Subsequently, the same approach could be found in various forms. One version appeared in the Third Action Programme, in which policy integration was related to the development of an ecological mapping system. The method recommended, which used cartography as a way of incorporating environmental knowledge into spatial organization, was regarded as desirable because it could 'make an important contribution to the preventive action by the authorities of environment related data, including pollution, in decision making processes linked with physical planning and environmental policy'.[70] It was believed that the data provided would allow for a preventive approach because of the role it could play in policy integration. Thus, linking the two in this way was the first step towards an integrated preventive approach.

The authors of the Third Action Programme clearly believed that the integration of environmental concerns into economic activities was essential if a preventive policy was to be effective. They pointed to the way in which EU funds were often used for activities that seemed to contradict the EU's environmental objectives, demonstrating a coordination gap that could have serious implications.[71] The potential dangers were highlighted by the Council in its resolution on the Third Action Programme. Here, they pointed to the benefits of integrating environmental concerns into the EU's economic and social activities.[72] Indeed, the Council recognized the development of EU thinking in this respect when it listed integration and environmental impact assessments as the two main priorities out of the thirteen identified in the Action Programme.[73]

While the First Action Programme talked only of balanced development, the Second Action Programme included references to the limits of economic growth and the damage that such growth could cause both to the environment and to future development.[74] Such sentiments indicate an early acknowledgement of the need for a form of development that is sustainable, i.e. for economic growth that does not degrade the environment to the extent that it prevents growth in the future. This is an approach that was not evident in the emphasis upon the quality of life in the First Action Programme. The anticipation of sustainable development was picked up by the Council in its resolution on the Third Action Programme; this also mentioned improvement in the quality of life as a continuing goal, but included 'making the most economical use possible of the natural resources offered by the environment' as one of the fundamental challenges facing the EU.[75] The Third Action Programme further highlighted the need for development and economic growth to be tied into environmental considerations, recognizing that 'the common environmental policy is motivated equally by the observation that the resources of the environment are the basis of—but also constitute the limits to—further economic and social development and the improvement of living conditions'.[76]

The evolution of this strand of policy thinking within the Action Programmes can best be illustrated by the Third Programme's anticipation of the theme of intergenerational equity in the Brundtland Report, when it stated that the objective of the EU environmental Action Programmes was 'to guarantee the quality of life for present and future generations'.[77] This is certainly a much wider remit than that of the 1973 Action Programme, which stemmed from a desire to avoid the consequences of independent national environmental policy-making on the common market, and which concentrated on ways of reducing disparity and harmonizing standards of living throughout the EU.

Despite these clear intentions, in practice policy integration did not seem to be a priority at this stage. It may have been a stated principle, but it was not one that was translated into concrete policy or action. Why was this? One answer was given by Nigel Haigh, in evidence to the House of Lords Select Committee on the European Communities in 1992:

The subject of integration has had quite a long history. For at least 12 years there has been talk about it. It has grown with a crescendo, culminating in the Fifth Action Programme. But for the first ten years of the Community's environment policy, which began in 1973, there was not much talk of integration and certainly it was not part of Community policy. The directorate-general, which was then called a service, concentrated its activities on drawing up pieces of legislation on things like drinking water, bathing water, the protection of birds and so on which did not touch on any of the other directorates-general. I think that was entirely right, because they were a very small directorate-general and there were plenty of people in the Commission who thought that the environment was a fashion that would disappear. Had the environment people gone and poked their fingers into the affairs of the big and powerfully established directorate-generals they would have been wiped out.[78]

In short, whatever the intellectual merits of the principle of policy integration, the conditions for its implementation were simply not in place for many years. The problems of achieving integration relate in part to the sectoralized nature of policy-making within the Commission and in part to the intrinsic difficulties of bringing it about, given the inertia, entrenched habit, and vested interests among policy-makers in general.

One way of achieving a measure of external integration is to enforce the polluter-pays principle, thereby providing those responsible for pollution with an incentive to change their behaviour. Acceptance of the principle can be found in the First Action Programme; and a 1983 Memorandum by Directorate-General XI to the House of Lords inquiry into the polluter-pays principle makes it clear that, in the Commission's thinking, acceptance of this principle rests upon economic grounds associated with the optimal allocation of resources.[79] The 1987 Fourth Action Programme took as one of its priority areas the 'development of efficient instruments such as taxes, levies, State aid, authorization of negotiable rebates', with the aim of implementing the polluter-pays principle;[80] and the 1992 Fifth Action Programme asserted the importance of getting market prices right and the need to create market-based incentives for environmentally friendly economic behaviour.[81]

During the 1980s, policy-makers in a number of countries began to show increasing interest in the use of economic or financial instruments to advance environmental standards. In some countries such instruments have sometimes had an important place in pollution control policy, as the example of the Danish, Dutch, French, and German water pollution charges goes to show;[82] and in the USA interest in air pollution grew after the failure to meet the air quality targets set down in the 1970 Clean Air Act.[83] These examples suggested to some policy-makers that it might be possible to expand their use.

The Task Force report *'1992': The Environmental Dimension* picked up the theme and made a plea for the use of more market-based instruments within the environmental policy of the EU and its member states.[84] Aiming at the efficient allocation of resources, the report stated that instruments such as emission charges, effluent fees, transferable discharge permits, and strict liability represent an approach that is fully consistent with the single market, since economic incentives provide a continuous motive for environmental improvement and so help to shape economic development towards environmentally clean technologies.[85] The market-based incentives approach was contrasted with the direct ('command-and-control') regulatory approach, which involves the setting of environmental standards enforced by legislation without the aid of market-based incentives.

The Dublin Environmental Council of May 1990 defined its own position and invited the Commission to work out concrete proposals in the areas of climate change, solid waste, environmental policy integration, and water pollution.[86] During that year the Commission presented a report in which it expressed itself in favour of more widespread use of economic instruments for environmental policy.[87] The design of such instruments was to be based upon the polluter-pays principle, and the Commission favoured pricing instruments such as charges and taxes.

The EU had its first experience in the application of economic incentives in the framework of the directive on the lead-free petrol.[88] This directive has been a necessary step for the widespread introduction of catalytic converters. As it specified only targets and not instruments, member states defined their own instrument mix. The creation of price differential between leaded and unleaded petrol largely accelerated the compliance with direct EU regulations, although coordinated action among member states would have enabled a more efficient and timely spread of unleaded petrol throughout the EU.

In the Fifth Action Programme there was a commitment to ensuring that economic and fiscal instruments would 'constitute an increasingly important part of the overall approach'.[89] 'The fundamental aim of these instruments will be to internalise all external environmental costs incurred during the whole life-cycle of products through production, distribution, use and final disposal', states the programme. The part of the programme on the use of economic instruments notes that '[it] will be important to study the extent to which possible options such as tradeable permits could be utilised to control or reduce quantities [of pollution]'. It also states that the charges and levies—well understood and used in the field of water pollution—should be 'progressively reorientated towards discouraging pollution at source and encouraging clean production processes, through market signals'.[90]

Taken to its logical conclusions, the emphasis on policy integration leads to a consideration of the principle of sustainable development, which can be regarded as an attempt to ensure that environmental considerations reshape the entire fabric of the social order. This was clearly the way in which the issues were presented in the Fifth Action Programme. However, the unambiguous formal acceptance of the principle of sustainable development had to wait for the Amsterdam Treaty. In the Maastricht Treaty the principles was expressed in the following formula:

The Community shall have as its task . . . to promote throughout the Community a harmonious and balanced development of economic activities, sustainable and non-inflationary growth respecting the environment. . ."[91]

This could be said to leave it unclear whether 'sustainable' is to be read as 'continuing' or 'in accordance with the principle of sustainable development'. After Amsterdam, this ambiguity was cleared away and there is now a commitment to achieve 'balanced and sustainable development'.

Looking at the way in which the principle of sustainable development began to influence policy thinking, we can find an example in the Commission Communication of 3 November 1994 to the European Parliament and the Council on economic growth and the environment, by which it hoped to promote the better integration of environmental protection requirements into the EU's economic policy.[92] This was an important communication, in which the Commission analysed the consequence of the principle of environmentally sustainable development for economic and fiscal policy-making and presented some first conclusions for discussion. According to the Commission, a convergence in political thinking was taking place, so governments and particularly the EU were coming to regard the 'Malthusian' view as seriously biased since it related to only one of the links between environment and economic growth, whereas, according to the Commission, there are three mechanisms that jointly determine the environmental impact of economic growth.[93]

First, economic growth entails increased pressures on the environment if there are no changes in the way the economy operates. Under such circumstances, an expansion of economic activities is likely to lead to decreases in environmental quality via a scale effect.[94] This is what occurred after the Second World War, when Western European economies experienced rapid economic growth. However, this rapid growth, based on quantitative criteria and on the uncontrolled exploitation of natural resources, caused widespread environmental degradation. This in turn gave rise, starting from the early 1960s, to increasing concern about the negative impact of economic development on the natural environment and on human health and safety.[95] A similar situation was to be found in Asia, where half the world's population is crowded into a sixth of its land, and where noxious gases and dust in the air of conurbations are at choking levels.[96]

Secondly, on this analysis, the composition of economic activity changes with the various stages of economic development. When economic growth takes off, economies move out of agriculture and into manufacturing, thereby increasing the resource and pollution intensity per unit of production. As income levels grow even higher, service activities increase their share in the economy. Because services are generally characterized by low pollution levels per unit of production, this slows down pollution. The European Union is in this last phase.[97]

Thirdly, technology changes as economies expand and this is likely to reduce pollution per unit of product. This is partly because in market economies the drive to produce at low costs puts a premium on energy efficiency and on reducing material intensity.[98] The analysis continues by noting that, as GDP reaches a certain level, the willingness to pay for environmental quality grows and policies are developed in the fields of clean air and drinking and bathing water. These policies affect technology, both by stimulating certain options and by imposing others. There is no shortage of technical technologies for smog, vehicle emissions, and water purification, although they come at a cost. Furthermore, as these policies favour clean activities and penalize pollution-intensive branches (by requiring abatement efforts, which raise the cost of production), the sectoral composition of the economy is also affected.

Consumers and pressure groups may also directly affect this trend by increasing their demand for environmentally friendly products.[99] For example, economic growth is one of the best routes to increase energy efficiency. The intensity of energy use in West German and American manufacturing fell as rapidly between 1960 and 1973, when their economies were expanding and energy prices were low, as it did after the oil shock, when growth was slow and conservation was increasing.[100]

An interesting element in this analysis of the relationship between economic growth and policies on environmental protection is to be found in the claim that the relation between economic development and environmental quality is strong for local forms of pollution (e.g. suspended particulate matter), but is not found in the empirical data on some of the global environmental issues, such as global warming. The inference drawn is that as countries become richer they first clean up the most pressing environmental problems that pose direct health hazards and fall exclusively under their national sovereignty. Given this tendency, it is essential, according to the analysis, that there is nothing automatic about the fact that many forms of pollution seem to decrease as economies grow. It is only because policy action is taken that pollution is brought down. Although economic growth by itself generates the means for pollution abatement and so the possibility to improve the quality of the environment, this will happen only if an essential prerequisite is met, namely a sound policy framework.[101]

In many ways, the concept of sustainable development is less a clear and distinct principle in its own right, and more a general orientation of thinking about the environment, indicating a broad encompassing objective for public policy. The concept itself has been variously defined and elaborated since the Brundtland Report. Some of these definitions locate the concept clearly in its original home of environmental protection and the ability to maintain resource extraction and use at a level that does not jeopardize future use. Other definitions extend the concept so widely that sustainable development comes to mean the good society taken in all its dimensions. In our context, however, these definitional issues are less important than the relationship between the idea of sustainable development and that of ecological modernization. It is to ecological modernization that we turn in the next section, when we come to look at the changing pattern of justification for EU policy principles.

THE JUSTIFICATION OF POLICY:
ECOLOGICAL MODERNIZATION

When the issue of environmental protection first came on to the political agendas of European countries in the 1970s, the attention of policy-makers was almost exclusively focused on the pursuit of economic and industrial reconstruction and regeneration, with the Rome Treaty's rationale making the prospect of a future (West) European war both unthinkable and materially impossible. The creation of a European common market was only one strand in a broader strategy which might allow these postwar priorities to be achieved. The introduction of environmental concerns did not originally mark a sea-change in these attitudes. Rather, it served to buttress the trade arguments that persisted, and placed the logic of environmental action clearly on a supranational level. This did not necessarily imply any activism on the part of the European institutions, but it did demonstrate the extent to which member governments saw the transnational institutionalization of environmental governance as being in line with their policy preferences.

The 1972 Stockholm Conference on the Human Environment, set up initially to address the issue of acid rain, offered the environmental movement a global platform. Institutionally, this led to the setting up of the UN Environment Programme (UNEP).[102] The 1972 Club of Rome study, which took as its agenda the limits to growth, provoked Commissioner Mansholt's so-called 'last will and testament', in which he demanded a U-turn on European economic policy and the construction of a 'centrally planned recycling economy'. This radical call for an extreme line to be taken by the Commission was rejected both by the Commission itself and by the Council.[103] It did, however, for the first time, cast the Commission in a rather different role, that of a potential agenda-setter. Although in this case the Mansholt line was too out-of-step with the rest of the Commission, it does illustrate the extent to which the environment as an issue could pose a challenge to dominant assumptions about the priority to be given to increasing economic growth as conventionally measured.

However, along with the increasing sophistication in the development of policy principles, we can also see a change in the conception of the underlying rationale of environmental policy, directed at modifying the assumption that there is an automatic trade-off between economic growth and environmental protection. This reconceptualization was important both intellectually and strategically, because the principal reason for the slow-down in environmental policy developments in the 1970s was the high priority given to improving economic growth in the wake of the oil price rises of 1973–4. Thus, if the tensions between economic development and environmental protection were to remain dominant in policy thinking, those arguing for a higher priority for environmental protection would always face an uphill struggle.

During the 1980s it became common for policy-makers—and not only in the EU—to argue for the role of environmental policy in promoting a new sort of economic competitiveness. The argument ran that, with the advent of global markets, the standard of product acceptability for international consumers would be determined by the country with the most stringent pollution control standards, so that the future of the post-industrial economy would depend upon its ability to produce high-value, high-quality products meeting high environmental standards. Thus, on this argument Europe would be able to take full advantage of economies of scale in globally competitive markets only if it legislated for high environmental standards on a par with those to be found in Japan and the USA.

This argument can be found in many places as it became diffused around European policy elites.[104] However, it was crisply expressed by Laurens-Jan Brinkhorst, as the head of DG XI, in testimony to the House of Lords Select Committee on the European Communities in their investigation of the Fourth Action Programme:

Secondly—and here it is the old Japan hand who is speaking—I have become very much concerned—and I think this is a view largely shared by other departments—that environment and technology, environment and competition, have become brothers and sisters. It is not because of the low prices of Japanese products that the Japanese are making inroads in all kinds of areas (whether we speak about cars or computers), but it is largely because of the quality of their products and, in the field of cars for instance, the very high emissions standards.[105]

Although the claim that this was a view shared by other departments was perhaps rather over-optimistic at the time it was made, it is certainly true that it was one that received widespread and increasing support in a number of circles during the late 1980s and early 1990s.

The significance of this argument was that it turned on its head the most familiar objection to stringent environmental policy, namely that there was always a trade-off between the imposition of environmental standards and the protection of economic interests, most notably the protection of employment. As Hirschman has argued, one of the most important rhetorical devices in the armoury of those arguing for 'progressive' causes is the claim that what appear to be conflicting goals (equality and freedom, or economic prosperity and social protection) are really consistent with and may even reinforce once another, just as it is a feature of 'reactionary' discourse to stress the conflicts that are involved.[106] In the case of environmental policy, it became almost an article of faith that environmental protection was a precondition of the economic success that was associated with the European project.[107]

It is clear that these arguments were developed extensively within the Commission and that they surfaced in relation to the Commission's White Paper on growth, competitiveness, and employment.[108] The background to the document is well known. Amid the growing public and political anxiety about recession and rising unemployment in Europe, the Copenhagen European Council in June 1993 invited the Commission to prepare a document on the subject outlining a diagnosis and discussing possible policy solutions. Given the origins and context of the document, positive mentions of environmental protection show the extent to which the fundamental argument of ecological modernization had entered the policy arena.

In terms of environmental policy, there is a clear formal recognition within the White Paper of the role of environmental projects and concerns in promoting enhanced growth and competitiveness. According to our interview evidence, this acknowledgement of the fundamental tenets of ecological modernization was mediated through the work of Jacques Delors's *cabinet*, which became convinced during 1992 of the potential of environmental measures in stimulating economic activity and thus employment. Chapter 10 of the Commission's report is titled 'Towards a New Development Model', and it advocates fiscal and other policy instruments as devices for moving costs away from the employment of labour and towards the use of resources. Existing policy instruments, the chapter argues, will have to be reorientated to encourage the more efficient use of resources (thus leaving open the possibility of eco-taxes), and priority should be given to environmentally friendly innovation both by means of subsidies for technical improvement and by funds for research and development.

However, this last section is only the conclusion to a series of points made throughout the document. Thus, in the context of the need to develop new forms of work and new employment opportunities, environmental protection is one of the sectors where expansion is said to be possible.[109] Although an improvement in physical transport links is said to be important, mention is made of the dangers of environmental damage.[110] Mention is also made of adjusting the tax base to resource use.[111] The argument is also used that there may well be a 'first mover' advantage to the developing of eco-industries.[112]

The strategy of ecological modernization was thus used as a legitimating discourse by the Commission in its attempt to reconcile the goals of the single market and the imposition of high environmental standards. These examples of policy advocacy might suggest that environmental policy-makers within the Commission were successful in articulating a legitimating discourse in terms of which the institutional expansion of European environmental policy could be justified. However, some caution needs to be exercised in drawing this conclusion. Within the new discourse, there were divergent elements that contained politically important ambiguities which blunted the effectiveness of the arguments that were advanced.

The elements of the discourse that we have set out above are complex even in summary form, and it always remained possible for policy-makers with their own interests and perspectives to stress some elements and downplay others. Perhaps the most important possibility here is the inherent tension between simply justifying environmental policy in terms of a 'market failure' rationale, in which the essential task is for the political authorities to correct for the divergence between social and private costs, and the 'global competitiveness' rationale, which implies a more interventionist line. This conflict was merely a local example of a more general conflict that occurred throughout the 1980s between ideological proponents of 'Rhineland capitalism', who favoured a partnership between economic enterprises, and the political authorities and proponents of neo-liberalism, who favoured a less interventionist role for the political authorities.[113]

This issue is important because it parallels an ambiguity to be found in the internal market project itself, between those, like Lord Cockfield in the 1985 White Paper,[114] who stressed the liberal component of the internal market programme and those who saw the internal market as creating a more interventionist regime at the European level, a view sometimes described as 'Fortress Europe'. Indeed, there was an ambiguity built into the position even of those who thought of the internal market in essentially liberal terms; for they could either stress the import- ance of reducing non-tariff barriers to trade created by national regulations, or stress the dangers of 'market failure', especially in the area of the environment, where there is a long established tradition of analysis that sees externalities as an espe- cially important source of market failure. As Majone has pointed out, the market failure argument suggests re-regulation at the European level.[115]

These issues also become entangled with broader questions about the role of *European* political authorities, as distinct from national political authorities. Thus, as the Commission Communication of 1994 pointed out, there is a perfectly good case, from a number of different premises, for the development of a European strategy towards issues of global warming involving the development of a carbon/ energy tax. But it is impossible to consider these arguments in the abstract with- out also becoming involved in broader arguments about the tax-levying powers of the EU. To accept a European carbon/energy tax—whatever its theoretical rationale and consistency with the new stress on the importance of economic instruments —would have involved conceding new tax-levying competence at the European level, an alternative to which the British government, among others, was always opposed.

From a quite different point of view, the strategy of ecological modernization could always be questioned by those who held to a different view of the relation- ship between environmental protection and economic cost. For northern countries like the Netherlands and Germany, with highly developed industrial capacity and the need to search for new markets in high value added sectors, the strategy of ecological modernization seemed to make a lot of sense; but the same was not true from the point of view of the Spanish government, which was highly productivist in its general ideology (in the sense of wishing to promote growth as convention- ally understood) and also saw that it had some absorptive environmental capacity. Of course, it is a central tenet of the ideology of ecological modernization that in the process of development latecomers do not have to repeat the mistakes of those who came before. The more developed country need not merely show to the less developed the image of its own future. But this claim always remained something of a promissory note, and there was little demonstration that it held true in general. In any case, even in developed northern states, environmental standards were never allowed completely to override cost calculations. As we shall see in discussing the principles of national policies, even distinctively German approaches to pollution control, which relied upon setting standards according to the 'state of available tech- nology', implicitly reckon on the economic consequences of their decisions. No standard is ever set solely by reference to environmental considerations and with- out considering its economic effects.

What then is the relationship between the approach of ecological modern- ization to the justification of environmental policy principles and the concept of sustainable development? Much of course depends on how narrowly or broadly the concept of 'sustainable development' is defined. However, even in relatively narrow definitions, much less in broader approaches, the principles of ecological modernization capture only a part of what advocates of sustainable development are seeking. Ecological modernization rests crucially on the claim that economic growth can take new, more environmentally friendly, forms. Sustainable development seeks to set the pursuit of economic development within the context of principles of intergenerational equity, social justice, and democratic participation. That it was the discourse of ecological modernization, rather than that of sustainable development, that could most easily be attached to the justification of EU environmental policy measure probably reflects the continuing importance of the origins of European integration in the Monnet method of economic interdependence.

NOTES TO CHAPTER 2

1. For a cross-section of work, see: M. M. Blyth, 'Any More Bright Ideas? The Ideational Turn of Comparative Political Economy', *Comparative Politics*, 29:2 (1997), pp. 229–50; J. Goldsmith and R. Keohane, (eds.), *Ideas and Foreign Policy: Beliefs, Institutions and Political Change* (Ithaca, NY: Cornell University Press, 1993); M. A. Hajer, *The Politics of Environmental Discourse* (Oxford: Clarendon Press, 1995); P. A. Hall (ed.), *The Political Power of Economic Ideas* (Princeton: Princeton University Press, 1980); P. A. Hall, 'Policy Paradigms, Social Learning, and the State', *Comparative Politics*, 25:2 (1993), pp. 275–96; H. C. Jenkins-Smith and P. Sabatier, 'Evaluating the Advocacy Coalition Framework', *Journal of Public Policy*, 14:2 (1994), pp. 175–203; R. Little and S. Smith (eds.), *Belief Systems and International Relations* (Oxford: Basil Blackwell, 1988); G. Majone, *Evidence, Argument and Persuasion in the Policy Process* (New Haven and London: Yale University Press, 1989); G. Majone, 'Public Policy and Administration: Ideas, Interests and Institutions', in R. E. Goodin and H.-D. Klingemann, *New Handbook of Political Science* (Oxford: Oxford University Press, 1996), pp. 610–27; C. Radaelli, 'The Role of Knowledge in the Policy Process', *Journal of European Public Policy*, 2:2 (1995), pp. 159–83; P. A. Sabatier, 'Knowledge, Policy-Oriented Learning and Policy Change: An Advocacy Coalition Framework', *Knowledge: Creation, Diffusion, Utilization*, 8:4 (1987), pp. 64–92; P. A. Sabatier and H. C. Jenkins-Smith (eds.), *Policy Change and Learning: An Advocacy Coalition Approach* (Oxford: Westview Press, 1993).

   For some earlier work that anticipates some of these themes, see H. Heclo, *Modern Social Politics in Britain and Sweden* (New Haven and London: Yale University Press, 1974); A. King, 'Ideas, Institutions, and the Policies of Governments: A Comparative Analysis, Parts I and II', *British Journal of Political Science*, 3:3 (1973), pp. 291–313, and 'Ideas, Institutions, and the Policies of Governments: A Comparative Analysis, Part III', *British Journal of Political Science*, 3:4 (1973), pp. 409–23; D. Winch, *Economics and Policy* (London: Fontana, 1972).

2. See, in particular, Hall, 'Policy Paradigms'; Jenkins-Smith and Sabatier, 'Evaluating the Advocacy Coalition Framework'; Majone, *Evidence, Argument and Persuasion*;

Sabatier, 'Knowledge, Policy-Oriented Learning and Policy Change'; Sabatier and Jenkins-Smith, *Policy Change and Learning*.

3. For the use of the term 'ecological modernization', see, *inter alia*, Hajer, *Politics of Environmental Discourse*, and A. Weale, *The New Politics of Pollution* (Manchester: Manchester University Press, 1992), ch. 3.
4. *Official Journal of the European Communities*, C112, 20.12.73, p. 5.
5. N. Haigh, 'A Green Agenda', paper for the UACES Conference, 'A Green Agenda for the Intergovernmental Conference: The Future of Environmental Policy', London, 29 March 1996.
6. N. Haigh, *EEC Environmental Policy and Britain* (London: Longman, 1989, 2nd edn), p. 9; E. Rehbinder and R. Stewart, *Environmental Protection Policy* (Berlin and New York: Walter de Gruyter, 1985), p. 17; and R. Wurzel, 'Environmental Policy' in J. Lodge (ed.), *The European Community and the Challenge of the Future* (London: Pinter Press, 1993, 2nd edn), pp. 178–99.
7. *Official Journal of the European Communities*, C112, 20.12.73, p. 5.
8. Ibid. 1.
9. Ibid. 5.
10. Ibid. 8.
11. *Official Journal of the European Communities*, C139, 13.06.77, pp. 40–1.
12. *Official Journal of the European Communities*, C112, 20.12.73, pp. 9–11.
13. Ibid. 13.
14. *Official Journal of the European Communities*, C139, 13.06.77, p. 9.
15. *Official Journal of the European Communities*, C112, 20.12.73, p. 14.
16. Ibid. 15.
17. Ibid. 16–17.
18. *Official Journal of the European Communities*, C139, 13.06.77, pp. 9–12.
19. *Official Journal of the European Communities*, C112, 20.12.73, p. 18.
20. *Official Journal of the European Communities*, C139, 13.06.77, pp. 13–16.
21. *Official Journal of the European Communities*, C112, 20.12.73, p. 20.
22. Ibid. 21.
23. Ibid. 22.
24. Ibid. 23.
25. Ibid. 26.
26. Ibid. 28.
27. Ibid. 29.
28. *Official Journal of the European Communities*, C139, 13.06.77, pp. 21–2.
29. *Official Journal of the European Communities*, C46, 17.02.83, p. 2.
30. Ibid. 10.
31. See also the comment in P. M. Hildebrand, 'The European Community's Environmental Policy, 1957 to "1992": From Incidental Measures to an International Regime?' *Environmental Politics*, 1:4 (1992), p. 22.
32. D. Vogel, 'The Making of EC Environmental Policy', in S. S. Andersen and K. A. Eliassen (eds.), *Making Policy in Europe: The Europeification of National Policy-Making* (London: Sage, 1993), pp. 116–17.
33. Hildebrand, 'The European Community's Environmental Policy', p. 34.
34. *Official Journal of the European Communities*, C70, 18.03.87.

35. Lodge states that the UK tried to cut these: J. Lodge, 'Environment: Towards a Clean Blue-Green EC', in J. Lodge (ed.), *The European Community and the Challenge of the Future* (London: Pinter, 1989), at p. 322.
36. Commission of the European Communities, *The Greenhouse Effect and the Community/ Commission Work Programme Concerning the Evaluation of Options to Deal with the 'Greenhouse Effect'*, COM (88) 656 final, 16.11.1988.
37. Lodge, 'Environment', p. 321.
38. *Official Journal of the European Communities*, C70, 18.03.87, p. 3.
39. Commission of the European Communities, *Towards Sustainability: A European Community Programmme of Policy and Action in Relation to the Environment and Sustainable Development*, COM (92), 23 final (Luxembourg: Commission of the European Communities, 1992). For some of the background, see World Commission on Environment and Development, *Our Common Future* (Oxford: Oxford University Press) and Second Chamber of the States General, *National Environmental Policy Plan: To Choose or Lose* ('s-Gravenhage: SDU uitgeverij, 1989).
40. For a discussion of the Dutch National Environmental Policy Plan, see Ch. 5.
41. Wurzel, 'Environmental Policy', p. 190.
42. Ibid.
43. For these examples, see N. Haigh, *Manual of Environmental Policy: The EC and Britain* (London: Cartermill International, 1992), pp. 3.7–8.8.
44. L. Krämer, *Focus on European Environmental Law* (London: Sweet & Maxwell, 1992), pp. 32–3.
45. See Ch. 5 for further details.
46. N. Haigh and F. Irwin (eds.), *Integrated Pollution Control in Europe and North America* (Washington: Conservation Foundation, 1990).
47. For the latter, see Weale, *New Politics of Pollution*, ch. 4.
48. See the discussion in Ch. 5 for more detail.
49. Mr J. Rowcliffe (then director, Central Directorate on Environmental Pollution, Department of the Environment), giving evidence to the Select Committee on the European Communities: see House of Lords Select Committee on the European Communities, *Fourth Environmental Action Programme* (London: HMSO, 1987), 1986–87 Session, HL 135, p. 4.
50. Most notably in the definition of sustainable development as 'development that meets the needs of the present without compromising the ability of future generations to meet their own needs': see World Commission on Environment and Development, *Our Common Future*, p. 43.
51. Single European Act Article 130r(1).
52. For general treatments, see: Department of the Environment, *A Guide to Risk Assessment and Risk Management for Environmental Protection* (London: HMSO, 1995); K. von Moltke, 'The *Vorsorgeprinzip* in West German Environmental Policy', Royal Commission on Environmental Pollution, Twelfth Report, *Best Practicable Environmental Option*, Cm. 310 (London: HMSO, 1988), app. 3, pp. 57–70; T. O'Riordan and J. Cameron (eds.), *Interpreting the Precautionary Principle* (London: Earthscan, 1994); E. Rehbinder, 'Vorsorgeprinzip im Umweltrecht und präventive Umweltpolitik', in U. E. Simonis (ed.), *Präventive Umweltpolitik* (Frankfurt/New York: Campus Verlag, 1988).
53. Hajer, *Politics of Environmental Discourse*.

54. See the discussion in Ch. 5.
55. von Moltke, '*Vorsorgeprinzip*', pp. 57–8.
56. Nigel Haigh in House of Lords Select Committee on the European Communities, *Fourth Environmental Action Programme*, p. 18.
57. Cf. L. Krämer, *EC Treaty and Environmental Law* (London: Sweet and Maxwell, 1995), p. 54.
58. For an attempt to reconstruct sympathetically the meaning of the principle that none the less concludes that no interpretation comes close to being a determinate guideline for environmental policy, see R. Malnes, *Valuing the Environment* (Manchester and New York: Manchester University Press, 1995), pp. *xi–xiv*.
59. See, *inter alia*, F. McGowan and P. Seabright, 'Regulation and Subsidiarity: Finding the Balance', in D. G. Mayes (ed.), *Aspects of European Integration* (London: National Institute of Economic and Social Research, 1993), pp. 45–53; E. Noam, 'The Choice of Government Level in Regulation', *Kyklos*, 35:2 (1982), pp. 278–91; A. Ogus, 'Standard Setting for Environmental Protection: Principles and Processes', in M. Faure, J. Vervaele, and A. Weale (eds.), *Environmental Standards in the European Union in an Interdisciplinary Framework* (Antwerp: MAKLU, 1994), pp. 25–37, esp. p. 33; J. Pelkmans, 'The Assignment of Public Functions in Economic Integration', *Journal of Common Market Studies*, 21:1–2 (1982), pp. 97–121; S. Peltzman and T. N. Tideman, 'Local versus National Pollution Control: Note', *American Economic Review*, 62:5 (1972), pp. 959–63; and J. Rothenberg, 'Local Decentralization and the Theory of Optimal Government', in J. Margolis (ed.), *The Analysis of Public Output* (New York and London: Columbia University Press, 1970), pp. 31–64.
60. Single European Act, Article 130R(4).
61. Treaty on European Union, Article 3b.
62. A. Jordan, 'European Community Water Policy Standards: Locked In or Watered Down?' *Journal of Common Market Studies*, 37:1 (1999) pp. 13–37.
63. B. Flynn, *Subsidiarity and the Rise of Soft Law* (University of Essex: Human Capital and Mobility Network, 1997), Occasional Paper no. 40.
64. A. Underdal, 'Integrated Marine Policy: What? Why? How?', *Marine Policy*, 4:3 (1980), at p. 162.
65. Weale, *New Politics of Pollution*, ch. 5. See also Ch. 5 below.
66. Single European Act, Article 130R(2).
67. Treaty on European Union, Article 130R(2).
68. *Official Journal of the European Communities*, C112, 20.12.73, p. 5.
69. Ibid. 7.
70. *Official Journal of the European Communities*, C139, 13.06.77, p. 20.
71. *Official Journal of the European Communities*, C46, 17.02.83, p. 13.
72. Ibid. 1.
73. Ibid. 2.
74. *Official Journal of the European Communities*, C139, 13.06.77, p. 5.
75. *Official Journal of the European Communities*, C46, 17.02.83, p. 1.
76. Ibid. 3.
77. Ibid. 4
78. House of Lords Select Committee on the European Communities, *Fifth Environmental Action Programme: Integration of Community Policies*, HL Paper 27, (London: HMSO, 1992), p. 9.

79. Commission of the European Communities, 'Memorandum: The "Polluter Pays" Principle', in House of Lords Select Committee on the European Communities, *The Polluter Pays Principle*, Session 1982–3, 10th Report (London: HMSO, 1983), pp. 102–3.

80. Cited in House of Lords Select Committee on the European Communities, *Fourth Environmental Action Programme*, p. 28.

81. Commission of the European Communities, *Towards Sustainability*, p. 67.

82. See M. S. Andersen, *Governance by Green Taxes: Making Pollution Prevention Pay* (Manchester and New York: Manchester University Press, 1994).

83. T. H. Tietenberg, *Emissions Trading: An Exercise in Reforming Pollution Policy* (Washington: Resources for the Future, 1985).

84. Task Force on the Environment and the Internal Market, '1992: The Environmental Dimension', (mimeo, Commission of the European Communities, 1989), p. 8.12.

85. Ibid.

86. J. Delbeke, 'The Prospects for the Use of Economic Instruments in EC Environmental Policy', in *Economic Instruments in EC Environmental Policy*, Report on the LMO/EEB Conference in The Hague, September 1991, p. 44.

87. Commission of the European Communities, *Communication on the Use of Economic and Physical Instruments in EC Environmental Policy* (Luxembourg: Commission of the European Communities, 1990).

88. Council Directive 82/884/EEC.

89. Commission of the European Communities, *Towards Sustainability*, p. 67.

90. Ibid.

91. Treaty on European Union, Article 2.

92. Commission of the European Communities, *Economic Growth and the Environment: Some Implications for Policy-Making*, Communication from the Commission to the European Parliament and Council, COM(94) 465, final, 3.11.94.

93. Ibid. 5.

94. Ibid.

95. A. Liberatore, 'Problems of Transnational Policymaking: Environmental Policy in the European Community' *European Journal of Political Research*, 19, (1991), p. 283.

96. The UN Environmental Programme estimates that traffic congestion in Bangkok cost $1 bn a year in medical and other side-effects. On cold winter days, the smog blanketing China's northern cities is between 6 and 20 times the highest levels in the West. (*The Economist*, 18 June 1994, p. 16).

97. Commission of the European Communities, *Economic Growth and the Environment*, p. 5.

98. Ibid.

99. Ibid.

100. *The Economist*, 18 June 1994, p. 17.

101. Commission of the European Communities, *Economic Growth and the Environment*, p. 7.

102. Wurzel, 'Environmental Policy', p. 180.

103. SEC (72) 596 of 14.2.72.

104. See Weale, *New Politics of Pollution*, ch. 3, and A. Weale, 'Ecological Modernization and the Integration of European Environmental Policy', in J. D. Liefferink, P. D. Lowe, and A. J. P. Mol, *European Integration and Environmental Policy* (London and New York: Belhaven Press, 1993), pp.196–216.

105. House of Lords Select Committee on the European Communities, *Fourth Environmental Action Programme*, pp. 53–4.
106. A. Hirschman, *The Rhetoric of Reaction* (Cambridge Mass.: Belknap Press, 1991), pp. 149–54.
107. In conducting interviews in the Commission, we often found ourselves listening to anecdotes about how firms that had reluctantly taken up environmental measures found after a short while that they had profited thereby.
108. Commission of the European Communities, *Growth, Competitiveness, Employment*.
109. Ibid. 20.
110. Ibid. 28.
111. Ibid. 62.
112. Ibid. 63.
113. See M. Albert, *Capitalism versus Capitalism* (London: Whurr, 1993).
114. Commission of the European Communities, *Completing the Internal Market*, COM(85) 310 final, 14.6.1985, pp. 4–8.
115. G. Majone, 'Market Integration and Regulation: Europe after 1992', *Metroeconomica*, 43:1–2 (1992), pp. 131–56.

3

Actors and Institutions in
Environmental Governance

Policy-making is an institutional process as well as an intellectual activity. In the previous chapter we examined the intellectual component of policy-making by looking at some of the principles that have been adumbrated by the EU in the choice of policy. But principles do not exist in thin air. They have to be employed by institutions in the task of formulating policy and devising solutions to environmental problems. Governance, then, involves institutions and institutional actors. Before choices can be made and strategies formulated, institutions have to be established and responsibilities defined.

When nation states first started to respond to environmental problems in the late 1960s and early 1970s, they initiated the process by fashioning institutional arrangements for the making of policy.[1] Yet institutionalization and policy-making interact in an ongoing process of adaptation and reformulation so that policy-making feeds into processes of institutionalization, just as institutions shape policy-making. Within the EU, where task expansion and issue redefinition is intrinsic to political integration, this interaction of policy and institutional development is even more marked, as we shall seek to show in this chapter.

European institutions and institutional actors thus occupy a pivotal position in the European environment policy narrative. As we have seen, the creation of environmental rules and the involvement of the European institutions in environmental rule creation has been an incremental and cumulative process, characterized by the gradual formalization and elaboration of what was originally little more than a disparate body of unrelated legislative acts. As part of this process, institutional proliferation also occurred, by which environmental concerns became a feature not just of a narrow range of EU institutions but also of the work of a significant set of actors.

The European system of environmental governance thus involved not just a development of policies, but also an extension of the range and character of various institutional actors. In charting the institutionalization of environmental regulation at the European level, we seek to explain how the role of the European institutions has altered and adapted as European environmental governance has evolved. In what follows we shall treat institutions primarily as organizational actors while recognizing that they derive their powers and place in the EU's system of environmental governance from the complex of rules and practices within which they are embedded.

THE MAIN INSTITUTIONAL ACTORS

The European Commission

The European Commission performs a wide range of functions and is involved in many ways in environmental governance. As an agenda-setter, consensus-builder, manager, and the formal initiator of legislation, its presence is largely taken as a given at all stages in the European environmental policy process. The institution has frequently been characterized as a hybrid mixture of European civil service, international secretariat, and embryonic government. Its functions have similarly been defined as both political and administrative, though these dichotomies hardly do justice to the uniqueness of the institution.

Structurally, the Commission is headed by an executive and collegiate decision-making organ, the College of Commissioners. These are the twenty commissioners who collectively decide Commission policy. Each commissioner is responsible for one or more portfolios, and voting is on a consensus or simple majority basis and is confidential. The division of tasks among the commissioners has as much to do with political expectations and national lobbying as with the competence and administrative or political experience of individual commissioners. As with any ministerial-type post, commissioners are expected to operate on a fast learning curve and to pick up the fine detail of the portfolios on the job. The names and associated details of those who have held the environment portfolio are given in Table 3.1.

Over the course of this study, Carlo Ripa di Meana was perhaps the most high-profile and controversial of the environment commissioners, although he held the post for only two years; in some ways then he was not typical, and an analysis of his term of office can distract attention away from the solid successes of his predecessors. Ripal di Meana presented himself as a 'true believer', and perhaps luckily for him his term of office coincided with a sharp rise in the European-wide issue attention cycle towards environmental issues. Emboldened by the pace of events

TABLE 3.1 *Environment commissioners and their terms of office*

Years	Name	Nationality	Party affiliation	President
1973–77	Scarascia Mugnozza	Italian	Christian Democrat	Ortoli
1977–81	Natali	Italian	Christian Democrat	Jenkins
1981–85	Narjes	German	Christian Democrat	Thorn
1985–89	Clinton-Davis	UK	Labour	Delors I
1990–92	Ripa di Meana	Italian	Socialist[a]	Delors II
1992	Van Miert	Belgian	Socialist	Delors II
1993–95	Paleokrassas	Greek	Socialist	Delors III
1995–99	Bjerregaard	Danish	Social Democrat	Santer

[a] Later Green and then United European Left/Nordic Green Left.

in the late 1980s, he was unafraid of drawing controversy to himself, attempting at times to bounce issues on to the collegiate agenda by preemptive force of a popular press conference or other such publicity. As a result, his often tense relationship with Commission President Jacques Delors was public knowledge. Personal and professional tensions ran particularly high over the controversial carbon tax proposal during the run-up to the June 1992 Rio Earth Summit, leading ultimately to di Meana's resignation over the refusal of the collective Commission to back his position. In hindsight, this policy style of 'forcing' the issue through high levels of publicity may have been less effective than the steady slow work of creating coalitions within the collective Commission as a whole, and with other institutions.

After Ripa di Meana's resignation, Karel Van Miert took over during an interregnum of six months. However, Van Miert was keen to make clear that he did not see his function as rolling back what he described as 'one of our most successful policies, and one of the best understood', even in the context of the demands for a repatriation of environmental competences.[2] After the interregnum, Ripa's long-term successor, Yannis Paleokrassas, marked a shift to a more traditional, cautious style. While as a former Greek minister of finance he was not known for his environmental convictions, it should be emphasized that much of DG XI's work continued—the normal review of out-of-date directives, the drafting of measures required as a corollary of the single market legislative bulge, and so on. Thus, it would be misleading to see the pace of environmental proposals emanating from the Commission as largely a function of the leadership qualities of a given environment commissioner.

Paleokrassas's successor, appointed in 1995, was Ritt Bjerregaard. A former schoolteacher and minister of education and social affairs in successive Social Democratic administrations in Denmark, she was once described as combining 'a hectoring, school-mistressy tone with a frosty charm that has earned her the nickname "Ice Maiden"'.[3] She, like Ripa, soon gained a reputation for outspokenness, publishing a diary early in her term that was openly critical of her fellow commissioners. As a result, the suggestion has been made that she was marginalized within the collective Commission, whose interest in pursuing environmental measures waned as other projects, such as EMU, came to dominate.

Whether personalities play such a central role is an open question. There is a case for caution in arguing for the centrality of the commissioner's role. To some extent, commissioners are only as good as their support staffs. The informal working groups of *cabinets* of various commissioners can be extremely important, as not only do such advisers to the commissioner have their master's or mistress's ear, but they frequently have excellent contacts beyond Brussels with Whitehall, Paris, and so on.[4] More generally, they provide a form of policy leadership and agenda-setting. Their interactions with the various personnel on committees is vital for transmitting and receiving information flows. It is the *cabinets* that keep commissioners informed of general policy developments and are responsible for specific briefs.

The *cabinets* also liaise between the commissioners and the Commission services. The Commission comprises twenty-four directorates-general (DGs), which, like mini-ministries, are responsible for specific sectoral and horizontal policies, reflecting the policy competences of the Union. These DGs are headed by director-generals, senior Commission officials who can themselves have an important effect on policy priorities. It was said for example that, when Laurens-Jan Brinkhorst was director-general of the environment DG, he was able to influence the department's agenda and was especially good with respect to those aspects of policy concerned with external relations. Within this general structure, horizontal services provide across-the-board facilities for all DGs. For environmental matters, the Legal Service is one of the most important. Since it is responsible for ensuring that legislation being developed within the DGs is compatible with the Treaty and is legally sound, it examines all draft environment texts, though it rarely interferes with the substantive aspects of draft legislation.

Whereas a number of DGs, such as those dealing with energy, research and development, and industry for example, have an interest and some involvement in environmental matters, it is DG XI (environment, nuclear safety, and civil protection) that is ultimately responsible for the drafting of environmental legislation and the implementation of policy. DG XI is divided into directorates dealing with general and international affairs, environment, industrial nuclear safety and civil protection, and environmental quality and natural resources. It is still a relatively small DG, though it has grown by a whole order of magnitude since the mid-1980s. Whereas before the Single European Act it managed with only 40–60 full-time personnel, this had risen to some 500 staff by the mid-1990s. Even so, Sbragia noted in 1996 that there are only 15 officials in DG XI dealing with the supervision of chemicals, as against 55 in the US Environmental Protection Agency.[5]

DG XI has a distinctive character within the Commission. Still viewed by many as a 'fringe' or 'science' DG, or as extreme in its advocacy of environmental causes, its leadership, particularly when Laurens-Jan Brinkhorst was director-general, has consciously sought to transform it into a more 'mainstream' institution.[6] Its image within the Commission is important, as it is necessary for the DG to build coalitions of support for its proposals. Alone, it can achieve little, as it is not one of the Commission's political heavyweights. Without inter-service consultation, there is no hope of commissioners agreeing to any draft environment proposal. However, disagreements among DGs, and among commissioners, have occasionally become acrimonious; it was said, for example, that the only reason that the Danish bottles case ended up in the European Court was because of an unresolved internal Commission dispute.

The change in ethos sought by DG XI's leadership remains contentious. As yet, it has had little impact on external perceptions of the DG, though environmental groups clearly see DG XI as an integral part of the Commission, and not as a defender of or voice for their interests. From their point of view, the 'mainstreaming' of DG XI has already gone too far.

Even so, there are close contacts between environmental interest groups and DG XI, if only because the Commission is dependent on outside expertise for scientific and policy advice. With the setting up in 1994 of the European Environment Agency, an advisory body designed to manage and filter information on the European environment, this dependence may well begin to weaken, though it is extremely unlikely that it will disappear altogether.

One domain of the Commission's activities that is frequently forgotten about is its duty to produce detailed delegated secondary legislation as mandated under parent directives and regulations that have been approved by the Council of Ministers. To assist them in this function, a host of specialized committees[7] with distinctive rules have been set up; indeed, at present some several hundred such committees meet on and off to assist the Commission in a system that is known as 'comitology'. These committees are composed of experts, typically nationally approved scientists from each member state, who provide detailed advice to the Commission on the rules and regulations associated with a major directive. Since much of the precise costs of an environmental measure turn on such details, the work of such committees is by no means trivial, even if it is often complex or obscure.

Several sources suggest that reliance by DG XI on these committees is quite extensive and detailed.[8] According to Demmke, DG XI relied during the 1990s on some thirty-six implementing committees, although the budget for 1996 rather confusingly lists only thirty-two in the environment sector.[9] Demmke suggests that just over half the implementation committees in the environment sector were active in 1995, producing the main positive proposals for the Commission's proposed secondary legislation. While this assessment suggests a relatively low reliance on implementing committees by DG XI (some 36 out of 400 committees for the whole Commission), this view needs to be put in context. In 1989, for instance, DG XI involved a total of some 3,157 experts (of which 1,397 were government experts and 1,760 were private experts) in their committee deliberations, making them the fifth largest users of committees measured in this way. (DG VI, with its responsibility for the Common Agricultural Policy, predictably came first.)[10] We also know that, measured in terms of total numbers of meetings for 1989, DG XI sponsored some 411 in total, which places them sixth in a table of DGs' committee use.[11] Of course these statistics relate to only a limited amount of time, and they also tell us little about their actual influence on proposals for Commission secondary regulation. But they are at least suggestive as to aggregate importance.

Comitology in environmental policy can be vital because, under a variety of complex rules, the so-called 'regulatory committees' in particular may actually refuse to approve Commission plans and thus leave policy in limbo. Alternatively, they can send issues back to the Council, thus reopening the terms of the original agreement. For these reasons, if for no other, the European Parliament has been keen to be given a greater say on comitology, while environmental groups have been prone to worry aloud about the scope for opaque and secretive deals being done between national representatives and Commission officials—a point that further illustrates the possibility of permeation of the supposedly supranational Commission by member states' representatives.

If we ask what is the typical sort of committee associated with the environmental brief, the answer is that they include the committees to oversee the application of the directive on waste (75/442/EEC), and the directive on integrated pollution prevention and control (94/61/EC).[12] These are distinctive because in most cases they involve member state experts who vet or advise the Commission's proposal. They are also distinctive in so far as some can effectively block Commission proposals or effectively demand that such proposals be referred back to the Council. This means that the Commission is subject to the influence of a web of national actors who shape the details of Commission proposals. Notice too that this highly complex method of producing secondary legislation also keeps the involvement of the generally pro-environment Parliament at arms' length, a fact that has provoked occasional bouts of inter-institutional guerilla warfare.[13]

The case of the pesticides authorization directive (91/414/EEC) is an example of how complex and controversial the operation of comitology can be in practice. The directive was intended to create a streamlined and harmonized procedure for the authorization of pesticides and related products, and it required daughter directives to be brought into force setting down the technical details. Crucial to this process was the securing of an agreement on common scientific principles which member states were to apply to products that contained specified pesticides or related ingredients. The task was left to the Standing Committee on Plant Health, an expert regulatory committee that took decisions on the basis of qualified majority voting.[14] The task took some time, and by 1994 had become quite politicized, the European Parliament challenging the procedure on the grounds of its implications for pesticide residues in ground water. The Parliament saw the regime being negotiated by the intergovernmental expert committee as a form of backdoor law-making. The result was a successful legal challenge by the Parliament to the European Court of Justice that struck down the putative directive.[15] Politically speaking, therefore, comitology is interesting as it illustrates the extent to which intergovernmentalist actors have become close working partners with supranational actors in the evolving system of European environmental governance. Institutional walls in Brussels are thin and allow for much permeation by nation state actors, in this case national experts, to the extent that distinguishing the 'national' from the 'European' becomes extremely difficult.

The European Parliament

The European Parliament often sees itself, and is seen by others, as the defender of environmental interests. Indeed, it is often to the Parliament that environment groups turn as a first port of call when seeking to lobby the European institutions. The Parliament's capacity to influence the European policy process is now well documented, although there is controversy about its extent and character.[16] As we shall see, particularly in the discussion of legislation on vehicle emissions, the Parliament's ability to alter environmental legislation has been enhanced since the Single European Act and the extension of qualified majority voting in environment matters. After Maastricht, and with the introduction of the co-decision procedure in some areas of environment policy-making, this influence has further increased, a trend that has been confirmed by the Amsterdam Treaty. Amendments proposed by the Parliament can lead to substantial changes in legislative outputs, as happened in the car emissions case. In this instance, the Parliament was able to persuade the Commission and the Council to accept stricter emission standards than those originally planned (see Chapter 11).

Most of the Parliament's formal work takes place in committee sessions. The twenty parliamentary committees debate and investigate draft proposals, produce reports on the Commission's legislative proposals, and propose amendments which are ultimately voted on in the Parliament's plenary sessions. Directly elected, the members of the European Parliament (MEPs) are the most obvious link between the European institutions and the citizens of Europe. As the EU becomes increasingly aware of the urgent need to reduce the democratic deficit, by increasing its legitimacy and by working towards a more open and transparent system of governance, the Parliament is sure to become an even more pivotal actor within the EU polity.

Much of the Parliament's pro-environment reputation is largely due to the work of its Environment Committee, which has traditionally had one of the heaviest workloads of any Parliament committee.[17] Under the effective leadership of the UK Labour MEP, Ken Collins, the Environment Committee became one of the more respected committees in the Parliament. One reason for this success stemmed from the fact that the Committee has been able to develop close relations with its partner institutions, and especially with DG XI, to the extent that '[a]t all stages of the EC policy process the footprints of the Environment Committee can be traced'.[18] The Committee is also the place where the Parliament's Green MEPs, to the extent to which they have been able to act as a unified group, have sought to advance their views.[19] Moreover, many members of the Committee have taken it upon themselves to initiate their own expert reports into environmental issues, and the Environment Committee has embarked on a great many more own-initiative reports than most other committees.[20]

In short, the Parliament's Environment Committee has attempted to become a serious parliamentary working committee, somewhat in the mode of the committees of the German Bundestag. Its own-initiative reports provide a key resource which can occasionally challenge the expert status of the Commission or evidence presented by the lobbies of interest groups. Thus, it has pursued 'a proactive policy role in agenda-setting'.[21]

Note however that considering the Parliament as a unified actor may be as misplaced as was that view of the Commission; for, while the Environment Committee may advise the Parliament as whole in plenary, a majority of MEPs may not agree with their conclusions. Clear overall majorities are needed from the Parliament as a whole if it is to exercise any control in the co-decision and cooperation procedures in opposition to the Council of Ministers. Conversely, there are cases where the Environment Committee has urged acceptance of a Commission and Council proposal only to find that the Parliament as a whole has different ideas and is intent to prove its green credentials by demanding some further change.

Some MEPs may wish to specialize in the environment brief for reasons of symbolic politics. Clearly, the Parliament is more likely to propose an amendment that raises questions involving visceral feelings rather than the more staid fare of technical harmonization that tends to concern the Commission. Hence some MEPs are prone to specialize in 'emotive environmentalism' concerning such issues as leg-hold traps, whaling, and baby seal fur. On the latter, the Parliament scored an early victory with directive 83/129, which prohibits the importation of seal pup skin; this was largely at the instigation of a few MEPs and a plenary majority receptive to such emotive issues.

While there has clearly been an official growth in competences, which reflects its role as a conditional agenda-setter, the Parliament's influence is more often informal and covert than open and institutionalized; or, to put it more accurately, the relationship between its formal and informal functions tend to become blurred. This is not to deny that the Environment Committee has been extremely effective in making use of formal treaty changes as a means of maximizing its influence throughout the policy process, but rather to emphasize how a politics of institutional expertise has brought the environment committee members in particular inside the policy network. As one source suggests, 'a shared inter-institutional ethos between Committee members and Commission staff has served to enhance the informal exercise of parliamentary influence over EC environmental legislation'.[22]

However, there are other reasons why the Parliament has developed a pro-environment reputation. One is the influence of the Green MEPs within the Parliament, where their representation may be proportionately larger than within a member state. (Ireland for example at one time had two Green MEPs but only one national Green MP.) Another reason is that the environment is one of the truly transnational issues dealt with by the EU. As such, European elections, commonly fought on a domestic agenda, have in the environment a distinctly European issue which is appropriately addressed by the Parliament. This was certainly the case in the 1989 European elections, though it has been a less obvious trait in European elections in the 1990s.

The Council of Ministers and the European Council

Despite the relatively novel legislative powers now in the hands of the European Parliament, the Council of Ministers remains to a large degree the legislating body of the European Union. What we identify as the Council depends on the policy sector under scrutiny. In the present context we are largely, though not exclusively, interested in the Council of Environment Ministers. This was created in 1973 as a response to the general rise in public concern about environmental issues. By the 1990s it was holding at least four Council meetings each year, more if we include informal meetings. As the Councils are not standing bodies, they are assisted by national officials, holding ambassadorial or deputy ambassadorial positions, who collectively form the Committee of Permanent Representatives (COREPER). COREPER can play a pivotal role in the development of environment policy. It steps in after the more technical committees and working parties have surveyed the draft legislation and does much of the groundwork for the Council meetings, sifting out controversial sticking-points and seeking agreement wherever possible.

The importance of the Council derives from the fact that it is the last port of call for European environment legislation, which, unless appealed against, must subsequently be implemented and enforced. The Council is made up of national ministers, one from each member state, and is chaired by the country holding the EU presidency. Depending on the issue and consequently the treaty base, votes on legislation are taken either by unanimity, with every state effectively holding a veto over new legislation, or by a system of qualified majority voting (QMV). QMV is a weighted voting system which gives the larger states more votes than the smaller ones (though not in a strict proportionate sense).

The significance of the decision procedures in the Council of Ministers stems from the fact that it is in this forum that differences of national policy preference are expressed. Given the institutional centrality of the Council, and its significance as the archetypical intergovernmentalist institution of the EU, its pattern of decision-making is dominated by the pattern of preferences that member states bring to Council discussions. In this context, the hypothesis that has dominated both journalistic and academic accounts of the Environment Council is that its divisions take a 'leader–laggard' form.[23] According to this view, we can categorize member states into 'leaders', who press for high environmental standards, and 'laggards', who for a variety of reasons oppose the raising of standards.

Among proponents of this view, there is more consensus on the composition of the leader group than there is on the make-up of the set of laggards. Usually Denmark, Germany, and the Netherlands, together with the three new members (Austria, Finland, and Sweden) who joined in 1995, are placed in the leader category, although some commentators question Germany's right to be included in this group.[24] One favourite candidate for a laggard is the UK, which during the 1980s earned among many members of the attentive public the unenviable reputation of the 'dirty man of Europe'. The cohesion countries and Italy are also sometimes said to belong to the laggards. A slightly more nuanced classification is a threefold one, with Denmark, Germany, and the Netherlands (joined since 1995 by Austria, Finland, and Sweden) in the leader category, then the UK, France, and Italy in an intermediate category, and everyone else in a third, laggard, group. The discrepancy in classification by observers suggests that the identification of countries according to their stance may not be well defined, or perhaps that assignment may depend upon the issues that are considered or on changing preferences over time.

If the leader–laggard hypothesis is to mean anything, it should pick out fairly stable patterns of member state policy preference over time and across a range of issues. To test this hypothesis, we have examined controversies in the Council of Ministers between 1980 and 1996.[25] We do not pretend that these reported disagreements are representative of Council decision-making in general. There are a great many issues of a non-controversial kind in environmental policy where there is no dispute at ministerial level. Thus, many accounts of the Council stress that, as often as not, policy-making is achieved in a highly consensual manner, without formal votes being taken after the *tour de table*. Moreover, any source, no matter how reliably it reports events, is liable to selection bias and error. None the less, examination of the position that member states take when there is a disagreement provides some indicator of the characteristic orientation that member states bring to decision-making.

Classifying the position that member states take is not a mechanical exercise. We cannot simply assume, for example, that opposing an environmental directive indicates a laggard position, since a member state government might want an even stricter standard than is implied in the draft directive—as was true of the Danish position on car exhausts, for example, in the 1980s. Hence we need to consider not just the fact of opposition, but also the reasons for opposition. Generally speaking, we can say that a member state is laggardly in respect of an environmental measure when it wants to weaken the stringency of the proposed standard.

There are various reasons offered by member states as to why any standard should be weaker than proposed, and the type of reason helps us to classify the various forms that opposition can take. They may oppose the measure on grounds of economic cost, as did a number of countries on the issue of car exhaust emissions in the 1980s. They may believe that there are technical constraints or other barriers, derived from administrative complexity, to a measure's being successful, as with the latter sort of argument pleaded by Germany over integrated pollution control. They may argue that the proposed standard is too inflexible, that the timetable is too fast, that the permitted pollution levels are too strict or that they are phrased in the wrong terms (for example as an emission limit rather than an environmental quality standard). It may also be argued, as it has been by Spain and the other cohesion countries on a number of measures, that their economic status means that they should be allowed to increase their pollution, within a certain margin, as the price for economic growth. Or it may be asserted that the EU is simply the wrong body to seek to regulate in a certain way, as a number of countries argued in connection with the proposal for a carbon-energy tax.

We can count the frequency with which, when expressing a position in a controversial matter, countries take a position in favour of raising environmental standards without expressing any reservations of the sort expressed above.[26] We set out these frequencies in Table 3.2. Some care must be taken in interpreting this table. It does not refer to a member state's position on all issues, but only on those issues

TABLE 3.2 *Support for more stringent environmental standards in the Council of Ministers, 1980–1995*[a]

Country	For	Against	Total	For (%)	Rank
Belgium	2	3	5	40	5=
Denmark	13	0	13	100	1=
Eire	1	4	5	20	10=
France	4	9	13	31	9
Germany	26	3	29	90	3
Greece	4	6	10	40	5=
Italy	3	6	9	33	8
Luxembourg	2	2	4	50	4
Netherlands	16	0	16	100	1=
Portugal	1	4	5	20	10=
Spain	0	8	8	0	12
UK	6	11	17	35	7

[a] Study countries in bold. Own categorization of support.

Source: ENDS *Reports* for various years.

where some clear view was expressed. Moreover, during the course of negotiating a complex directive, sometimes extending over half a decade, member state preferences can change, and it is difficult to capture these modulations in a simple 'for or against' classification. Some judgment, therefore, has to be exercised. Finally, although expressed as percentages, the numbers can be small (the percentages for Eire and Portugal are based on only five issues, for instance), and indeed this is one reason why we do not present data for the post-1995 three. However, bearing all these limitations in mind, we hope that the data do provide some systematic basis against which to test impressions, impressions that might otherwise have been gained from considering only a limited number of issues.

The results presented in the table confirm the position of a group of environmental leaders made up, until 1995, of Denmark, Germany, and the Netherlands. Their common position was characterized as wanting tight emission standards in air pollution, both from stationary and from mobile sources, favouring stringent controls on discharges to water, and pressing for international leadership to be shown by the EU on matters like ozone depletion. Germany's 'defections' from this group were principally over the administrative implications of measures such as eco-auditing and integrated pollution control. However, on a whole range of measures— vehicle emissions, sulphur dioxide control, titanium dioxide control, packaging, landfill regulations, waste water treatment, restrictions on discharges of dangerous substances to water, and investments in hazardous waste control—these countries occupied a leader position within the Council of Ministers.

By contrast, it is not possible to identify a core group of laggard countries. Spain stands out as the country most keen to push the case for conventional economic growth against the demands for stricter environmental standards, and often with the implication that low standards may be appropriate for countries with a margin of environmental quality to exploit. Although sometimes joined in this position by the other cohesion countries, Spain was clearly, in its expressed positions, the most productivist of the member states after its accession in 1986. The position of Greece contrasts with that of Spain, although in both cases the absolute number of issues is small. Thus, Greece was in the leader group on unleaded petrol, vehicle emissions, waste exports, and civil liability, but it was a laggard on the large combustion plant directive, proposals on the sulphur content of fuel oils, measures to combat ozone depletion, co-disposal to landfill, the carbon tax, and integrated pollution control.

Does the UK deserve its reputation as the 'dirty man of Europe'? On many issues it was clearly laggardly. These include the large combustion plant directive, control of titanium dioxide emissions, vehicle emissions, co-disposal to landfill, the carbon tax, packaging and packaging waste, and the carbon tax. On the other hand, it can be regarded as a leader on eco-audits, integration pollution control, and, latterly, control of carbon dioxide emissions. To some extent, its laggardly reputation is derived as much from the style with which its opposition was expressed as from the substance of the position that it took. To some extent also, its placement in the middling group of countries, with France and Italy in particular, reflects the averaging of a laggardly set of positions in the 1980s with a leaning towards more leadership in the 1990s.

How far, then, has there been a leader–laggard dynamic at work in the Council? Clearly, there have been leaders, and undoubtedly this conclusion would be reinforced if we were also to consider the non-controversial issues where pressure from the greener member states played a role in developing policies. However, we cannot infer from the existence of a clear leader group that there is an equally coherent laggard group. Those who favoured less stringent standards often did so for a variety of reasons, and by virtue of that fact there was no underlying principle at work to bind different member states together in broad opposition to the development of environmental policy. Thus, with the cohesion countries, the issues were often less to do with the justification of the proposed standard itself, and more to do with securing the resources to finance the investment that the standard would require. Arguments of economic feasibility also played a role for countries like France, Italy, and the UK, who were often highly sensitive to the cost implications of the measures that the leader group proposed. It is not difficult, therefore, to see the influence of comparative economic standing in the varying national preferences as they were expressed.

The varied preference patterns of the member states therefore account for two otherwise contradictory features of EU policy development since the early 1980s. On the one hand, there have been some significant innovations in EU environmental policy. On the other hand, there have also been some issues on which potential developments have been stalled or restricted. No developments could have taken place had there not been a willingness on the part of some countries to lead and enough other countries (on particular issues) to follow. Conversely, the constraints and restrictions would have been less had more countries shared the policy preferences of the leaders.

In this context, the voting rules and the number of votes per member state are not matters of mere detail. Before the 1995 enlargement, France, Germany, Italy, and the UK had ten votes each; Spain had eight votes; Belgium, Greece, the Netherlands, and Portugal had five; Denmark and Ireland had three, and Luxembourg had two. Out of a total of 76 votes, 54 constituted a qualified majority. Since the 1995 enlargement and the accession of Sweden, Finland and Austria, 62 out of 76 now constitutes a qualified majority.

Such figures are crucial as they affect the ways in which coalitions are built in favour of legislation, and the extent to which blocking minorities can be constructed in opposition. For example, could an alliance of Belgium, the Netherlands, Germany, Sweden, Finland, Austria, and Denmark force through an environmental law against the wishes of the UK, Ireland, and the Mediterranean states? For them to do so, they would need at least 62 votes for a qualified majority and at least ten members states would have to vote for the measure.[27] Taking the coalition suggested above together with Luxembourg would still give only 36 votes for the putative 'eco-leaders' coalition. The conclusion is that this might be enough for them to block legislation aiming to weaken environmental standards, but it would be very hard to get a winning coalition together to force stringent environmental legislation through against determined opposition.[28]

Equally, we may conclude that a blocking coalition of environmental 'laggards' can slow down the pace of environmental laws should they choose to. In fact it is relatively easy to construct a blocking majority against environmental laws with QMV. A coalition of the UK, Spain, Greece, and Portugal would together form a blocking group of 28 out of 87 in total; or the 'big three' of Germany, France, and the UK could together stop a proposal dead in its tracks. Even if France and Italy were to join the hypothetical 'leader' alliance suggested above, this delivers only 56 votes, leaving the coalition still 6 short of the number needed. In this case a combination of two more states would be needed: either the UK and Ireland together, with 13 votes against the Mediterranean recalcitrant states, or a combination of the Irish and one or more Mediterranean states would be needed. Thus, in practice coalition building is fraught with complexity, and in fact more than ten states may be required. Note also this exercise assumes that one can confidently predict member state preferences on a particular issue with some degree of certainty. In practice, on particular issues coalitions may be more fluid and dynamic.

Yet voting mechanisms are crucial in determining whether environmental legislation will be blocked by one or more states. The use of qualified majority voting in the Council has increased since the mid-1980s. With the 1992 Maastricht Treaty, QMV has been extended to cover almost all aspects of environment policy. Now only fiscal policy, land use and town and country planning matters, and energy supply legislation are subject to the unanimity principle. But these are important areas, and account, for example, for the problems in developing economic instruments at the European level.

The Secretariat of the Council is frequently overlooked in many institutional accounts of environmental governance. Yet it exerts a powerful role, and especially with regard to environmental policy one must note the creation in 1995 of a new Directorate-General I within the Secretariat General of the Council, which specializes in environmental matters. Interestingly, however, it has the lowest number of staff, with just fifteen persons.[29] It is simply too early to say what impact this special committee within the Council secretariat will have on COREPER and the Council's views on environmental policy, but it is clear evidence of the more extensive institutionalization of environmental policy within the EU. As the policy sector grows, there is a clear trend towards greater functional specialization on the environmental brief and less 'ad hoccery'. For functionalists, this suggests a future of more complex environmental policy advocacy coalitions between perhaps competing specialized environment policy actors inside Brussels, whereas intergovernmentalists may view such developments as yet another sign of the intergovernmentalist actors at work to ensure that they are well prepared defensively to control and, if necessary, stem the tide of environmental proposals.

The Council also includes the bureaucratic network of the various COREPER special committees, which in practice vet and agree proposed legislative points (so called 'A' points) prior to the deliberations of environment ministers. This leaves the ministers free to address the most important and contentious matters. To our knowledge, there is as yet no detailed account of COREPER's workings with regard to environmental policy, yet in general they must be considered vital in policy-making terms, as they are, as the *Financial Times* memorably dubbed them, 'the men who run Europe'.[30] The latter is not hyperbole on the part of journalists, considering that the COREPER processes routinely take care of about 85 per cent of proposed directives or regulations before the environment ministers ever get to do a *tour de table*.[31] We cannot even say with certainty if there are special environment working groups in COREPER II, as no official list is available.[32] However, and perhaps more importantly, what has not been explored are the non-hierarchical venues created through the regular working group meetings attended by Council Secretariats and the Commission's General Services Secretariat. One wonders how information and policy debate in this 'club-like atmosphere'[33] affect environmental policy debates. We just do not know how, and if at all reliably, Parliament learns, what is being talked about in COREPER II, or if they have ways of communicating their views back to COREPER working groups, although personal and informal contacts between permanent representatives and MEPs may well be the more important channel of communication.

Yet there can be no doubting that the staff of COREPER must exert some influence on the details of environmental directives and regulations. While we know comparatively little about their workings in specific instances of environmental legislation, one can note with confidence that the style of policy-making here is deeply technocratic. While national log-rolling and intergovernmentalist approaches would logically seem to predominate, the fact that such a close informal working relationship exists between these senior and mid-ranking national civil servants may in fact mean that a greater willingness to co-operate and agree legislation is much more evident than might be thought possible.[34] Thus, COREPER and the Council may be more consensual in their policy style with regard to the many mundane environment proposals than simple accounts of a north–south or 'leader–laggard' split would suggest. Sbragia adds to this observation the interesting point that a certain degree of solidarity can exist when the fifteen national environment ministers get together in council, which may well be at odds with the feelings of marginality from which they might often suffer inside domestic cabinets.[35] Hence, lest we should automatically assume the Council of Ministers to be always the most cautious of the European institutions on the environment, Sbragia suggests that the Council experience may well grant leverage to isolated environment ministers who, acting in concert, can then carve out an agenda that suits their own interests and reputations.

Of course, one should not overestimate such suggestions, for the council of environment ministers meets infrequently and any attempt at 'solo runs' on environment policy will quickly attract the attention of more senior councils and national cabinet members, typically finance or treasury members. Note also that a great deal of diversity exists in the composition of national environment ministers' portfolios.[36] Spanish, Irish, British, and Greek ministers have a large policy sphere which can include local government spending control, transport, and even housing. Such ministers may be less disposed to pursue environmental legislation than, say, a German or Danish minister who is preoccupied with environmental policy issues alone. Thus, what may matter is the relative cross-institutional coalition for a given environmental proposal, and not whether any one actor can confidently be labelled 'pro-environment'. At all times, environment proposals will demand support from other sectors either in Council or in the Commission.

There are clearly areas of policy affecting the environment which are the responsibility of Councils other than that dealing specifically with the environment: the energy policy, agriculture, transport, and research and development portfolios all have strong environmental implications. In order to overcome some of the problems of coordination in this area, joint councils may be held as a way of promoting consistency across what institutionally seem to be discrete policy areas. Although relatively rare, these joint council meetings can be high-profile events. For example, the new UK Labour government marked its Council presidency in 1998 by holding a joint council meeting between environment and transport, focusing on issues of car pollution and global climate change.

The supreme decision-taking body of the European Union is however the European Council, an institution with an identity distinct from that of the Council of Ministers. Composed of the heads of government (and heads of state in some cases) of the member states, the European Council sets agendas and filters information and demands for policy from the domestic political arena through to the European level. However, only the most controversial and politically sensitive of issues will come to the attention of the European Council. In the twice yearly meetings (with additional informal or extraordinary meetings also possible) there is time only to discuss and deal with issues unresolvable at Council level.

It is rare for environmental issues to take centre stage in European Council business, although the Dublin Council in 1990 stands as an exception to this rule. Its prioritization of issues of high politics—foreign policy matters, constitutional and institutional questions as well as economic affairs—meant that the environment was only one of many internal policy issues that rose sporadically to the top of its agenda, usually as a reaction to intense public or media attention. This does not mean that the European Council never deals with particular policy concerns. It often has little choice in the matter, as blockages at the level of the Council have frequently led to the transferring up of what might at first sight seem quite specific legislative proposals. However, in the large majority of cases it is the Council of Environment Ministers that is the legislating body.

One way in which the European Council did touch upon environmental policy was through its decision, championed by Helmut Kohl and John Major at the Essen summit of December 1994, to set the special *ad hoc* MOLITOR committee to examine ways of changing the Commission's working style to make it less interventionist and intrusive on national administrative regimes. Its influence on environmental policy is not immediately evident, but it certainly has developed an interest in the area and attracted the ire of environmentalists and the Parliament. The MOLITOR Group issued its report to the Commission in June 1995,[37] in which it recommended the simplification of existing environmental rules across the board, including the adoption of framework legislation that would clarify the environmental *acquis*. This, to a large extent, brought to a head a process that began in the 1992 Edinburgh Council, at which it was agreed that something had to be done to make the EU more transparent to its citizens.

While some of the recommendations of the MOLITOR Group have been well received (most notably those that encourage and increase the consultation and contacts between the EU institutions and those implementing policy in national environmental authorities and 'on the ground'), there was a great deal of concern about the assumptions under which the Group was operating. The European Environmental Bureau (EEB), the umbrella organization for environmental NGOs in Brussels, criticized the MOLITOR Group for directing its energies towards a neo-liberal inspired critique of environmental policy, suggesting that it articulated a view of environmental directives as making life hard for European business. As the Group was set up to consider administrative simplification from the perspective of job creation and competitiveness, it is perhaps not so surprising that it should adopt such a line. However, the European Parliament was keen to make clear its opposition to any assumption that simplification necessitated deregulation. In calling for new 'soft law' approaches in environmental policy-making, as well as for the use of more voluntaristic agreements, the Group seemed to be suggesting such an association. For the EEB, it was the process as well as the substantive aspects of the report that provoked anger, because they thought that 'Environment Ministers, Environment Ministries, and the advisory Committee set up by DG XI [of environmental NGOs—see above] were kept out of things. The whole system was by-passed so that the top of the hierarchy could impose a new environmental policy philosophy'.[38] While it is beyond the scope of this chapter to evaluate such claims, the institution watcher interested in environmental policy can note the continuing ability of new institutional practices to develop and to become in themselves politically charged.

The European Court

Situated outside the legislative institutional triangle, the relationship of the European Court of Justice to its partner institutions means that it plays a rather different role from that of Commission, Parliament, and Council. This does not alter the fact that the Court is one of the most important institutions of European environmental governance. It is the Court that sets the limits within which policy is made and, in confirming or rejecting the legality of European-level legislation, affects and even alters the focus and priorities of environmental policy.

There are in fact two European Courts: the Court of First Instance (CFI), and the European Court of Justice (ECJ). The CFI was set up in 1989 to reduce the backlog of cases that had built up in the ECJ. This backlog had been exacerbated by the increasing litigiousness of groups and individuals within the member states. Only cases involving 'legal or natural persons', that is cases not brought by the member state governments or the European institutions, are initially referred to the CFI. However, this applied to environmental appeals only from 1993. Thus, our focus of attention remains with the European Court of Justice, the court of last instance. Through the medium of both direct actions (appeals) and referrals from domestic courts asking for specific rulings, the ECJ is responsible for clarifying and interpreting European environmental law. Its impact on environmental governance since the early 1980s must not be underestimated.

It is possible to identify a number of distinct roles that the Court has come to play. The most obvious of these is that of hearing infringement proceedings brought by the Commission against a member state or by one member state against another for failure to implement an agreed piece of EU legislation. As we shall see in Chapter 8, the issue of implementation is an important one for EU environmental governance, and the role the Court can play, while not the only way in which compliance can be secured, is none the less important. The powers of the Court in such matters are defined by the treaty articles, and their exercise in the environmental sphere goes back to issues of implementation of measures passed in the 1970s.

Early cases were against Italy and Belgium.[39] The Italian cases were concerned with the implementation of two directives, one on detergents and the other on the sulphur content of liquid fuel oils. In those cases the Court confirmed, in a pair of judgments in 1980, that environmental measures could be passed under Article 100 of the Treaty of Rome. And, in a series of six judgments in 1982 against Belgium for infringements, the Court confirmed that environmental measures could be taken under the 'catch-all' Article 235 of the Treaty.

Another role of the Court is to clarify the legality of EU measures, and in this context it is important that the jurisprudence of the Court is teleological. This means that its decision-making is based upon considerations of policy, and in particular on a view that sees one of the primary functions of the Court as enlarging not only the scope and effectiveness of EU law, but also enlarging the powers of the EU itself.[40] This teleological jurisprudence has been important in shaping Court decisions that have permitted an expansion in the policy competence of the EU. Thus, in a judgment given in 1985 on the provisions of the waste oil directive, the Court argued that environmental protection was one of the EU's essential objectives, even though, at that time, there had not been a formal treaty revision.

The waste oil case also saw the Court introduce the idea that the objectives of the EU had to be balanced against one another. This was, of course, to be one of the principal points at issue in the Danish bottles case to which we referred in Chapter 1. What was notable in that case was the Court's willingness to envisage restrictions on the principle of freedom of trade, provided that the measure in question was not disproportionate to the environmental objective being sought.

The final important role of the Court in connection with environmental governance arises from the need to adjudicate on disputes among EU institutions about the application and interpretation of rules. In a case in 1991 concerning a directive aimed at the reduction of titanium dioxide waste, the Court had to decide whether the measure should have been passed under Article 130s of the Single European Act as an environmental measure, or whether it should have been treated as a single market measure under Article 100.[41] The Commission had argued that the directive should have been treated as a single market measure, whereas the Council had argued that it was an environmental measure. The Court's judgment is interesting from a number of points of view, not least its argument that Article 100 should have been used because that provided for greater democratic input from the Parliament; but in the present context its noteworthy feature is the extent to which it illustrates the role of the Court in adjudicating in disputes between other EU institutions. (See the next chapter for further discussion.)

As can be seen from these examples, part of the importance of the Court comes from the doctrines of direct effect and the pre-eminence of EU law under which it operates. These two principles together mean that European legislation takes priority over domestic law in cases where they conflict, and that any decision of the Court is directly applicable to citizens of the member states. There are question marks however over the capacity of the ECJ to *make* as well as to interpret environmental law. Whether this is indeed what the Court is doing is itself a matter of interpretation. The judicial politics or judicial activism of the Court is controversial, as it suggests that it acts as an unaccountable source of policy-making. However, given that environmental interest groups are increasingly willing to use legal challenge as a policy tool, the Court may well be judged more as a way of increasing citizen involvement in the European policy process than as a way of making environmental policy-making less transparent and accountable. The Court's role in the policy process is particularly important as the Commission has no environmental inspectorate, something that effectively bars the Commission from taking a proactive role in environmental enforcement. As such, the Commission–Court relationship is pivotal in ensuring the effective application of European environment law.

The European Environment Agency

The European Environment Agency is a more recent addition to the EU's system of environmental governance. While the Agency's establishment was delayed for some years as the result of complex political wrangling, it is slowly beginning to have an impact. In the course of its establishment, there were some voices calling for it to be given powers of supervision over national environmental inspectorates to ensure that they were correctly implementing and enforcing environmental legislation. However, this function was deleted from the final directive. None the less, its current role of disseminating and regularizing the production of environmental statistics and information is far from insignificant. As Majone has argued, the mere production of such information can have unintended regulatory effects by indicating implementation gaps and deficits and thus creating pressure for action.[42]

The fact that the Parliament scored two key victories on the content of the directive setting up the European Environment Agency (EEA) is relevant in this context. These gave the Parliament the right to choose two expert nominees to sit on the management board of the EEA,[43] and the supervisory competence of the EEA was to be reviewed before 1998. This leaves open the potential for institutional expansion (but perhaps contraction too). Thus, while it is too early to evaluate the contribution of the EEA to environmental policy, we can note that its creation marks a greater degree of institutional responsiveness to environmental concerns at the European level, and that an increase in the competences of the EEA in the future is a possibility.

OTHER INSTITUTIONS

Although the Commission, the Parliament, the Council and the Court are the central institutions in the making of EU environmental policy, with the Agency coming to be a part of the institutional mosaic, there are other institutional actors that are also important.

The *European Court of Auditors* has increasingly shown an ability and willingness to get drawn into environmental policy debates. In particular, its practice of responding to regular European Parliament requests to investigate the cost effectiveness of various environmental measures has led to a series of influential and authoritative special reports.[44] In these, the Court of Auditors can play its trump cards to the maximum: a high degree of credibility in policy debate, owing to its legal guardianship role, allied with the judicious use of pointed financial information to drive home its observations. While all institutions can produce arguments, few can do this so readily with clear price tags attached. Equally, the Court's powers are legally significant, and, should a hostile verdict of maladministration be recorded, this will provide the Parliament with powerful ammunition and leverage in its approval of the budgetary process in which it holds a veto. Thus, a number of the Court's special reports have had a significant impact, as in the recasting of the structural funds during the early 1990s to ensure that greater regard was given to environmental considerations. Note how such a change in policy arose from what in effect was a nexus between the Court of Auditors and the European Parliament.

Conversely, the Court has not for instance engaged in the type of financial analysis that might be damaging to environmental legislation, for example by showing how many jobs have been lost because of some environmental measures. Instead, the approach has been to ensure greater accountability in EU transfers for environment measures, in particular highlighting that there is little point spending money under one heading (cohesion) if it will cost the EU money to redress the effects of the spending under another (environment). Thus, it is the Court of Auditors more than any other actor that has done the most to ensure that the aim of integrating environmental considerations into other policies areas should be taken seriously and acted upon.

The *Committee of the Regions*, as one of the chief institutional innovations of the Maastricht Treaty, has also shown itself eager and capable of entering into the environmental policy fray. Firstly, it set up within its own working procedures a subcommittee (so called Commission Five) to examine issues of land use planning, environment, and energy. In plenary sessions environmental opinions have formed a substantial part of the committee's work; between September 1994 and November 1995 it issued some six environmental opinions, usually in response to a Commission legislative proposal.[45] With its unique make-up of subnational delegates, the Committee of the Regions has also allowed certain states, where the subnational tier of government is most developed, to have a louder and more effective voice, a voice that in some cases has had an environmental dimension.

Obviously, because of its composition from regional Europe, the regional policy profile of DG XVI is of paramount concern. Moreover, like the Court of Auditors, the Committee of the Regions has focused on the environmental components of European Regional Development Fund and the Cohesion Fund, at times demanding more integration and reflecting the desire of some regional subnational elites to be free from environmental 'fetters' on development. Nor is this a simple north–south split, as both Catalan nationalists and Bavarian conservatives can find common cause in arguing for deregulation, relaxation of rules, and in some cases even less environmental legislation.[46] However, the majority of contributions of the Committee of the Regions to environmental policy debate may be confidently characterized as 'pro-environment'. Witness its hostile view of the Commission proposal to amend the EU rules on environmental impact assessment, or its demand for action on drought in southern Europe, and its views on proposed reforms of the drinking water regime, which argued that parameters and tests of water quality should be extended while funds should also be made available for the removal of lead from water.[47]

In contrast to the relative newness of the Committee of the Regions, the older *Economic and Social Committee* has been part of the institutional architecture since the Treaty of Rome. Redolent of European Christian and Social Democratic thinking, it was originally designed to reflect the views of the so-called social partners (capital and labour), and to institutionalize interest aggregation at the European level. Yet this has not stopped the ESC developing an interest in environmental policy. In this regard, the work of the Committee in its plenary session for 1993 is instructive, with about five or six of its opinions concerned with environment measures. In particular, two substantive interventions were made on the carbon tax debate, with the tone and gist of the ESC's opinion favouring greater research and development into alternative fuels, while expressing anger at delays in the setting up of the European Environment Agency. On the crucial issue of support for a carbon tax, the ESC was broadly favourable, and certainly hedged its position with no more qualifications than most other institutions.[48]

It is also important to recognize the place of environmental non-governmental organizations. The most important umbrella group for environmental interests, with around 150 member organizations, is the *European Environmental Bureau* (EEB).[49] This is an extremely small office which must content itself with general tasks such as ensuring that environmental matters are recognized and discussed within the European institutions.[50] It tends to play a rather reactive role, though it does help to facilitate dialogue between NGOs and national governments, aided usually by DG XI. Meetings are held in Brussels each year with the president of the Commission and the president of the Environment Council. It would be wrong, however, to consider the EEB as part of the Commission's decision-making network, though there have been occasions on which EEB input has led to small amendments; examples include that of the eco-audit logo, and assistance given to MEPs in the drafting of the EP's response to the Fifth Action Programme.

Of perhaps greater relevance is the *General Consultative Forum*, which was set up in December 1992 as a response to the requirements of the Fifth Action Programme, and to contribute to the effective implementation of that programme. This is a thirty-two-member body which includes representatives from consumer groups, trade unions, and local authorities, as well as from environmental groups and industry. It seeks to provide a framework for the exchange of information with the Commission.[51] So far it has defined twelve principles for sustainable development, including statements on population issues, bio-diversity, and resource use and regeneration.[52] Resembling the UK's Advisory Council of the Business Environment, it is perhaps not the most important body to emerge from the post-1992 restructuring, but it is likely to serve a function that until then had not been catered for.

More important still is the *Environment Policy Review Group*, a meeting of top environmental civil servants from each of the member states. Set up early in 1993, it holds four meetings every year, allowing for a regular exchange of ideas between the European institutions and national officials. This is less a lobby group than the Consultative Forum, although it is clear that member state representatives often act almost simultaneously as policy-makers and lobbyists at different stages in the policy process.

CONCLUSIONS

Since 1972 environmental institutions have become more important within the general context of EU institutional actors. The establishment of DG XI and its subsequent expansion in size, the growth in the frequency of meetings of the Environment Council, and the central importance of the Environment Committee to the work of the European Parliament all testify to the rise of environmental issues on the public policy agenda and the salience that environmental policy has come to acquire in the process of European integration. In this sense, European environmental governance has reflected the 'inherently expansive' character of environmental policy in general.

Another aspect of the inherent expansiveness is the proliferation of institutional actors. Although the central institutions of European environmental governance remain the Commission, the Council of Ministers, the Parliament, and the Court, other bodies, most notably the European Environmental Agency, have come to play a role. Moreover, the interest shown in environmental policy by the Court of Auditors suggests that the cross-cutting character of environmental questions is important in shaping institutional forms, since environmental considerations raise questions about the appropriateness and side-effects of policies, such as agriculture or regional development, that are housed in parts of the policy-making machine that have traditionally lacked an environmental focus.

Specifically we can note here a number of trends. Firstly, between the period after the ratification of the SEA (1987) and the Treaty of Maastricht (1993) there has been a continual growth evident in the number of institutions that now take on board an 'environmental brief'. Equally, it is evident some of these have done so in more than a superficial way, having become potentially important contributors to environmental policy debates. Thirdly, this growing complexity provides greater scope for inter-institutional bargaining and policy advocacy coalitions—not just between different European institutions, but also, say, between national, subnational, and EU actors. What increasingly matters is the way the circus of actors fits together and the particular coalitions that persist and retain power and influence.

The multi-level character of the EU means that the institutions that mediate between national governments, including COREPER and national expert committees as well as the Council of Ministers, are particularly important. The extent to which policy preferences are rooted in domestic processes, and the form in which they can be transmitted and pursued at European level, are likely to be strongly conditioned by the place that institutional actors have within the overall system of governance.

All of this presupposes that actors are willing and able to use the power that rules, conventions, and practices bestow upon them. To be an actor is one thing; to play a part is another. In the next chapter we examine the extent to which the processes and procedures of European environmental governance are changing and thereby altering the role that actors can play.

NOTES TO CHAPTER 3

1. A. Weale, *The New Politics of Pollution* (Manchester and New York: Manchester University Press, 1992), p. 14.
2. See D. Gardner, 'Brussels: Green Activism Goes On', *Financial Times*, 22/3 August 1992, p. 2.
3. L. Boulton, 'A More Sustainable Commissioner', *Financial Times*, 13 November 1997, p. 3.
4. F. Hayes-Renshaw and H. Wallace, *The Council of Ministers* (London: Macmillan, 1997), p. 182.
5. A. Sbragia, 'Environmental Policy: The "Push–Pull" of Policy-Making', in H. Wallace and W. Wallace (eds.), *Policy-Making in the European Union* (Oxford: Oxford University Press, 1996), p. 244.
6. See K. Middlemas, *Orchestrating Europe* (London: Fontana, 1995), p. 251, for one example of the extremist characterization.
7. Confusingly, committees with the title 'expert' also exist in the Commission. The Commission appoints representatives, very often of peak interest bodies, for up to three years in informal consultative *ad hoc* committees. These may be not experts, certainly not in the neutral scientific sense, but lobbyists brought formally into the Commission's otherwise very wide 'open door' policy. Although it must be stressed that these groups cannot vote on proposals, they can make their opinions clear. Obviously,

such informal expert groups must play a not insignificant role in environmental policy-making as they tease out particular questions.

8. C. Demmke, 'National Officials and their Role in the Executive Process: "Comitology" and European Environmental Policy', in C. Demmke (ed.), *Managing European Environmental Policy: The Role of the Member States in the Policy Process* (Maastricht: European Institute of Public Administration, 1997), pp. 23–39; and G. J. Buitendijk and M. P. C. M. van Schendelen, 'Brussels Advisory Committees: A Channel for Influence?' *European Law Review*, 20:1 (1995), pp. 37–56. See also T. Bainbridge and A. Teasdale, *The Penguin Companion to the European Union* (Harmondsworth: Penguin, 1995).

9. Demmke, 'National Officials and their Role in the Executive Process'. The budget frequently underestimates the number of committees operating, because the Commission publishes a financial review only for those committees where consultation in mandatory; other *ad hoc* or purely advisory committees do not require a financial report, so that commentators are agreed that we cannot be sure how many committees are in operation at any one time. Cf. Buitendijk and van Schendelen, 'Brussels Advisory Committees', p. 40.

10. Ibid. 41.

11. Ibid.

12. O. Brouwer, Y. Comtois, M. van Empel, D. Kirkpatrick, and P. Larouche, *Environment and Europe: European Union Environment Law and Policy and its Impact on Industry* (Deventer: Stibbe Simont Monahan Duhot, 1994), p. 189.

13. This ongoing institutional guerilla warfare over comitology saw the Parliament reject the 1993 Voice Telegraphy Directive on comitology grounds and, later, remove some £17.5 m from the 1995 budget appropriations for committees in 1994. They maintained this drastic action until the Commission eventually gave in and provided the Parliament with information on the way in which various committees were operating. This in turn led to a 1993 inter-institutional agreement on comitology which modified earlier 1987 legislation.

14. N. Haigh, *Manual of Environmental Policy: The EC and Britain* (London: Cartermill International, 1992), p. 7.16–4.

15. *ENDS Report*, 'Uniform Principles Setback to Stall Approval of Pesticides', 261 (1996), pp. 45–7.

16. See D. Judge, D. Earnshaw, and N. Cowan, 'Ripples or Waves: The European Parliament in the European Community Policy Process', *Journal of European Public Policy*, 1:1 (1994), pp. 27–52; C. Hubschmid and P. Moser, 'The Co-Operation Procedure in the EU: Why was the European Parliament Influential in the Decision on Car Emission Standards?' *Journal of Common Market Studies*, 35:2 (1997), pp. 225–42; and G. Tsebelis, 'The Power of the European Parliament as a Conditional Agenda Setter' *American Political Science Review*, 88:1 (1994), pp. 128–42. The specific issue of car emissions legislation is discussed in Ch. 11.

17. F. Jacobs, R. Corbett, and M. Shackleton, *The European Parliament* (Harlow: Longman, 1992, 2nd edn), p. 115.

18. Judge *et al.*, 'Ripples or Waves', p. 32.

19. See E. Bomberg, *Green Parties and Politics in the European Union* (London and New York: Routledge, 1998), p. 132.

20. Jacobs *et al.*, *European Parliament*, p. 115.
21. Judge *et al.*, 'Ripples or Waves', p. 32.
22. Ibid. 33.
23. D. Liefferink and M. S. Andersen, 'Strategies of the "Green" Member States in EU Environmental Policy-Making', *Journal of European Public Policy*, 5:2 (1998), pp. 254–70; and Sbragia, 'Environmental Policy'.
24. See H. Pehle, 'Germany: Domestic Obstacles to an International Forerunner', in M. S. Andersen and D. Liefferink (eds.), *European Environmental Policy: The Pioneers* (Manchester and New York: Manchester University Press, 1997), pp. 161–209.
25. As reported in what is generally agreed is a reliable and well informed source, the *ENDS Report*.
26. This measure is thus the reciprocal of expressed opposition in cases where a view is expressed.
27. Bainbridge and Teasdale, *Penguin Companion to European Union*, pp. 378–83. An abstention is treated as a vote against a proposal. The QMV procedure applies at the first stage of the Council's 'Common Position' of any measure brought forward under the Article 189b co-decision procedure and the Article 189c cooperation procedure. It may apply thereafter. The system works in favour of the small states and a blocking minority has remained very stable, at about 29.9% of the votes from 1995 onwards. In theory therefore the position of the large states has been weakened. However, most measures are bargained for and are still achieved without a formal vote but with unanimity instead. Bainbridge and Teasdale suggest that, of 272 legislative acts undertaken between December 1993 and February 1995, only some 38 were actually adopted with abstentions or votes against. In fact, where alliances have been created, they have not followed the big-state-versus-small-state pattern but rather are often alliances of small and big state views.
28. Compare Liefferink and Andersen, 'Strategies of the "Green" Member States', pp. 260–1.
29. Hayes-Renshaw and Wallace, *Council of Ministers*, p. 102.
30. *Financial Times*, 11–12 March 1995.
31. Hayes-Renshaw and Wallace, *Council of Ministers*, p. 77.
32. Ibid. 97.
33. Ibid. 81.
34. Ibid. 77.
35. Sbragia, 'Environmental Policy', p. 247.
36. For more extensive discussion of different administrative structures within a selection of member states, see Ch. 6.
37. Commission of the European Communities, *Report of the Group of Independent Experts on Legislative and Administrative Simplification: Summary and Proposals*, COM (95) 288, final, 21.06.95.
38. European Environment Bureau, *Review of the Fifth Action Programme* (European Environment Bureau: Brussels: 1996), p. 36.
39. See I. J. Koppen, 'The Role of the European Court of Justice', in J. D. Liefferink, P. D. Lowe, and A. P. J. Mol, *European Integration and Environmental Policy* (London and New York: Belhaven Press, 1993), pp. 126–49, from which much of this section draws.

40. T. C. Hartley, *The Foundations of European Community Law* (Oxford: Clarendon Press, 1988), p. 77.

41. *Commission* v. *Council*, Case 300/89.

42. G. Majone, *Independence vs Accountability? Non-Majoritiarian Institutions and Democratic Government in Europe*, EUI Working Papers in Political and Social Sciences, SPS No. 94/3 (1994), pp. 13–14.

43. The first two appointees were Brian Wynne (Lancaster University) and Michel Scoullos (University of Athens).

44. See in particular Court of Auditors, 'Special Report No. 3/92 Concerning the Environment together with the Commission's Replies', *Official Journal of the European Communities*, C245, Vol. 35 (1992), pp. 1–30; see also Court of Auditors, 'Special Report No. 4/94 on the Urban Environment together with the Commission's Replies', *Official Journal of the European Communities*, C383, Vol. 37 (1994), pp. 1–14; Court of Auditors, 'Special Report No. 1/95 on the Cohesion Financial Instrument together with Commission's Replies', *Official Journal of the European Communities*, C59, Vol. 38 (1995); and Court of Auditors, 'Special Report No. 1/93 on the Financing of Transport Infrastructure accompanied by the Replies of the Commission', *Official Journal of the European Communities*, C69, Vol. 36 (1993), pp. 1–23.

45. See Committee of the Regions, *Two Years of Consultative Work 1994–1995: The Contributions of the Committee of the Regions to the Construction of Europe* (Luxembourg: Office for Official Publications of the EC, 1996).

46. For a good example of this type of lukewarm environmentalism, see Committee of the Regions, 'Opinion of the Committee of the Regions on the Proposal for a Council Directive concerning the Quality of Bathing Water, COM(94), 36 final', CDR 182/94, *Official Journal of the European Communities*, C210/95/07, Vol. 38 (1995), pp. 53–5. The opinion concerns the review of the bathing water directive and suggests, among other things, relaxation of implementation dates and a more flexible approach for testing. Note that none of these positions are straightforwardly 'anti-environmentalist', however. (Access to reports of the Committee of the Regions can also be obtained at: http://www.cor.eu.int/CorAtWork/com4.html.)

47. See Committee of the Regions, 'Opinion of the Committee of the Regions on the Proposal for a Council Directive amending Directive 85/337/EEC on the Assessment of the Effects of Certain Public and Private Projects on the Environment, COM(93)575, final', CDR 245/94, *Official Journal of the European Communities*, C210/95/12, Vol. 38 (1995), pp. 78–80; Committee of the Regions, 'Opinion on the Proposal for a Council Regulation (EC) amending Council Regulation (EEC) No. 1973/92 establishing a Financial Instrument for the Environment (LIFE), COM(95)135, final', CDR 301/95, *Official Journal of the European Communities*, C100/96/23, Vol. 39 (1996), pp. 115–18; and Committee of the Regions, 'Opinion on the Proposal for a Council Directive concerning the Quality of Water Intended for Human Consumption, COM(94)612, final', CDR 304/95, *Official Journal of the European Communities*, C100/96/26, Vol. 39 (1996), pp. 134–6.

48. See Economic and Social Committee of the EC, 'Opinion on a Proposal for a Council Decision for a Monitoring Mechanism of Community CO_2 and Other Greenhouse Gas Emissions, *Official Journal of the European Communities*, C89/97/03, Vol. 40 (1997), pp. 7–8; Economic and Social Committee of the EC, 'Opinion on the Proposal for a

Council Directive introducing a Tax on Carbon Dioxide Emissions and Energy, COM(92)226, final', *Official Journal of the European Communities*, C108/93/06, Vol. 36 (1993), pp. 20–4.

49. Interview with senior DG XI official, September 1993; C. Grant, *Delors: the House that Jacques Built* (London: Nicholas Brearley, 1993), p. 42.

50. R. Hull, 'Lobbying Brussels: A View from Within', in S. Mazey and J. Richardson (eds.), *Lobbying in the European Community* (Oxford: Oxford University Press, 1993), p. 89.

51. Members are appointed for three years; see *Eur-op News*, 3:1 (1994).

52. *Eur-op News*, Environment supplement (Summer 1995).

4

Patterns of Environmental Governance in the European Union

In the previous chapter we looked at the development of European policy institutions, and we noted the proliferation and associated institutional complexity that
now constitutes the European system of environmental governance. In this chapter
we look at the functioning of that system of governance in terms of the decisions
that are taken and the forms of behaviour that are characteristic, given those institutions. While Chapter 3 was concerned with the institutional actors that make
the rules, this chapter is concerned with the processes that are characteristic of
primary rule-making in the environmental field. This topic touches on some of
the major theoretical issues that were dealt with in the Introduction to Part I. There
we outlined the major theoretical controversies about European integration. It is
in looking at the operation of institutions of the European system of environmental
governance that we begin to see how far that system has transcended the constraints
of the nation state.

The complexity of the European policy process makes life difficult for those
attempting to unpack the sources and influences on environment policy. Policy-
making takes place not only horizontally, through the interaction of institutions
and policy actors operating at the European level, but also with the participation
of vertical channels of influence, involving a number of tiers of government at the
European, national, and in some cases regional levels. In exploring patterns of
European environmental governance through the medium of the European policy
process, we are clearly interested in the interactions between policy actors and institutions, as policy proposals become translated into law. These relationships lie at the
heart of the EU's legislative capacity in environmental matters, as they do in other
policy areas. However, we must be careful not to take formal relationships at face
value, as it is often through informal interaction that patterns of governance emerge.
To this extent, analyses of agenda-setting, policy formulation and decision-taking
must take on board the fact that governance can often be an extremely arcane
process.

The chapter begins by looking at environmental agenda-setting, and in particular at how actors influence the European policy agenda. It then turns to assess
the more formal initiation and formulation of policy, and the instruments available to the Commission at this stage in the policy process. We also encounter the

intra-institutional wrangling and bureaucratic politics that often have a dramatic effect on the Commission's policy outputs at this point. The third section of the chapter focuses on decision-taking, placing emphasis less on the role of the Commission and more on the involvement of the European Parliament and the Council at this last but crucially important stage of policy-making.

SETTING THE AGENDA:
PROBLEMS, ISSUES, AND SCIENCE

The role of the European institutions in setting the agenda for environmental policy-making varies from case to case. Policies do not emerge out of thin air; nor are they based solely on the fundamental beliefs and values of those who are involved in policy-making. Environmental issues emerge from a wide range and intermingling of moral values, interests, and crises. Indeed, the unintentional role of institutions can be the internalization and institutionalization of problems, and this can be one of the prime causes of the non-integration of one set of policy concerns into others.[1] As such, the agenda-setting phase can shape and determine the future path and the future success of a proposal, even before it has been drafted. As the questions asked invariably colour the answers received, it is important to consider who is asking the questions, and who (or what) causes environmental issues to be placed on the European agenda.

The questions themselves, or rather the assumptions underpinning the questions, often determine the shape of a particular policy. For example, is the function of European environment policy to tackle environmental problems to the best of one's ability, given the present technological (and cost) limits, or is environmental problem-solving worthwhile only when scientific research offers 'objective' answers about the most effective policy avenue?

These fundamental undercurrents to policy preferences at national level make the formulation of policy, and not least the agenda-setting stage, fraught with difficulties. It is not in the Commission's interest to produce strategies and formulate policies when they have no hope of being accepted by the Council of Ministers. In any case, it is only in exceptional cases that the Commission itself has set the agenda (such as on Environmental Impact Assessments (EIAs) and wild birds), in spite of its precautionary rhetoric. The issue is not that the Commission is heavily influenced by national interests, but *which* national interests capture its attention. Goncalves goes so far as to claim that policy agendas in the environmental field are rarely established at the European level, though legislation may well appear there first; with a need for regulation already having been recognized at the national level or in another international forum, 'the knowledge base for the technical decision by the EC is already available to a certain extent'.[2] Therefore the European institutions often have little option but to be reactive to agendas set, issues raised, and problems identified elsewhere.[3]

It is clear that the European policy agenda is set not only by the European institutions. Input into environment policy comes from a wide variety of sources, giving a somewhat pluralist colour to the policy process. As a result, it is not always easy, even in the best documented cases, to identify from where agendas emerge. The complexity of the European policy process, the intermingling of a large number of institutions, agencies, and groups at different levels of government, make the identification of policy sources difficult to sustain. It also makes outcomes in the environmental policy sector extremely difficult to predict.[4] Regional governments, for example, may use the European institutions to further their own institutional and political ends *vis-à-vis* their national counterparts. This crowded policy space can mean that messages are often blurred and that policy-makers are faced with a babble of scientific, technical, interest-orientated, and political argumentation, out of which they have to draw conclusions and formulate policy and specific pieces of legislation.

It is this attempt to balance what for simplicity's sake we may call the political and the technocratic that is at the heart of the difficulties for the European legislator. This distinction is nothing new, of course. Jean Monnet, one of the founding fathers of the European integration process, strove to create in the Community a depoliticized organization whose legitimacy would be based upon apparently objective technical criteria, and where politics would be subsumed under a wealth of sector-specific expertise, though this expertise was to be of a legal–economic rather than scientific kind. This exercise in modernity, based largely on the French experience, has been impossible to sustain. Increasingly, it seems, there has been a move away from placing absolute faith in the European 'technocrat–legislator', towards a separation of the functions of scientific and technical judgment from political decision-making.[5] Peterson claims that at the European level '[t]echnocratic rationality, based on specialized or technical knowledge, often dominates at the meso-level',[6] implying that politicization comes either at a later stage in the process or at a different level of analysis.

Of all the European institutions, it is the Commission that plays the pivotal role in initiating European legislation and establishing policy priorities, a process that can itself have a bearing on the more specific task of setting environmental standards. The Commission is the formal policy initiator of the Union, and as such can rightfully take the lead in pushing forward its own policy agenda—if it has one. Policy leadership may not be the same as political leadership, however, as the latter usually assumes some prioritization of policy agendas. Although Jacques Delors became increasingly interested in environment policy during the last few years of his presidency, there was little to suggest that the environment was ever a Commission priority. This was especially evident in light of its virtual exclusion from the 1992 programme. Only on the issue of the energy/carbon tax did Delors push a specific environmental agenda (initially at least), though even here support for the proposal was sacrificed to more general institutional and political needs.[7]

The involvement of organized interests in the Commission's internal decision-taking process is well documented.[8] From one point of view, it might seem as though there was relatively little lobbying capacity in relation to the environment. From another point of view, it might seem that in the case of environmental policy there is still a relative dearth of group involvement in the policy process. The number of such groups is small. Butt Philip for example has noted that in 1991, out of a total of 744 Euro-Groups identified, only 19 dealt with environmental matters. Webster identifies seven groups that are in a privileged postion.[9] However, the number of groups does not necessarily reflect their policy influence. Moreover, environmental measures often have wide-ranging implications and carry potentially large economic costs for different economic sectors. So lobbying on environmental issues has become increasingly more institutionalized and professional, as environmental groups have had to compete with the well funded industry groups for the DG XI's attention. The Packaging Directive, for example, has been described as the 'most lobbied in EU history'.[10] Previously, industry would really seek to lobby on environmental issues only through their influence with DG III. This is no longer the case.

Legislators are in any case aware of the need to balance the information presented by interest groups. Within the Commission, it seems to be acknowledged that, while environmental groups often 'go too far', to quote one senior official, industry groups also have their own more specific axe to grind. However, there have been some occasions (on CFCs, for example) on which environmental NGOs have virtually been excluded from the policy communities established by the Commission.[11]

Interests also participate through the internal network of advisory committees, such as the Advisory Committee on Measures to Protect the Environment in the Mediterranean Region, and the Advisory Committee on the Control and Reduction of Pollution caused by the Discharge of Hydrocarbons and Other Dangerous substances at Sea. The Commission does provide lists of committees in its *Official Journal*, but as yet no thorough analysis of members has taken place. It has been argued generally that the voice of the voluntary sector on advisory committees is low. Environmental interests are not, for example, represented on many important agricultural committees.[12]

The Commission's reliance on outside expertise has frequently been criticized by those who feel that this can all too easily lead to a situation in which the Commission loses its capacity to distance itself from the interests around it. The inadequacy of the scientific information available to the Commission as it seeks to formulate its policy and draft its environmental legislation is acknowledged, though there is some subliminal tension in raising these matters. Criticism from one senior DG XI official that the 'old' (i.e. pre-1988) environment policy was based on data alone implies that the 'new' policy is founded much more on a political reality that places scientific information *in context*. Whether this means an undermining of the scientist in favour of the political policy-maker, or simply the adoption of a less quantitative, more qualitative approach to policy-making, is not clear, however. While it appears that 'policy-making is about policies',[13] legislating and standard-setting is perhaps where the 'experts' come into their own.

Despite the extension of its influence over the Commission's powers of initiation, there are still substantial constraints upon the European Parliament when it attempts to influence the environmental policy agenda. This does not mean that it fails to do so, however. Although there is little evidence of this being put to great effect so far, this has not stopped the Parliament from wielding a certain amount of influence over the Commission. Participation in the environmental policy process at the earliest opportunity is essential if the Parliament is seeking to define the character of the policy debate. Influence at this pre-legislative stage is crucial, though the Parliament's capacity to act effectively rests upon the resources available to its Environment Committee (in particular). The most important resource, in that it is the resource most lacking, is information, and especially scientific and technical information. So, even though environmental *rapporteurs* are increasingly chosen for their scientific knowledge, it is clear that scientists or engineers are not in abundance among the Parliament's members.

The European Parliament (EP) and its committees are generally not equipped to scrutinize technical proposals within which there are often complex and subtle scientific as well as moral judgments to be made.[14] There are few scientific staff in the Parliament, either among the MEPs or on the staff. This is highlighted by the fact that the EP's information and research resources amount to only two grade A administrators in DG IV (research), and one A grade administrator, two fellows and four researchers on temporary contract based in the EP's Scientific and Technological Options Assessment (STOA).[15]

POLICY FORMULATION AND STANDARD-SETTING

Although the Commission is not the only actor or institution involved in environmental agenda-setting at the European level, it is the only institution endowed with the formal right of legislative initiative implying the practical task of policy formulation. Only the Commission staff draft the legislative proposals that form the basis of eventual regulations, directives, and decisions.[16] There has been a tendency for environmental legislation to be drafted in the form of directives which establish goals but leave the means for achieving those goals up to the member states. This gives more leeway to states when they come to implement, though it has, as Huelsdorff and Pfeiffer point out, limited the opportunity of individuals to bring cases to the European Court.[17]

In the eyes of a number of observers, one problem with the regulatory approach adopted by the Commission is that the focus of attention is on constructing directives, but with a lack of concern about issues of effectiveness and implementation.

Regulatory measures tend to operate in a top-down fashion, focusing attention on the policy formulation and legislative process, with little regard to outcomes. This stress on the creation of legal instruments suggests that the success of a policy rests on the enactment of a piece of regulation rather than on its capacity for enforcement or its potential as an effective reaction to environmental problems. Supporters of European legislation will refer to some 12,000 pages of existing legislation, with less attention paid to levels of implementation. Implementation under the Fifth Action Programme was prioritized. As a result, in place of the creation of new pieces of legislation, much of the recent work of the Commission during the 1990s has involved the consolidation, simplification, and updating of directives and regulations already in existence.[18]

The formulation of legislation of this sort is a process that takes place within the Commission, though not without a great deal of input from interest groups, European institutions, and governments outside it. Nevertheless, the Commission has, at this stage in the process, an autonomy that it has at no other time.[19] Generally speaking (though there are exceptions), a middle-ranking official within DG XI (or whichever DG responsible) is given responsibility for the drafting of a proposal; this individual (the *rapporteur*) will follow its progress not only through the relevant Commission channels, but also when it leaves the Commission to be considered by the Parliament and the Council.[20]

While in the Commission however, the draft will be subject to numerous checks and balances. Vertically, it will be transmitted up and down the Commission hierarchy until all grades are satisfied with it. Horizontally, the proposal must follow a process of consultation which involves the circulation of the draft to all potentially interested DGs so as to elicit responses and reactions to it. It is only when this process is exhausted that the proposal can be considered firstly by a meeting of the *cabinets* (personal staff) and subsequently by the College of Commissioners.[21] The Commission's structure is different from that of the national administrations in that the services' opinions can be ignored if the *cabinet* and the commissioners disagree with them.

But this account of the passage of a proposal through the Commission does not do justice to the more informal political channels through which it must also pass. Formal channels provide helpful check on a piece of draft legislation, but the reality is much more complex. Decisions initially have to be made as to which DG has control of a proposal. In many cases this will be a straightforward matter, but there are exceptions. During the consultation process, opposition to a proposal from within the Commission can be intense. DGs clearly have their own policy agendas to satisfy. Their interests, and even their basic values, are often quite different, and perhaps even incompatible. During Jacques Delors's presidency of the Commission between 1985 and 1994, attempts were made to ensure consistency of approach within the Commission. While strong leadership helped to give the impression of central control, the process of fragmentation that has been apparent within the Commission since the late 1960s has continued.[22]

In the environmental policy field, however, there has been a conscious top-down effort to counter this trend. Attempts to integrate environmental concerns into other European policy arenas have led to attempts to achieve organizational and structural integration.[23] Indeed, it should be remembered that it is not only DG XI that is responsible for environment policies:[24] coordination with other DGs and other agencies (Eurostat, for example[25]) is crucial. Institutional change was one of the key elements within the Fifth Action Programme, though previous action programmes had also had this as an objective. The process of integration has been rather slow, however, although progress has been made in the setting up of networks and channels of communication, and in the appointment of senior staff in all DGs to deal with environmental matters. Of course, as one senior DG XI official commented, this does not necessarily mean that there is any action on the environmental front.[26] Some have suggested that a more confrontational approach may be necessary. Several DG XI officials, for example, suggested that Community funding be blocked if environmental considerations are not taken into account.[27] This would penalize the member states more than the DGs but might also put pressure on the Commission services to take environmental matters more seriously.

There are a number of interesting practical examples of how this process of organizational (and policy) integration has been initiated, and what the policy's impact has been. A new relationship between DG XI and DG XVII (energy) after 1988 began with coordination on matters of energy efficiency, renewables, taxation, and industrial codes of conduct.[28] When the Fifth Action Programme was to be drafted, the two DGs were together responsible for drafting the energy chapter. This was more a collection of objectives than a substantive change in the relationship, however, as the mechanisms for considering the environmental impact of DG XVII proposals were already up and running.

Cooperation between DG III and DG XI has by contrast been rather tense in the past, with DG III often speaking for industry and against environmental legislation. Disagreements over the 1988 Task Force, for example, meant that the report it produced could not be published as a Commission document, something that has led at least one commentator to imply that the Commission placed the market before the environment.[29] A unit dealing with industry and environment was nevertheless set up in June 1993 to deal with coordination between the two DGs, and a high-level inter-service task force on the impact of environment policy was also established to improve liaison.[30] The fact that several senior DG XI officials, including Tom Garvey, the assistant to the director-general, previously worked in DG III is likely to help the relationship, though one official suggested that this will only mean that the DG is forced to compromise to a greater degree.

In the agricultural DG, too, a new unit was established specifically as a result of the Fifth Action Programme, although there are also regular informal contacts between the two DGs. Here, as in many DGs, the common complaint from co-ordinating staff is that, although *they* see the merits of considering environmental concerns (of integration, that is), the rest of their DG remains to be convinced.

In the case of DG VI (agriculture), the official in charge of liaison stated that it was often impossible to convince directors and unit heads in charge of market regulation of the merits of injecting an environmental input into their work.[31]

The image of DG XI producing outlandish and unworkable proposals has been deeply entrenched at times despite the organizational changes that have taken place. In the transport DG (DG VII), for example, one official remarked that DG XI staff do not live in the real world; they simplify issues and are overly optimistic.[32] Ironically, in the DG VII case the unit coordinating the transport–environment relationship was disbanded in 1991 in favour of more sectorally specific units acting as liaison. Nevertheless, DG VII consults and negotiates with DG XI at unit level, though coordination has been made more difficult as a result. Conflicting policies continue, with recent reference having been made to the DG's involvement in the trans-European networks (TENs) programme, involving extensive motorway construction.[33]

Cooperation with DG XII, the research DG, is crucial because of the dependence of DG XI on scientific research. Since the Fourth R&D Framework, environmental aspects have become more prominent. The scientific work on climate change, for example, has fed directly into DG XI policy.[34]

The relationship between DG XI and DG XVI, the regional policy DG, is perhaps the most enlightening example. In the past, the relationship has been much criticized, in particular in a well publicized Court of Auditors' Report in 1992,[35] which demonstrated the existence of conflicting policy goals between the two organizations. Not only have regional policies contributed to the degradation of the environment, but the conflicts have also led on many occasions to 'territorial clashes between commissioners and *cabinets*'.[36] However, there has been a pattern of change since the mid to late 1980s, and it is interesting to note how this has come about.

A reform of the Regional Funds, togther with the other Structural Funds (the non-price support element of the European Agricultural Fund and the European Social Fund), led to a system in which allocations were made in multi-annual programmes. From some points of view, this gave the Commission greater responsibility for the allocation, since the programmes had to be agreed with the member states rather than, as with the previous system, allowing the member states much greater discretion. But as Scott pointed out, the Commission's monitoring of the implementation of the operational programmes did not extend to a close scrutiny of individual projects.[37] The problem was compounded by the fact that in 1991, for example, only six people were responsible for ensuring a consistency of approach between regional policy and environmental policy.[38]

However, the greater formal involvement of DG XVI in the allocation of funds gave environmental groups a handle in terms of which they could criticize the Commission for a failure to act according to their own announced principles. Mazey and Richardson, for example, show how the World Wide Fund for Nature (WWF) was able to use the report of the Court of Auditors, connections with the European Parliament, and the Danish presidency of the time to create circumstances in which a shift of opinion began to take place about the desirability of greater integration.[39] A major turning point was the convening of an experts' group meeting in the middle of 1992, which brought together officials from various DGs to discuss the incorporation of environmental objectives into a range of EU policies. The resistance of DG XVI to greater integration was therefore weakened through a process of political embarrassment and a diffuse sense that something needed to be done on the issue. Interestingly in this context, Lenschow has argued that the crucial move in the better integration of the Cohesion Funds with environmental policy came with their relocation, under the Santer Commission, from DG XIX (Budgets) to DG XVI, suggesting that the organizational and political changes inaugurated by policies on the Structural Funds had wider effects.[40]

DG XI distinguishes itself from nearly all other DGs whose concerns are largely sectoral, and whose clientele is readily identifiable. DG XI is not clientelistic in this sectoral sense, and it has even moved away from any close identification with the environmental lobby outside the Commission. This has given the DG space to create alliances within the Commission on specific proposals (although the ultimate objectives of the different DGs may not of course be the same). The effectiveness of policy integration objectives is difficult to assess, however, especially as integration can operate on an informal as well as a formal level. One DG official dealing with energy policy noted that 'a lot of contacts are made informally. You get to know people working in your field.'[41] Relationships between middle-ranking individuals in different DGs are important, just as they are at more senior levels. It is clear for example that the relationship between the environment and energy commissioners, Ripa di Meana and Cuhna, was important in the early 1990s, though there is no suggestion that it was decisive. Yet real integration would take more time than the services have. At the end of the day, telephone conversations and meetings are perhaps the most effective way of cooperating.

Policy integration has to be a two-way street. The integration of environmental concerns into other European policies, through the establishment of organizational networks and new coordination structures, can be effective only if DG XI is prepared to compromise. DG XI must itself act as an agent of integration. Structurally this may be a problem, with one official criticizing the fact that DG XI is too divided vertically for effective coordination. It may also mean that DG XI should keep a watchful eye on other DGs, though this may be difficult, given resource constraints. It is not only organizationally that there must be adaptation within DG XI: it must also take into consideration the concerns, fears, objectives, and policy lines of other DGs, as the environmental identity of DG XI, from the point of view of those outside, is crucial. Environmental policy was for a long time considered something separate from the Commission mainstream, which was essentially about economic integration. This made it extremely difficult for DG XI to compete within the Commission. In this sense, it is interesting to note that a senior DG XI official commented that since the late 1980s there had been a conscious attempt to alter the 'culture' of DG XI, to make it much more 'mainstream'.[42]

General accounts of agenda-setting, policy formulation, and the integration of environmental concerns into other policy domains do not, however, help us to understand the more specific and often informal processes through which environmental standards are set at the European level. Clearly, we can consider only part of the story at this stage, for much of the process of European standard-setting takes place beyond the formulation stage, once the proposal has entered the inter-institutional European arena. Nevertheless, policy, legislation, and, more specifically, standards are initially developed within the Commission, and are agreed and advanced by the College of Commissioners, before consideration in the Parliament and the Council. It may be useful therefore to consider an empirical case, one that has gained a great deal of media attention, and has occupied much time and effort within the Commission: namely, that of the carbon tax.

This example is interesting as it exemplifies the relationship between scientific information and policy-making in the European policy process, while at the same time demonstrating the importance of alliances between DGs within the Commission at the formulation stage. It was clear that there were to be disagreements within the Commission on the relevance, workability, and desirability of introducing a carbon/energy tax. For DG III, questions of competitiveness were paramount. This meant that the issue of reciprocity, and in particular what the USA and Japan would do, would dominate much of the early discussion. Scientific uncertainty was used to back up more political arguments about the implications and potential impact of the tax. One DG VII official claimed that there could be no scientific justification for the DG XI stance on this subject, and that elasticity studies had demonstrated, for example, that the tax would in any case have little effect on car-users' habits.[43] However, Skjaerseth notes that Intergovernmental Panel on Climate Change conclusions were generally 'taken for granted' within the Commission.[44] The Commission set up an inter-service group on climate policy for those likely to be affected.[45]

At the heart of the DG XI campaign in favour of the tax, however, was the energy DG, DG XVII. A senior official in DG XVII outlined the different forums within which discussion took place in the run-up to the drafting of the proposal. DG XVII itself was involved in the IPCC (Intergovernmental Panel on Climate Change) climate change process. Within the Commission there were three working groups, which were used as sources of information for those involved in the drafting process. Among the working groups was one on science/policy, in which scientists and policy-makers discussed options and the practical application of scientific knowledge. In DG XII, modelling work was done on climate research. Advice was sought from the Environment Institute at Ispra, whose researchers were asked to review the state of play. Eurostat provided relevant figures, and use was made of statistics, booklets, and scenarios that were generated internally within DG XVII. While DG XI tended to concentrate on economic studies, DG XVII looked at the energy implications, and DG II gave macroeconomic advice.[46]

While DG XVI and DG XI worked well together, the relationship between Ripa di Meana and Delors was not so good, especially by 1992, when Delors was keen to keep a low Commission profile, that is not to rock the post-Maastricht European boat. Although Delors, backed by the Forward Studies Unit, supported the tax in principle, the only way agreement could be reached among the commissioners was for Ripa di Meana to accept the conditionality principle, which would make the EU tax depend on the acceptance of a similar measure in the USA and Japan. And even then, Council refused to sanction the tax in time for the Rio Summit of June 1992. After Ripa di Meana, however, DG XI, with the help of environmental NGOs, has managed to keep alive the idea of a carbon tax since 1993.

DECISION–MAKING AND
INTER–INSTITUTIONAL RELATIONS

The European policy process is shaped by inter-institutional relationships which guarantee checks and balances within European-level governance, as the passage of legislation proceeds. As such, it is the inter-institutional triangle of Commission, Parliament, and Council that provides a focal point for European decision-making in the environmental sphere as in other policy spheres. As supranational institutions, the Commission and Parliament do not simply act as adjudicators among the member states, though this may indeed be an element of their function: they are in fact policy actors and policy advocates in their own right.

Coalition-building among the European institutions at all stages of the decision-making process bids up the final outcomes and, in the jargon of European integration, 'upgrades the common interest'. Indeed, where institutions compete to advance innovative and radical solutions to environmental problems, the results can be dramatic.[47] There is clearly scope for European institutions to empower themselves by playing these inter-institutional games, and in so doing to form alliances and isolate opposition. There have even been cases in which environmental interest groups, ostensibly outside the European institutional arena, have played a crucial brokerage function, bringing officials and other policy actors together for the first time.

Once a Commission proposal reaches the Council Secretariat, it is transmitted directly to the relevant Council working group, which will deal with the legislation at this first Council stage. The sponsoring Commission service is usually present at these meetings. Individuals involved here may be the same as those who participated in advisory groups within the Commission earlier in the formulation process. Here, however, they will be performing a rather different function. They will be seeking to work through some of the more controversial technical questions, with an eye to the national positions likely to emerge once the proposal is sent on to COREPER, the Committee of Permanent Representatives. The changes made in the working groups can be serious.

COREPER is important in the development of environmental policy. Here, for the first time, national interests can come blatantly to the fore. And it is here that it is possible to distinguish the different policy positions taken by national governments. There are clearly going to be differences of opinion on legislation among the member states. At this stage, the differences and points of friction are less of a scientific nature than of a financial, economic, and political kind.[48]

Unanimity may still be required to get environmental legislation through the Council. Proposals may not get through at all, or they may be severely watered down, undermining the original message of the legislation.[49] Formal contacts between the member states are made in the Council when the government representatives are in 'negotiating mode'.[50] This shapes the nature of the agreement reached. The essence of the EU policy process is effectively the combining of objectives in order to find a language of consensus and ultimately to reach a decision. The existence of a range of procedures involving different configurations of institutional and policy actors and relationships means that environmental governance will vary between issues, and as a result can be unstable and unpredictable.

Formally, the specific roles performed by each of the European institutions in the decision-making process depends largely on the legal base and procedure used. After Maastricht there were four distinct groups of procedures, though in all more than twenty different procedural avenues were identified as operative in this period. This was undoubtedly a messy and unsatisfactory situation which was the source of much confusion and argument. Notably, the decision about which procedure to use in the event of a new proposal being issued can be a real source of contention. While in certain circumstances the choice is relatively clear–cut, there are many occasions on which such a decision falls in a grey area.

Although the characteristics of each of the decision-making procedures are well documented elsewhere, it is worth noting the main distinctions among the four types of procedure. While the *consultation* procedure allowed the EP to give its opinion on draft legislation, and required that the Council vote on it using the unanimity principle, the *cooperation* and *assent* procedures gave the EP a second reading, and introduced qualified majority voting in the Council. The Maastricht Treaty introduced the *co-decision* procedure, which forces the EP and Council to cooperate on draft legislation within a Consultative Committee, allowing the EP a potential veto if no agreement is reached. The use of the co–decision procedure was then extended in the Treaty of Amsterdam.

The choice of procedure in most cases is clear-cut. However where there are grey areas, much of the Commission's task involves second-guessing the European Court, assessing its likely stance should the matter be referred to it at a later date. Usher has attempted to fathom the logic of the Court in these cases, suggesting rather tentatively that the Court is now more likely to rule in the Parliament's favour, all other things being equal.[51]

Procedural differences may seem arcane but they are nevertheless extremely important when considering the relative position of the European institutions in the European environmental policy process. Whereas many policy areas are subject to only one decision-making procedure, with disputes occurring only at the margins, several procedures affect the environmental domain, depending on the specific policy matter under consideration. Procedural difficulties do not end there, however. European-level competence in environment policy is often concealed by the fact that many 'environmental' directives are initiated under different policy headings, such as agriculture, where, for example, the consultation procedure might apply. This further complicates the procedural underpinnings of the policy process.

As we noted in the previous chapter, the importance of qualified majority voting (QMV) in the Council is high, and more important still is the way that QMV dictates inter-institutional relations, and ultimately shapes outcomes. The European Parliament's input into legislation is in this sense constrained or extended, depending on the extent to which intergovernmentalism characterizes the decision-making process. Where unanimity is required among members of the Council, the Parliament's formal input is minimized. Where QMV applies, there is more opportunity for the EP to take advantage of it. Indeed, QMV allows both Commission and Parliament the option of exploiting divisions among the member states as the Council looks to reach some form of agreement. Under the cooperation procedure, the Council can limit the influence of the EP by reaching a unanimous common position at the first reading,[52] but this is not easily achieved. Under the co-decision procedure, it is more in the Council's and Commission's interest to 'court' the Parliament.[53]

The introduction of co-decision in some areas of environment policy has had a major impact on the way in which legislation emerges and on the respective roles of the European institutions in the policy process. There is no doubt that the policy competence of the Union in this area has extended dramatically since the middle of the 1980s, to the extent that there has even been talk of a process of 'federalization' in the environmental policy domain.[54] Yet there are difficulties associated with the fact that environmental policy is one policy area in which the member states and the EU institutions hold a shared competence.

Not surprisingly, however, disputes between the institutions are fairly common. These disagreements often involve procedural as well as substantive matters, creating a source of tension that some recognize as unnecessary. This does not always make for a generally harmonious relationship between institutions, even if it does little to prevent cooperation where this is mutually beneficial. The process leading to the adoption of the titanium dioxide directive provides an excellent example of such interactions, involving not only the Commission, Council, and Parliament, but also the European Court of Justice.

Agreeing a directive to limit pollution from the titanium dioxide sector was one of the priorities of the 1988 German Council presidency. The original proposal stemmed from 1983, but following the Single European Act the Commission attempted to base the directive on Article 100a, which would have allowed it to be adopted by qualified majority in the Council. However, the Council chose to use Article 130s of the Single European Act, specifically designed for legislation devoted to environmental protection, and requiring the unanimous agreement of all member states in the Council. Article 100a was appropriate, according to the Commission, because the legislation was designed to reduce disparities between national industries in the titanium dioxide sector. Ministers, however, were not convinced, and argued that 130s should be the relevant article because the primary aim of the directive was to protect the environment.[55]

The Commission took the Council to the European Court of Justice disputing the ministers' conclusion. The Court judged that the ministers should have used Article 100a. In upholding the Commission's complaint, the Court agreed that price differences in the sector, which had been between 10 and 20 per cent in 1984, had made harmonization a priority. Although it was clear that environmental protection was also an aim of the directive, the Court felt that the stress that its wording laid on the harmonization of pollution control measures within the member states warranted the use of Article 100a over and above 130s.

Perhaps the single most important precedent set by this case was that it suggested the possibility that environmental protection could be a joint goal of legislation without necessitating the use of Article 130s, with its requirement for unanimity. Such a conclusion was clearly possible in the light of the Single European Act's Article 130r, which stressed that environmental protection must be a component of all Community policies. The Court judgment also made reference to the fact that Article 100a meant a more significant role for the European Parliament through the cooperation procedure. The Court's comment that this should be encouraged for democratic reasons was unusual, given its normally objective legal line, and it has not been repeated since.[56] Nevertheless, it is interesting that the Court felt it necessary to underline its reasons for finding against the Council. Following the annulment of the titanium dioxide directive by the Court's judgment, it was re-adopted by the Council, this time under Article 100a, at the Environment Council on 26 May 1992.[57]

Success in the above case gave the Commission encouragement and it promptly took the Council to the Court with the same argument over the new framework waste directive, using the same argument, this time bolstered by the fact that the original 1975 directive had been adopted under Articles 100 and 235 of the Treaty of Rome, which the Commission argued had been replaced by 100a in the Single European Act.[58] However, in this case the Council's view was upheld by the Court.[59] As the primary aim of the directive was to enact the principle that waste should be disposed of as close to source as posssible, and as it did not seek to facilitate the free movement of waste (defined as a good), the Court stated that the single market implications of the directive were ancillary, and therefore the Council had been right to use Article 130s.[60] Although the Court was prepared to sanction restrictions on free trade when environmental protection was likely to be achieved on the basis of a measure that would harmonize national regulation, it became clear that the Commission would have to provide a strong case for the importance to the single market of any environmental measure if it was to be successful in similar challenges to the Council.

The following year saw the Commission take the Council to the Court yet again on this issue. This time the directive in question was one that amended the 1978 hazardous waste directive.[61] The Parliament's support for the Commission was understandable, as Article 100a would have given it more influence under the co-operation procedure. However, following the signing of the Treaty on European Union at Maastricht, the Commission's zeal was harder to understand: under the Maastricht amendments, most legislation put forward under Article 130s would be subject to qualified majority voting anyway.

It might be argued that these inter-institutional wrangles between the Commission and the Council belong to a particular phase of European environmental policy. With the coming into force of the Treaty on European Union, environmental policy acquired an even firmer basis within the legal and institutional competence of the Union, in particular with the procedure by which both single market measures and environmental policies are decided within the Council by qualified majority voting. As far as the relationship between the Council and the Commission is concerned, this is correct. However, when we turn to the relationship between the Parliament and the Council, a relationship in which the Commission is itself often involved, we can see that the separation of powers that is built into the EU's system of environmental governance creates the possibility for conflicts over environmental measures in which the Parliament has the opportunity to assert a distinct point of view.

One important procedural change under the Single European Act was the shift in legislative process for environmental policy with a single market component from the consultation procedure to the cooperation procedure. The most important part of this procedure is that it provided the Parliament with second reading powers that meant it could reject, by an absolute majority, the position of the Council arrived at through a qualified majority, so that the Parliament's position could then be reversed only by a unanimous decision of the Council. The first occasion in relation to any single market measure on which the Parliament exercised its new-found powers was on vehicle emissions policy in 1989, when it in effect put pressure on the Council to adopt more stringent standards than the Council had originally intended by rejecting the Council's common position on the second reading. Nine years later the Parliament was able to strengthen vehicle emissions policy again, but this time using the co-decision procedure that had been introduced for such measures under the Treaty on European Union. (The full story is told in Chapter 11.)

A similar pattern of the Parliament rejecting Council measures can be seen in the making of landfill policy, where legislation has been held up with the council finding it difficult to adopt a measure favoured by a qualified majority, because the cooperation procedure, under which the measure is taken, has allowed the Parliament to reject the measures the Council has proposed. In particular, the

Parliament has argued that the derogations proposed under the Council's favoured position make the policy too lax.

Given these examples, it might be thought that the secondary rules that have co-evolved with the development of environmental policy have placed great power in the hands of the Parliament, and in one sense this would be true. The measures on vehicle emissions are certainly thought to be demanding by manufacturers, and for the proposals agreed in 1998 this is particularly important, since the proposals that the Parliament insisted on modifying emerged from a long process of joint consultation between the Commission and representatives of industry.

However, it is easy from these examples of positive action on the part of the Parliament to overestimate its role. To have a proper estimate of its influence, we need to consider not only the cases where it exercised its power, but also those cases where it might have exercised its power but for one reason or another chose not to.

Looking at environmental directives since the coming into force of the Single European Act in 1987 and 1998, it has been estimated that there are some twenty-six examples where the Parliament had the opportunity to intervene under the cooperation or co-decision procedures, and some fourteen cases where it was relatively quiet, that is to say where the final directive shows little sign of Parliament's activity.[62] To some extent, the lack of influence is a consequence of the rules, since amendments by the Parliament to the Council's position typically require an absolute majority of MEPs. However, there are also occasions on which the Parliament appears to back down in its struggle with the Council because it fears that the measure may be lost. This was true with a dispute over the control of vehicle emissions in 1994. (See chapter 11 for details.)

One significant aspect of the institutional and procedural struggle is the centrality of the role of the European Court of Justice. Precisely because environmental issues trace their origins to the otherwise legitimate interests of other policy sectors, questions will always arise over the balance to be struck between the demands of environmental protection and the goals of trade liberalization. In this context, the Court is likely to play a continuing role in determining the scope and implications of environmental policy, and this could be particularly important if it is asked to rule on, say, the principle of subsidiarity.

However, the relative influence of the European institutions in relation to one another and the inter-institutional relationships that characterize the environmental policy process vary not only according to formal procedures, but also in line with more informal factors. It is difficult to generalize about the influence wielded by the EU institutions, member states, and interest groups in the making of environmental policy. However, focusing on less formal roles played by the European institutions with the decision-making process, as well as on the less tangible aspect of inter-institutional relationships, can be instructive.

Thus, even though one might imagine that the bulk of the Commission's work is completed once a proposal is agreed to by the College of Commissioners, this is not the case. The Commission's function may alter somewhat, in that it now seeks to facilitate agreement among the European institutions, including the member states in the Council, rather than merely pushing its own policy line. But to some extent the Commission was already taking this into consideration as the proposal was being drafted.

Even though the Commission's relationship with the EP is generally a good one, the two European bodies do not always see eye-to-eye. For example, in the run-up to the 1994 EP elections, it was believed by MEPs that the Commission might hope to profit from the naïvety of the new Parliament. With up to 50 per cent of the Environment Committee replaced after the elections, one MEP warned of the need to be vigilant in order to prevent the Commission from sneaking though draft legislation which it knew might be seen as contentious.[63]

The high-profile role of the European Parliament in the policy process has meant that it is essential for it to keep a close watch on developments within the Commission. In environment policy, perhaps more than in any other policy area, the Parliament has pushed the boundaries of its own competence to the very limit. The Environment Committee's presence is now acknowledged at all stages of the European policy process, playing an activist role and seeking to influence the policy line adopted by DG XI as the latter mediates agreement in the Council and in the conciliation committees.[64] Because the introduction of the co-decision procedure for many areas of environmental policy gave the Parliament greater blocking power at first readings, the Commission has had more frequently to anticipate the reaction of the Parliament, making close relations between the *rapporteurs* in both institutions imperative. In this sense, there has developed a 'shared inter-institutional ethos between Committee members and Commission staff'.[65] However, the formal powers of the EP have been used to even greater effect as a way of strengthening its informal influence. As a result, the Environment Committee has found itself in a stronger position *vis-à-vis* both Commission and Council at the first reading stage of both the cooperation and co-decision procedures.[66]

Informally, the influence wielded by the EP is less visible and more difficult to document and identify. So, as Judge notes, while it is possible to assess the quantitative increase in legislative input from the EP since the Single European Act, it is almost impossible to define its influence in any qualitative sense.[67] Judge goes on to note that in the biotechnology directive ten out of seventeen proposed amendments were originally worked into the Commission's revised proposals, while in the municipal waste water treatment directive none were incorporated.[68] But, while this tells us something about the EP's effectiveness, it does not give us the full parliamentary story. It ignores, for example, the involvement of the Parliament at the pre-legislative stage, and the fact that the Commission will now take into consideration the EP's views much earlier in the decision-making process. This has become all the easier since *rapporteurs* can now be appointed on the basis of the Commission's annual programme, rather than only after the appearance of the proposal. It also ignores the ability of the EP to 'interpose itself on the consciousness of other institutions, and into the formal Commission–Council dialogue'.[69]

It is not surprising, then, that environmental groups now consider the Parliament as a key forum for influence. They are also aware that the lobbying of the EP can be less costly that the lobbying of the Commission or Council (at national level). The sympathetic ear offered to environmental groups by the Environment Committee provides a focal point for these groups, who now find that within the Commission, and even within DG XI, they must compete for attention with industrial groups with more political clout and greater resources.

Relations between Council and Parliament are more difficult to assess. There is no direct contact between the EP and the national administrations for example,[70] and the Environment Committee is largely dependent on the Commission to keep it informed of progress in the Council's working groups and in COREPER. When the European Council cut out the goal of environmental protection from the Maastricht Treaty objectives, it was making a statement about its own priorities as an institution. As institutions go, the Council of Ministers is clearly in a different league from both Commission and Parliament. It remains the most important institution in terms of the legislative process. Even with the changes made in the Maastricht Treaty, in a large majority of cases the Council continues to be the privilege decision-maker. As the institution representing collectively the interests of the member states' governments, it provides a crucial link between the European and the national levels of environmental policy-making, between formulation and implementation. After all, the governments agreeing to legislation in the Council are the same governments whose responsibility it is to oversee the implementation of the policy at the end of the day.

CONCLUSION

The evolution of European environmental policy has been characterized by the cumulative expansion of European-level competences and an increasingly proactive role for the European institutions in the governance process. From the early years of environmental legislation, when national governments clearly dominated the policy game, to the post-Maastricht period, in which Commission, Parliament, and Court each can be shown to have influenced purposively European environment policy, the relationship between national and European actors has fundamentally altered. After taking a passive or quiescent role in the 1960s, by the mid-1970s the European Commission had demonstrated its capacity to make use of symbolic and informal policy instruments (the Action Programmes in particular) in order to shape the norms and principles that would henceforth underpin a distinctly European system of government.

From the mid-1980s, Commission, Parliament, and Court demonstrated how, whether together or at odds with one another, they could influence the environmental agendas and play a leadership role in environmental governance. However, rather than claiming this to be evidence of a move from passive to purposive institutionalism, we might see it more as recognition of the adaptability and malleability of the European institutions. Although they have the capacity to act purposively, they do not always do so. They have at their disposal a range of strategies and roles that they might adopt in order to achieve their ends. While it would be wrong to see national governments as anything other than the most important actors in the environment policy game, establishing the limits within which the European institutions can flex their muscles, there is no contradiction in defining the European institutions as purposive. However, this purposiveness remains subject to constraints imposed nationally. The European institutions may be able to act purposively, but this is not the same as claiming that they are able to act independently.

It is clear then that neither supranational nor intergovernmental interpretations of European environmental governance are in themselves particularly helpful. Together, however, they do give us some feeling for the intermingling of the national and European norms, rules, priorities, and goals that knit together to form a type of governance that is novel and difficult to pin down. As such, it does not fit easily into a simple dichotomy of intergovernmental or supranational, but instead forms a distinctive system of governance that has its own evolving logic.

Clearly, inter-institutional relationships and interactions among a wide range of policy actors shape patterns of environmental governance at the European level. Yet, the European institutions are not the only actors involved, even if they do have a noteworthy role to play. Interest groups and national and subnational governments are also important sources of influence. However, this chapter has shown that the patterns of environmental governance that begin to emerge top-down from an examination of the European policy-making process are extremely arcane. And, while they are in part a function of the procedural and institutional framework within which environment policy is made, and which acts as a constraint upon the legislative process, they also vary according to the political salience and technical obscurity of the issues being addressed.

What becomes all too clear, as we assess the way in which policy is made, is how the technical and scientific inputs into the policy merge and blur with the political discourse, the character of which is established institutionally. Thus, issue dynamics may be important in shaping policy outputs, but inter-institutional wrangling also has an extremely important role to play. In a sense, then, we are confirming and extending the conclusions of Chapters 2 and 3 to argue that, in European environmental governance, institutions and principles are important, and that it is a combination of structural and procedural contexts, the values and belief systems that underpin them, as well as the substantive issues themselves that frame the patterns of governance that define European environmental policy.

NOTES TO CHAPTER 4

1. See S. Mazey and J. J. Richardson (eds.), *Lobbying in the European Community* (Oxford: Oxford University Press, 1993), pp. 11–12.
2. M. E. Goncalves, 'Scientific Expertise and European Union Regulatory Problems', paper presented at the Conference on Scientific Expertise in the European Public Policy Debate, London School of Economics, 7 September 1994.
3. In the case of motor vehicles by the European Parliament, and seals by the general public, for example.
4. J. Peterson, 'Decision-Making in the European Union: Towards a Framework for Analysis', *Journal of European Public Policy*, 2:1 (1995), p. 77.
5. See D. Taylor, G. Diprose, and M. Duffy 'EC Environmental Policy and the Control of Water Pollution', *Journal of Common Market Studies*, 33:3 (1986), pp. 225–46.
6. Peterson 'Decision-Making in the European Union', p. 74.
7. See e.g. G. Ross, *Jacques Delors and European Integration*, (Cambridge: Polity Press, 1995).
8. See e.g. Mazey and Richardson, *Lobbying in the European Community*; B. Kohler-Koch, 'Changing Patterns of Interest Intermediation in the European Union', *Government and Opposition*, 29:2 (1993), pp. 166–80.
9. A. Butt Philip, 'David versus Goliath? The Challenge for Environmentalists in the Making and Implementation of EU Environmental Policy', paper presented at the ECSA–US Biennial International Conference, Charleston, SC, May 1995. R. Webster, 'Environmental Collective Action: Stable Patterns of Cooperation and Issue Alliances at the European Level', in J. Greenwood and M. Aspinal (eds.), *Collective Action in the European Union* (London: Routledge, 1998), pp. 176–95.
10. For more discussion, see Ch. 13.
11. Mazey and Richardson, *Lobbying in the European Community*, p. 18; Butt Philip, 'David versus Goliath?'. The author notes that, in the case of the packaging and packaging waste directive, the Commission was keen to harness the technical expertise of industry, and that in the first stages the environmental groups were not involved in discussion in the Commission.
12. 'Consultative Committees within the Commission', *European Citizen*, 6, Feb.–Mar. 1991.
13. Interview with senior DG XI official, September 1993.
14. Proposals on BSE, ozone depletion, and AIDS research are good examples of such areas.
15. See G. Lake, 'The Utilisation of Scientific and Technical Expertise in a European Policy Context', paper presented at the Conference on Scientific Expertise in the Public Policy Debate, London School of Economics, September 1994, for a full account of the European Parliament's scientific information gap.
16. A distinction has to be made between regulation as an approach to environmental problems, and regulations as contrasted with directives, the specific policy instruments in the hands of the Commission policy-makers.
17. M. G. Huelsdorff and T. Pfeiffer, 'Environment Policy in the EC: Neo-Functionalist Sovereignty Transfer or Neo-Realist Gate-Keeping?' *International Journal*, 47:1 (1991–2), p. 143.
18. See e.g. the amendment to the EIA directive and the consolidation into one of the texts on the classification, packaging, and labelling of different substances. For more on implementation, see Ch. 8.

19. Goncalves, 'Scientific Expertise', p. 7.

20. See e.g. M. Donnelly, 'The Structure of the European Commission and the Policy Formulation Process' in Mazey and Richardson, *Lobbying in the European Community*, pp. 74–92.

21. The *cabinets* meet firstly as the special *chefs*, dealing with the technical content of the proposals in some depth. After this, they meet in the *chefs de cabinet* meeting, a forum that does much of the groundwork for the commissioners' meeting, and which under certain circumstances can effectively take decisions on the College's behalf.

22. See e.g. L. Cram, *Policy-making in the EU: Conceptual Lenses and the Integration Process* (London: Routledge, 1997), ch. 6.

23. There is also a lot of discussion about the need to integrate environmental concerns into production processes at all stages. One way of doing this is to extend the use of EIAs. J. Scott, *Development Dilemmas in the European Community: Rethinking Regional Development Policy* (Buckingham: Open University Press, 1995), p. 84, notes that in the 1980s EIAs were thought of as the route to integration of environmental consideration, though this proved inadequate because of the nature of the instrument.

24. Mazey and Richardson, *Lobbying in the EU*, p. 3, note that DGs III, V, VI, VII, XII, XVI, XVV, XVVV, and the European Investment Bank also have responsibilities in this field.

25. A four-year programme (1994–7) took place within Eurostat on the development of statistics on the environment.

26. Interview with senior DG XI official, September 1993.

27. Ibid.

28. Interview with senior DG XVII official, September 1993.

29. Huelshoff and Pfeiffer, 'Environment Policy in the EC', p. 146.

30. Interview with DG III official, September 1993.

31. Interview with DG VI official, September 1993.

32. Interview with DG VII official, September 1993.

33. *Eur-op News*, Environment supplement, 4:2 (1995).

34. Interview with senior DG XI official, September 1993.

35. Court of Auditors, *Annual Report No 3/92 concerning the Environment, Official Jounral of the European Communities*, C241/1, 1992.

36. Mazey and Richardson, *Lobbying in the European Community*, p. 174.

37. Scott, *Development Dilemmas*, p. 82.

38. Ibid.

39. S. Mazey and J. Richardson, 'Policy Co-ordination in Brussels: Environmental and Regional Policy', *Regional Politics and Policy*, 4:1 (1994), p. 32–7.

40. A. Lenschow, 'The Greening of the EU: The Common Agricultural Policy and the Structural Funds', *Environment and Planning* C, 17:1 (1999), p. 99.

41. Interview with senior DG XVII official, September 1993.

42. Interview with senior DG XI official, September 1993.

43. Interview with DG VII official, September 1993.

44. J. B. Skjaerseth, 'The Climate Policy of the EC: Too Hot to Handle', *Journal of Common Market Studies*, 32:1 (1994), p. 27.

45. Skjaerseth, 'Climate Policy', p. 27, notes that those involved were DGs I, II, III, VI, VII, VIII, XI, XII, XVII, and XXI.

46. Interview with senior DG XVII official, September 1993.

47. Peterson, 'Decision-Making in the European Union', p. 74. Peterson quotes S. P. Johnson and G. Corcelle, *The Environmental Policy of the European Communities*, (London: Graham & Trotman, 1989), pp. 127–34, on auto emissions.
48. Goncalves, 'Scientific Expertise', p. 6.
49. Interview with DG XI official, September 1993.
50. Interview with senior DG XI official, September 1993.
51. J. Usher, 'The Commission and the Law', in G. Edwards and D. Spence (eds.), *The European Commission* (Harlow: Longman, 1994), pp. 146–68.
52. D. Judge, D. Earnshaw, and N. Cowan, 'Ripples or Waves: The European Parliament in the European Community Policy Process', *Journal of European Public Policy*, 1:1 (1994), p. 45.
53. Ibid. 47.
54. Mentioned in N. Haigh and D. Baldock, *Environmental Policy and 1992* (London: Institute for European Environment Policy, 1989), p. 24, and repeated by Judge *et al.*, 'Ripples or Waves', p. 44.
55. 'Waste Management into the 1990s: A Strategy from Brussels', *ENDS Report*, 175 (1989), pp. 16–18.
56. 'European Court Shakes Up Legal Basis of EEC Environmental Policy', *ENDS Report*, 197 (1991), pp. 15–16.
57. 'Environment Ministers Fail Again to Agree Waste Shipment Rules', *ENDS Report*, 208 (1992), p. 35.
58. 'Brussels in New Legal Challenge on Framework Directive on Waste', *ENDS Report*, 199 (1991), pp. 34–5.
59. See *Commission* v. *Council*, Case C-155/91.
60. 'Legal Basis for EC Environmental Laws', *ENDS Report*, 221 (1993), pp. 44–5.
61. 'Legal Tussle over EC Environment Rules Continues', *ENDS Report*, 208 (1992), p. 37.
62. R. Schaltz, *EU Environmental Policy Process: A Role for the European Parliament?* MA dissertation, University of Essex, 1998.
63. Interview with chair of the European Parliament Environment Committee, September 1993.
64. Judge *et al.*, 'Ripples or Waves', p. 32.
65. Ibid. 33.
66. Ibid.
67. Ibid.
68. Ibid. 35–8.
69. Ibid. 45.
70. Interview with the chair of the European Parliament Environment Committee, Ken Collins, September 1993. Collins states that informal contacts are the norm, however, with relations existing e.g. through party groups.

Part II

Comparative Environmental Governance

Introduction to Part II

In Part I we were concerned with the development and functioning of the system of multi-level environmental governance in the EU. We argued that a system of European environmental governance had emerged, consisting of recognized rules, conventions, norms, and practices for dealing with environmental problems at the European level. In the space of two decades, environmental protection has developed within the EU from an unacknowledged and peripheral sector of public policy to one of the central components in the strategy for European integration. The pace of policy development has been particularly marked since the early 1980s, coinciding with, though, as we have seen, not integrated with, the single market programme.

Four main features characterize this system of environmental governance: it is evolving, it is incomplete, it is complex, and it is multi-level. The latter two features in particular suggest a privileged position for member states within the overall system. For example, the complexity of the system, resulting from decision rules that operate on the principle of concurrent majorities, implies considerable power for member states within the Council of Ministers. The expressed preferences of member states are often crucial in determining the form and content of environmental policy decisions, as well as being responsible for decisions not to pursue certain decisions. To be sure, the member states operating through the Council of Ministers and institutions such as COREPER are not the sole decisive actors within the system (if they were, it would not be so complex); but they are clearly privileged, not simply as veto players, capable of frustrating initiatives, but also as initiators of policies themselves.

Just as the complex nature of the decision system gives a privileged position to the member states, so the multi-level character of European environmental governance means that member states are important. Member state preferences emerge from domestic political processes and are shaped by the pattern of economic interests, public opinion, existing policy commitments, and so on that is typical of each country. With its important role in the setting of agendas and the definition of problems, the Council of Ministers is one important channel by which these domestic influences are brought to bear on policy-making within the EU, a trend reinforced by the EU having little by way of own resources for the development of policy. Moreover, the practice according to which EU directives are implemented indirectly according to the legal and political systems of member states also contributes to the privileged position of the latter.

In short, complexity and multiple levels of government together give some substance to Bulmer's claim that 'the lower decisional tier of the EU is rooted in policy environments which differ between member-states and within them, according to the policy area concerned'. He concludes that 'the policy-making process does not follow the logic of integration but rather that integration follows the logic of decision-making processes', which 'have their roots in the power structures of the member states'.[1] Given this ineliminable core of national policy-making, we need then to consider the comparative politics of environmental policy in the member states of the European Union. This is the task we undertake in Part II.

How best can we understand the complex domestic politics of member states? We suggest that one central issue is the extent to which countries converge or diverge in their environmental policies and domestic systems of governance. How far have secular pressures towards a common politics of environmental policy operated in the member states? How far have such pressures been reinforced by the emergence of the European system of environmental governance, transforming the domestic environmental politics and policies of member states so that they have come to resemble one another in certain crucial respects? Scholars of comparative politics and policy have for some time been interested in the issue of policy convergence.[2] As Bennett points out, such convergence can take a variety of forms, ranging across policy goals, policy content, policy instruments, policy outcomes, or policy styles.[3] We suggest that, in the context of the emergence of a European system of environmental governance, the question of convergence acquires a heightened significance across all these dimensions.

We might expect *a priori* that moves towards mutual recognition or even harmonization would be easier at the European level if they were founded on convergences at the national level, since with such convergence member states would have less cause for disagreement. Moreover, if the EU itself were to become the focal point of convergence, particularly in diffusing certain policy principles, countries should begin to adopt a policy paradigm that resembled in some respects at least the perspective of ecological modernization. The direction, if not the pace, of policy development would be similar. By contrast, if there persist significant divergences of approach—rooted in distinct histories, institutional arrangements, and policy styles—then we should expect agreements at the European level to be less easy to achieve and the old catch-phrase about European 'unity in diversity' will carry less conviction, especially given the transnational nature of many environmental problems among Europe's mutually contiguous and often densely populated countries. We might also expect the implementation of EU policy measures to be less than uniform in scope and quality.

In the following five chapters, therefore, we survey the comparative politics of European environmental governance in six countries (Germany, Greece, Spain, Italy, the Netherlands, and the UK) in order to examine these questions. In the next section of this chapter we look at some theories in the policy-making literature to assess the sources from which we should expect either convergence or persisting divergence. We identify four main classes of variables that might be thought relevant: those related to issue characteristics; state-related variables, especially institutional features of policy-making; society-related features, encompassing broader social trends and currents of opinion; and the downward influence of pressure from the EU along with other international influences. The assumption here is that, although issue characteristics and state structures are important, the development of a system of environmental governance takes place within the context of broader social pressures as well as within the institutionalized system of political authority represented by the EU. We are thus implicitly hypothesizing that the overall changes we see in environmental policy within member states are the sum of autonomous state-related changes plus society-based pressures for change plus international pressures for change operating on the patterns of policy formation that the issue gives rise to. The question is, to what extent, if any, are these changes pushing member states significantly towards more convergent policy measures and strategies?

CAUSES OF CONVERGENCE AND DIVERGENCE

Issue Characteristics

The theory that policy sectors are of basic importance in studying public policy may begin with a remark by Lowi that 'policy creates politics'.[4] Putting this point less gnomically, we may say that the character of issues is a fundamental determinant of the policy process. That is, issues have a logic and dynamic of their own. Thus, to take one obvious and major contrast, regulatory politics, involving the setting of standards for economic products and processes, is different from redistributive politics, involving the transfer of cash from contributors to beneficiaries: different types of actors are involved, the type of available solutions to policy problems will vary from issue to issue, and the constellation of actors will therefore vary from issue to issue.

Why should we expect different policy sectors to develop in these distinct ways? From one point of view, this has to do with the character of the issue itself and the types of interest that it usually affects. Social security policies, for example, affect a large number of people in tangible ways, particularly in such matters as pensions. The costs are typically dispersed and the benefits highly visible, both to recipients directly and to their friends and family. Environmental benefits, by contrast, are often intangible and dispersed, taking the form of public goods like clean air, or problems forestalled, such as preventing the bio-accumulation of pesticide residues. Costs, by contrast, are often concentrated. They fall on particular sectors of industry, some of which may be affected substantially by seemingly small 'technical' changes in control parameters, such as the precise level at which an emission limit value is set.

If issues affect interests in different ways, then we should expect this pattern to be reflected in the politics of those issues. If the benefits of environmental policy are often dispersed and intangible, with costs concentrated and visible, this will provide greater incentives for certain interests to mobilize more forcibly than others, punctuated only by those occasions when public opinion at large is focused on a particular environmental problem. Thus, in the field of environmental politics, some analysts have stressed the extent to which the policy-making process across a range of countries is dominated by economic interests, presumably affecting the logic of collective action arising from the pattern of dispersed benefits and concentrated costs.[5] In so far as the issue determines the politics, we might expect this form of interest articulation to be replicated in all countries and policy-making systems in which environmental measures affect similar sorts of interest.

Another reason for holding to the proposition that 'policy determines politics' is connected with the organizational division of labour in political life. Governments are organized in specific ministries and agencies, so that responsibility for developing and implementing policies falls to particular bodies within the complex organization of government. Behind this phenomenon lie the fundamental constraints of bounded rationality and organizational process that condition any complex task undertaking.[6] Moreover, specific policy networks are associated with that part of government holding responsibility for the issues in which members of the network are interested. While policy networks can be closed and rather exclusive (a 'policy community') or open and fluid (an 'issue network'), we would expect there would be an equilibrium prevailing in the policy system, including an agreed understanding of how issues are to be dealt with.[7] The policy sectors approach might thus imply types of belief system that have developed within policy sectors. Most importantly, policy understanding—the way problems are conceptualized, the preference for certain types of policy instruments, and the criteria that define the solution to a problem—will be related to the type of problem being dealt with. Closely related policy sectors might develop similar approaches; for example, concepts of risk management may be shared between policy-makers in the fields of environmental protection and occupational health and safety. But more distantly related sectors in the same country are likely to share little with one another.

In accordance with the logic of the policy sectors approach, it has been argued that there are good reasons for thinking that administrative structures for environmental policy will follow a particular pattern of development. For example, Martin Jänicke has argued that a measure of the institutionalization of environmental policy is captured by four indices: the establishment of an independent ministry; the creation of an environmental agency; the passing of an environmental framework act, possibly leading to constitutional protection for the environment; and the production of an environmental report.[8] Two of these features, it will be noted, are institutional.

Majone has developed a parallel organizational argument suggesting that problems dealt with by the new social regulation, including environmental policy, lend themselves to an agency approach in which the technical competence of regulators is encouraged to work in the public interest.[9] If Majone is right, then policy learning should lead to countries adopting similar organizational reforms to deal with a similar range of problems, adapting institutions only in so far as it is necessary to deal with local circumstances. The implicit logic of this approach is that a policy problem will, by its character, impose certain constraints on the range of possible policy solutions. It is thus an implication of the policy sectors approach that countries facing similar problems will often converge in the way in which they are treated. For example, it can also be shown that the sequencing of problem recognition in the early 1970s across different political systems was surprisingly similar, with a pattern in which air and water pollution were accorded priority, with control of soil protection and chemicals regulation following later.[10] This is what one would expect if the characteristics of the policy sector were an important determinant of policy process.

However, even if it were empirically well established, the principle that policy determines politics is not by itself sufficient to enable us to conclude that policy convergence in any of its various forms was occurring. Even in the same policy sector, issue characteristics can vary. Arguably, this is particularly relevant in the field of environmental policy. Although we may categorize an issue as a problem of water pollution, say, its significance within a political system will depend upon the physical forms that it takes (does it affect sluggish, slow-moving rivers or fast-moving streams?) which are likely to vary from country to country. More generally, what counts as an environmental problem is likely to vary depending upon geographical conditions; problems of water supply, for example, will be more important in hot dry climates than in wet temperate ones. We should therefore be open to the thought that the exact significance of issue characteristics is something that can vary from place to place.

Although issue characteristics may exert an important influence on the politics of environmental policy, there are other important influences at work. Within the literature on comparative politics and policy there is a familiar controversy between those analytic approaches that place a great emphasis upon policy sectors and those that place a great emphasis upon policy styles.[11] The notion of styles is one that leads directly to the next category of variable, the state-related variables.

State-Related Variables

There is now a well established analytic tradition which stresses the importance of the autonomy of the state from social forces, and hence the importance of state characteristics, to the understanding of public policy.[12] One way of bringing out these distinctive features is by the notion of national policy styles and the forms of institutionalization that policy can have.[13] Each political system might be said to develop its own general policy style, which is fundamentally determinative of how different issues are handled. Instead of emphasizing the character of the issue in question, and the associated pattern of interest articulation to which it gives rise, the theorist of national styles stresses the distinctive ways in which policy conflict and debate are institutionalized in different countries. For example, in comparing policy-making styles in different countries, analysts have contrasted informal nego-tiated styles of rule-making with formalized and rigid styles of rule-making across different policy sectors, a contrast that can hold generally. Thus, it is claimed, the environmental policy of a country bears a closer resemblance to the policy-making process in, say, occupational health and safety or social security in that country than it does to the policy-making style on environmental issues in other countries. In an earlier study on European environmental policy, Rehbinder and Stewart related national policy diversity in particular to state structures and differ-ent levels of decision-making, certainly with respect to policy implementation.[14]

The notion of an independent effect from policy styles implicitly assumes that the institutional arrangements of a country do more than simply describe the 'how' of policy. They also prescribe to a significant extent the substance of policy. Within the EU context, this perception is potentially very important. The legal instru-ment whereby most EU environmental policy is made is the directive. This oper-ates on the assumption that the 'how' is relatively unimportant in policy-making, for the implementation of directives is left to the institutions of the member states. However, we shall see in our chapter on implementation that this legal fiction is not always as plausible as standard practice presupposes.

In fact, the national styles approach goes beyond issues of implementation, asserting that in policy-making the structure and pattern of institutions has an independent effect. In other words, within the same issue area, and controlling for differences in popular preferences, we should expect different institutional arrangements to lead to substantive differences in policy content. Institutions mat-ter, at least in so far as they are intervening variables. Thus, analysts of tax pol-icy or health policy have sought to explain important and substantive differences between tax regimes or health policy between the USA, the UK, and other coun-tries solely on the basis of the type of institutions that prevail in those countries.[15] Similarly, it has been argued that differences in the policy stances of the UK and Germany in the early 1980s in environmental policy owed much to the political institutions of the two countries rather than to any deep cultural difference in atti-tudes to nature.[16]

Why might we expect there to be distinctive national styles of policy-making? One answer refers to the recruitment and socialization of policy elites. On this view, each country develops its own distinctive way of recruiting and training key policy-makers, and the traditions of thinking and administrative culture that are estab-lished are transmitted from one generation to the next. Thus, in France there have been well-known patterns involving the *grandes écoles* that have led policy-makers in different policy sectors to favour centralized and 'rationalistic' solutions to prob-lems. British policy elites, by contrast, have traditionally been socialized into the ethos of amateurism and the co-option of specialists as and when necessary.

The same general features of bounded rationality and organizational process that led to the division of labour in policy sectors could, with equal merit, be taken as a premiss of the national styles approach. The initial institutionalization of a problem will create a framework within which subsequent policy-makers will work. This will be especially important in terms of the *intellectual* assumptions that are built into policy paradigms. Within a limited time and attention span, the whole basis upon which a particular national system is constructed is unlikely to be re-examined, except under the influence of the most acute periods of crisis. Hence, historically given solutions and institutions will tend to persist. By the same token, policy-makers within a national system in one sector looking for solutions for problems they face will easily turn to solutions developed in other sectors.

The notion of a policy style therefore implies 'a durable, persistent, and systematic approach to public problems' that characterizes a number of policy sectors within one country.[17] The implications of this approach for the comparative analysis of different national systems is easy to understand: in contrast to the stress on policy sectors, a national styles approach predicts persistent differences in the way that countries handle the same problem.

Society-Related Variables

One particular sort of society-related factor that might be thought important in leading to convergent trends is the *level of economic development*. The argument runs as follows. Environmental quality, in economic terms, is a superior good; that is to say, it is a good for which demand rises as income grows. (Demand elasticity with respect to income is greater than unity.) Hence, as the average income of a society grows, so we should expect the demand for environmental quality to increase.[18] This is a standard argument from economists.

This argument has also been given an interpretation within political sociology by its appeal to the notion of post-materialist values.[19] On this account, as people become richer, so the pattern of their needs changes. In particular, they become less interested in quantitative improvements in their material standard of living and more interested in values such as self-actualization, participation, and environmental protection. It follows on this account that, as a society becomes more wealthy, the proportion of its electorate containing post-materialists grows, particularly among the young who are likely to be active in social movements, and this in turn leads to political demands for environmental improvement. Though not cast in the economic language of demand theory, the core of the reasoning in the theory of post-materialism is the same: as people get richer their wants change, and one of the things they want more of is environmental quality.

The pattern of reasoning in either case leads to an interesting claim about the similarities and differences that we should expect in the case of environmental policy in our six countries, given that they span a sample from the wealthiest countries in the EU to some of the poorest. The prediction is that the political commitment to environmental protection will be stronger in the richer countries than in the poorer ones, but that as the poorer countries become richer they will come to favour stronger measures of environmental protection. Broadly speaking, therefore, we should expect initial divergence to be replaced with convergence. Of course, the convergence cannot be expected to be complete, since some differences in levels of wealth as well as national cultural differences will remain and can be expected to have an effect. None the less, the overall trends on these two accounts should be clear: initial divergence increasingly replaced by convergence, at least in terms of the political importance of environmental policy.

Despite these arguments for convergence drawn from economics and political sociology, indicating the importance of an underlying pattern of economic development, there are some society-related features of environmental policy that might be expected to lead to divergence. The *institutions of civil society*—the media, non-governmental organizations, and economic interests—vary from society to society and may have quite distinct historically conditioned roles within national systems of government. Moreover, the *institutions that mediate between civil society and the state*, in particular political parties and the party systems in which they are embedded, will also vary considerably from place to place. Even if there is an underlying pattern of economic growth that is a force for homogenization is different societies, its effects may well be small by comparison with these variations in the institutions of civil society and the patterns of interest intermediation to which they give rise. An appeal to the influence of society-related variables is therefore likely to throw up discrepant initial expectations.

The International Context

A priori, one might expect that international pressures for change, particularly those arising within the EU, are likely to have the effect of promoting convergence. This is most clearly seen in the issues that have arisen in the formal implementation process within the EU, where traditional national forms of administration are found wanting and have to undergo a process of adaptation, as we shall see in Chapter 8. Beyond these questions of administration, as the EU has also raised the challenge of ecological modernization and has come to press in recent years for a policy of sustainable development in its Fifth Action Programme, such new and ambitious policy objectives are likely to question settled policy principles and paradigms for two reasons. Firstly, the new approach to environmental policy entails a long-term perspective that may not sit easily with some forms of national policy style. Secondly, as we have seen in our discussion of the conflicts and complementarities between environmental policy and the single market, it is difficult to isolate the setting of specific environmental standards from broader questions about the scope and purposes of regulation, and this may have implications for the ways in which some countries take up the challenge of ecological modernization.

The potential for policy convergence in member states may also be related to their role in the EU and perhaps to the length of their EU membership. Hypothetically, long-standing member states which took an active part in pushing EU environmental policy are less likely to diverge from its approaches than passive member states, which are also recent entrants. This dichotomy overlaps considerably with the northern countries on the one hand and the southern ones on the other. The northern three examined in this book were either founding members or joined in 1973, just when the EU was taking its first steps towards defining an environmental policy. Two of the three southern cases joined the EU in the 1980s, around the time it adopted a more vigorous line on the environment. Italy is, of course, an exception here, being a founding member state, although one somewhat inactive in the environmental area before the mid-1980s. If length of EU membership is important, we should expect a clustering of countries in so far as they converge,with the three longest serving showing the greatest similarity, the UK showing some convergence, and Spain and Greece showing the least similarity to the others.

Moreover, a similar push in a more convergent direction might also be expected to come from the diffuse influences that are represented by the international currents of thinking that circulate among policy elites. Thus, given the influence of wider international institutions and processes, most notably those associated with the Brundtland report and the OECD's interest in environmental performance, we should generally expect international pressures to lead to convergent patterns of policy-making.[20] These similarities of process can take place without those involved being conscious of what policy-makers in other countries are doing. Obviously, if policy borrowing from one national system to another does occur, this will reinforce the distinctive character of a given policy sector and create pressures for convergence.[21] Thus, in the field of environmental policy, certain policy, instruments, most notably the tool of environmental impact assessment, have been consciously borrowed from the USA in which the technique was first developed.[22] Such borrowing is therefore likely to increase the similarities in the ways different countries deal with the same problem.

We have assumed so far that the international pressures pushed generally in the direction of convergence. As a first-order effect this is indisputable: there would be no point in an international system of governance that simply allowed its member states to continue in their old ways. On the other hand, possible second-order effects make the theoretical expectation a little more complex. For example, decision-makers in the southern countries may have allowed their policies on the environment to be determined to a considerable extent by the EU, as we show below, but this does not have to mean that their approach has drawn upon an active consensus across a range of domestic actors. On the contrary, the fact that Brussels has tended to be ahead of these countries in policy-thinking if not policy action suggests quite some scope for domestic tensions in the south. International pressures may well create reactive second-order patterns of political organization at the national level that reinforce patterns of divergence, for example by leading important economic actors to organize against a particular measure. Bulmer's claim that the logic of integration is rooted in domestic political circumstances may well hold true through these second-order effects. So, as with our other types of variables, the implications for convergence and divergence of international factors are ambivalent.

COMPARING THEORIES OF CONVERGENCE AND DIVERGENCE

Unless we think *either* that the character of an issue has no effect upon the policy process, *or* that the institutions of a country have no independent effect, *or* that economic growth does not affect societal preferences, *or* that the influence of international organizations is unimportant, it should be clear that we are here faced with competing empirical hypotheses about what influences policy outputs and national systems of environmental governance.[23] In the accompanying table we summarize the discussion so far and the influence that we expect different types of variables to have.

It is important to note from this model that what is at issue here is convergence in policy patterns *not* an identity of policy strategies and principles. At any one time we might well expect differences of policy, most obviously related to the level of economic development of the country in question. However, although *at any one time* forces acting on the policy system might lead to differences, *over time* we might expect convergence. The focus in this approach is therefore on developing

TABLE II.1 *Summary of main models of convergence and divergence*

Type of variable	Causes of predicted effect	
	Convergence	Divergence
Issue characteristics	Interest patterns	Geographical diversity
State-related	None	Policy styles Party systems Political culture Administration
Society-related	Economic growth; post-materialism Environmental groups	Economic interests Media
International	Implementation demands International opinion	Second-order effects

trends within policy patterns rather than on determining which stage has been reached within one policy system. A poorer country may well be content with lower environmental standards than would a richer country at any one time, but if there are converging trends within the system we would expect its standards to be rising. Moreover, to the extent to which there is an independent influence on policy patterns from converging non-economic factors, for example pro-environmental currents of international opinion, we should expect that, if convergence is really occurring, we should observe a stronger commitment to environmental measures from countries at a relatively low level of economic development than were observed in richer countries at a comparable stage of their own development.

Thus, a tension potentially arises between Europeanizing and other pressures for policy convergence and rooted national constraints on policy change arising from cross-national divergence. This tension may be overlaid by basic cross-national differences concerning the process and purpose of European integration itself, ranging from the intergovernmentalist to the integrationist or even the federalist, with different implications for the legitimate role of the EU in the environmental area. Such disputes about the scope of EU environmental policy also affect views about appropriate standards to be applied.

In the end, the balance between the different elements is a question that can only be answered empirically. In this Part, we aim to characterize the distinctive principles of environmental protection that different countries adopt, and we seek to relate them to the institutional processes and contexts in which these principles are embodied. The chapters that follow look beyond the policy preferences of national systems by identifying the kinds of pressures and influences to which policy-makers are subject in their domestic contexts. We have a particular concern about how far such political dynamics assists or inhibits the process of European legislation. How much, for instance, do domestic pressures account for a firmer line taken in Brussels over specific sectors of environmental policy? At the other end of the policy process, do such pressures tend to enhance (or not) the prospects for compliance with European directives? It is hypothesized that the combination of 'top-down' pressures from Brussels and 'bottom-up' pressures within member states, which we identified in the pressures for convergence, is likely to prove a powerful incentive for national policy-makers to act and choose. But this simple model needs to be modified in various ways.

This kind of two-way dynamics dictates the focus of successive chapters in this Part. Thus, Chapters 5 and 6 look at the diversity of environmental governance at the national level in reference to both policies and administrative structures and procedures. Chapter 7 then turns to the range of significant bottom-up pressures operating in domestic systems which may affect the prospects for policy convergence at the European level. Chapter 8, on the other hand, is concerned with top-down pressures for convergence from Brussels, with particular attention to the implementation of EU policies on the environment. Finally, the balance of European and national influences is assessed in Chapter 9.

In pursuing these themes, we draw upon the experience of six member states within the EU: Germany, Greece, Spain, Italy, the Netherlands, and the UK. The range is deliberately wide, posing a severe test for the thesis that there are convergent trends. The countries differ not only in their policies and institutional arrangements in respect of environmental policy, but also in their economic development and cultural dispositions. Hence any signs of convergence are important, since the starting points are so different.

NOTES TO PART II INTRODUCTION

1. S. Bulmer, 'Domestic Politics and European Community Policy-Making', *Journal of Common Market Studies*, 21:4 (1983), p. 353.
2. For a good review, see C. J. Bennett, 'What is Policy Convergence and What Causes It?' *British Journal of Political Science*, 21:2 (1991), pp. 215–33.
3. Bennett, 'What is Policy Convergence', p. 218.
4. T. J. Lowi, 'American Business, Public Policy, Case Studies and Political Theory', *World Politics*, 6 (1964), pp. 677–715.
5. C. H. Enloe, *The Politics of Pollution in Comparative Perspective* (New York and London: Longman, 1975).
6. The best introduction to this 'organizational process' view of government is still G. T. Allison, *Essence of Decision* (Boston: Little, Brown, 1971), ch. 3.
7. For a good review of the policy networks literature, inclusing its terminological niceties, see M. J. Smith, *Pressure, Power and Policy: State Autonomy and Policy Networks in Britain and the United States* (New York: Harvester Wheatsheaf, 1993), ch. 3. See also the studies in D. Marsh and R. A. W. Rhodes (eds.), *Policy Networks in British Government* (Oxford: Oxford University Press, 1992).
8. M. Jänicke, 'Erfolgungsbedingungen von Umweltpolitik im Internationalen Vergleich', *Zeitschrift für Umweltpolitik*, 3 (1990), pp. 213–32.
9. G. Majone, 'Cross-National Sources of Regulatory Policymaking in Europe and the United States', *Journal of Public Policy*, 11:1 (1991), pp. 79–106, and 'The European Community between Social Policy and Social Regulation', *Journal of Common Market Studies*, 31:2 (1993), pp. 153–70.
10. A. Weale, *The New Politics of Pollution* (Manchester and New York: Manchester University Press, 1992), ch. 1.
11. G. P. Freeman, 'National Styles and Policy Sectors: Explaining Structured Variation', *Journal of Public Policy*, 5:4 (1985), pp. 467–96.
12. P. Evans, D. Rueschemeyer, and T. Skocpol (eds.), *Bringing the State Back In* (New York: Cambridge University Press, 1985); E. A. Nordlinger, *On the Autonomy of the Democratic State* (Cambridge, Mass.: Harvard University Press, 1981); S. Steinmo, K. Thelen, and F. Longstreth (eds.), *Structuring Politics: Historical Institutionalism in Comparative Analysis* (New York: Cambridge University Press, 1992).
13. J. J. Richardson (ed.), *Policy Styles in Western Europe* (London: Allen & Unwin, 1982)
14. E. Rehbinder and R. Stewart, *Environmental Protection Policy* (Berlin and New York: Walter de Gruyter, 1985), pp. 207, 232.

15. For taxation see S. Steinmo, *Taxation and Democracy: Swedish, British and American Approaches to Financing the Modern State* (New Haven: Yale University Press, 1993), who presents a particularly clear view of the institutionalist perspective. For health see E. M. Immergut, *Health Politics: Interests and Institutions in Western Europe* (Cambridge: Cambridge University Press, 1993), and T. R. Marmor and R. Klein, 'Cost vs Care: American's Health Care Dilemma Wrongly Considered', *Quaterly Journal of Health Services Management*, 4:1 (1986), pp. 19–24, reprinted in part as ch. 6 of T. R. Marmor, *Understanding Health Care Reform* (New Haven and London: Yale University Press, 1994). For a good general introduction see B. Rothstein, 'Political Institutions: An Overview', in R. E. Goodin and H.-D. Klingemann (eds.), *A New Handbook of Political Science* (Oxford: Oxford University Press, 1996), pp. 133–66.
16. Weale, *New Politics of Pollution*, ch. 3.
17. Freeman, 'National Styles and Policy Sectors'. p. 477.
18. See e.g. W. Beckerman, *Small is Stupid* (London: Duckworth, 1995), pp. 39–40, and F. Hirsch, *The Social Limits to Growth* (London: Routledge, 1977), ch. 3.
19. R. Inglehart, *The Silent Revolution: Changing Values and Political Styles among Western Publics* (Princeton: Princeton University Press, 1977), and *Culture Shift in Advanced Industrial Societies* (Princeton: Princeton University Press, 1990); and R. Inglehart and P. R. Abrahamson, 'Economic Security and Value Change', *American Political Science Review*, 88:2 (1994), pp. 336–54.
20. For a discussion of OECD performance reviews in a wider context, see O. S. Stokke, 'Environmental Performance Review: Concept and Design', in E. Lykke (ed.), *Achieving Environmental Goals* (London: Belhaven Press, 1992), pp. 3–4.
21. Bennett, 'What is Policy Convergence?', pp. 220–3, stresses 'emulation' as a source of policy convergence.
22. On the spread of environmental impact assessment, see S. Taylor, *Making Bureaucracies Think* (Stanford, Calif.: Stanford University Press, 1984).
23. *Outputs* are laws, regulations, and other policy measures that are the product of political decision. *Policy outcomes* are the changes in the world that policy outputs make.

5

National Policies on the Environment:
Evolution, Principles, and Style

In this chapter we compare the environmental policies of our six member states, sketching the background to the development of environmental policy and setting out the policy principles and policy style characteristic of each country. By the term 'policy principles' we refer to the basic conceptualization of environmental policy as encoded in legislation and practice. Although, as we shall see, such principles are often set out at a high level of generality, this does not detract from their importance in defining the content of environmental policy and the policy stances of different countries as witnessed, for example, in conflicts over environmental measures in the Council of Ministers or other international bodies. By 'policy styles' we refer to the distinctive processes of policy-making within which these principles are worked out. These processes may be consensual or adversarial, reactive or anticipatory, participatory or exclusive.[1]

From one point of view, in examining policy principles and policy styles, we are looking at *dependent* variables, that is to say the summary characteristics of what makes for differences between our six member states on the assumption that these characteristics reflect underlying institutional and other influences. From this perspective, the different policy regimes characteristic of each state are defined by reference to their policy principles and policy styles, and we expect convergence or divergence of policy regimes arising from the issue-related, state-related, society-related, and international independent variables that influence each country.

On the other hand, policy principles and styles can also be regarded as *independent* variables, falling within the state-related category, since the adoption of policy principles or the processing of issues at one time is likely to leave an historical legacy that will shape how issues are dealt with in subsequent periods. In this chapter we confine ourselves largely to the task of describing distinct national policy principles and styles, defining them primarily as dependent variables; but we also note the extent to which historically established national patterns influence contemporary developments in our six countries.

CROSS-NATIONAL POLICY EVOLUTION AND PATTERNS

Environmental policy first began to emerge in its modern form in Europe (as well as North America, Australasia, and Japan) in the late 1960s and early 1970s.

However, although modern environmental politics can be said to begin at this time, there is a history of environmental measures in each of our countries that pre-dates the measures adopted in the 1970s, and which therefore to some extent has shaped them. Similarly, since the emergence of modern environmental politics in the 1960s and 1970s, new issues and new ways of thinking have developed, as we saw in connection with the development of ecological modernization in the European Union in the 1980s.

For our purposes, therefore, we can thus distinguish three phases of environmental policy: (i) the pre-modern, going back to the nineteenth and early twentieth centuries, in which the focus is on limited measures largely at a local level and primarily for the purpose of maintaining public health; (ii) the modern, emerging in the 1970s, in which the focus is on the development of measures at a national level to control specific pollutants, largely through end-of-pipe controls; and (iii) the 'new' politics of pollution, which developed in the 1980s and 1990s, where there is a growing acknowledgement of the complexity of environmental policy and the need to integrate environmental measures with other sectors of public policy.[2]

The pre-modern history of environmental legislation stretches back well into the nineteenth century, and in some cases even to the middle ages. Much of the focus of this earlier legislation was mainly on the public health issues that arose from poor drinking water quality, or the potential for contagious disease transmission that environmental hazards present. In *Britain*, for example, water pollution became an issue in the wake of the development of the great industrial towns of the nineteenth century, with public health pioneers like Sir Edwin Chadwick campaigning for reform from the 1840s. By the 1870s, the problems of river pollution in London were so serious that disinfected sheets had to be hung over the windows of the Houses of Parliament in order to overcome the stench from the River Thames. Public health legislation in the 1870s gave powers to local authorities to control pollution and redevelop slums. Legislation in the field of air pollution also established the world's first national pollution control agency, the Alkali Inspectorate, in 1863.[3] So by the end of the nineteenth century there had developed a centralized regulatory authority for the control of pollution from major manufacturing sources, but local control for matters of water pollution.

In *Germany*, the earliest legislation dealing with environmental matters can be found in the Prussian General Trade Ordinances of 1845, which created a permit system for productive processes and enabled local authorities to place conditions on manufacturing methods where there was likely to be a problem of air pollution.[4] This form of regulation was taken up by the North German Confederation in its 1869 trade regulations, although the legislation remained permissive in character, and the Civil Code of 1873 included a duty of toleration upon individuals where pollution was seen as an essential accompaniment of economic development. In essence, then, the policy regime that was to govern German environmental policy until the reforms of the 1970s were in place before the First World War.

There are examples of *Dutch* attempts to control for environmental damage going back to the end of the middle ages, when local authorities were already attempting to regulate the disposal of wastes and discharges to water.[5] As early as 1810, when the Netherlands was still under Napoleonic rule, a decree was issued aimed at controlling the hazards and damage caused by industry.[6] Later in the nineteenth century, legislation was passed to further control the hazards and nuisance from industrial sites in the form of the 1875 Nuisance Act (*Hinderwet*), which remained the framework for policy until its revision in 1952.[7] The Dutch case also confirms the public health orientation of nineteenth-century attempts to control for environmental pollution.

In *Italy* too it is possible to look back to nineteenth-century legislation, passed in 1865, on the control of water supply, an instance of environmental legislation with a public health rationale. Moreover, during the Fascist period laws were passed on such matters as the country's artistic and archaeological heritage and on urban waste as evidence of early concern about environmental matters. The law of 1939 on 'natural beauties' (*bellezze naturali*), which among other things instituted landscape architecture plans, was one of the most advanced pieces of conservation legislation in its time.[8] Other main issues for legislation have been toxic and nuclear waste, coastal pollution and national parks (for example, in the Galasso Law of 1985).

Even Greece and Spain, which as relatively under-industrialized countries one might expect not to come under the same pressures to develop environmental regulation, show instances where early legislation on environmental matters was developed. For example, in *Greece* there were laws in the 1920s on water supply and on the disposal of wastes.[9] In *Spain* the early legislation of 1879 is concerned with water quality, and in 1918 there were attempts to protect nature, with the establishment of two national parks.

We can see therefore that environmental policy was not an entirely new phenomenon in the 1970s. However, it did take a new form under a conjunction of social and political developments that created the pressure for more extensive measures. Internationally, the event that came to symbolize the response to these developments was the United Nations Stockholm conference on the environment in 1972. In Part I we saw that it was this event that catalysed action at the European level, but it can also be seen as a symbol of the common concerns experienced by many countries in the years prior to the conference.

Comparing policy developments across different countries, the precise role of the varying elements in the emergence of environmental policy at this time is subject to debate and interpretation. Nevertheless, the following can be seen as generally important: the emergence of new environmental problems as techniques of industrial production developed; growing scientific understanding of the character and extent of environmental problems; the cultural transformation and emergence of post-materialism that followed over two decades of unparalleled economic growth and affluence; higher standards of education among mass publics that provided a ready audience for critiques of capitalist development; and the inconsistencies between the narrow improvement in material circumstances on the one hand

and the failure to secure improvements in the quality of life to keep up with these material developments on the other, most famously summarized in Galbraith's criticism of capitalism as promoting private opulence and public squalor.[10] These various elements comprised a common set of circumstances operating on all developed countries, although it is reasonable to suppose a significant degree of cross-national variation in the balance of these different elements, in terms of their influence as well as their timing. This is not to say that there were no modern policy developments prior to the upsurge of interest in the 1970s. For example, in Germany important legislation on the management of water was passed in 1957, and in the UK the 1956 Clean Air Act marks a significant development. However, the pace and scale of activity becomes more extensive in the late 1960s and early 1970s.

Thus, in *Germany*, by common consent among expert observers, the modern phase of environmental policy began in 1969 with the Social Democratic–Free Democratic (hereafter, Social–Liberal) government elected in that year. In 1970 the government reorganized the administration of environmental protection, bringing sections of the bureaucracy together in the Interior Ministry, and it also produced its Immediate Programme for Environmental Action. In 1971 there followed a more fully developed Environment Programme, and in 1974 important legislation in the field of air pollution. Here the model of US policy developments was particularly important in shaping the response.[11]

In *Italy*, a first serious attempt at an autonomous approach to environmental issues occurred with the law on atmospheric pollution of 1966, followed a decade later by the Merli law of 1976 on the protection of water from pollution.[12] Although Italy showed legislative initiative on environmental policy at about the same time as the northern countries, organizational change in environmental management did not follow until a decade later. Rome's espousal of environmental concerns as a more central component of government policy occurred in the first half of the 1980s, under the Craxi government, formed in 1983. This was marked by the establishment of the new Ministry of the Environment in 1986. (This is commonly seen, however, as a largely symbolic turning-point in Italian policy on the environment.)

Similarly, it was in the late 1960s and early 1970s that a wave of public and political concern swept across the *Netherlands*, to create the climate of opinion within which environmental policy could be systematically developed. The Netherlands is a country that is open to international currents of opinion, and the Club of Rome report, *The Limits to Growth*, appears to have been influential among many people.[13] Among the social and economic conditions that seemed to have created the conditions for the receptiveness of Dutch public opinion to issues of environmental concern were the breakdown of pillarization in Dutch politics as secularization made less salient the confessional distinction between Catholic and Protestant, and the rapid rate of economic growth in the postwar period which had led to problems of air pollution, particularly in the area of the Rhine Delta.[14]

In the *United Kingdom*, the sinking of the *Torrey Canyon* oil tanker in 1966 proved a catalytic event, as did press exposure of poor hazardous waste management practices in some parts of industry. This led to legislation in the early 1970s as well as significant organizational restructuring with the creation of the Department of the Environment. However, as we shall see below, one of the striking features of UK developments is the attempt to put new wine into old bottles and to seek to build the modern response to pollution along traditional approaches.

Both *Spain and Greece* are commonly viewed as latecomers on the environmental scene, in the sense of granting serious attention to, and beginning to produce policy on, the environment in this modern phase. Undoubtedly, this may be attributed in large part to the existence of their authoritarian regimes and to the fact they were not yet member states of the EU—Greece joined in 1981 and Spain in 1986. As a result of their absence from mainstream European politics, they did not experience to the same degree the policy engagement of the 1970s on which to build as a basis for further policy development. For these countries, the 'new politics of pollution' were almost literally new in the 1980s.

The right-wing dictatorships were not attitudinally well disposed towards environmental concerns, for their policy strategy in both cases was dominated by a priority for economic growth. None the less, environmental legislation of a kind was decreed, although largely as a result of international pressure. The UN conference at Stockholm in 1972 was influential in Franco's Spain, now more sensitive to European opinion for reasons of regime maintenance and in order to further closer links with the EU. The Franco regime chose to emphasize nature conservation. The birth of Greek environmental law has similarly been placed by one study in the mid-1970s, shortly after Stockholm; and the military junta passed laws on national parks, the protection of game, and the control of shipping.[15]

Several international conventions were signed by these authoritarian regimes, but their policy shift was very limited, legislation being a piecemeal response for economic or diplomatic reasons. It was usually technical in its focus on particular environmental problems, and it lacked any integrated approach.[16]

The arrival of democracy and their emergence from international isolation opened up the prospects for environmental policy in both Spain and Greece. Controls on public information (as on the environment) ceased, just as the surfacing of environmental groups pointed to a new domestic pressure. However, in practice environmental matters did not automatically move up the policy agenda. Standard ideological concerns focusing on familiar socio-economic issues became central to political debate once the newly established democracies settled down. Moreover, international concern with the environment had receded from the mid-1970s in the face of recession, which became the commanding policy issue in Western Europe. It was not until the mid-1980s that international and especially EU action on the environment brought this area back on to the visible agenda. Furthermore, by this time environmental degradation in southern Europe had become rather more pressing.

Greece began to develop environmental policy in a more conscious way from the early 1980s, this being marked by the creation of a ministry bearing in part the name 'environment' in 1980. The arrival of PASOK in office in 1981 gave an impetus to environmental concerns, for by this time the Athens pollution cloud (*nefos*) had become an issue in its own right and this has tended to lead the way in pushing the environment up the policy agenda. Other main concerns have been coastal pollution, forest fires, and national treasures. The following years saw new activism on environmental matters, culminating in the Framework Law of 1986, which sought to coordinate approaches to the environment and to facilitate the adoption of EU directives.

The beginning of Spanish policy broadly paralleled the Greek case. As in Greece, there is a constitutional mandate for environmental protection, but this was not, for a while, followed by much significant legislation. In 1983 a modification of the penal code introduced environmental crimes and set penalties for emitting or dumping polluting substances in the physical environment and for threatening public health or natural resources. There followed regulations on standards for soil and water use, the rehabilitation of natural open areas, and the protection of coastlines.[17] If there has been any continuity of emphasis within environmental policy, this has related to not only urban air pollution, forest fires, and coastal pollution (as in Greece), but to also water supply (an increasing concern) and to soil erosion and desertification.

Thus, by the time of the Rio Conference in 1992, twenty years on from the Stockholm Conference, environmental policy had emerged as an autonomous policy area in all six of our countries. All governments could provide a detailed account not only of their environmental legislation and policy, but also of the thinking that was supposed to inform policy. To be sure, there was considerable variability, both in the extent and the quality of this policy thinking and in the extent to which the statement of principles was operationally significant as well as rhetorically deployed. In the next section we look in detail at these principles and at the accompanying policy style of each country.[18]

POLICY PRINCIPLES AND POLICY STYLES

Germany

Policy principles. The German approach to environmental policy and legislation needs to be seen in the context of the German legal tradition, which, in common with many continental systems, places a great emphasis on the formulation of general principles. Moreover, this is reinforced in the case of Germany both by the federal constitutional system and by the reaction to absence of the rule of law under the Third Reich.

By the time of the Rio Conference, Germany could claim to have well established legislation in many fields of pollution control, of which the following is but a sample. Legislation in 1957 had provided a framework for the management of water resources; in 1974 there was major legislation effectively nationalizing the setting of air pollution control standards; 1976 saw the establishment of legislation on water pollution charges; chemicals control legislation came in 1980; and in 1986 there was a major updating of waste control legislation. Moreover, a significant further reform of waste legislation was to take place in 1993, with the introduction of the 'Circular Economy' law, which was an attempt to reduce the production of waste. In addition to this sectoral legislation, there was legislation on environmental impact assessments and other 'procedural' environmental laws.

Behind the legislation, there was a serious attempt to spell out principles for environmental policy. In large part, these principles were formulated in the period following the Environment Programme of 1971, when the federal government first sought to secure the constitutional changes necessary to give it the powers to regulate environmental standards. The principles then spelt out included: the polluter-pays principle; the common burden principle, to deal with cases where the polluter could not be identified; the cooperation principle, to ensure that social actors and groups collaborated in the making and implementation of environmental policy; and the principle of international cooperation. In addition to these principles, which in broad terms are common either implicitly or explicitly across many economically developed countries, one other principle has come to occupy a central role in German environmental policy and to be the *leitmotiv* of German environmental strategy: the so called *Vorsorgeprinzip*, or principle of precaution. Although not included in the original statement of environmental policy, the principle of precaution was mentioned in the German federal government's 1976 Environmental Report. It was also incorporated into the 1974 legislation on air pollution.

In its 1992 submission to the Rio Conference, the German government picked out three of these principles in particular as defining its approach to policy: the precautionary principle; the polluter-pays principle; and the cooperation principle.[19] The polluter-pays principle is of course widely accepted by many governments (as well as widely flouted in their policy measures), and the principle of cooperation is perhaps especially important in a political regime that attaches very high importance to constitutional procedures. However, much of the distinctiveness of German environmental policy is given by the importance placed on the principle of precaution.

This principle has played a particularly important role in German domestic environmental policy, since it enabled the German government during the 1980s to legislate for higher and more costly standards on air pollution control from large stationary sources. Despite its importance, it is not easy to see a uniform core in the development and application of the principle. Indeed, one leading German legal scholar, writing in 1988, identified no less than eleven different senses in which the term had been used in legal judgments or policy discourse.[20] However, it is clear that the thrust of the principle is to legitimate more stringent standards of pollution control than would otherwise be required, where there is some ground for thinking that without the higher standard environmental damage would be done. The case of forest damage in the early 1980s illustrates this point well. Although there was no clear evidence linking forest damage with sulphur dioxide emissions from stationary sources, the government was prepared to legislate to control these emissions, citing precaution as the ground of action.

The principle of precaution cannot be understood, however, without also understanding the long-standing principle of control in German environmental policy of regulating in accordance with the so-called *Stand der Technik*, or state of the art. This occupies more or less the same logical space in German environmental discourse as the principle of best practicable means occupied in British discourse (see below). In the 1974 air pollution legislation, the principle of *Stand der Technik* was defined as follows:

the level of development of progressive procedures, installations/equipment or methods of operation, which appear to assure the practical suitability of a measure for the limitation of emissions. In determining the *Stand der Technik*, comparable procedures, installations/ equipment or methods of operation, which have been successfully tried out in practice, are especially to be taken into account.[21]

As this principle has been developed and refined, it has come to mean in practice that regulators ask what is technically feasible in engineering terms, leaving operators free to determine how to achieve those standards. They then see whether controls that are technically feasible can be applied to an emission, making some judgment about the economic costs of such control. Among those that are responsible for formulating standards in accordance with the principle of *Stand der Technik*, there is therefore always an economic, as well as a technical engineering, assessment involved.[22] It is therefore not true, as is sometimes claimed, that Germany in the 1980s was prepared to legislate for higher standards whatever the cost. It is however true that Germany, being a relatively rich country with considerable strength in engineering and process control, could afford to legislate for high environmental standards.

How does the notion of *Stand der Technik* relate to the principle of precaution? Perhaps the simplest answer is that, except in cases of special danger such as to do with nuclear technology, a precautionary environmental policy in the German context is one that always takes advantage of the available state of the art in dealing with an environmental problem.[23] The emphasis, therefore, is less upon the assimilative capacity of the environment, as in the British policy approach, and more upon the technical capability of dealing with an environmental problem. One important consequence follows from this emphasis. Since technical capability rather than assimilative capacity is the starting-point, uniformity of emission standards occupies a central place in framing regulations. Emission standards do not typically take into account where the emission is occurring, but rather state a general requirement for processes of a particular type. A further justification for this approach that is sometimes cited in Germany is the importance that the private sector places on economic calculability in its obligation to meet environmental standards and therefore on the desirability of reducing discretion in the application of standards.

The net effect of the appeal to the precautionary principle is therefore to make standards of pollution control more stringent than they would otherwise be. This has been an important element in the evolving German discussion about the priority to be given to environmental protection and its relationship to economic development. Germany was thus the site of some of the earliest arguments about ecological modernization, in particular the view that environmental protection and economic growth were not opposed but could form a partnership, particularly in the competition of global markets for clean technology. Within the framework of the development of the Large Combustion Plant Ordinance, these arguments could be used as a way of justifying the otherwise expensive retrofitting of power stations with flue-gas desulphurization equipment, since it was thought by some proponents of the policy that the technical advance could form the basis for future exports to other countries (including the UK, which resisted the policy at European level). Similar arguments were used about catalytic converter technology for cars.

Another theme of those who argued for a policy based on the principles of ecological modernization was that waste was costly. This is in turn led to arguments for closing off waste run-off and the development of the so-called circular economy. Although the idea of a circular economy, in which waste is minimized through reduction and re-use, is ambitious, Germany certainly managed a decoupling of economic growth and pollution flows in the late 1980s.[24] It might seem therefore that by the end of the 1980s an elaborate set of policy principles had been integrated into a more general account of the positive role of environmental policy in the development of a modern economy. However, this would be something of a premature conclusion, for a number of reasons.

Firstly, some representatives of industry began to question the stringency of pollution control measures within the context of the debate on *Standort Deutschland*, or the national competitiveness of the German economy within the international economic system. The argument was that the spate of environmental measures in the 1980s had imposed disproportionate costs on German industry which were not incurred by other countries, and that this was working to the disadvantage of German economic performance. This argument was taken seriously by proponents of environmental policy, and the Ministry of the Environment went to the length of commissioning independent studies by research institutes to counter the accusations. Much of the debate was also affected by the measures surrounding the unification of Germany. As part of the reconstruction of the former German Democratic Republic, laws were passed to allow for a speeding up of the planning processes for such projects as road building. For constitutional reasons, the laws had to apply in both the east and the west of the country, and some observers felt that the effect was to tip the balance more in favour of conventional economic development than had been the case before. Since the early 1990s, the debate about *Standort Deutschland* appears to have shifted from the questioning of environmental policy to the costs to employers of Germany's social security system.

Secondly, although German principles of pollution control might be embedded in a more general account of the relationship between the economy and the environment, there has been a reluctance among German policy-makers to use 'new' policy instruments sometimes associated with ecological modernization. Legal and administrative regulation of polluting substances are still the norm; the adoption of measures such as environmental impact assessments has been slow, although the take-up of eco-audit, which was initially resisted, has been among the highest in Europe. Moreover, the integration of environmental concerns into other areas of policy has not been easy, with the most spectacular example being the government's failure to impose a national speed limit on the motorways; indeed, in March 1994 the government announced that it would contest any attempt by the European Union to impose a common speed limit.[25] The German Council of Environmental Experts, in one of its general reports, has also been critical of the lack of use of economic instruments.[26]

A third qualification to the view that German policy principles can be characterized in terms of ecological modernization concerns the absence of a general framework for environmental legislation. Although there is a clear statement of policy principles, the legislation in which they are embedded is large and diverse, and does not necessarily provide a coherent basis for policy-making. A project commissioned from the University of Trier by the Federal Environment Office and published in 1986 looked at the possibilities for harmonizing environmental law.[27] Since 1990, successive draft environmental codes have been published, but there have been no legislative developments.[28] There has also been a long discussion about the incorporation of a requirement of environmental responsibility in the German Constitution (the Basic Law), and this resulted in 1994 in an amendment that made environmental protection a state duty, although it did not go so far as to make it a right of citizens.

One way of summarizing these rather disparate elements is to say that policy principles, and their legislative outcomes, have been well developed in so far as they have built upon traditional regulatory techniques of a legal and administrative kind. The emphasis is on technical possibilities of control rather than on a pragmatic search for results. Other instruments, including economic instruments, have been less well developed, despite the existence of the polluter-pays principle in policy discourse and the high salience that environmental issues have in Germany.

Policy style. In many ways the German environmental policy style can be regarded as the polar opposite of the British style. It is highly legalistic, seeking to reduce administrative discretion to a minimum and incorporating explicit statements of principle into its legislation and policy approaches. Thus, instead of informality and administrative discretion, German environmental standard-setting is highly formalized. One observer has pointed out that the degree of legalism in German environmental regulation is matched only by the United States among OECD countries.[29] This formalism of regulation is most marked in the tendency to ensure that standards, and the procedures that accompany them, are clearly stated in legislative and administrative documents. The major pieces of legislation in Germany on environmental protection—governing discharges to air, water, or land—take the form of framework legislation, within which specific standards have to be set by regulators in the Federal Environmental Office and the Environment Ministry and propagated through ordinances. It is also one of the reasons why those setting standards favour uniform emission limits, despite the criticisms that can be made of such standards from the point of view of economic efficiency and cost effectiveness.

With its elaborate constitutional safeguards under the postwar constitution, it is a matter of considerable importance in Germany that the administrative process of determining standards should be formalized. There is thus an elaborate structure of German administrative law, which requires administrators to be explicit about the standards they are setting and the duties these standards imply to those who are subject to them. No one who has tried to work their way through a German environmental ordinance could fail to be impressed by its exhaustive (and exhausting) quality. It has been argued that, despite its legal form, the German policy-making style actually imposes little by way of genuine procedural restriction upon the higher levels of policy-making and that, by comparison with the US Administrative Procedures Act, German standard-setting is highly discretionary. Moreover, this argument continues, German administrative and constitutional courts do not have the power to declare particular pieces of legislation unconstitutional on general grounds, although they do have the power to scrutinize the way in which legislation affects particular individuals.[30]

There is undoubtedly some truth in this argument if the standard is made one in which legal control can constrain the policy-making process of governments that enjoy parliamentary confidence. However, this is in some ways to go beyond the norms of parliamentary government, in which the administration is expected to implement the collectively determined policy goals of the governing party or coalition. Moreover, by comparison with other European systems, the German processes are highly legalistic.

Although formal, there is none the less a cooperative element within the German regulatory style. There are widespread processes of consultation between administrators and industry about the setting of standards. Susan Rose-Ackerman, for example, points to the close negotiations between the federal ministry and representative of the chemical industry in the drafting of the 1980 Chemicals Act.[31] Much of the detailed work in setting standards is carried out by the Federal Environment Office, which expects to consult regularly with industrial representatives. Moreover, the Association of German Engineers has long taken an interest in environmental standards; it has promulgated over two hundred environmental norms and, together with the German Institute for Norms, has taken an active part in formulating standards.

German policy-making is also characterized by its high degree of specialization. Some people even speak about a 'cult of expertise' in German public policy. Within the Environment Ministry and the Federal Environment Office, the division of labour is highly specialized. Traditionally, the dominant professional background has been in engineering and the law, reflecting the need to draft technically competent and legally sound standards, but one of the changes in recent years has been a growth in the number of economists employed. This highly specialist and expert style has led to criticism of the exclusive and closed character of the German system of regulation. This can make horizontal coordination among different ministries difficult. It also means that parliaments can sometimes play only a residual role in the development of environmental policy, even though standards have to be approved in most cases by the Bundesrat. Indeed, the Large Combustion Ordinance, which marked a resurgence of environmental policy-making in 1983, was a purely administrative matter.

Greece

Policy principles. The Greek government's national report for the Rio conference of 1992 made suitable reference to all the standard concepts current in EU and international circles. It said:

Recent evolution at the international level constitutes at the same time challenges and constraints for the designation and implementation of environmental strategy and policies in Greece. The following major principles are to guide such environmental policies for the future: the standstill principle, the precautionary principle, integration of environmental aspects into sectoral policies, respect of national/local special environmental conditions and features, application of most appropriate technologies, individual responsibility and international cooperation and solidarity. It is expected that such environmental strategy will be harmoniously implemented as a result of parallel sustainable development policies.[32]

In its conclusion, the report listed in full all the principles that would direct future policy strategy on the environment. Apart from those just mentioned, they also included abatement at source, the polluter-pays principle, more stringent source-oriented measures on the basis of effect-oriented quality standards, and international cooperation and solidarity.[33]

This was the first time a major Greek policy document on the environment—itself a rare occurrence—stated in bold terms the principles that motivated Greece's policy approach—indeed, more boldly than the Italian and Spanish governments have ever done on environmental matters. Several aspects of this statement are evident: the principles are essentially imports from abroad; it is rhetorical, aimed among other things at pleasing partner governments, especially in the EU; and it argues that less developed countries (like Greece) require external financial assistance to rehabilitate the environment. It thus implies that economic growth remains Greece's principal policy concern.

In practice, Greek policy has not really been guided by any specific principles of the kind found in the northern member states. When a 'new' environmental policy was introduced in the early 1980s, its main features were simply described as the rational use of natural resources, balanced and uniform regional development, environmental protection, and increased public participation.[34] Between such bland objectives and rhetorical overkill, policy has in fact been overshadowed by considerations of economic development as in Italy, only more strongly so. If principles have been highlighted in Greek policy, this has been due to an individual minister's commitment and, more consistently, to external pressure above all from the EU.

The one concept that has come to feature most around policy circles has been the overarching one of sustainable development. Laliotis, appointed Minister of the Environment in 1993, used this concept much in his public statements, but there is a suspicion that this is cosmetic to some degree. There are doubts as to how far it has really penetrated the world of policy-makers. An official with long experience in the management of environmental policy in Athens noted on sustainable development that:

people [in government circles] are informed, they know what it is; people have this kind of consciousness and there are some heroic efforts to care for the environment, to allocate funds, but when you come to implementation, when you come to management . . . then everything breaks down.[35]

As one of the main advisers to the deputy minister noted, his ministry had developed a five-year plan called 'Attica-SOS' to turn Athens into a sustainable city; but it was the complexity of applying the concept that marked policy approaches. For this reason, the plan was designed by different people, for 'there is a need for so many different actions to be taken at the same time at the same level'.[36]

By far the dominant policy concern in the Greek environment ministry (YPEHODE) has been its other responsibility of public works. The values of development have carried great weight in policy considerations since the 1960s, when industrialization began. A general secretary in the Ministry of Agriculture had this to say about the conflict of interests within YPEHODE:

As you understand, in a country which has an elected government, the balance is [towards] public works. People, for example, in the mountainous communities demand a road and they want the road quickly. If the road cuts through the forest in a more or less barbaric way, this is a secondary concern for them. Therefore, when the two elements are judged within that Ministry—and similar contradictions exist in the Ministry of Agriculture . . .[37]

Clientelism clearly lies behind the powerful pull of economic interests. Despite ideological differences between New Democracy and PASOK (which alternated in power in 1981, 1989, and 1993), there was a *de facto* consistency between the main parties in this respect.[38] As one high official of the Ministry of Environment remarked, the problem at the political level is always that of 'saying no to developers' and pressure not to do so was rather greater under New Democracy than under PASOK ministers.[39] Given this situation, it is no surprise that policy principles have not had any profound impact on policy formulation. Once again, as elsewhere in southern Europe, the economic imperative has acted as a negative or veto principle.

Although the EU and other international organizations have been the principal source for policy principles on the environment, in reality, Brussels' influence has tended to exacerbate the conflicts noted above. The first Integrated Mediterranean Plan, granted to Crete, was formulated preponderantly in terms of developmental objectives, with environmental measures constituting only a fraction of the total funding. Then there was the pilot scheme for Prespa National Park, which went wrong environmentally because of a lack of coordination in planning, and caused persistent controversy.[40] In the eyes of Athens, Brussels is an important source of developmental funding and there is a desire to spend funds as quickly as possible once they arrive. The only apparent change has come when a particular minister has a personal commitment to environmental quality. The first such case was Tritsis, in the first half of the 1980s, who, unlike his successors, was prepared to challenge economic interests. For him, European models of environmental policy, such as the Dutch and Swedish, were influential. Indeed, as his main policy adviser later said, Tritsis was responsible for a virtual 'internationalization' of environmental policy in Greece.[41]

This dependence of strategy on individual ministerial commitment in Greece was also its weakness, for it did not guarantee policy consistency. An official in the Greek ministry complained: 'the government might change; maybe there won't be this minister but another minister who'll change everything, or the priorities will be reversed by another politician'.[42]

Policy style. When looking at Greek environmental legislation, the profusion of measures over time is striking. This has resulted in intense sectoralism and an absence of coherence, which became a problem during the process of harmonizing with EU directives in the 1980s. The predominant characteristic of Greek legislation has been the regulatory approach, using restrictions, limitations, licensing and the setting of standards. In recent years, there has been a new willingness to adopt economic incentives to facilitate environmental programmes, for example concerning the discharge of waste and the use of clean fuels; but these constitute a small part of environmental policy in Greece overall.[43]

Greece has adopted a reactive policy style, with little evidence of the kind of shift in style that occurred in Italy in the early 1990s. The increasing frequency of pollution episodes since the 1970s—with the Athens *nefos* as the main focal point—has resulted in a predominance of emergency actions. These crises in the capital have led to a variety of short-term 'extraordinary' measures, including a complete ban on private cars on days when meteorological conditions are critical.[44] Such an approach is commonly called 'fire-extinguishing', as one environmentalist explained: 'in policy and legislation, there are long-term concerns, but the way in which programmes have been structured . . . one can see that this is not possible really, it is very much the approach and ad hoc as far as specific action is concerned'.[45] The counterpart to this was an implicit absence of policy strategy. By this is understood a policy that is anticipatory, long-term in its perspective, and rationally conceived.

More concretely, the absence of a strategic approach is shown in the lack of environmental planning and in prevalent attitudes to that idea. A high official in the Greek Ministry of the Environment noted that her country's policy approach was 'not that close to strategic planning', and that 'in most cases, most people dealing with environmental problems are not very willing to participate in strategic planning, either because they don't know how or because they consider it is futurism, since things are changing so easily in this country this will be meaningless work'.[46] Similarly, the weaknesses of technical infrastructure make the application of specific policy principles very difficult. As one study of air pollution in Athens noted, those like the polluter-pays principle cannot be applied 'because of the inadequate network of surveillance'.[47]

The EU does, of course, provide the most important pressure for changing traditional practices. As a director-general in the Greek environment ministry explained, institutional change was necessary 'because if something comes from the EU all the ministries have to face it; and, after all, the Minister for the Environment is the one who is going to give the explanation to the Community; this is quite understood by the other ministries'.[48] However, Brussels pressure on Athens to engage in strategic planning evidently can run up against resistance from public administration there. One official explained:

Another problem of EU development policy is that it involves long-term planning compared to what it used to be when we planned for ourselves . . . Many of these programmes are on a five to six-year basis. For an economy like ours, where we hate planning, and where we cannot really plan ahead, because we don't have many studies and many research facilities and we don't have planning procedures on every level, to plan for six years is almost impossible. So, you've to absorb the money and sometimes you make the wrong decision today for 1998. A further reason is the frustration on the part of the EU, because we didn't follow their instructions. What we did is, we went on with our patterns of planning of the past. One of the problems is that you had already some programmes going on . . . so, you had some obligations towards different regions . . . this is one of the factors that the bureaucrats in Brussels cannot take into account.[49]

In short, while the EU has been by far the most significant factor behind Greek environmental policy in the past decade and more, its impact on policy principles has been largely superficial and that on policy style minimal.

Spain

Policy principles. When those in Madrid policy circles use the political discourse of developing a 'new strategy' on the environment, this really begs the question of what principles lie behind this strategy, apart from the promise of longer-term perspectives in policy-thinking. Clearly, in the last few years there has been some effort to develop a new approach to environment issues. Undoubtedly, EU influence has been decisive here. But, compared with Italy, this has not produced the kind of determined change initiated by Ruffolo (see below); while, compared with Greece, there has been less rhetoric.

As in the other two southern countries, economic development has traditionally been a greater priority than the environment. The Spanish State Secretary for the Environment, Cristina Narbona, commented that in her country 'too little importance was given to the environment in the broad spectrum of sectoral policies during the period of intense economic growth following Spain's transition to democracy'; and that, as a result, 'the volume of legislation enacted at central government level is insufficient and, worse, there are no models for coordinating decisions between one area of administration and another'.[50] In fact, the overriding priority in Spain of economic concerns has persisted into the 1990s. The top policy issue of high unemployment has, it was acknowledged in the annual report of the Ministry of Public Works for 1988, 'made it difficult to break the traditional view that environmental protection and employment generation stand in an antagonistic relationship to each other'[51] Efforts to redirect policy thinking have not been helped by statements from top politicians. Prime Minister Gonzalez's dismissive reference to the environment, and much greater stress on the habitual Spanish preoccupation with water provision on the tenth anniversary in 1992 of PSOE's election to power, is one such instance.

The tendency in official circles to see environmental protection as an obstacle to economic growth remained through out the 1980s and beyond, although it has gradually come to be qualified by ideas of sustainability, especially under international pressure. Above all, the question of public works has held sway. As Minister Borrell remarked in 1992, there is an 'extraordinary impatience' in Spain to carry out public works, and this priority has made 'us victims of our success'.[52] In this respect, it is relevant to note that basic policy conflicts between public works and the environment are worked out within the same ministry; if difficult, they are resolved by the minister. But the automatic priority given to the former has been modified in two ways: by enhancing the bureaucratic status of the environment within the Ministry, and through the new emphasis on using strategic plans to reconcile these different interests in a way that is less *ad hoc*,[53] although it must be said that such strategic plans are more pragmatic in origin than conceptually derived.

At any rate, judging by government statements at least, there was a rather more vigorous response to the Rio summit of 1992 from Spain than from the Greek government. The Spanish government acknowledged that the Earth Summit obliges it to 'redesign its model of development, to explain it and discuss it with all social and economic actors in every forum, in the form of a national strategy for the environment and sustainable development'.[54] The idea of sustainable development was more often mentioned in elite interviews for the project carried out in Madrid in the spring of 1994 than in those carried out in 1992. A high official in the Ministry of Public Works, Transport, and Environment noted that he had been hearing the concept of sustainable development around the corridors of power in Madrid for 'some years' and that 'the influence of Brussels has furthered this concept at the national level'.[55]

Another high official in the same ministry took a more sceptical line. He recognized that the idea of sustainable development was present in government circles, but only 'at the theoretical level'; for 'all are talking about sustainable development' within the national government, as well as in regional governments and at official conferences on the environment since the Rio summit, but the problem was to follow the theory up with effective action.[56] The government has included in its policy lines strategic planning and the integration of environmental concerns with economic policy for the purpose of promoting sustainable development.[57] Nevertheless, it is difficult to see how this umbrella concept can be applied effectively, for reasons similar to those identified in Greece—the very complexity of the concept, and the need for institutional reform to carry it through. Significantly, answers in interviews about the possibility of integrated pollution control invariably dwelt on deficiencies of cross-ministerial policy coordination.

While, as in Greece, public debate about policy principles is to a large degree imported discourse, Spain has been rather too busy implementing European directives to give much thought or time to particular policy concepts on the environment, particularly as Spain was a new EU entrant in the mid-1980s. While Madrid initiated important new laws on water as well as on toxic or hazardous waste before acceding to the EU in 1986, Spanish environmental policy was still not really very advanced. Spain's dependence on Brussels has been pronounced, as the whole corpus of EU legislation (more than 90 laws) was adopted after Spain's entry in 1986—in contrast to Portugal, which deferred adoption, and unlike Greece, which was slow in adopting European legislation. Spain took the decision to enter in 1986 for high political and historical reasons, to mark its overcoming the international isolation of the Franco period.[58] But little attention was paid at this point to the economic cost of adopting this EU legislation, and the process took two years, causing severe administrative blockage.[59] The costs of implementation, however, could not be ignored by Madrid and, occurring just when the EU was becoming proactive in environmental policy, apparently contributed to the Spanish government's new harder policy line towards Brussels.[60] Nevertheless, the impact of European legislation on Spanish policy has been described by a party leader prominent in this area as having caused an 'environmental revolution'.[61]

Policy style. Although Spanish policy style on the environment has, tended over time to be reactive, it has recently become more anticipatory. This has been helped, more than in Greece and even Italy, by improvements in policy procedure. Traditionally, the same lack of planning has been true of Spain's policy on environmental questions as of Greece's.[62] But in recent years this has begun to change, with greater attention given to the idea of environmental planning, and the development of a series of national sectoral plans such as for industrial waste, urban waste, and treating air pollution.[63] The director-general of the environmental policy department of the Spanish ministry saw this as 'orchestrating policy through plans' and developing a process called 'environmental strategic evaluation'.[64]

Otherwise, Spanish policy style may traditionally be described as exclusive rather than participatory. For instance, there has been little consultation in the past with industry, although that has now begun to change, again under pressure from Brussels. Moreover, a cooperative element is guaranteed by the fact that environmental policy is shared with the 'autonomous communities' (regions) in Spain's quasi-federal system. Centre–periphery coordination on environmental matters has indeed become better institutionalized from the early 1990s. In fact, focusing just on the national level is misleading, for, as the 1992 report of the Ministry on the environment in Spain stated in its introduction, 'the role of the central administration of the state and of the political will expressed through the General Cortes [the Spanish Parliament] are very circumscribed by, on the one hand, what are the Community's initiatives and by, on the other, the management carried out by the Autonomous Communities'.[65]

Italy

Policy principles. It is difficult to speak of particular guiding principles that have motivated Italian environmental policy in the way that is evident in the northern countries, either historically or since the environment gained international recognition as a concern around the late 1960s and early 1970s. And even during the past decade, while it is possible to identify certain principles as providing policy direction, these take a bland form, such as that of the preventive or programmatic approach (*programmazione*). In fact, the guiding or overarching principle has in effect been that of international cooperation, reflecting the EU influence which has been crucial in driving Italian policy.

Although Italian policy has a long history of environmental legislation somewhat similar to the northern countries discussed here, this has been mainly known for its profuse, complex, and often uncoordinated character as well as its absence of strategic approach. The abundance of measures (some 535 laws up to 1986, not counting regional ones), their lack of clarity and bad drafting, not to mention lack of correlation, tended to create confusion.[66] The very term 'strategy', commonly used for instance in Italian party politics, was notably missing in the field of Italian environmental policy, which in recent times has been criticized not merely by environmentalists but also openly in governmental circles as lacking a 'unitarian approach'.[67]

Moreover, Italian policy has been traditionally marked by the superior economic imperative compared with the environmental one.[68] This has been evident in a frequent concern among politicians not to confront economic interests or 'place in difficulty economic development which remains the fundamental objective in the heads of the majority of parliamentarians'.[69] This has meant that the production of environmental laws has been strongly conditioned by economic factors. Market reasons or those to do with energy policy have acted as a virtual negative principle, notably over the anti-smog law (delayed by years for this reason) and regulations on car emissions and industrial plants.[70]

Although the establishment of a Ministry of the Environment in 1986 might be thought to have been a significant departure in giving environmental policy more salience and purpose, the establishment of the Ministry was more important for its symbolic role as a response to Chernobyl. The law providing for this proclaimed the environment as a 'fundamental interest of the community' and as such worthy of legal protection. It also set out national principles of environmental protection, with a comprehensive scheme of rules, including preventive action and sanctions, and established a fault-based system of responsibility. According to the latter, any environmental damage was considered as unlawful damage to the state, so that whoever caused such damage was required to restore it to the *status quo ante* or to repair it.[71]

The traditional absence of clear guiding principles was not really surprising, given the long-standing emphasis in environmental policy on emergency action. Even Minister Giorgio Ruffolo, in his statement attached to the first national report on the state of the environment (1989), noted that Italian policy actions 'are principally understood as *ex post facto*, for repairing damage and reducing destructive and polluting effects'.[72] In a country that is not only densely populated (above all in the coastal zones), but also strongly industrialized (especially in the north), and at the same time heavily dependent on tourism, the incidence of, and motivation for overcoming, emergencies is obvious. The first really serious and subsequently symbolic case of such an emergency was the well-known Seveso crisis of 1976, following an explosion at a chemicals plant in a densely populated area just north of Milan. A survey of Italian legislation on the environment for the first 10 months of 1989 showed that, of some 80 measures, about 40 were for emergencies and only ten could be described as innovative (primarily in the application of EU directives).[73] Looking back over the decade of the 1980s, much Italian legislation, especially on drinking water, bathing water, and industrial waste, owed its inspiration to emergency measures.[74]

The reluctance to espouse environmental policy strategy persisted even in the face of growing degradation. The economic priority has been challenged only over the past decade. This began with the attempt of Ruffolo, as Minister of the Environment in 1988–92, to give policy a more long-term perspective. At the same time, the EU has acted as an important external force for policy change, particularly since it became more active in environmental affairs from the mid-1980s.

In the first national report on the state of the environment of 1989, Ruffolo at last confronted the predominant concern in Italian government with economic issues that made the environment a low priority. He spoke bluntly of his country's obsession with the gross national product, arguing that 'environmental policy is conceived still, to a large degree, as something external, peripheral and sectoral with respect to the production and consumption processes'.[75] With good reason, therefore, Ruffolo saw economic policy indifference towards the environment as a major constraint on his own policy initiative, not least because this represented a cultural value both within and outside government circles.[76]

By the 1990s, however, some sense of questioning the assumed incompatibility between economic and environmental interests had begun to influence Italian policy thinking. According to one source, environmental policy also 'gives birth to economic interests', involving economic activity that is more reconcilable with the environment, made possible by reorganization and restructuring in the economy.[77] It was at this time, too, that the EU embraced sustainable development as the theme of its 1992 Fifth Environmental Action Programme. This certainly provided external stimulus to the discussion that had just begun in policy circles in Rome. Thus, the way was opened for developing Italian policy with a longer-term perspective.

Ruffolo insisted on operationalizing the preventive approach, and to this end developed three- and even ten-year plans. These were a novelty in attempting to establish policy priorities and criteria for legislation. For instance, the Triennial Programme of 1989 included general programmes and strategic projects as well as provision for programme agreements with other ministries and also regions and other subnational authorities.[78] To further support his intention, Ruffolo argued for increasing environmental expenditure, enlarging environmental legislation, and imposing a more activist line for Italy at the international level to confront problems of ozone depletion and the greenhouse effect.[79] The Italian government soon afterwards started planning to adopt eco-taxes, which involve a new type of environmental policy towards sustainability. Italy has also experimented with taxes on such items as plastic shopping bags, although the schemes have been poorly implemented.

Critics say that these plans were marked more by a general sense of strategy than by a strict adherence to any particular environmental principles. While they hoisted 'preventive and programmatic action' to the mast of government policy, as an intended departure from the predominance of emergency-oriented policy, this bore only a vague resemblance to the German precautionary principle. In another sense, the three-year plan introduced in 1989 was more an action plan with strategic projects for different environmental sectors. The idea of integrated pollution control (IPC) is known in policy circles in Italy, but it has not been given much attention in policy debate. If at all, it is viewed in a narrow sense as a problem concerning organization and policy planning.[80] Nevertheless, Ruffolo's initiative over environmental programmes represented a significant shift in Italian environmental policy.[81] His relatively long tenure, by Italian standards, of the environment portfolio in various successive governments made for some continuity of purpose. However, this has not been replicated since, with fairly regular changes in the minister concerned. Also, sharp reversals in policy line are not impossible, as has been shown by Matteoli, the rather anti-environmentalist neo-Fascist minister of the environment (1994–95), whose appointment was described as 'like putting Saddam Hussein in charge of Amnesty International'.[82] To some extent, therefore, Italian environmental policy has lost some of its drive, even though Ruffolo did set a precedent for new policy approaches.

If there has remained a constant force for policy change in Italy, undoubtedly this has been the EU. The latter's influence is not always stated explicitly or prominently, but it colours if not pervades key policy documents. It was in fact highlighted in the country's first report (1989) on the state of the environment; [83] while the second report (1992) spoke of 'adapting strategic directions recently emerged at the international level to the Italian case' and the importance of learning from more environmentally advanced Western countries.[84] According to Bianchi, the impact of the EU is all the greater 'because the lack of a previous general legal framework relating to the environment rendered the Italian legal system particularly receptive' to policy from Brussels.[85]

Policy style. Italian policy style concerning the environment is very largely implicit in the policy features just discussed. Thus, it has been overwhelmingly reactive (with the concentration on emergency action), and only in the early 1990s did it attempt a major shift towards an anticipatory style. This pattern has been underlined by the lack of clear guiding principles. At the same time, the rather obvious dependence on initiative from the minister has detracted from policy continuity, given short-lived coalitions and the fact that Ruffolo, with his commitment and relevant expertise, was more an exception than the rule.

Policy action has placed a strong emphasis on regulation and has tended to be highly legalistic, with, as noted, a pronounced number of laws. In this respect, Rome's policy style fits well with that of the EU and is similar to that of other member states such as Germany. However, the crucial role played by the EU with respect to both policy motivation and policy content has also revealed a certain passivity on Italy's part as a member state in environmental affairs, as indeed in other areas of policy.

In other ways, the Italian approach approximates to the consensual rather than adversarial style and to the exclusive somewhat more than the participatory. In the first instance, the consensual approach fits with traditional habits in other areas of Italian policy. It has been expressed, for example, in a tendency to agree on informal environmental pacts with industry, especially the large companies. In the second instance, Italy has been slow in implementing provisions for public information. This has been seen in the considerable delay in publishing each volume on the state of the environment. However, the main environmental groups are influential, although the degree to which they get a hearing in the Ministry has depended very much on the personal willingness of individual ministers. Ruffolo succeeded in creating more openness in policy circles in the environmental area, although this has not been true of all his successors.

Finally, it should be noted that inefficiency also characterizes Italian policy style. This is clearly reflected in the fragmented nature of legislation, but is evident also in the slowness in completing some legislation. That problem became marked with mounting difficulties over incorporating EU directives into Italian legislation until a law of 1989 introduced a new yearly procedure for carrying into effect outstanding EU measures.[86]

The Netherlands

Policy principles. During the 1970s various pieces of legislation were passed with respect to controlling water pollution (1970), air pollution (1971), chemical waste (1976), waste materials (1977), and noise nuisance (1979) In many ways there is nothing at all distinctive about this response to environmental problems at the time, since many countries passed similar pieces of legislation.[87] What the different pieces of Dutch legislation had in common was that they all employed the same technique of control, namely the use of a licence for productive activities granted by the appropriate authorities. However, the existence of different regulations controlling discharges to different environmental media, and the fact that different authorities were involved in applying the licensing procedure, led to pressures for consolidation in the General Environmental Policy Act of 1980.

The General Environmental Policy Act created more simplified procedures for pollution control but did not represent an innovation in environmental policy principles itself. Under the Act, the regulation of economic activity still uses the instrument of the licence. In effect, Dutch environmental policy operates on the principle that no one can perform an environmentally damaging activity without a licence. Various principles can then be employed to govern the terms under which the licence is granted. Two principles have been particularly important here: that of best practicable means, and that of best technical means. Until recently, it has not been common for policy-makers and legislators in the Netherlands to spell out the meaning of these key policy principles. Instead, the implications of principles were spelt out in guidance notes, most notably from the Ministry of Transport and Communications over water pollution control.[88]

The principle of best practicable means (BPM) has been defined in a guidance note as the means to be used to create the largest reduction in pollution, taking into account the economic consequences for a normal profitable concern.[89] Until recently it was this principle that was regarded as that underlying Dutch environmental law and regulation. The best technical means (BTM) principle is one that has been applied in practice to pollution sources where the pollutant is potentially more serious. Unlike the BPM test, which requires that the reduction in pollution should be achieved at acceptable cost to an individual plant, the BTM test requires only that the cost be acceptable to an entire branch of industry. It therefore allows the regulators to set higher standards.

Since the Dutch reform of environmental law in 1993, the basic principle has become the so-called As Low As Reasonably Achievable (ALARA) principle. According to section 8.11 of the 1993 Dutch Environmental Management Act (Wet

Milieubeheer), the ALARA principle implies that agencies granting permits have to make sure that, 'as far as negative consequences for the environment cannot be prevented by subjecting licences to conditions, licenses must be subject to conditions which offer the largest protection possible against these consequences, unless the request would be unreasonable'.[90] In order to assess whether there is compliance with the ALARA principle, the intention seems to be to use the BTM test. BPM is now to be used only as a minimum standard where application of BTM would be unreasonable. The 1993 Act therefore marks an increasing stringency in the principles used to assess the appropriate standard to be applied to an operator.

Financial instruments remain less important, with the exceptions of water effluent charges and tax differentiation, which were used to support the introduction of cleaner cars.[91] Water effluent charges were based on the principle of the polluter-pays in the 1970 Surface Waters Pollution Act, which prescribed a detailed system of levies for financing measures of water pollution control. The basic principle of the levy is that all polluters pay the same charge irrespective of the source into which they are discharging, so that those discharging into a water course or canal pay the same as if they were connected to the public sewerage system.[92]

The legislation of the 1970s, as consolidated and reformed in the 1980 General Environmental Policy Act and the 1993 Environmental Management Act, thus provides the legal framework within which pollution control policies can be developed. However, the principles of this development have been worked out more explicitly in the 1980s in a series of plans for environmental protection, first in the so-called Indicative Multi-Year Programmes (IMPs), the first one of which was published in 1984, and then in the the National Environmental Policy Plan (NEPP), published in 1989.

The IMPs were a further response to the problem of how to deal with the fact that pollution often is not simply a problem for one receiving medium (air, water, or land), but can affect all three media. Sulphur dioxide emissions may be typically thought of as an air pollution policy, for example, but they also create problems of soil contamination. A simple focus upon the form of the pollution can disguise these more widespread effects. The response to this problem, developed through the IMPs, was to move from a focus on the forms of pollution to a focus on effects, moving back from the effects to an identification of the variety of causes. Thus, in the case of sulphur dioxide, the strategy that was developed was to treat the control of emissions as part of a more general problem of acidification. This is the intellectual basis of the notion of *themes* in environmental policy.[93]

This thematic basis for organizing environmental policy emerged in the NEPP as the basis for setting environmental objectives.[94] The themes were related to the scale and level at which they occurred, with the following as the principal categories: climate change at the global level; acidification at the continental level; eutrophication and diffusion at the river basin level; waste disposal and disturbance at the regional level; and dyhydration and squandering at the local level.[95]

Within this broad policy framework, the NEPP sets out quantitative targets for reductions in pollutants over a twenty-year period. It does this within a frame of reference within which different environmental problems are seen to occur at different levels of social and political organization (the global, continental, national, regional, and local levels), and it provides an account of pollution as involving the 'run-off' from substance cycles that would otherwise occur within the overall mass balance of nature (an approach that should be compared to German thinking on the 'circular economy'). On this sort of account, the protection of the environment has implications for the economy at large, since it involves the restructuring of production in order to minimize the run-off that is potentially damaging.

An important element of the NEPP is that responsibility for bringing about improvements in environmental quality is assigned to many different groups in society, and in this context it develops the idea of 'target groups'. The crucial elements of the approach include an explictly articulated theory about the origins and nature of pollution, the development of quantitative targets for the reduction of pollution, the identification of target groups responsible for achieving the targets, and a stress upon the cooperative character of the social action that is required.

The idea of cooperation was developed in an original way under Winsemius as environment minister. The Dutch term for this, used by Winsemius, is *verinner-lijking*, which means an internalization of responsibility for the environment. The NEPP itself was consciously produced as a cooperative policy document, with four central ministries (environment, transport, agriculture, and economics) as signatories, although there were different degrees of cooperation from the partner ministries, with the economics ministry being least accommodating.[96] Another aspect to the idea of cooperation that is important in Dutch policy thinking is that of international cooperation. Given its relatively small size and geographical position, the Netherlands is vulnerable to imported flows of pollution, particularly down the Rhine and the Scheldt, as well as being unable by itself to exert a great deal of influence on action to prevent or mitigate global problems. This has led Dutch policy-makers to stress the importance of the European Union in making environmental policy.

Policy style. As we have seen, the early institutionalization of environmental policy in the 1970s led to medium-specific legislation under the principles of the licensing system. Within the structure of Dutch environmental administration, there is a difference between those who set the regulations in the central government ministry and those who apply the regulations at provincial government level. According to Bressers and Plettenburg, this has had two consequences: firstly, there was a tendency for those setting the standards to have rather negative attitudes to industry; and secondly, there was too little communication between those setting the standards and those implementing them. It has been argued that there has been a significant change in policy style in the Netherlands during the 1980s. In particular, under Winsemius as minister there was a serious attempt to produce an ethos of cooperation and a greater degree of self-regulation, which in many ways fits in with the predominant Dutch national style of consensual policy-making.[97]

The most visible manifestation of this consensual style is the development of the idea of 'target groups' in policy planning, mentioned above. This target group approach was built upon changes in the organization of the Ministry that had taken place some years before the NEPP was produced. By 1985 four priority target groups had already been identified: agriculture, transport, energy generation, and refinaries. Under the approach of the NEPP, a wide range of groups is targeted as having special responsibility for a particular segment of policy. In the first place, these are social actors who have the potential to play a large part in causing pollution—industry, agriculture, and the transport sectors. But the idea is extended to include all consumers and citizens who have to take responsibility for the part they can play in improving environmental quality. Within the Dutch ministry, there is an explicit allocation of responsibility among officials for liaison with the target groups.[98] Moreover, there has been a growth in the importance of voluntary agreements, or covenants, between industry and government, as a way of seeking to ensure environmental improvements.

This notion of target groups also highlights another feature of the Dutch environmental policy style, namely its tendency to moralize policy issues. An important line of argument in the NEPP is the insistence on the responsibility that individuals have to make their contribution to environmental improvement, even if one person's contribution is only a drop in the ocean. Thus, the NEPP refers to the individual citizen as 'a *de facto* manager of the environment', and citizens in their various capacities (as consumers purchasing products or as householders disposing of waste) have a responsibility to constrain their actions to protect the environment.[99]

In relation to industry, this notion of the internalization of responsibility has fed into the preference during the 1990s for the greater use of voluntary agreements, known usually in the Netherlands as covenants, in pursuit of improvements in environmental quality. After the elections of 1989, an extension to the plan was developed, the so called NEPP-plus, which focused upon issues of implementation. In the choice between a strict regulatory approach and a more cooperative style, it was decided that negotiated agreements with industry were preferable. They were adaptable over the long planning horizon, and they avoided the legal need to acquire regulatory competence in some cases, while aiming at the decision centre of the relevant organizations.[100]

These covenants cover important matters, such as the reduction of phosphates in detergents, mercury in alkaline batteries, CFCs, packaging, and the reduction in waste in various industrial sectors including steel, chemicals, and the paper industry.[101] To some extent, this move away from a simple reliance upon regulation towards 'softer' instruments was a general trend in many countries in the 1990s, as policy-makers discovered the complexity of the regulatory tasks they faced and as the effects of the economic recession were felt in the field of environmental politics. However, even within this context, it seems reasonable to say that the extensive use of covenants, of which there are now over one hundred, does express the cooperative nature of the Dutch environmental policy style. But it should be noted that in the Netherlands there is considerable debate about the effectiveness and public accountability of covenants as a policy instrument.

How far has the Netherlands succeeded in achieving an anticipatory, rather than reactive, policy style? In the 1970s the policy style was clearly reactive, with policy-makers tending to formulate policies and legislation to deal with problems that had become generally manifest, for example detergent foam in water courses. The development of the environmental planning system in the 1980s was an attempt to swing the style of policy in the opposite direction, seeking to define pollution reduction targets over a twenty-year period and fitting specific measures into a forward-looking process of decision making. Moreover, this planning style was consistent with the role of planning in the Netherlands more generally, and in particular with the role of the Central Planning Bureau, an economic planning agency first established in 1945 whose first director was the Nobel Prize winning economist Jan Tinbergen, as well as the paradigmatic role that the *Deltaplan*, adopted as a measure of flood protection after the inundations of 1953, has within the Dutch policy process.[102] The plan-based approach reaches down from the national to the subnational level, with environmental protection plans being developed by the various regulatory and other authorities.

The policy style in the Netherlands is also a highly rationalistic one. Dutch environmental statistics are well collected and extensive. Emission inventories, environmental quality standards, and other environmental data are plentiful and widely available. However, this should not be mistaken for a great emphasis upon the scientific character of the policy process. Thus, the document that galvanized public and policy attention on environmental issues from the RIVM, a national scientific institute for public health, was distinctive in going beyond scientifically well established relations of cause and effect to larger projections about the damage that was likely to arise from a failure to deal with pollution.[103]

Finally, it is worth noting the openness of the Dutch policy system to international influences in parallel to its stress in terms of policy principles on international cooperation. As befits a relatively small country with a language that few foreigners learn and with access to a variety of international media, the Netherlands is an outward-looking country, receptive to ideas from abroad. Observers agree, for example, on the importance of Rachel Carson's *Silent Spring* in the original upsurge of environmental interest in the late 1960s, and the Netherlands quickly adopted the idea of sustainable development from the Brundtland Report as the basis for its own thinking. Indeed, in some ways the NEPP and its successor documents can be seen as one of the most ambitious attempts to operationalize the idea of sustainable development.

United Kingdom

Policy principles. From one point of view, it can be argued that it is difficult to identify specific principles in the development of UK environmental policy. Commentators have noted, for example, that in the UK government structures and legislation relating to environmental protection have been 'an accretion of common law, statutes, agencies, procedures and policies'.[104] One of the striking features of UK environmental policy documents, for example, is the extent to which policy problems are translated into issues of policy process or the machinery of government. (For specific examples of the way that administration has been extensively modified since 1980, see the next chapter.) None the less, it is possible to identify a core of intellectual commitments that run through the UK discussion of environmental policy principles, and it can be argued that contemporary approaches owe much to the historical legacy derived from the nineteenth century.

By the early 1990s, UK pollution control policy was based on the central principle of integrated pollution control (IPC) This had been incorporated into the 1990 Environmental Protection Act, which codified and reformed much of the pre-existing environmental legislation, but it was also a principle that was widely discussed and debated within the environmental policy community. Moreover, it was the approach to pollution control that the UK sought to promote within the European Union.

The essence of the IPC approach is that the pollution standards set and enforced in one medium, say air, should be consistent with the standards set for another medium, say water. Thus, the basic requirement for integrated pollution control is that the *totality* of emissions from a given process be considered by the regulatory authorities. Within the 1990 legislation, the approach to integrated pollution control was accomplished by specifying certain prescribed processes for which pollution standards were to be set using the principle of 'best available technology not entailing excessive costs' (BATNEEC). This approach was linked, however, to another important principle in the legislation, namely that of 'best practicable environmental option' (BPEO). What do these two ideas mean, and what is the relationship between them? In order to answer this question, it is necessary to look at the intellectual history of UK thinking about approaches to pollution control.

Current UK thinking about pollution control has been conditioned by a long process of historical development, which has been important in setting the distinctive style and operating characteristics of British pollution control legislation. As Hajer has shown, policy elites have pointed to this long history as part of the 'proud record' of British pollution control.[105] The argument has been that, from the nineteenth century onwards, Britain has been developing flexible, efficient and effective strategies for reducing pollution.

The first chairman of the Royal Commission on Environmental Pollution, Lord Ashby, himself did much to state what was taken to be the operative policy principles of British pollution control. The central idea, according to Ashby, was that pollution control policy should not seek in principle to minimize the state of pollution, but instead should aim to optimize it.[106] This approach was intended to be a statement both about how pollution control policy had developed in Britain and about what an intellectually justifiable principle of pollution control would amount to. In order to accomplish this goal, inspectors for air pollution (the so called Alkali Inspectorate) were given the power under nineteenth-century legislation to require the 'best practicable means' on operators to reduce their emissions.

In its *Fifth Report*, published in 1976, the Royal Commission summarized the way in which the British approach to air pollution control had developed since the mid-nineteenth century. It pointed out that 'best practicable means' in effect meant 'best practicable means to the satisfaction of the Alkali Inspectorate' (a good example of how issues of principle and machinery are conflated in the UK approach). The Royal Commission also noted that the Inspectorate looked at three sorts of factors in making their judgment: local conditions and circumstances, the current state of technical knowledge, and the financial implications for a firm of a prescribed abatement strategy. Each of these conditions has been important in defining the principles of British pollution control regulation.

The importance of local conditions rested upon recognizing that the natural environment possesses an absorptive capacity. Air pollution in an enclosed valley may be a more serious problem than in a location where prevalent winds can disperse the pollution. In consequence, it would be unnecessarily restrictive, according to the traditional conception of air pollution legislation, to impose the same emission limits in all parts of the country. Therefore, the Alkali Inspectorate worked with 'presumptive limits' for emission standards. That is, for a range of prescribed processes, the Inspectorate laid down standards that it presumed ought to apply, unless there were local circumstances to the contrary. Those responsible for local inspection were therefore allowed considerable scope for administrative discretion, and they operated within a legal context in which moving forward on a case-by-case basis was a fundamental norm. Without that discretion in standard-setting for particular plants, it would have been impossible for the Alkali Inspectorate to take into account local circumstances.

The second element of the 'best practicable means' test was the prevailing state of technical knowledge. In essence, this meant engineering knowledge about suitable abatement technologies. In other words, if there was operating a process that emitted pollution, the pollution inspectorate was always supposed to ask of the process whether the operator was using the most effective pollution abatement technology, given the current state of knowledge.

The third element of the 'best practicable means' approach was the financial implications of using technology in accordance with the current state of technical knowledge. This was part of what was meant by the notion of 'practicable'. The Royal Commission report recognized, for example, that, where it would have been prohibitively expensive for an operator to install a piece of pollution control equipment, the best technical means need not be required by the public authorities.[107] It is important to note that in the traditional conception of regulation this was a strictly financial judgment, supposedly reflecting the state of the company balance sheet, rather than a more broadly based judgment of economic welfare.

The 1976 Royal Commission report was important not simply because it provided a summary of the traditional principles of air pollution control, but also because it advocated an extension of this approach, an extension that was to prove influential in subsequent policy and legislative developments. The Royal Commission noted that one problem with traditional air pollution control was that it could in practice—and, they argued, had in fact—lead to a situation in which an air pollution problem would be solved, but only at the cost of increased pollution in another environmental medium; for example, they argued that sulphur dioxide emissions from a London electricity generating station were solved, but only at the cost of increasing water pollution in the Thames. In order to solve this kind of problem, the Royal Commission advocated generalizing the approach used in air pollution control to the control of discharges into all receiving media, and suggested that the appropriate principle should be that of 'best practicable environmental option'.[108] It was this principle that eventually was to become so important in defining what should be understood by integrated pollution control.

Before looking at the development of this idea, however, we need to consider the other principle introduced by the 1990 legislation, the BATNEEC principle. This is the principle by which, according to the legislation, standards are to be set. It can be seen as a domestication of the principle of 'best available technology' that is found in the EU's framework directive on air pollution.[109] It can also be seen, however, as a logical development of some aspects of the old 'best practicable means' test. In effect, that test has been made more stringent by requiring that pollution control technology be available in the sense that 'the operator of a process would be able to procure it from at least one supplier'.[110] A specific implication of the principle, however, is that it allows for the possibility that small firms could be driven out from a sector if the costs of applying BATNEEC were too stringent.[111] In this sense, the development of the principle follows the logic of Dutch developments in moving from plant-specific standards to standards that might apply to a whole industrial sector.

Even with this degree of stringency, however, it does not follow that, if an emission meets the BATNEEC standard, it is, thereby, permissible. This is precisely the force of insisting that emissions need to be looked at in the round. Emissions in one medium may meet the BATNEEC standard, but if they do not represent the best environmental option, according to the judgment of the regulating authorities, then operating permission can in principle be refused.[112] What is best from one point of view may not be best when the emissions are considered in totality.

It might look as though what is happening in the development of the BPEO principle is that standards are being made more stringent by the requirement that the operation of a process be made consistent with a judgment about what is best for the environment. Thus, just as the principle of precaution was used by German regulators to impose more stringent emission requirements, so it could be argued that the UK's BPEO principle also had that effect. However, this interpretation needs to be treated with some caution, because the form of the two principles is different, as we can see if we look at how BPEO has been applied.

The BPEO principle was defined by the Royal Commission on Environmental Pollution in its 1988 report, as follows:

A BPEO is the outcome of a systematic consultative and decision-making procedure which emphasises the protection of the environment across land, air, and water. The BPEO procedure establishes, for a given set of objectives, the option that provides the most benefits or least damage to the environment as a whole, at acceptable cost, in the long term as well as the short term.[113]

It was the application of the BPEO principle in this sense that led the British government to give its initial permission to Shell to dispose of the Brent Spar oil rig in the Atlantic, rather than bring it to shore for land disposal.[114] The argument was that, considering the risks of land disposal, the best option would be deep sea disposal where effects would be limited. However, the Brent Spar decision was seen by a number of commentators and other governments at the time as being inconsistent with the principle of precaution, since sea disposal lacked the capacity to control for untoward effects. Does this mean that the BPEO principle is somehow inconsistent with the principle of precaution? Putting the matter the other way around, how has the principle of precaution been domesticated into the UK's general approach to pollution control?

In the UK government, ministers first began to speak positively about the precautionary principle in 1986, and the earliest statement to Parliament that the government accepted the principle was in January 1988, in a statement by the Earl of Caithness in the House of Lords. Two months prior to this statement, the British government had accepted the precautionary approach in principle, under pressure from Germany, in the declaration of the Second Conference on the North Sea in November 1987.[115]

Formally, there has been acceptance of the principle of precaution at least since 1990 in the government's statement of its policies on sustainable development. The form in which the principle is accepted is highly qualified, but there is acceptance none the less, and this has been reinforced by subsequent accounts from the Department of the Environment. The original statement reads as follows:

Where there are significant risks of damage to the environment, the Government will be prepared to take precautionary action to limit the use of potentially dangerous materials or the spread of potentially dangerous pollutants, even where scientific knowledge is not conclusive, if the balance of likely costs and benefits justifies it. This precautionary principle applies particularly where there are good grounds for judging either that action taken promptly at comparatively low cost may avoid more costly damage later, or that irreversible effects may follow if action is delayed.[116]

The 1990 Environmental Protection Act also contains provisions for a regulatory system to control the release of genetically modified organisms into the environment, and the relevant part of the Act is introduced with the words: 'This Part has effect for the purpose of preventing or minimising any damage to the environment which may arise from escape or release from human control of genetically modified organisms.'[117] The establishment of a system of control had been recommended by the Royal Commission on Environmental Pollution, which had suggested a precautionary approach, and the provisions of the Act can be regarded as implementing those recommendations.

Putting these various elements together, UK policy principles have something like the following structure. Two elements of the traditional 'best practicable means' test, originally applied to air pollution control, have been developed. BATNEEC makes it clear that 'best' is to be interpreted in the light of available technical possibilities for a particular type of process, while BPEO makes it clear that the controls are to be exercised in the light of effects on the environment taken as a whole. The notion of 'best' is further qualified by the recognition of the principle of precaution, which may entail that emissions or substances should be restricted even where firm evidence of harmful effect is missing. There is thus both the development of a traditional way of thinking, through the BATNEEC and BPEO concepts, and an attempt to domesticate an internationally promulgated principle of precaution.

How has this way of thinking absorbed the discourse of sustainable development? The answer to this question provides a clear example of the tendency in UK pollution control policy to translate issues of policy choice into questions about policy process and the machinery of government. The centre-piece of the first government document on sustainable development was a series of proposed changes in the workings of government such that cross-departmental committees and ministerial responsibilities were established. Similarly, in 1994, in the government's statement of its formal sustainable development strategy, the main recommendations were for new advisory bodies (see below), although there was, as Carter and Lowe have pointed out, a significant reversal of the government's previous stance with the admission that unlimited traffic growth would be incompatible with the government's environmental goals.[118] The conflation of policy issues with process and machinery of government issues takes us to questions of policy style.

Policy style. In terms of policy style, the British approach to environmental regulation has usually been characterized as cooperative rather than adversarial. It has also traditionally relied upon the exercise of considerable administrative discretion in a context of a policy-making process that rests upon a closed and expert policy community. It is clear that the principles that we have discussed have borne a close relationship to these features of policy-making style.

The usual measure of cooperative regulation often cited is the traditionally low level of prosecutions for breaches of pollution control regulation that the administrative authorities have been prepared to bring. But for various reasons, this is not a good or reliable measure. Studies of implementation have shown that for enforcement officers the question of compliance with regulations is never a mechanical matter, but involves complex assessments of fault and intention.[119] Prosecutions are only one means by which compliance is induced where there is a continuing relationship between polluter and enforcement authority. Moreover, even in the USA—which is often regarded as the epitome of an adversarial system dependent upon legal enforcement—prosecution is not the primary instrument of control, and much of the legal controversy occurs not over enforcement but over the judicial review of the setting of standards.

Hence, a cooperative style should not be confused with an unwillingness to pursue control through legal enforcement. Rather, the traditional style of cooperation has rested on a willingness to treat the process of regulation as a sharing of information. Ashby and Anderson, in their study of the history of air pollution control in Britain, cite the first Alkali Inspector, Angus Smith, as saying that he resisted the ambition to teach 'by the cane instead of through the intellect', and they quote the *Chemical News* of 1875 as saying of Smith: 'He does not seek to lay down at once a hard and fast line, but as a truly practical man he aims and effects gradual improvement.'[120] It is clear that for many years the pollution inspectorates, and in particular the Alkali Inspectorate and its successors, laid more stress on securing improvements through an attempt to educate industry than by seeking a legal means of enforcement.

The second feature of the policy style has been a pattern of considerable administrative discretion in setting and applying standards. Given the stress upon the assimilative capacity of the environment in the traditional principles of regulation, it is inevitable that the system administering these principles is allowed considerable discretion, since there is no other way by which variable standards could be applied in different parts of the country. Moreover, administrative discretion in this sector of public policy has been consistent with a similar policy style across other sectors of public policy.

The third traditionally important feature of the British style of environmental regulation is that of 'club government', resting upon tacit and informal agreements among a limited number of people.[121] Whatever may be true in the general case, there is certainly good reason to think that this has traditionally applied to the issues surrounding the setting of environmental standards. Because the area was seen to be one where scientific standards applied, requiring professional experts, the number of generalist public officials involved has been small.

How much have these three features of cooperation, discretion, and specialization changed in recent years? In terms of cooperation, there have been periods when it seemed as though regulators like the HM Inspectorate of Pollution and the National Rivers Authority were pursuing a more adversarial style. However, the cooperative mode of working is still well established in many respects. So, although it would be correct to talk about some change in the cooperative character of the regulatory style, it would be implausible to say that the style has changed to one of confrontation. Similarly, there have been recent moves away from the tradition of administrative discretion, but these too have been limited. For instance, there has been a growth of judicial review of administrative action; but this has had relatively little impact specifically in the field of environmental policy and law.

Perhaps the greatest challenge to the system of administrative discretion has arisen from the impact of EU legislation. The setting of emission standards for urban wastewater treatment plants, quantitatively prescribed reductions in sulphur dioxide emission levels, and changes in procedures for environmental impact assessments are merely some examples where a more formal style of regulation has become part of British practice. But the pressure from the EU has combined with other new developments on the UK scene. The rather closed and specialist character of British policy style has undergone some change. A growing public concern about environmental questions has played a part in opening up the standard-setting system to scrutiny. Moreover, the development of House of Commons select committees and the interest shown in environmental matters by the House of Lords Select Committee on the European Communities in environmental questions has also raised levels of public awareness. It is interesting in this connection that the focus of the Royal Commission report on the setting of standards in environmental policy in fact spends a great deal of time on issues of public consultation and on the way in which public views may be better articulated in the policy process.[122]

One significant reason why there has been a greater public discussion of standard-setting arises from institutional changes in the economic regulation of the privatized utilities, particularly the water industry. When the utilities were privatized, a series of regulatory agencies were established to control their monopoly aspects and to implement a regime of price controls. The water industry regulator, the Office of Water Services (OFWAT), was faced with a particular problem in controlling the prices of the water companies. It was recognized that the water companies needed to invest in waste-water treatment facilities, partly to compensate for the neglect of investment in the 1970s and 1980s and partly to enable the water authorities to meet EU emission standards. In consequence of this role, OFWAT has conducted investigations into the affordability of environmental standards. It has broached the question in public of what the appropriate balance should be between environmental quality and economic cost. In effect, there is now an institutional tension established within the British policy system, between those responsible for price regulation and those responsible for environmental quality, that has served to open up public debate on the setting of standards.[123]

Although the style of British environmental policy has changed in some respects in recent years, there are elements of its traditional approach that are still very influential. This can be seen most clearly in the tendency to displace questions about policy into questions about the structure of the policy process. The UK's sustainable development strategy in effect had as its centre-piece the establishment of various advisory bodies: a Panel of Sustainable Development, consisting of five experts reporting to the prime minister; a Round Table on Sustainable

Development, consisting of thirty representatives from business, local government, environmental, and other organizations; and a 'Going for Green' programme, aimed at local communities and individuals. In other words, unlike the Dutch National Environmental Policy Plan, the UK approach has been to focus on changes in policy process and machinery rather than to concentrate on the development of an elaborately calculated set of planning targets.

CONCLUSION: CONVERGENCE AND DIVERGENCE IN CROSS-NATIONAL PERSPECTIVE

Our survey of the six member states of the European Union has identified a rich variety of policy principles and policy styles. These tend to relate to—indeed, reflect—general national approaches to policy-making, and national elite cultures to some extent. This is not so surprising when we consider that, for the most part in these countries, environmental legislation has a relatively long history. At the same time, changes in national policy patterns—especially since the mid-1980s—indicate some departure from traditional approaches.

No country has fully adopted the principles of ecological modernization, let alone sustainable development, in its environmental policy principles and practices. Even in Germany, which is sometimes taken to be an international model (and where those in the relevant policy networks sometimes talk of it as such), there are clear indications that ecological modernization has encountered resistance and inertia. The relative lack of interest in economic instruments, the lack of interest in procedural instruments such as environmental impact assessment, and the failure to achieve a framework within which environmental goals inform wide areas of public policy all testify to the limits of the modernization process.

However, it is also clear that, seen in a relative light, both Germany and the Netherlands have developed and transformed their principles and style in ways that have responded to key elements of new demands for environmental protection. In Germany, emission limit values have been tightened, as they have in the Netherlands, to the point where end-of-pipe techniques are ineffective, and there is a need to look at cleaner technologies and waste reduction at source. Although the principle of precaution often remains operative at a purely rhetorical level, one can also find cases where the principle has at least strengthened the case for higher standards of performance. The requirements of integrated pollution control are taken seriously, particularly in the Netherlands, which has also pioneered the attempt to integrate environmental concerns into other areas of policy via the National Environmental Policy Plan.

The UK stands as an interesting case in this context, suggesting that it is difficult to make an easy or too simple contrast between north and south in Europe. From one point of view, it can be regarded as more resistant to ecological modernization than either Germany or the Netherlands, in many ways sharing with Spain an emphasis on the priority of economic growth, conventionally understood, over environmental protection. For this reason, it has been cautious about greater stringency in emission limits, often questioning the scientific basis for the limits proposed and sometimes insisting that issues of economic cost always need to be borne firmly in mind when a proposal for environmental protection is made. Moreover, its leading policy principles, in particular the notion of 'best practicable environmental option', are such obvious developments of its traditional approach, as is its consensual style of regulation, that it is easy to see it as a 'laggard' in terms of ecological modernization.

However, this conclusion would also be too simple. It is clear that in Germany too there is a balancing between economic cost and environmental standards, just as there is in the UK. In Germany the principle of 'state of the art' is taken always to include an implicit reference to cost. The difference is the extent to which state of the art requirements are taken to apply to whole branches of industry rather than to particular plants, as is still true in the UK. Moreover, the discussions about *Standort Deutschland* in Germany in the early 1990s can be seen to parallel the discussions about the cost of environmental regulation in the UK.

The UK has certainly not made the effort to integrate environmental concerns into wide areas of public policy, as has been such a feature of the Dutch approach, and it is implausible to draw too detailed a comparison between the Dutch National Environmental Policy Plan and the UK's key principles of sustainable development as revealed in *This Common Inheritance*. However, at least at the level of policy discussion, the UK does accept the need for policy coordination, so that all policy measures are scrutinized for their environmental impact, even if the practice often falls short of this anticipatory ideal.

One element that does appear to be common to all three northern countries is that the policy-making style has remained predominantly exclusive. Standards are negotiated between bureaucracies and interested parties, with little contribution from the public in general or even from parliaments. It is certainly true that the Dutch idea of 'target groups' includes public interest organizations, but the extent to which it has been possible to include such groups in the detailed setting of standards has been limited, and the experiments with voluntary agreements has reinforced the exclusive nature of the agreements between government and industry.[124] The same is true in Germany, where less effort has gone into questions of public participation (standard-setting being seen predominantly as a technical matter), and where groups often have to wait until the implementation phase of policy before making their voices heard.

The other three countries—Italy, Spain, and Greece—show some similarities with the northern countries, especially Germany and the Netherlands, in their preference for regulation, their inclination towards consensual and exclusive styles, and their rhetorical, if not principled, movement towards ecological modernization. The latter is quite a significant change in the environmental policy strategy of these countries in the 1990s. The differences lie most in the priority given to economic development and in policy styles in so far as they reflect on how their systems operate. The concern, if not obsession, with economic growth has tended to act as a powerful constraint on environmental initiatives. Thus, we see an aspect of policy legacy operating as a determinant of policy choice. At the same time, it is the (worsening) environmental legacy—combined with EU policy and growing public sensitivity—that has begun recently to challenge this historical policy precept.

It is possible in practice to read a general lack of priority for the environment in political statements in the southern countries. Yet, some particular environment issues in these countries cannot be seen as low in priority—such as air pollution in all three, coastal pollution in Italy, and water supply in Spain. Nevertheless, the overriding priority in these countries has remained economic development and growth to the extent of subordinating the environment (a much later policy concern), although this is less true in Italy than in Spain and Greece. This is hardly surprising in countries that modernized late in the postwar period (with the partial exception of Italy); and where industrialization and urbanization were largely precipitous and unplanned, creating serious environmental degradation.

In all three southern countries, the question of environmental costs in applying EU legislation has gained in salience recently and illustrates the continuing importance of the economic imperative in the south. Costs have hit these countries severely, both because they tend to be the poorer member states and because they have to make greater strides to keep pace with this European legislation than northern partners. This has become an issue particularly for Madrid, concerned about the effects on industry, although the same concern is present among policymakers in Greece and to a lesser extent Italy.

Considerable difficulties have remained in the ability of the southern countries to respond to the demanding agenda of the new politics of pollution. Until the 1990s, their policy styles were to a large extent reactive to crisis or emergency. Clearly, responding to environmental emergencies is part of any country's policy in this area. But in the south this has been raised to the status of a policy approach, and not necessarily because emergencies are more common there than elsewhere: it arose from problems of inefficiency and the lack of planning and coordination. Hence, the only effective way of acting is when the situation is compelling, in the full glare of publicity, whereby crisis management temporarily overcomes bureaucratic sloth.

It is relevant here to point out that strategic approaches in the southern countries have owed much to individual ministerial commitment to environmental interests. This is more true of Italy and Greece than of Spain. But this pronounced dependence of policy strategy on the personal commitment of a minister has also made it vulnerable to ministerial turnover. The Spanish case seemed different, where the ministry's weight counted and there was a greater political continuity in contrast to Italy's temporary and varying coalitions. Thus, Borrell's talk of a 'new strategy' towards the environment in the mid-1990s[125] is probably less linked to his continuance as minister, a conclusion underlined by the development of sectoral plans for the environment. It would seem that there has not emerged any policy style peculiar to the environment in these countries. Policy-making has been very much determined by established procedures and traditional structures, generally reflecting national system characteristics. This is now less true of Spain, where institutional reform has been more effective than in the other two southern countries. It should also be noted that individual ministerial commitment has been important in the northern countries, with individuals like Winsemius in the Netherlands or Töpfer in Germany playing an important role in developing the environmental agenda.

Undoubtedly, the EU has exerted a distinct influence in environmental affairs, although the effects on individual countries have varied. Generally, this influence is evident in the pressures to adopt ecological modernization as well as some modest changes in style, such as a more formal approach in the UK, the introduction of planning in the south (mainly Italy and Spain), and signs of greater openness in several of these countries. Germany and the Netherlands are clearly those member states most advanced in relation to EU developments. On the other hand, the two southern countries of Spain and Greece developed their environmental policies only fairly recently but have been particularly open to the requirements of Brussels.

None of this entails strong patterns of policy convergence among the member states. There is evidently a balance, if not some tension, between the pull of traditional approaches and national history on the one side and the push or challenge of international trends among advanced economies, and the institutional and policy imperatives of the EU in particular, on the other. It should not be forgotten that the latter and its effects is a fairly recent development for Spain and Greece, and that the UK also found itself under strong pressure from the EU. In other words, the new dynamism of EU environmental policy from the mid-1980s only really began to have some qualitative impact on national policies from the early 1990s, especially in southern Europe. The continuation of this new policy scenario does of course depend on wider developments in the EU in the future, with respect not just to the single market but also to monetary union and EU institutional reform and enlargement. If the outcome of these developments is more positive than negative for EU environmental policy-making, then theories of policy sectors may become more applicable to national policies than they are at present.

NOTES TO CHAPTER 5

1. For the concept of a policy style, see J. J. Richardson (ed.), *Policy Styles in Western Europe* (London: Allen & Unwin, 1982). For a specific application to environmental policy, see J. J. Richardson and N. S. J. Watts, *National Policy Styles and the*

Environment, Discussion Paper no. 85–16 (Berlin: International Institute for Environment and Society: Wissenschaftszentrum Berlin, 1985), and D. Vogel, *National Styles of Regulation* (Ithaca, NY, and London: Cornell University Press, 1986).

2. A. Weale, *The New Politics of Pollution* (Manchester and New York: Manchester University Press, 1992).

3. E. Ashby and M. Anderson, *The Politics of Clean Air* (Oxford: Clarendon Press, 1981), ch. 2.

4. For this early German period, see G. Hartkopf and E. Bohne, *Umweltpolitik* (Opladen: Westdeutscher Verlag, 1983); G. Spelsberg, *Rauchplage* (Aachen: Alano Verlag, 1984); and K.-G. Wey, *Umweltpolitik in Deutschland* (Opladen: Westdeutscher Verlag, 1982).

5. D. Liefferink, 'The Netherlands: A Net Exporter of Environmental Policy Concepts', in M. S. Andersen and D. Liefferink (eds.), *European Environmental Policy; The Pioneers* (Manchester and New York: Manchester University Press, 1997), p. 211.

6. H. T. A. Bressers and L. A. Plettenburg, 'The Netherlands', in M. Jänicke and H. Weidner (eds.), *National Environmental Policies: A Comparative Study of Capacity-Building* (Berlin: Springer Verlag, 1997), p. 113.

7. D. Liefferink, *Environment and the Nation State: The Netherlands, the EU and Acid Rain* (Manchester and New York: Manchester University Press, 1996), pp. 73–4; Liefferink, 'The Netherlands', pp. 211–12.

8. D. Alexander, 'Pollution, Policies and Politics: The Italian Environment', in F. Sabetti and R. Catanzaro (eds.), *Italian Politics: A Review* (London: Pinter, 1991), pp. 90, 101.

9. *European Environmental Yearbook* (London: DocTer International UK, 1990), p. 780.

10. J. K. Galbraith, *The Affluent Society* (Harmondsworth: Penguin, 1970, 2nd edn), p. 212.

11. See, on these developments, A. Weale, T. O'Riordan, and L. Kramme, *Controlling Pollution in the Round: Change and Choice in Environmental Regulation in Britain and Germany* (London: Anglo-German Foundation, 1991), pp. 102–14.

12. A. Bianchi, 'Environmental Policy', in F. Francioni (ed.), *Italy and EC Membership Evaluated* (London: Pinter, 1992), p. 87.

13. M. Hajer, *The Politics of Environmental Discourse: Ecological Modernization and the Policy Process* (Oxford: Clarendon Press, 1995), p. 176; A. Jamison *et al.*, *The Making of the New Environmental Consciousness* (Edinburgh: Edinburgh University Press, 1990), p. 136.

14. Hajer, *Politics of Environmental Discourse*, p. 176; Jamison *et al.*, *The Making of the New Environmental Consciousness*, pp. 130–1.

15. G. Timagenis and P. Pavlopoulos, *The Law and Practice Relating to Pollution Control in Greece* (London: Graham & Trotman, 1982), p. *xxxi*.

16. M. Estevan, *Implicaciones Economicas de la Proteccion Ambiental de la CEE: Repercusiones en España* (Madrid: Ministerio de Economia, 1991), p. *xix*.

17. M. Del Carmen, 'Spain's Accession to the EC: Repercussions on Environmental Policy', *European Environment Review*, 1:1 (1986), p. 14.

18. As noted in the Introduction, we take the countries in the order in which they are classified in EU documents.

19. Bundesumweltministerium, *Umweltschutz in Deutschland* (Bonn: Economica Verlag, 1992), pp. 74–6, trans. as Federal Ministry for the Environment, *Environmental Protection in Germany* (Bonn: Economica Verlag, 1992), pp. 74–6.

20. E. Rehbinder, 'Vorsorgeprinzip im Umweltrecht und präventive Umweltpolitik', in U. E. Simonis (ed.), *Präventive Umweltpolitik* (Frankfurt/New York: Campus Verlag, 1988), pp. 129–41.
21. Federal Immission Control Act, cited in S. Boehmer-Christiansen and J. Skea, *Acid Politics* (London and New York: Belhaven, 1991), p. 169.
22. A point that was stressed in interviews at the Federal Environment Agency by those whom we interviewed.
23. The more stringent principle of *Stand der Wissenschaft und Technik* applies in the case of nuclear regulation.
24. H. Weidner, *25 Years of Modern Environmental Policy in Germany: Treading a Well-Worn Path to the Top of the International Field* (Berlin: Wissenschaftszentrum, 1995), FS II 95–301, p. 49, citing OECD, *OECD Environment Performance Reviews: Germany* (Paris: OECD, 1993), p. 205.
25. Weidner, *25 Years of Modern Environmental Policy*, p. 14.
26. Cited in Weidner, *25 Years of Modern Environmental Policy*, p. 45.
27. M. Kloepfer and K. Messerschmidt, *Innere Harmonisierung des Umweltrechts* (Berlin: Erich Schmidt Verlag, 1986).
28. M. Kloepfer *et al.*, *Umweltgesetzbuch* (Berlin: Erich Schmidt Verlag, 1990).
29. K. von Moltke, 'The *Vorsorgeprinzip* in West German Environmental Policy', Royal Commission on Environmental Pollution, Twelfth Report: *Best Practicable Environmental Option* (London: HMSO, 1988), Cm. 310, app. 3, p. 61.
30. S. Rose-Ackerman, *Controlling Environmental Policy* (New Haven and London: Yale University Press, 1995), esp. chs. 4–6.
31. Ibid. 30.
32. Ministry of Environment, *National Report of Greece: UN Conference on Environment and Development, Brazil, June 1992* (Athens: Ministry of the Environment, 1991), p. 17.
33. Ibid. 127.
34. OECD, *Environmental Policies in Greece* (Paris: OECD, 1983), p. 14.
35. Interview with Dimitra Katochianou, Centre of Planning & Economic Research (KEPE), Athens, November 1992.
36. Interview with Constantinos Cartalis, adviser to the Deputy Minister for the Environment, Athens, March 1995.
37. Interview with Dimitris Katsoudas, Ministry of Agriculture, Athens, November 1992.
38. C. A. Vlassopoulou, *La Politique de l'environnement: le cas de la pollution atmospherique à Athenes*, Ph.D. thesis, University of Picardy, 1991, pp. 42, 48.
39. Interview with Ioannis Vournas, Ministry of Environment, Athens, November 1992.
40. D. Baldock and T. Long, *The Mediterranean Environment under Pressure: The Influence of the CAP on Spain and Portugal and the IMPs in France, Greece and Italy* (London: Institute for European Environmental Policy, 1987), pp. 17–22.
41. Interview with Evangelos Raftopoulos, University of Athens and legal adviser to UNEP, Athens, March 1995.
42. Interview with Maria Kritikou, Ministry of Environment, Athens, December 1992.
43. G. Pridham, S. Verney, and D. Konstadakopulos, 'Environmental Policy in Greece: Evolution, Structures and Process', *Environmental Politics*, 4:2 (1995), p. 259.
44. Ibid.

45. Interview with George Tsekouras, environmental consultant and 'Nea Oikologia', Athens, November 1992.
46. Interview with Athena Mourmouris, Ministry of Environment, Athens, November 1992.
47. K. Pelekasi and M. Skourtos, *Atmospheric Pollution in Greece* [in Greek] (Athens: Papazisi, 1992), sec. 8.1.
48. Interview with George Kardassis, director-general for environment, Ministry of the Environment, Athens, November 1992.
49. Interview with Michalis Modinos, Ministry of National Economy and 'Nea Oikologia', Athens, November 1992.
50. C. Narbona, editorial in *Naturopa*, 74 (Strasbourg: Centre Naturopa: Council of Europe, 1994).
51. Ministerio de Obras Publicas, *Medio Ambiente en España 1988* (Madrid: Ministerio de Obras Publicas, 1989), p. 220.
52. *El Pais*, 19 October 1992.
53. Interview with Domingo Jimenez Beltran, director-general for environmental policy, Ministry of Public Works, Madrid, March 1995.
54. Ministerio de Obras Publicas, *Medio Ambiente en España 1992* (Madrid: Ministerio de Obras Publicas, 1993), p. 27.
55. Interview with Jose Gonzalez-Nicolas, directorate-general for water quality, Ministry of Public Works, Madrid, April 1994.
56. Interview with Joaquin Ros Vicent, environmental policy directorate, Ministry of Public Works, Madrid, April 1994.
57. Ministerio de Obras Publicas, *Medio Ambiente en España 1992*, p. 17.
58. Interviews with Ros Vicent, Madrid, October 1992; and Carmen Diez de Rivera, PSOE MEP, Madrid, October 1992.
59. Interview with Teresa Mosquete, environmental policy directorate, Ministry of Public Works, Madrid, October 1992.
60. Interview with Liam Cashman, European Commission, DG XI, legal unit, Brussels, April 1992.
61. Interview with Angel Del Castillo, PSOE party organization, Madrid, October 1992.
62. Del Carmen, 'Spain's Accession to the EC', p. 13.
63. Ministerio de Obras Publicas, *Medio Ambiente en España 1989* (Madrid: Ministerio de Obras Publicas, 1990), sec. 9.
64. Interview with Beltran, Madrid, April 1994.
65. Ministerio de Obras Publicas, *Medio Ambiente en España 1992* (Madrid: Ministerio de Obras Publicas, 1993), p. 13.
66. A. Capria, 'Formulation and Implementation of Environmental Policy in Italy', paper for 12th International Congress on Social Policy, Paris, October 1991, pp. 10–11.
67. Ministero dell'Ambiente, *Rapporto al Ministro sulle Linee di Politica Ambientale a Medio e Lungo Termine* (Rome: Ministero dell'Ambiente, 1989), sec. 1.1.
68. Bianchi, 'Environmental Policy'.
69. Lega per l'Ambiente, *Ambiente Italia 1990* (Milan: Arnaldo Mondadori, 1990), p. 577.
70. Capria, 'Formulation and Implementation', p. 13.
71. Bianchi, 'Environmental Policy', pp. 88–9.
72. Ministero dell'Ambiente, *Nota Aggiunta del Ministro Giorgio Ruffolo* (Rome: Ministero dell'Ambiente, 1989), p. 37.

73. Lega per l'Ambiente, *Ambiente Italia 1990*, p. 548.
74. Capria, 'Formulation and Implementation', p. 6.
75. Ministero dell'Ambiente, *Nota Aggiunta*, p. 37.
76. Ibid.
77. Interview with Vittorio Silano, Ministry of Health, Rome, May 1992.
78. Ministero dell'Ambiente, *Relazione sullo Stato dell'Ambiente* (Rome: Ministero dell'Ambiente, 1992), pp. 25, 416–23.
79. Ibid. 4–5.
80. Capria, 'Formulation and Implementation', pp. 35–6.
81. Bianchi, 'Formulation and Implementation', p. 93.
82. *Sunday Times*, 28 August 1994.
83. Ministero dell'Ambiente, *Rapporto sullo Stato dell'Ambiente* (Rome: Ministero dell'Ambiente, 1989), pp. 14 ff.
84. Ministero dell'Ambiente, *Relazione sullo Stato*, sec. 1.2.13.
85. Bianchi, 'Formulation and Implementation', p. 94.
86. Ibid. 90.
87. Weale, *New Politics of Pollution*, pp. 10–23.
88. M. Faure and M. Ruegg, 'Environmental Standard Setting through General Principles of Environmental Law', in M. Faure, J. Vervaele, and A. Weale (eds.), *Environmental Standards in the European Union in an Interdiscplinary Framework* (Antwerp and Apeldoorn: MAKLU, 1994), p. 45.
89. Ibid. 47.
90. Ibid. 46.
91. Bressers and Plettenburg, 'The Netherlands', p. 115.
92. M. S. Andersen, *Governance by Green Taxes: Making Pollution Prevention Pay* (Manchester and New York: Manchester University Press, 1994), p. 152.
93. Weale, *New Politics of Pollution*, p. 137.
94. Second Chamber of the Estates General, *National Environmental Policy Plan: To Choose or Lose* ('s-Gravenhage: SDU uitgeverij, 1989).
95. See Weale, *New Politics of Pollution*, p. 130, table 5.1.
96. Interview information.
97. Bressers and Plettenburg, 'The Netherlands', p. 116. Compare Liefferink, 'The Netherlands', pp. 223–34.
98. Interviews VROM, The Hague, 10–12 March 1993.
99. See e.g. *National Environmental Policy Plan: To Choose or Lose*, pp. 115–18.
100. Interview information.
101. J. Eberg, *Waste Policy and Learning: Policy Dynamics of Waste Management and Waste Incineration in the Netherlands and Bavaria* (Utrecht: Uitgeverij Eburon, 1997), p. 43.
102. On the latter, see Hajer, *The Politics of Environmental Discourse*, p. 178, and Jamison et al., *The Making of the New Environmental Consciousness*, pp. 124–5.
103. See Rijksinstitut voor Volksgezondheid en Milieuhygiene, *Zorgen voor Morgen: Nationale Milieuverkenning 1985–2021* (Bilthoven: RIVM, 1988).
104. N. Carter and P. Lowe, 'Britain: Coming to Terms with Sustainable Development?' in K. Hanf and A.-I. Jansen (eds.), *Governance and Environment in Western Europe: Politics, Policy and Administration* (Harlow: Addison Wesley Longman, 1998), p. 22.
105. Hajer, *The Politics of Environmental Discourse*, p. 115.
106. Ashby and Anderson, *The Politics of Clean Air*, p. 136.

107. Royal Commission, *Fifth Report: Air Pollution Control: An Integrated Approach*, Cmnd. 6371 (London: HMSO, 1976), p. 26.
108. Ibid. 76.
109. Framework Directive on Combatting Air Pollution from Industrial Plants (84/360/EEC), *Official Journal of the European Communities*, L188, 16.7.84.
110. See the exposition in Royal Commission on Environmental Pollution, *Twenty-First Report: Setting Environmental Standards*, Cm. 4053 (London: The Stationery Office, 1998), p. 38.
111. Ibid. 39.
112. Ibid.
113. Royal Commission on Environmental Pollution, *Twelfth Report: Best Practicable Environmental Option*, Cm. 310 (London: HMSO, 1988), p. 5.
114. For a discussion of the issues arising from the Brent Spar incident, see A. Weale, 'The Kaleidoscopic Competition of European Environmental Regulation', *European Business Journal*, 7:4 (1995), pp. 19–25.
115. N. Haigh, 'The Introduction of the Precautionary Principle in the UK', in T. O'Riordan and J. Cameron (eds.), *Interpreting the Precautionary Principle* (London: Earthscan, 1994), pp. 229 and 237–8.
116. UK Government, *This Common Inheritance: Britain's Environmental Strategy* Cm. 1200 (London: HMSO, 1990), p. 11. See also Department of the Environment, *A Guide to Risk Assessment and Risk Management for Environmental Protection* (London: HMSO, 1995), ch. 5.
117. Environment Protection Act, 1990: sec. 106.
118. For the two key documents, see UK Government, *This Common Inheritance*, and UK Government, *Sustainable Development: The UK Strategy* (London: HMSO, 1994). For the significance of the admission about traffic growth, see Carter and P. Lowe, 'Britain', p. 33.
119. K. Hawkins, *Environment and Enforcement* (Oxford: Clarendon Press, 1984).
120. Cited in Ashby and Anderson, *The Politics of Clean Air*, p. 35. The quotation from Smith himself is at p. 136.
121. D. Marquand, *The Unprincipled Society* (London: Jonathan Cape, 1988), ch. 7, and S. Brittan, *A Restatement of Economic Liberalism* (Basingstoke: Macmillan, 1988), pp. 80–92.
122. Royal Commission, *Setting Environmental Standards*.
123. See S. Cowan, 'Regulation of Several Market Failures: The Water Industry in England and Wales', *Oxford Review of Economic Policy*, 9:4 (1993), pp. 14–23, and A. Weale, 'Environmental Regulation', in P. Vass (ed.), *Regulatory Review* (London: Centre for the Study of Regulated Industries, 1997), pp. 201–16.
124. Eberg, *Waste Policy and Learning*, pp. 43–4.
125. Ministerio de Obras Publicas, *Informacion de Medio Ambiente*, November 1993, p. 5.

6

The Institutionalization of Environmental Policy

In the previous chapter we looked at the development of policy styles and principles in our six countries. However, policies have to be developed through organizational processes, so in this chapter we look at the organization of environmental policy. In what ways has environmental policy been institutionalized in our sample of six countries? What forms of administration have they adopted, and how does environmental administration relate to other facets of the machinery of government?

Why consider questions of administrative organization in relation to environmental policy? Firstly, while it is clear that alterations in the machinery of government generally take place for a number of reasons, the desire of policy-makers to give weight to a policy area and to symbolize new priorities is often an important consideration.[1] Thus, when environmental issues first began to arrive seriously on the agenda of liberal democracies in the late 1960s, the most common response of governments was to establish a separate part of the bureaucratic machinery to deal with the problems.[2] A number of countries, including Sweden and the USA, even established specialist agencies to take responsibility for environmental protection; while others, such as Britain and the Netherlands, restructured a central ministry to provide a focus for environmental policy. Italy eventually created a special ministry although one with very restricted powers in the governmental machinery at Rome. At the same time, even those countries, like the Federal Republic of Germany, that did not immediately establish environmental ministries nevertheless concentrated environmental functions in an existing ministry.

We saw in Part I that this organizational response to environmental issues was also a feature of the way in which the EU first sought to develop its own policy capacity. However, that story highlighted another feature of the administrative politics of the environment. Over time, within the EU the pattern of organization became more complex, and organizations with an interest in environmental issues began to proliferate. As the issue of external integration—the coordination of environmental issues across several sectors of policy—came to be appreciated, so a wider range of administrative bodies within the Union came to acquire some environmental interest or responsibility and the institutional space became more crowded.

In comparative terms, therefore, we can think of issues of administrative organization as providing some measure of policy salience. There are two ways of looking at this proxy for salience. On the one hand, some centralization of environmental policy-making functions, within an identifiable ministry or its equivalent, provides a measure of the initial importance of the governmental response to environmental issues. On the other hand, the more extensive the range of institutions with some environmental responsibility, the more this suggests that environmental policy is not only established as a policy field in its own right, but is also expanding in ways that are required by the problems that environmental issues pose. Patterns of institutionalization thus provide some measures, if only indirect ones, of the extent to which environmental concerns are taken seriously by governments.

In this context, looking at policy organizational structures also allows us to compare empirically the relative importance of issue-based explanations of the developments of environmental policy with the importance of explanations based on national institutional patterns and policy styles, a comparison that we have taken to be one of the central purposes of this part of the book. As we saw in the Introduction to this Part, the general drift of arguments about issue characteristics is that the nature of an issue brings about certain common patterns of response, implying a convergence among policy systems. Against this approach, we may put the arguments that identify the importance of national styles and institutions of policy-making, and which stress how historically conditioned institutional arrangements limit or determine what political actors are able to do. Such national policy-making styles are likely to preserve a divergence between different national systems dealing with the same problem. Therefore, proponents of the theory of national styles of regulation hold that it is contingent historical events distinctive to each country that are generally important in shaping policy responses to problems. In so far as administrative arrangements provide a measure of policy salience, the patterns to which they give rise provide us with some evidence for testing the predictions of these two approaches.

Our assessment of the evidence relies upon an analysis of how environmental protection is organized within our six countries in two main respects, the national and the subnational. Firstly, we consider the pattern of organization in central government and in particular the extent to which functions are concentrated in an environment ministry. Is one ministry given responsibility for most environmental functions, or are functions assigned to a number of ministries? In general, types of environmental administration vary considerably, with models ranging from the concentration of competences in one environmental ministry, through partial concentration with the ministry playing a coordinating role, to the dispersal of competences (alleviated by some inter-ministerial bodies), and finally to what is called 'hyper-sectoralization', where policy competence is widely dispersed.[3] What models are followed in our six countries, and how far, if at all, have central administrative structures changed in the last twenty years in the light of public concern about environmental issues and other pressures, especially from the EU, making for administrative change?

Within this context, we also consider the organization of technical advice. Although many environmental issues have a great deal of salience and emotional resonance in the public's mind, it is equally true that, in virtually all pollution control issues, technical questions concerned with the setting of emission limits or quality standards, the restructuring of production processes, or the diagnosis of cause and effect relationships come to be prominent in making policy choices. In this context, we need to consider how expert bodies are constituted and what their relationship is to policy-makers.

Secondly, attention is given to how central structures relate to subnational structures. Clearly, policy-making takes place at more than one level of government, and when we turn to issues of implementation, subnational structures often come to be of crucial importance. It is sometimes argued, for example, that policy integration on environmental matters is more problematic in federal political systems than in unitary political systems.[4] How far is administrative responsibility for environmental issues devolved to subnational bodies, and how far is it concentrated at the national level?

In this chapter we consider these questions first by looking at comparative trends in relatively easily measured comparative indices. We argue that it is very difficult to discern strong common trends across the six countries that could be said to reflect issue-based phenomena within the field of environmental policy. Instead, we have to look at the legacy of specific institutional arrangements within each country, and in particular at the ways in which both the shadow of the past and the specific problem characteristics that each country faces shape the structure of administration.

ADMINISTRATIVE CONCENTRATION AND ENVIRONMENTAL POLICY: TOWARDS SECULAR CONVERGENCE?

Central Government

In this section we consider the question of how environmental policy-making is organized within central government and in particular the extent to which there has developed a centralization of functions across our six member states. We have seen already that some analysts take this to be an important measure of the institutionalization of environmental policy, arguing that the creation of an environment ministry is an important measure of institutionalization. The presence or absence of a ministry, by itself, is an inadequate measure, however, since it ignores the extent to which environmental functions are actually assigned to such a ministry. Hypothetically, a ministry might be called a ministry and yet have relatively few relevant functions, those being assigned to, say, an agriculture or a public works ministry. Accordingly, we need to measure not simply whether a ministry exists, but also the extent of its environmental functions.

In order to measure concentration, we compare the extent to which functions have become concentrated in an environment ministry. By a 'function' we mean

TABLE 6.1 *Relation of environment functions to ministries*

Environment function	Environment ministry	
	Yes	No
Yes	(*a*)	(*c*)
No	(*b*)	(*d*)

an activity carried out to achieve a particular purpose. Examples of functions in this sense include: controlling polluting discharges to water, air, or soil; regulating the marine environment; developing policy on environmental impact assessments; formulating policies on alternative policy instruments; conducting or commissioning research on environmental problems; or controlling radioactive emissions. We do not suppose that there is any canonical list of functions. The ones we identify have been inductively derived by examining the standard functions of environmental ministries from a survey of listings in government state almanacs and public service guides. Of course, in certain respects it may be disputed as to whether a given function is properly characterized as being environmental. For example, is the regulation of drinking water an environmental function or an issue of consumer protection? There is obviously no single right answer to these definitional questions, so we have chosen to stipulate a particular answer and apply it as consistently as possible across the different national systems.[5]

The logical possibilities for the concentration of environmental functions can be set out in a two-by-two matrix as in Table 6.1. We first define any particular function as to whether or not it is an environmental function, and then ask which such functions are located in the environment ministry and which are located elsewhere. Perfect concentration will be represented when all the environmental functions are clustered in cell (*a*) and all the non-environmental functions are clustered in cell (*d*). By analogy with the logic of statistical testing, false negatives are those environmental functions outside of the environmental ministry in cell (*c*), and false positives are those non-environmental functions located in the environment ministry, cell (*b*). (This classification is not, of course, intended to carry any prescriptive judgment about whether environmental functions *should* be entirely concentrated in an environment ministry.)

From the logic represented in Table 6.1, we can construct an index of the concentration of functions. This index is defined in terms of the environmental functions located in the environment ministry as a proportion of all environmental functions, wherever located, plus all non-environmental functions located in the environment ministry. (The non-environmental functions not located in the environment ministry are irrelevant in this context.) The index can thus be expressed as follows: $(a)/[(a)+(b)+(c)] \times 100$. This index will take a value of zero when there is no environment ministry, a value of 100 per cent when all environmental functions

TABLE 6.2 *Administrative concentration in six countries, 1982–1992*

	Germany	Greece	Italy	N'lands	Spain	UK	Avg.
1982	0	24	0	75	0	64	27.2
1987	100	40	75	64	0	59	56.3
1992	100	40	85	79	0	65	61.5
Avg.	66.7	34.7	53.3	72.7	0	62.7	

are located in an environment ministry, and values in between for concentrations of environmental functions between these two extremes. (In-house functions such as personnel and research are included in our list in order to constrain the index to take the value of 100 per cent when there is a complete concentration of environmental functions.)

The measures of concentration for our countries over the decade for which we have data are set out in Table 6.2. A word of caution is necessary in connection with the data. Minor administrative reorganizations take place all the time in government ministries, as sections are amalgamated or divided. Thus, too much attention should not be focused upon small changes in percentages, given the relatively low numbers that we are dealing with overall. With that warning in place, let us look at the trends.

We can assess the effect of general trends leading to structural convergence by comparing the variance in averages over time with the variance of national averages, which involves comparing the marginal percentages of the columns with the marginal percentages of the rows. Clearly, the national variations are more important than the time trend. Although there is an obvious upward trend over time, it is not large by comparison with the variations between nations at any one time, including the end of the period we are examining. The percentage gap between the average concentrations at the beginning and the end of the period was 34.3 per cent, whereas the extreme values for the national averages range from zero to 72.7 per cent. An exploratory data analysis of the residuals (not reported here) as suggested by Tukey[6] showed that the residuals from the time trend were large by comparison with the residuals from the national averages, thus confirming the importance of national factors.

There is another piece of reasoning that leads us to suggest that the time trend, although significant, is not the more important of the two effects. One of the reasons why the time trend increases is the position of Germany, which created its environment ministry in 1986, so raising its index of concentration from zero to 100 per cent in one go. A similar point can be made for Italy. Unlike Italy, however, before 1986 Germany already had a significant concentration of environment functions within an already existing ministry (the Interior Ministry). So we need to acknowledge the special effect of this case on the time trend average. If we remove Germany from the analysis, the time averages range from 32.6 per cent in 1982 to 53.8 per cent in 1992, whereas the average national differences for the whole period show a range of 72.7 per cent. This suggests that we need to look less at general patterns affecting all countries and more at factors specific to each.

Looking at the figures for 1987 and 1992, these tend to confirm the conventional wisdom about the environmental commitment of the different countries. In the context of EU negotiations on environmental objectives, as we saw in Chapter 3, Germany and the Netherlands can properly be regarded as 'leaders' and Spain as one of the 'laggard' countries. The relatively high degree of concentration of functions within the Dutch and German ministries is consistent with this perception (supposing that greater commitment leads to greater administrative concentration), just as the 'productivist' policy stance of the Spanish government is symbolized by the location of environmental functions within a ministry of public works and transport. The relatively stable position of the UK is consistent with its early start in environmental policy in 1970 followed by a stalling process, as the politics of economic decline, so typical of the whole postwar period, became sharper in the 1970s and 1980s.

What conclusions can we draw from the above analysis about the relative significance of national versus structural trends in the shaping of environmental administration? The patterns of concentration that we observe are clearly the effect of national policy dynamics and of trends towards some convergence operating across systems, but the latter effect appears far weaker than the former.

If we look at the functions that are assigned to environment ministries, the details elude any simple cross-national generalizations. For example, the place of water pollution control or nature protection within the bureaucratic lego depends crucially on the historic responsibilities that other ministries have held. The counter-example to this assertion is Germany, but this is perhaps the exception that proves the rule. It took something as large and politically significant as the national panic over Chernobyl to dislocate the strong historical attachments of environmental functions to the ministries of the interior and agriculture. The final decision to create an environment agency in Italy is a less clear-cut example, for this owed something to a crisis over institutional reform at home.

There is one specific reason why the comparative patterns of concentration reflect national factors, and it is related to the origin of new bureaucratic structures. Looking at the experience of public administration in European countries, few government departments or offices are created *ex nihilo*. Typically, the creation of a new ministry or specialist agency arises from the amalgamation of existing units. The wrenching of these units from their existing position within the bureaucratic structure provides an occasion for turf disputes and resistance from those bodies that are in danger of losing some of their functions. Thus, the German Interior Ministry engaged in a sustained battle to retain its environmental functions, even though it was clear by the early 1980s that the whole range of functions for which it was responsible was too extensive. In Italy, the Ministry of the Environment was established in 1986, but only after long-standing ministries had conducted a largely successful defence of their roles, thus limiting the functions of the new ministry. Similarly, the Department of Employment struggled with the Department of the Environment in Britain to retain the Industrial Air Pollution Inspectorate, despite the Inspectorate itself wanting to move to Environment.[7]

In some countries, political pressures add to the bureaucratic inertia, particularly in systems in which government coalitions engage in delicate balancing acts among the parties, each of whom is keen to retain its portfolio. For example, one of the factors that led to the delay in creating an environment ministry in Germany was the fact that the interior ministry was held by politicians from the Free Democrats, and changing the composition of the ministries would also change the balance of portfolios in the cabinet. Similarly, the strong hold of the Dutch agriculture ministry on issues of nature protection reflects the traditionally strong hold throughout most of the twentieth century that the Christian parties have wanted to retain on agricultural affairs.

Sometimes these pressures of bureaucratic and political rivalry are so strong that only an influential external actor is capable of inducing the agreement necessary for reorganization. Thus, Christofilopoulou reports that the management of water and waste water in Greece was reorganized only under pressure from the European Investment Bank;[8] the Bank was prepared to provide loans for water and waste-water treatment plants only if there was a suitable institutional structure to implement the programme. In Spain, as we shall see, the EU proved to be a persistent influence in enhancing the status of environmental management and especially in improving the mechanisms for centre–periphery cooperation.

Despite the importance of these national differences, we can observe some elements of cross-national patterning. Greece and Spain fall fairly clearly into the less concentrated mode of administration, in that no significant concentration of environmental functions has occurred in either of these countries. In Italy, the creation of a proper ministry of the environment has to be interpreted in context, given the resistance from established ministries. There was limited symbolism and even less substance in the sense of administrative concentration, a conclusion that holds more generally in terms of the impact of environmental challenges on decision-making in all three countries. For this reason, one may possibly speak of a distinct continuity within discontinuity.

In comparison with the three northern countries, two differences may be noted. Firstly, the northern ministries are generally larger than their opposite numbers in the south, even taking account of the fact they have not been entirely 'environmental'. This suggests greater bureaucratic weight, though that is not necessarily the same as policy priority. Secondly, the fact that in two of the three southern cases responsibility for the environment has been combined with public works is particularly significant. In countries that are concerned about their economic development —and are also known for their clientelistic practices—it follows that there have been special reasons why environmental administration has been held back from ready expansion.

One feature that does stand out is the symbolic role that the creation of an environment ministry reveals. In the cases of Germany and Greece this was particularly evident, and a similar point can be made in respect of Italy. The UK and Spain illustrate the negative symbolism of the dog that did not bark, or in Madrid's case did not bark for quite some time. The location of environmental responsibility in the public works ministry in Spain for a long time symbolized the government's failure to establish an independent environmental organization; and the stasis of the UK is equally symbolic. In the latter case the continual prevarication over the creation of a fully integrated pollution inspectorate seems an apt symbol of political dithering. Although John Major announced on 8 July 1991 the desire to establish a unified pollution control agency, there was no immediate organizational change as a follow-up, and the agency came into being only in April 1996.[9]

The most interesting case in this respect is the Netherlands. Despite the protestations of those Dutch bureaucrats whom we interviewed, we attach symbolic significance to the move of the ministry to the centre of The Hague. However, a far more important policy symbol was the 1989 National Environmental Policy Plan, which reflected an attempt by the planners involved not to allow turf disputes over organizational competences to displace substantive coordinated policy-making. Their argument was simple. To spend time and energy reorganizing the bureaucracy detracts from the process of negotiating improved polices between ministries. If this argument were to gain greater weight in decision-making in other countries, it would further reduce the common incentives to reconfigure environmental bureaucracies and would reinforce, even further, the importance of the distinctive national political and institutional contexts within which each environment ministry is located.

Subnational Administration

Subnational administration and its relationship to the machinery of central government is important for a number of reasons. The institutionalization of environmental policy in the 1970s and 1980s, which we described in looking at the reorganization of central government, was in many respects a nationalization of activities that had taken place before at the local level. Thus, new laws on pollution control gave to national bodies powers of administration and standard-setting that had previously been confined to subnational authorities. However, the adoption of certain responsibilities at the national level often accompanied, rather than simply replaced, continuing local responsibility. The nationalization of much pollution policy in some ways therefore compounded the problems of central–local relations.

The emerging public administration of pollution also transformed the character of the subnational bodies that remained. New responsibilities, for example in the areas of monitoring or solid waste control, were often assigned to subnational authorities, and old responsibilities shifted from being merely permissive to being mandatory. Moreover, one important responsibility typically carried out by subnational bodies is the inspection of licensed plant and premises to ensure that standards are being maintained in accordance with the licence. Given the need for local knowledge, it is not surprising that subnational bodies are assigned to take on this task, even when the standards have been set at the national, or perhaps even international, level.

Broadly speaking, there are two patterns of subnational/national relations that may exist in the administration of environmental policy and which are found in various forms and combinations in our six countries. The first pattern rests on the principle of splitting the *policy functions* that are related to any specific area of activity, by making policy-making and standard-setting a national responsibility but policy implementation and compliance monitoring a subnational responsibility. The second is to split responsibility according to criteria that relate to *substantive issues*. Thus, responsibility for hazardous chemicals may be made the responsibility of central government, but some forms of waste disposal may be made the responsibility of local or subnational government. In this latter approach there may be various bases for demarcation, including the receiving medium (air, land, or water), the specific polluting substance being controlled, or the scale of potential damage that a pollutant might cause.

Naturally, this two-fold categorization of ways in which policy responsibility might be assigned is clearer in analytical terms than it is in practice, especially in a case like that of Spain, where centre–periphery relations have continued to be reformed since the constitutional settlement of 1978. Although Germany may be said, for example, to approximate to the pattern in which responsibility is assigned on the basis of policy functions, with the federal government making policy and setting standards and the *Länder* governments implementing policy, there is still within the German system some assignment of responsibility on the basis of substantive issue. Conversely, in the UK, where on some substantive issues there has historically been a centralization of responsibility (e.g. air pollution from major sources), the central authorities have always tried to make due allowance for the assimilative capacity of the local environment in the exact standards that were enforced. Nevertheless, despite recognizing that the two different ways in which responsibility might be assigned is clearer in theory than in practice, the significance of the distinction is still noticeable.

How might we classify our six countries in respect of this distinction, and what have been the patterns of change in the last few years? Looking across the range of countries, it is difficult to see a clear pattern to the way in which administrative responsibilities are divided between different levels of government, and it is also difficult to observe any common secular trends since the early 1970s. Indeed, national distinctiveness, rather than common patterns, appears to be the rule. As Box 6.1 shows, the patterns vary from country to country. Moreover, where there have been changes, they have often revealed divergent rather than convergent trends.

This point is well illustrated in the case of the UK, which since the middle of the 1980s has undergone extensive administrative changes affecting the division

Box 6.1 Division of Responsibility between Central and Subnational Authorities

Germany. There is a functional division, with the federal government setting standards in areas where it has responsibility and subnational authorities responsible for implementation, and subnational authorities having responsibility in areas where federal government only has framework powers.

Greece. Central government has primary responsibility for legislation and standard-setting, but in a context of divided central authority. Regional and prefectural authorities have some policy-making as well as administrative responsibilities. Local authorities share policy-making in some areas and have exclusive control in others.

Spain. National government legislates and sets standards. However, the autonomous communities also have standard-setting powers, though these vary depending on the autonomous community in question. Local authority powers depend upon the population administered.

Italy. National government has legislative and standard-setting responsibility. There is also legislation at the regional level. Provinces with important responsibilities in water management and municipal authorities can also set local standards.

Netherlands. Central government has main responsibility for setting standards, and provincial authorities have responsibility for implementation. Water boards are also important actors.

United Kingdom. Central government takes responsibility for setting standards and for implementation in those areas of pollution control in which it has powers. Local authorities control less serious pollution.

between central and local responsibility. The principal changes that we detail below —in particular, first the creation of Her Majesty's Inspectorate of Pollution and the National Rivers Authority and then their merging in the creation of the Environment Agency—reinforced the tendency towards a relatively high proportion of issues being dealt with by a centralized body.

What then might account for these persisting divergent trends? The simplest and most obvious explanation is that environmental administration cannot be considered on its own, but needs to be placed in the legal and institutional context of each country. This is clearly the case with Spain's evolving quasi-federal system.

But it is Germany that provides the paradigm. For obvious historical reasons, there is a great deal of stress in the postwar German constitution and in postwar German political practice on the importance of the decentralization of power. This has been achieved principally through a form of federalism that divided policy competences functionally rather than by issue area, as in the USA. Moreover, the same constitutional anxieties that led to Germany's vertical federalism also make it difficult to establish independent agencies that might escape adequate parliamentary scrutiny. It is hardly likely that the structure of environmental administration would be an exception to these constitutional norms.

The legacy of historical tradition can also be important, as is illustrated by the centralist tendencies in Greece and Italy. In the case of the UK, its tendency to conform to a principle for the assignment of responsibility that stresses substantive issues rather than policy functions can be traced back to the nineteenth Century, when Sir John Simon, when head of the Local Government Board, lost the battle to have the responsibility for major air pollution control lodged with the local authorities instead of with a national body, the Alkali Inspectorate.[10]

Finally, the geographical circumstances of a country can be important in shaping the pattern of central–local environmental administration. This is especially true in a country like the Netherlands, where the importance of the canals and the vulnerability of much of the land to sea flooding has meant that the management of water is an important central government function in its own right. This is not to say that the need to manage water means that no other body can play a role in controlling polluting discharges to water, as we shall see in the next section. However, it does impose constraints on what is possible, and certainly means that there has to be some sharing of authority at different levels of government.

Thus, the differences among the six countries and the lack of common features across them mean that the idiosyncrasies of the individual countries are important in understanding the specific role that institutions play. Accordingly, in the next section we look at each country in turn, examining its institutional arrangements in terms of the organization of central government, the provision of technical advice, and central–subnational relations.

ENVIRONMENTAL ADMINISTRATION IN THE SIX STATES

Germany

Central government. As we have seen in the comparative analysis, Germany stands out as having a high degree of concentration of functions. This reflects the creation of the environmental ministry (Bundesministerium für Umwelt, Naturschutz und Reaktorsicherheit) in June 1986, which brought together in one organization the main pollution control functions. There are of course a number of functions apart from pollution control that are relevant to the environment—most notably those concerned with land use planning and nature protection—which are still outside the environment ministry. Even so, the creation of the environment ministry was a major break from the prior arrangements under which most environmental functions had been carried out by the Interior Ministry since 1969.

The reconfiguration of functions in 1969 had been part of the response to the upsurge of political interest in environmental questions that occurred in the late 1960s. The FDP politician Hans Dietrich Genscher had been made interior minister in October 1969, and he took a special interest in the development of environmental policy. On 11 November, departments concerned with the control of water, air, and noise pollution were moved from the health ministry to the interior ministry.[11] Other ministries, however, still held on to environmentally relevant functions. The agriculture ministry retained responsibility for human and veterinary medicine and control of chemical substances, the housing ministry retained responsibilities for planning, the transport ministry kept control of transport policy, and the ministry of research and technology kept control of environmentally relevant research.

However, in the wake of the Chernobyl accident in spring 1986 the interior minister Dr Zimmermann was held responsible for the mishandling of public information about radiation exposure. In the absence of federal radiation limits for milk, the Ministry of the Interior failed to step in quickly, prompting the *Länder* to issue contradictory standards, thus causing public anxiety. To quell the disquiet about this incident, Helmut Kohl, the West German chancellor, issued a decree creating the environment ministry. Water and waste management, clean air policy, noise abatement, reactor safety, and radiation protection were moved from the interior ministry. Nature protection was moved from agriculture, and sections dealing with the medical aspects of environmental protection, radiation hygiene, and chemical substances were moved from the Ministry of Health.[12]

There seems to be general agreement among policy experts interviewed shortly after the creation of the ministry that the move was largely driven by the political need to symbolize a change of priorities, although it has been observed by a member of the Christian Democratic Union (CDU) that there was a widespread expectation that a ministry would be created after the federal elections of 1987, and the main effect of Chernobyl was to bring the date forward.[13] However, given the symbolic need to demonstrate a commitment of a strong policy of environmental protection in the wake of the perceived crisis of Chernobyl, it is not surprising that it was possible in 1986 to overcome the long and well entrenched bureaucratic resistance, particularly from the interior ministry, to the loss of environmental functions. (In defending its position, the ministry had even pointed to its fleet of low-flying aircraft as being particularly suitable to defend German borders from cross-boundary threats!)

Although bureaucratic turf disputes obviously play a role in the decision about the location of environmental functions, it is also worth noting that there has been a long-standing intellectual debate in Germany about the most appropriate organizational form for environmental policy since the creation of the first environmental ministry at *Land* level in Bavaria in 1970. Roughly speaking, the debate has been between those who favour the concentration of environmental functions in a single ministry and those who favour making environmental functions part of a larger and more powerful ministry with some influence across the wide range of policy sectors that bear upon environmental quality. In favour of concentration, proponents have pointed to the incentives that an environment minister has to improve policy, and to the fact that a separate ministry is less prone to compromise in the specification of environmental goals. In favour of lodging the environment functions in a larger ministry have been those who have been aware that the environment ministry has little power compared with those with whom it would have to negotiate and that it is inhibited by a sensitivity to the difficulties of always having to demand compliance from others. Analysis after the event suggests that these tensions have continued.[14]

Even without these intellectual disputes, however, the creation of an environment ministry was made difficult in late 1970s and early 1980s by the dynamics of coalition politics in Germany. During the last years of the Social–Liberal coalition, which ended in 1982, the Social Democratic Party came to favour the creation of a separate environment ministry after a party inquiry chaired by Volker Hauff recommended its establishment. However, it was not possible to act on this recommendation without upsetting the delicate balance of party portfolios in the coalition cabinet.

The first holder of the environment portfolio was Walter Wallmann, who was largely seen as both a safe pair of hands and a caretaker on his way to prime ministerial office in Hessen, a post he moved to in 1987. He was succeeded by Klaus Töpfer, who had an academic background in the economics of land use planning and was a former environment minister in Rhineland-Palatinate.[15] He brought to the post an understanding of the complex dynamics of environmental policy which was reflected in early organizational changes within the ministry. These strengthened the waste control functions by upgrading two administrative sections into a sub-department, boosting central planning functions, and adopting a matrix approach, in which sectional responsibilities were related to cross-cutting themes.

The difficulty of adapting the traditional bureaucratic structure of the German ministry to the cross-cutting demands of environmental management, in which problem solutions have to be seen holistically, has been a long-standing feature of academic and policy discussion. It is hardly accidental that Max Weber developed his account of the technical superiority of bureaucratic organization through specialization in the context of the German culture of administration. The organization of German ministries follows a pattern of departments, sub-departments and sections (*Referate*), the last often being relatively small, involving about six people, and highly specialized. At various times experiments have been tried with working groups that cut across the sections, but their influence has been low, and some of the difficulties that the German government had in implementing the EU's environmental impact assessment directive[16] sprang from the fact that its scope affected some sixteen sections.

Another aspect of the attempt to secure greater integration of environmental measures into the broad range of public policy is the creation of so-called 'mirror sections' in relevant ministries and the environment ministry, which are supposed to liaise with one another and coordinate their activities. However, their effectiveness is weakened by their being understaffed in the environment ministry, where one section is responsible for liaising with more than one ministry, and by divided loyalties on the part of those in the mirror section in the corresponding ministry.

The main work of the environment ministry involves drafting the legislative measures that are necessary in order to implement policy. Legislative measures are not taken in isolation of the considerations involved in their implementation; for example, working groups of *Länder* officials are set up to look at the feasibility of proposed measures. However, the administrative component of policy-making is important, since the broad framework legislation in each of the main areas means that significant policy developments occur as a result of administratively drafted measures. Moreover, since there is a strong emphasis on constitutionality in the drafting of German legislative measures, there is a need to ensure drafting that is highly competent in technical terms, and this reinforces the pressure towards specialization.

That brings us to the role of technical advice in the drawing up of legislation and technical standards.[17] The ministry is aided in the formulation of environmental regulations by the independent Federal Environment Office (Umweltbundesamt, UBA). UBA takes responsibility for the technical tasks of researching standards and drafting potential regulations, while the ministry has the legal and the technical task of formulating the regulations in a way that is legally and constitutionally sound. Founded in 1974, UBA's function is to provide technical advice to the ministry in the setting of standards and the drafting of legislation. Strong technical support is particularly important in a system of environmental policy in which the principle of *Stand der Technik* plays a central role. Our interviews in both the ministry and UBA itself suggested that there was not a regular established pattern of practice between the two bodies, but that one or the other took the lead in standard-setting discussions, depending on the topic at hand and the issues that it raised. (It is also worth noting that, whereas UBA was located in Berlin during the period of our study, the ministry was in Bonn.)

UBA has also played a role in monitoring environmental pollution, particularly on issues of intercalibration. For example, during the 1995 smog alerts in Germany, UBA discovered that the *Länder* authorities were not all using EU-approved measuring methods, and the UBA sought to give advice about standardizing the procedure. Moreover, since issues of expertise go beyond the setting of standards to wider questions of environmental policy, UBA has also sought to explore these; for example, in the middle of the 1990s it was conducting research projects on the role that international trade agreements might have in securing environmental protection and on what the appropriate rules of international trade might be. UBA also funds out-of-house research, for example on the introduction of improved techniques of production in industry.

UBA is relatively large—larger even than the ministry—in terms of the number of staff that it employs, having over six hundred staff working for it. Until September 1994 it was organized primarily according to the focus of regulation, but at that date, as a result of organizational change, a new cross-media approach was instigated. A good example of this is the section organized to look at issues of soil protection, where pollutants can come from a variety of sources. Reunification put the issue of contaminated land on to the policy agenda, and Klaus Töpfer's successor, Angela Merkl, took a particular interest in the issue of soil clean-up. The reorganization of UBA was therefore occasioned by the need to deal with such problems.

Although UBA is clearly important in providing expert advice from within government, it is also clear that the German environment ministry uses other sources of specialist advice, often located in federally funded research institutes. For example, in the field of water regulation, the ministry would expect to consult, among others, the Federal Institute of Hydrology in Koblenz, the Federal Institute for Navigation and Hydrography in Hamburg, the Federal Institute for Hydraulic Engineering in Karlsrühe, and the German weather service at Offenbach. Similarly, when the environment ministry was drawing up the technical instructions for waste disposal in urban areas, it asked the German medical research council to undertake a study of the risks associated with waste incineration.[18]

The environment ministry has also set up joint working parties with the Federation of German Industry, for example on the technical possibilities of various soil clean-up methods. The importance of such joint working parties also has to be seen in the context of the principle of *Stand der Technik*. The view has been held by some observers that in the 1970s industry operated a 'cartel of silence' on the possibilities of flue-gas desulphurization for large combustion plants, as a way of frustrating the attempts by the government to require higher standards of air pollution control. The use of a joint ministry–industry working party in the mid-1990s is some indication of how far the assumptions of policy, and in particular the assumptions about the relationship between economy and ecology, have altered.

Another important component of the advice network is the Council of Environmental Experts.[19] Established in 1972 on the model of the US Council of Environmental Quality, it is an independent advisory body made up of experts from both the natural and the social sciences as well as engineering. It produces both general and specific reports and has been responsible for raising a number of issues on the policy agenda, including the problems of implementation failure in its 1978 report on the subject, the protection of the North Sea and the case for the increased use of economic instruments in the control of pollution.

A distinctive German advisory institution is that of the inquiry commission, a mixture of parliamentarians and experts set up to investigate and report on a particular topic. Looking at the 'large' questions, for example global climate change or the management of product cycles, the reports of such inquiry commissions are less important for their strict technical content than for keeping the discussion of certain issues on the policy agenda. One striking example of the influence of an inquiry commission arises from the one established by the Bundestag in 1987 on climate change, consisting of eleven members of the Bundestag and eleven scientists. The commission played an important role in prompting action and filled a political vacuum left by the government. Its activity appears to have been decisive in establishing the urgency of the problem and the need to set stringent targets for carbon dioxide reductions of 30 per cent of the 1987 figure by 2005.[20]

Subnational administration. Germany is a federal state. This simple statement of constitutional fact opens up a complex world of subnational environmental policy and politics, a world that has become more complex since reunification in 1990 and the incorporation of the five new *Länder* into the federal republic. Moreover, even in formal terms, and without the complication of moving from eleven to sixteen *Länder*, the administrative situation is complex. The *Länder* are responsible for the implementation of environmental measures; they have their own forms of administrative organization and in some sub-sectors of environmental policy can set their own environmental standards independently of the federal government. Indeed, it was only with a constitutional change in 1972 that the federal government came to have significant powers in the environmental policy sector. Since that constitutional change, the federal government can override the standards of the *Länder* where it has 'concurrent' powers, as in air pollution control, but not where it has only 'framework' powers, as with much water pollution control. Thus, although in formal terms Germany's federalism rests largely upon the distinction of policy functions, it also relates to substantive issues of policy.

The importance of the federal constitution is also shown in the way in which it has allowed the German Greens to have an influence in the making of public policy. In a number of *Länder* the German Greens have been in coalition with either the Social Democrats alone (the red–green coalition) or Social Democrats and the Free Democrats (the 'traffic light' coalition). These coalitions began with a tentative period of political cooperation between the Greens and Social Democrats in Hamburg after 1982 through the Hesse coalition of 1985–7 to others in Brandenburg, Bremen, and North-Rhine Westphalia.[21] Although in this section we shall focus on the relationship between the federal government and the *Länder* governments, the importance of local environmental administration, particularly on such issues as traffic management, can be extremely important.

For the period of our study, the formal constitutional division of responsibility between the federal government and the *Länder* is reflected in the legislative and standard-setting procedures in which the *Länder* are represented both formally, in particular in the Bundesrat, and informally, in such institutions as working parties convened by the ministry. There is an important distinction in Germany between the passing of legislation bestowing standard-setting powers and the setting of standards under such legislation. Legislative measures are drafted by the ministry in consultation with the UBA. They first go to the federal cabinet, and are then passed to the Bundesrat, the parliamentary body of the *Länder* governments, for an opinion. The cabinet then forms an opinion and puts the proposal to the Bundestag. The legislative committee in the Bundestag then consults the *Länder* governments before the matter is decided. Standard-setting, by contrast, does not involve the Bundestag, but is undertaken through processes in which only the government and the Bundesrat participate.

In this context, various non-legally mandated processes of consultation and decision-making become important, involving various bodies representing the *Länder* governments. The Conference of Environment Ministers (Umweltminister-konferenz, UMK) includes representatives of *Länder* ministers with environmental responsibilities as well as the federal environment minister. After its first meeting on 6 October 1972,[22] the UMK has subsequently met regularly about twice a year. It is complemented by a parallel meeting of civil servants, the Permanent Committee of Departmental Heads of the Federation and Federal States (Ständige Abteilungsleiterausschuß-Bund, STALA), which plays a role in preparing the business for the meetings of the ministers.

At *Land* level itself, various forms of organization are to be found. The earliest experiment with the creation of a unified environment ministry was in Bavaria in 1970, when a new ministry was formed by bringing together the sections responsible for nature protection from the economics ministry, waste disposal from the interior ministry and noise control from the labour ministry. In North Rhine Westphalia, by contrast, the creation of an integrated environment ministry had to wait until 1985, and there is some suspicion that the unwillingness to form such a ministry was due to the fear from local politicians that the ministry would be too strong in the face of the local coal industry, which was such a large supplier of jobs. In the end, the public pressure was such that it was necessary to have a ministry that featured the word 'environment' in the title.

Below the level of the *Land* authorities, there are the municipal authorities, which are also important in themselves, partly because they have important pollution control functions such as waste disposal, and partly because they have licensing functions in respect of plants that are sources of pollution. Moreover, in terms of preventing or offsetting environmental problems, the municipal authorities can be very important. For example, the city of Freiburg was able for some time to cross-subsidize its public transport from the profits it made on its ownership of the electricity generating plant, and other authorities have experimented with economic instruments in fields where the federal government has not dared to tread.

It can be seen, therefore, that the institutionalization of environmental policy-making in Germany takes many and varied forms. In part this is a consequence of the country's constitutional structure. In part, however, the institutionalization reflects the emphasis given to the search for technical solutions to environmental problems under the principle of *Stand der Technik*, the logic of which requires the creation of forums of discussion, interest articulation, and policy deliberation among a wide range of parties.

Greece

Central government. In Greece, there was an agreement in principle in the constitution to protect the environment as part of the desire to give the new regime a more modern and caring image on the country's return to democracy in 1974. This bore fruit with the creation in 1980 of a new Ministry of Physical Planning, Housing, and the Environment. (Its predecessor was the National Council for Physical Planning and Protection of the Environment, set up in 1976.) However, the origins of this change suggest that environmental management was slotted into the pre-existing state machine rather than it involving any serious institutional reform.[23]

The ministry's main environmental responsibilities were vaguely defined and included preparing environmental programmes and coordinating their implementation.[24] Following the change of government in 1981 from the conservative New Democracy to the socialist PASOK, a major review of environmental administration led to the new ministry acquiring new functions and services, such as responsibility for cooperation with international organizations and with the agency for the Athens Environment Pollution Control Programme (PERPA).

As of today, there has been a symbolic change, in that 'environment' now comes first in the ministry's title. This came about in 1985, when the physical planning and environment sectors were combined with the powerful Ministry of Public Works (and became known as YPEHODE). This change has, however, been criticized for subordinating environmental protection to expensive developmental projects.[25] In substance, its responsibilities now include: coordinating various public and private agencies for environmental monitoring; protecting the atmosphere and controlling industrial emissions (sewage as well as atmospheric); imposing quality controls for recreational waters; and overseeing the national parks.

But despite its name, the new ministry is hardly dominant in environmental administration, for Greece is an example of extreme fragmentation of environmental functions. To give just several examples, the Ministry of Merchant Marines covers protection of the marine environment; the Ministry of Health tests seawater quality and classifies beaches; the Ministry of Agriculture is responsible for protecting forests and monitoring rivers; and the Ministry of Transport monitors car emissions. As a former director of environmental planning in YPEHODE remarked, 'we are not the only branch of government dealing with the environment—there are many branches; from some points of view we aren't even the most important'.[26]

Although the Ministry of the Environment is supposed to coordinate environmental policy in Greece under the Framework Law of 1986, in practice this has not happened to any significant degree. The absence of effective coordination in the past still mattered, for different ministries had developed the habit of muscling in on environmental matters;[27] for example, the Ministry of Agriculture enjoyed considerable bureaucratic weight through its control over resources and personnel. Given these problems of effective inter-ministerial coordination, environmental policy-making has been subject to the vagaries of political interest or environmental crisis. Furthermore, there has been some tendency for officials from other ministries to hide behind YPEHODE on anti-pollution matters, while looking to the interests of their own clienteles.[28] Undoubtedly, this kind of bureaucratic buck-passing tends to inhibit policy effectiveness which in the environmental area depends so much on inter-ministerial cooperation.

Such cooperation is further inhibited by the lack of a clear division of labour. There are numerous cases of overlapping tasks, such as national parks, where both YPEHODE and agriculture have responsibilities. This kind of intrasectoral co-involvement certainly makes for bureaucratic confusion, while demonstrating problems of differential political weight. For instance, one major weakness of YPEHODE's environmental work is that it lacks a presence on the ground in the form of field-staff. In contrast, the agriculture ministry boasts a large forestry service.[29]

The failure to delimit clearly environmental responsibilities is marked with respect to air pollution. The Ministry of Industry has a concentration of competences over industrial pollution, making it open to conflicts of interest between industry and the environment. At the same time, the Ministry of National Economy holds some responsibility for industrial pollution. (Three of its directorates authorize industrial installations, following impact assessments carried out by the Ministry of Industry.) But YPEHODE, which controls industrial emissions, has to get permission from the National Economy Ministry to ban an industrial firm; and it is the latter that finances anti-pollution programmes, thus making YPEHODE dependent on it for achieving its own anti-pollution programme.[30]

Environmental administration clearly suffers from its brigading with public works, lacking as a consequence real autonomy and political weight. The environment has been described as 'the third leg' in the ministry.[31] In the early 1990s, for example, YPEHODE was divided into 88 directorates, of which 54 were related to public works and 32 to physical planning, while only 2 covered the environment; the latter had been allocated only 290 out of 3,354 civil servants.[32] The political superiority of public works was also indicated by the structure of the ministry's budget; as a former senior official in YPEHODE explained, 60 billion drachmas were devoted to public works, compared with only 2 million drachmas for the rest of its tasks, including the environment.[33] It should be noted, too, that the ministry functions in effect as two rather separate units, housed in two buildings some distance apart in central Athens. The environment is not located in the main part of the ministry. Coordination between the ministry's separate parts is weak, occurring mainly at the top level, so there is little integration of civil servants at lower levels. As one senior official on the environment side commented, 'practically, we have more problems with our colleagues from public works than we have with other ministries'.[34]

These various structural and bureaucratic problems within YPEHODE, and affecting its relations within the machinery of government, have been modified only when the minister in charge has shown determination on environmental matters. One such minister was Antonis Tritsis, PASOK's first minister of the environment from 1981, who sought albeit with limited success to control building development and to deal with Athens' notorious pollution cloud. Another, Stefanos Manos, made a spirited attempt after New Democracy returned to power in the early 1990s to confront the issue of car emissions, noting in reference to some of his predecessors that all it needed was 'a government that goes ahead to do things rather than just talk'.[35] Individual ministers from both parties have made more of a difference than a political party as such. But the main lesson is that, whatever progress there has been in environmental administration, it has been unable to overcome a history of fragmented centralization.

The extent to which traditional administrative patterns have persisted, in particular the weak state of policy coordination, does not bode well for Greece's position in relation to the EU. YPEHODE is responsible for defining Greek policy overall and for the country's representation in the EU Environmental Council. In this respect, it is buttressed by the 1986 Framework Law. Some officials in YPEHODE have claimed that the EU factor has strengthened environmental priorities within the ministry *vis-à-vis* public works.[36] But in practice these formal functions have not cut seriously across the bureaucratic power of some other ministries.

EU membership certainly creates pressures for stricter policy coordination and response. This seems to have produced more intensive contacts between YPEHODE and local authorities in order to take advantage of EU programmes in the environmental area.[37] But it does not seem to have produced much improvement in Athens and is a source of frustration with Commission officials in Brussels. In some cases, EU pressure has even exacerbated inter-ministerial tensions. A high official of YPEHODE remarked that recent EU programmes had not enhanced the political or bureaucratic standing of her ministry:

The peculiar thing in this story, especially for the two major programmes, ENVIREG [a regional action programme on the initiative of the Commission concerning the environment] and the Framework Assistance Programme, is that the coordination of each of these programmes is *not* the Ministry of the Environment: it is the Ministry of National Economy. Any why? Because within these two programmes there are many other activities in addition to the environment protection activities. So, since they are mostly dealing with development, it is another ministry coordinating these activities. *But*, since it is another ministry coordinating the activities, the approach to environmental problems is totally different in some cases from ours. And, this means that in some cases we do not have the needed credit. . . .[38]

In short, there are strong continuities in Greek public administration despite the evolution of the relatively new policy area of the environment and despite EU membership. Many familiar problems of the Greek state have been reflected here.

Environmental management in Greece has suffered too from weak infrastructural support and expertise. The main exception has been the PERPA agency, which, together with some planning services, was incorporated into the ministry. But there has been no independent environmental agency, although plans for one have been voiced since the early 1980s.[39] The Framework Law of 1986 provided for such an agency (to be called EFOP), but it was not established, for reasons of bureaucratic power. Inter-ministerial rivalry has been activated. As one high official in YPEHODE explained, the reason was 'political' in that this agency would be 'too strong and unique an organization', and 'power would have been transferred to this organization'.[40]

Attitudes have persisted whereby environmental expertise is seen as the preserve of each ministry; hence it has remained dispersed across Athens.[41] This is certainly true of the agriculture ministry with its specialist resources but it is also true of the Ministry of Health, which draws on the skills of the Athens School of Hygiene. Interviews on the role of scientific expertise tended to show that this was usually available to ministers in decision-making not from active scientists, but rather from bureaucrats with a scientific or other form of specialist background. Yet scientifically trained officials in YPEHODE have felt weighed down by bureaucratic tasks. As one remarked, 'most of the time, 90–95 per cent is applied to the routine job, is not research'.

There is also the question of how far the personnel involved are beholden for political or patronage reasons, given the nature of the Greek governmental system. For instance, while professional expertise in environmental matters—e.g. in research institutes or universities—has grown in Greece in past years, very little of this has been fed into the policy process, because of ministerial preference for in-house expertise. Thus, it may be said that expertise has become institutionalized to the extent of its losing any autonomous merit.

YPEHODE has found it difficult to battle with such vested bureaucratic interests in the Greek government machinery. These are all the more powerful as environmental management is still very centralized in Greece. Indeed, a further reason for opposing an environmental agency was 'the idea that this organization was not only governmental: other factors of society would have been able to participate in the decision-making—the local authorities, social organizations such as the technical chamber, the association of scientists'.[42]

Subnational administration. The Greek political system is highly centralized. With a prefectural system, a large number of small local authorities, and a legislative framework that provides for a great deal of power at the centre, subnational administration has not played a major role in the development of Greek environmental policy, even in respect of issues of implementation. In 1986 Greece was divided into thirteen administrative regions. These play a role in the planning of European programmes, but in the environmental area at least they are not very influential bodies. In 1989 there was a reorganization of field services which established directorates for physical planning and the environment in each of the regions, but the regions themselves remain largely intermediaries in the process of economic planning.[43] Similarly, although environmental quality inspection teams could have been set up ever since 1986, there has been a requirement for environmental units in the prefectures only since 1990, and their staffing is mostly inadequate.[44]

Within local government, the larger municipalities have usually been responsible for sewage networks and treatment plants, the management of household waste, and the supply of drinking water. They also share responsibility with the central administration over such matters as air and water pollution and the application of traffic regulations.[45]

Some local authorities have shown initiative on environmental questions in recent years, but this has not greatly altered patterns of policy-making. Centre–periphery coordination has varied and has of course been affected by difficulties of horizontal coordination at the national level. Often, political and personal links fostered in Athens by local leaders helps. In short, subnational administration is underdeveloped in Greece.

Spain

Central government. The main characteristic of environmental administration in Spain is to a large degree its virtually federal structure. While the centre retained responsibility for basic legislation on environmental protection, in the mid-1980s the Autonomous Communities (regions) acquired many environmental competences. At the national level, environmental management has evolved over several decades in a very gradual way. In the course of this change, the environmental area has acquired more and more bureaucratic status. For a long time, it was similar to the Greek situation, with environment being combined with a large ministry (i.e. public works), although there is less horizontal institutional fragmentation in Spain than in Greece. Latterly, there has been a shift towards the Italian model, with the institution of a separate environment ministry.

Environmental management began seriously with the creation of a directorate-general for territorial action and the environment within the Ministry of Public Works and Urban Affairs (MOPU) in 1977, although it could be traced back in some minimal form to the early 1960s. Later changes led to the ministry being called Public Works and Transport (MOPT), and this was renamed Public Works, Transport, and the Environment in the summer of 1993. The final addition of 'environment' to the ministry title was attributed to the fact this ministry had progressively acquired many of the environmental functions at the national level.[46] In 1996, the new Popular Party government created the separate Ministry of the Environment.

From 1982 until 1996, the ministry in question included the General Directorate for the Environment, which among other tasks represented Spain in international organizations. This unit gradually increased in weight within MOPT and
in 1990 was elevated in status to a General Secretariat (SGMA) headed by a state
secretary (the only case in the ministry); but this was not accompanied by any change
in its functions.[47] Officially, the SGMA acted as coordinator of all national environmental policy and was responsible, for instance, for data collection and analysis,
environmental planning and programming, and the preparation of environmental
legislation. It also had some sectoral functions such as over waste and atmospheric
pollution.

This gradual addition of bureaucratic weight to the environment area has increased
SGMA's strength over conflicts with other policy areas in this ministry. In the
past, such conflicts have presented a serious challenge for the environment, given
the traditionally pronounced emphasis on public works in Spanish developmental
policy. While such intra-ministry conflicts may be easier to resolve than inter-
ministry ones, they are referred upwards to the minister when resolution is difficult
among high officials.[48] In this sense, there is a difference from the Greek model, where
the environment has remained weakly represented in the bureaucratic structure.

The other main ministries to hold important environmental functions have been
agriculture (nature conservation and forestry), industry (environmental impacts of
industry, industrial waste management), and health (including health monitoring
with regard to air and water pollution).[49] Coordination between these ministries
and the Ministry for the Environment has become more complicated over time.
Originally, this was handled by the Inter-Ministerial Committee of the Environment (CIMA), established in 1972, but this was abolished in 1987. The reason given
for its abolition was the greater everyday complexity of environmental business
combined with the emergence of the regions as an actor, as well as the growing
importance in Spain of the EU.[50] CIMA has therefore not been replaced, although
various special inter-ministerial committees aim to facilitate coordination. Coordination has in the past been rather inefficient, so there has been a predominance of
separate sectoral approaches in solving problems. According to Lopez Bustos, this
deficiency of coordination was not reduced by the 1990 reform, for the MOPT
still did not 'have a structure adequate for imposing environmental discipline exactly
where it is necessary to exercise control'.[51]

The role of specialist agencies is more developed in Madrid than in Athens, with
the ministry responsible for the environment better serviced. At the same time,
there is a similarity with the Greek case in that these agencies are institutionalized along separate ministerial lines. The absence of a national environment agency
seems to relate to the very gradual and belated emergence of environmental management in Madrid. On the other hand, the existence of environment agencies in
most regions clearly reflects the quasi-federal structure of the state.

The Ministry of Public Works has enjoyed various support structures, such as
the National Water Council, a council overseeing the National Waste Plan, and

the Geographical Council.[52] Other ministries draw on their own specialist agencies, in particular the Ministry of Industry on the Centre for Energy, Environment, and Technology Research (CIEMAT), and the Ministry of Health on the Carlos III Institute. CIEMAT's role is to provide technical policy advice. In an interview in 1992, its director remarked on 'a lack of sympathy' between decision-makers and policy advisers, although the situation had improved as Spanish policy came to be based more on technical knowledge and with a growing precautionary rather than reactive focus in CIEMAT's work.[53] The Carlos III Institute is large and well-funded, and its basic purpose is to carry out research on such topics as toxicology and transmissible diseases in order to improve knowledge and the control of health risks.

While better managed than in Athens, these mechanisms for the input of expertise into policy still tend to illustrate the closed procedures of the Madrid bureaucracy. The head of the directorate-general for environmental policy in MOPTMA himself acknowledged that 'the Spanish administration is not an administration very accustomed to working with the universities, with centres of research . . . this is, I think, one element that is one of the major difficulties'.[54] A prominent figure in an environmental organization criticized more pungently the habit of

resorting to a certain type of 'expert', very professionalized but with very clear political connections . . . there has been a traditional mistrust, as much in the previous UCD [governments as in the present PSOE] one, towards experts who are even minimally independent —for them, an expert is someone that you control, of the same party. . . .[55]

What has been the effect, however, of EU membership on Spanish environmental management? Three influences are apparent on the basis of interviews with high officials in MOPTMA and other ministries responsible for the environment in Madrid. Firstly, the gradual increase in bureaucratic status of the environment part of MOPTMA—indeed, the belated creation of an environment ministry as such —is among other things due to EU engagement in the environment area. According to an official in the environmental policy section of MOPTMA,

Yes, the EU has changed things: when we entered the EU in 1986, within this ministry there only existed one directorate-general [for the environment] . . . now we have a secretary of state for water policy and the environment. Undoubtedly, yes, the status has been raised of the department that is responsible for representation in Brussels.[56]

Secondly, EU membership forced Madrid to reassess its relations with the Autonomous Communities in the environment area, for previously they were not regulated.[57] The institutionalization of vertical coordination, described above, took place with particular reference to strengthening Spain's role at the EU role.[58]

Thirdly, Brussels has had some effect in helping to open up Spanish administration to consultative procedures at the national level. Moreover, the EU has been quite crucial in urging Spain to develop an environmental information system.[59]

In this connection, the development of scientific transnational networks has been important. As the head of the environment institute at CIEMAT in Madrid put it,

It is not a matter so much of funds, because in one way or another funds come and go. It is not a quantitative matter, rather that in general Spain has, notably, been opening up to an external relationship in every way since 1975, following the change of regime in Spain. And this has allowed also an opening from the scientific point of view which now safeguards a better understanding of the frontiers of knowledge, through participating in well integrated projects that guarantee the quality and competitivity of such research.[60]

In Spain, it has been recognized that the relative lack of research and development in the environmental field requires an even greater involvement of Spanish scientists in international environmental programmes, and not just those of the EU.[61]

Subnational government. While the central administration is broadly responsible for basic legislation, international relations, and coordination, the Autonomous Communities enjoy wide competences in legislating for and managing the environment. But the situation is complex, in so far as the central and regional administrations have concurrent powers and as the actual competences of the seventeen communities vary; for example, only half of them have legislative powers on air pollution control. Furthermore, the powers of the regions has been subject to intermittent institutional reform over the years. In 1991 five regions reformed their environmental administrations, the pattern of change generally being one of reinforcing environmental protection structures.[62] The structure of environmental management varies, with many regions following the national model of dividing environmental responsibilities among several departments, although Catalonia has concentrated all environmental functions in one single department. While most regions have environmental agencies, in six of these the agency is autonomous and contains most environmental competences, along the American model.[63]

Despite this complexity, centre–periphery coordination has been reformed with the establishment of the Sectoral Conference consisting of the minister together with the heads of the environmental units from the regions. This meets twice yearly, while the director-general for environmental policy from the Madrid ministry meets his regional counterparts on a quarterly basis. Working groups covering specific themes prepare these meetings.[64] These new bodies, set up in the early 1990s, illustrate the ability of the Spanish administration to adapt, although horizontal coordination in Madrid has become less institutionalized than that between centre and periphery.

These new mechanisms for vertical coordination have, for instance, improved the means for consultation between Madrid and the regions over forthcoming environmental proposals from Brussels, including specific directives in the pipeline.[65] The leading role in representing Spain in the EU Environment Council has been played by MOPTMA. Despite institutional fragmentation in the environmental area, enhanced by the quasi-federal structure, the relative efficiency of Spanish administration allows Spain to have a more determined policy as a member state than, for example, Greece.

Italy

Central government. In Italy the formal model of administration is somewhat different from the other two southern countries, but in practice the diffusion of environmental functions and deficient coordination make it not so dissimilar to the Greek case, for example. With around 400 employees, the Italian Ministry of the Environment is also small, especially when compared to such established ministries as interior (140,000), education (194,000), labour (16,000) and even agriculture (4,000).[66] Italian administration is further complicated by a decentralization of some responsibilities, as well as by the general uncertainty over Italian structures in the 1990s with increased pressure for institutional reform.

When it was established in 1986, the environment ministry replaced the Inter-Ministerial Committee for the Environment created by a decree of 1979. It was granted limited powers as over air, water, and soil pollution as well as nature reserves. The latter was the only transfer of a function from another ministry (agriculture), for the established ministries fought an effective campaign to keep their powers in the face of the challenge presented by the formation of the new ministry.[67] Despite the high-minded declarations in Article 1 of the law establishing it (e.g. 'ensure, within an organic framework, the promotion . . . of environmental conditions'), key powers were retained by such ministries as public works, health, civil protection, and cultural heritage.[68] In the course of time, however, the Ministry of the Environment has acquired further functions, notably for industrial waste, recycling, emergency clean-up programmes, powers of short-term intervention for immediate threats to the environment, and preparing a general plan for improving water quality.[69]

While this represented some improvement in the new ministry's standing, it should not be forgotten that many of its environmental functions are shared with other ministries. These include atmospheric pollution (shared with public health, energy, transport, and industry), industrial risk (shared with public health), marine pollution (shared with the merchant navy ministry), and environmental impact (shared with cultural heritage).

Although the Ministry of the Environment has gained some additional sole powers, such as over waste disposal, this has done little to overcome considerable constraints on its action. This is because inter-ministerial coordination has been weak, and has not allowed the ministry to gain more bureaucratic muscle. Coordination mechanisms have reflected necessity rather than normative choice, and generally have not worked well.[70] But the ministry has also suffered from inadequate infrastructure. The report of the ministry on its first five years mentioned not only the problem of its small staff, but also the lack of resources and logistical problems. (Its offices were located in four different parts of Rome.) Furthermore, it continued to depend heavily on external collaboration from local agencies for so many areas of operation (e.g. data collection and evaluation), and this proved difficult and slow.[71]

Old practices die hard in Italian public administration. One study of policy-making in Rome referred to 'the many technical and bureaucratic hindrances of the Italian legal and administrative system, especially in the field of environmental protection, where many overlaps of interests and procedures occur'.[72] Typical of Italian government, such bureaucratic lethargy (sometimes called *lentocrazia* or 'slow-ocracy') has only been countered, and then only temporarily, when a committed and proactive minister like Ruffolo has expended unusual energy to push for policy change.

In his policy statement attached to his ministry's first report on the state of the environment in Italy in 1989, Ruffolo argued strongly for reinforcing and restructuring environmental administration and for a rethinking of inter-ministerial co-ordination to make 'government of the environment' more effective.[73] In that same year, a law was passed initiating a three-year programme that included provisions for better coordination, but it did not produce a radical departure.

One plan to rectify institutional deficiencies in the environmental area was to set up a national environmental agency, linked to a reorganization of the Ministry of the Environment, which was first proposed in 1990. But this was blocked by several other ministries, especially industry.[74] Eventually the National Agency for Environmental Protection (ANPA) was established in 1994. This decision may be seen as one outcome of general pressures for institutional reform (in particular the 1993 referendum), but it was also influenced by the creation of a European Environment Agency in Copenhagen.[75] Its functions include data collection, information diffusion and the promotion of research; making proposals on standards and promoting innovative technology; and cooperating with international bodies. With over 600 personnel envisaged, ANPA was placed under the supervision of the Ministry of the Environment but with independent authority.[76] Formally, this represented an important departure in environmental management; in reality, much depended on how it developed its role.

In the past, the Ministry of the Environment has depended heavily on other more established and larger ministries for expertise. For instance, the Ministry of Health has traditionally been supported by the work of the reputable Istituto Superiore di Sanita (ISS). The Ministry of Agriculture also benefits from some special agencies with an environmental dimension; while an important role is played by the National Agency for New Technologies, Energy and the Environment (ENEA), which is responsible to the Prime Minister's Office.[77] This dependence on other ministries' expertise was notably true in the environment ministry's production of the first national reports on the state of the environment in 1989 and 1992. As one way of escaping this institutional dependence, the environment ministry has resorted to external expertise in private organizations and especially universities.[78] The ministry has been quite active in furthering official support for environmental research, although this has entailed cooperation with the Ministry for Scientific Research. In general, Italy has been ahead of Greece and Spain with respect to research policy and programmes.[79]

The outcome for managing government machinery for EU purposes is rather more akin to the Greek than the Spanish case. While the Ministry of the Environment is represented in the EU Environment Council, it has only a small staff in its international affairs department. In fact, a key role in coordinating Italian policy is played by the Ministry of Foreign Affairs.[80]

The effects of EU membership on Italian administration have been altogether weaker than in the case of Spain. The new dynamism of Brussels in environmental affairs seems to have been one influence, probably a secondary one, in the establishment of a separate Ministry of the Environment in 1986. As a high official (secretary to the head of the minister's cabinet) explained, the creation of his ministry was 'a clearer sign, a consequence of the pulling activity of the EU'.[81] However, there was little indication that the need to coordinate policy for Brussels was having any moderating effect on inter-ministerial conflicts in the environment area.[82] Evidently, Rome showed less adaptability than Madrid in this respect.

The major exception, noted above, was the belated formation of an environment agency, in part arising from the creation of the European Environment Agency. This fits with evidence from interviews that the EU has been, and is regarded as, a major source of support for environmental research. As in Spain, this is much appreciated in scientific circles attached to the government. As the director of the environment section of the Istituto Superiore di Sanita (ISS) in Rome agreed, the EU has been important not so much for funds for research as for 'bringing together groups of scientists of different countries' with the opportunity 'for increasing experience, enlarging skills and for extending those things previously carried out with one's own internal budget'.[83]

Subnational government. There are three main levels of subnational government in Italy: the regional, the provincial, and the municipal. Historically the municipalities have had a wide-ranging interest in environmental questions, but their activities are constrained by a highly centralized system of public finance.[84] The provinces have some important responsibilities, particularly in the field of water pollution control. And the regions, established originally in 1970 but acquiring significant powers only in 1976, have come to play a significant part in environmental policy, with Lewanski reporting that some 30 per cent of legislative output in some regions are concerned with environmental matters.[85] Yet the dominant pattern at the subnational level is one of understaffed administration, underuse of the full range of policy instruments, and overlapping and partially conflicting responsibilities.

As to centre–periphery relations, the bias is rather more towards central administration than in the Spanish case. While Rome is responsible for such functions as policy frameworks, coordination, planning and safety standards, the regions' powers are uneven but as a whole include regional plans, data collection, emission control, and a variety of technical matters (depending on the environmental problem).[86] It remains to be seen what effect the granting of further autonomy to the regions (e.g. over taxation) in institutional reform plans will have in the environmental area. Vertical coordination has not generally worked well, either in terms of formal structures or in practice. The then shadow minister for environmental affairs remarked: 'the problem is that the Italian regions operate at very different speeds: some respond well, others don't respond at all; and the mechanism for co-operation is not very efficient'.[87]

The Netherlands

Central government. Environmental protection first became institutionalized within a ministry in 1971, in a directorate-general in the Ministry for Public Health and Environmental Quality.[88] Prior to that date, a Public Health Inspectorate had been established in the Ministry of Social Affairs and Public Health. Responsibility for physical planning, however, was vested in the Ministry of Housing and Physical Planning. In 1982, the two functions of pollution control and physical planning were brought together in the Ministry of Housing, Physical Planning and the Environment (VROM).[89] This pattern of institutional development thus nicely captures the evolution of a certain pattern of thinking about environmental policy. First seen primarily as an issue of public health, where the emphasis is upon the control of the effects of pollution, the understanding shifts to understanding how the causes of the problem might be addressed through better planning.

By 1982, therefore, the basic institutional pattern was that VROM had responsibility for four main functions: housing, physical planning, public buildings, and the environment. In 1982 there were between 500 and 600 people working in the environmental protection section; by the early 1990s there were about 1,100 people.

Alongside this growth in numbers, there have been other changes in the ministry. For example, although officials when interviewed in early March 1993 were rather coy about the subject, it was difficult not to see the then plush new ministerial building close by the main railway station in The Hague (instead of, as formerly, in Leidschendam in the suburbs) as anything other than a symbol of the growing importance of environmental policy in the Netherlands.

At the same time, important environmental functions are performed outside VROM, of which nature protection (in the Ministry of Agriculture) is one, and water pollution control located in a directorate-general in the Rijkswaterstaat, an operational arm of the Ministry of Transport and Public Works, is another. The Rijkswaterstaat is particularly important, as it is responsible for general management of the Dutch canal system and waterways, in terms of both quantity and quality. Given the historic importance of waterways in the Netherlands, it would be surprising if a relatively junior ministry like the VROM, which only during the 1980s assumed an important position in government, could challenge the Rijkwaterstaat for control of water pollution. Although some observers have noted that the Ministry of Transport and Public Works has a higher status in the Dutch environmental policy community than VROM,[90] our interview evidence suggested that the relationship between VROM and the Rijkswaterstaat did not appear to be antagonistic.[91] However, there is a formal covenant between the two bodies on water quality policy, an interesting example of adapting the policy instrument of the voluntary agreements to the cause of environmental coordination when it is usually employed between governments and private actors.

VROM does not always see eye to eye with the agricultural ministry, which for most of the century has been under the control of the Christian parties. As with most West European agricultural ministries, the Dutch minister is powerful and has adopted a more conservative view of exact details of pesticide regulation (for which it has primary competence, even though it is groundwater that is mainly polluted) than the VROM. In a typically Dutch way, however, the VROM has sought to cultivate links with farmers and the chemical organizations as part of its target groups.[92]

There has been much discussion in the Netherlands about the organization of environmental policy in central government, and various suggestions have been made for reforming its structure. Some think that the environment ministry should be merged with the traffic and water ministry and some that the environment ministry should be made very small, on the lines of a coordinating unit, with the various specialist functions dispersed to other ministries such as agriculture. As we have already noted, issues of administrative structure were left to one side in the development of the National Environmental Policy Plan, in order to concentrate on issues of policy substance.

Because the National Environmental Policy Plan was a joint product of the environment, economics, agriculture and transport ministries, there was a commitment to following up its implementation through a steering committee at the level of the director-generals in each ministry.[93] In addition, there is a joint coordinating body between agriculture and environment on the issue of manure policy, as an alternative to establishing a formalized covenant between the two bodies. With other ministries there are also formalized working relationships. Moreover, there is a unit in the environment ministry with responsibility for the issues that arise in collaboration with other ministries, and it has a specialized interest in both environmental impact assessment and social policy instruments, especially education and communication. There is also a formal reporting structure on the extent to which other ministries have achieved the targets contained in the National Environmental Policy Plan.

During the period of our study, the main body responsible for giving policy advice was the Dutch Central Council on Environmental Issues.[94] This emerged from the bringing together in 1981 of the Temporary Central Council for Environmental Quality, first established in March 1974, and the Temporary Council for Air Improvement, which had been set up in 1970 and became operational in 1972.[95] The Central Council was set up in such a way that it is intended to be broadly representative, including members from industry, employees, and nongovernmental organizations. However, with the development of the idea of the internalization of responsibility and the identification of target groups by the ministry, it appears to have lost its influence in recent years.

An important body within the system of specialist advice is the Government Institute for Public Health and Environmental Quality.[96] This was the body that in 1989 published the report known as *Concern for Tomorrow*, which provided much of the background documentation for the National Environmental Policy Plan.[97] It sought to take evidence about existing levels of environmental pollution and damage and to project them forward in order to ascertain what would occur without adequate policy response. For example, it turned out to be important in the public discussion of the National Environmental Policy Plan that *Concern for Tomorrow* had claimed that half of Dutch woodland had suffered damage from acidification.[98] Although in many ways the report went beyond what could strictly be shown in scientific terms, since the prediction of environmental trends over a period of twenty years is as much of an art as a science, it was clearly important as an example of what has been called 'trans-science'.[99]

An interesting and distinctive feature of the Dutch organization of technical advice stems from the close links between government and the universities through the existence of environmental study centres.[100] When they were founded between 1970 and 1975, the idea of the environmental studies centres was to bring together different disciplinary specialists to work on problems of environmental management. According to Copius Peereboom and Bouwer, at least half the members of such study centres in the mid-1980s were undertaking research paid for by either the government or government organizations, a higher ratio than is found in other departments.[101] Such centres therefore provide a more institutionalized expression of environmental policy-relevant research than is found in most other countries.

Subnational government. The Netherlands is a unitary state with three main levels of government: national, provincial, and municipal. There is not the same tradition and culture of local autonomy that one finds in Germany; for example, municipal mayors are appointed by central government rather than being elected by municipal citizens, and there is a high dependence upon centrally raised revenue. However, there is an interesting pattern of water resource management under the independent and self-financing water boards. Both policy development and its implementation therefore depend upon a complex interaction among various institutional actors.

The water boards date back to the Middle Ages, when peasants and landholders carried out the drainage and reclamation of land.[102] They are run by those who use water resources, for purposes of both abstraction and discharge. In 1970 the Netherlands had more than 800 water boards, some of them very small. Many were merged, so that today just twenty-seven water boards carry out water quality management.

As recipients of a large volume of transboundary pollution carried down the Rhine and the Meuse, the Dutch for many years were not interested in devoting an enormous quantity of resources to water clean-up. In the postwar period more attention began to be paid to the issue, though it was not until 1970 that the permitting of discharges on a comprehensive basis was introduced in the Surface Waters Pollution Act. The Act also distinguished between provincial waters, to be managed by the provinces and the water boards, and the state waters, to be managed by the Rijkswaterstaat.

The provinces are important in the implementation of pollution control standards and in drawing up plans for environmental protection. In relation to water pollution management, therefore, there is a complex relationship between province and water board. In some cases, for example Gelderland, it is the province that sets the water quality standards and also the quantity levels, but it is the water boards that set the emission levels that will be necessary to meet those standards.

The provinces play a more central role in the regulation of soil protection, the permitting of chemical and other waste treatment facilities, the control of air pollution, and the setting of noise standards. Since inspection is a provincial responsibility, the provinces also play an important role in implementing the policy of internalizing environmental responsibility among key actors, particularly the firms whose pollution is regulated.

Although the municipalities are not traditionally strong in the Netherlands, it is clear that they are anxious to play a distinctive role. One striking example of how they can use such freedom of manoeuvre as they have is provided by the Port Authority of the city of Rotterdam, which some years ago implemented a programme to persuade German polluting firms on the Rhine voluntarily to reduce their polluting discharges.[103] The first of these voluntary agreements or covenants dates from 1991 and the second from 1995 running to the year 2000. Some observers have expressed the view that originally the initiative was not looked upon favourably by the central government ministries in the Netherlands.

Perhaps more importantly, it has been argued that, though there has been investment on the part of the companies discharging into the Rhine, not all the clean-up can be ascribed to the effectiveness of the action undertaken by the Rotterdam Port Authority. For example, it seems clear that German companies reduced their cadmium discharges as a result of German legislation,[104] and it can also be argued that it is too easy to infer causation from the engagement of the Dutch subnational authorities.[105] On the other hand, it is clear that the German companies concerned did not originally welcome the Rotterdam intervention, and according to one Dutch observer did not even give them a cup of coffee.[106]

This extensive reliance upon the instrument of voluntary agreements in co-ordinating activity among various bodies is well illustrated in the stimulus given to renewable energy. Under a covenant, the central government, the provincial authorities, and the electricity producers have agreed to meet a certain proportion of the country's needs from renewable sources and each province has to make its own contribution to this target.[107] In one particular instance, the municipality of Eemsmond in Groningen won the contract for the location of subsidized wind farms on the north-west coast of the country, having overcome local opposition. In this sort of instance, the system of voluntary agreements operates as a framework within which the various actors can converge on innovative solutions to environmental problems within overlapping spheres of interest.

United Kingdom

Central government. For the period with which we are concerned, the main ministry responsible for environmental protection and pollution control was the Department of the Environment. This was the successor to a number of bodies concerned with environmental issues, going back to the Local Government Board of the nineteenth century. Established in 1871, the Local Government Board had the task of overseeing local authorities with the responsibility for sanitation and slum clearance in English cities.[108] These health-related functions were consolidated in 1919 with the transformation of the Local Government Board into the Ministry of Health, the association of health and housing in the same ministry being 'a hangover from Victorian sanitarianism'.[109] With the establishment of the National Health Service in 1948, the administration of health care ceased to be a matter of liaising with primarily local organizations and became instead a matter of administering a nationally controlled and funded system of health care. The gap between the local government wing of the department's work and the health wing became increasingly wide, and in January 1951 the ministry was split into two component parts, with the local government functions, including the responsibility for pollution control, going to the newly created Ministry of Local Government and Planning, renamed the Ministry of Housing and Local Government on the Conservative's accession to power later the same year.[110]

The situation remained stable until Edward Heath came to power as prime minister in 1970. Keenly interested in questions to do with the machinery of government, and responding to the wave of public concern about environmental issues at the time, he transformed the Ministry of Housing and Local Government into the Department of the Environment (DoE). This brought together the Ministry of Housing and Local Government and the Ministry of Transport, the theory being that the institutional brigading of the various functions contained within these ministries would make possible a more comprehensive assessment of the needs of the environment. In 1974, with the accession of a Labour government, this mega-ministry was broken up, and the transport functions were given their own ministry again. The incoming Labour government of 1997 completed the circle, by once more linking transport and environment in a new Department of Environment, Transport and the Regions, headed by the deputy prime minister.

Despite its name, the department created by Edward Heath was never a ministry whose sole, or even primary, purpose was the protection of the environment. With its continuing responsibilities for local government, much of its work was connected with local government finance, a function that became particularly important in the later 1980s with the politically mismanaged reform of local government finance introduced under Mrs Thatcher.[111] Indeed, between 1974 and 1987 the DoE did not even have departmental responsibility for the national air pollution inspectorate. Nevertheless, the department did have responsibility both for pollution control and for nature and countryside protection, and some of the junior ministers, i.e. below the level of the secretary of state, have always been assigned special responsibility for the functions of environmental protection.

The low concentration of environmental functions in the DoE was not challenged by successive secretaries of state. The Thatcher government was throughout most of its long period of office hostile to, or at best uninterested in, what may be regarded as the modern constellation of environmental problems: acid precipitation, ozone depletion, pollution of the seas, river quality, and waste management.[112] Secretaries of state like Michael Heseltine, Kenneth Baker, and Nicholas Ridley either displayed an interest in other aspects of the department's work, for example urban renewal in the case of Heseltine, or demonstrated hostility to the growing consciousness of environmental problems, as in the case of Ridley. William Waldegrave as a junior minister was able to make some progress on key environmental issues such as acid precipitation,[113] but his secondary position obviously precluded him from being able to take the lead on questions of ministerial organization. Christopher Patten showed a genuine interest in issues of environmental protection and pollution, but during his brief term of office his attention was absorbed by the controversy surrounding the community charge, leaving him little opportunity to focus consistently on environmental questions.

The Department of Environment shared its responsibilities for environment functions with four other departments of state: the Ministry of Agriculture, Fisheries, and Food, the Department of Transport, the Scottish Office, and the Northern Ireland Office. The Ministry of Agriculture, Fisheries, and Food had pollution control responsibilities in respect of some marine pollution, and the Department of Transport had responsibility for vehicle emissions control. The two territorial ministries were, and still are, responsible for environmental matters within the areas for which they are responsible. Despite this rather untidy set of relationships, the political focus of pollution control policy was centred within the Department of the Environment.

A major change in the administration of environmental policy took place with the creation of the Environment Agency, formally established in April 1996. From that date, primary operational, as distinct from policy, responsibility for environmental protection has rested with the Environment Agency (in Scotland the Scottish Environment Protection Agency). This comprises a board appointed by the government to implement policy. In England and Wales the new agency brings together two bodies: Her Majesty's Inspectorate of Pollution (HMIP) and the National Rivers Authority (NRA), as well as some inspectors from local authorities concerned with waste management.

HMIP had been created on 1 April 1987 and brought together specialized inspectorates within the Department of the Environment responsible for air pollution (which, by a quirk of administrative history, had been the responsibility of the Department of Employment since 1974), radiochemicals, hazardous waste, and water quality. HMIP had administrative responsibility for the setting of standards in the fields for which it was responsible. Traditionally HMIP and its precursor, the Alkali

Inspectorate, has been small: around the time of its creation it had some 230–50 inspectors; in 1993/4 it had about 450, but it was due to reduce these numbers, under public-sector so-called 'efficiency savings', to some 434. The consequence of these small numbers is that site visits were—and still are—relatively infrequent, even to complex plants. The single largest category of visit in recent years has entailed the pre-licensing discussions with operators.

By contrast with HMIP, the NRA was a non-departmental public body, meaning that it operated at arms' length from the ministry. It was created in 1989 in the wake of the privatization of the previously public Regional Water Authorities. The NRA had its own board, made up of part-time members, as well as a full-time director-general. At its inception it had some 7,000 staff, and so was significantly larger than HMIP. In bringing HMIP and the NRA together into one body, the intention was to create the organizational structure needed to operate integrated pollution control, aided as well by the transfer of some functions from local authority waste regulatory authorities.[114]

Another non-departmental public body with some environmental responsibility is the Health and Safety Commission, the prime responsibility of which is worker health and safety, but with obligations regarding residual emissions affecting the public. It works through an executive, and has responsibility for such matters as the control of pesticides and the labelling of hazardous chemicals.

The Royal Commission on Environmental Pollution (RCEP) is a long-standing part of the environmental policy advice system. The original decision to set it up was made under the Labour government in 1969. The late Anthony Crosland was made secretary of state for local government and regional planning, with an urgent remit to improve the machinery for dealing with problems of pollution. Along with a new unit within the department, the Central Scientific Unit on Pollution, it was decided to establish the Royal Commission on Environmental Pollution as a standing body capable of giving independent scientific and policy advice to government.[115] In formal terms, its responsibilities are defined as follows:

to advise on matters both national and international, concerning the pollution of the environment; on the adequacy of research in this field; and the future possibilities of danger to the environment.[116]

In practice, it has always taken a wide view of its responsibilities, as captured in the opening of its first report: 'We are authorised to enquire into any matters on which we think advice is needed.'[117]

To date, the RCEP has produced nineteen reports, covering not only problems of pollution (air and water pollution, waste management, lead in the environment) but also questions of administrative organization (it was behind the establishment of HMIP) and policy principles and approaches.

In addition to the RCEP, governments have drawn in scientific experts in a variety of ways to provide advice on specific issues. Examples of such bodies include the Expert Panel on Air Quality Standards and the Quality of Urban Air Review Group. These bodies have the function of identifying problems and advising on appropriate responses. Two particularly important advisory bodies are the Government Panel on Sustainable Development and the Advisory Committee on Business and the Environment. Both have wide-ranging remits to advise on the development of policies for sustainable development, and in its first report, for example, the former advocated a substantial shift in taxation away from labour and towards taxes on pollution and resource use.

Other parts of the 'discursive space' for the discussion of environmental policy are provided by parliamentary committees. Although such committees do not have legislative power, their reports can be influential and can lead to changes in policy. Three committees in particular have been important: the House of Lords Committee on Science and Technology, the Environment Sub-Committee of the House of Lords Committee on the European Committee, and the House of Commons Select Committee on the Environment.

Subnational government. Local authorities too have important pollution control functions. In Britain there are two broad types of local authority: those responsible for large urban areas, and those responsible for the rest of the country. In the large urban areas metropolitan districts have a full range of local authority functions, although no one authority covers more than a fraction of the conurbation in which it is located. (For example, London has thirty-two districts, with no government for London as a whole.) In the non-metropolitan areas there are typically two layers of government (although the structure is currently under review): county councils have been responsible for waste disposal policy, and district councils for some aspects of air pollution policy, with both operating within the framework of national legislation and standards.

Local authorities are creatures of statute in the UK and therefore do not enjoy constitutional autonomy. During the 1980s, Conservative governments under Margaret Thatcher sought both to limit their powers and to control their spending. A particularly important theme in these years was the attempt to turn local authorities from service providers into service regulators. This distinction was especially important in the field of waste disposal, where the functions of managing waste disposal were separated from those of regulating the standards of waste disposal.

Despite their lack of powers, a number of UK local authorities have sought to promote environmental protection, even though their resources are limited. Local Agenda 21 emerging from the Rio Conference has been a particularly important galvanizing influence, and many local authorities have sought to set high standards in the fields of recycling, alternatives to car use, and energy efficiency.

CONCLUSIONS

From the detailed description of forms of policy organization, and as we sought to establish in the earlier comparative discussion, there is no clear pattern of institutional development that emerges in our six cases. The manner in which environmental policy is institutionalized within the sample of six cannot be detached from the general institutional arrangements of each country.

The most obvious institutional variables in this respect are the constitutional ones. Thus, the pattern of institutionalization in a country like Germany is conditional upon the constitutional framework which in general secures a decentralization of power and considerable autonomy for subnational authorities. To be sure, the constitutional framework is not immutable, as the example of the national powers in air pollution legislation goes to show in Germany, but it does impose constraints on the speed and form of organizational development. The rapid, if interesting, experiments that were such a marked feature of the UK's experience depended upon British governments having the comparative freedom to ordain administrative changes very easily owing to the country's flexible constitition and the absence of a need to appease party sensibilities within a government resting on coalitions.

The variety in the way in which environmental policy is institutionalized has also to be placed in the context of the recognition that similar problems of institutional design are present in all systems, the most conspicuous of which is how to ensure that environmental concerns are diffused around all organizations whose policies have environmental implications and not just those parts of the machinery of government that have primary responsibility for environmental policy. The discussion of this problem, conceived as an issue in the organization of government, has been most intensive in Germany. To some extent, what is the most striking feature of the comparative experience is that the most successful way of resolving the dilemma, the solution adopted in the Netherlands, depends upon recasting the problem not as one about administrative organization, raising as it does all the issues about turf disputes between different departments, but as one about policy process. Whether this is an adaptable lesson on the part of other countries is an open question.

There are two respects in which there appears to be a clear distinction between northern and southern countries. The first is in the way that all the northern countries have sought to institutionalize policy advice in a body that was both expert and independent of government. This contrast should not be overdrawn, given the way in which the Central Council in the Netherlands seems to have declined in importance since the introduction of the National Environmental Policy Plan. But it may be symptomatic of the extent to which the southern countries are importers of policy concepts rather than possessors of the machinery to develop them.

The second noticeable contrast is the way in which a concentrated environmental policy function was institutionalized earlier in the northern countries than it was in the southern ones, if we allow that the German interior ministry contained a significant concentration of environmental functions before 1986. Essentially, the northern countries carved out environmental policy as a separate administrative sphere in the later 1960s and early 1970s. In the case of the southern countries, similar developments had to wait until the 1980s—or in the case of Spain the 1990s.

The national differences of administrative evolution appear to be fairly stable over time. The most obvious explanation for this is bureaucratic inertia, combined with an interest among ministers in maintaining their turf. It might have been reasonable to suppose that the coalition governments of the Netherlands and Germany would have revealed more stable patterns than that of the UK, since complex negotiations over portfolio allocations between hard-bargaining coalition partners might have the effect of stabilizing ministerial responsibilities. But the coalitional factor cannot explain the stability of the British case, where ministerial reshuffles are commonplace and the prime minister has the freedom to reorganize the machinery of government, often for purposes unrelated to functional requirements. This three-country comparison thus suggests that bureaucratic inertia is the primary cause of resistance to change, given that domestic or party politics has failed to push for change.

The three southern member states of Greece, Italy, and Spain have all created their formal environmental administrations during the 1980s, although, as elsewhere, sub-units responsible for environmental matters existed previously under other ministries. In none of these cases can we speak of an environmental crisis prompting an abrupt change in bureaucratic structures. The Chernobyl crisis certainly had a major impact on Italy, but plans were already completed for establishing the new Ministry of the Environment in July 1986 (by a law passed early 1984). Environmental administration evolved, and if there was any outside stimulus to buttress environmental policy that was provided by a combination of pressure from a more proactive European Union in this area as well as by growing public awareness.

The outcome is that Greece, Italy, and Spain present rather different models of environmental administration. Italy is the only one to have had an environmental ministry with some concentration of functions, although Spain has very recently moved in this direction. In Greece and Spain, the environment is combined with public works and one other portfolio (respectively, physical planning and transport), but the difference is the symbolic one of including 'environment' in the ministerial title (Greece) or not (Spain—until 1993). Common to them all, broadly speaking, is the considerable fragmentation of environmental functions between a range of ministries. And bureaucratic inertia has been as powerful as in the north if not more so, though rather less in Spain than the other two southern countries.

NOTES TO CHAPTER 6

1. For good discussions of the various causes and consequences of administrative reorganization, see P. Szanton (ed.), *Federal Reorganization: What Have We Learned?* (Chatham NJ: Chatham House, 1981); C. Pollitt, *Manipulating the Machine* (London: Allen & Unwin, 1987).

2. See A. Weale, *The New Politics of Pollution* (Manchester and New York: Manchester University Press, 1992), pp. 12–15.
3. F. L. Lopez Bustos, *La Organizacion Administrativa del Medio Ambiente* (Madrid: Civitas, 1992), pp. 114–21.
4. E. Rehbinder and R. Stewart, *Environmental Protection Policy* (Berlin: Walter de Gruyter, 1985), pp. 9 ff. and 232.
5. For further discussion and a listing of the functions, see A. Weale, G. Pridham, A. Williams, and M. Porter, 'Environmental Administration in Six European States: Secular Convergence or National Distinctiveness?' *Public Administration*, 74:2 (1996), pp. 255–74, esp. 260–2.
6. E. Tukey, *Exploratory Data Analysis* (Reading, Mass.: Addison-Wesley, 1977), pp. 363–400.
7. T. O'Riordan and A. Weale, 'Administrative Reorganization and Policy Change: The Case of Her Majesty's Inspectorate of Pollution', *Public Administration*, 67:3 (1989), pp. 277–94.
8. P. Christofilopoulou, 'Professionalism and Public Policy Making in Greece: The Influence of Engineers in the Local Government Reforms', *Public Administration*, 70:1 (1992), pp. 99–118, at 109–10.
9. See 'Major's Greening Starts Rush towards Environment Agency', *ENDS Report*, 198 (1991), p. 13.; A. Weale, 'Grinding Slow and Grinding Sure? The Making of the Environment Agency', *Environmental Management and Health*, 7:2 (1996), pp. 40–3.
10. E. Ashby and M. Anderson, *The Politics of Clean Air* (Oxford: Clarendon Press, 1981), pp. 37–43.
11. E. Müller, *Innenwelt der Umweltpolitik* (Opladen: Westdeutscher Verlag, 1986), p. 56.
12. See A. Weale, T. O'Riordan, and L. Kramme, *Controlling Pollution in the Round* (London: Anglo-German Foundation, 1991), pp. 125–6 and *passim.* for further details
13. Interview by Louise Kramme with Dr Laufs, member of the parliamentary party group section on the environment, 26 November 1987.
14. H. Pehle and A.-I. Jansen, 'Germany: The Engine in European Environmental Policy?', in K. Hanf and A.-I. Jansen (eds.), *Governance and Environment in Western Europe* (Harlow: Addison Wesley Longman, 1998), pp. 82–109 at 95–6.
15. See the interesting semi-autobiographical address given to the conference on Environment and Economic Ethics organized jointly by the Deutschen Netzwerks Wirtschaftsethik EBEN and the Wissenschaftlichen Kommission 'Umweltwirtschaft' des Verbandes der Hochschuellrer für Betriebswirtschaft (German Economic Ethics Network and the Scientific Committee on Environmental Economics of the Association of Teachers of Business Economics), 15 November 1996, and reprinted as K. Töpfer, 'Sustainable Development im Spannungsfeld von internationaler Herausforderung und nationalen Handlungsmöglichkeiten', in H. Steinmann and G. R. Wagner (eds.), *Umwelt und Wirtschaftsethik* (Stuttgart: Schäffer-Poeschel Verlag, 1998), pp. 93–103.
16. See Ch. 8.
17. Interviews at the Federal Environmental Office, Berlin, 10–14 July 1995.
18. Interviews at the Environment Ministry, Bonn, 23–4 June 1993.
19. Rat von Sachverständigen für Umweltfragen (SRU).
20. Pehle and Jansen, 'Germany', pp. 90–1, citing M. T. Hatch, 'The Politics of Global Warming in Germany', *Environmental Politics*, 4:3 (1995), pp. 415–40.

21. C. Lees, '*Red–Green' Coalitions in the Federal Republic of Germany: Models of Formation and Maintenance*, Ph.D. thesis (University of Birmingham, 1998), p. 98.
22. Müller, *Innenwelt der Umweltpolitik*, p. 73.
23. C. A. Vlassopoulou, *La Politique de l'environnement: le cas de la pollution atmospherique à Athenes*, Ph.D. thesis (University of Picardy, 1991), p. 31.
24. OECD, *Environmental Policies in Greece* (Paris: OECD, 1983), p. 13.
25. Hellenic Society for the Protection of the Environment and the Cultural Heritage, *The State of the Greek Environment* (Athens, 1991), p. 26.
26. Interview with Ioannis Vournas, Ministry of the Environment, Athens, November 1992.
27. Vlassopoulou, *La Politique de l'environnement*, pp. 57–61.
28. Ibid. 120–21.
29. G. Pridham, S. Verney, and D. Konstadakopulos, 'Environmental Policy in Greece: Evolution, Structures and Process', *Environmental Politics*, 4:2 (1995), pp. 244–70 at 253–4.
30. Ibid. 254.
31. Interview with Georgia Valaoras, head of WWF office, Athens, December 1992.
32. Vlassopoulou, *La Politique de l'environnement*, pp. 68–70.
33. Interview with Vournas, November 1992.
34. Interview with Vournas, March 1995.
35. *Sunday Times*, 14 Oct. 1990.
36. Interview with Vournas, March 1995.
37. Interview with Athena Mourmouris, Ministry of the Environment, Athens, November 1992.
38. Ibid.
39. OECD, *Environmental Policies in Greece*, p. 52.
40. Interview with Vournas, November 1992.
41. Interview with Dimitra Katochianou, Centre of Planning and Economic Research (KEPE), Athens, November 1992.
42. Interview with Vournas, November 1992.
43. C. Spanou, 'Greece: Administrative Symbols and Policy Realities', in K. Hanf and A.-I. Jansen (eds.), *Governance and Environment in Western Europe* (Harlow: Addison Wesley Longman, 1998), pp. 110–30 at 120.
44. Spanou, 'Greece', pp. 120–1.
45. Pridham, Verney and Konstadakopulos, 'Environmental Policy in Greece', p. 255.
46. Interview with Domingo Jimenez Beltran, environmental policy directorate, Ministry of Public Works, Madrid, April 1994.
47. Lopez Bustos, *La Organizacion Administrativa del Medio Ambiente*, pp. 45–6.
48. Interview with Luis Mas, environmental policy directorate, Ministry of Public Works, Madrid, October 1992.
49. Commission of the European Community, DG XI, *Administrative Structures for Environmental Management in the European Community* (Brussels: Commission of the European Community, 1993), pp. 69–71.
50. Lopez Bustos, *La Organizacion Administrativa del Medio Ambiente*, pp. 50–1.
51. Ibid. 49.
52. Commission of the European Community, *Administrative Structures*, p. 74.
53. Interview with Francisco Mingot, head of environment institute, CIEMAT, Madrid, October 1992.

54. Interview with Beltran, April 1994.
55. Interview with Humberto Da Cruz, Friends of the Earth, Madrid, October 1992.
56. Interview with Teresa Mosquete, environmental policy directorate, Ministry of Public Works, Madrid, October 1992.
57. Lopez Bustos, *La Organizacion Administrativa del Medio Ambiente*, pp. 37–8.
58. Interview with Anna Fresno, Ministry of Health, Madrid, October 1992.
59. G. Pridham, 'The Environmental Policy Process and Scientific Expertise in Southern Europe', paper for the Centre for Mediterranean Studies conference, Bristol University, December 1994, p. 39.
60. Interview with Mingot, October 1992.
61. M. Estevan, *Implicaciones Economicas de la Proteccion Ambiental de la CEE: Repercusiones en España* (Madrid: Ministerio de Economia, 1991), p. 519.
62. Commission of the European Community, *Administrative Structures*, p. 71.
63. Ibid. 71–2.
64. Ibid. 73.
65. Interview with Jose Diaz Lazaro, director-general of EMGRISA (industrial waste disposal company), Madrid, April 1994.
66. D. Hine, *Governing Italy: The Politics of Bargained Pluralism* (Oxford: Clarendon Press, 1993), p. 232.
67. A. Capria, 'Formulation and Implementation of Environmental Policy in Italy', paper for 12th. International Congress on Social Policy, Paris, October 1991, pp. 27–8.
68. Capria, 'Formulation and Implementation', p. 17.
69. Commission of the European Community, *Administrative Structures*, pp. 117–18.
70. Capria, 'Formulation and Implementation', pp. 26 ff.
71. Ministero dell'Ambiente, *Bilancio di un Quinquennio di Politiche Ambientali* (Rome: Ministero dell'Ambiente, 1992), pp. 74–5.
72. A. Bianchi, 'Environmental Policy' in F. Francioni (ed.), *Italy and EC Membership Evaluated* (London: Pinter, 1992), pp. 71–105 at 88.
73. Ministero dell'Ambiente, *Nota Aggiunta del Ministro Giogio Ruffolo* (Rome, 1989), pp. 43–4.
74. Ministero dell'Ambiente, *Bilancio di un Quinquennio*, p. 74.
75. E. Croci, M. Frey, and A. Molocchi, *Agenzie e Governo dell'Ambiente* (Milan: Franco Angeli, 1994).
76. Ibid. 277–80.
77. Commission of the European Community, *Administrative Structures*, p. 119.
78. Interview with Angelo Carere, Istituto Superiore di Sanita, Rome, May 1992.
79. Pridham, 'Environmental Policy Process', p. 16.
80. Commission of the European Community, *Administrative Structures*, p. 123.
81. Interview with Oliviero Mantanaro, Ministry of the Environment, Rome, May 1992.
82. Interview with Valeria Rizzo, Ministry of the Environment, Rome, May 1992.
83. Interview with Carere, May 1992.
84. See R. Lewanski, 'Italy: Environmental Policy in a Fragmented State', in K. Hanf and A.-I. Jansen (eds.), *Governance and Environment in Western Europe* (Harlow: Addison Wesley Longman, 1998), pp. 131–51 at 144.
85. Ibid. 141–2.
86. Commission of the European Community, *Administrative Structures*, pp. 119–20.

87. Interview with Chicco Testa, Shadow Minister of the Environment, PDS, Rome, May 1992.
88. See H. T. A. Bressers and L. A. Plettenburg, 'The Netherlands', in M. Jänicke and H. Weidner (eds.), *National Environmental Policies: A Comparative Study of Capacity-Building* (Berlin: Springer Verlag, 1997), pp. 109–31 at 113; D. Liefferink, 'The Netherlands: A Net Exporter of Environmental Policy Concepts', in M. S. Andersen and D. Liefferink (eds.), *European Environmental Policy: The Pioneers* (Manchester and New York: Manchester University Press, 1997) pp. 210–50, at 213. There are various ways of translating the name of the ministry Volksgezondheid en Milieuhygiëne. Literally, it would be 'environmental hygiene' or 'cleanliness'. Some use this literal translation. Some use 'health' or 'protection'. We have chose 'environmental quality' as that keeps the emphasis on the state of the environment, but seems the closest and most natural functional equivalent in English.
89. Ministrie van Volkshuisvesting, Ruimtelijke Ordening en Milieubeheer.
90. M. S. Andersen, *Governance by Green Taxes: Making Pollution Prevention Pay* (Manchester and New York: Manchester University Press, 1994), p. 149.
91. Interviews conducted in VROM and the Rijkswaterstaat, 10–12 March 1993.
92. P. Hurst, 'Pesticide Reduction Programs in Denmark, the Netherlands, and Sweden', *International Environmental Affairs*, 4:3 (1992), p. 246.
93. Interviews, VROM, 10–12 March 1993.
94. Centrale Raad voor de Milieuhygiëne.
95. Personal communication, Maarten Hajer.
96. Rijksinstituut voor Volksgezondheid en Milieuhygiene.
97. Rijksinstitut voor Volsgezondheid and Milieuhygiene, *Zorgen voor Morgen* (Alphen aan den Rijn: Samson H. D. Tjeenk Willink, 1989).
98. Rijksinstitut, *Zorgen*, p. 112.
99. For the concept of 'trans-science' see A. Weinberg, 'Science and Trans-Science', *Minerva* 10:2 (1972), pp. 209–22; cited and discussed in R. Williams, 'Innovation and the Political Context of Technical Advice', in L. Roberts and A. Weale (eds.), *Innovation and Environmental Risk* (London and New York: Belhaven, 1991), pp. 124–37.
100. See J. W. Copius Peereboom and K. Bouwer, 'Environmental Science "Milieukunde" in the Netherlands: A Review', *The Science of the Total Environment*, 129 (1993), pp. 157–70.
101. Ibid. 163.
102. This discussion relies upon Andersen, *Governance by Green Taxes*, pp. 149–54.
103. 'Good Neighbours', *Environmental News from the Netherlands*, 6 (1997), pp. 10–11 (available at http://www/minvrom.nl/enn).
104. W. M. Stgliani, P. R. Jaffé, and S. Anderberg, 'Heavy Metal Pollution in the Rhine Basin', *Environmental Science and Technology*, 27:5 (1993), pp. 786–93, suggest that this may have more to do with stringent national BAT policies, particularly in Germany, and the fact that of its own accord industry began to stop dumping cadmium and instead started using it as a side-product.
105. T. Bernauer and P. Moser, 'Reducing Pollution of the River Rhine: The Influence of International Cooperation', *Journal of Environment and Development*, 5:4 (1996), pp. 389–415. Quite apart from the point in the text, other accounts suggest a more favourable experience from such multi-lateral institutional innovations; see e.g.

K. Wieriks and A. Schulte-Wülwer-Leidg, 'Integrated Water Management for the Rhine Basin: From Pollution Prevention to Ecosystem Improvement', *Natural Resources Forum*, 21:2 (1997), pp 147–56.

106. Presentation by Professor Jan M. van Dunné, 'The Rotterdam Rhine Inquiry Project 1984–1994', Conference on Governing Our Environment, Copenhagen, 17–18 November 1994.

107. 'New Skyline for Dutch Coast', *Environmental News from the Netherlands*, 1 (1997), p. 8.

108. R. C. K. Ensor, *England 1870–1914* (Oxford: Clarendon Press, 1936), pp. 23, 127.

109. C. Webster, *The Health Services since the War* (London: HMSO, 1988), p. 166.

110. Weale, O'Riordan and Kramme, *Controlling Pollution in the Round*, pp. 52–3.

111. For the sorry story of the 'poll tax', see D. Butler, A. Adonis, and T. Travers, *Failure in British Government* (Oxford: Oxford University Press, 1994).

112. M. A. Hajer, *The Politics of Environmental Discourse: Ecological Modernization and the Policy Process* (Oxford: Clarendon Press, 1995), ch. 4; Weale, *The New Politics of Pollution*, ch. 3.

113. Ibid. 124, 166.

114. For details on the history behind the creation of the Environment Agency, see A. Weale, 'Environmental Regulation and Administrative Reform in Britain', in G. Majone, *Regulating Europe* (London and New York: Routledge, 1996), pp. 106–30, esp. 110–25.

115. P. D. Lowe, 'The Royal Commission on Environmental Pollution', *Political Quarterly*, 46 (1975), pp. 87–94 at 88.

116. Royal Commission on Environmental Pollution, *First Report* (London: HMSO, 1971), Cmnd. 4585, p. *iii*.

117. Ibid. 1.

7

Domestic Politics and Society-Related Variables

In the previous two chapters we have looked at the characteristic similarities and differences between environmental policy systems in our six countries. We have seen that the common issues, for example policy coordination and the integration of environmental considerations into a wide range of public policies, are played out in all the countries, but in quite distinct institutional and intellectual settings. State-related variables, in particular the historical legacy of national policy styles and principles, as well as the specific patterns of institutionalization, play a large role in determining the distinctive characteristics of each system.

In this chapter we turn to look at the society-related variables, or, in the case of political parties, a variable that mediates between state and society. Conceivably, it is in the domestic political environments that cross-national differences are most likely to be reinforced or reduced depending on the balance of actors, interests, and pressures. A central element of these domestic political systems is the role of electoral competition on the part of political parties vying with one another for votes from mass publics. Political parties and public opinion do not as such determine policy, but they may help to shape policy strategies and preferences over the environment on which governments act. Competition for votes by political parties means that they have to show some responsiveness to changes of popular opinion, so that if there is growing popular concern about an issue we should expect it to be taken up by political parties. However, the direction of influence should not be simply assumed to be one way. Political parties search for new issues and seek to sensitize mass publics to problems to which the parties purport to offer a solution. Public opinion is also important, not only for its direct effects in democracies through the ballot box but also in its indirect effects. The willingness of people to abide by norms and regulations for protecting the environment is obviously a significant element in the extent to which any policy strategy is feasible and successful.

Alongside the electoral system, there is also the system of pressure group politics, the functional representation that complements electoral representation. Although broad movements of public opinion, communicated by the media or influencing political parties, affect the salience of environmental issues on the policy agenda, detailed policy-making is typically the result of policy networks: collections of actors forming an element in the system of decision-making and linked by complex patterns of resource dependencies.[1]

In this chapter we look at two important groups of policy network actors: environmental pressure groups and economic interests. Environmental groups have a varied link with policy-makers. Their influence may well depend, for example, on whether their relationship with government is semi-institutionalized as 'insider', or more confrontational as an 'outside', pressure able to mobilize opinion. Different economic interests clearly play a vital part in formulating policy in view of the traditional predominance of economic development and the now current emphasis on integrating environmental concerns into the planning of production. How far have economic actors moved autonomously in this direction, allowing environmental policy-makers more scope for pursuing their policy aims?

The study of policy networks provides another dimension to our study. In addition to the simple balancing of the distribution of costs and benefits, to which any public policy issue give rise in the system of pressure group politics, environmental policy questions also gives rise to ideological and principled contestation about public policy. Sabatier has characterized the contest of interests and perspectives which thereby emerges as one between two 'advocacy coalitions', one stressing the protection of the environment through the imposition of high standards, and the other stressing economic feasibility.[2] Although this is played out in many forums and contexts, and although it is highly complex in any one national setting, we need to evaluate the balance of argument and interest that each of our national systems displays alongside the policy orientation that emerges from electoral competition. Clearly, the extent to which debate in a political system is able to transcend this dichotomy is a measure of the extent to which the discourse of ecological modernization has become established.

By focusing on the dynamics of these national environments, we can estimate the scope for variation in different actors' roles and influence among our six countries and hence explain the priority accorded the environment as a policy issue. Furthermore, we can explore the extent of convergence or divergence in environmental politics among member states of the EU. We thus have two main questions in mind: what factors make for a higher priority for environmental policy in our six countries? and, to what extent are these pressures convergent or divergent across the six? In this chapter we are essentially concerned with bottom-up pressures that help account for answers to these questions; in the following chapter we turn to top-down pressures emanating from the EU itself.

There is a sense, however, in which we cannot make an easy distinction between the internal domestic pressures and the external, international pressure, if we are really to retain our fundamental thesis that there is now in place a system of European environmental governance. Such a system of governance is unlikely to leave domestic political environments entirely untouched. Hence we are interested also in a third question: to what extent has there been a transformation of domestic political systems in the context of the Europeanization of environmental policy and politics?

Looking at the comparative patterns of political actors helps us to address in another context the central theoretical question in this study: are we to think of environmental policy in terms of policy sectors, policy problems creating their own distinctive politics, or in terms of national policy institutions and styles, varying from place to place with their own distinctive historical legacy? If policies really do determine politics, then it is in the pattern of domestic political dynamics that we should be most likely to see the effects at work. It also enables us to obtain a clearer picture of the role and place of national systems within the overarching system of European environmental governance.

PUBLIC OPINION

In studying public opinion on the environment, it is useful to bear in mind the distinctions that Almond identified many years ago between different elements of public opinion.[3] In particular, he distinguished between policy elites on the one side and the public on the other. However, among the public he further distinguished two categories: the general public and the attentive public. The attentive public comprised those members of the general public who are informed and interested about a particular set of policy issues. By contrast, the general public took only a sporadic interest in policy matters. Whereas we would expect to find the attentive public active in environmental groups and networks, this would not be true for the general public.

However, this does not mean that we can ignore the views of the general public. Policy is made within the context of a public opinion that, even though it is diffuse, may still act on policy-makers. In academic studies of public opinion and environmental attitudes, there has been great interest in the sources of attitudes towards environmental protection, looking at such factors as the degree to which demographic variables like class, age, and sex are correlated with different patterns of attitudes. Analysts have been particularly interested in the extent to which positive attitudes towards environmental protection are correlated with post-materialist values more generally, and thus with the extent to which environmental politics is indicative of a 'culture shift' within liberal democracies.[4]

In our discussion, however, we are more interested in the links between public opinion and the policy-making process within our six countries. Of course, this influence is neither direct nor mechanical. Politics in liberal democracies does not work by a simple translation of public opinion into public policy, in part because public opinion itself is diffuse and hard to measure. Public opinion is thus in many ways the most difficult contextual factor in the wider policy arena to assess, because it is less tangible than the other influences discussed in this chapter. Also, it tends to interact with or is dependent on them, and is not necessarily autonomous. Opinion poll patterns admittedly describe public inclinations in this or that country, and in doing so reveal cross-national differences. But this is no sure clue as to actual influence on the policy-making process. Still less can opinion polls capture the subtle but pervasive effects of deeply ingrained cultural orientations.

All the same, politicians take note of public moods and opinion trends to a greater or lesser degree. Politicians cannot afford to ignore public opinion, most obviously in periods when it is surging in a strongly pro-environment direction. The attention given to environmental issues in the 1990 Dublin European Council meeting after the 1989 European elections provides a clear example of this phenomenon. Although there is no clear and direct effect from public opinion on policy-making, it is part of the climate within which policy is made. This sensitivity to public opinion was also revealed in the responses of some of our interviewees. As one policy adviser in Athens put it, 'the sensitivity of the public has tremendously increased generally; and, now, under pressure of this sensitivity of the public, more or less, every type of government tries to conform with new legislation regarding the protection either of the environment or of health'.[5]

To explore these issues first in a cross-national context, we turn to the data gathered by Eurobarometer, a regular survey of public opinion in all member states financed by the Commission. These data are far from perfect. Consistent questions are not asked on a sufficiently regular basis to build up a reliable time-series, and question wording is often poor. There are also problems about the consistency with which the questions are asked across the member states, let alone with more subtle problems like the meaning of the term 'environment' itself in different cultural contexts. Despite these disadvantages, Eurobarometer does provide some quantitative evidence to set against other sources. Among the issues that can be addressed by looking at Eurobarometer, we pick out two main questions: what priority is accorded to environmental policy by European publics in contrast to other aspects of public policy? and what is the state of public opinion on patterns of European environmental governance? For neither of these questions does Eurobarometer have much evidence, but it does have some.

The issue of the priority to be accorded to environmental policy can be explored by looking at how much importance respondents give to environmental problems. One question sometimes asked has invited respondents to identify the most important problems facing Europe, so implicitly was asking people to rank the importance of the environment against other issues, such as the single currency; regional disparities; inflation; job initiatives; energy; agriculture; scientific research; aid to the Third World; consumer protection; dialogue between the USA and Russia; and the harmonization of qualifications. The test that this relative ranking requires is thus quite stringent as far as any one item is concerned, so that if there are changes over time we can be reasonably sure that they reflect significant changes in attitude. As Dalton has pointed out, in commenting on these data, by the mid-1970s most Europeans were aleady ranking the environment above many other public policy issues in importance.[6]

Figure 7.1 gives the results for our six countries for the two years 1974 and 1993 (1993 only, in the case of Spain and Greece), thus taking responses from the earliest stages of environmental policy development and comparing them with the 1990s. The results, both over time and across countries, are striking. Taking

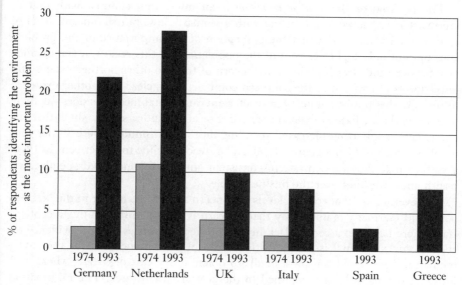

FIG. 7.1 Percentage of respondents who identified the 'environment' as the most important problem facing member states, 1974 and 1993
Source: Eurobarometer, 40 (1993), tables 1, A20 and A21.

the four countries that were members of the EU in 1974, the relative importance of the environment as an issue increased substantially. Over these four countries, the average proportion of respondents regarding the environment as the most important issue increased by nearly 13 per cent, a figure that is close to the EU average for all the relevant countries of 12 per cent. This places the environment among the top four issues that grew in importance between 1974 and 1993, along with the single currency (12 per cent increase), regional disparities (14 per cent), and job initiatives (12 per cent). Limiting ourselves to the nine member states of 1973, the environment has had the largest growth in importance among all the issues.

However, in addition to the general secular growth in the importance of the environment as an issue from 1974 to 1993, there are also interesting variations between countries. The surge in concern in both *the Netherlands* and *Germany* is remarkable, particularly in the latter, which at the beginning of the period lagged behind the UK in popular concern for environmental issues. Remembering that the question invited people to name what they thought was the *most important* problem, and that Germany was in the throes of coping with the economic problems of reunification, the priority ascribed by German respondents to the environment in 1993 is noteworthy. Equally noteworthy is the fact that the discrepancy in levels of concern between the old (23 per cent) and the new (18 per cent) *Länder* was relatively low.

The position of the *United Kingdom* is an interesting contrast with that of Germany over the period. Starting with a similarly low, but significant, level of concern in 1974, we find that the perception of the importance of the problem goes up, but only to 14 per cent of the population. In this regard, it stands midway between the clear high level of concern of the two other northern states and lower levels of concern of the southern countries. It is clear from other evidence in the UK that public support for stricter environmental measures does fluctuate over time. Thus, figures from the British Social Attitudes survey show that the percentages supporting increased spending on the environment were 34 per cent in 1985, a high of 61 per cent in 1990, and a steady decline to 41 per cent in 1996, a pattern that shows a contrast to consistent support for increased spending on health and education over the business cycle.[7]

However, to say that relative levels of concern seem to be higher in the Netherlands and Germany is not to say that concern is absent in the south. Except for Italy, there has been a certain lack in the southern countries of hard evidence on specific environmental issues as distinct from bland statements about the environment in general. This is most of all a problem in the case of *Greece*, where professional polling is largely confined to the greater Athens area. The information available tends to be spasmodic, often impressionistic, and sometimes ambiguous. For example, the OECD report of 1983 noted that public concern about environmental problems was fairly recent, albeit on the increase,[8] while subsequent reports have cast doubt on how far this has continued. Thus, the Greek government's 1991 report for the Rio summit concluded that 'environmental awareness is not yet highly developed in Greece', although efforts were being made to overcome this through programmes of environmental education.[9]

In *Spain* the state of opinion research is rather better, although as in Greece it is not possible to trace trends back beyond the 1980s because the relative newness of their democracies means that such research was not conducted in earlier times. Because of their preoccupation with matters other than the environment in the early years of their democracies, it did not emerge as an issue of public concern in either country until the 1980s. In Spain, nevertheless, environmental awareness has developed slowly according to what evidence is available. By the start of the 1990s there were distinct signs of a growth in public concern over the environment, although it was not as strong as in other EU states. The 1980s decade was seen as decisive in bringing about this change.[10]

Although there may be a diffusion of environmental concern, which was increasingly and regularly expressed in the 1990s, it may not run deep. It is striking, for example, how in the Eurobarometer figures Spain stands out from the other Mediterranean countries in terms of the priority accorded to the environment. A Demoscopia survey in late 1990 in Spain identified a growing awareness—86 per cent of the Spanish public thought pollution in the country was serious—but at the same time a firm reluctance to accept more taxes on cars and petrol.[11] The problem arises when environmental demands interfere with the conduct of individuals. In Spain, it has been observed, most people regard industry and not individuals as the main cause of pollution, creating a pressure for the imposition of fines but not for the alteration of individual conduct—as is more common, for example, in countries like Germany or Denmark.[12]

In *Italy*, environmental concern appeared and grew rather earlier than in Greece and Spain. This was partly because the democratic system allowed this to be expressed from the early 1970s, but also because a series of environmental scandals did much to stimulate concern. A notable instance was the Seveso crisis of 1976 which made a deep impact in the country. Resentment over this scandal persisted for years afterwards.[13] Of course, as elsewhere in Europe, one decisive event that spurred on environmental concern among the national publics of Italy and Greece (but not so much Spain, for geographical reasons) was the Chernobyl crisis of 1986. In Italy's case, this occurred at a time when the public was already becoming more sensitized to pollution, and it was followed by a series of other home-made scandals in the Adriatic and in other coastal areas concerning the transportation of toxic and refuse materials. From then on, environmental awareness in Italy began to accelerate. One report in 1989 noted that 'nowhere in Europe is the environmental pendulum swinging so fast, from neglect to acute concern, as in Italy'.[14]

If environmental issues show an increasing degree of salience among European publics, what are beliefs about the extent to which this is an item of policy that is internationalized? Richard Sinnott considers this question in the context of a more general discussion of public opinion and the internationalization of governance in Europe.[15] He shows from Eurobarometer data that between 1974 and 1991 a high proportion of respondents thought that the environment was an intrinsically international issue, and that this was one of a small number of issues in which internationalization was widely perceived to have taken place. Indeed, over the period 1974–1991, 72 per cent of respondents on average regarded the environment as an international issue. Similarly, a high proportion of respondents (66 per cent average) thought that the European Union had policies to deal with environmental problems, again one of the highest policy issues in the set of those asked.

This apparent willingness to accept international governance is also evidenced in a recent Eurobarometer survey from 1996.[16] Here respondents were asked which of a list of policy issues was a high priority for the European Union. Although the question is not relative, so that inter-country comparisons may be bedevilled by differential willingness to assign a high priority to a large number of objectives, it is nevertheless striking that joint efforts to protect the environment figures fifth overall on the list. Among our six countries, the lowest support comes from Germany, at 81 per cent of respondents assigning it a high priority, and the highest priority is 94 per cent from Greece. In other words, there appears to be a high degree of acceptance of EU action in this area, and therefore an acknowledgement that it is embedded in a system of European governance.

So far we have looked at opinions as measured through opinion polls. However, it can be argued that this is only to look at a superficial level of attitude, and that we need to consider the deeper cultural values out of which attitudes, and ultimately behaviour, grow. Here there is a particularly interesting question concerning our three southern countries. It is sometimes argued that there are persistent cultural features of the southern countries that are likely to predispose them towards a lack of environmental concern. The cultural syndrome, sometimes known as 'amoral familism', is said to bias behaviour towards private rather than public goals and to undermine the sort of civic culture that would be necessary for successful environmental policy.[17] It is therefore worth looking more closely at these southern countries as a test of resistance to convergent pressures on public opinion and the environment.

In this vein, one study of air pollution in Athens stressed the problem of developing environmental values in the face of the individualism, which was a distinctive trait of Greek society and 'excludes the real development of a collective consciousness'.[18] The same difficulty was encountered in the provinces. An official of the municipality of Rethimno in Crete remarked: 'everyone is talking about the environment, and everyone is interested in the environment, but when they have to take action for the protection of the environment many people turn their backs and they go'. He felt that the way to confront this problem was through activities, and 'the most important is to inform the public and especially school education'.[19]

Officials in the Environment Ministry (YPEHODE) in Athens referred to this attitudinal problem encountered when trying to promote environmental protection in Greece. One senior official commented:

You have to make people understand first the meaning of the environment and the importance of the environment, and you've to try to face some very personal problems of owners who didn't very much want to see an area they own characterized as protected. One of the difficulties for the protection of the environment of Greece is due to the fact that the big majority of Greek land is owned privately. We do not have vast areas of land owned by the public or local authorities. So this means that one needs to make expropriations for the protection of eco-systems, and this costs money. And it is not only a question of money, it is also a question of mentality. People consider that it would be much more profitable for them to have a small hotel, for instance, and manage it by themselves and derive a higher profit, than to accept expropriation or to participate in the management of a biotope or whatever. These are meanings they cannot understand yet. So, we need more time to persuade the many different people who are involved in the protection of each area.[20]

In Greece, moreover, people are generally not litter-conscious. The state of the countryside is often jarring to the eye (and offensive to the sense of smell in hot weather) with random dumping of municipal waste. This is in part a supply-side problem arising from a lack of collection services and treatment plants, and not solely an attitudinal problem.[21] However, the absence of public pressure on this matter contributes to the problem. Greeks are, however, for reasons usually linked to national pride, concerned about atmospheric and other effects on national monuments. Thus, public anxiety becomes easily aroused on this particular problem.

However, efforts to handle the wider impacts of atmospheric conditions encounter conflicting points of view. The public's response to the authority's attempts to control car use by making city centre access depend on the number of the car registration was to buy a second car with an alternative (even–odd) registration number; but older models were likely to pollute badly, and the police were lax in imposing fines because they did not want to become unpopular.[22] Over the years, air pollution in Athens has become decidedly worse and has forced public opinion to accept the greater likelihood of measures to combat it. In the spring of 1995, the main centre of the city was closed off to traffic in a new kind of experiment.

But generally, there remains a problem of public mentality which is difficult to overcome. According to an expert on environmental problems there,

Popular resistance is very big in Greece. The same in the countryside—you cannot implement an anti-pollution regulation or tax laws, for popular resistance is big. So, when we see the ineffectiveness of Greek administration, it is not so much because of vested interests of industrialists, capitalists—yes, there are some very big interests that dominate decisions—but also of the non-informed public that is resisting very much. Because the two parties in Greece are not purely class parties, they are interested in the popular response to their policy and especially to environmental policy, which is a policy that affects people's lives not directly, but only indirectly. So people resist.[23]

Despite this, local authorities can come under direct pressure from public opinion to act on environmental matters. There may also be issues where local authorities may be encouraged by concerned local opinion to pressurize national governments. One such case concerned the island of Milos in Greece, where plans for establishing a geothermal energy unit threatened tourism which had been growing steadily during the 1980s. Health incidents occurred following toxic emissions, and the national media covered the case. Under sustained local pressure, the Ministry of Industry in Athens suspended the project, although it was later resumed under specified environmental conditions.[24]

In Spain there is a similar lack of objection to the dumping of rubbish in the countryside. This has been explained by the fact that Spaniards see their country (one of the largest in Western Europe) as having much empty space.[25] On other matters, however, public anxieties can be readily mobilized, including concern about nature reserves, toxic waste, and industrial (especially chemical) contamination. These tend to be issues requiring not individual responsibility, but a response from particular interests. The cooking oil scandal in the late 1980s certainly aroused public ire, being an issue of public health that could notionally affect anyone.

At the same time, there remain cultural patterns that are difficult to dislodge. The widespread attachment to the importance of public works projects in Spain is a major case in point. In 1993 the national minister responsible went on record about the Spanish 'impatience' to institute public works projects—'we are the victims of success'—an impatience that was exacerbated by local rivalries.[26] However, some signs of a counter-influence to popular support for the economic imperative were evident by the late 1980s. The Ministry's annual report for 1988 on the environment in Spain noted a new attitude questioning indiscriminate economic development. In this respect, Spain was a good decade behind more advanced countries in Europe.[27]

The local dimension is important, because territorial attachment in these southern countries is a matter of tradition and therefore culture. That is particularly so in Spain, with the presence of seventeen different regions with important policy powers on the environment, not to mention distinct feelings of regional nationalism in some of them. Territoriality does, in fact, represent a potential source for furthering environmental values, since it usually combines with a concrete perception of environmental problems if they are pronounced in the area concerned. According to a survey conducted by the environment department of the Catalan regional government, the highest level of environmental awareness was found in small rural communities when there was an environmental problem: 'the small communities are the most sensitive to an unfavourable change and automatically generate agreement'.[28] Local feeling could also be mobilized on environmentalist grounds even when it concerned the economic interests of an area. A well-known example in Spain were the debates that surfaced for some time over the despoliation of the Costa Brava arising from mass tourism.[29] This touched public sensitivity about national parks, but also mobilized regionalist feeling, which is rather strong in Catalonia.

However, as in the other southern countries, a distinction should be drawn between environmental awareness and environmentalism, which points to some changes in lifestyle. As recently as the end of the 1980s, it was noted that in Italy 'a cultural barrier has formed against the concept of sustainable growth, and the result is slowness and rigidity in political, legislative and administrative acts concerning the environment'.[30] The basic problem is cultural, and comes from the difficulty of relating the collective to the particular.

In Italy, environmental values have nevertheless spread more than in the other two southern countries; and this change came about somewhat sooner. There were, even in the late 1980s, some signs of it, with a growth of the use of lead-free petrol, the appearance of bottle banks in rural towns as elsewhere, and the inauguration in some Italian cities of traffic-free zones.[31] But there was variation across Italy with, generally, more commitment to environmentalism in the north than in the south of the country.[32] This appeared to fit with political-cultural differences between the 'two Italies'. Also, geographical proximity of northern regions to central Europe, with strongly environmentalist countries like Austria and Germany, no doubt counted. This certainly affected north-eastern Italy where voluntary action was well established; while a region like Lombardy in the north-west had such severe environmental problems (especially industrial and urban) that the growth of environmental values was almost inevitable. This did not exclude their emergence in some regions of the south such as Calabria, where they related to a sense of natural inheritance.[33]

Italy is a more densely populated country than either Spain or Greece. This helps to explain why a now fairly wide range of issues have mobilized opinion—including air pollution in many cities, the nuclear issue, and industrial pollution of land, air, and water. The nuclear issue derives from the Chernobyl crisis of 1986, with a decisive vote in referenda the following year severely restricting the scope of nuclear planning and research.[34] Drinking water is another issue that arouses feelings, and has been highlighted in the context of Italy's defective implementation of the EU directive. As an environmental group leader put it, 'it is easier to get people mobilized [on this issue] than on, for example, the environmental impact of the *autostrade* and large public works'.[35] Again, the prospect of direct effects on individual health is obviously influential.

When territorial identity comes into play, then, as in the other southern countries, the chances of environmental commitment gaining ground in Italy are considerable. Thus, Tuscany has a strong tradition of naturalism and sense of '*il bel paese*', transmitted through attachment to locality—a phenomenon known as '*campanilismo*'. In many instances '*campanilismo*' has a distinctly historical source in the origins of many towns, some of which were independent communities in the Middle Ages. One such is the town of Montalcino in southern Tuscany, a classic hilltop fortress which is also well known for its high-quality Brunello wine. In 1989 there was a proposal to establish in the vicinity a large waste disposal facility. This caused intense local opposition, with concern that the plan would contaminate the soil in this wine-growing area, and the matter reached the national press. It also offended local opinion as it was seen as an affront to local identity.[36]

Thus, in the southern countries—especially Greece and Spain—there has been a general lack of the kind of civic culture that advances collective interests, and hence promotes environmental culture. Evidence from these countries suggests that a change is developing, but it is recent. It is rather more advanced in Italy than in the other two countries. Environmental awareness began to develop only in the 1980s and, perhaps inevitably, it has been slow. In other words, while environmental awareness has increased, environmentalism as such—embracing behavioural change—has not developed rapidly or very much. In recent years there has been a slow growth of post-materialist values in these countries, in line with the EU as a whole. However, such values tend to be more pronounced in the northern member states, while in the southern ones the ratings for such values are below the EU average.

Our analysis also shows, however, that in the southern countries some link with territorial culture may help to advance the environmental cause. This is particularly evident where local traditions and attachments may dovetail with environmental concerns. This seems to raise the question of how much environmentalism involves 'modernizing' society purely and simply.

However, it is possible to overdraw the contrast between north and south, particularly if it is associated with broader views about the influence of amoral familism on Mediterranean cultures. We should not draw too sharp a conclusion about the distinction between south and north in terms of civic attitudes. It is a matter of simple observation that the German love of the fast car means that most auto-bahn drivers are usually travelling more quickly than environmental concerns, and perhaps even personal prudence, would suggest desirable. The problems associated with translating expressed attitudes into environmentally compatible behaviour are not trivial even in northern countries. Thus, in a comparison between householders in Bern and Munich, Diekmann has been able to show that, although approxim-ately the same proportion of respondents in a survey (over 80 per cent) agreed with the view that people should behave in environmentally responsible ways, only 23 per cent of households in Bern said that they turned their central heating down in winter when they left their dwelling for more than four hours, whereas 69 per cent did so in Munich. If we seek the reason for this difference, it is to be found in the fact that, whereas 80 per cent of households in Munich were responsible for their own heating costs, with the remainder relying on district heating schemes, in Bern only 38 per cent of households were responsible for their heating costs. The inference is that subscription to general principles translates straightforwardly into behavioural change only when the costs of doing so are low.[37]

A similar argument that expressed attitudes, even in the north, are consistent only with low–cost environmentalism has been made by Sharon Witherspoon on the basis of a comparative survey of attitudes in five EU countries (Germany, Italy, Ireland, the UK, and the Netherlands).[38] Starting from the observation that the publics in these different countries appear to exhibit similar levels of concern about a variety of problems, Witherspoon argues that, if the measures of concern are set against an expressed willingness of respondents to bear extra costs, significant dif-ferences emerge between the countries. For example, respondents in the former West Germany and in Italy show similar levels of concern on a 'willingness-to-sacrifice' score, although German attitudes show greater consistency than Italian ones within the countries. Of course, it is not possible to draw too many infer-ences from one survey, but results such as these should at least caution against drawing too strong a set of conclusions about comparative levels of concern for environmental protection in different countries. Even so, we should acknowledge that there is little evidence of an homogeneous European set of public attitudes towards environmental policy.

POLITICAL PARTIES

Political parties first began to respond to environmental issues in West European countries at the time international concern began to grow in the early 1970s. Their reaction was conditioned by ideological affinity but also eventually by political com-petition, once (in some countries) green parties began to rise and public opinion began to display higher levels of interest according to the pattern described in the previous section. However, political parties have found it difficult to espouse whole-heartedly environmentalist positions, partly for reasons of political tradition and partly because they have rival or more compelling policy concerns. A more voluble concern for the environment has, more often than not, been dictated by immediate concerns, and above all by pollution crises. Thus, while it has become standard for all parties to include the environment in their menus of programmatic commitments, they are not a consistent source of pressure for increasing the priority given to environmental measures.

Nevertheless, although programmatic statements by political parties are often adopted less for reasons of policy substance than for reasons of political competition, the analysis of party programmes can give us some idea of the developing salience of environmental issues within the processes of party competition. One way of looking at this aspect of parties in more detail is to compare their manifestoes, which provide evidence, in a cross-nationally comparable form, on the salience of different issues. Such manifestoes have been conveniently collected and coded by the Manifesto Group, the data being available in usable and intelligible form.[39]

Manifesto data are available for all six of our countries, going back to the 1940s for Germany, Italy, the Netherlands, and Great Britain, and to the 1970s for Greece and Spain.[40] The assumption on which the data are collected is that parties do not tend to take up simple 'for or against' positions in respect of issues in order to avoid being cornered by their opponents. Thus, a party that is keen on higher defence spending will not say in its manifesto that it is for war and against peace, but instead will stress the need for national security and downplay themes of international cooperation and overcoming historic divisions. In other words, policy sectors generally are treated as *valence* issues, and the task is to identify the salience of issues by counting the occurrence of key terms.

If we take this approach in respect of the environment, the assumption is that all parties will seek to show that their programme or actions will contribute to the achievement of environmental goals. Thus, the priority the issue receives in public debate will to a large extent determine the comparative seriousness with which environmental questions are taken. Note, however, that we may expect the salience of environmental issues to vary over time as well as between countries.

This point is especially important when it comes to analysing manifesto data on environmental policies. Since parties are not going to take an 'anti' stance in respect of the environment as a value, we need some way of identifying the importance of the environment in their programmatic statements. The way that we have chosen to do this is to produce an index that subtracts from mentions of the environment mentions of conventional economic productivity. In this way, we hope to produce a measure of policy commitment to the environment in which what we can call *productivism* is set against *environmentalism*. Our index therefore measures the net number of mentions of environmental protection, after the number of mentions of economic productivity has been subtracted. (Clearly, this net value can be negative.)

The sort of picture this produces can be seen in Figures 7.2(*a*)–(*f*), where we plot over time the net environmentalism index for all six countries. The index is

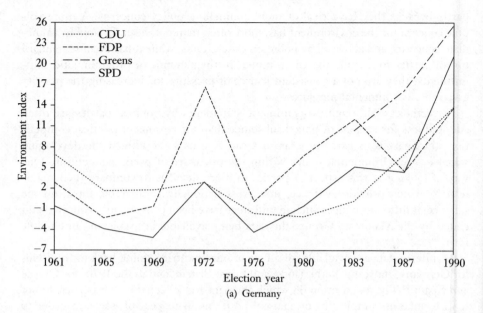

(a) Germany

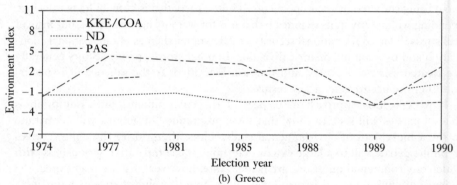

(b) Greece

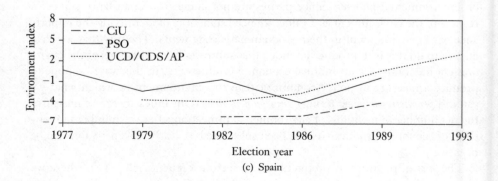

(c) Spain

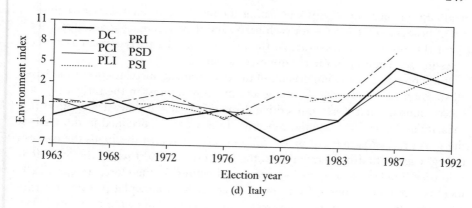

(d) Italy

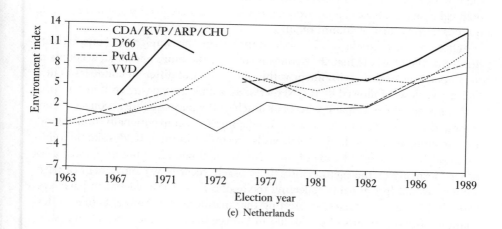

(e) Netherlands

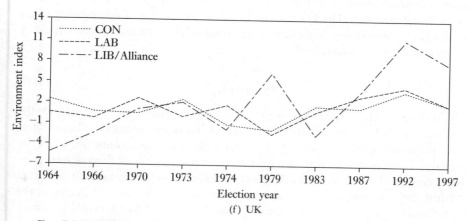

(f) UK

FIG. 7.2 Trends in environmentalism in party manifestos of six member states

made up for each country by calculating the mentions of environmental concern net of productivity concerns for each party, and then averaging across all parties.[41] What this produces is a picture of the priority that the party system as a whole gives in each country to the environment as an issue.

It can be seen that the importance of the environment fluctuates over time across all six countries. Although there was an upturn of interest in the early 1970s, for those countries that were competitive democracies at the time, it was offset to a substantial degree by economic concerns. In any case, it declined in the wake of the world recession induced by the 1973 oil price rises. In the 1980s the concern emerges again, first in Germany and the Netherlands and then in the other four countries. Looking across the average for all countries, therefore, we can clearly identify common trends. The priority given to environmental protection varies over time, largely in inverse relationship to the condition of the economy; when the economy is perceived to have been doing well for some years, there is higher political concern about the environment; when it is perceived to be in recession, there is a downturn of commitment.

When we turn to the differences, rather than the similarities, one striking feature of the charts is that they confirm some of the more anecdotal accounts of the importance of the environment within the politics of different countries. Thus, Germany, closely followed by the Netherlands, stands at opposite ends of the spectrum of concern from Spain, where for much of the period political concerns concentrated on the need for economic development, as conventionally understood. The upsurge in interest in the 1980s is also recorded in the UK, despite the reputation of the 1980s as a decade of materialism,[42] although it is not as marked as in either Germany or the Netherlands. Italy barely records any movement of party opinion overall (presumably reflecting the ossification of the old Italian party system), and Greece fluctuates, suggesting that manifesto commitments may be less bound by the constraints of credibility in Greece than in some other countries. In other words, although it is true that all countries are subject to a similar pattern of oscillation in political party concern, the extent and degree of that concern varies from country to country. We can examine some of these trends in more detail by looking at countries individually.

Germany

Undoubtedly, the country in which the party system has experienced the greatest effects from environmental influences has been Germany. These effects were originally felt in the early 1970s, along with many other countries, when the Social–Liberal coalition, with the Free Democrat Genscher as the relevant minister, enacted the first major piece of national legislation concerning air pollution control. Interestingly, the importance given to the environment is reflected in the manifesto position of the Free Democrats in the early 1970s which shifts from a middling to a more pro-environment position between 1969 and 1972. On the other hand, despite the importance that some commentators have given to their 'Blue skies over the Ruhr' campaign of 1961, the Social Democrats do not show up on the manifesto data as being particularly pro-environment between 1953 and 1972. This is presumably a reflection of their need to make promises of material economic growth to their traditional working-class constituents. Environmental commitment was set back by the recession induced by the oil price rises of 1973/4. In 1975, a meeting at Gymnich, organized by the Federal Chancellor's office, decided to give environmental issues a lower priority than economic development.[43] During the late 1970s, all the parties gave a lower place to environmental issues than to economic ones, and this can be seen in the dip in environmentalism in the manifestoes of all the parties between 1972 and 1976.

By 1980 the situation had begun to turn around, with the major surge of all three main parties between 1980 and 1983, years that included the replacement of the Social–Liberal coalition in 1982 by the Christian–Liberal coalition. With that transition, the German government moved from a cautious stance on environmental questions to a conscious espousal of certain environmental themes. There were two circumstances that led to this change of orientation. Firstly, the newly established Greens began to challenge the position of the Free Democrats as not only the third party, but also thereby as the pivotal party in coalition formation. In response, it was necessary for the governing coalition to look credible on environmental questions. Secondly, the Bavarian element of the Christian parties, the Christian Social Union, in particular saw the opportunity to use the issue of forest death to attack the heartland of social democracy in North Rhine Westphalia. The manifesto data show how the parties begin to stress environmental issues more strongly following party competition on the issues that are induced by these changes.

The rise of the Greens as a party has been attributed to the failure of the prevalent party system to respond to environmental issues, as well as to the influx of personnel from the ecology and peace movements.[44] During the 1980s all parties moved towards embracing the importance of environmental issues, at least as part of their rhetorical commitments. Although the Greens underwent a severe crisis in the latter part of the 1980s, their return to electoral politics at local and *Land* level has meant that their influence is still widely felt. By the end of the 1980s the manifesto data show all of the main parties giving considerable stress to environmental issues, thus exhibiting a consensus that is rare in other countries.

Greece

In Greece political parties embraced environmental issues later than in Germany, simply because democratic politics did not return to that country until 1974. In the first few years thereafter, overriding concerns with regime transition discouraged interest, and political leaders were reluctant to give any priority to this area. The constitution of 1975 provided for environmental protection, but there was no obligation to initiate immediate action.[45] The issue began to engage parties in the early 1980s, although PASOK had begun to emphasize environmental concerns from the late 1970s after it rose in popularity as an opposition party. The change of power in 1981, when PASOK was elected to government, gave the issue some impetus, and for several years thereafter it was a fairly regular subject of parliamentary questions. Both main parties developed lines on the environment, with that of PASOK being rather more rhetorically sympathetic than that of New Democracy.[46]

Subsequently, party-political interest in the environment has fluctuated usually in line with electoral deadlines or rising and declining public concern, although always as essentially secondary to developmental programmes. If there has been any one issue that has determined this pattern, it has been the Athens pollution cloud. Over the past decade this has been a regular item in electoral discourse, whether in national or municipal (Athenian) politics. This fits with a general pattern, whereby it has to be pollution crises that spur parties into giving greater attention to problems of the environment.

The manifesto data charted in (Figure 7.2(*b*)) confirm these trends during the first decade and a half after the return to democracy. Although there is some fluctuation of interest, especially in PASOK's case, it is difficult to detect trends over time that are significant in a major way. There is no real evidence of the party system addressing these issues in a sustained way. It is, therefore, relevant to note that green organizations have been politically very weak, and have not placed the established parties under any serious challenge on environmental questions. In 1989, 46 disparate environmental groups established a party called Ecologists-Alternatives, which managed to win one parliamentary seat; but internal differences in the party led to its losing this seat in 1993. Thus ended the attempt to form a green party.[47]

Spain

In Spain, as in Greece, parties have come late to the environmentalist cause because of a return to democracy only in the mid-1970s. But their reluctance to embrace green issues is also due to an overriding concern with economic issues since then, linked to the high rate of unemployment, the need to reconvert industry for the international market, and, of course, entry to the EU. Furthermore, it has been the common assumption among party elites that 'green measures do not win votes'.[48] This explains a rather passive line adopted by the main parties, notwithstanding rhetorical noise about prominent environmental matters when the occasion arises. The pattern suggested is one of following rather than leading public opinion.

This picture is reflected in the manifesto data charted in Figure 7.2(*c*). The evidence here not only shows Spain as the most productivist country in terms of overall ideological disposition, but also reveals that all of its major parties featured strong productivist tendencies until 1989, when by international standards there was a modest upswing. Altogether, the main Spanish parties have been preoccupied with the requirements of economic development to an extent that has inhibited any significant opening to environmentalist arguments. The lack of a serious challenge from green political organizations has reinforced this tendency. Nevertheless, the parties have evolved environment programmes over the past decade. In the PSOE's case, there was no attention to this area before 1982 (the year it came to power), when it began to give attention to environmental matters following controversy over nuclear power and growing industrial contamination; while, now, as with other political forces, the theme of sustainable development has come to the fore.[49]

Italy

The situation in Italy has been somewhat different from the other two southern countries, for environmental awareness developed slightly sooner, not least because democratic politics has a longer (i.e. postwar) history here. Nevertheless, the parties have largely continued to cater for consumerist values. The centre of gravity within Italian politics for most of the postwar period has balanced off environmentalism with productivist values, as is shown in Figure 7.2(*d*). The main Italian parties were for long remarkably similar in their stances.

It was only in the late 1980s that there occurred any general upsurge of interest in environmental issues. This has left a space for the small green movement to establish its position as distinctive from the other parties, though with little effect in terms of influence on public policy. From the early 1980s, the party of the Verdi began to increase its support in local elections, although it was not until 1987 that it entered the national parliament with 2.5 per cent of the vote and twelve deputies and two senators. In the three elections of 1992, 1994, and 1996 the level of support of the Verdi has remained consistent and modest, ranging between 2.5 and 2.9 per cent.[50] But they have not enjoyed the political standing or influence of the Greens in Germany.

At the beginning of this present decade, one study of the Italian environment noted that 'the country's main political parties still regard environmental protection as external, peripheral or only partially relevant to the production–distribution–consumption function of society'.[51] Certainly, the environment has featured in interparty battles as part of normal everyday politics, although usually with respect to very particular issues. The opposition spokesman of the PDS on the environment, interviewed in 1992, mentioned the following points on which his party had recently attacked the government: the faulty application of the EIA directive, the issue of the world exhibition in Venice and its environmental effects, and the matter of eco-auditing.[52]

In the early 1990s, the turmoil over widespread political corruption (the persistent Tangentopoli scandal) as well as the pressures for system reform monopolized party-political concerns. There followed a basic restructuring of the party system, initially not in a way to suggest stronger possibilities for environmental policy. Against a background of economic recession, the environment was pushed down the scale of priorities. In May 1996, however, the Prodi centre–left coalition took office, with the Greens as part of the coalition, obtaining seats in the cabinet. This coalition succeeded in passing a number of laws, as well as strengthening Italy's position in international negotiations on climate change.[53]

The Netherlands

Like Germany, the Netherlands has a party system in which environmental issues have come to play a strong role. All parties pay deference to environmental values. Despite the complexity of Dutch party politics, the evolving trend has been quite straightforward. During most of the postwar period until the early 1970s, the extent of environmental commitment was limited, with all parties balancing off references to environmental improvement and commitment to economic growth in more or less the same way. When the global concern with the environment developed in the early 1970s, the left liberal party, Democrats '66, made the most significant move, stressing environmental concerns more than any other party. However, the two main party blocs also made moves in that direction. As in Germany, there was a downturn of interest in the 1970s, to be replaced by a significant upturn of interest in the 1980s.

One interesting aspect of the Dutch situation is the position of the right-wing liberal party, the VVD. We have seen in Germany that it was the liberal FDP that stressed environmentalism first in the 1970s and consistently afterwards. In the Netherlands, with two distinct liberal parties, we can see how in the manifesto commitments the dual faces of liberalism are exhibited. The left liberals take a strong pro-environment line; the right liberals are more cautious, however, despite following the general trends over the period. One important consequence has been that VVD environment ministers, such as Winsemius and, more particularly, Nijpels, have sometimes found themselves torn between their party loyalties and their ministerial commitment, as was Nijpels in particular during the general election of 1989.

United Kingdom

In the UK, the predominant discourse of party competition has been concerned with the overriding problem of reversing the country's comparative economic decline. That has not allowed environmental values much place. This is reflected in the negative score on environmentalism recorded by the party manifestoes up to the late 1960s and the low scores of the two main parties during the 1980s, when party competition turned on issues of material well-being. To be sure, in the late 1960s and early 1970s the UK shared the general upsurge of interest in environmental questions. However, neither major party at the time found a way of adapting its ideological commitments easily to the demands of environmental policy. The Labour Party of the 1970s was too preoccupied with the problems of economic policy to find it easy to adopt environmental issues; in 1979 it recorded the lowest scores of all the three main parties on our environmentalism index.

During the 1980s, with the long hold on power of the Conservatives, the dominance of neo-liberal ideology in their thinking meant that deregulation was seen as taking priority. It was difficult to square this emphasis with what were seen as the demands of environmental policy for greater regulation. However, towards the end of the decade there were some in the Conservative Party who became prone to cite the privatization of the public utilities like water and electricity as providing the right institutional context within which pollution externalities could be regulated.[54] And there were also those who saw the fiscal advantages in green taxation, so that measures of domestic fuel taxation were sometimes defended in terms of their environmental advantages. However, despite reference to a 'green Conservatism', there has been no successful attempt to create a strong body of environmentalist opinion within the party.

Meanwhile, for much of the 1980s the Labour Party was preoccupied with resolving its own internal organizational affairs. It thus often found it difficult to give adequate attention to matters of policy. There are those within the Labour Party who speak of the continuity between the modern green agenda and the traditional social democratic concern with matters of public health and housing. However, there has remained a tendency to see environmental and economic imperatives as opposed to one another, whether these take the form of employment losses resulting from environmental restrictions on economic activity, or adverse effects on the distribution of income from increasing green taxation. Indeed, a leading edge of the Labour Party's attack in opposition on the Conservative government was its critique of the imposition of VAT on domestic fuel.

Among the smaller political parties in the UK, two should be mentioned in particular. The first of these is the Liberal Democrats, the result of a merger between the Liberals and the Social Democrats after the 1987 general election. The Liberal Democrats have consistently argued for greater priority to be given to environmental issues, following in part the lead given by the Liberals in the 1970s when still a separate party. This is reflected, for example, in their strong environmentalism in their 1992 election manifesto.

The Green Party has also been committed to an environmental agenda, varying over time in its degree of fundamentalism. The Green Party enjoyed a surge of popularity in the late 1980s, partly as a result of the general interest in environmental questions at the time, and partly as a result of their being residual beneficiaries of the unpopularity of the Liberal Democrats in the wake of their somewhat cantankerous birth. Thus, in 1989 the Green Party secured 15 per cent of the popular vote at the European elections, and this undoubtedly affected the thinking of the other parties. However, internal squabbles of the familiar realist/fundamentalist kind quickly split the party, while in any case the UK electoral system punishes severely any party that recruits only a relatively small percentage of the vote without geographical concentration.[55] But the Green Party does have some elected members on local councils, and one Plaid Cymru (Welsh nationalist) MP arguably owes his seat to an election bargain with the local Green Party.

So far we have considered the role of the political parties domestically. How far has this role been changed by the European system of environmental governance? To this question we can offer a brief reply. The answer is: almost not at all. National party systems remain quite distinct from one another and immune from outside influences, except in so far as they have to take up a definite stand on international issues and have representation in the transnational party groups in the European Parliament. However, parties at the European level remain weak. As Rudy Andeweg has pointed out, they lack the organizational structure to link them to the grass roots, their staffs are small, they are poorly financed, and they do not nominate their own candidates.[56] Moreover, European elections and even referendums on European questions produce results that are as likely to reflect the standing of national governments in popular opinion as they are to provide a collective judgment by the peoples of Europe about the acceptability of proposed institutional changes.[57] We should not therefore look to the party systems to see a significant source for the Europeanization of environmental policy.

ENVIRONMENTAL ORGANIZATIONS

A general feature of environmental politics is the number of voluntary organizations and pressure groups that it attracts. In all six of our countries environmental organizations encompass an enormous diversity, ranging from small, localized groups through national bodies up to national branches of the major international organizations such as the World Wide Fund for Nature (WWF), Friends of the Earth, and Greenpeace. There are all kinds of groups involved in preserving local culture and heritage and in promoting local development. Not only are there a great many groups, but some of the larger ones in particular straddle a great variety of activities. Organizations like the WWF or Greenpeace may be involved in policy networks at the same time as they are commissioning their own research, running campaigns, or providing commercial services. Moreover, environmental issues are capable of providing the basis for a great variety of interests, particularly when they involve large infrastructural projects such as road building, where local, national, and even international organizations may be mobilized in opposition.

From a sociological point of view, the interest of environmental organizations relates to their origin and character. How far are such organizations to be seen as expressions of new social movements engaged in the process of transforming the politics of bargained interests in liberal democracy into a politics of identity and meaning, as distinct from organized interests faced with certain collective action dilemmas? Dalton has shown how the tension between identity politics and the organizational imperatives arising from the logic of collective action is related to the ideological outlook of different types of group.[58] In particular, he argues that there is a distinction between the conservation orientation of traditional groups like bird protection societies, whose aim is to secure improvements in legislation, and ecologically oriented groups, usually of more recent foundation, where the aim is a more fundamental restructuring of society. This distinction is important in terms of studying environmental policy, since which category a group falls into is likely to affect the extent to which it is concerned to become a participant in policy networks. Even groups that do not fundamentally reject the prevailing norms of the political order can find themselves in the dilemma of having to choose between ideological purity with minimal policy influence on the one hand and some policy influence with ideological compromise on the other.[59]

In so far as environmental groups do become participants in the policy process, they have to face the fundamental dilemma of how to deal with the problem of mobilizing disparate and dispersed individuals to take action to protect a collective interest. For the larger and more established groups, even those who have an ecological ideology, the answer lies in a combination of high profile publicity campaigns and the efficient management of credit card membership. For smaller and more radical groups, the answer is more likely to lie in an appeal to existential commitment that draws upon deeply held sentiments. Either way, the manner in which the fundamental organization dilemma is resolved will have implications for the political role of the different types of group.

A number of environmental organizations are international in character. Although they may have national branches, they think of themselves as operating across national, and sometimes even continental, boundaries. In some cases, as with the UK's Royal Society for the Protection of Birds, an international orientation amounts to the forming of alliances with partner organizations in Europe, providing expertise and even funding. Even small and more radical organizations, engaged in direct action campaigns against road building or atomic power, will often be able to draw upon the support of like-minded groups in other countries through informal networks of communication. A particularly striking type of international organization is exemplified by Greenpeace: highly centralized and professional, and with no clear national identity, but none the less participant in national policy-making systems and tailoring their activity to the issues that are specific to individual countries.

Within the context of our general concerns about the Europeanization of environmental governance, this international aspect of environmental organizations is especially important. It suggests that, rather than the shifting of loyalties, expectations, and activities predicted by neo-functionalist integration theory, we are seeing a politics of multiple participation in national and international networks that may themselves interpenetrate. In looking at the political engagement of environmental organizations in our six countries, we should be sensitive not only to the specific history and context of national environmental politics and the common dilemmas of collective action to which all organizations are subject, but also to the way in which the growth of European environmental governance may have implications for participation in national policy networks and national processes of policy-making.

Germany

Organized societies for nature protection in Germany go back to the nineteenth century, but during the late 1960s and early 1970s new types of political organizations grew up. Of these, the most important were the citizens' inititatives (*Bürgerinitiativen*), whose origins were to be found in contests between citizens' groups and planning authorities, as well as the important anti-nuclear protests of the late 1970s and early 1980s. The citizens' initiatives began to organize themselves federally in 1972 by founding the Federation of Citizens' Groups for Environmental Protection (BBU), a development supported by the newly established environmental administration in the interior ministry.[60] By the end of the 1970s there were about 11,500 projects stemming from the citizens' initiatives in the former West Germany and Berlin, and estimates suggest that the movement included 300,000–400,000 people including friends and sympathizers.[61] The groups were important in part because of their willingness to mobilize candidates in elections; they were behind the breakthrough of the Greens into the party system.

Alongside the growth of the citizens' initiatives, there are a large number of other local and national environmental organizations, some of which, like the German Association for the Protection of Nature and the Environment (BUND), have a long history. In addition, at a national level the following have large memberships: Greenpeace; the WWF; the German Nature Protection Association (NABU); and the Bavarian branch of the BUND, the Bund Naturschutz in Bayern. The umbrella organization is the German Ring for Nature Protection (DNR), which has over ninety member organizations covering a broad range of interests including animal protection, local history, and angling.[62] Estimates suggest that there are some four million members of nature protection and environmental associations in Germany.[63]

Despite their size and popular appeal, a number of observers concur that traditionally there have been few opportunities for environmental groups to participate in the policy process. To some extent, the lack of exchange between representatives of the environmental movement and policy-makers reflects the closed and technical orientation of the ministry, which, as Pehle has pointed out, tends to look on the environmental movement as opponents rather than partners.[64] Looking at the matter from the other side, Dalton's survey of European environmental representatives in the early 1980s showed that environmental groups in Germany gave an unusually low rating to the performance of the environment ministry (though this was still at the time when environment functions were lodged in the interior ministry).[65] Moreover, the corporatist style of policy-making in Germany reinforces a distinction between insiders and outsiders, and this division is further reinforced by the fact that formative experiences for many participants in the policy process would have been over nuclear energy policy, which is an exclusive and closed policy sector in all countries.

Despite this background, Pehle does suggest that changes may be taking place in attitudes, pointing in particular to the interest of the BUND in questions of ecological tax reform.[66] Brand goes even further and points to a transformation in the institutionalized relationship between environmental groups and the policy process between the early 1980s and the mid-1990s.[67] In part this would seem to be due to a familiar dynamic of environmental politics, in which ministers and the ministry look to environmental organizations to articulate a sense of public opinion that can reinforce the standing and position of environmental policy-makers in their negotiations with other colleagues in government. This is not to say that the German system has been transformed from a corporatist policy-making style into a pluralist one—Brand, for example, reports participants from environmental groups in policy networks saying that they have felt marginalized in meetings where business or industrial organizations were present. But it is to say that the German corridors of power became more open to environmental groups as the policy field became more institutionalized.

An interesting feature of German environmental organizations is the effort and resources they put into research, a striking example of the way in which the practice of environmental organizations borrows much from a national policy style in which expertise is important, a style that is such a notable feature of the German system. The clearest example of this investment in expertise is provided by the establishment of the Öko-Institut at Freiburg in 1977.[68] Brand also reports the growth of specialist appointments in environmental organizations in the late 1980s.[69]

Greece

In Greece there were few environmental groups in the early 1980s, and they had little political influence.[70] Traditionally, the weakness of Greek civil society has inhibited the emergence of autonomous pressure groups, for the larger political parties have tended to monopolize such activity. The environmental movement is a striking exception to this pattern of party-political colonization. However, while establishing some independence, their lack of party links has very much restricted the influence of such groups over the policy-making process.[71]

There is now a great diversity of environmental groups in Greece, often with a very specific or sectoral focus to their activities. They include the Society for Ecological Agriculture of Greece, the Society for the Protection of the Nature of Epiros, the Sea Turtle Protection Society, the Society for the Protection of the Monk Seal, and HELMEPA (Hellenic Marine Environment Protection Association), which provides training schemes for Greek shipowners.[72] A particular strength in the movement is the presence of grass-roots organizations with a capacity for mobilizing communities against specific threats, as has been shown by a number of cases from the late 1980s. Local distrust of authorities, especially national ones, seems to play a part in this process.[73]

While this diversity of groups has made their national coordination rather difficult, the standard large organizations are also present in Greece. The WWF, for instance, has placed much emphasis on information campaigns, including for tourists, and on lobbying local governments and international bodies to legislate for protection of the natural environment.[74] A major recent issue in Greece was the proposed diversion of the River Acheloos for irrigation of the Thessaly plain. For two years several environmental organizations, including WWF and the Greek Bird Society, campaigned against this project because of its repercussions on the natural and human environment, and in 1995 success was won when the State Council decided against the project.

Relations between environmental groups and the government have not really improved in Greece. Frustration over attempts to contact government authorities and at the lack of consultation was expressed strongly by leaders of the main organizations. The head of WWF in Athens complained that the Fund was consulted even when it had had the relevant expertise (e.g. on wetlands) relating to a particular item of government policy.[75] Particularly confusing is the problem of having to deal separately with so many different ministries in the environmental field in Athens.

Furthermore, institutional fragmentation inhibits the effectiveness of environmental organizations. One smaller group noted that, for a proposal on environmental education, it had to seek approval from three different ministries in turn —education, agriculture, and environment and public works (YPEHODE). In doing so, they had had to wait for an answer from one ministry before proceeding to the next: 'every ministry has another responsibility on the environment, and this makes for a lot of work and a lot of time for each agreement'.[76] Inter-ministry rivalry, especially that between YPEHODE and agriculture, did not help. The head of the WWF mentioned an announcement by the former that NGOs would be invited to tender for contracts to manage protected areas; almost at the same time, the latter officially denied the right of NGOs to do anything in protected areas unless they operated via the forestry services under its control.[77]

Spain

In Spain environmental organizations developed slowly after Franco, but they grew particularly from the late 1980s. These have included national federations, groups that operate in certain regions, and the Spanish sections of international environmental organizations.[78] According to a 1987 survey, the Spanish groups concentrated their efforts on the defence of animal species, flora and natural spaces, while only 30 per cent of them focused on urban or industrial themes and 3 per cent were on public education about the environment. While the 'lack of interest shown by Spaniards in ecological matters is a historical phenomenon', by the early 1990s it was noted 'this trend seems to be changing'.[79] At this level, therefore, Spain is a late developer at a time when the environment had clearly become a matter of broad international concern.

In Spain relations between government and pressure groups were traditionally weak or non-existent, a state of affairs that persisted well into the democratic period after Franco. This was seen as being due to a policy style in Madrid that was closed and bureaucratic.[80] However, this changed in the environmental field in the 1990s, with Greenpeace now acknowledging that the government is more open to dialogue.[81] Relations have also improved with the Friends of the Earth, to the extent that agreements have been made with the Ministry (MOPTMA) on collaboration over such matters as biodiversity and climate change, a common interest being the furtherance of environmental education.[82] At the same time, the new Advisory Council on the Environment, established by MOPTMA early in 1994, included representatives from the major environmental groups as well as other non-governmental organizations.[83]

Italy

Environmental organizations have a somewhat longer history in Italy than in Greece or Spain, with the very first groups going back to the turn of the century. They are able therefore to draw on a more vibrant tradition of collective action than in the other two southern countries, developing more as a political force from the 1970s as part of a growing movement for civil rights and against nuclear tests.[84] Furthermore, in Italy there is more of a practice of access by these organizations to government decision-makers than in Spain and Greece, where until recently government remained rather closed to such contact.

There are Italian branches of international organizations; for example, Amici de la Terra (Friends of the Earth) was founded in 1977, while WWF has been present in Italy since 1966. Also, some large national organizations, such as the Lega per l'Ambiente, formed in 1979, enjoy a mass membership; other national bodies include Italia Nostra (with a special interest in historical and artistic heritage), Federnatura (with its support for natural resources), and hundreds of local ecological associations.[85]

The main focus of these organizations has thus been on public campaigns in their particular areas of concern. The largest organization in Italy, the Lega per l'Ambiente, has concentrated much energy on the quality of bathing water. Using its own monitoring facilities, the Lega has annually tested the state of Italian beaches and has contested data issued by the Ministry of Health. Its results have been made public and have forced the government to tighten up its own monitoring.[86] The impact of this campaign has been obviously enhanced by the importance of the tourist industry in Italy, although we are clearly looking at an environmental organization that is exceptionally well provided for in infrastructure and expertise.

The larger organizations have tended to have close relations with political tendencies or even particular parties. Thus, Amici della Terra was initially close to the Radical Party, while the Lega has been broadly linked with the New Left.[87] Nevertheless, relations with the national administration have not always been satisfactory for environmental organizations, even though they are significantly better than in Spain and especially Greece. In Italy, a country where pressure groups are more developed and have enjoyed more political legitimacy than in the other two cases, contacts with government are more established.

At times, the Ministry of the Environment, small as it is and with limited expertise, has looked to environmental organizations for specific advice and information. This was so, for instance, with preparations of the Italian delegation for the Rio summit on the question of nuclear power.[88] Much depends, however, on the interest of individual ministers so far as the regularity of such links is concerned. According to one informed source, relations with Minister Ruffolo were 'conflictual but good, based on mutual regard', and clearly benefited from Ruffolo's own expertise and personal commitment to environmental affairs and the fact that he was 'intellectually honest'.[89] The atmosphere was very different with Minister Matteoli, a neo-Fascist appointed to the Berlusconi government, who showed distinct signs of being anti-environmentalist. However, a spokesman for one major environmental organization argued that in practice his appointment made little difference, as his very ignorance of environmental affairs made him all the more dependent for advice on these organizations.[90]

Netherlands

In the Netherlands there is a long tradition of environmental organization dating back to the turn of the century, with a focus largely upon the protection of ecologically valuable areas.[91] However, in the period 1968–72 a new environmental movement grew up, partly rooted in the traditional organizations but with a new focus on pollution and the destruction of natural resources generally and with a willingness to engage in more confrontational political action. Towards the end of the 1970s the popularity of extra-parliamentary political action began to wane, and there was a growth in the willingness to negotiate with governments around the table. The Netherlands has seen a considerable increase in the size of such organizations, particularly those like Greenpeace and WWF that have an international organization.

Within the Netherlands, an important role is played by the Stichting Natuur en Milieu (SNM, Foundation for Nature and the Environment), which acts as a think-tank for the environmental movement. SNM was established in 1972 and represents some 120 environmental organizations, with similar federations being set up at provincial and local level.[92] Among other activities, it houses the National Environmental Consultation (LMO), to which all environmental movements are united in national and regional federations.

Dalton's survey from the early 1980s showed that the representatives of the environment movement rated the environment ministry highly favourable—in striking contrast with the views of similar groups in Germany.[93] In keeping with the consensual and inclusive norms of the Dutch political order, the ministry reciprocates these warm feelings and regards the Foundation as an important ally. Hanf and van de Gronden point out that Dutch governments surround themselves with an 'iron ring' of advisory councils through which private organizations have an opportunity to influence government policy. An important part of the Dutch government's environmental policy strategy is to identify 'target groups' to be consulted in the formulation and development of policy. SNM acts as an important intermediary between the government and the environmental movement in this respect, supplying many of the representatives for consultation and committee work. It is also important in this regard that the government has played a part in funding these groups. The Dutch policy system has thus, from an international perspective, developed a high degree of institutionalization of the environmental movement.

United Kingdom

Environmental pressure groups in the UK go back to the late nineteenth century with the formation of the Commons, Open Spaces and Footpaths Preservation Society. Other groups were to follow: the Society for the Protection of Ancient Buildings in 1877 and, in the 1880s, the Coal Smoke Abatement Society and the Royal Society for the Protection of Birds. The 1920s and 1930s saw the formation of other groups, including the Pure Rivers Society and the Council for the Preservation of Rural England (later the Council for the Protection of Rural England).

The surge of interest in environmental matters in the late 1960s and early 1970s led to some newer groups being established but often with international credentials, of which the two most important are Friends of the Earth, established in 1971, and Greenpeace, established in 1977.[94] There has also been a process at work by which some long-standing groups, most notably the Council for the Protection of Rural England, have taken up new issues and transformed their campaigning style. Since the mid-1980s membership of the principal environmental groups has grown considerably,[95] with some organizations, for example the National Trust and the Royal Society for the Protection of Birds, growing spectacularly. Thus, there has been both an expansion of the range of groups and an increase in membership.[96] A significant number of UK environmental organizations are concerned with the protection of the countryside, wildlife, and historic buildings, rather than with pollution control, although Friends of the Earth, Greenpeace, and the National Society for Clean Air have been among the principal groups concerned with the latter.

The principal significance of the growth in membership has been pointed out by Stephen Young: it has enabled the groups to expand the range of their activities and employ more staff for research, campaigning, and fund-raising.[97] This has been particularly important as the policy process has taken a more open and discursive form. Thus, with the development of parliamentary select committees and the elaboration of the advisory committee structure, the ability of groups to influence policy depends upon their technical competence and their intellectual persuasiveness. An increase in membership, even when there are high turnover and fluctuating fortunes, enables environmental groups to be respected participants in the policy process, submitting memoranda and other notes of advice to select committees, advisory bodies, and the government itself.

In this context, there is an important distinction often made with respect to pressure groups in the UK: that between insider and outsider groups. As Grant has pointed out, the distinction is that insider groups are regarded as legitimate by government and are consulted on a regular basis, whereas outsider groups do not wish to become enmeshed in the consultative relationship with government.[98] Insider groups thus seek to use the formal and informal methods of consultation to influence public policy, shunning publicity stunts in order to achieve their goals. Outsider groups adopt a less compromising attitude to the public authorities, and seek to achieve their goals through public pressure or direct action. This theoretical distinction should not be confused with a description of any particular group, however, since some groups, like Friends of the Earth, have moved from being an outsider group in the 1970s to being an insider group. It would also be a mistake to see insiders as always being more influential than outsiders. Greenpeace's campaign against the disposal of the Brent Spar oil facility at sea in 1995, for example, was a classic case of 'outsider' tactics paying off, although some have seen this incident as a throw-back to an earlier form of campaigning.[99]

Size is not necessarily a good indicator of effectiveness. One of the more influential groups of the 1980s was the Green Alliance, with a membership of no more than five hundred people, but with the status and contacts to gain access to Westminster and Whitehall. Not only does the Green Alliance supply parliamentary briefings and propose parliamentary questions, but it is credited for example with prompting a meeting in 1987 in the prime minister's office to address problems in relation to agriculture and the environment. In 1992 the director of the Alliance, Tom Burke, was appointed as adviser to the then secretary of state, Michael Heseltine. There are also groups that seek to promote dialogue between government, industry, and the environmental movement. One of the leading groups in this category is the Centre for Environment and Economic Development. The London-based office of the Institute for European Environmental Policy has a similar clientele. It should also be noted that 'green capitalist' organizations are strong in the UK.

Influence on policy is not always solely a matter of influencing governments. There can be indirect influence as well. Thus, groups can also exercise indirect influence through discussions with think-tanks, like the Centre for Policy Studies or the Institute for Public Policy Research, which themselves may have an influence on policy. Moreover, pressure to improve the environment comes from groups other than those solely devoted to environmental protection. For example, growing concern over the effects of air pollution on asthma sufferers has been prompted in part by the concerns of the British Medical Association. UK environmental groups have also increasingly sought a direct dialogue with industry, or alternatively have sought to put pressure on industry, for example by campaigns to expose misleading claims about the environmental credentials of products.

EU environmental policy has been of considerable significance for UK environmental groups, in providing an alternative channel through which to pursue campaigns and seek to influence domestic governments. Lowe and Ward point out, however, that contacts with EU organizations vary considerably among environmental groups, with 47 per cent of those they sampled having no contact with European institutions and only a small elite of groups (14 per cent) having consistent and long-term connections with European forums.[100] When asked about the focus of their lobbying efforts in the EU, most groups gave priority to the Commission.

Comparative Features

Setting the individual country experience in a comparative framework, it is clear that there are both common and divergent trends at work. In terms of their historical legacy, present-day organizations in some countries are more able to rely upon their past achievements than others. Germany, the Netherlands, the UK, and, to a lesser extent, Italy have strong environmental organizations that go back to the nineteenth century. In a number of these cases, the organizations were able to adapt themselves readily to the new politics of the environment that began to emerge in the 1970s by transforming their own policy priorities, modes of working, and membership profiles. By contrast, Spain and Greece lack such long-standing and relatively autonomous groups capable of playing a part in the policy process.

Here patterns of interaction between government and environmental groups are important, and we can identify a spectrum of such interaction. At one end of the spectrum is a country like the Netherlands, in which environmental groups benefit (though perhaps they also suffer some loss) from the inclusive, and financially supportive, national policy style. At the other end of the spectrum is Greece, in which the centralized party system tends to work in an exclusionary way. In between these extremes we find interesting variations. In the UK, for example, there is clearly a well established pattern of inclusive consultation, provided that the group has insider status. Some organizations in this context will find it worth their while to transform themselves from outsiders to insiders. Conversely, in Germany the policy-making machine has found it worth its while, for reasons of its own, to make itself more open to environmental groups. In this regard, contrasting Spain and Greece on the one hand with the Netherlands and the UK on the other might suggest that we were here seeing an effect of the establishment of democratic norms. However, the German example also suggests that there are irreducible features of national policy style that vary independently of the existence of democratic norms.

Environmental organizations are a major channel through which international influences affect domestic policy decisions. In this respect, environmental groups contrast markedly with political parties, which, as we have already pointed out, maintain a domestic focus and for whom European political competition is a secondary activity.

Undoubtedly, the most striking illustration in recent years of the internationalization of political strategy is provided by the Greenpeace campaign against the planned deep sea disposal by Shell of the Brent Spar oil storage buoy in the North Sea in 1995. Here was a case in which the company that owned the buoy had been in discussion with the UK government for two and a half years in connection with the disposal, which was due to be carried out in accordance with the UK's policy principle of 'best practicable environmental option'. Within two months of Greenpeace launching its campaign, the agreed decision was reversed by Shell, with the UK government having come under very strong pressure from the German government, and with the company having come under equally strong pressure from the spread of consumer boycotts of its products in Europe. The difference between the incentives that environmental groups have to go international and that political parties have to stay domestic is thus highlighted by this example. It clearly reflects the fact that for environmental groups international political actors can be a source of countervailing power within a context in which they might otherwise have difficulty securing their goals.

In this context, the EU provides a unique forum of appeal, in part as a result of the purely formal fact of the direct effect of EU legislation, which enables groups to point to breaches of requirements, and in part because the EU can be a useful political ally more generally. Perhaps the clearest examples in which the formal powers of the EU have been invoked by environmental groups have arisen from the application—or, more accurately claimed, lack of application—of the directive on environmental impact assessment. This was important in the campaigning activities in the UK of those opposed to the building of a road at Twyford Down. Similarly, organizations in southern Europe have sought to use Brussels as a reference point in some of their campaigns. Indeed, they have generally benefited from a strengthening of transnational links between environmental groups in different countries.

For southern environmental groups this has increasingly become a major activity of the major organizations, with inevitably a pronounced attention to links with Brussels and with other member-states. The tendency to look to the EU as an outlet for their activity and influence has arisen from the more active role of the Commission in environmental affairs and its encouragement (for instance, under Commissioner Ripa di Meana). As one environmental consultant in Athens put it in reference to Brussels, 'we've got friends, we know exactly where to go; we've discovered who is effective and who is going to listen to you in an official manner, and who is going to do something about it and take it a little further'.[101] This type of contact is a welcome relief from the frustration of trying to deal with national bureaucracies in the southern member states.

Feelings towards the Commission as a whole tend, nevertheless, to be ambivalent because of the record of environmental damage caused by European developmental programmes in the past. Groups in Spain and Greece, in particular, have been acerbic in their accusations against Brussels over the effects of the Structural Funds.[102] As the head of the WWF in Greece put it succinctly,

The EC is the big ally and it is also a big threat. On the one hand, there is a very small DG XI [for the environment] in the EC, which is extremely influential in Greece, because it uses NGO material and information and bounces it back . . . On the other hand, 80 per cent of the EC's money goes to structural and agricultural funds. Both of these things are absolutely devastating to Greece's environment. And now, we have of course tried to influence DG XI to influence DG XVI [for regional policy] . . . There is a case to be made for the fact that DG XVI is putting through programmes that are contradictory to EC [environmental] directives.[103]

The WWF has gained a reputation as a respected critic of some of the EU's policies, especially its Cohesion Fund, which places an emphasis on improving environmental infrastructure. The WWF has laid down a series of benchmarks for judging Cohesion Fund performance in communicating with the Commission. In its 1994 report, it proposed improvements for the final regulation that would govern the use of the Fund until 1999.[104]

In general, the difference here between the Commission and national administrations is significant. The former has often actively sought at the national level outside advice and expertise of a critical nature, a mentality that is difficult to find among bureaucrats in the southern countries. Major environmental organizations have participated in some EU research programmes on the environment; and their provision of detailed information on environmental degradation in their own countries is only welcome in DG XI, with its own limited resources. The Lega per l'Ambiente, for instance, has provided the Commission with dossiers on problems of applying the EIA directive and on the environmental effects of public works in Italy. The Lega's contacts with the Commission intensified from the late 1980s, helped by the fact that the Environment Commissioner (Ripa di Meana) was Italian.[105]

Thus the environmental organizations in the south have distinctly benefited from their countries' entry to the EU, both in terms of enlarging their scope for influence on policy-makers and also in enhancing their own legitimacy.[106] As a result, their impact on national governments has become indirect (via the Commission) as well as direct. Recent improvements in direct relations between the two sides, as in Spain, have also owed something to the experience of participating in the EU.

ECONOMIC INTERESTS

Economic interests play an important role in environmental policy. As we saw in Part I, a significant element in the development of environmental policy in the EU was the need to coordinate environmental regulation with the growth of the single market. Increased costs, or the perception of increased costs, arising from policies of pollution control provide an incentive for firms to lobby governments in the setting of standards, as well as the ability of economic actors to meet the standards once they have been set. Moreover, once responsibility for the environment ceases to be seen solely as the external imposition on companies by the political authorities and comes to be seen as a set of principles to be internalized within the culture and working practices of organizations, as has happened with policies on eco-auditing for example, then the role of economic actors in the pursuit of environmental quality is enhanced.

This last point is of particular importance. We have seen that during the 1980s there emerged a new paradigm of thinking about environmental measures, in which the antagonism between economic success and environmental protection was attacked as being one-sided and short-sighted. At the micro level of the firm, a number of organizations began to explore the validity and significance of the principle espoused by the 3M corporation that pollution prevention pays. According to this principle, by reducing the consumption of raw materials as inputs, eliminating wastes, and recycling materials, firms have important tools for lowering their production costs. At the macro level of economic policy, greater emphasis came to be placed by policy-makers in some countries upon the potential of environmental measures to promote new forms of economic activity.

Although economic interests are central to the successful pursuit of environmental policy, the pattern of interests potentially affected by environmental measures is highly complex. They include firms of all sizes and in all sectors of the economy. At one end of the spectrum, the businesses involved may include large, international firms in the vehicles or chemicals sectors who will have specialist departments dealing with environmental management and public policy regulation. At the other end, there will be small local enterprises, like a garage, where pollution outputs are significant but relevant expertise within the organization as to how to handle the problem may be lacking. An important source of many environmental problems is agriculture, which is itself a highly differentiated sector. Moreover, pollution control measures stimulate economic activity as firms develop pollution control equipment in markets secured by regulatory standards or rising consumer demands.

Such complexity suggests that we should not anticipate a straightforward relationship between rising per capita national income and higher environmental standards. Even if environmental quality is thought of as a superior good for which demand is likely to rise faster than the growth in national income, any such demand has to be secured through public policies that are themselves subject to the normal lobbying processes of economic agents. Since such lobbying takes place within an established network of relationships, we should expect that the influence on environmental policy from economic interests would be highly variable.

There is, none the less, an underlying logic to economic activity and the lobbying behaviour to which it gives rise. Measures that lower demand for particular products or that significantly raise costs to producers can be expected to encounter organized resistance. As with the study of environmental groups, our concern is with the way in which specific national policy-making processes play variations on an underlying common logic of action.

Germany

The German economy is characterized by a number of large, world-class, and highly productive firms in sectors such as engineering, chemicals, and vehicles. In addition, it has a large number of smaller firms, the so-called Mittelstand, themselves often involved in complex supply arrangements with the large firms. Its public utilities have strong elements of both public and private control, and it also has a large, dispersed agricultural sector involving in many instances small-scale, part-time farmers. This economic structure is housed within a corporatist framework of policy-making in which much wage-bargaining is conducted centrally by large organizations representing employers and employees within different sectors. There is heavy dependence on the banks as sources of capital investment. During the time of our study, prior to EU economic and monetary union, there was a dispersal of policy-making authority through the central bank and the *Länder*. Post-war government policy has been strongly committed to continuity and economic growth through policies involving the concertation of economic activities.

Finally, because international competitiveness is important to large sectors of the economy, the implications of policy measures for the relative costs of German products compared with those of other countries cannot be ignored. By implication, given that EU membership has been a central plank of German foreign policy since 1957, the opportunities that the EU offers for the regulation and stabilization of the international economic context are not likely to be ignored by policy-makers.

The role and influence of economic interests is revealed in the course of German policy developments since 1969. As we saw in Chapter 5, the German public and government participated actively in the upsurge of activity that marked the dawn of the modern phase of environmental politics in the late 1960s and early 1970s. However, the oil price rises of 1973/4 put severe pressure on the German economy, and at a meeting in Gymnich in 1975 business and trade union representatives put great pressure on the Social Democratic–Liberal government to soften its regulatory stance as a way of continuing to secure economic growth. Here we have a clear example of the way in which corporatist economic arrangements of concertation seemed to entrench a productivist paradigm of policy.

However, the corporatist arrangements took a different form in the 1980s with the new wave of policy measures. Indeed, Germany was one of the first countries to attempt to recast the traditional opposition between prudent economics and stringent environmental protection in the early 1980s, with the discussions surrounding the Large Combustion Ordinance. Boehmer-Christiansen and Skea have shown how the implementation of the ordinance drew upon much of the corporatist framework of economic policy-making in coordinating manufacturers to produce pollution control equipment as part of counter-cyclical economic policy.[107] Similarly, the car industry accepted the need for higher emissions standards for vehicles. An important element arising from the corporatist style of Germany's industrial policy was the way the German government, having accepted the need to legislate domestically, then sought international measures, particularly within the EU, to ensure that the competitive disadvantage was not too great for German firms.

One of the most tangible ways in which a new approach developed was in spending on environmental protection. The share of total investments accounted for by investments in environmental protection rose from 3.5 per cent in 1980 to 4.4 per cent in 1984 and to 5 per cent in 1991.[108] Germany has also seen a large expansion of funds going from the government into environmental research and development —another example of the way in which the traditional corporatist pattern has adapted to new environmental demands. One of the effects of the renewed interest in environmental protection in the 1980s was the growth not only of pollution control industries (the 'eco-industrial complex'), but also of the development of environmental consultancies and other research-based activity concerned with the greening of industry. Moreover, there have been some interesting alliances between environmental organizations and business, of which examples include cooperation between BUND and Tupperware and Greenpeace's endorsement of the East German company Foron for marketing a CFC refrigerator.[109]

During the late 1980s the environment minister, Klaus Töpfer, a former professor of environmental economics, sought to provide an intellectual rationale for environmental measures by appealing to the notion of the 'circular economy'. The fundamental idea here was to think of material flows through the economy in terms of their effect on the environment and to ensure that there was as little leakage from these flows as possible. Gerd Wagner has shown that the Circular Economy Law, which came into effect in October 1996 and sought to regulate waste management by reference to the principle of product stewardship, can be seen as a way of seeking to internalize environmental risk management into the decision-making calculus of firms.[110] Similarly, looking at the experience of eco-audits in German industry, Steger points out that, whereas the requirements for formal auditing processes have not proved difficult to implement in large firms like those in the chemical industry, there have been problems for small and medium-sized enterprises, the Mittelstand, in which accounting patterns are often informal and implicit.[111]

The reorientation of the coroporatist system to the principles of ecological modernization and the attempt to reconceptualize the environmental responsibilities of business management have clearly been important. Brand also reports the growth of constructive dialogue between environmental groups and industry, with representatives from the environmental groups saying that their conversations with industry are more exciting than those with policy-makers.[112] However, it is difficult to know how far these trends amount to a fundamental realignment away from the underlying conflict between economic and environmental interests. In 1993 there was a heated debate initiated by industrialists in the midst of the recession on the economically harmful effects of purportedly strict environmental regulation. The response of the environment ministry was to commission independent research institutes to assess this claim. Their conclusion was that, although there had been some negative effects, the overall result in stimulating modernization was positive.[113] From the political point of view, however, the most important feature of the episode was the fact that German industrialists felt compelled to challenge publicly what many recognized as the new orthodoxy on the relative priority to be given to environmental protection. It is also worth noting, however, that the debate about Germany's competitive position has now moved away from the question of environmental regulation to that of social costs.

There are other criticisms that suggest even deeper problems, some connected with economic cost and some connected with the influential position of key interest groups. Thus, it is claimed that attempts to deal with nitrate pollution in the North Sea have focused on expensive investment in upgrading sewage treatment plants, to the relative neglect of agricultural polluting sources.[114] Through the German Farmers' Union agricultural interests have normally had significant influence on public policy, and in the postwar period German farming underwent significant concentration, specialization, and intensification. It has been argued that, in response to the environmental criticism of agriculture, the Farmers' Union faces a difficult organizational trilemma: balancing its claims to protect its special interests with the claims of the general interest; protecting the price support that farmers receive; and meeting the challenge of the environmental critique.[115] If Germany has managed to achieve environmental targets without always following the polluter-pays principle in the agricultural sector, there is a similar point made by critics about water pollution control. Thus, the 1994 decision to revise wastewater treatment charges, it has been claimed, will lead to a substantial reduction in the incentive effect of the charges, which prior to the revision encouraged the installation of clean-up technology.[116]

Greece

In Greece, industry has traditionally been cosseted by the widespread belief that the state rather than the private sector should carry the onus of environmental protection.[117] The practice, however, of Greek governments of whatever party avoiding strict environmental controls for private producers on the grounds that these would hinder industrial development has hardly encouraged the private sector to adapt to new environmental demands. As a 1992 survey of large industries showed, some have made a token effort and others none.[118]

In Greece, a similar hostility between the Ministry of the Environment and industry developed during the tenure of Tritsis in the first half of the 1980s. This was at first a period of dynamic change in launching Greek policy on the environment at the time of EU entry. But economic interests began to mobilize against Tritsis, whose personal commitment to environmental interests was blatant, and these contributed among other things to his eventual retirement from this position. One of his major achievements, the 1986 Framework Law, was much complicated and delayed by the pressure of economic interests concerned at how much this might really encourage a more effective implementation of EU directives.[119]

Business interests, such as those of the construction industry, have exerted a powerful pull over government circles when renewed efforts have been made to resolve the growing problem of atmospheric pollution in Athens.[120] During the initial period of concern over this issue, up to the early 1980s, industrialists had been made the scapegoat for the Athens pollution cloud, but they had learned to mobilize in defence. Subsequently, laws concerning industrial pollution were formulated in such a way as not to 'embarrass' industrial activity; e.g., findings from monitoring would be confidential, this being all the more possible because of the decisive role here of the Ministry of Industry.[121]

A significant key to the power of industrial interests is the institutional fragmentation of responsibility for environmental policy in southern Europe and especially Greece. This has allowed such interests to exploit inter-ministerial rivalry —such as between Industry and the National Economy, not to mention YPEHODE and other ministries in the Greek case—and in effect to divide and rule when industrial interests are directly threatened.[122] In fact, one special reason for industrial obstruction of the 1986 Framework Law was its basic aim to improve inter-ministerial coordination in environmental management. More recently, the contribution of growing traffic to pollution in Athens has drawn some attention away from industry. This has in turn mobilized a new pressure group, the taxi drivers of Athens, whose influence comes from the inadequacy of public transport in the city.[123] However, to complete the story, growing public concern in Athens has come to weigh more in the considerations of politicians on air pollution, whether at the local or the national level.

Greece, by comparison with other member states, is less industrialized and, for instance, has no car industry of its own. However, an initiative was taken in the mid-1980s to regulate its shipping industry to protect the marine environment of the Mediterranean, following a series of oil tanker disasters.[124] This is a case, again, where bad publicity—with international pressure for still more measures— serves to stimulate a commitment to environmental protection.[125] Shipowners have developed environmental training courses in conjunction with the Hellenic Marine Protection Association (HELMEPA).

The other sector in Greece, as in the other countries, that has reacted on similar grounds of the threat to its own economic interests from environmental degradation has been tourism, which includes many small businesses. Here, programmes have developed, invariably in cooperation with responsive local authorities and sometimes with European funding, to improve the quality of tourist facilities, clearly with an eye to changing demands in the international market.

Spain

Small companies may be assisted by economic programmes geared towards small and medium-sized enterprises (SMEs) in the form of subsidies in order to improve their environmental infrastructures. Spain in the 1990s has become quite active in this respect. In the region of Madrid, for instance, subsidies are awarded after environmental auditing has taken place.[126] This procedure has been followed in that region since 1989; and, although expensive, by the end of 1992 over a hundred industrial units there had been audited.[127] Similar programmes had been instituted in most Spanish regions by the mid-1990s.[128]

Spain in particular has been fairly enterprising in providing support programmes for industry as a whole. In 1989, the Ministry of Industry in Madrid launched its programme to facilitate through investment the adaptation of Spanish industry to EU environmental regulations for a four-year period, 1990–4.[129] Another programme called PITMA focused on developing environmental technology.[130]

In Spain, the Confederation of Entrepreneurial Organizations (CEOE) has established an environmental committee, as has the Council of Chambers of Commerce.[131] A trend that has developed over the past few years is for conferences to be had on industry and the environment with government support and participation; in the same period, generally, relations between government and industry have improved with respect to policy consultation. This is a marked change from the time when government remained closed to such contact.

Italy

In Italy the power of economic interests has been evident in the fortunes of environmental legislation, where direct conflict has resulted in the obstruction or at least the delay of draft laws.[132] Influence has been exerted either through personal contacts with relevant ministers or through party-political channels closely linked with business interests. With the EU directive on bathing water, for example, considerable pressure came from interests affected—above all, beach operators—operating via local and regional channels, this being not unconnected with Italy's request for exceptions and postponements.[133]

The problem has also been one of deeply rooted mentalities on the side of industry. A 1990 report on environmental policy and socioeconomic planning in Italy noted a conflict between growing environmental consciousness and industrial secrecy, as featured in attacks on the Seveso law, for fear that it would force the revelation of industrial secrets.[134] Such conflicts were likely to increase with growing pressure from European legislation, especially in certain sectors. A distinctly defensive attitude was apparent in the Italian chemical industry towards environmental protection in the face of accusations that it was a great polluter. Its position ranged from arguments appealing to consumer interests i.e. (that without chemical products the 'fine life' enjoyed by Italians would not be possible) to exploiting the absence of reliable data on the state of pollution.[135] Conflict with policy options tended to come to the fore most often when initiatives were taken by a pro-environment minister of the environment seen as being not sufficiently committed to industrial interests. Thus, industrialists lobbied powerfully against Ruffolo's idea of a new energy tax in 1992, and also made an issue of the government's monopoly of Italian representation at the Rio summit.[136]

With other large Italian companies, environmental scandals have been a significant motivation behind their conversion to environmental protection. A number of scandals from the 1970s received wide media attention, such as the export of toxic wastes and grave industrial accidents, notably at Seveso (Icmesa), Priolo (Enichem), and Massa Carrara (Farmoplant).[137] Such major firms as Ferruzzi-Montedison, ENI, and ENEL as well as FIAT have come to invest considerable sums in environmental protection in response to environmental regulations; and Confindustria too gives environmental protection a high priority. A practice has developed of seeking voluntary agreements with government authorities at regional or national levels.[138]

Netherlands

Dutch commercial culture is historically well established. The Netherlands has a highly developed economy and is the location for international firms such as Shell. It is one of the main transport hubs for Europe, especially through the port of Rotterdam. It has an agricultural sector that is highly concentrated on intensive production. Exposure to the international market is extensive for many sectors. With a bourgeois class that has endured an embarrassment of riches since the late sixteenth century, the Netherlands is also a society in which the state has historically supported and fostered the development of commerce. Perhaps even more than the USA, the business of the Netherlands is business.

The industrial and economic policy style for much of the twentieth century has been corporatist, with high levels of organization for employers and employees superimposed upon the traditional 'pillars' of Dutch politics: the Protestant, Catholic, and secular groupings. Just as Dutch pillarization began to break down in the 1970s, so the corporatist style of policy-making also changed, particularly under the first Lubbers government elected in 1982. Yet, although the importance of the peak organizations waned, sectoral organizations strengthened, combining quasi-compulsory membership and an increased prominence in the policy process.

Within the Netherlands, we find a similar pattern to that of Germany, in the sense that there is a widespread attempt to reconceptualize the relationship between environmental protection and economic performance. Mol has provided extensive evidence of how parts of the Dutch chemical industry responded to growing pressures for ecological modernization.[139] The Dutch chemical industry is varied, having both small and large firms, but it is dominated by a relatively few large producers who are both capital-intensive and exposed to international markets. For example, 90 per cent of Dutch polymer sales in 1991 were from exports.[140] The chemical industry is also one that has come increasingly under a more sceptical gaze from the public and the media, particularly over such issues as waste disposal, plastics, packaging, and pesticides.

Mol shows that during the 1980s the paint industry, for example, came to pay increasing attention to questions of pollution control; in particular, there was a professional debate in the industry about moving the focus of control away from end-of-pipe techniques towards recycling and closed production systems in which waste run-off was minimized.[141] In this context the main sectoral organization for the industry became more important because it provided a channel through which negotiations could take place with the environment ministry on such matters as the establishment of a voluntary programme to reduce the emission of hydrocarbons.

The increasing prominence of the environment ministry in relation to leading economic interests is a measure of the growing salience of environmental issues during the 1980s. As a result, the chemical industry had to learn how to negotiate with a ministry that, unlike the ministries of economic affairs or agriculture, did not necessarily take a developmental or protective attitude towards their concerns. Mol shows that the effects of this complicating of government relations involved not only the increased prominence of the sectoral organizations, but also a narrowing of the policy network in the debate on chemicals and the environment as the discussion between industry and the environment ministry became more technical and focused on issues of implementation.

The increased sensitivity of the chemical industry to environmental concerns had a number of causes. They were partly internal to the industry itself, as professionals within it began to raise questions about its environmental effects and the possible technical remedies to the problems that were thrown up. They were also a response to public and media concern, on which the environment ministry was able to rely in its policy discussions with the industry and with other ministries. The causes also included the need to respond to EU directives in the area of chemicals and a perception that consumers in international markets were demanding more environmentally friendly products.

To observe such changes in the relationship between the chemical industry and the government is to see some of the background for the developments contained in the 1989 National Environmental Policy Plan, which aimed to persuade target groups to internalize responsibility for environmental protection. The Plan sought to set targets for the reduction of leading pollutants over a twenty-year period, polluting industries being an important target group in this process. In fact, in setting the targets the environment ministry engaged in direct negotiation with sectoral organizations from industry about the stringency of the Plan's standards and found that they were sometimes more amenable than the economics ministry, the traditional guardian of industry, had been. Moreover, the development of the Plan itself opened up the possibility for interesting new political alliances between industry and the environmental cause. This was true not simply of the obvious potential created by the Plan for the pollution control industries and associated consultancies: there were also some surprising alliances. For example, the road hauliers were keen on the idea of moving more traffic from road to rail, in order to avoid the delays their vehicles encountered from commuter cars on Dutch motorways.

The major sector in which corporatism does not appear to have broken down is that of agriculture, in which it is alleged, for example, that organic farmers have been marginalized in the negotiations between government and producers.[142] There may be many reasons for this exception, but one possible explanation is that there have traditionally been strong links in the Netherlands between the agricultural sector and the Christian Democratic parties, and so the corporatistic arrangements are likely to be reinforced by more than the functional necessities of bargaining.

The internalization of responsibility as a theme of Dutch policy has had two implications with respect to the way that government regulates for environmental protection. The first is that inspectors take a different view of the process of regulation in companies where there are well developed internal systems of control. And this has led many companies to develop such systems. Secondly, it has become part of government policy to rely more upon voluntary agreements (covenants) with industry in order to achieve environmental objectives. These are not simply tacit understandings, but are formal documents available for public inspection.

The origin of this strategy goes back to the period when the minister for the environment was the Liberal Winsemius in the first Lubbers government (1982–86). However, it was carried on by his successor, Nijpels, also a Liberal, and even by the Labour minister Alders when he came to office in 1992. From the point of view of industry, the advantage of regulation through voluntary agreements is that industry itself retains control over the process of implementation in a way it would not do if it were confronted with an impersonal mechanism such as a pollution tax. In the Dutch discussions on the implementation of a policy for the control of greenhouse gases, for example, the option of voluntary agreements, particularly in sectors that were exposed to international markets as well as in those that were vulnerable to increased costs, was much preferred to the tax alternative. Indeed, some representatives from industry voiced the view that they would move production to Belgium if a carbon tax were introduced on producers.[143]

In summary, then, we can say that, in respect of economic interests in the Netherlands, the development of environmental policy has transformed the traditional patterns of government–industry interaction, and also that the policy strategy itself has been transformed by the political relations within which it has been worked out. The target group strategy has brought to the fore the sectoral organizations that can speak as representatives of producers at a certain level of aggregation, but the close relations that exist have provided the context within which the strategy of voluntary agreements and the internalization of environmental responsibility have been stressed.

United Kingdom

By contrast with Germany, the UK has traditionally had an industrial structure that is both less technically strong and more dependent upon equity capital. It can be argued that this has made the UK less receptive than Germany to the ideas of ecological modernization, since there is not the corporatist infrastructure within which priorities can be renegotiated and coordination on economic activities built. Moreover, an essential part of the Thatcher government's economic programme consisted in creating the institutional and legal climate in which business managers would be freer to pursue profitable activities.

Despite this, there have been important institutional and policy developments in recent years that have sought to realign the relationship between business and environmental protection. As part of its plans to implement the programme of *This Common Inheritance*, the government established the Business and Environment Council, with the task of spreading environmental awareness among industrialists and businesses. The industry standard BSI 5750 has been established by the semi-independent British Standards Institute to provide a benchmark against which companies can measure their environmental performance. Moreover, there are attempts to promote environmental technology among learned organizations and other public bodies. The Royal Society has been important in promoting the public discussion of risk perception, while the Royal Society of Arts has sought to promote the importance of environmental awareness in industrial design and manufacture. A further way in which technical innovation is encouraged is through the so-called 'Queen's Award', a special section of which was established in 1993 to promote environmental achievement.

Among business organizations, the Confederation for British Industry, the main employers' organization, has sought to develop awareness of the commercial importance of environmental quality among its members through an environment department. But it is a body with a varied membership, requiring it to balance its environmental awareness with concerns among its members about costs, particularly those arising from regulation. The Chemical Industries Association has also sought to develop codes of conduct for the chemical industry and is a regular participant in policy forums.

The retail sector is a relatively strong part of the UK economy, so it is not surprising that retail organizations have sought to respond to public concerns about the environment, in part to attain a competitive advantage. The foremost example is the Body Shop, which has since the 1970s aimed to be environmentally responsible in the purchasing and marketing of its products.

The circumstances among industries traditionally regarded as the main polluters has changed considerably in recent years. In the early to mid-1980s one of the principal actors was the Central Electricity Generating Board, a nationalized undertaking responsible for electricity generation. It was this body, for example, that was one of the principal sources of opposition to greater UK participation in international action to control acid emissions.[144] In 1988 the electricity industry was privatized, and subsequent policy by the electricity generators has been to replace the burning of coal with the burning of gas. Partly in consequence, the coal industry, formerly a powerful actor, has been severely reduced in size and scope.

The water industry has undergone a similar transformation.[145] Between 1974 and 1989 responsibility for water supply and waste-water treatment, as well as pollution control, rested with the regional water authorities, which were virtual monopolists in their areas of operation. With the privatization of the water industry, the roles of 'poacher and gamekeeper' were separated. In anticipation of the increased costs of installing water treatment facilities arising from EU directives, the water industry was allowed a special factor in the formula used by the price regulator to regulate permissible price increases. It should be noted that the price regulator, a public body known as OFWAT, has been critical of the cost of EU directives, arguing that they are detrimental to the customer and unjustified by evidence of environmental and other benefits.

Overall, then, we may say that in the UK there has been a shift in the traditional perception of a built-in opposition between environmental protection and economic performance. But there are clearly limits as to how far this has gone, and there are still considerable reservations within the world of business about the costs of environmental protection. Moreover, the Department of Trade and Industry—a strong ministry within British government and closely aligned with business interests—is pushing for more comprehensive cost–benefit assessments of proposed regulation on business.

Comparative Trends

Among important economic interests, there have clearly been major adaptations to increasing environmental requirements. These have been most visible in cases where there are large, capital-intensive industries, like chemicals, that are exposed to international markets and have the organizational capacity to introduce procedures for environmental auditing and management. In some measure, these changes have been brought about through policy and regulation, but the extent of autonomous change from within key industries should not be underestimated. Moreover, as environmental policies have had their effects, they have offered economic opportunities for the development of eco-industries. The perception that such opportunities are important has been more prevalent in the Netherlands and Germany than elsewhere, but it none the less plays a role in the structuring of environmental politics more generally.

If the structure of industry is important, then this has been a constraint in the southern countries on the prospects for adapting to environmental demands. The predominance of SMEs, with a very high proportion of small businesses, has created two problems. In the first place, it is much more difficult to monitor the activity of a profusion of small businesses than it is a number of large or even medium-sized companies. And secondly, the former do not have the resources or the skills to support such adaptation, many small businesses being family concerns. They have, as in the Spanish case, very limited investment scope and weak technology.[146] In Greece it was noted that sometimes small industries built treatment plants, but they did not operate them, for 'they are not easily controlled'.[147]

Clearly, environmental costs are a major factor in the way of SMEs responding to growing demands for environmental quality. But this is not merely a practical problem of resources, for there are also cultural factors at work. The idea has been widespread, and somewhat unquestioned, in these southern countries that costs occasioned by environmental issues should be met by the state and not the private economic actor. The case is quoted of heavy lorries, the main cause of pollution in the area, being banned from using the coastal roads along the Adriatic in Italy and required to use the motorways instead. This ban proved impractical because of the lack of funding for policing the ban at night. Only when the regional government agreed with the lorry-owners' association to assume the burden of fares paid by lorries on the motorway was the matter resolved.[148]

Spain is, in this respect, well ahead of Greece, where generally the shortage of public funding, combined with the absence of industrial wealth, has been a major problem. Even with the addition of EU funding, adaptation by Greek industries is inhibited by the need to rely on bank loans for which the interest rate is very high. On the other hand, some larger industries, e.g. in the cement and food sectors, have invested in environmental protection.[149]

One main exception in Greece to the lack of a strategy has been the organization of industrial estates under the Greek Bank for Industrial Development (ETBA). Operating on the principle that environmental protection is easier to apply where there is a concentration of industry, this programme started as long ago as 1969 and included such projects as a large treatment plant in the Thessaloniki industrial area, set up in 1977. By 1992 there were eight industrial estates with such treatment plants, and they function on the basis of strict application of EIAs. Early projects under this programme were funded by the European Investment Bank (EIB) and the World Bank, but now the EU has become more important through its programmes like MEDSPA.[150] Although limited, the ETBA programme for industrial estates is a pertinent example of the lesson pinpointed by the OECD report on environmental policy in Greece (1983):

Industrial development in Greece is still at a relatively early stage. This creates an opportunity to pursue a policy of prevention that would avoid the heavier, future costs of curative measures and other ensuing costs to health, property and the environment. Greece may thus avoid many of the environmental problems and costs afflicting other OECD member countries.[151]

The European Commission's Task Force's report on the environment and the Single Market recorded the low level of environmental markets in the southern member states.[152] At around the same time, a survey of four European countries noted that the Italian market was far less ready than the German to follow tighter standards over car emissions, and that this affected the attitude of companies.[153] However, during the 1990s the situation began to change gradually although unevenly. Even at the start of the decade a certain change of attitude was becoming evident, for instance in Spain. There, it was noted, 'until recently industry considered the protection of the environment as an extra cost, without any productive yield', but now 'it was beginning to perceive the environmental variable as an element capable of introducing notable improvements in the productive process' and generally as a stimulant to modernization.[154]

The pattern of state–industry relations varies across our six cases. Among the northern countries, for example, there have been long-standing corporatist patterns of economic policy-making in the Netherlands and Germany by comparison with the UK, in which corporatist experiments have been tried at various times but have had to compete with alternative approaches as well as organizational structures of labour and industry that made corporatist styles of negotiation difficult. In the southern member states, there are certain patterns and similarities in the relations between industry and the state that have constrained choices in environmental policy; these too tend to demarcate those member states from the northern ones. The extensive role of the state in the economy, deriving from authoritarian or totalitarian rule, has had a number of consequences. One of these is of course the extent of clientelism based on this close link between state authority and economic interest. Furthermore, the former has tended to cushion industry from pressures for environmental quality. Finally, the overriding concern with economic growth in these countries has weighed heavily against ecological modernization. This has allowed business and industry a privileged position and considerable influence in the corridors of power.

To the extent that there has been a greening of economic actors, it is not easy to associate this with styles of economic policy-making. There have been general discussions in the literature on comparative environmental policy about the role of corporatism as a facilitating or inhibiting condition of environmental policy change.[155] To be sure, it is possible to point to corporatist features, particularly in the Netherlands and Germany, that may be said to help ecological modernization, not least the ability to use sectoral organizations to coordinate environmental action.

Conversely, however, one can argue that it has been the protective attitude of the state towards industry in the south that has prevented ecological change. One also has to reckon with the fact that it has been the liberalization of the UK economy that appears to have created the conditions under which environmental investments, especially in water quality improvements, have been made possible.

In all our countries, the special place of agriculture is worth noting. Although there have been a number of measures, like set-aside, that have been promoted by the EU, there have been strong structural constraints, largely to do with the way in which interests are organized in the agricultural sector, that have preserved a bias in favour of large-scale intensive agriculture. As we saw in the case of the Netherlands, for example, the transformation of practices was less marked in the agricultural sector than in other sectors of the economy.

The growing pressures from the international market for environmental quality have had an effect on all our countries, both north and south. In the north, for example, it has proved impossible for plastics or vehicle manufacturers to ignore rising consumer demands in the USA or Japan. In the south, similar pressures have begun to have some effect, though predictably much more in some quarters than in others. Most of all, large companies have felt this pressure; in particular, the large multinationals with subsidiaries in the southern countries have been at the forefront of this change. These were seen as the 'motor of change in Spanish industry', in reference to such companies as Volkswagen.[156] In Italy, Fiat has led this new approach of responding to green demands. As long ago as the mid-1980s, Fiat signed an agreement with the Ministry of the Environment on promoting environmental quality (atmospheric and acoustic) in metropolitan areas and publicly supported the implementation of EU directives on car emissions.[157]

For the southern countries these trends amount to an evolving situation which represents a loosening of traditional constraints from economic interests on policymakers with respect to environmental policy. This new situation is due only in part to the impact of policy itself, especially of the EU, and probably more to movement in the international market. In essence, though, it is explained by a combination of different factors. As was recently concluded in a survey of nine European countries, 'In all countries of the study the picture is the same: the environment becomes an issue for industry through the combination of regulations adopted by the administration, the pressures from the environmental movement and from the attention paid to pollution by the mass communication media.'[158]

CONCLUSIONS: DOMESTIC POLITICS AND ENVIRONMENTAL ISSUE DYNAMICS

If we seek to summarize the above analysis of domestic political systems in the EU in the light of our original questions, then a pattern of common trends and national distinctiveness emerges. Looking at the general nature of public opinion, it is clear that there has been a common upward movement of concern across all six countries in the last twenty-five years. However, the extent of the similarities is limited, and it is unclear how far these attitudinal differences are likely to translate into behavioural changes. It is sometimes thought that behind these attitudinal differences there lurks a 'southern syndrome' showing a pattern of 'amoral familism'. Although interview respondents in the south sometimes volunteered such thoughts, they too have to be interpreted in the light of the evidence that in northern countries there are behavioural patterns that are at odds with an expressed concern for the environment.

To some extent there is a similar story about common trends to be told with respect to other elements of the domestic political system, apart from public opinion. The party manifesto data show a generally upward movement in the salience of environmental issues, and the growth in the number and strength of environmental groups is also important. Moreover, though stronger in the Netherlands and Germany, the growth of ecological modernist attitudes among certain economic actors elsewhere is also striking.

However, despite these underlying common trends upwards in the salience of environmental issues, there are still considerable differences among the six countries. Indeed, cross-national differences between our six countries are in several respects quite marked. Such differences are apparent when examining all the main elements of the domestic political systems. Public opinion may display increased salience of environmental concerns, but at significantly different levels across the six countries. German and Dutch political parties are in general much less productivist than their counterparts elsewhere, particularly in Spain. The specific economic structures and different levels of economic development in the six countries affect both attitudes of economic interests and the governments' ability to implement changes in the production practices. Even environmental groups display distinct national patterns.

Thus, the role of and pressures from these elements vary as one would expect, and there are often identifiable reasons for cross-national differences. In particular, there are differences as to timing with respect to the environment gaining more priority in domestic politics. This is most evident when we compare the two new democracies of Spain and Greece with the more established democracies of northern Europe and also the other southern country, Italy. Thus, one should avoid comparing these six member states too statically at any given point of time.

How can we understand this pattern of similarities and differences? One simple model that is often invoked at this point is that the differences that we observe are to be accounted for largely in terms of differences in levels of economic development. We saw in the Introduction to Part II that both economists, in the notion of superior goods, and sociologists, with the appeal to post-materialist values, sought to explain differences in environmental commitment to an underlying cause that was in essence economic. As national income rises, so we should expect societal preferences to move increasingly in a pro-environment direction. The primary place where such differences would show is in public attitudes; but we might also expect that it would be revealed in party position statements in manifestoes, the fate of environmental groups, and the willingness of economic actors to embrace ecological modernization.

Some of our findings are consistent with this view. For example, it is an implication of this approach that the six countries should really fall into three groups: Germany and the Netherlands as the richest countries emerge as most concerned about the environment; Italy and the UK fall somewhere in the middle; and Greece and Spain appear the least concerned. Certainly the data on public opinion about the relative priority that environmental issues should receive are consistent with that view, as is the prominence given to environmental issues in the manifesto positions of the German and Dutch political parties.

Other features of these society-related variables are, however, less susceptible to such an analysis. For example, one important feature of the trends is that they are far from smooth. The German party system, for instance, shows a decisive move towards environmental concerns in the early 1980s. Similarly, the impact of democratization in Spain and Greece in the 1970s is a discontinuous process that is distinct from that of the relatively steady economic growth that the two countries have experienced. Moreover, it is clear that specifically political factors, for example in the case of the UK the strength and longevity of the environmental groups, can have a significant effect. In addition to the underlying economic variable of national income growth, therefore, we need also to look at the political and other factors that are likely to be important.

The most obvious point to consider is the significance of green parties within national party systems. This is not to say that green parties are a necessary condition for political priority to be given to the environment—after all, Denmark does not show such influence—and it has always to be noted that institutional as well as party-political factors are at work. Moreover, much determines the fortunes of green parties and therefore helps to account for cross-national variation in their presence. These include: the type of electoral system, the nature of political competition, the ability of traditional parties to respond to new demands and their occupation of political space, and general disaffection towards traditional parties where the greens assume a protest or even anti-party position.[159]

Germany displays their clearest influence, with the Greens having occupied a potentially pivotal role in the formation of federal governments for much, though not all, of the period. The clear connection between the rise of the Greens in the early 1980s and the decisive shift of parties' stances on environmental questions suggests the significant influence of the Greens as an important precipitating factor in the transformation of German party politics. This is not to say that the rise of the Greens was the sole, or even the main, cause of such transformation of policy orientation. Firstly, the change of orientation, having taken root in the Christian–Liberal coalition, was consolidated and built upon in the late 1980s when the Greens were declining in significance. Secondly, we see a marked shift in policy orientation in the Dutch party system, where the influence of the green political parties is significantly less. Hence, although Germany stands out among the six countries in having a strong green party, it would be wrong to assign too much significance to this fact alone.

In the southern member states, the main parties have tended not to give a priority to environmental policy save on an *ad hoc* basis. They have at least been slow to respond to environmental issues, for a number of reasons. Firstly, except in Italy, the lack of democratic systems and hence of competing parties meant the first wave of international concern made no impact at this level in the 1970s, which in any case came to be dominated by the politics of regime transition. Secondly, if any policy concern predominated in party circles it was economic development and modernization—a tendency reinforced by economic interest links of many of these parties and by the general pattern of clientelistic practices in these southern countries. Thirdly, green parties presented no serious challenge to the established parties, save eventually for the Italian Verdi. In fact, it was not until well into the 1980s that parties began to take the environment seriously. This did not precede the arrival of environmental policy at governmental level, and thus suggests that the parties were not protagonists of the environmental cause.

It is in local politics in the southern countries that parties have pressed more fervently for environmental causes, although that has been highly variable from area to area. In some Italian and Spanish regions, parties of different political leanings have espoused local environmental concerns; and this goes also for parties in some localities in all these countries. Mounting pressure over local degradation combined with a strong local presence from the greens have helped to account for this phenomenon. Additionally, touristic interests have often completed local arguments for giving the environment a priority.

Among the most important ideological trends in the 1980s was the growth of neo-liberalism, which should have some bearing on party thinking and strategy. In relation to environmental questions, neo-liberalism is somewhat ambiguous. On the one hand, the typical neo-liberal stress upon deregulation as part of the need to improve economic performance might be thought to place obstacles in the way of strong environmental measures, since environmental measures often involve some form of regulation. On the other hand, much pollution is induced as a result of state subsidies (with agriculture being the most conspicuous example), and a neo-liberal policy of controlling public expenditure might well reduce the public support of polluting activities. Moreover, the increasing fiscal stringency of the 1980s, in which governments under the influence of neo-liberal thinking felt the need to balance public budgets, might have encouraged green taxes as an attractive way of raising revenue.

Neo-liberalism was felt most strongly the UK's Conservative Party, but in practice it turned out to be difficult for environmentally orientated neo-liberals to convince their ideological colleagues that the control of environmental pollution ought to be a centrepiece of the neo-liberal agenda. Hence the British case would suggest that neo-liberalism had a negative effect upon the saliency given to environmental issues. However, the example of the Netherlands provides some counterweight to this as a general interpretation of the influence of neo-liberalism. Although the influence of neo-liberalism was felt in the CDA, the VVD has been the typical holder of the neo-liberal position. As environment minister, Nijpels was able to combine neo-liberal commitments with a strong commitment to environmental planning, suggesting that it is less the influence of neo-liberalism itself than its particular interpretation that is important.

By contrast with both the UK and the Netherlands, German parties remained largely insulated from the effects of neo-liberal ideology. Although there have been voices in Germany arguing, for example, the superiority of economic instruments over regulation, these have tended to come from research institutes rather than the political parties. And in the southern European countries, as seen, traditional economic concerns dominated party thinking, whether on the left or right, although the centre-right parties have at times genuflected rhetorically in the direction of neo-liberal ideology. (This has not however had a marked effect on their positions on the environment.)

In general, it is difficult to distinguish between parties and their leaders in government, primarily because it is certain of the latter and not the former who have determined the discourse on environmental matters. As we have seen in Chapter 5, action in government has depended not least on environmental 'champions' such as Töpfer in Germany, Ruffolo in Italy, and Nijpels and Winsemius in the Netherlands. And such figures are usually not typical of their parties. Environmental specialists tend to be a rather exclusive and small group within party structures, and unrepresentative of party attitudes as a whole.

In conclusion, it is evident that parties *qua* parties—as distinct from their political role in government—have not played any significant part in pushing the environmental cause or in affecting the fortunes of European legislation. They have also shown little sign of being profoundly affected by the discourse of environmental matters at the EU level. However, they have in the customary manner acted as channels for political opinion and demands, including green ones; and it is now a convention that they express these across the political spectrum in EU member states.

As the most explicit proponents of environmental quality at the national level, the presence and impact of environmental groups is clearly relevant. On the one hand, their growth over the past decade, especially in the southern countries, underlines their quantitative importance. On the other hand, the degree of their influence on policy-making varies considerably cross-nationally. It is most evident in those countries where they have acquired some 'insider' status and use their political muscle on decision-makers, as in Germany, the Netherlands, and also Britain to some extent—and, to a lesser degree, in Italy. Their influence is weakest in Greece, and also in Spain, until recent institutional changes began to integrate them in the policy consultation process. However, one significant trend is the growing habit of European networking and pressure activity by the larger organizations, allowing those in southern Europe in particular some alternative influence in Brussels compared with their national capitals.

Given their centrality to policy effectiveness, any significant shift in the thinking and behaviour of business and industry towards ecological modernization could be crucial. There is such evidence, although it is much more marked in the northern than the southern member states. As we have seen, the reasons behind any such shift tend to be cross-nationally variable. Thus, in Germany traditional patterns of corporatism have been turned to good advantage, while in the Netherlands a systematic conceptually based approach for target-setting has been adopted. And in Britain some change in the perception of the environment and its relationship with the economy has occurred, but in a less formal and more haphazard way than in the Netherlands. It is in the south that belief in, as distinct from rhetoric about, ecological modernization has advanced much less. The reason has been the traditional pull of the economic imperative (as seen above in our discussion of policy patterns). As of late, there have been some signs of this mind-frame becoming less rigid, with perhaps most change occurring in Italy, especially among large companies. The effects of the international market have begun to show in the south as elsewhere in western Europe.

Given the limits of our analysis here, in concentrating on special characteristics that might affect perceptions of environmental policy, it is not possible to draw any systematic conclusions about deep change. However, it is noticeable that all countries have shown gradual but increasing pressure from national publics over the past decade—a change of which policy-makers are only too aware. There are also signs of a potent impact by opinion on politics. For instance, the link with territoriality is again evident, as is that between certain environmental issues and public health. Furthermore, it seems that a combination of environmental scandals (one might say a traditional phenomenon in public impacts) and cultural predisposition (deriving from value change in society) is most likely to force decision-makers to act.

Finally, what does our analysis of these influences suggest about the relationship between the growth of a system of European environmental governance and the domestic politics of our six countries?

Rather than simply asking whether EU membership has made a difference—which it undoubtedly has in terms of policy content—we should be trying to assess whether the changes identified in this chapter make for a more favourable context in which the EU may impact. Several broad trends suggest a positive answer here, and they include the greater saliency of environmental issues compared with a decade ago and the persistent growth of public concern or sensitivity. This begins to describe a scenario in which the EU may come to interact with other influences to produce ever more sustained pressure for environmental considerations in policies across the board. Formulated schematically, we are talking about a scenario in which bottom-up pressures combine dynamically with the top–down pressures exerted by the EU. Conceivably, in this situation it would become decreasingly possible for national authorities to resist or avoid policies of ecological modernization.

Is this prospect unrealistic? The answer depends of course on future developments beyond the speculation of this book, not least on international economic tendencies, but for our purposes we confine our discussion to the four actors on which this chapter has concentrated. This does at least help to relate our future scenario to political realities as of the moment.

Political parties are central actors in the systems of our six countries. Our finding here however is that they do not play a significant autonomous role with respect to the EU. One suspects that if anything they are reactive to rather than promotive of the discourse emanating from Brussels about sustainability. But it is necessary to judge parties in relation to their political roles, particularly that of government. Admittedly, parties in EU member states have developed their own transnational links along loosely ideological lines, but there is no sign that this activity has had any special impact in the environmental field, notwithstanding the commitment of different MEPs. It should be said here that the institutional structure of the EU is perhaps too complex for party-political pressures to operate easily.

Environmental organizations seem to be another matter. Undoubtedly, their own transnational operations have been more effective, but then they benefit here from their single-issue focus. Their lobbying activity in Brussels is presumably a pattern that will continue, perhaps even grow, in the future, and it is one further example of the growth of European networking, one of the less visible and sometimes underrated dimensions of European integration.

With *economic interests*, evidence points to their accepting the reality of the EU as an actor of increasing importance, including in the environmental field. The pressures of accommodating European legislation, together with genuine anxiety about consequent environmental costs, do not essentially detract from this conclusion. The only matter of analytical dispute is how much industrial adaptation to the dictates of ecological modernization is due directly to the EU or in one way or another to the general requirements of the international market.

When we turn to *public opinion*, it becomes much more difficult to draw conclusions about EU impacts beyond the vague points at the outset of this final comparative discussion. The media certainly take note of the reality of European integration, but they are not necessarily clear in identifying its particular impacts, because their concerns—whether commercial or nationally inclined—do not easily allow this. In the message of the media, the EU and other international factors often become a matter for confusion. And, public opinion is rather too far removed in its perceptions of Brussels, notwithstanding long membership of most of the countries examined here, to speak of particular impacts. This does not however have to mean there is no influence at work, and we refer here to the receptivity of EU action for cultural or other reasons.

NOTES TO CHAPTER 7

1. For a good summary of this literature, see M. J. Smith, *Pressure, Power and Policy: State Autonomy and Policy Networks in Britain and the United States* (New York: Harvester Wheatsheaf, 1993), ch. 3, building on, *inter alia*, D. Marsh and R. A. W. Rhodes (eds.), *Policy Networks in British Government* (Oxford: Oxford University Press, 1992) and R. A. W. Rhodes, *Beyond Westminster and Whitehall* (London: Unwin Hyman, 1988).

2. P. Sabatier, 'Knowledge, Policy-Oriented Learning and Policy Change: An Advocacy Coalition Framework', *Knowledge: Creation, Diffusion, Utilization*, 8:4 (1987), pp. 649–92.

3. G. A. Almond, *The American People and Foreign Policy* (New York: Praeger, 1960), p. 138.

4. See e.g. M. Nas, 'Green, Greener, Greenest', in J. W. van Deth and E. Scarbrough (eds.), *The Impact of Values: Beliefs in Government*, iv (Oxford: Oxford University Press, 1995), pp. 275–300.

5. Interview with Papadakis, December 1992.

6. R. J. Dalton, *The Green Rainbow* (New Haven and London: Yale University Press, 1994), pp. 53–5. Questions of an absolute sort have also been asked. For example, *Eurobarometer* 16 (1981) asked people to agree or disagree with the statement 'Stronger measures should be taken to protect the environment against pollution'. But this is clearly a question without any constraints, and the results are therefore difficult to interpret with any sense. For what it is worth, the environment as an issue consistently scores high ratings on importance across all countries when measured in this way.

7. B. Taylor, 'Green in Word . . .', in R. Jowell *et al.*, *British Social Attitudes: The 14th Report* (Aldershot: Ashgate, 1997), pp. 111–36, at 113.

8. OECD, *Environmental Policies in Greece* (Paris: OECD, 1983), pp. 12–13.

9. Ministry of Environment (YPEHODE), *National Report of Greece, UN Conference on Environment and Development, Brazil, June 1992* (Athens: Ministry of the Environment, 1991), p. 17.

10. Ministerio de Obras Publicas, *Medio Ambiente en España 1989* (Madrid: Ministerio de Obras Publicas, 1990), p. 165; and *Medio Ambiente en España 1990* (Madrid: Ministerio de Obras Publicas, 1991), pp. 119–21.

11. *Pais Internacional*, 8 Oct. 1990.

12. A. La Spina and G. Sciortino, 'Common Agenda, Southern Rules: European Integration and Environmental Change in the Mediterranean States', in J. D. Liefferink, P. D. Lowe, and A. P. J. Mol (eds.), *European Integration and Environmental Policy* (London: Belhaven Press, 1993), pp. 217–36, at 232–3.

13. *The Guardian*, 6–7 Mar. 1993.

14. *Financial Times*, 24 Apr. 1989.

15. R. Sinnott, 'Policy, Subsidiarity and Legitimacy', in O. Niedermayer and R. Sinnott, *Public Opinion and Internationalized Governance* (Oxford: Oxford University Press, 1995), pp. 246–76, esp. at 262–9.

16. *Eurobarometer*, 45 (1996).

17. For the concept of amoral familism, see E. C. Banfield, *The Moral Basis of a Backward Society* (Chicago: Free Press, 1958).
18. C. A. Vlassopoulou, *La Politique de l'environnement: le cas de la pollution atmospherique à Athenes*, Ph.D. thesis (University of Picardy, 1991), p. 167.
19. Interview with V. Archontakis, Municipality of Rethimno, Crete, October 1994.
20. Interview with Athena Mourmouris, Ministry of Environment, Athens, November 1992.
21. Hellenic Society for the Protection of the Environment, *The State of the Greek Environment* (Athens, 1991), p. 38.
22. Vlassopoulou, *La Politique de l'environnement*, p. 150.
23. Interview with Leonidas Louloudis, Agricultural University of Athens, Athens, November 1992.
24. G. Pridham, S. Verney, and D. Konstadakopulos, 'Environmental Policy in Greece: Evolution, Structures and Process', *Environmental Politics*, 4:2 (1995), pp. 244–70 at 260.
25. *The European*, 28–31 May 1992.
26. *ABC*, 19 Oct. 1993.
27. Ministerio de Obras Publicas, *Medio Ambiente en España* (Madrid: Ministerio de Obras Publicas, 1989), pp. 286 ff.
28. Interview with Joan Puigdollers, Directorate for Environmental Promotion, Generalitat, Barcelona, October 1992.
29. A. Morris, 'A Sea Change in Spanish Conservation: With Illustrations from Gerona Province', *Journal of the Association for Contemporary Iberian Studies*, 5:2 (1992), pp. 23–30.
30. D. Alexander, 'Pollution, Policies and Politics: The Italian Environment', in F. Sabetti and R. Catanzaro (eds.), *Italian Politics: A Review*, v (London: Pinter, 1991), pp. 90–111 at 106.
31. *Die Zeit*, 17 Jun. 1988.
32. Alexander, 'Pollution, Policies and Politics', p. 105.
33. Interview with Antonio Cianciullo, *La Repubblica*, Rome, April 1995.
34. Alexander, 'Pollution, Policies and Politics', p. 104.
35. Interview with Mauro Albrizio, Lega per l'Ambiente, Rome, May 1992.
36. Interview with R. Cappelli, founder of Montalcino Ambiente, Montalcino, May 1991.
37. A. Diekmann, 'Moral oder Ökonomie? Zum Umweltverhalten in Niedrigkostensituationen', in H. Steinmann and G. R. Wagner (eds.), *Umwelt und Wirtschaftsethik* (Stuttgart: Schäffer-Poeschel Verlag, 1998), pp. 233–47.
38. S. Witherspoon, 'Democracy, the Environment and Public Opinion in Western Europe', in W. M. Lafferty and J. Meadowcroft (eds.), *Democracy and the Environment* (Cheltenham, Glos.: Edward Elgar, 1996), pp. 39–70.
39. The Manifesto Group Research Group, under the direction of Ian Budge, commenced work in 1979 with the support of the European Consortium of Political Research. For examples of the use of the manifesto data see: I. Budge, D. Robertson, and D. J. Hearl (eds.), *Ideology, Strategy and Party Change in 19 Democracies* (Cambridge: Cambridge University Press, 1987); H.-D. Klingemann, R. I. Hofferbert, I. Budge *et al.*, *Parties, Policies and Democracy* (Boulder Colo.: Westview Press, 1994); and M. Laver and I. Budge, *Party Policy and Government Coalitions* (London: Macmillan, 1992).

40. Data on Northern Ireland are collected separately, so that the results we report in the text are only for Great Britain.

41. There is a case for producing a weighted average based on the proportions of popular support that each party receives, but for our concerns this would unnecessarily complicate the analysis.

42. A reputation that is almost certainly inaccurate as an account of public opinion is I. Crewe, 'Values: The Crusade that Failed', in D. Kavanagh and A. Seldon (eds.), *The Thatcher Effect* (Oxford: Clarendon Press, 1989), pp. 239–50.

43. E. Müller, *Innenwelt der Umweltpolitik* (Opladen: Westdeutscher Verlag, 1986), pp. 97 ff.

44. T. Poguntke, 'Between Ideology and Empirical Research', *European Journal of Political Research*, 21:4 (1992), pp. 337–56, cited in H. Weidner, *25 Years of Modern Environmental Policy in Germany: Treading a Well-Worn Path to the Top of the International Field* (Berlin: Wissenschaftszentrum Berlin für Sozialforschung gGmbH, 1995).

45. Vlassopoulou, *La Politique de l'environnement*, pp. 22–3.

46. Ibid. 32–4, 38–48.

47. Pridham, Verney, and Konstadakopulos, 'Environmental Policy in Greece', p. 146.

48. *The Economist*, 27 April 1991.

49. Interview with Carlos Davila, PSOE deputy and member of the environment committee of the Spanish Congress (Parliament), Madrid, October 1992.

50. R. Lewanski, *Governare L'Ambiente: attori e processi della political ambientale* (Bologna: Il Mulino, 1997), p. 149.

51. Alexander, 'Pollution, Policies and Politics', p. 106.

52. Interview with Chicco Testa, shadow minister of the environment, Rome, May 1992.

53. R. Lewanski, 'Italy: Environmental Policy in a Fragmented State', in K. Hanf and A.-I. Jansen (eds.), *Governance and Environment in Western Europe* (Harlow: Addison Wesley Longman, 1998), pp. 131–51 at 137.

54. See e.g. N. Ridley, *Policies against Pollution: The Conservative Record—and Principles*, Policy Study no. 117 (London: Centre for Policy Studies, 1989).

55. G. Evans, 'Hard Times for the British Green Party', *Environmental Politics*, 2:2 (1993), pp. 327–33.

56. R. Anderweg, 'The Reshaping of National Party Systems', in J. Hayward (ed.), *The Crisis of Representation in Europe* (London: Frank Cass, 1995), pp. 58–78.

57. A conclusion amply demonstrated by M. N. Franklin, C. van der Eijk, and M. Marsh, 'Referendum Outcomes and Trust in Government: Public Support for Europe in the Wake of Maastricht', in J. Hayward, *The Crisis of Representation in Europe* (London: Frank Cass, 1995), pp. 101–17.

58. Dalton, *Green Rainbow*.

59. For an exploration of this dilemma with green political parties, see E. Bomberg, *Green Parties and Politics in the European Union* (London and New York: Routledge, 1998).

60. S. Boehmer-Christiansen and J. Skea, *Acid Politics*, (London and New York: Belhaven, 1991), p. 85.

61. H. Pehle and A.-I. Jansen, 'Germany: The Engine in European Environmental Policy?', in K. Hanf and A.-I. Jansen (eds.), *Governance and Environment in Western Europe* (Harlow: Addison Wesley Longman, 1998), pp. 82–109 at 87.

62. H. Weidner, *25 Years of Modern Environmental Protection in Germany: Treading a Well-Worn Path to the Top of the International Field* (Berlin: Wissenschaftszentrum Berlin, 1995), FS II 95–301, p. 71.
63. D. Rucht and J. Roose, 'The German Environmental Movement as a Crossroads?' in C. Rootes (ed.), *Environmental Movements: Local, National and Global* (London and Portland: Frank Cass, 1999), pp. 59–80 at 63.
64. H. Pehle, 'Germany: Domestic Obstacles to an International Forerunner', in M. S. Andersen and D. Liefferink (eds.), *European Environmental Policy: The Pioneers* (Manchester and New York: Manchester University Press, 1997), pp. 161–209 at 177, citing C. Hey and U. Brendle, *Umweltverbände und EG: Strategien, Politische Kulturen und Organizationsformen* (Opladen: Westdeutscher Verlag, 1994).
65. Dalton, *Green Rainbow*, pp. 158–59.
66. Pehle, 'Germany', p. 178.
67. K.-W. Brand, 'Dialectics of Institutionalisation: The Transformation of the Environmental Movement in Germany', in C. Rootes (ed.), *Environmental Movements: Local, National and Global* (London and Portland: Frank Cass, 1999), pp. 35–58, esp. 51–2.
68. Rucht and Roose, 'The German Environmental Movement', p. 62.
69. Brand, 'Dialectics of Institutionalisation', p. 47.
70. OECD, *Environmental Policies in Greece*, p. 13.
71. Pridham, Verney, and Konstadakopulos, 'Environmental Policy in Greece', p. 261.
72. *The Athenian*, April 1992.
73. P. Fousekis and J. Lekakis, 'Greece's Institutional Response to Sustainable Development', *Environmental Politics*, 6:1 (1997), pp. 131–52 at 146.
74. *The Athenian*, October 1993, article by G. Valaora, head of WWF office in Athens.
75. Interview with Georgia Valaoras, head of WWF, Athens, December 1992.
76. Interview with Julie Vlachavas, Pan-Hellenic Centre of Environmental Studies (PAKOE), Athens, November 1992.
77. Interview with Valaoras, December 1992.
78. J. La Calle Dominguez *et al.*, 'On the Origins of the Environmental Question in Spain', unpublished paper, Madrid, October 1991, pp. 4–5.
79. A. de Esteban Alonso and A. Lopez Lopez, 'Environmental Policy', in A. Almarcha Barbado (ed.), *Spain and EC Membership Evaluated* (London: Pinter, 1993), pp. 60–8 at 63–4.
80. See S. Aguilar-Fernandez, 'Spanish Pollution Control Policy and the Challenge of the European Union', *Regional Politics and Policy*, 4:1 (1994), pp. 102–17.
81. Ministerio de Obras Publicas, *Informacion de Medio Ambiente*, November 1993, p. 7.
82. Ibid., May 1993, p. 7.
83. Ibid., May 1994, p. 5.
84. Lewanski, *Governare L'Ambiente*, p. 143–4.
85. A. Postiglione, *Manuale dell'Ambiente: Guida alla Legislazione Ambientale* (Rome: La Nuova Italia Scientifica, 1984), pp. 69–76.
86. Interviews with Mauro Albrizio, of Lega per l'Ambiente, and with Enrico Fontana, journalist attached to AIGA, both in Rome, May 1992. See also issues of *Panorama* for summer 1993, e.g. 1, 22 and 29 August.
87. Lewanski, *Governare L'Ambiente*, p. 146.
88. Interview with Valeria Rizzo, Ministry of the Environment, Rome, May 1992.

89. Interview with Antonio Cianciullo, journalist, *La Repubblica*, Rome, May 1992.
90. Interview with Mauro Albrizio, Lega per l'Ambiente, Rome, April 1995.
91. This draws upon H. T. A. Bressers and L. A. Plettenburg, 'The Netherlands' in M. Jänicke and H. Weidner (eds.), *National Environmental Policies: A Comparative Study of Capacity-Building* (Berlin: Springer Verlag, 1997), pp. 109–31.
92. K. Hanf and E. van de Gronden, 'The Netherlands: Joint Regulation and Sustainable Development', in K. Hanf and A.-I. Jansen (eds.), *Governance and Environment in Western Europe* (Harlow: Addison Wesley Longman, 1998), pp. 152–80, at 157.
93. Dalton, *Green Rainbow*, pp. 158–9.
94. See P. Lowe and J. Goyder, *Environmental Groups in Politics* (London: George Allen & Unwin, 1983), pp. 15–17; and S. C. Young, *The Politics of the Environment* (Manchester: Baseline Books, 1993), pp. 17–19.
95. T. O'Riordan, 'Stability and Transformation in Environmental Government', *Political Quarterly*, 62:2 (1991), 167–85.
96. See G. Jordan and W. Maloney, *The Protest Business? Mobilizing Campaign Groups* (Manchester and New York: Manchester University Press, 1997), p. 12, for the importance of this distinction.
97. Young, *Politics of the Environment*, p. 19.
98. W. P. Grant, *Pressure Groups, Politics and Democracy in Britain* (Oxford: Philip Allan, 1989), pp. 14–15.
99. P. Rawcliffe, *Environmental Pressure Groups in Transition* (Manchester and New York: Manchester University Press, 1998).
100. P. Lowe and S. Ward, 'Domestic Winners and Losers', in P. Lowe and S. Ward (eds.), *British Environmental Policy and Europe* (London and New York: Routledge, 1998), pp. 87–104, at 100.
101. Interview with George Tsekouras, 'Nea Oikologia' and environmental consultant, Athens, November 1992.
102. *Pais Internacional*, 24 Aug. 1992.
103. Interview with Georgia Valaoras, head of WWF, Athens, December 1992.
104. WWF briefing paper, February 1994.
105. Interviews with Mauro Albrizio, Lega per l'Ambiente, Rome, May 1991 and May 1992.
106. Compare the general discussion of enhanced legitimacy of interest groups through EU membership in D. Sidjanski, 'Transition to Democracy and European Integration: The Role of Interest Groups in Southern Europe', in G. Pridham (ed.), *Encouraging Democracy: The International Context of Regime Transition in Southern Europe* (Leicester: Leicester University Press, 1991), pp. 195–211.
107. Boehmer-Christiansen and Skea, *Acid Politics*.
108. Weidner, *25 Years*, p. 74.
109. Ibid. 60.
110. G. R. Wagner, *Betriebswirtschaftliche Umweltökonomie* (Stuttgart: Lucius & Lucius, 1997), pp. 44–8.
111. U. Steger, 'Umwelt-Auditing', in M. Junkerheinrich, P. Klemmer, and G. R. Wagner (eds.), *Handbuch zur Umweltökonomie* (Berlin: Analytica, 1995), pp. 245–50 at 249.
112. Brand, 'Dialectics of Institutionalisation', pp. 52–3.
113. Weidner, *25 Years*, p. 52.
114. Pehle, 'Germany', pp. 28–9.

115. R. G. Heinze and H. Voelzkow, 'Der Deutsche Bauernverband und das "Gemeinwohl"' in R. Mayntz (ed.), *Verbände zwischen Mitgliederinteressen und Gemeinwohl* (Gütersloh: Verlag Bertelsmann Stiftung, 1992), pp. 122–61, at 145–54.

116. Pehle, 'Germany', p. 9.

117. Pridham, Verney, and Konstadakopulos, 'Environmental Policy in Greece', pp. 259–60.

118. *To Vima*, 8 Nov. 1992.

119. Interview with Athena Mourmouris, Ministry of the Environment, Athens, November 1992.

120. Vlassopoulou, *La Politique de l'environnement*, p. 23.

121. Ibid. 103, 105.

122. Ibid. 106.

123. Ibid. 155.

124. E. Rehbinder and R. Stewart, *Environmental Protection Policy* (Berlin and New York: Walter de Gruyter, 1985), p. 212.

125. N. Lowry, 'Sos: Muddy Waters', *The Athenian*, April 1993, pp. 16–18.

126. Interview with Jose Hortas Perez, Environmental Agency, Madrid, April 1994.

127. M. Garcia-Ferrando *et al.* (eds.), *Ecologia, Relaciones Industriales y Empresa* (Bilbao: Fundacion BBV, 1994), p. 315.

128. Interview with Hortas Perez, April 1994.

129. Estevan, *Implicaciones Economicas de la Proteccion Ambiental de la CEE: Repercusiones en España* (Madrid: Ministerio de Economica, 1991), pp. 228–33.

130. Ministerio de Obras Publicas, *Informacion de Medio Ambiente*, December 1992, p. 7.

131. Esteban Alonso and Lopez Lopez, 'Environmental Policy', p. 65.

132. Postiglione, *Manuale dell'Ambiente*, p. 40.

133. Fondazione Agnelli, *Manuale per la Difesa del Mare e della Costa* (Turin: Fondazione Agnelli, 1990), p. 120.

134. Lega per l'Ambiente, *Ambiente Italia 1990* (Milan: Arnaldo Mondadori, 1990), p. 510.

135. Ibid. 200.

136. *Panorama*, 24 May 1992.

137. OECD, *Environmental Performance Review, Italy* (Paris: OECD, 1994), p. 106.

138. Ibid.

139. A. P. J. Mol, *The Refinement of Production* (Utrecht: Van Arkel, 1995).

140. Ibid. 216.

141. Ibid. 146.

142. *Joint Environmental Policy Making (JEP): New Interactive Approaches in the EU and Selected Member States*, research report under the European Union's Environment and Climate Research Programme (1994–8) (Wageningen, 1998), i. 96.

143. Ibid. ii. 24.

144. Boehmer-Christiansen and Skea, *Acid Politics*, ch. 11, and M. A. Hajer, *The Politics of Environmental Discourse* (Oxford: Clarendon Press, 1995), pp. 112–17.

145. See D. Kinnersley, *Coming Clean: The Politics of Water and the Environment* (Harmondsworth: Penguin, 1994), chs. 4–7; W. A. Maloney and J. Richardson, *Managing Policy Change in Britain: The Politics of Water* (Edinburgh: Edinburgh University Press, 1995).

146. Estevan, *Implicaciones Economicas de la Proteccion Ambiental de la CEE*, p. 475.

147. Interview with Philoktitis Veinoglou, Greek Bank for Industrial Development (ETBA), Athens, December 1992.

148. La Spina and Sciortino, 'Common Agenda, Southern Rules', p. 234.
149. Interview with Zacharias Mavroukas, Ministry of Industry, Athens, December 1992.
150. Details on industrial estates from interview with Philoktitis Veinoglou, ETBA, Athens, December 1992.
151. OECD, *Environmental Policies in Greece*, p. 17.
152. Task Force on the Environment and the Internal Market, '*1992: The Environmental Dimension*', mimeo (*c.* 1989), sec. 9.3.
153. H. Arp, 'Interest Groups in EC Legislation: The Case of Car Emission Standards', ECPR paper, Essex, 1991, p. 13.
154. Estevan, *Implicaciones Economicas de la Proteccion Ambiental de la CEE*, p. 476.
155. For contrasting discussions of the effects of corporatism on environmental policy performance, see e.g. J. Hukkinen, 'Corporatism as an Impediment to Eclogical Sustenance: The Case of Finnish Waste Management', *Ecological Economics*, 15 (1995), pp. 59–75; D. Jahn, 'Environmental Performance and Policy Regimes: Explaining Variations in 18 OECD-Countries', *Policy Sciences*, 31 (1998), pp. 107–31; and L. Scruggs, 'Institutions and Environmental Performance in Seventeen Western Democracies', *British Journal of Political Science*, 21:1 (1999), pp. 1–31.
156. Interview with Cristina Alvarez, WWF, Madrid, October 1992.
157. Lega per l'Ambiente, *Ambiente Italia 1990*, pp. 179–80.
158. Garcia-Ferrando *et al.*, *Ecologia, Relaciones Industriales y Empresa*, p. 194.
159. Lewanski, *Governare L'Ambiente*, pp. 150–1.

8

National Systems and Multi-level Governance: Convergence through Compliance?

In the previous chapter we have looked at the extent to which the politics of our six countries provides the context and pressures for a distinctive process of policy-making in each case. Although there are common, secular forces at work across each member state, reflected for example in trends in public opinion, the institutional and political differences remain strong. Domestic political forces—political parties, interest organizations, and voters—themselves led to national variations as well as to the sharing of some common features.

In this chapter we place these national systems in the context of EU multi-level environmental governance. We consider the role that the EU plays in harmonizing, or at least reducing the variation of, national policy strategies and practices, as well as looking in particular at the problems raised by the implementation of EU environmental measures with their associated difficulties of compliance. If we can identify the circumstances under which countries find it easy or difficult to comply with EU environmental measures, we shall begin to understand the extent to which international pressures make for convergence among national systems.

In looking at the issue of compliance, we are looking primarily at the direct effects of the EU's system of multi-level governance. Exactly how much we can conclude about international influences on the domestic systems by looking at the issue of implementation and compliance is limited, however. To be sure, the problems of compliance raised by the implementation of EU measures provide some indication of the effect of EU governance on national systems. If there were no effects from such governance, the national systems could simply continue as before. If we observe countries changing substantive laws or altering administrative procedures as part of their efforts to comply with EU measures, then we gain some estimate of the importance of the EU and the pressures for change that it sets up. On the other hand, the extent to which we should expect direct influence is itself limited. The principal instrument of EU environmental policy is the directive, the legal force of which explicitly allows countries to implement measures in accordance with the practices of their own legal systems. Therefore compliance does not of itself imply convergence in any straightforward way. Moreover, as with all studies of implementation, particularly in the field of environmental policy, there are typically multiple influences that can affect a country's ability to meet an environmental objective. For example, a downturn in the economy normally makes it easier to reach an emissions target, independently of any change in policy or administration.

The nature of international policy-making also precludes any easy assessment of international influences. As Laffan has pointed out, 'the discretionary element in any policy implementation process may be substantial as goals must be spelled out and the initial decisions may require resteering to make them more effective'.[1] Secondly, it is intrinsically difficult to identify an international policy process as such. A qualitative difference from national systems is evident in that policy-making at the international level is typically 'not embedded in stable structures'.[2] While the EU possesses more established and rather more powerful institutional structures and procedures than other international organizations, its systemic nature is one open to reform, creating, as we saw in Part I, a situation in which secondary rules change along with developments in primary rules within a system of shared political authority. Whatever the effects of the Single European Act, the Maastricht and Amsterdam Treaties, and further reforms to come, it is still true and is likely to remain so that 'policy-making is shared between the international and national levels, while policy execution is in practice primarily concentrated at the national level or even subnational level'.[3]

All that having been said, compliance arising from the implementation of EU measures provides us with some relevant empirical evidence on the extent to which the EU's system of environmental governance has affected national systems. In particular, where there are difficulties with compliance, these are normally indicative of some features of the national policy system that is at odds with the requirements of the EU system. What is more, the issues of implementation and compliance are clearly important in their own right and have been receiving increasing attention in recent years. Moreover, the implementation of EU environmental measures is something that is susceptible to comparative evaluation (though we note some methodological problems later). We shall also see that hypotheses that have been advanced about the causes behind implementation failure coincide with the general framework within which we are looking at convergence and divergence in our six countries.

In what follows, we first look at the issue of implementation as it has arisen in the EU, before going on to compare compliance rates among our six countries and the possible explanations for variation. We then look in detail at each of the six countries before drawing conclusions.

IMPLEMENTATION, COMPLIANCE, AND EU ENVIRONMENTAL GOVERNANCE

The issue of effective implementation of EU environmental policies was not a high priority for some time, and certainly not one that occasioned much open dispute about policy mechanisms and the policy process in general. However, over time this issue has steadily gained in importance. The Fourth Environment Action Programme of 1987–92 put a new emphasis on problems of implementation, while the Fifth Programme devoted a full chapter to implementation and enforcement.

Jordan has drawn together the literature on why this change occurred and has offered the following list of possible causes: the drive towards the single market, which led states to realize that creating the conditions of fair competition required giving greater emphasis to implementation; the growth of the environmental *acquis*; MEPs putting pressure on the Commission from 1983 to report on implementation; an increasingly common policy agenda among members states; the consequences of landmark rulings by the ECJ; the continuing pressure of embarrassing incidents like the disappearance of several drums of toxic waste from the Seveso plant; growing public interest in environmental issues; increasing pressure from environmental groups at the national level; greater academic interest in the effect of EU law at the national level; and the growth of environmental legislation itself, which led to a number of deadlines for implementation being missed.[4] In short, a cocktail of causes began to come together from the mid-1980s, the cumulative effect of which was to raise the importance of implementation as an issue.

Although policy implementation has surfaced as a general issue in the EU, the record in the environmental area is one of the worst. During the 1980s there was a considerable increase in infringement proceedings brought against member states for the non-implementation of EU environmental legislation, covering different categories (including partial compliance, non-notification, and poor application), with a marked rise in these occurring from the mid-1980s.[5] Undoubtedly, this was linked to the more activist line on the environment adopted by the European Commission during this period, suggesting difficulties of policy overload, not to mention the complexity of much environmental legislation. The Single European Act, and above all the process of establishing a single market, gave prominence to the issue of implementation, for failures here were seen as a potential barrier to free and fair trade.[6] By the 1990s regular reviews of how member states were implementing environmental legislation had become established, and the European Parliament had begun to investigate problems of compliance in the environmental area out of dissatisfaction with the inability of member states to carry out legislation.[7]

What does 'implementation' mean in this context, however? The term may be defined in a number of ways. 'Legal implementation' relates to the transposition of European legislation (directives) into national law, involving the redrafting of existing national legislation and the issue of new statutes that fulfil the requirements of the directive. 'Practical implementation' is what occurs at street level, that is the putting of policy and law into practice.[8] While the executive functions of the Commission can affect in various ways what goes on at ground level, implementation in the legal and practical senses is the preserve of national and subnational actors. Even if European institutions had the legal powers, they lack the resources to oversee the implementation of the policies they produce.

In place of control or influence over practical policy implementation, the Commission is responsible for the enforcement of compliance in terms of transposition. But although the Commission has a formal function to perform in this respect, Commission staff cannot easily obtain accurate information on breaches of European legislation. The small size of DG XI and the Commission's lack of environmental inspectors has meant that ensuring or even checking the correct transposition of European legislation is extremely difficult. It is hardly surprising that officials in DG XI are jealous of the powers of the competition directorate-general, with their 'dawn raids' and investigators.[9] The Commission does not even have a procedure by which it can discuss the content of draft national legislation after a directive has been agreed,[10] thus highlighting the past emphasis placed on formulation at the expense of implementation.

Under the heading of enforcement, staff working within Commission's services follow procedures common to most European policy areas. In this task, they are largely reliant upon the accuracy of information provided by those responsible for implementing policy, that is, those who may be breaching the rules. In recent years, however, officials have been assisted by interest group representatives. Their dependence on complaints made by interests and frustrated governmental actors means that public awareness of environmental policy is encouraged almost as a substitute for comprehensive enforcement mechanisms. Public awareness of environmental issues and responsibilities has made it somewhat easier for the Commission to identify the more important implementation gaps. So, in the absence of more extensive formal enforcement measures, public opinion, as mediated through environmental non-governmental organizations, has come to fill a gap.

Since the revisions of the Treaty of European Union, complaints about non-compliance can be raised not only by the Commission itself, but also by legal persons, including natural persons, under Article 173, by member states under Article 170, and by national courts under Article 177. The Commission's powers under Article 169 have led it to develop a standard procedure for handling issues of non-compliance, which begins with an informal exchange of correspondence, goes through an Article 169 letter of warning and a reasoned opinion concerning non-compliance, and may eventually issue in a reference to the ECJ. All this is a long drawn out process that can take more than two years, and sometimes up to four to five years, to complete. The initiation of infringement proceedings by means of an Article 169 letter begins a chain of events that are by definition adversarial and confrontational.[11]

Interest in compliance has usually focused on formal implementation or incorporation of EU directives into national legislation. Though requiring resources to collect, achievement is susceptible to comparative analysis, since rates of compliance are collected by the Commission and published regularly for the European Parliament. To be sure, the comparative measures have to be treated with some caution. Their recording may be influenced by a variety of factors that vary from country to country but may not be closely related to the degree of compliance with a measure that a country may be achieving. Thus, documenting this stage of the policy process has been complicated by differences in national procedure—and hence in identifying the exact form in which EU directives are adopted—as well as deficiencies in information on national processes.[12]

The more problematic area to evaluate is that of practical application and the enforcement of European legislation in member states. This matter of policy outcomes has now come to be the source of greatest disquiet, producing some controversy between certain member states—usually to the detriment of the south. But it is also the area in which it is particularly difficult to produce hard or consistent evidence. Attention has been given to such methods as public complaints and infringement procedures, with warning letters from the Commission or referrals to the European Court of Justice. But data on infringements is not a very satisfactory measure of practical application problems, as no clear distinction is made between these and success with enactment. Also, such evidence is marred by a common reluctance by member states to admit policy failure (with some national differences in this respect). Other independent variables may intervene to varying degrees cross-nationally. For example, environmental associations may be more assiduous in reporting breaches in one country than in another, although there may be more serious problems of enforcement in the latter. Thus, if country A has a larger number of more active environmental groups willing to use the infractions procedures than country B, country A will look worse on the measures than country B, without there necessarily being any real difference between their compliance rates.

Despite these drawbacks, it is necessary to start with official data for want of alternative evidence on national tendencies. As Macrory has noted in his study of the enforcement of European environmental laws, such data 'probably reflected a reasonable approximation of the relative levels of compliance'. How far cross-national variation in environmental group activism accounts for variations in the figures is impossible to estimate, though Macrory argues that it is not generally a decisive factor in the environmental context.[13]

It is difficult to determine the significance of the issue of compliance for the more general question of the degree of convergence in European environmental policy. It is necessary to view implementation not in isolation, but contextually as part of the longer process of policy development, and to examine the implications of the contradictory logics of supranational governance and national implementation. If, as we have already argued, member states occupy a privileged position within the EU's system of environmental governance, when we turn to implementation and compliance, we are looking at the pre-eminent privilege of the privileged.

Comparative Compliance Rates in Member States

Table 8.1 presents figures for the formal transposition of environmental legislation into national law between 1990 and 1994. The figures refer to the percentage

TABLE 8.1 *Transposition of environmental directives into national law, by country and year*[a]

Country	% of directives transposed			
	1990	1991	1992	1994
Belgium	86	81	94	85
Denmark	99	98	99	100
Germany	92	92	92	91
Greece	79	76	92	85
Spain	92	93	91	86
France	92	89	96	94
Eire	87	84	90	97
Italy	63	59	83	76
Luxembourg	89	86	92	93
Netherlands	97	95	97	98
Portugal	95	94	89	82
UK	91	85	93	82
Median	91.5	87.5	92	88.5
Median	91.5	85.5	92	85.5

[a] Study countries in bold.

Sources: Commission of the European Communities, *The 10th Annual Report to the European Parliament on the Application and Monitoring of EC Law* (1993); *The 12th Annual Report on the Monitoring and Application of Community Law* (1995).

of total eligible legislation that should have been transposed that was actually transposed. Entries in bold relate to our sample of six countries, while other figures refer to the remaining six countries that were also members of the EU at the time. It will be seen that the median figure each year for the six and the twelve countries do not differ from one another very much, and fall within the range of 85–92 per cent over the period.

Relative to the median figure for each year (which we may take as some sort of average performance for the EU countries taken as a whole), there are four distinct groups in our sample of six countries. Firstly, there is the pair of Germany and the Netherlands, which in each year always return at least as good a performance as the average, and usually one that is better. Secondly, there is a pairing of Spain and the UK, which are generally about the average, sometimes falling below and sometimes scoring above. Thirdly, there is Greece, which is considerably below the median figure in 1990 and 1991, but which picks up in 1992 and 1994. Finally, there is Italy, in a group of its own and consistently below the median throughout the period. Categorizing countries in this way suggests that it is political, rather than economic or social, variables that are likely to be most important in understanding compliance. Italy's poor performance may in part be due to economic costs and the absence of a strong post-materialist culture in parts of the country, but clearly economic conditions cannot be the whole story, since otherwise Spain

TABLE 8.2 *Article 169 (Warning) letters, 1988–1992*[a]

Country	1988	1989	1990	1991	1992
Belgium	11	5	10	13	10
Denmark	4	2	5	4	4
Germany	6	2	5	4	4
Greece	7	8	26	11	14
Spain	5	11	18	15	14
France	4	4	14	5	12
Eire	6	11	13	10	16
Italy	8	12	21	10	13
Luxembourg	7	2	8	5	10
Netherlands	8	6	13	6	3
Portugal	3	4	15	4	17
UK	8	2	17	10	14
Median	6.5	4.5	14.5	8	12.5
Median	7.5	7.5	17.5	10	13.5

[a] Study countries in bold.

Sources: Commission of the European Communities, *The 10th Annual Report to the European Parliament on the Application and Monitoring of EC Law* (1993); *The 12th Annual Report on the Monitoring and Application of Community Law* (1995).

and Greece would be more closely bracketed with Italy. So, the most obvious cause of Italy's poor implementation performance is the low quality of Italian governmental performance since 1947.

We can shed further light on the comparative aspects of compliance by looking at complaints. Although affected by the differential rates of activity of environmental groups, this has the advantage of identifying actual problems of implementation, rather than the purely legal process of transposition. The figures also have the advantage that they are tied to a now routinized process within the Commission, which includes the three stages referred to earlier: the issuing, after an informal exchange of correspondence, of a formal Article 169 warning letter; the statement of a reasoned opinion regarding non-compliance; and finally, a reference to the ECJ.

Table 8.2 provides the figures during the period 1988–92 for the number of Article 169 warning letters written. Here the same pattern that we observed in the case of transposition is in part discernible, though some with modifications. Spain and the UK again seem to perform at about the average level, although with some variation from year to year. The Netherlands usually does better than average and Italy usually does worse. Germany, however, does even better than its transposition rates might lead one to expect, while Greece does better relative to the average, though with some poor years.

When it comes to reasoned opinions, the pattern changes again somewhat, as shown in Table 8.3. Germany, the Netherlands, and the UK perform at about the

TABLE 8.3 *Reasoned opinions, 1988–1992*[a]

Country	1988	1989	1990	1991	1992
Belgium	11	3	9	4	2
Denmark	1	1	0	0	0
Germany	9	3	2	2	1
Greece	16	4	4	9	6
Spain	1	2	7	4	4
France	6	3	1	3	0
Eire	16	2	3	5	4
Italy	27	2	7	13	0
Luxembourg	12	1	1	5	2
Netherlands	1	0	5	2	4
Portugal	0	2	1	1	1
UK	8	2	2	2	2
Median	8.5	2	2.5	3.5	3
Median	8.5	2.5	4.5	3	3

[a] Study countries in bold.

Sources: Commission of the European Communities, *The 10th Annual Report to the European Parliament on the Application and Monitoring of EC Law* (1993); *The 12th Annual Report on the Monitoring and Application of Community Law* (1995).

average level, with some years above and some below. Spain is somewhat worse. Greece slips somewhat relative to its position in the earlier tables, recording four out of five years in which it performs worse than the average of the six and five years for the average of the twelve. Although Italy has two years for where its performance is at or about average, it also has two years when the number of reasoned opinions is considerably above average.

The number of references to the ECJ is normally too small in any year to make year-by-year analysis plausible. However, if we take the cumulative figures, a striking picture emerges as Table 8.4 shows. Germany and Italy together account for some 40 per cent of the total references made during this period, with the other four countries in the sample accounting for only about a third of total references made. What is it that leads to this apparently unusual bracketing of Italy and Germany, which in other respects show up as being so different in terms of implementation? The answer to this question is less likely to be found in the characteristics of the two national systems than in the characteristics of the interaction between the national systems and the EU within the European system of environmental governance, as we seek to show in our discussion of the individual cases below.

How far do the data suggest a clear-cut divide between northern and southern member states? Certainly there is no absolute north–south dichotomy in the EU over the enactment and enforcement of environmental legislation.[14] Differences emerge between southern states, while some northern states have worse records than is generally believed. Despite this, the poor reputation of the southern countries

TABLE 8.4 *References to the ECJ and Judgments, 1988–1992*[a]

Country	1988	1989	1990	1991	1992	Cumul. no.	Cumul. %
Belgium	4	4	7	2	3	20	19.6
Denmark	0	0	0	0	0	0	0.0
Germany	3	3	3	5	5	19	18.6
Greece	0	1	0	4	3	8	7.8
Spain	0	1	2	1	0	4	4.0
France	2	1	5	3	0	11	10.8
Eire	2	0	1	0	1	4	4.0
Italy	3	7	5	6	1	22	21.8
Luxembourg	1	1	0	2	2	6	5.9
Netherlands	0	0	2	1	2	5	5.0
Portugal	0	0	0	0	0	0	0.0
UK	0	1	1	0	1	3	2.9

[a] Study countries in bold.

Sources: Commission of the European Communities, *The 10th Annual Report to the European Parliament on the Application and Monitoring of EC Law* (1993); *The 12th Annual Report on the Monitoring and Application of Community Law* (1995).

in enforcing European environmental legislation has persisted. Much concern has been expressed by the northern countries about the lack of effective monitoring in the south (in fact, with some justification); and, there has been some debate there over the lack of linkage made between tighter standards and problems of enforcement.[15] However, given the absence of hard or reliable information on practical implementation, it is difficult to show exactly what happens in this respect 'on the ground', and how much differentiation there might be not only between but also within member states according to environmental sector. Since there are limits to general lessons that may be extracted from the official data, our six country cases are now examined more closely in turn to identify patterns and problems and to determine where the main obstacles to practical implementation lie. In this way, we may see how much cross-national variation is really important.

NATIONAL PROBLEMS OF IMPLEMENTATION

Germany

Implementation has been a recurring theme of domestic German environmental policy, quite apart from concerns about EU measures. In Germany the first active phase of environmental policy in the 1970s was followed by a period of concern about 'implementation deficit' that was initiated by the Council of Environmental Experts.[16] The problems arose in part because of the federal administrative structure, which separates the formulation of environmental standards from their implementation, with the federal government often devising regulations that are then enforced by *Land* authorities. However, the debate that was sparked off by the Council's report itself did much to improve the quality of implementation, and observers speak about the generally compliant nature of those affected by regulations. Even so, problems have not been entirely eliminated. There have been criticisms of the enforcement of the 1980 Chemicals Act[17] and also of measures to speed up planning consents in the wake of unification. Some of the critics allege that plans for new roads and other infrastructure, for example, have not been properly scrutinized for their environmental implications in the attempt to ensure the prompt rebuilding of the economy of the former German Democratic Republic.

There are, however, clear successes of practical implementation that can be pointed to in the case of Germany. One such example is provided by the air pollution control measures introduced in 1983 for large combustion plants, which between 1983 and 1988 led to sulphur dioxide emission reductions of 88 per cent and to nitrogen oxide reductions of some 76 per cent for a somewhat longer period.[18] As the originator of the EU large combustion plant directive, Germany was thus ahead of many other countries in terms of implementation. Similarly, in the field of cadmium reduction there has been a similar dramatic decline in use, in the wake of the ban on cadmium products introduced in Sweden in 1980. By the end of the 1980s cadmium use was approximately half of the volume that it was in the late 1970s. The only effect of the EU directive on cadmium (91/338/EEC) was not to alter cadmium use in Germany, which already conformed to the provisions of the directive, but to ensure that imported items also were free of cadmium.[19]

Yet this is not to say that the implementation of EU measures is without problems. Implementation of the environmental impact assessment directive was delayed by the German government for two years, being acted on only in February 1990. More importantly, the German government also came under criticism from the Commission for the way in which standards were set under routine administrative procedures called 'technical instructions', according to which measures were implemented only by rules that were binding on the public service. These problems were manifest in the cases that found their way to the ECJ. In these cases, difficulties in implementation appear to owe much to the complexity of the German federal structure and to the difficulty that German civil servants have had in accepting that merely relying on administrative measures is insufficient to provide an effective legal instrument for transposing most directives.

In a sequence of cases that the Commission fought relentlessly during the early 1990s, this point was to crop up again and again. For example, in the case of *Commission* v. *Germany*,[20] the practice of using administrative circulars to transpose directives, which the Germans argued had the force of binding law, was challenged by the Commission. In this instance what was at stake was the need to introduce clear and precise mandatory limit values for sulphur dioxide in air for the whole national territory (directive 80/779/EEC). According to German practice, a number of very detailed, and in many cases technical administrative circulars were addressed to the *Länder* and various other parties, under the 1974 air pollution legislation. However, these clearly were deficient in so far as they frequently referred to neighbourhood effects (in keeping with the terminology of the Federal Immision Control Act of 1974) or addressed themselves to industrial plant only, potentially missing other sectors such as transport. Despite contested evidence, the ECJ ruled that such administrative circulars were not clearly capable of being binding in giving legal persons, beyond just administrative staff, enforceable legal rights. Furthermore, the German 1974 Air Pollution Act empowered the *Länder* to take action on air pollution, but created no mechanism through which a general mandatory rule linked to the specific limit values for the whole state could be articulated— which was what the Commission wanted.

In another case that same year, the complexities of the German federal system were to reveal how in particular it presented challenges for the proper implementation of environment directives.[21] This time what was at issue was a water quality directive (75/440/EEC) which demanded a plan of action from member states to combat pollution. A number of interesting conclusions emerged from this case.

Firstly, the problem of coordination within a federation expressly evoked comments, with the ECJ indicating that a federal state ought to make due allowance in securing proper implementation. In other words, Bonn ought to take its federal nature into account and actively plan for coordination between and within *Länder*.[22] In this regard, one classic example of the loopholes in a federal system in respect of implementation was the revelation that, while Bavaria did indeed draw up a required improvement plan for the Danube with a sampling point inside Bavaria, the place where the required improvement was actually needed lay in Baden-Württemberg, because the Danube river flows from east to west for a section. The issue of coordination was broadened to include the international dimension as well, with Bavaria pleading its difficulties with Lake Constance and the Danube. However, the Court was unsympathetic and used the fact that some progress had been made in creating an international regime for the latter to demand that German authorities actively seek cooperation with their Czech counterparts if the directive's provisions were to be met.[23]

Moreover, a number of derogations, either inapplicable or improperly made, were also rejected. In particular, an attempt to secure a derogation *post hoc* on certain waters on the grounds that they were polluted by soil types was flatly rejected on a literal reading of the directive. Equally, the repeated German attempt to use administrative measures as a means to transpose directives was criticized, with the Court rejecting the argument that the combined effects of water management law and a licensing system were together sufficient to meet the classification standards of the directive.

These examples suggest that problems of implementation within the EU system of multi-level environmental governance need not reflect inadequate or undeveloped institutional arrangements. Indeed, the spate of problems revealed in the ECJ actions suggest that it is precisely because German domestic institutions and practices were so developed and elaborate that they were inconsistent with the requirements of the internationalized system of governance. We should not confuse 'leader' status in a comparative sense with compliance to an internationally agreed set of rules. However, it can also be argued that, at least in one respect, the problems of adaptation that Germany has experienced reflect not just institutional but also cultural factors. Such cultural factors were manifest when, in deference to the German love affair with the fast car, the government in March 1994 repeated its opposition to an EU-imposed national speed limit.[24] Although this threat has never been tested in practice, it would be interesting to see whether it would be put into effect should the need ever arise. The technical and institutional adaptation required by other aspects of policy implementation seem less important in this one regard than the lifestyle change that one environmental measure might require.

Greece

As we saw in the comparative statistics, Greece improved its formal implementation in the early 1990s, though the record on its practical implementation is still poor. Its achievements at the formal stage have to do with the absence of the kind of intricate political problems that so inhibit effective government in Italy. There is also no real difficulty concerning centre–periphery cooperation, given that the Greek state is still largely centralized. Institutional fragmentation has, however, certainly created some problems at the national level. It was precisely to overcome this, for the sake of speeding up the adoption of EU directives, that the 1986 Framework Law was passed; but it has remained largely a dead letter.

If there are any political obstacles, these relate to policy priorities, since the strong developmentalist and productivist elements in Greece's line towards Brussels have tended to dominate for much of the time.[25] This persistent interest in EU resources explains the fairly prominent attention given to the environmental costs of implementing directives. Moreover, the umbilical link between the state and economic interests has meant that any lowering of priority of the environment by governments has in effect tipped the wink to business and other interests, discouraging compliance with EU rules.[26]

There is thus a similar preponderance, as in Italy, of the public sector in determining the outcome of implementation. But it is precisely here and because of this that the main problems arise. Bureaucratic slowness and delay, lack of personnel or those with the requisite skills and general inefficiency mark the public administration in Greece. It is an inefficiency that is widely acknowledged in Greece, all the more so given the pressures on it from Brussels. As one prominent environmentalist commented,

What happens today is that we have a system which is not efficient. This system is accepted as such by the European Union, yet they load on to this system the kind of decisions, mechanisms, and procedures the system is not prepared to accept or able to administer. And this is the problem! You have an old car, and before you drive it [you have] to change the engine or do something in the engine you loaded or overloaded . . . So, this is the misery . . . I am very pessimistic.[27]

According to the experience of an environmental adviser to the Ministry of Agriculture, the weak administration in the environmental area, as in other areas, 'cannot implement difficult and complex policies; it is very bureaucratic without reason . . .'[28] It was inefficient practices that largely accounted for the delay with which EU directives were adopted in Greece in the 1980s following entry to the EU. The lack of reforms in public administration since membership has meant that such problems have persisted. One high official described the difficulties with which the EIA directive was implemented, involving many years of painstaking procedures, inter-ministerial shuffling, and endless delays:

This was a very difficult task we had in recent years. After the directive from the Commission, we had a period of very hard negotiations with other ministries, which was more than two years, and we arrived at a compromise and legal texts of more than 100–200 pages. Nobody was satisfied with this compromise. With the new government this compromise was never legalized. It was signed by some ministers, but then we had elections, so the proceedings were stopped. And in 1990, Mr Manos (who was minister at that time) very quickly formulated another piece of legislation without negotiation; and this was finally approved, in the form of a multi-ministerial decision, i.e. a decision signed by eight or nine ministers. So, we had legislation. But, because this legislation was done very quickly, it is very difficult to apply it. It has many problems . . . mainly time-consuming procedures, and I am afraid it is not very efficient in practice.[29]

There are several particular problems related to inefficiency that have a direct effect on practical implementation. Firstly, a traditional lack of openness in Greek bureaucracy has been underlined by pressures from Brussels over environmental directives. This came to the fore over environmental impact assessment, for satisfactory evaluation has proved almost impossible owing to the refusal of civil servants to provide relevant information, as shown in a study of the agricultural sector.[30] This closed mentality has also inhibited the diffusion of official information on EU directives.

A series of interviews with environmental officials in Crete late in 1994 revealed complaints that such information did not percolate down to the local level. An official of Chania remarked: 'I do not know what is happening in other municipalities; messages originating from the EU either do not reach us . . . or take a long time to reach us; I have heard from colleagues from other municipalities that they say that "if you do not have your connection in Brussels then you can achieve nothing"'.[31] Large cities like Salonica, Larissa, and certainly Athens have relatively easy access to Brussels, but not the average Greek town. An official in the prefectural office for the environment at Heraklion in Crete pointed out how this problem could inhibit implementation:

Unfortunately, we do not have any contact with Community legislation . . . Community legislation goes to the region; here we get nothing. This is very negative because we do not know what is going to happen. Also, we cannot recommend to the central services [YPE-HODE—Ministry of the Environment] how adaptation of Community legislation should be carried out. This issue is creating a lot of problems, because adaptation of Community legislation brings a situation which is unrealistic for the Greek situation.[32]

Secondly, environmental management is particularly weak so far as mechanisms of control and enforcement are concerned. It is this that was most commonly seen by interview respondents as the main single cause of the discrepancy between practical and formal implementation. A senior environmentalist explained the problem:

We are not so bad at introducing legislation into Greek law and in areas where control is relatively easy . . . when you need to have regular controls, some measuring or sending out to collect samples, check and go back, there we have very poor implementation; and this is partly expected because the staff we have in some of these public services, the particular section of controls, is very small, very poorly staffed.[33]

This was noticeable, for instance, over implementation of the bathing waters directive, which, according to a senior government adviser, 'was difficult because it needed specific scientific data analysis, and cooperation with the National Marine Centre with respect to the very high level of analysis that was needed for determining the quality of waters'.[34] On air quality there have been failures of compliance on some directives, as in other member states; but monitoring practices here have improved under EU influence, and in any case Greece does not have a major problem (apart from Athens) because there are few heavy industrial areas in the country and no car industry.[35] A major problem, however, is household waste, for managerial and financial reasons including lack of cooperation between different local authorities; and this is likely to remain unresolved for some time.[36]

Thirdly, the problem of costs featured quite prominently in interviews on the question of implementation (more so than in the Italian case, for instance). A round-table discussion with officials in the Ministry of Agriculture in Athens identified lack of money as well as of trained personnel as the principal practical problem here. In confronting environmental problems, it was noted,

time and again, the EU exerted more pressure on the application of various regulations and directives, and it created for us a problem. Whereas in the beginning they gave us money, later on the money became less and more participation was required . . . at the present moment we find ourselves in the situation where we need some financial backing from the EU in order to materialize all these legislative measures that the EU imposes on the country.[37]

Environmental costs have now become a central consideration in environmental policy-making. An official concerned with environmental matters in the Ministry of Industry explained:

you cannot say that you are going to have a policy without having the money. Probably in the past you would say that, and say that industry probably can carry the whole cost, but nowadays it is very difficult; you must have a figure . . . the Ministry of Industry, and probably industry, is on the defensive, trying to convince everybody that before you take action on a certain environmental directive, you must know the figures.[38]

One official in the Ministry of the Environment ventured to say that costs were sometimes used as an excuse for not taking action, and that invariably economic interests lay behind this line.

Fourthly, and finally, public attitudes towards observance of the law have often affected practical implementation, although it is difficult to measure this factor. A senior official in YPEHODE related this to general state/society relations: 'traditionally, the people, the majority of people . . . society has a sort of solidarity against the state due to the history of the country, to the "Colonels" period, due to the dictatorship, things like that'.[39] An environmental expert with long experience of working for the government stressed attitudes as the main basic problem in implementation:

what happens in Greece is that nobody—and when I say nobody, I mean no ministry, no minister, no public service, no private interests or any other, not even the citizen—feels obliged to follow any kind of directive, any kind of law; and this is even more difficult for the environment, because it is a new concern.[40]

Funds from Brussels attached to environmental actions could help to persuade, he continued, but even then people 'try to discover what is the kind of minimum obedience to the directives'.

Illustrating how attitudes could actually affect behaviour, a survey conducted on the view held by farmers of environmental directives concluded that:

Since we have not implemented any serious measures on the environment in rural areas, farmers are almost ignorant of the problem; they speak about the seriousness of pollution, of environmental hazards, they accept that some measures should be taken, but they think that the problem is in another area. There is really no experience in taking measures: the only measures we take are something that concerns pesticides and some regulations of local significance, some regulations of the Greek administration . . . normally, nobody controls the implementation of these small rules, except [when] some of the farmers have some damage, and their neighbours go to the administrators and say there is this problem. Then, they take some measures in that respect, not systematically . . . we have not implemented a nitrate directive yet. It is almost ready to be implemented.[41]

Until the 1990s, the Greek failures of implementation had not resulted in a large number of references to the ECJ. However, the situation began to change and Greece's implementation record came under greater scrutiny. For example, in Case C-96/329 the Greek state was held to have failed to have given effect to the directive on conservation of natural habitats and flora and fauna (92/43/EEC).[42]

Greece has also shown how the implementation 'game' has changed after Maastricht through the empowering of the Commission to seek from the Court substantial daily fines for non-compliance with Court judgments under the so-called

Article 171 procedure. This was first used in the environmental policy sphere with regard to Germany,[43] but as of late 1997 it was also being deployed against Greece for its neglect of the waste situation on the island of Crete.[44] Other Greek implementation failures (largely shared by many other states, it has to be said) include the framework waste directives (75/442/EEC and 91/156/EEC),[45] the nitrates directive (91/676/EEC), where no designation of a single nitrate vulnerable zone had been made,[46] the directive on access to environment information (90/313/EEC), and, more seriously, failures to deal with hazardous waste through a lack of national implementing legislation[47] and the omission (along with the supposedly environmentally virtuous Dutch!) of fixing binding water quality objectives for pollution reduction plans under directive 76/464/EEC.[48]

Spain

The general picture in Spain is rather different from the other two southern countries. As we have seen in the comparative analysis, Spain often seems to be closer to the UK in its compliance record than the other two, although the partial evidence on practical implementation suggests a mixed picture. The limited data show a high number of environmental complaints, and hence a significant number of warning letters; but the energy of environmental groups has apparently contributed to this result.

This record has to be seen in the context of Spain's being the most recent entrant (1986) to the EU of the six countries under study. Its decision upon entry to incorporate all EU legislation enacted before 1986 caused a severe administrative blockage. In the environmental area this process was slow, lasting more than two years. An official of the Ministry of Public Works, Transport, and the Environment (MOPTMA) responsible for it pointed out that it was impossible to work out so many laws to effect EU directives, so that recourse was made to royal decrees to speed up matters.[49]

In one sense, Spain's lack of much environmental legislation before membership in effect facilitated this process, for there has been much less of a problem of harmonizing European with national laws compared with, say, Italy. Nevertheless, the speed with which Spain adopted so much environmental legislation had a disrupting effect in some sectors.[50]

Spain's efficient adoption of EU directives at this time contrasted with Greece's delays in doing the same over a much longer period, although there are, of course, fewer ministries to negotiate with than in Athens or Rome. However, evidence from interviews suggests that the incorporation process is often complicated. On the whole, Spain's difficulties here have arisen from a lack of experience as a new member state and are not really exceptional, being familiar to most other countries in the EU.

Spain's *de facto* federal system, on the other hand, with as many as seventeen different autonomous communities or regions, presents a potential difficulty so far as implementation is concerned, as we might expect from looking at the case of Germany. It is important to remember that as a rule central government is concerned only with formal implementation, and that practical implementation is a subnational responsibility particularly of the regions. Generally, the autonomous communities operate within framework legislation set by Madrid, although there is some ambiguity over the division of competences; to confuse matters further, the regional statutes vary in specific environmental functions. Inevitably, their performance varies, with some being rather efficient and others less so. Undoubtedly, this makes for variation in regional patterns of implementation in certain environmental sectors. As an official of MOPTMA complained,

difficulties [over implementation] have existed from the moment we had a regional system for controlling the application process . . . countries like Spain have special difficulties through having competences very divided between different administrations on environmental matters.[51]

Environmental protection agencies in the regions offer some mechanism of control on the implementation of environmental regulations. While national governments in Spain have tended not to place a high priority on the environment, this cannot be said of several of the regions. This must be considered a significant influence on practical implementation and enforcement. An incentive to carry through European legislation is particularly strong when such a priority combines with economic interests, especially tourism, and also with a strong sense of territorial identity. This is found, for instance, in regions like Andalusia, Catalonia, and the Balearic Islands.

Centre–periphery coordination is, therefore, crucial in the link between formal and practical implementation, since Madrid is formally responsible to Brussels for results that are essentially in the hands of regional authorities. Now there is a coordination mechanism for the enactment of EU legislation on the environment in the sectoral conference (with sectoral conferences on other policy areas).[52] Information flows in the environmental area between centre and periphery have improved over the years, but there is frustration when Brussels demands, often at short notice, information on implementation rates, for which Madrid relies almost entirely on the different regions, some of which are tardy in responding.[53]

If there are any particular obstacles to effective implementation at the practical level, these tend to be administrative inexperience, the problem of environmental costs, and public attitudes towards legislation. The first problem has varied somewhat according to environmental sector, and has, for example, been especially evident over the carrying out of impact assessments because of lack of practice and necessary skills.[54] Also, serious problems have existed over industrial pollution, bathing water quality on Spain's Mediterranean shores, and drinking water (where the country's lack of water *per se* has tended increasingly to dominate considerations in this sector). A major factor in all these cases is the cost of implementing directives to the full.

Environmental costs have become more of an issue in Spain, undoubtedly acting as a disincentive to carrying through EU regulations. This is especially found in some sectors where the costs of meeting them are particularly high, notably controlling industrial emissions and waste water. Thus, the question of costs is a sensitive and fairly major issue, but it is not merely a material problem. There is a problem of policy priority and with it conflict over resources, with much greater attention being given in Spain to matters of public works, some of which (such as road-building) have deleterious environmental effects. Also, it appears that attitudinal and behavioural factors present some obstacles to effective implementation.

Public attitudes come into play over implementation, and tend not to act as a force to strengthen its prospects. An official in the Ministry of Economy contrasted the situation in Spain with countries like Denmark and the Netherlands, where public reliability was much greater and derived from a tradition of confidence in public authorities. Hence in Spain—where such confidence was not strong—there was often not a great readiness to understand the purpose of EU regulations on the environment.[55] Nevertheless, environmental groups operated as a counter-influence to this tendency. Although state–society relations present some problems, influenced—as in Greece—by authoritarian experience, the existence of viable regional and local authorities helps to counter the effects of executing environmental policy. It emerges, therefore, that these authorities are crucial in the process of practical application.

One way in which we can see the form that implementation problems take in Spain is by looking at issues that have come before the ECJ. In one leading case the Commission successfully won an Article 169 action against Spain. In this case the directive in question was in relation to wild birds (79/409/EEC) and concerned the failure of the Spanish authorities to protect the habitats of many species found in large populations of the Santona marshes.[56] The crux of the Spanish failure here lay in the way in which they interpreted the directive's flexibility about choosing Special Protection Area (SPA) sites. The Court ruled that, while member states had some discretion over the choice of exact territory for an SPA, the classification as such was not open for debate but depended on where and when certain species were found. Perhaps hoping for an administratively easier route, the Spanish authorities sought instead to classify the marshes as a 'nature reserve', using an existing Spanish legal categorization. However, this category was one that the directive did not mandate. More substantively, the Court's finding pointed beyond mere administrative sloppiness, since it found that there was also clear evidence that the Spanish authorities had failed to prevent pollution of the marshes. The judgment thus highlighted a substantive failure in implementation, and not just a problem of institutional or administrative dissonance with the European legal order.

Spain has seen a shift away from its traditionally relaxed view on the enforcement and implementation of environmental laws in general, following a notable supreme court case of 1990 which visited a prison sentence on a major polluter, heralding an about-face.[57] More significant legal teeth have been given to private

Spanish citizens seeking redress under the doctrine of direct effect through both a new Criminal Code (1996), which clearly expands the sanctions for environmental offences, and a new reformulation of administrative law, which creates a system of binding fines and remedies for legal persons whenever administrative ordinances are breached. This goes a long way towards addressing the usual objection of the ECJ to the use of administrative measures to implement directives, in so far as it creates a generalized redress for citizens. In other ways, the enforcement capacity has been built up, albeit with some regional differentiation evident. Catalonia for instance has notably created an environmental police force to improve its field agency side of enforcement.[58]

Italy

Political factors have undoubtedly weighed heavily in explaining Italy's somewhat notorious problems in the implementation process, both formal and practical. Judging by available statistics, Italy has the worst overall record among member-states. More than in the other southern countries, the marked tendency for short-lived governments has often played havoc with this process. As Rehbinder and Stewart noted, rapid changes made it difficult to comply with deadlines set in environmental directives.[59] Political changes and systemic crises in recent years have not improved the duration of governments. Faced with such chronic difficulties in getting detailed legislation through the Italian Chamber of Deputies and Senate, Italian executives have occasionally even attempted to argue, unsuccessfully, that old 1950s and even earlier workers' and health protection legislation might serve as a legal basis to implement various environment directives.[60]

As for the operation of political structures, the weak role of the environment ministry and the lack of effective inter-ministerial coordination over environmental questions creates basic difficulties. Furthermore, the regions and their problematic cooperation with Rome have long been identified as a serious obstacle to implementation, given the common practice among regions of not following national directions as to the content, information requirements, and deadlines for environmental regulations.[61] Matters have not been helped by controversy over the role of the regions in the execution of EU directives in general.[62] The overall effect has been to retard regularly and considerably the process of implementation. As Ruffolo, minister of the environment, remarked in his statement for the first official report on the state of the environment in Italy (1989), 'the decentralised structure of the Italian state, with vast competences in the environmental field attributed to the regions, provinces and municipalities has checked and slowed down the process of our legislation'.[63] However, in recent years some efforts at centralization have with partial success been made by the Ministry of the Environment precisely to overcome this problem.[64]

In addition, administrative and procedural problems account significantly for Italy's poor record over implementation. These include the practice of implementing

EU directives by means of new laws even when these are not required (adding to the already existing confusion over Italy's profusion of environmental legislation); and parliament's delegation of legislative competence to the government, creating in reality further delay.[65] The procedure for receiving EU directives is laborious and slow, involving elaborate multilateral consultation backwards and forwards between a range of ministries (the exact ones depending on the environmental sector).[66]

The legislative procedure has been notoriously slow too, given the strict bicameral system and multi-party dealings, a source of some frustration on the part of the more efficient agencies of environmental management. Senior environmental officials of the national energy agency ENEA complained that the legislation that ensues is 'the result of many interventions, very often ending up as legislation rather pulled in all directions which therefore pays little respect to the practical problems [of the environment]'.[67] The dominance of party-political considerations in this as in other areas of policy was commonly quoted by interview respondents in different ministries as a major obstacle to effective formal implementation of environmental directives.

Pressure on Italy over its much criticized record has on occasions been influential. An instance is the new procedure under Law 86 of 1989 to tighten up the legislative process, requiring an annual law (known as the 'Community law') for dealing with the backlog of outstanding laws.[68] However, it has not necessarily helped with the confusion arising from the failure to sort out contradictions between EU regulations and existing national legislation, a labour of Hercules in itself, given Italy's plethora of laws on environmental matters. In this way, genetic problems of European legislation have become magnified at the national level at the start of the implementation process.

The European Court of Justice has also been firm in its insistence that the problems of the Italian state cannot stand as an excuse for failures of implementation. One clear example is provided by the case concerning the directive on the sulphur content of fuel oils (75/716/EEC), which was adopted under the technical programme to eliminate trade barriers.[69] The directive harmonized standards in such a way as to prohibit fuels that did not meet minimum standards. In the case of Italian implementation, what was involved was a classic case of *lentocrazia*. There was simply too much of a delay in the Ministry of Health's production of the required legislation. In response to the Italian state's plea of slowness owing to sudden government collapse, the Court reiterated a long line of case law,[70] emphasizing that no state can give administrative problems as an excuse for non-implementation, even if the problems are constitutional in nature. Transposition in this case was made also difficult by the relatively short implementation phase required (nine months).

Public administration has not in any significant way improved. Its ponderous and inefficient procedures are a general Italian problem, affecting the environmental area as much as any other. Several factors came to light in interviews with senior officials involved in that area. These included the lack of a complete and efficient information system, the absence of financial resources, and difficulties relating to Italy's particular legal culture.[71] While there have been some limited recent improvements in official environmental information,[72] the lack of adequate resources has been highlighted in specialist studies as seriously affecting the operation of implementation agencies around the country.[73]

Cultural complications have been apparent, for instance, in the difficult introduction of environmental impact assessment. The EU directive of 1985 represented in effect the starting-point of EIA in Italy. But its provisions conflicted with the ethos of the country's public administration and its closed procedures because of the requirement for public accountability. As a legal adviser to the Italian Greens in the European Parliament explained,

this problem of failings in the formal implementation and then the substantial problems over EIA, is seen as a dialectical relationship between the public administration and the citizens . . . and this is a phenomenon foreign to Italian legal culture, something that in the Anglo-Saxon countries is already there. Therefore, the administration experienced difficulty in living with this requirement of responding to citizens who presented issues and provided opposition. A cultural problem, of the cultural roots of the institution. This added to the lack of agencies, means and personnel for instruction on environmental impact assessment in a significant way.[74]

It is small wonder that certain mentalities have prevailed in Italian government over the implementation of EU directives. These in turn have tended to detract from the prospects for practical implementation. Rehbinder and Stewart observed that Italy stood out among member states for agreeing to rather strict EU measures, anticipating they would not have to be fully implemented, this being a root cause of a large implementation gap.[75] Furthermore, the problems for implementation are compounded by the lack of practice of administrative review, and by a procedural approach that emphasizes the pure execution of norms over the actual achievement of results.[76] Hence, as one journalist expert in environmental matters remarked, 'in Italy directives are applied in a rigorous manner on paper', but often 'they are not put into practice, or derogations, prorogations are requested'.[77]

A basic problem in Italy is the tradition whereby nearly all rules depend for their implementation on public intervention and public administration, with no recognized principle of responsibility on the part of the private sector.[78] It is not surprising, therefore, that rationalization is a strong motive behind the formal adoption of EU directives. An environmental expert working for the Ministry of Health explained:

It is very important to have a common reference. That a decision is not only one at the national or local level, but is agreed at the international level—this is most useful precisely for the purposes of rationalization. I would say a series of directives have been very useful for rationalizing, in so far as there is acceptance on the part of public opinion of what happens at the EU level even if there may be criticism.[79]

The Italian record has varied somewhat between environmental sectors. On air quality, there have been failures in implementing directives over detailed discrepancies in national regulations and because of lethargy in some regions. But on matters such as standards for fuels and vehicles, Italian provisions are now in line with EU legislation, despite earlier problems; and air monitoring networks have been much extended throughout the country.[80] Italy has been much criticized in the past for failing to implement the bathing and drinking water directives, with lack of resources being one major cause.[81]

But on these issues (so directly impacting on personal health) public pressure has come to the fore through the activism of environmental organizations. It has on some issues been a vital influence in helping to secure compliance with EU regulations. A notable case has been over the bathing waters directives, where the Lega per l'Ambiente has persisted in its regular campaigns to secure effective monitoring and to expose government deficiencies.[82]

Another notable case in which Article 169 proceedings have been driven by Italian civil society is that of *Pretora di Salo* v. *Persons Unknown*.[83] Here a local group of environmentally conscious anglers (the Ecological Association of Fishermen for Safeguarding the River Chiese) managed to get the peculiarly Italian office of investigative magistrate to begin a form of unusual investigative criminal proceedings. The institutional prerogatives enjoyed by this office meant that the magistrate in question also had the power to seek an Article 177 reference, thus pushing the whole issue upwards to the European Court. While the ECJ discounted the attempt at criminal proceedings in the absence of any such measure within the directive in question and/or domestic Italian legislation which allowed for such criminal charges, the plaintiffs none the less managed to score an important victory against the Italian state in getting a clarification that the 1978 directive on water quality (78/659/EEC) also included by implication issues of quantity of water.[84]

Netherlands

Issues of implementation in Dutch environmental policy need to be seen in the general context of the Dutch policy style and approach to environmental problems. In particular, there are three features of the Dutch style that interact with one another to give rise to the characteristic pattern of implementation: the administrative separation between standard-setting at the national level and enforcement at the subnational level; the framework of the National Environmental Policy Plan (NEPP) within which policy is now developed; and the instrument mix that has come to dominate policy, in particular the use of voluntary agreements, or 'covenants' to use the Dutch term, to achieve certain goals. These are not separate influences on implementation, but they work together to define the process of implementation. For example, the use of covenants as a device is tied to the notion of target groups developed through the planning process, and administrative organization has been adapted to orientate the process to the target groups.

In simple terms, the standards that are set at the national or EU level have to be enforced by regulators in the provinces or by the water boards responsible for the waterways. Since the main instrument of Dutch policy is the licence, the implementation process is one in which licence conditions are enforced. Some implementation slippage occurs when operators function without a licence, an inherently difficult activity to quantify, though there have been cases of the unauthorized dumping of chemical waste or operators of plant not having the appropriate licence.[85] However, even when simple criminal behaviour of this sort is not an issue, the application of the licence terms raises its own complexities.

Some commentators have noticed how in the past the administrative separation of national standard-setting and subnational implementation had behavioural consequences, with national policy-makers being relatively uninterested in issues of implementation and subnational regulators being understaffed and with little motivation.[86] However, since the mid-1980s the situations has changed considerably, for three reasons.

Firstly, at the subnational level, those responsible for enforcement began to take a more positive attitude to regulation, seeing it as a means by which those that are to be regulated can be helped to realize the policy goals. At the provincial level, in the 1980s local regulators were already undertaking their task in a different way; firms that had installed satisfactory environmental management systems were still visited regularly, but there was a greater emphasis in these visits on matters of process, rather than on straight compliance.[87]

Secondly, although the development of the NEPP always placed a greater emphasis on the specification of environmental quality goals and standards and less on the way in which those goals and standards were going to be achieved, the team responsible for drawing up the NEPP were always aware of implementation problems. Indeed, those issues affected their own planning process, not in the setting of the standards, but in establishing the timetables for their implementation.[88]

Moving from the planning stage to the implementation of the NEPP saw greater attention being focused on issues of implementation, and in 1992, there was a reorganization within the ministry which involved clustering the directorates into named groups, making it easier for the target groups (e.g. construction, the energy industry, and consumer groups) to identify the section that they needed to deal with. These changes were made on the understanding that, as the policy tasks shifted from legislation to implementation, so the functions of the ministry would change.[89] In addition, a more regular structure of reporting on environmental performance was introduced.

In many ways these consensual arrangements work well, but they do give rise to some of the characteristic issues of implementation in respect of EU environmental policy. For example, with their close links to target groups, Dutch policy-makers are well aware of the economic implications of environmental measures. Indeed, one of the reasons that policy-makers give for being interested in ensuring international environmental action is the need not to put Dutch industry at a competitive disadvantage.[90] The close links between policy-makers and target groups may also go some way towards explaining why it is that the most successful instrument of Dutch environmental policy—the hypothecated system of water charges —has not been more replicated in other sectors of environmental policy.[91]

The consensual and well developed nature of the implementation community may also serve to explain why, as in Germany, it is the administrative processes of implementation that have often been at issue when the Netherlands has faced legal action over implementation. For example, the case of the *Commission* v. *Netherlands* concerned the poor implementation of the directive on bathing waters (76/160/EEC), which had been made the responsibility of the Ministry of Transport.[92] In that event, national actors, confident and familiar with a well developed and comprehensive corpus of national measures, appear to have felt that the transposition of European directives required little more than administrative measures, although the Dutch also accepted the principle that it would be ideal to introduce clear legal provisions as well. But in this regard a law to amend the Law Relating to Hygiene and Safety in Bathing Places (Wet Hygiëne en Veiligheid Zweminrichtingen) by means of the values and parameters described in the directive still existed only in draft form. Indeed, the Commission was happy only when the Dutch did eventually modify their surface water pollution law (Wet Verontreiniging Oppervlaktewateren) in 1982, when it felt they had finally gone some way towards ameliorating the situation. This latter modification allowed the Dutch to do two things that none of the previous measures had permitted, and with which Dutch practice was previously unfamilair: (1) introduce binding nationwide discharge limits; and (2) create a general nationwide legal obligation for a minimum standard for various uses of surface waters.

In this case, the Dutch also pleaded (to no avail) the complexity of their national implementation system, pointing to the fact that a high degree of delegation to regional, specialized, and local agents meant that national legal provisions were of only limited application: what mattered more was to be able administratively to communicate effectively to the various tiers. Attempts to invoke the practice of multi-annual targeted anti-pollution programmes as evidence of good implementation was swiftly rebutted by the Court on the simple point that such agreements failed to generate legally enforceable rights under the doctrine of direct effect. Interestingly, the Commission was prepared to admit that it was not necessarily quarrelling with the Dutch over a substantive breach of limit values within the directive or a shortage of information: what it was keen to press home was that the correct specified procedure must be followed for giving information. In other words, the performance goal was not enough: the process aspects of the directive were also crucially important.

However, it would be perhaps wrong to characterize Dutch difficulties with implementation as merely a clash of legal cultures, for concrete examples can be pointed to where substantive breaches with directives are evident. In the case of *Commission* v. *Netherlands*,[93] the Netherlands' strong agricultural lobby showed its power in the manner in which the wild birds directive was improperly implemented under as many as five complaint headings. In this case Dutch administrative measures were shoddy, displaying poor integration with their domestic hunting law (Jachtwet). Moreover, they attempted to plead a derogation for species of carrion (magpies, etc.) on the grounds that they caused damage to farmland. Such derogations had not been notified properly to the Commission, nor were they in any event permissible upon a close reading of the directive. In that event, because the directive set out a common heritage approach for the entire EU (arguing that national bird populations were in effect a common resource), it was particularly important to have a detailed exact implementation of the facts.

Finally, in this context it is also worth noting how the European context for the domestic implementation of environmental measures can lead to the phenomenon of 'over-implementation', in the sense that the taking of measures to bring about an improvement in the quality of the environment can run into opposition from Brussels. In the wake of the Council decision of 1985 that established the framework within which subsequent measures on emissions controls for cars were negotiated, the Dutch government introduced a subsidy to encourage the purchase of cleaner vehicles.[94] This stimulated opposition from other member states, most notably France, which protested to the Commission about the measure. In 1989 there was even the threat of an ECJ reference by the Commission, though it was a threat not acted on in the end. The example is important as a reminder that international action at the European level, while it may be a force for keeping member states in some sort of line, is not always a force for high environmental standards.

United Kingdom

The UK stands out from the other countries in our study by having a traditional form of inspection and implementation located in a central government body (or, more accurately, successive government bodies). Called at various times the Alkali Inspectorate, the Industrial Air Pollution Inspectorate, and Her Majesty's Inspectorate of Pollution, it was responsible for controlling emissions from complex and large industrial processes. In 1974 the Health and Safety Executive was established with some environmental responsibilities, particularly in the field of nuclear power and chemicals. Then, in 1989, another national inspectorate was created in the form of the National Rivers Authority. Under the 1995 legislation, the National Rivers Authority was merged with Her Majesty's Inspectorate of Pollution to form the Environment Agency, also acquiring some powers in the field of waste control.[95] In addition to these central government bodies, however, subnational authorities, both local authorities and water authorities, have had responsibilities for implementation, usually for the less complex processes.

As we noted in Chapter 5, the traditional account of the style of implementation in the UK stresses its informal and consensual character. Legislation has typically been cast in terms that bestow broad discretionary powers on regulatory bodies, leaving them considerable freedom to vary the stringency of pollution control depending upon local circumstances. Certainly until the 1980s the style of regulatory negotiation was consensual, with inspectors and industry discussing together the relevant standards.[96] Although it is possible easily to overstate the national distinctiveness of these informal elements, many of which manifest themselves even in more traditionally formalized systems such as the USA and Germany, the informal and discretionary elements of traditional UK practice were at odds with EU demands for much of the 1970s and 1980s.

In this context, the UK presents an interesting case in respect of issues of implementation of EU measures. Rhetorically it has been prone to argue that it places a high priority on implementation, often stressing that it bargains hard about the formulation of directives precisely because it takes implementation so seriously (presumably carrying the tacit implication that other countries are less fussy at the formulation stage because they are more lax about implementation).

This argument was put with characteristic panache by Mr Michael Heseltine, when he was secretary of state for the environment, giving evidence to the House of Lords inquiry into implementation:

The British Government's view is absolutely clear. It carefully evaluates the Directives to which it is asked to give its name. If it is persuaded that they are desirable, it goes along with its support and it does all that is within its powers to implement those Directives and then it has to follow through the commitment that it has made. There is inevitably an occasion on which the Commission, in discharge of its proper responsibilities, will question (or others may raise with the Commission the need to question) whether this country or other countries are fulfilling their commitments.

. . . our view is that, as I said at the very beginning, we do take seriously these Directives. We do try to implement them as rapidly as possible and we do then try to ensure the administrative follow up is effective. The tables that are produced by the Commission on implementation show this country favourably; there is no question about that. We are not always at the top of every league table but we are always close to the top of the league tables and that is precisely because of the way we conduct the business of this country. . . .

He went on later in his testimony to say (with perhaps more enthusiasm than accuracy):

I think we are a nation that is very preoccupied to carry through the commitments we make and to introduce systems and penalties to uphold the law that then has to be enshrined in the statute books. There are other European countries which take just as careful a view of their commitments. It is interesting if one looks at the league table that there are other countries which seem to share the lead spots with us on a consistent basis.[97]

However, quite apart from the fact that, as we have seen, the UK can hardly be said to have consistently occupied the 'lead spots' in the implementation tables, the record is slightly more complex than this argument would suggest.

There are some cases where the UK has simply been slow in the legal transposition of measures agreed at the European level or in meeting the obligation to inform the Commission of the arrangements put in place to implement a measure. For example, local authorities were not even notified until April 1978 of their obligations under the waste framework directive (75/442/EEC) agreed in 1975. The 1975 directive on the disposal of waste oils (75/439/EEC) has not been implemented at all (though the UK is not alone in this regard). There was no formal compliance until March 1989, nearly two years late, with the terms of the 1984 framework directive (84/360/EEC) on emissions to the atmosphere from industrial plants, and full implementation had to await the 1990 Environmental Protection Act. In addition, the government was five months late in designating sensitive areas under the urban waste water directive (91/271), and full implementation was a year late.[98]

Another problem of implementation, which the UK shared with other member states including the Netherlands and Germany, was the use of established legal powers and instruments, even though the EU measures seemed to require more. This was compounded in the case of some directives by the fact that the relevant domestic legislation, the 1974 Control of Pollution Act, had provisions that had themselves not been fully implemented.[99] This was particularly true in the case of directives dealing with water pollution control and the control of waste disposal. Indeed, it was not until the 1989 Water Act and the 1990 Environmental Protection Act that the UK had provided the appropriate statutory framework for the setting of water and air quality standards, quite apart from the issue of implementing EU measures purely by means of departmental circulars.

However, the form of implementation deficit that most clearly challenges the thesis expressed by Mr Heseltine has involved exploiting imprecision or loopholes in the directives as drafted. Thus, under the sulphur content of fuel oils directive, the whole of the road system was designated as an area where low sulphur fuels could be burnt, and the rest of the country was designated as an area where fuel oils of a higher content could be burnt.[100] Similarly, exploiting a loophole in the way in which bathing beaches were defined, only twenty-seven beaches were originally designated under the bathing waters directive, a list that managed to exclude the major resorts of Blackpool and Brighton.[101]

The bathing waters case is interesting, since it was clear during the whole course of negotiation over the directive that the traditional British principles of coastal water control were at odds with what was being proposed. As Andrew Jordan has shown, there was a clearly established principle of bathing water pollution control that has been built upon a 1959 Medical Research Council study, which rested on the distinction between hygiene and aesthetic distaste.[102] Although there is no direct evidence that bears upon the question, we might suppose that measures that were approached with a sense of scepticism when they were being formulated would not always receive enthusiastic support when it came to their implementation.

The cases that have come before the ECJ reveal various forms of implementation failure and underline the extent to which the shortcomings are not simply procedural but also substantive. For example, in the case of the *Commission* v. *UK*,[103] the UK suffered a heavy defeat in the Court on three substantive grounds. Firstly, the Court decided there was a failure properly to create legally effective regulation for Scotland and Northern Ireland, in this case showing that coordination is not just a problem for federal states. Indeed, echoing Dutch and Italian claims of administrative difficulties, the UK pleaded the legal complexities of transposing law through direct rule for Northern Ireland. Secondly, no provision in regulations had been made for the food processing industry. Thirdly, and most significantly, the Court squashed the rather dubious UK argument that substantive breaches on the maximum allowable concentration for nitrates in twenty-eight locations should not be seen as a breach of the directives, as all it required the UK to do was to show that it had tried as far as was practicable to reduce such pollution. Interestingly, however, a Commission complaint about measuring lead in water was rejected by the court in so far as it was not contested that the British had broken from the practice described for measuring such concentrations.

Again, substantive environmental bad faith, in contrast to just administrative incompatibility, was shown in the case of *R* v. *Secretary of State for the Environment, ex parte Royal Society for the Protection of Birds*.[104] This basically limited the discretion of the secretary of state for the environment to apply a derogation under the Special Protection Area of the Birds directive. The facts concerned a previously designated SPA near Sheerness which was de-categorized by the secretary of state in order to ensure the commercial viability of the port. This was not however a sufficient economic interest to override the general interest of environmental protection; and it was not done subject to Commission approval, or by reference to public health concerns or even to improve some broader environmental aim.

UNDERSTANDING IMPLEMENTATION IN A SYSTEM OF MULTI-LEVEL GOVERNANCE

In terms of the general approach that guides our discussion in Part II, we might expect the process of enactment and enforcement of EU legislation on the environment in the six European states to illustrate only too well the dictum 'that the policy-making process [in the EU] does not follow the logic of integration, but rather that integration follows the logic of decision-making processes', which 'have their roots in the power structures of the nation states'.[105]

The literature on EU legislative implementation has also tended to give prior attention to domestic factors in explaining deficit problems, if only because, officially, responsibility for implementation lies at the national level. Laffan listed (in a study on social policy) the following variables as affecting the implementation of policies: communication, information, control, adequacy of resources, the nature of the policy instrument, bureaucratic structures, and the existence of feedback mechanisms.[106]

According to Collins and Earnshaw, the key factors inhibiting the implementation of environmental legislation are the range and complexity of existing national laws, the variety of national and subnational structures, different definitions of concepts contained in directives, legislative culture in member states, and, finally, deliberate non-compliance on grounds of political expedience.[107] Furthermore, in a general study of EU policy implementation, Helen Wallace has noted national diversity in the form of language, culture, economic preferences, administrative methods, political emphasis, and priorities, 'all of which tend to be magnified by the intense and often conflictual bargaining process of Brussels'. However, such diversity has to be set against a number of commonalities among member states: broadly similar and highly interdependent political systems and economies; some common values and objectives; and relative mutual familiarity, shared knowledge, and similar administrative and legal practices.[108]

Understanding implementation difficulties in a system of multi-level governance in fact requires us to pay attention to all three categories of variable that we have identified in terms of our general concern about convergence and divergence in European environmental policy, the international as well as the state-related and the society-related. Implementation is not simply a problem of domestic resistance to internationally agreed commitments: it is also a consequence of how those international agreements are entered into and formulated. In our analysis we look at each category of variable in turn.

International Level

At first sight it might appear that international variables are always likely to push countries towards compliance and hence towards convergence. To be sure, we noted the possibility of second-order effects, according to which domestic reactions to international pressures were likely to reinforce resistance to international efforts at compliance, but our general expectation was that the overall direction of the international level of governance was one that would lead countries to converge.

However, it is clear from the empirical evidence that the situation is more complex than this simple model would suggest, even if we leave aside the cases where the EU delays environmental progress, for example regarding the attempt by the Dutch to speed up the introduction of cleaner cars. In the first place, implementation concerns arise to some extent during policy negotiations. As Haigh has shown in a four-country study of the implementation of water and waste directives,

the process of negotiation in the Council is to some extent an attempt by the member states to ensure that a directive is agreed in such a form that it is compatible with existing national legislative and administrative practices. Inevitably, compromises have to be made and countries may well find themselves accepting commitments before they are ready for them . . . the question must nevertheless be asked as to whether, in the negotiations leading to the adoption of a directive, countries admit to themselves and to others that they know they cannot meet the date for implementation.[109]

Moreover, the overall policy process in the EU is highly complex for two reasons: the nature of decision-making structures, which are multiple and involve a diffusion of executive power; and a forward-and-backward movement in the dynamics of policy formulation, defying any neat identification of separate and successive stages by which policy is, rationally speaking, carried through from conception to completion.

The genesis of environmental directives might often be said to encode implementation failure into their character. Such genetic factors refer most of all to the nature and content of EU policy decisions. In the environmental area, the regular use of the directive allows for flexibility in the means of implementation, but it also necessarily creates scope for opportunities to delay and even avoid commitments made at the European level. This may not always be intentional, but the absence of effective supervision from the EU itself is a form of inducement in this respect. In fact, there are very few environmental pressures that operate from the EU level, apart from the emphasis placed on environmental protection by the European Parliament, given that the Commission is dependent on information from the national levels and is in any case overloaded, while the environmental lobby at Brussels is weakly organized.[110] Furthermore, the question needs to be explored how far the method of direct regulation, so far favoured in the environmental area, conflicts with the legislative cultures of member states, particularly those with a long tradition of extensive and consensual consultation over legislative proposals.

In addition, EU directives are often unskillfully drafted, imprecise, and basically complex, hence contributing to problems of their application at both formal and practical stages of implementation. Jan Pentreath of the UK's National Rivers Authority argued, in giving evidence to the House of Lords inquiry into the implementation of EU environmental policy, that terms like 'eutrophication' were often used in an imprecise way in directives:

The words which occasionally give us difficulties are simple words like 'eutrophication' and 'sensitive areas' and so on. These words are easily rolled off the tongue, I think, in reading a Directive. When we then have to implement it on the ground, we within the United Kingdom have to define what we mean for operational reasons by 'a risk of eutrophication' or by 'sensitive areas', and how that compares with a 'vulnerable zone' in another Directive of a similar nature. This takes quite a while to work out; and it is probably fair to say the interpretation would differ from one country to another.[111]

Imprecision in regulations has sometimes allowed member states to delay or make exceptions at these stages, depending on the case in question. This was true, for instance, of the directive on bathing water which was ambiguous in its provisions, just as that on drinking water was criticized for being too rigid and hence difficult to apply in terms of quality control.

Lack of adequate information is particularly a problem here.[112] But complexity does not stop there, for there remains the problem of adapting standing national laws on specific environmental sectors. Over twenty items of legislation were required, for instance, to implement the directive on environmental impact assessment in the UK, and even then implementation was still regarded as incomplete by the Commission.[113] It must be remembered, too, that the environmental area is particularly technical and thus outside the expertise of most legislators. It is thus clear that genetic factors, essentially deriving from the EU level, can aggravate implementation considerably.

Indeed, at one time there was a tendency for implementing authorities to use EU directives as little more than guidelines.[114] As Ludwig Krämer noted, EU laws without adequate national legal and administrative measures are insufficient.[115] It would be very wrong, therefore, to imagine that the introduction of consistent and comprehensive implementation, or of a much stricter enforcement regime, would necessarily help to guarantee the application of a strong environment policy. Indeed, more effective implementation may well have an adverse knock-on effect on policy formulation, since it may reduce the willingness of some representatives on the Council to agree to more environmental legislation. There is a certain irony in the possibility that consistent policy implementation might lead to a slowing down of decision-making or a dilution of environmental standards. Nevertheless, a commitment to investigate all complaints would in any case shift attention and resources away from policy-making.[116]

Problems arising out of stricter enforcement should not be used as an excuse for deficient implementation, however, although it may well act as a justification for those who wish to see the introduction of a more flexible regime, one that might take into consideration regional characteristics, for example.[117] The Fifth Action Programme did attempt to address the serious problem of non-implementation. Organizationally, among the new structures established under the programme, an Implementation Network was set up to consider relevant issues. Bringing together representatives from national authorities and from the Commission, it provides a forum for an exchange of experiences, with the ultimate aim of encouraging consistent implementation across the board.[118]

Enforcement depends in the last resort on the European Court and the European rule of law. But the cases that reach this stage in the enforcement procedure are really only the tip of the iceberg. Court cases are time-consuming and costly, and merely give member states the opportunity to delay, albeit temporarily, the application of a particular policy. Referral to the Court is a treaty obligation placed on the Commission, though in practice, given the scale of non-implementation, priorities have to be established, and cases chosen with care. The Commission can usually be sure of one thing: that the court has little sympathy with member states who blame their failure to implement environmental legislation on domestic constitutional or political factors.[119]

This now distinct trend casts some doubts on the credibility of EU environmental policy, but also, more seriously, on the overall policy process leading to enactment. There are always general problems of measuring policy effectiveness, relating outputs and outcomes to policy intentions. But in the case of the EU we are looking at a hybrid and rather incomplete policy system, where decision-making is conducted at one major level (European) and implementation at another (national)—or, rather, a multiplicity (precisely, now fifteen) of the latter. The strong cross-national variation among member states with respect to compliance with EU environmental legislation only underscores this complexity in the policy process.[120]

State-Related Variables

As we have seen, problems of institutional fragmentation in most member states also cause difficulties of coordination both horizontally and vertically (relating to centre–periphery). It is to be expected that such problems have a significant impact on implementation, especially of the practical kind, notably where environmental regulations depend heavily on local implementation, such as for instance concerning atmospheric pollution. Matters are complicated by the fact that formal account-ability to Brussels lies with national governments, while practical implementation is often shared with if not located at regional and local levels, depending on the national system and the environmental sector. EU directives are not directly bind-ing on subnational authorities, for the latter have only derivative tasks and, of course, are not involved in the formulation of EU policy.[121]

Thus, a considerable onus is placed on effective, not to mention harmonious, cooperation between centre and periphery. In fact, the pressures in this direction have been such that in given cases central–local government relationships have been affected. As Haigh has shown in his study of water and waste directives, this has produced a shift of decision-making power from local to national level in the Nether-lands though less in France, where local authorities were already at the service of central government.[122]

Political factors otherwise include such problems as whether there may be a clash between national policy styles, and the approach to environmental policy followed by Brussels. That would have serious implications for implementation, affecting the willingness to bear political and economic costs of agreed policy measures. For example, the EU's preference for a regulatory style or the articulation of policy principles as a essential element in policy style have not always been compatible with national styles.[123]

Problems of efficiency, infrastructure, and control that may affect the imple-mentation process vary from the formal to the practical. Thus, legislative proced-ures can well influence the manner in which, and dispatch with which, European legislation is translated into national law. In their study of the implementation of EU legislation in member states, Siedentopf and Ziller see the administrative capacit-ies of national public administrations as quite crucial in contributing to or detracting from implementation. Analysing a series of project reports on different member states, they conclude that both the quality and the quantity of administrative resources are significant in the enforcement of EU legislation, and that 'the personal, technical and financial capacities of the responsible agencies have to be recognized as a decisive factor in the implementation of Community legislation'.[124]

In general, it was found in their 1988 study that the implementation of EU legislation 'follows the same patterns and meets the same obstacles as the implementation of the respective national legislation'. In other words, EU law 'shares the fate of the remaining national law with regard to the administrative style and administrative culture of a member state'. Hence, the former had become part of the 'normality' of policy implementation at the national levels, countering any expectation that the unique character of Community legislation with its regulatory form and specific aims might lead to the evolution of particular administrative procedures for its application.[125] Our own analysis of environmental policy implementation confirms this judgment.

This effect is most clearly seen in the case of Italy. Its problems of formal transposition related directly to the general difficulty that the Italian state has in passing laws in a political system that has been poorly served by the wayward power traditionally enjoyed by both houses of the Italian parliament, fuelled as they have been by an average government duration of a year since the Second World War, and complicated by arcane secret voting and bill reading practices.[126] However, such general difficulties of legislation can be seen in other member states as well. For example, British governments have crowded legislative timetables. Securing the passage of environmental legislation in order to meet the timetable of an EU directive may not always be possible, and particular difficulties arise in a state where there are two separate legal systems and three ways of passing legislation, depending on whether the legislation applies to England and Wales, Scotland, or Northern Ireland.

It remains to be seen, though, whether or not further experience with environmental legislation has produced even secondary or marginal reforms in national administrations for the sake of improving implementation. Other features of an administrative or procedural kind that may impinge on implementation would include mechanisms of control and communication. The former refer to checks and audits relating to finance in particular but also policy evaluation.[127] Also pertinent are monitoring systems and technical expertise, which are crucial in establishing how far legislative requirements are carried out on the ground. Problems of communication have also been identified as a central feature of the implementation process, clearly involving a two-way procedure between European and national levels.[128]

Moreover, policy understanding among national elites or networks involved in the environmental area can be crucial in determining how EU directives are interpreted. Conceptual approaches to environmental questions may be read into legislation coming from Brussels, just as—a related but different problem—there might simply be genuine differences of understanding as to what the agreed measures involve. In other words, the flexibility over applying EU regulations allows quite some scope for misunderstanding to enter the policy process. Undoubtedly, attitudes to the EU may in some way influence willingness to comply, although Siedentopf and Ziller found that member states did not consider the implementation of EU directives as the application of 'foreign imposed law'.[129]

Sometimes directives have furnished a rationalization or opportunity for policy initiative. As Haigh has noted, they have 'on occasion provided the impulse for change, particularly when arguments were needed to justify expenditure'. Similarly, directives 'have also strengthened the hands of the authorities when negotiating with industrialists, since they provide standards which are not negotiable —standards which have a higher status than national standards since in theory they are being applied in all member states'.[130]

From a quite different angle, divergent attitudes at different levels may hamper the prospects for environmental legislation. Thus, in the same study of implementation, Haigh identifies as a major reason for failure in practical implementation

the contrasting perspectives on environmental management prevailing in the local and regional implementing authorities in the member states from those prevailing among the policy-makers in the Community. While the Commission is concerned with the formation of a broad environmental policy applicable across the Community, the preoccupation of environmental control officers is the resolution of local problems. As such, the general principles of control reflected in the directives are not as a rule the primary concern of the officers in carrying out their day-to-day duties.[131]

It has also been found that ignorance of directives and their provisions 'was not unusual'; indeed, that ignorance is 'the Commission's biggest handicap in enforcing its rules'.[132] Such weaker familiarity with European compared with national legislation reflected the sense of remoteness of local actors from Brussels which was likely to undercut commitment to EU objectives. However, informal channels of communication can help to overcome this mental gulf. While much more developed on the part of national elites and administrators, close ties have also evolved with some localities. Invariably geared to EU assistance or research and development programmes, these offer a potential for altering perceptions and expectations.

Society-Related Variables

Most political pressures in the environmental field operate at the national levels, such as interest lobbies (environmentalist or industrial), the media, and public opinion. Their scope for influencing implementation is potentially strong, but in practice depends much on the issue and situation at hand.

The first sort of variable we might expect in this category is the problem of costs in applying EU legislation on the environment. This category, which also relates to economic interests that may be affected by it, should not be neglected in studying implementation in the EU. Until recently the problem has not been openly discussed; but clearly, the increased momentum of EU legislation on the environment has helped to bring the matter to the fore. Furthermore, there had been a lack of attention to costs in early European legislation, such as in the case of the 1975 bathing water directive, since member states had ten years to comply.[133] A report late in 1992 on the success rate of member states in implementing directives stressed lack of money as 'one reason why present compliance is so patchy'; it related ability to implement high environmental standards, such as in Denmark, Germany, and the Netherlands, to national wealth.[134] Evidently, the entry in the 1980s of several poorer member states was a major reason why this problem has come to be recognized openly, for some Mediterranean states have tended to say to Brussels: 'we would comply but we can't afford to.'[135] Greater acknowledgement of funding constraints on environmental legislation is likely to keep the economic dimension of policy implementation very much alive, just as will—from another angle—greater readiness to use economic instruments alongside regulatory approaches.

It is however also clear that, even in the well-off member states, the influence of particular economic interests is an important constraint on compliance. Probably the most important group here is agricultural interests. This is not simply the familiar argument that, whereas environmental benefits may be dispersed, the economic costs of securing those benefits will typically be concentrated: it is also that the political practice of member states has for many years incorporated the interests of farmers into the policy-making process and into the ideologies of political parties that have been prominent in government. The domestic political practices of member states are thus bound to provide obstacles to the implementation of measures where agricultural interests will have been less involved in their formulation.

To what extent are cultural attitudes a barrier or a facilitating condition for the implementation of environmental measures? Whatever the variations in general public opinion as measured by opinion polls, these are unlikely to play a significant role in implementation. Issues of compliance with internationally agreed commitments are simply not salient enough for a widely diffused public opinion to play a significant part in affecting the behaviour of the relevant parties. However, it is clear that public opinion as organized into environmental groups can play a significant role. As we have seen in the empirical evidence from each country, the role of environmental groups has often been crucial in initiating proceedings over non-compliance. Furthermore, the importance of such groups shows that there is not a simple north–south difference in this respect. Indeed, in Italy a great deal of the credit for effecting implementation has to go to environmentally concerned groups.

CONCLUSIONS

On certain specific issues the EU has had a beneficial effect, such as in promoting monitoring and impact assessment in individual countries—and, in Italy's case, improving the legislative procedure—just as the EU accounts for so much of the environmental legislation on the books of the southern member states in particular. Even taking that into consideration, however, it must be acknowledged that the difficulties facing a common policy on the environment are considerable. These are in part general across the EU and relate to genetic factors in European environmental legislation. But they also derive in particular from individual member states and the way they process this legislation.

While this chapter has concentrated on the range of difficulties at the national level, it has nevertheless shown that records on formal implementation and also problems of practical implementation vary significantly. Predictably, such differences reflect on the different political and administrative systems in these countries. Thus, Spain emerges as altogether more effective than the other two southern countries, especially on political/structural grounds compared with Italy and on administrative/procedural ones compared with both Italy and Greece. Common to the south is the problem of environmental costs, although this is highlighted more in Spain and Greece than in Italy, because developmentalist motives are stronger in the former than in Italy, where modernization occurred at an earlier stage in the postwar period. It should, finally, not be forgotten that these same two countries are relatively recent entrants to the EU (Greece 1981; Spain 1986). They have, therefore, had greater problems in coping with the inundation of European legislation in this area over the past decade. With time, these problems might even out.

Differences also emerge over environmental sectors, these being linked to some extent with the differing salience or impact of particular environmental problems in the countries concerned. Macrory suggests from his figures that sectoral variation relates to 'the focus of attention of national environmental interests'.[136] This is broadly correct, but his judgment here underrates the complexities. The southern countries have difficulties with water quality (a common problem relating to the Mediterranean environment), but this too is a sector that particularly engages environmental groups and it is one that relates to an important economic interest, the tourist industry. There is in addition some evidence that sectoral variation relates to differences in efficiency between different ministries in the environmental area. Furthermore, one should not ignore the differential impact of costs between different environmental sectors when considering the southern member states of the EU.

Given the cross-national variation that exists over the enactment and enforcement of environmental legislation, it is too simple to speak of a basic north–south dichotomy over the environment in the European Union. There are some grounds for arguing there are different tendencies between the two areas of the EU, but there are other grounds for painting a differentiated picture. Furthermore, there are other problems over implementing environmental directives between some of the northern member states.

Seen in general terms, environmental legislation is an extremely complicated business, as is indicated by difficulties across the EU in this respect. Problems of implementation are therefore endemic in the environmental policy arena. They are also closely related to the European institutions' lack of capacity to enforce effectively the legislation they formulate. In a survey of the literature, Jordan has noted that top-down models are in some ways relevant to the EU since directives tend to have defined goals and strict standards and timetables for compliance, although the 'top' is hardly unified and in fact includes actors from 'below' (i.e. national governments).[137] 'Bottom-up' models are less obviously applicable to the EU, but they are relevant because of the discretionary element and they have the virtue of drawing attention to national political dynamics; just as the bargaining and also policy network models serve to highlight the different interactions that take place between the two main levels.[138] However, perhaps the main message to emerge from the study of implementation is that both bottom-up and top-down approaches are likely to be one-sided in a multi-level system of environmental governance in which there is interaction between the different levels.

NOTES TO CHAPTER 8

1. B. Laffan, 'Policy Implementation in the European Community: The European Social Fund as a Case Study', *Journal of Common Market Studies*, 21:4 (1983), pp. 389–408 at 391.
2. H. Wallace, 'Implementation across National Boundaries', in D. Lewis and H. Wallace (eds.), *Policies into Practice: National and International Case Studies in Implementation* (London: Heinemann, 1984), pp. 129–43 at 131.
3. Ibid.
4. A. Jordan, 'The Implementation of EU Environmental Policy: A Policy Problem without a Political Solution?' *Environment and Planning* C, 17:1 (1999), pp. 69–90, at 75–7.
5. K. Collins and D. Earnshaw, 'The Implementation and Enforcement of European Community Environment Legislation', *Environmental Politics*, 1:4 (1992), pp. 213–49 at 216.
6. F. Snyder, 'The Effectiveness of European Community Law: Institutions, Processes, Tools and Techniques', *Modern Law Review*, 56:1 (1993), pp. 19–54 at 21.
7. *The Times*, 27 Jun. 1990; *The European*, 20 Jul. 1990.
8. For this distinction, see N. Haigh, *Manual of Environmental Policy*, (London: Cartermill International, 1992), p. 1.5. Implementation can also mean the 'filling out' or execution of framework legislation. This task, where necessary, is delegated by the Council of Ministers to the Commission, requiring that the Commission issue regulatory decisions which will enable the legislation to be implemented. Although it might seem here that the Commission has some scope for administrative discretion, this must be considered in the light of constraints on its autonomy imposed by the member state governments through the Council.

9. Interview with Ludwig Krämer, 1993.
10. R. Macrory, 'The Enforcement of Community Environmental Laws: Some Critical Issues', *Common Market Law Review*, 29 (1992), pp. 347–69 at 355.
11. Interview with David Hull, September 1993.
12. G. Pridham and M. Cini, 'Enforcing Environmental Standards', in M. Faure, J. Vervaele, and A. Weale (eds.), *Environmental Standards in the European Union: An Interdisciplinary Perspective* (Antwerp: MAKLU, 1994), pp. 251–77 at 259.
13. Macrory, 'Enforcement of Community Environmental Laws', p. 365.
14. Pridham and Cini, 'Enforcing Environmental Standards', pp. 259–60.
15. *The European*, 5 Aug. 1994.
16. R. Mayntz *et al.*, *Vollzugsprobleme der Umweltpolitik* (Wiesbaden: Rat von Sachverständigen für Umweltfragen, 1978).
17. H. Weidner, *25 Years of Modern Environmental Policy in Germany: Treading a Well-Worn Path to the Top of the International Field* (Berlin: Wissenschaftszentrum Berlin für Sozialforschung gGmbH, 1995), p. 18
18. All these figures refer to the territory of the former West Germany. See L. Metz, 'Reduction of Exhaust Gases at Large Combustion Plants in the Federal Republic of Germany' in M. Jänicke and H. Weidner (eds.), *Successful Environmental Policy: A Critical Evaluation of 24 Cases* (Berlin: Edition Sigma, 1995), pp. 171–86, at 174.
19. K. Bätcher, 'Reduction of the Calculated Use of Cadmium in German Industry', in M. Jänicke and H. Weidner (eds.), *Successful Environmental Policy: A Critical Evaluation of 24 Cases* (Berlin: Edition Sigma, 1995), pp. 325–41, esp. 326–7 and 340.
20. *Commission* v. *Germany*, Case C-361/88.
21. *Commission* v. *Germany*, C-58/89. Not all of the Commission's arguments were successful. For example, the Court rejected the argument that, because a member state has to use a system of classification of surface waters according to water quality, this imposes a corollary obligation to produce a formal act of law which indicates whether every measuring point is of a given quality.
22. *Commission* v. *Germany*, C-58/89.
23. All Bavaria had done regarding the Danube was to classify waters as demanded by the directive, but the Court rules that there was a need to go further and show evidence of having sought cooperation: *Commission* v. *Germany*, C-58/89.
24. H. Pehle, 'Germany: Domestic Obstacles to an International Forerunner', in M. S. Anderson and D. Liefferink (eds.), *European Environmental Policy: The Pioneers* (Manchester and New York: Manchester University Press, 1997), p. 200; Weidner, *25 Years*, p. 14.
25. G. Pridham, S. Verney, and D. Konstadakopulos, 'Environmental Policy in Greece: Evolution, Structures and Process', *Environmental Politics*, 4:2 (1995), pp. 244–70 at 264–5.
26. Ibid. 259–60.
27. Interview with M. Skoulos, head of Elliniki Etairia, Athens, and member of board of European Environment Agency, March 1995.
28. Interview with Leonidas Louloudis, Agricultural University of Athens and environmental adviser to the Ministry of Agriculture, Athens, November 1992.
29. Interview with Ioannis Vournas, Ministry of the Environment, Athens, November 1992.

30. L. Louloudis *et al.*, 'Environmental Impact of Agricultural Structures Policy in the European Community: The Case of Greece', mimeo, Athens, 1991.
31. Interview with Chrissoula Moniaki, municipality of Chania, Crete, October 1994.
32. Interview with Leonidas Papadakis, prefecture of Heraklion, Crete, October 1994.
33. Interview with Skoulos, March 1995.
34. Interview with Constantinos Cartalis, adviser to the Deputy Minister of the Environment, Athens, March 1995.
35. G. Bennett, *Air Pollution Control in the European Community: Implementation of the EC Directives in the Twelve Member States* (London: Graham & Trotman, 1991), pp. 59, 164–5 and 197.
36. Elleniki Etairia, *The State of the Greek Environment* (Athens: Elleniki Etairia, 1991), p. 38; interview with Cartalis, March 1995.
37. Round-table discussion with Dimitrios Koumas, Charalambos Tsafaras, and Tzortzis Georgios, Ministry of Agriculture, Athens, November 1992.
38. Interview with Zacharias Mavroukas, Ministry of Industry, Athens, December 1992.
39. Interview with Ioannis Vournas, Ministry of the Environment, Athens, March 1995.
40. Interview with Dimitra Katochianou, Centre of Planning and Economic Research (KEPE), Athens, March 1995.
41. Interview with Leonidas Louloudis, Agricultural University of Athens, Athens, March 1995.
42. Rapid Text Press release, IP/97/114, 1997/12/15.
43. Rapid Text Press Release, IP/97/63.
44. Rapid Text Press Release, IP/97/571, 1997/06/26.
45. Rapid Text Press Release, IP/97/890, 1997/10/17.
46. Rapid Text Press Release, IP/97/843, 1997/10/02.
47. Rapid Text Press Release, IP/97/578/, 1997/06/30.
48. Rapid Text Press Release, IP/97/577, 1997/06/30.
49. Interview with Teresa Mosquete, Environmental Policy Department, Ministry of Public Works, Madrid, October 1992.
50. Interview with Joan Puigdollers, Environment Directorate, Generalitat, Barcelona, October 1992.
51. Interview with Mosquete, October 1992.
52. Ministerio de Obras Publicas, *Medio Ambiente en España 1992* (Madrid: Ministerio de Obras Publicas, 1993), p. 241; interview with Joaquin Ros Vicent, Environmental Policy Directorate, Ministry of Public Works, Madrid, April 1994.
53. Interview with Mosquete, October 1992.
54. Ministerio de Obras Publicas, *Medio Ambiente en España 1988* (Madrid: Ministerio de Obras Publicas, 1989), p. 357.
55. Interview with Jose Antonio Gallego, Ministry of Economy, Madrid, April 1994.
56. *Commission* v. *Spain* [1993] 1 ECR 4221.
57. X. Junquera and E. Pujol, 'Environmental Regulation in Spain', in T. Handler (ed.), *Regulating the European Environment* (London: John Wiley, 1997, 2nd edn), pp. 177–200 at 197–8.
58. Ibid.
59. E. Rehbinder and R. Stewart, *Environmental Protection Policy* (Berlin and New York: Walter de Gruyter, 1985), p. 235.

60. See *Commission* v. *Italy*, Case C-240/89. This case related to a directive on protect-ing workers from asbestos, 80/1107/EEC, of 27 November 1980. The directive had set a deadline of 1987 for administrative measures of implementation to be taken. The Italian government not only failed to take these measures, but also failed to reply to the Commission's complaints. When challenged, the Italian government argued that an older 1956 law could be relied upon to offer protection, because the relevant draft law existed but was still blocked in the Parliament. The Commission argued that such laws were far too general and did not have the same philosophy concerning the determination of a maximum level of asbestos in the air. What is interesting in these cases is the relative ease with which Italian authorities admitted a failure to imple-ment, whereby often the Commission's argument was only weakly contested. For examples of the standard Italian delay and lateness with regard to water directives, see the case of *Commission* v. *Italy*, Joined Cases 30 and 34/81. In these cases some five directives were at found to be improperly or not at all implemented: wastes oil disposal (75/439/EEC), surface drinking water (75/440/EEC), waste (75/442/EEC), bathing water (76/160/EEC), and PCBs (76/403/EEC). Again, owing to legislative difficulties, the Italian position was little better than to plead delay.

61. H. Siedentopf and J. Ziller (eds.), *Making European Policies Work: the Implementation of Community Legislation in the Member States*, i, *Comparative Syntheses* (London: Sage, 1988), pp. 59–60; A. Capria, 'Formulation and Implementation of Environmental Policy in Italy', paper for 12th International Congress on Social Policy, Paris, 1991, pp. 9–10.

62. A. Bianchi, 'Environmental Policy', in F. Francioni (ed.), *Italy and EC Membership Evaluated* (London: Pinter, 1992), pp. 71–105 at 91.

63. Ministero dell'Ambiente, *Nota Aggiunta del Ministro Giorgio Ruffolo* (Rome: Ministero dell'Ambiente, 1989), p. 22.

64. R. Lewanski, 'Environmental Policy in Italy: From the Regions to the EEC, A Multiple Tier Policy Game', ECPR paper, 1993, pp. 22–4.

65. Bianchi, 'Environmental Policy', p. 88.

66. Interview with Anna Villa, Ministry of the Environment, Rome, May 1992.

67. Interview with Riccardo Luppi and Cesare Silvi, ENEA, Rome, May 1992.

68. Bianchi, 'Environmental Policy', p. 90.

69. *Commission* v. *Italy*, Case 92/79.

70. E.g. *Commission* v. *Italy*, Case 100/77.

71. Interviews with Anna Villa, Ministry of the Environment; Valeria Agostini, Com-mittee on the Environment, Senate; Corrado Carruba, Green group, European Parliament—all in Rome, May 1992.

72. G. Pridham, 'National Environmental Policy Making in the European Framework: Spain, Greece and Italy in Comparison', *Regional Politics and Policy*, 4:1 (1994), pp. 80–101 at 89–90.

73. B. Dente and R. Lewanski, 'Administrative Networks and Implementation Effect-iveness: Industrial Air Pollution Control Policy in Italy', *Policy Studies Journal*, 11:1 (1982), 116–29 at 118–19.

74. Interview with Carruba, May 1992.

75. Rehbinder and Stewart, *Environmental Protection Policy*, p. 263.

76. Ibid. 153; Lewanski, 'Environmental Policy in Italy'.

77. Interview with Antonio Cianciullo, *La Reppublica*, Rome, May 1992.
78. Capria, 'Formulation and Implementation of Environmental Policy in Italy', pp. 8–9.
79. Interview with Giovanni Zapponi, Istituto Superiore di Sanita, Rome, May 1992.
80. Bennett, *Air Pollution Control in the European Community*, pp. 32–3, 68–70.
81. Capria, 'Formulation and Implementation of Environmental Policy in Italy', p. 40.
82. Interviews with Carruba and with Mauro Albrizio, Lega Ambiente, Rome, May 1992.
83. *Pretora di Salo* v. *Persons Unknown*, Case 14/86.
84. P. Federici and A. G. Galeotti, 'Environmental Regulation in Italy', in T. Handler (ed.), *Regulating the European Environment* (London: John Wiley, 1997, 2nd edn), pp. 125–33 at 132.
85. Ken Hanf, 'Politics of Regulatory Compliance', lecture delivered University of East Anglia, 16 October 1989.
86. H. T. A. Bressers and L. A. Plettenburg, 'The Netherlands', in M. Jänicke and H. Weidner (eds.), *National Environmental Policies* (Berlin: Springer-Verlag, 1997), pp. 109–31 at 116.
87. Interview with George Meuders and Bernard Enklaar, Province of Gelderland, Environmental and Water Division, September 1989.
88. Interview with Paul de Jongh, VROM, September 1989.
89. Interview, VROM, 10–12 March 1993.
90. Ibid.
91. On the success of the water charges, see M. S. Andersen, *Governance by Green Taxes: Making Pollution Prevention Pay* (Manchester and New York: Manchester University Press, 1994), and H. T. A. Bressers, 'The Impact of Effluent Charges: A Dutch Success Story', in M. Jänicke and H. Weidner (eds.), *Successful Environmental Policy: A Critical Evaluation of 24 Cases* (Berlin: Edition Sigma, 1995), pp. 27–42.
92. *Commission* v. *Netherlands*, Case 96/81.
93. *Commission* v. *Netherlands*, C-339/87.
94. This story is told in G. J. I. Schrama and P.-J. Klok, 'The Swift Introduction of "Clean Cars" in the Netherlands, 1986–1992: The Origin and Effect of Incentive Measures', in M. Jänicke and H. Weidner (eds.), *Successful Environmental Policy: A Critical Evaluation of 24 Cases* (Berlin: Edition Sigma, 1995), pp. 203–22.
95. For the story of these changes, see A. Weale, 'Environmental Regulation and Administrative Reform in Britain', in G. Majone, *Regulating Europe* (London and New york: Routledge, 1996), pp. 106–30. Strictly speaking, the story relates only to England and Wales; there have always been quite separate administrative arrangements in Scotland and Northern Ireland.
96. See D. Vogel, *National Styles of Regulation* (Ithaca, NY, and London: Cornell University Press, 1986).
97. Rt Hon. Michael Heseltine, giving testimony to the House of Lords Select Committee on the European Communities (Sub-Committee F), *Implementation and Enforcement of Environmental Legislation Volume II—Evidence* (London: HMSO, 1992), HL Paper 53-II, at 184, 186 and 189.
98. All these examples are documented under the appropriate measures in Haigh, *Manual*.
99. For the story of the failure to implement the provisions of the Control of Pollution Act, see R. Levitt, *Implementing Public Policy* (London: Croom Helm, 1980).

100. Haigh, *Manual*, p. 6.3–3.
101. The best comment on this tactic was provided by the Royal Commission on Environmental Pollution in its 1984 report, which under a full colour picture of a crowded Blackpool beach on a bank holiday printed the caption: 'Blackpool beach. Not an area of traditional bathing as designated by Her Majesty's Government.'
102. A. Jordan, *Post-Decisional Politics in the EC: The Implementation of EC Environmental Policy in the UK*, Ph.D. thesis (University of East Anglia, 1997).
103. *Commission* v. *UK*, C-337/89.
104. *R* v. *Secretary of State for the Environment, ex parte Royal Society for the Protection of Birds*, Case C-44/95, 21 March 1996.
105. S. Bulmer, 'Domestic Politics and European Community Policy Making', *Journal of Common Market Studies*, 21:4 (1983), pp. 349–63 at 353.
106. Laffan, 'Policy Implementation', p. 391.
107. Collins and Earnshaw, 'Implementation and Enforcement', p. 217.
108. Wallace, 'Implementation across National Boundaries', p. 136.
109. N. Haigh with G. Bennett, P. Kromarek, and T. Lavoux, *Comparative Report. Water and Waste in Four Countries: A Study of the Implementation of the EEC Directives in France, Germany, Netherlands and Unitied Kingdom* (London: Graham & Trotman, 1986), pp. 87–8.
110. H. Arp, 'Interest Groups in EC Legislation: The Case of Car Emission Standards', ECPR paper 1991, p. 16.
111. House of Lords Select Committee on the European Communities, *Implementation and Enforcement of Environmental Legislation*, ii, *Evidence* (London: HMSO, 1992) HL Paper 53-II, p. 82.
112. *The European*, 26 Mar. 1992.
113. Collins and Earnshaw, 'Implementation and Enforcement', p. 217.
114. Interview with Krämer, 1993.
115. L. Krämer, *EC Treaty and Environmental Law* (London: Sweet & Maxwell, 1995), p. 131.
116. Macrory, 'Enforcement of Community Environmental Laws', p. 363.
117. The notion of a more flexible policy has been accepted by the environment commissioner, Ritt Bjerregaard. She links it to the notion of a 'green dialogue', i.e. of getting as much information from citizens as it is possible before decisiona are taken (*Eur-op News*, Summer 1995 suppl.).
118. Interview with David Hull.
119. Macrory, 'Enforcement of Community Environmental Laws', pp. 349–54.
120. Collins and Earnshaw, 'Implementation and Enforcement', p. 218.
121. K. Hanf, 'The Impact of European Policies on Domestic Institutions and Politics: Observations on the Implementation of Community Environmental Directives', ECPR paper 1991, p. 9.
122. Haigh *et al.*, *Comparative Report*, pp. 101–2.
123. H. Buller, 'Supra-National Policy Making and Local Implementation Practice: Perspectives of an Anglo–French Comparison of Environmental Management', paper for Anglo-French conference, University of Bristol, December 1991.
124. Siedentopf and Ziller, *Making European Policies Work*, pp. 61–2.
125. Ibid. 58, 179–80.

126. See R. C. Macridis (ed.), *Modern Political Systems* (Hemel Hempstead: Prentice-Hall, 1990, 7th edn), p. 238.
127. Laffan, 'Policy Implementation', pp. 401–4.
128. Ibid. 399–400.
129. Siedentopf and Ziller, *Making European Policies Work*, p. 178.
130. Haigh *et al.*, *Comparative Report*, p. 92.
131. Ibid. 93–4.
132. Ibid. 94; Bronwen Maddox, 'High Cost of a Cleaner Europe', *Financial Times*, 3 Nov. 1992, p. 18.
133. Maddox, 'High Cost of a Cleaner Europe'.
134. Ibid.
135. Ibid.
136. Macrory, 'Enforcement of Community Environmental Laws', p. 365.
137. A. Jordan, 'Implementation Failure or Policy Making? How Do We Theorise the Implementation of European Union Legislation? ECPR paper, 1995, p. 18.
138. Ibid. 20 ff.

9

Convergent and Divergent Trends in European Environmental Policy

The European system of environmental governance is both complex and multi-level. In Part II we have been looking at six member states and observing the complexities at country level. Whatever may be emerging at the European level, the member state level is one that shows tremendous diversity, under the influence of well established historical legacies and highly variable current influences. Transplant a policy-maker from one system to another, and he or she would take months, perhaps even years, to learn the rules of the local environmental politics game. What would the Dutch policy-maker do in Spain or Greece without the familiar target groups? Could a British civil servant persuade the German regulator of the virtues of flexibility and administrative discretion? How would a Spaniard persuade a northern European of the importance of desertification? Who outside of Italy would know how to redefine and reconceptualize the ethos and ideology of an Italian political party to make environmental priorities seem more attractive?

These questions give some illustration of the difficulties of generalizing across our six countries or of identifying practical rules for the improvement of policy and policy-making. And all this is before considering the genuinely contextual and tacit knowledge on which political decisions are really made. 'All politics is local', runs the adage. Who should sit on which committee? Who is sympathetic to environmental concerns in the transport or agriculture departments? Which research institute delivers reports that are accurate and useful? How is the governing coalition likely to change after the election? These are the sorts of questions that national policy-makers have to deal with day after day. It is small wonder that they have little incentive to engage in the difficult and often fruitless task of lesson-drawing from abroad. Still less wonder is it that they scarcely refrain from seeking to impose their own solutions on to the European level.

None of this is to say, however, that there are no similarities and common trends across our systems. Nor is it to say that we cannot construct an account that will make sense of both the differences and such similarities as there are. Before looking at the comparative trends, however, we seek to summarize the experience of each country, even at the risk of riding roughshod over the complexity of domestic politics described in detail above.

Germany

Germany experienced an early upswing in environmental awareness in public opinion and in the party system in the early 1980s. Despite subsequent fluctuation, this concern became consolidated by the mid-1980s in that the green message was spread by an enlarged and influential world of environmental groups; but—even more significantly—it became rooted in the party system at different levels. Undoubtedly, public opinion and behind it cultural predisposition—drawing on both some traditional values (romanticism about the German forest) and new social movement activity—gave special weight to environmentalist pressure from other actors. Although the aftermath of reunification and the need to deal with the consequent economic problems to some extent reduced the political weight given to environmental concerns, environmental protection now figures as a public policy goal on which there is a high degree of consensus. This is not to say that environmental protection is uncontentious, but it is to say that, as a goal, it is not likely to be challenged in the same way as, say, the high costs of the social security system.

The institutionalization of environmental policy concerns in a separate ministry had to wait until 1986. In another sense, however, the German system of environmental protection has been institutionalized for some time. With legislation going back to the nineteenth century, a system of cooperative federalism and a policy style that stresses concertation, institutional *immobilisme* is a feature of German environmental policy, and one of the causes of its difficulties over the implementation of EU directives.

As a large and well established player in the EU game, Germany's switch of policy stance in the early 1980s inevitably had significant effects at the European level. Concerns in the 1980s over air pollution from stationary sources and vehicles were followed by the packaging legislation that also had European ramifications. Apart from these specific measures, however, Germany pressed for the advantages of a certain national style across a whole range of issues, a style in which a conservative (precautionary) attitude to pollution risks was linked with an insistence on high technical standards of pollution control equipment. Moreover, a concern that Germany's high environmental standards should not be diluted by environmentally less advanced member states has combined with an industrial sensitivity to international competition.

Greece

In Greece the pattern is in many respects almost the opposite of the German case. Greece has a relatively new although consolidated democracy, is a much later entrant to the EU, and is still at a stage of economic development that does not easily allow post-materialist values to penetrate society. It follows that the system dynamics do not strongly favour the emergence of environmentalism: political parties have usually been opportunistic in their response to environmental issues, invariably because of crises or public pressure (often in a local setting). Environmental groups there certainly are, but with limited political impact. They are in no position to challenge the extensive influence enjoyed by economic interests within the world of government. And there are no major indications of a break in this rather unmovable situation in the foreseeable future.

Nevertheless, the EU is an important outside influence in Greece, all the more so after Athens (specifically, PASOK) abandoned its populist reservations about European integration in the mid-1980s. If anything, Brussels is viewed as a welcome source of assistance in meeting environmental challenges. But, at the same time, that demonstrates how limited are the internal dynamics in the Greek case.

Spain

As with Greece, the approach in Spain to EU environmental policy has been determined by a still fairly recent transition from authoritarianism, inhibiting the emergence of democratic pressures, as well as even later membership of the EU. However, Spain embraced this ambitiously, with positive feelings about further integration in Europe, combined nevertheless with an abrasive pursuit of economic modernization. In this context, domestic politics have been more dynamic than in Greece, in environmental matters at least. This has been most evident in the ability of the system to adapt, such as in the opening up of government to both economic interests and environmental organizations. However, the parties are not under any serious challenge from green parties, and public opinion is rather less advanced over environmental matters than in the northern countries. Nevertheless, a link with territoriality reveals one way in which opinion can be mobilized.

Italy

Italy is neither very typically 'southern' nor all that 'northern' in its approach to environmental matters. Undoubtedly, this different position is explained to a significant extent by its being one of the founder members of the EU and having a decidedly positive view of European integration—among other reasons, as a compensation for its national system incapacity. In this context, some system dynamics have emerged over environmental matters, although too often with diffuse effects. A green challenge has emerged in the party system, but it is not compelling. More serious has been the challenge from a fairly vibrant environmental movement, while industry has in part begun to adapt more than in other southern countries.

A particular feature of the Italian case is the continuing dissatisfaction with and uncertainty about the political system, which has nevertheless managed to effect a number of institutional reforms. Meanwhile, pressure from the public and the media on the environment is now a constant factor, although it may vary in intensity across the country in line with the traditional north–south dichotomy.

The Netherlands

The Netherlands is one of the countries traditionally pushing for high environmental standards within the EU. The domestic politics underlying this position stems from a meshing of public opinion and a party system, both of which have been strongly influenced by the rise of post-materialist values, as well as a general perception that, as a small country, the Netherlands is vulnerable to cross-boundary pollution against which international action is the only effective safeguard. It is also noteworthy that in the Netherlands environmental protection was seen to be important during the 1980s, even under the strong influence of neo-liberal values in public policy more generally.

The institutionalization of environmental policy in the Netherlands captures the general tendency of environmental policy to move from a preoccupation with human health to a more general concern with ecosystem integrity. The institutionalized interests of agriculture and the traditional system of waterways management have been important constraints on the influence of the environment ministry. More importantly, however, it is impossible to consider the institutionalization of Dutch environmental policy without also considering a policy style in which cooperative working with target groups is seen as vital. In this sense, Dutch environmental policy-making is rooted in a more general Dutch national policy style.

It is this style, rather than any particular policy measure, that the Netherlands has sought to export to the EU, most clearly in the fashioning of the Fifth Framework Programme, with its emphasis on collaborative working by the political authorities and the major social actors. The Netherlands is also important in the EU as a central member of that bloc of countries that are likely to support the strengthening of environmental measures in the Council of Ministers.

United Kingdom

In the UK domestic support for environmental protection shows many signs of being strong in the long term, but it has not displayed the growth and dynamism of its northern neighbours. Although membership of environmental groups is high and UK political parties have adapted their policy stances over time, the dominance of the two-party system, reinforced by the first-past-the-post electoral system, has meant that environmental concerns have had to be placed inevitably in the context of the more general programmatic commitments of the political parties, and these in turn were dominated by the issue of how to reverse the UK's relative economic decline in the postwar period. Moreover, the dominant neo-liberalism of the Thatcher and Major governments never satisfactorily made up its mind about the role that the regulation of economic externalities should play in the system of government.

During this period the UK lost an institutional tradition and failed to find an alternative paradigm. The traditional system of regulation had been based on an informal process of standard-setting administered within a context of discretion and flexibility. Under EU pressure in the 1980s, the system necessarily became more formal, with a greater emphasis on more explicit and uniform standard-setting. Within EU deliberations, the UK continued to insist upon the importance of scientific evidence, cost effectiveness and subsidiarity. At the level of specific measures, it successfully exported its concerns over integrated pollution control and eco-auditing.

COMPARATIVE TRENDS

The above summary of the current state of environmental politics and policy in individual countries inevitably draws attention to their specific and distinct experiences. In looking at comparative trends, however, we shall begin with the common elements. In all six countries, environmental issues achieved greater salience in the period since the mid-1980s than they had during the decade between 1975 and 1985. In terms of general public perceptions this trend is evident in the data from public attitude surveys, where there was a general upward trend in the priority accorded to the protection of the environment. From the other side of the political market-place, similar trends are evident in the party manifestoes. To be sure, there are differences as well as similarities among the countries, with Germany and the Netherlands registering stronger shifts than elsewhere as well as registering such shifts earlier and more quickly. But, as a general trend, it is clear that by the end of the 1990s environmental issues were showing a greater prominence on the political agendas of all these countries than they had at the beginning of the 1980s. Even modulations of opinion show not dissimilar trends over time, with the high point of the late 1980s and early 1990s giving way to the drop in interest during the mid-1990s. These common patterns across such diverse countries suggest a strong common cause, most likely the fluctuations of the business cycle.

Before the 1980s, the traditional policy paradigm stressed both the potential for conflict between economic growth and environmental protection and the extent to which pollution control and environmental regulation was a technical matter of primary concern to experts and specialists. Internationally dispersed currents of thinking associated with ecological modernization and sustainable development have called into question these central assumptions, and none of our sample countries has been entirely immune from their influence.

In some cases the attempted reconceptualization of the relationship between the economy and the environment has gone further. The idea of sustainable development, for example, has been particularly influential in at least the way that major policy strategy documents have been formulated, for example *This Common Inheritance* in the UK and the National Environmental Policy Plan in the

Netherlands. Interestingly, the specific idea of sustainable development seems to have come relatively late to Germany, whereas Germany can be seen as a pioneer in the ideology of ecological modernization. Even in the southern countries, where all too often it seems that the references to sustainable development more usually take the form of mouthing pieties than guiding action, it would not be possible for a policy-maker entirely to ignore the challenge that environmental questions pose. What we *can* say is that in all six countries previous policy paradigms have not remained intact. In each case there is, at the least, a willingness to acknowledge that the relationship between the economy and the environment is a complex one rather than a simple binary opposition between the two. Moreover, the greater political salience of environmental protection in the politics of mass publics means that the former assumption that environmental regulation is predominantly a technical matter for specialists no longer holds.

The organizational changes in government structures that we have documented also revealed some common elements. Here again, there were significant differences in structure, but the common trend was towards a more integrated environment ministry holding stronger powers than in the early 1980s, though trends in Spain are some exception to this generalization. Although difficult to measure in accurate cross-national terms, it also is plausible to say that one of the ways in which the environment ministry has become stronger is through a tendency for its portfolio to be held by more senior politicians than previously—or, at least, by politicians whose voices are likely to carry more weight in cabinet discussions. Moreover, there has grown up a pattern of increasing advisory bodies around these central ministries, so that the institutional space has become more crowded.

We might even see a coming together in environmental policy with the convergence of non-decisions, or at least the common problems that all the political systems have found it difficult adequately to confront. Pollution from farming is common across all six states, as is consumption-induced pollution. The latter in particular has been a problem; all six countries have had to confront the problems of how to deal with consumption-induced pollution—and with the associated difficulties of how to change lifestyles—arising from traffic, tourism, and waste. This is true whether we speak of the *nefos* in Athens, high levels of tropospheric ozone in Germany, the Netherlands, and the UK, or the problems of water use in Spain, Italy, and Greece. Whereas traditional production-related pollution was primarily a matter of regulation, consumption-induced pollution involves more complex problems of combining moral, economic, and legal incentives to change the everyday behaviour of large numbers of people, in situations in which there is seldom a simple 'technical fix'. However large the variation among the countries in their general willingness to promote environmental goals, they all have yet to succeed in finding the right mix of instruments and policies to cope with these complex problems.

These similarities, of course, are buried in a mass of differences, as was brought out in our country profiles in the previous section of this chapter. The scope and range of legislation, and more particularly the depth of policy thinking, is more developed in the Netherlands and Germany than elsewhere, and these two countries have been keen to pursue higher emission standards both domestically and in Europe. A similar story can be told about institutionalization, in particular if we look at the range of depth of specialist support that is available in the northern three countries by comparison with the southern three, especially Spain and Greece. The party systems in the Netherlands and Germany have given greater scope to environmental concerns than those in the other four, and key interests in both have to pay much more attention to the pollution implications of their activities. Greece and Spain have to find ways of balancing the demands of economic growth and environmental protection in circumstances that are more challenging than in the other countries. Moreover, the extent to which national differences among member states are smoothed out by the effect of EU measures is limited, both by the legal form that directives take through reliance on the legal and administrative procedures of the different countries, and by the shortcomings of the persistent implementation deficit, present to some degree or another in all member states.

Thus, we have a picture that involves a complex combination of similarities and differences. How then can we account for this picture?

In the Introduction to Part II we set out a categorization of the variables affecting the development of national policies from which we were able to extract a simple model of convergence. According to this model, converging policy trends were to be accounted for by a mixture of top-down international pressures and bottom-up society-related pressures combined with autonomous state-related developments working on the issues to which environmental concerns gave rise. Thus, the pressures of implementation from the EU and the diffuse climate of international opinion formed the basis for the top-down pressures, whereas increasing economic growth and the associated development of post-materialism, along with the pressures coming from internationally linked non-governmental organizations in civil society, formed the basis for the bottom-up pressures. Issue characteristics, combined with the place of policy champions in the political sphere, then formed the basis for the state-related pressures for convergence in at least certain aspects of national policy.

As we noted in presenting the model, the prediction of convergence in policy patterns is not a prediction of identity in policy strategies and principles. The model of policy convergence does not apply to environmental policy-making in an unchanging way. For example, it may be possible to distinguish the stages of the policy process in terms of their susceptibility to influence from national styles or issue characteristics. Similarly, it is quite possible to hold that historically national styles have been important but that, under the pressure of common problems and increasing influences from international environmental policy regimes such as the EU, policy convergence is taking place within sectors. How does this relate to the complex picture of similarities and differences that we have observed?

Society-Related Effects

In terms of society-related factors and, in particular, the level of economic development, it is not surprising that Germany should have been keen to push for high environmental standards internationally in those spheres in which its world-class engineering industry could gain a competitive advantage. Conversely, it is not surprising that the poorer countries of Spain and Greece have been resistant to calls for higher environmental standards when these have been perceived to pose barriers to economic development. For this reason, the receptiveness of the policy elites of different countries to the principles of ecological modernization has an obvious material basis. For a portion of German industry it has been economically advantageous to press for higher environmental standards, because this created a market for high-quality German engineering. Moreover, to the extent that environmental regulations on products form a barrier to trade, one would expect the highly regulated German economy to favour stringent regulations on packaging to protect its own domestic industry.

However, the structural features of the economy by themselves go only part of the way to explaining the differences. There is no one-to-one association between innovation in environmental policy and economic development, as is illustrated by the issue of instrument use. As we saw in connection with the selection of policy instruments, there remain intriguing and important differences between the countries.

The explanation for these persisting differences is to be found in the continuing influence of national regulatory styles, that is the modification of society-related effects by state-related effects. Here the German example is most striking. Despite the willingness of Germany to set higher environmental standards, the form in which policies have been developed has borrowed much from the trade regulations that go back to nineteenth-century Prussia, with a strong legalistic bias and a commitment to detailed regulation. Moreover, a strong culture which stresses the importance of economic calculability in the German business community means that uniform emission limits legally encoded have an important place. Contemporary culture thus reinforces historic legacy.

The contrasting case, in terms of policy style, is the UK, where the historical legacy is one of considerable administrative discretion adapted to the economic and natural environments within which the regulation of a specific site is occurring. Many of the changes that have been induced in this traditional policy style in recent years have come from the EU. The domestic political structures in many cases have reinforced the inherited approach.

Even where there is not a strong legacy of environmental protection institutions and practice on which to draw, as in the case of Spain, we can still see that national policy-making structures—in the case of Spain the pressures for decentralization—play an important role.

Moreover, we cannot see the differences in environmental commitment reflecting levels of economic development in a simple way because there is much greater discontinuity in environmental policy than the linear progression of economic growth would allow for. By and large European economies grow year by year; but environmental policy changes can be rapid. Here, again, Germany provides an interesting example. The switch on policy priorities by the German government in 1982 reflected not a particular level of economic development, but the rise of the Greens to a pivotal position in the party system. Hence we cannot identify the direct influence of society-related effects on policy strategies and stances, but rather see them as mediated in important ways through political institutions and practices.

Although, in the light of new paradigms, a serious case can be made for the claim that sustainable economic growth can occur only within the limits of the carrying capacity of the environment, there is no doubt that, in the short term, certain groups or collections of interests will suffer disadvantages from the pursuit of particular environmental measures. This was true of electricity supply companies in the UK and Spain in relation to the large combustion plant directive, of that part of the car industry responsible for small vehicles in the UK, Spain, and Italy (as well as France) in relation to proposed controls on vehicle emissions, and of the wide variety of energy-intensive industries in relation to proposals for a carbon-energy tax.

As the example of the opposition to the carbon-energy tax shows, certain types of group turn out to be important in all countries, suggesting that the source of their power is economic rather than institutional, even though they have to find a way of translating their economic assets into political influence. Confirmation of the importance of the place of potential oppositional groups comes from the most striking exception: in Greece, where there is no car industry, the Greek government was able to take a much firmer line on emission limit controls than Spain, Italy or the UK.

In drawing attention to the importance of certain groups, we are not saying that there are certain sorts of interests, for example industry, that always play the same oppositional role wherever they are located. Indeed, we note below that one of the significant points of non-convergence among our six countries is the attitude of business groups to environmental protection. Nevertheless, where there are significant adverse economic implications attached to environmental measures, we should expect those groups on whom the costs of the measures are concentrated to be most active in opposition, whatever country they are in.

A particularly important group in this respect is farmers, especially those engaged in a relatively intensive form of agriculture. Their political influence derives in part from their economic role pure and simple (as well as their ability to engage in direct action in certain countries), and in part from the way in which the representation of their interests in public policy formulation has been institutionalized through agriculture ministries. In all six of our countries, the agriculture ministry plays a vital role in supporting and buttressing the agricultural interest. Moreover, the representation of agricultural interests and opinions is typically cemented through links with particular political parties; for example, in the period since 1917 it is only recently that the agriculture minister in the Netherlands has not come from the Christian faction of the governing coalition.

Although the position of potential oppositional groups within the policy system was a common feature across all six countries, the composition and degree of opposition varies, and this is an important differentiating feature. In the case of business, for example, much depends upon the particular composition of the business community. Thus, in economies where a significant part of business is made up by pollution control industries, opposition to stringent environmental controls can be expected to be lower from business. There may also be more diffuse sources of variation coming from differences of culture and belief system. Thus, it is difficult to believe that the call for a more environmentally sensitive economy, launched by the Association of Young Entrepreneurs in Germany, did not reflect the influence of more general social attitudes and pressures.

State-Related Effects

This brings us to the distinctively state-related elements in our categorization. In our initial discussion of possible sources for convergence, we stressed the importance of issue characteristics as possible sources for convergence, and the persistence of non-decisions in the fields of agricultural pollution and traffic pollution might suggest that issue characteristics are important. Any policy paradigm would come under pressure from the effects that an observer would notice by standing on any busy street corner at rush hour. Moreover, for all our states, coastal pollution also causes serious problems.

Yet, despite these pressures for convergence from the issue characteristics, there are also different ways in which issues of sustainable development are constructed within different policy systems. For rural communities in Greece, the problems of traffic congestion are some way off as they struggle to have the road to their village improved to a higher standard. The international language of sustainable development needs to be mapped on to the specifics of each country, and in this process of mapping differences inevitably emerge.

Within this process of political construction, there is a place for politicians to influence the interpretation of ideas and priorities. One possibility that we canvassed was that the role of politicians is important not just as a symbol of or evidence for greater salience, but also for the role that as individuals they play in championing environmental policy developments. In particular, when an able and committed politician enjoys a long term of office, his or her role in the policy process can be very important, a phenomenon we observe within these different countries.

We also see here a connection to the international dimensions of change. Within the EU, committed politicians can pursue their goals not only domestically but also at the European level. The committed have included Italian socialists like Ruffolo as well as Christian Democrats or Conservatives like Töpfer or Patten and liberals like Winsemius or Nijpels. Other members of the same party or ideological grouping may have occupied the post of environment minister without bringing the same sense of policy direction. Thus, the obvious way to account for this highly individualized feature of the role of politicians is by noting that political attitudes on the environment tend to cut across existing political and ideological tendencies.

International Effects

We originally conjectured that the least ambiguous effects would come from international influences, including both the formal pressures for implementation and the more diffuse pressures coming from the international climate of opinion.

Implementation rates vary, as we have seen in our discussion of the problem. However, it is equally clear that there is no country that has been without problems of implementation. The UK provides an interesting example at this point. Although its rhetoric is that it is an assiduous implementer of EU policy once it has been agreed, even if it contested the formulation of the policy in the first place, it is striking that it has been involved in a number of serious disputes over implementation, ranging from the bathing waters and environmental impact assessment directives to issues where the actual implementation of the policy did not accord with what was envisaged by the negotiating parties at the time, as with the large combustion plant directive. We might think from the variance that length of EU membership was an important factor, but though Germany and the Netherlands, long-standing members, have relatively good records of implementation, the same cannot be said for Italy, an equally long-standing member.

In the cases of both Germany and the UK, difficulties of implementation are in part related to state-related factors such as administrative traditions or existing policy paradigms. This suggests that there is no linear pattern of policy development reinforced by international pressures. Instead, it may well be a disadvantage, given the international pressures, for a country to have been early in the development of an environmental policy strategy when that strategy is out of accord with prevalent international currents of opinion.

It is none the less revealing that the institutionalization of international environmental policy within the EU has created a form of interactive dynamics, involving national and European levels. Given the importance of decisions taken within the Council of Ministers, the dual position of environment ministers, both as members of their own government and as participants in the Environment Council, has also provided an opportunity for policy championing by committed southern politicians. The pressure coming from the EU for higher environmental standards has provided a bargaining counter for disputes within their own political systems. A good example is provided by the way in which, in the 1980s, Tritsis in Greece was able to use EU environmental policy as an argument for securing greater prominence for environmental measures by the Greek government. Similarly, Ruffolo was able to draw upon the international climate of opinion in his campaign to have the environment taken more seriously in Italian politics.

If we consider these various elements of convergence together, we can see that international influences play a key role, but they are by no means the only sort of element at work. The international influences are diffused through formal processes of implementation, but they also arise from less formal means of diffusion such as climates of opinion among internationally mobile policy elites. These influences combine with domestic sources of change that incline policy systems towards convergence. The increase in pollution from consumption relative to production, for example, itself a product of rising affluence, is something that is observable in all six countries. Moreover, certain common features of social and political structure, such as the position of farmers in the economy and the political system, will reproduce a common pattern of political contestation.

On the other hand, the persisting variations from country to country, even allowing for differences in level of economic development, are considerable. Such differences among the six countries include: variation in the willingness to pursue stringent standards of environmental protection; variations in the willingness to experiment with new policy instruments; differences in the support from public opinion for environmental protection; and differences in the attitudes of key groups. These differences in turn lead to a differential ambition to take a lead role in international efforts to control pollution. Thus, just as international measures, particularly those from the EU, could lead to pressure for changes in domestic policy arrangements and strategies, so domestic sources of policy can lead to some countries seeking to use international institutions to achieve their own goals. Just as society-related influences are mediated through political relationships, so international influences have to be mediated through individual state and political structures. Multi-level governance is not uniform multi-level governance. Europe will still enjoy, or suffer, its diversity, even in its increasing unity.

Part III

Case Studies in the Policy Process

Introduction to Part III

So far we have been concerned with the processes that shape policy within the European system of environmental governance. In Part I we traced the emergence of EU environmental policy and institutions and saw how the original pressures of spillover from the creation of the single market, combined with the constitutional bargain struck in the Single European Act, created an emergent set of institutions, principles, and practices that constitute the European system of environmental governance. However, it was clear that, for a number of reasons, these developments could not be considered separately from environmental policy dynamics in the member states. Those states themselves occupy a privileged place within the European system of environmental governance through their role in the Council of Ministers. Their priorities at the European level reflect their domestic politics and they have a crucial role with respect to the implementation of policies. Moreover, the emerging system of EU environmental governance is incomplete, so that many important matters are left to member states to pursue. For these reasons, we examined the comparative politics of environmental policy in six European states in Part II.

However, although we cannot avoid looking at the processes on these two different levels, there is a problem with the approach we have adopted so far. To present the European and nation state levels in terms of their distinctive characteristics risks disconnecting what should really be considered together. After all, it is the content and effects of policies that we are interested in, and these emerge and are fashioned by processes that operate simultaneously at all levels. In this sense European environmental governance is a *system*, perhaps not an integrated one, but nevertheless one in which the components are related to one another. Our aim in Part III therefore is to show how the different elements of the system are related to one another by examining a number of EU directives. Our approach here is chiefly illustrative. We are not so much seeking to test hypotheses about the specific workings of the system of governance as to exhibit its workings in some of their complexity.

In pursuing this goal of illustration, we look at a range of directives across the three receiving media of water, air, and soil. To attempt to illustrate the European system of environmental governance through directives, and in particular through directives that were politically salient and controversial, to some extent risks observation bias. It could be argued that we are mistaking the distinctive for the typical.

Many environmental directives are uncontroversial. They involve arrangements for the sharing of information, the specification of maximum allowable concentrations or exposures of particular substances according to technically agreed criteria, or the incremental development of standards with which everyone agrees. No one is likely to find much to dispute in such measures. We may have the wrong focus if we do not see the evolution of the system of European environmental governance through the steady accretion of non-controversial technical matters. The tip of the iceberg does not reveal the whole.

Although observation bias is a problem, this does not mean that we can avoid looking at issues where controversies have taken place. Precisely because they are distinctive, the controversial issues reveal features of the EU's system of governance that could not be seen in any other way. Moreover, as we seek to show, some important changes in rule-making and practice have occurred through the processes by which controversial decisions were taken. In this sense, the issues that we examine are often landmarks in the development of the EU's system of environmental governance and deserve to be noted as such.

In the examples we discuss in this section, we look at articulated expressions of policy preference on the part of key actors, but we do not treat them as being based exclusively on interests. They may stem from scientific research, principled concerns about the state of the environment, the mobilization of domestic and international social movements, or the perception of collective risks. Correspondingly, non-decisions—which imply the failure to deal with certain problems—can have a variety of roots. Our discussion in this Part leads on to an analysis in Part IV according to which the main reason for non-decisions in European environmental policy is the form and pattern of the policy-making process itself.

We take the development of directives in the field of water policy first, because water pollution control was the first area in which EU policy began to be formed. Because of these early developments, water pollution control is one area where we might expect there to be a significant influence on the development of national systems. Consequently, as well as looking at the dynamics of EU water pollution directives in their own right, we also pose the question of what influence the EU's policy regime has had upon the practices and institutions of the member states.

We then look at the two major air pollution directives in the 1980s, one concerned with the control of pollutants from large, stationary sources and the other concerned with pollution from vehicles. In both cases we shall see that the original concerns have been taken up and transformed in the EU system of multi-level governance. In the case of vehicles there is a clear connection to single market concerns, and the EU's involvement in pollution control in this sector goes back a long way. Stationary sources present a different set of issues, and the EU's involvement represented both a clear case of political contestation between member states and an attempt to fashion policy on acidification at a time when the relevant scientific analysis was still in its early stages of development. Interestingly, however, we find in both cases that policy in the 1990s has moved from a concern with end-of-pipe solutions to an attempt to set standards in the light of ecological evidence. How far this process of policy learning has taken place inside the EU is an important part of our analysis.

Finally, we look at packaging and packaging waste. From many points of view, policy-making here shows similar features to those we find in other areas. To what extent were the political dynamics at work typical of the richer and more complex policy processes of the 1990s? To be sure, there was a much wider range of interests involved in policy-making, and the arguments among policy analysts were also complex. However, much of the original impetus for the policy came from a combination of single market concerns and the unilateral action of one member state, and the bargaining in the Council of Ministers resembled a pattern that we find in the debates in the 1980s about air pollution.

As we have already noted, looking at a relatively narrow range of policy decisions will not enable us to be decisive in choosing among rival hypotheses about EU decision-making. They are suggestive, however. We also hope that they reveal the effect of some of the general practices, processes, patterns, and trends that we have looked at in Parts I and II.

10

Water Quality and European Environmental Governance

In this chapter we examine a core subset of EU water directives as a way of illustrating the operation of the EU's system of environmental governance in respect of water policy. We first describe the EU's approach to water pollution policy, and in particular the significance of a particular set of directives, including the drinking water directive (80/778) and the bathing water directive (76/160). We then turn to the process leading up to the directive on urban waste water (91/217). Finally, we seek to evaluate how far national policies and approaches have been changed, if at all, by EU developments in clean water policy. Our conclusion is that, while EU water directives had an undoubted impact on national policy systems, there is little clear evidence of an outright Europeanization of policy. Instead, national norms and peculiarities prove resilient, though they are often suffused by EU approaches. Conversely, there is scope for EU policy initiatives to originate within national regimes.

THE EARLY WATER DIRECTIVES

Water pollution was one of the first concerns of the nascent EU environmental policy, with important legislative developments taking place between 1975 and 1980. In relation to drinking water, there are a number of directives that address quality standards. Directive 75/440/EEC laid down requirements to ensure that surface freshwater for use as drinking water meets certain standards and is treated adequately before being introduced to the public supply. Directive 80/778/EEC laid down standards for the quality of water intended for human consumption, both directly and after processing. It has the dual purpose of promoting the free circulation of goods in the European Union and of protecting human health and the environment. Directive 80/68 provides protection of the groundwater from pollution caused by dangerous substances. Member states must monitor compliance with the conditions of authorization and the effects of discharges on groundwater, keep an inventory of authorizations, and supply the European Commission with any relevant information at its request.

The main legislation concerning the quality of bathing water is directive 76/160/EEC, which now applies to more than 10,000 bathing areas in the EU. The directive lays down nineteen physical, chemical, and microbiological parameters for the quality of bathing water (fresh or seawater) and establishes a system of monitoring bathing water quality by the member states.

In addition to the bathing water and drinking water directives, the directive on the discharge of dangerous substances into water (76/464) was passed as part of the early phase of legislation. As Haigh has pointed out, the directives adopt different standards for the control of pollution.[1] The bathing water directive is a water quality standard, setting maximum concentrations for nineteen physical, chemical, and microbiological parameters. The drinking water directive is based on the approach of an exposure standard, again setting parameter values (including maximum allowable concentrations and minimum required concentrations) for certain substances. The directive on the discharge of dangerous substances into water, by contrast, allows countries to adopt one of two approaches: either standards can be set by reference to emission values, or they can be set by reference to water quality. The choice under this directive arises from the desire of the UK, at the time at which it was drafted, to preserve its own traditional approach to the control of water pollution.

Many of the implementation battles that the Commission would later wage with various member states in the late 1980s and early 1990s would be largely over the failure to implement this early corpus of 1970s law. Directive 80/68 has been the subject of numerous violations, for instance by Belgium, the Netherlands, Italy, and Germany.[2] The transposition of the bathing water directive took between two and eight years, and Belgium, the Netherlands, Italy, and the UK have all been condemned by the Court of Justice for failing to comply with it. In view of this, it is striking that there is little evidence on how the standards that the bathing water directive contains were formulated. It is also notable for example that the regulatory committee established by the directive had not met by the time of a House of Commons inquiry into bathing water policy in 1989/90, so that some of the outstanding technical questions about the standards had not been addressed.[3]

Similarly, the approach adopted in the dangerous substances directive has given rise to a number of problems. Even today, this early legislative corpus of the 1970s has proven to be highly controversial, and EU clean water policy is still dominated by complex debates over the essence of the regulatory approach that was taken in these original laws. For example, under the dangerous substances directive a number of daughter directives were enacted which took a substance reduction focus, setting strict limit values. Lists of dangerous chemicals were to be drawn up according to priority: 'black' list chemicals were the most damaging (typically, heavy metal and organochloride chemicals), while a 'grey' list was to cover those substances whose health effects were less proven. In practice however it can be hard to draw such hard and fast distinctions among chemicals, and some member states, especially the UK, protested that the directive was not based on a serious scientific evaluation of risk.

Few member states have successfully implemented all the demands made by the dangerous substances directive, in particular the demand under Article 7, which required member states to set up 'programmes for reducing water pollution by certain substances'.[4] In other words, the directive required member states to go further than just implementing control and stabilization through emission limits, relying on best available technology notices: they should actively ameliorate any waters to which damage had been done by dangerous substances. Even Germany, which had been an original supporter of the directive, was by 1996 facing court action from the Commission, on the grounds that its authorization system in particular did not cover diffuse sources of dangerous substances in water (such as from agriculture). As a result, it is perhaps no surprise that, in a recent work on deregulation in EU environmental policy, Grant suggests that European industry sources consistently identify this directive as one of the more demanding and unpopular ones with which they have to work.[5]

The drinking water standards were set by reference to World Health Organization promulgated standards, though even here there was controversy, as the UK wanted a more lenient standard for lead than was proposed as a maximum allowable concentration, since the proposed value (50 μg/l) was half the WHO-recommended value.[6] The position on pesticides in water is another good illustration of how politically charged and complex implementation was to prove. The British and Italian governments felt that the stringent Maximum Allowable Concentrations for pesticides were too strict and in effect were a surrogate zero. Consequently, their policy was in effect to disregard the limits.

The standards set in the drinking water directive can be seen as quite strict applications of the precautionary principle. This directive was not based on a toxicological scientific basis, but rather on whether one could measure and detect pesticides in water. Therefore the position of EU law at the time was to place a general prohibition on levels of pesticides wherever they could be detected. This did not coincide with WHO guidelines, which set various levels above 0.1 μg/1, for example 1.7 μg/1 for atrazine, a pesticide that was causing some severe pollution incidents in Italy by the mid-1980s. As a result, the Italian government attempted to pass decrees based on WHO standards rather than EU ones, arguing that these were more realistic. Equally, in 1986 the UK's DoE ordered water authorities to ignore the EU standards set out in 1980; these were suggested to be 'unworkable', and the DoE instead issued guidelines based on WHO and domestic toxicological data. The German and Dutch, however, appeared to endorse the original zealous approach, on the grounds that as a matter of principle drinking water should never have pesticide residues, and that water should be as close to its natural state as possible.[7] More recently, the focus has switched to product authorization legislation in an attempt to eliminate dangerous pesticides at source before they reach the market. In this regard, such legislation in 1991 and 1994 has attracted widespread controversy and hostility from the European Parliament and environmentalists. Indeed, in 1994 the European Parliament successfully took legal action against Commission regulations under these pesticide product directives, on the grounds that the methodology for approval could undermine the strict standard set in 1980, which is basically a prohibition on detectable residues.[8]

With the general move away from command and control approaches, and under the political pressure arising from the 'no' vote in the first Danish referendum on Maastricht, there was pressure on the Commission to innovate. This originally expressed itself through the language of subsidiarity. The European Councils of Edinburgh in 1992 and Brussels in 1993 requested that the Commission specifically review the existing EU water legislation in the light of the principle of subsidiarity and scientific and technical progress. The British government, in particular, argued for an outright repatriation of the clean beaches policy back to the national authorities. But the review did not yield a repatriation of clean water policy. Instead, the exercise has been one of redrafting and simplification. The main product of such a review process has been a draft framework directive on water policy in 1997.[9]

This draft directive has emerged as the single most vital document guiding future policy on water for the early years of the twenty-first century. It aims to review a variety of 1970s legislation, repealing and replacing in one swift move the old dangerous substances directive, the surface water directive, the fish water directive, and the information exchange decision, all within a single framework directive originally intended to come into force in 1999.[10] The regulatory direction that this new approach appears to be taking is towards an exploration of 'soft law' instruments, involving flexibility in the use of either ambient quality or emissions-based standards, with an added re-emphasis on river basin management, as the key to providing a more integrated legislative programme for clean water.

At first glance, then, it would appear that the old battle between German- and Dutch-style emission standards, relying on BAT notes, and British background water quality standard-setting appears to be resolved, suggesting an end to the era of political confrontation over water directives that marred the early 1980s. On closer examination, however, it is largely a continuation of the mutual recognition tactic; indeed, environmental quality standards still attract the ire of the European Parliament's environmental committee, and, even on specific details, the Dutch in Council continue to express reservations. Hence clean water policy still has a capacity to provoke a charged political debate at Brussels level.

There does however appear to be more agreement on a regulatory environment that is softer and is based on a more sophisticated line of thought than the approach of the 1970s. As a result, a number of distinctive plans to review legislation have now been shelved and encompassed within the framework directive, notably the reviews of the ecological quality of water directive, the groundwater directive, and the drinking water directive. These will not now be rewritten as separate laws, but will find their way into the new framework directive.

Why should the attempt to roll back EU water policy have proved so fruitless? Jordan has offered the most plausible answer to this question.[11] The difficulties of overturning the *acquis* in this particular area can be found in the institutional logic of the EU's system of environmental governance. Having initially passed much water legislation almost in a fit of absent-mindedness, expectations of key actors began to converge around the standards that had been set. Even though some of these standards are literally unattainable (for example, droppings from birds make the salmonella targets unattainable for the bathing water directive[12]), the fact that they existed as agreed international standards gave them a life of their own. In addition, in the case of bathing waters, economic interests, for example construction companies, could see advantages in the standards.

Moreover, the fact that there is EU legislation setting out limits for certain dangerous substances is of considerable political salience in the majority of member states, especially when formerly closed policy communities have become more open to public scrutiny. The high profile of the issue in political and public life can be attributed partly to the regular publication of monitoring results, particularly of bathing waters, which provide newsworthy material. Environmental groups also try to keep the issue of pure water on the public and political agenda. In addition, the fact that several member states have been brought before the European Court of Justice for non-compliance with EU water directives has substantiated the claims by environmentalists that national, regional, or local administrations were not complying with EU standards. Therefore EU clean water policy has been importantly 'political' as opposed to just being merely 'technical', a fate that has befallen many other environmental laws. This politicization of water policy is evidenced by the fact that the Commission at one stage received some 12,000 letters from Germany alone concerning the revision of the drinking water directive.[13] Evidently, the unattainable ambition of eliminating risk has considerable political power.

THE URBAN WASTE WATER TREATMENT DIRECTIVE

The initial approach to the control of water pollution, discussed above, was based on the principles of setting standards according to end-use. This approach was also incorporated in a number of more minor water policy areas in the late 1970s. For example, water for freshwater fish was covered by directive 78/659, and water for shellfish by directive 79/923. Subsequently, with the EU Fourth and Fifth Action Programmes, the emphasis shifted slowly to a source-based approach as opposed to the final-use approach. This demanded that pollution should be traced to its source and dealt with there, a shift that can be illustrated with regard to the urban waste water directive.[14]

The urban waste water directive (91/217) marks a shift towards a more demanding preventive approach in tackling water quality at source. It provides for the treatment of urban waste water and waste water from certain industrial sectors, both of which are responsible for large quantities of pollution in all surface waters. The directive reflects the increasingly detailed nature of European environmental legislation, and it entails significant and costly improvements for the treatment of waste waters in many of the member states. Despite a trend towards greater investment in such infrastructure, there is still wide variation in their provisions for sewage treatment.[15]

The basic content of the directive is to require secondary treatment for sewage (that is, treatment to reduce the oxygen demand of the effluent through biological filtration or aeration) for inland waters for populations of over 10,000 persons or their equivalent in waste load terms, and primary treatment (which removes solids) for populations of over 2,000 persons. For coastal waters it generally demands primary treatment only for populations of between 10,000 and 15,000, and for coastal communities below 10,000 persons a regime is put in place by which member states can determine the adequacy of their own treatment practices provided that water quality standards are met.[16] This regime allows for the possibility that in less sensitive areas long sea outfalls are an acceptable technology under the directive, a concern that was particularly important to the UK government in the negotiations over the directive, and a matter that seems to have been settled at a meeting of experts in April 1989.[17]

The origins of the directive are interesting. The forces behind it were threefold. Firstly, it was affected by the regime for regulating pollution in the North Sea under the Oslo and Paris conventions. Secondly, there was a process of reflection and policy learning within the Commission and the Council, suggesting a move away from the 'end-use' legislative approach of the 1970s and towards the target group/problem theme approach of the 1980s. Targeting municipal waste water works was seen as start in this problem-solving approach, especially as progress to reach the standard already agreed in the water directives of the 1970s and early 1980s was being undermined by poor sewage effluent control in many states—a feature largely unforeseen in the 1970s. Thirdly, what was politically crucial in securing support for the urban waste water directive was the parallel decision, taken in 1987, to double the structural funds available for cohesion in the southern states and Ireland.

The starting point for the first of these influences was the 1987 meeting of member states under the Oslo and Paris conventions, which, at a high point in the issues attention cycle, and with a little help from the Prince of Wales speaking out in favour of the principle of precaution, agreed on significant cuts in polluting inputs into the North Sea. The subsequent meeting in March 1990 saw the UK government, in a surprise move (with Chris Patten as secretary of state), agree to the phasing out of sewage sludge dumping at sea by 1998.[18] The ending of the UK's opposition to such a phasing out inevitably implied that major investments would be needed in the UK whatever was decided in the EU. Moreover, it seems that the forces pushing for an improvement in waste water quality were not met by vigorous opposition. The European water industries association, EUREAU, was dominated by those concerned with the supply of water, rather than with waste water treatment. Indeed, the passing of the directive prompted the creation of an industrial association, the European Waste Waters Group, which orginally attracted members from France, Spain, Portugal, and the UK but then came to embrace all member states, and is concerned to highlight the implications for pollution control of dealing with the sludge that is inevitably created.[19]

Secondly, at Frankfurt in June 1988 a meeting of the EU ministers responsible for water policy was set in train with the then commissioner, Clinton-Davis, chairing what was to turn out to be an example of a reflective moment in the EU's water policy process. At this meeting widespread dissatisfaction was expressed with the 'end-use' approach of the 1970s. Equally, there was little enthusiasm for the whole dangerous substances approach, with some states favouring an emission-based removal at source approach, and others a more discretionary approach which grouped families of pesticides and dangerous chemicals together for action. It is interesting that, although by then waste water had reached the agenda, it was not greeted with widespread acceptance. Indeed, the Frankfurt meeting of 1988 ended on a tame note, suggesting only that agreement *in principle* could be reached that waste treatment was something that should be harmonized at Community level.

What moved the issue then to its being accepted by all as a legislative proposal? It is worth noting in this regard that the directive proceeded to develop very quickly, being first proposed in an October 1989 draft, and accepted, without major amendment by the Council and Parliament, in March 1991.[20] The basic aim of the directive was that all municipalities across the EU should have secondary sewage treatment facilities by 2005, and tertiary treatment, where waters were damaged or 'sensitive', by 1998.

Most states were remarkably agreeable to such a demanding schedule, although Germany tried to make secondary treatment of all sewage a basic norm and failed, and various UK positions could be construed as negative. Yet overall, the urban waste water directive is notable for a high degree of consensus, in contrast to the charged politics concerning dangerous substances in the early 1980s. The central reason why such a coalition prevailed must be the existence of associated structural funds for investment in sewage plant and infrastructure. More generally, one might add that couching the issue as one of infrastructure modernization and not merely risk regulation helped to make the policy more attractive.

This suggests the third reason for agreement: that the passing of the directive could be linked with a politics of distribution, a politics that lies at the heart of the EU process in policies such as the CAP. The funds available for water infrastructure were considerable during the 1989–92 period, and indeed remain so— Greece for example received about 35 million ECU for various water and sewage infrastructure projects in 1998.[21] By September 1989 both Portugal and Spain were making joint bids to Brussels for massive subsidies (*c.* 1,300 million ECU) for sewage plant construction, tailored to maximize the level of EU support.[22] By November 1989 the Council had also approved a dedicated regional and coastal environmental fund, ENVIREG, with a budget of 500 million ECU for the period 1990–3 and a specific focus on sewage infrastructure.[23] In particular, its focus on coastal Mediterranean regions meant that southern states had a funding source by which to meet the terms of the bathing water directive as well, albeit much later than the supposed 1985 deadline. Equally, they also had in this an important incentive to keep any bathing waters directive 'alive' at the European level, in order precisely to justify such transfers. Additionally, the political future of such funds looked solid when newly unified and politically pivotal Germany began in 1991 to receive financial support from the structural funds which they could use to partially fund clean water measures in the new *Länder*.[24]

We can suggest therefore that, while for the leader northern states the issue was one of essentially technical harmonization, for the southern states and, interestingly, some northern states such as Ireland and Belgium (which leaves 70 per cent of its urban waste water untreated) the issue was one of modernization and investment. The expectation was that cohesion funding and transfers would be made available for a wave of sewage plant building and associated developments. We have in mind a miniature version of the 'log-roll' that we earlier argued underlay the co-evolution of the Single European Act and the growth of environmental competences, so that the policy had much to commend it to various national interests. Yet, as with many European initiatives, national interests do not simply dominate the content of policy. Where the nation states proved decisive in Council was in slowing down the time scale envisaged for investment, originally six to seven years. The split in Council showed the leader states lined up against the rest: the Netherlands, Germany, and Denmark argued for a short time-period of implementation, and the rest were more cautious if not actually hostile to this. In the end, an Italian presidency brought the negotiations to maturity and substantially widened the discretionary scope of the directive, lengthening the implementation periods significantly.[25]

Despite these disagreements and the experiences of the 1970s directives, the member states were able to agree on a measure that involved improvements in water quality, but at considerable extra costs. This suggests, at least, that EU environmental policy is sometimes perceived as an important device for raising national standards of pollution control. But how far does the reach of the EU's system of environmental governance extend into national policies on water pollution? It is to that issue that we turn in the next section.

HAS THERE BEEN A EUROPEANIZATION
OF NATIONAL WATER POLICY?

So far it might seem as though we were arguing that the EU's system of environmental governance had come to play a dominant role in the various national systems of water pollution control. How far can this conclusion be justified? To answer this, we need to look at the experience of the member states.

Germany

On first impression it is not immediately obvious that German clean water policy has been substantially influenced by the EU process. Indeed, the German obsession with a technology-driven emission standard approach has positively thrived in the face of the EU's distinctive water use approach. Contrary to the norm in German pollution control, water pollution is one area of German policy that, like the Dutch approach, uses fiscal instruments. The German water charges vary according to the volume and the waste load. There is a 50 per cent rebate if the BAT option (*Stand der Technik*) is applied, and there is even an extra incentive built in for companies that want to go above the recommended standard and reduce pollution by a further margin: such companies are exempted from paying waste water charges.[26]

Yet the German experience of charges has not been entirely without problems. These have been revealed for example in the allocation of the revenue raised from such charges in so far as it is not always reinvested in pollution control but rather has been co-opted into general expenditures.[27] Otherwise, the German Waste Water Charges Act of 1976 and the Washing and Cleaning Agents Act of 1975 find elements of both resonance and dissonance with EU themes. Indeed, it is interesting to note that, while domestic legislation was certainly in place early, one source suggests that these domestic laws may not have been as significant in changing actors' approaches on the ground.[28] Therefore the German approach to EU clean water directives instances an important principle: the Europeanization of water policy can occur at the same time at which distinctive national innovation also occurs.

The other limit on a Europeanization of German clean water policy has been Germany's unique institutional structure—and its associated problems. For example, the distinctive German problem of administrative regulations that do not satisfy the EU legal principle of 'direct effect' continues to undermine the proper implementation of directives.[29] Then there is the problem of institutional coordination, which is really of course a manifestation of the failure to achieve an integrated type of environmental policy across sectors, notably with agriculture. Thus, while the federal Ministry of the Environment estimated in 1991 that Germany would need to spend some DM4–6 billion on sewage infrastructure, partly in response to the urban waste water directive, some 50 per cent of nutrient enrichments discharged into coastal seas still comes from non-point agricultural sources.[30] In fact, German clean water policy has been persistently beset by a problem of coordination with agricultural institutions, a trend that is observable even in German inputs to EU policy-making. An example of this is the proposed amendment to the Guidelines on Drinking Water during the early 1990s. In this instance it was only through an alliance with the powerful health ministry that the environment ministry was able to place suitable pressure on the agriculture ministry to be more accommodating on the risks of agricultural pesticides.[31]

Perhaps the clearest example of how Europeanization has proceeded unsteadily in Germany is with regard to pesticides. For, as Rüdig and Kramer explain, directive 80/778 clearly created difficulties for the German administration, with transposition occurring for pesticides quite late in 1989, a fact that provoked Commission complaints.[32] They attribute this to a fear of upsetting domestic policy compromises with the German farming sector and agricultural policy network.

Another feature that influences German approaches to EU clean water policy is the federal–*Länder* battle for competences and leadership in water policy. There is some evidence that, despite the undoubted importance of the *Länder* in water policy, the federal dimension of clean water policy may be more clear-cut, and thus there is less of a trend towards Bonn using Brussels to outmanoeuvre the *Länder*.[33] In theory, while the *Länder* enjoy a concurrent competence with the federal government, which is supposed to draw up only framework legislation, in practice, in relation to water, the federal laws have been drawn up so tightly as to provide only limited discretion to the *Länder*.[34] In theory, this should allow European directives in the sector of water to be transposed uniformly across Germany.

More generally, we can say that the structure of German institutions for the provision of water and water disposal are unusual and should be contrasted with the more unified type of organizational structure found in the Netherlands and Spain, where water supply and disposal are typically within one single unified institution. In Germany the twin functions of water supply and water purity are usually not integrated, and furthermore they are still very much left to the local level of municipality and city government, in contrast to a regionalist drift discernible elsewhere.[35] It is hard to say what definitive impact this has had on EU policy implementation, but it does seem to suggest a continued dilution of any expected 'Europeanization' trend. For example, whereas in the UK privatization of the water industry was a national-level policy, in Germany it has emerged only as a trend in subnational innovation. In Lower Saxony, and generally in coping with former GDR water institutions, there has been some experimentation in this direction, but it has led to fears about underinvestment and market failure, with incentives to delay and offset construction of new waste treatment infrastructure, or to inflate construction costs. Moreover, such private utilities will not enjoy the access to favourable fiscal borrowing rates that German municipalities currently enjoy.[36]

Finally, it is interesting to consider the structure by which domestic and EU water laws are enforced. In this regard the Germans do appear to have a better system for the enforcement of EU clean water policy than most of the other member states studied here. For instance, in Germany visits by regulators are usually annual if not more frequent.[37]

Spain

Through the key innovation of water management boards, Spanish legislation since the domestic Water Act of 1986 has aimed at the creation of meso-level super water agencies. These have the virtue of being linked to the geographical reality of the resources through the river basin concept.[38] Such boards integrate all issues, allocating consumption and supply together with the enforcement of environmental objectives. Therefore Spain has developed its own quite distinctive institutional pattern for water governance at the same time as it has started to transpose and implement EU directives on clean water policy.

The 1986 water law (Ley de Aguas) shows clear signs of the coexistence of Europeanization and domestic modernization in Spain, as it replaced the previous water law of 1879 but conformed to EU legislation. This law is one of the most important pieces of legislation in Spain and is the subject of a passionate debate regarding the competences of the central state and the autonomous communities, in particular when river basins runs through more than one region. According to Bermejo, this legislation effectively nationalized the water resources of Spain and reduced tensions among public organizations.[39] Further innovation occurred with a royal decree of 1988 which introduced the National Hydrological Plan. This coordinated a variety of sectoral and regional water projects into a unified schema through a domestic 'Hydrological Confederation'. In addition to this indigenously inspired framework, a substantial monitoring force was built up in the form of three monitoring networks: the Basic Monitoring Network, the Monitoring Network of Surface Drinking Water, and the Monitoring Network of Continental Fisheries Water. These have focused on issues of quality and trends in surface water.

The Spanish regions have of course proved powerful and have moved assertively into the water policy field notwithstanding the existence of the water/river basin management boards. Even so, policy also receives inputs from the General Directorate for Water Quality within the Ministry of Public Works, Transport, and the Environment.[40] While this domestic legal regime appears impressive, doubts have been raised about the predictable question of implementation. For example, with regard to Spain, the Dutch Ministry for the Environment in a 1990 evaluation makes the point that although the Spanish 1986 water law was actually quite advanced, by 1990 it had still not been widely implemented.[41]

With regard to compliance with the bathing water directive, so vital for domestic tourism, Spanish particularism is also evident. For example, the Shores Act (Ley de Costas), Law 22 of 1988, is innovative in many respects and has incorporated new concepts and techniques in order to provide solutions to the problems arising from tourism and the degradation of the coast.[42] Bathing waters have also been protected under Royal Decree 1471 of 1989 on the disposal of solid waste and raw sewage, which prohibits such dumping within 500 metres of the shoreline. Yet bathing waters and coastal water quality are very much under severe pressure in Spain. Some 82 per cent of all visitors concentrate on the coastal regions, where a third of the Spanish population already lives. Equally, some 80 per cent of industrial effluents from more than 2,000 sources go into the sea. The implementation of the urban waste water directive is hence challenged by such a 'coastal crisis' in Spanish water quality policy. In fact, some 478 coastal municipalities discharge their often untreated waste waters directly into the sea.[43] Additionally, more than 40 per cent of waste waters are not subject to any treatment,[44] and like Italy a large part of the existing municipal water purification plants are not operating properly. The situation for industrial sewage appears to be even more acute.[45]

For these domestic reasons, the Spanish have been broadly supportive of both the bathing waters and urban waste waters directives, the latter attracting large transfers from the EU. Indeed, the Spanish have emerged as enthusiastic supporters of the 'European Blue Flag' campaign symbol for uncontaminated beaches, as it clearly provides a standard that has acceptability and credibility among European tourists. Data for 1991 indicated that 170 beaches from a total of 250 were awarded the Blue Flag, and in this regard one simple unintended consequence of the scheme is that it provides a very high level of visibility as to whether or not policy is being met. Thus, administrators are very mindful of losing or winning Blue Flag status.[46] Accordingly, the number of areas monitored under the directive has increased substantially since 1991, and the quality of coastal bathing waters has improved substantially as the compliance rate in areas sampled rose from 89 per cent in 1991 to 96 per cent in 1993. However, for inland waters the compliance rate for 1993 decreased slightly in comparison with the 1992 level.[47] The Spanish authorities have identified the discharges that could impair water quality in each bathing area, and improvement plans have been drawn up.[48] Only in 1990 was legislation enacted that allowed for the use of fiscal instruments. It is noticeable, however, that in the Spanish case subnational innovation is a striking feature. Catalonia, for instance, introduced water charges for waste water before the other regions did.

To conclude the Spanish case, the main political issue is the management of water rather than the quality of water. As consumption has risen with expanding urban populations and enlarged agricultural areas under irrigation, water has become increasingly scarce, and is now a serious political issue. Growing competition for water is leading to conflicts between users, the so-called *guerras del agua*.[49] Indeed, the central government had to act as mediator between the regional governments of Castilla-La Mancha, Valencia, and Murcia over water for the Segura Basin, one of Spain's richest fruit growing areas.[50] Therefore Spanish water policy is politically charged more for domestic reasons than for the effect that EU water quality directives have had. Yet into this fray has stepped the EU with its water quality guidelines and limits, offering legal resources to competing actors, who can then add quality issues to questions of water quantity and distribution.

Greece

In Greece we again see a pattern of Europeanization. Before entry into the EU the quality of drinking water was regulated by a decision of the Minister of Social Services (Sanitary Regulation of 1968). Since then the focus has been on transposing EU water law and lobbying hard for fiscal transfers to meet such standards. For example, as early as 1986, the Joint Ministerial Decision 46399/1352 transposed the bathing water directive into Greek national law. This also incorporated EU directives on quality standards for drinking and bathing water, and waters suitable for fish farming and aquaculture. A Ministerial Council Act (144/1987) and further decisions (18186/2171/1988 and 55648/2210/1991) have set limit values and quality objectives for specific substances discharged into the sea, in clear conformity with several EU directives. Fianancial transfers have of course played an important part in allowing for Greek compliance with EU water law, and indeed for building a domestic constituency in support of higher water quality standards. For example, Greece recently received 94 million ECU, which will mainly aid a dam and a tunnel project increasing the availability of water resources to Athens, and this demand for transfers has in turn led to specific tailored EU legislation.

How far have Greek institutional arrangements permitted Europeanization? In contrast to the other six states, Greece has an administrative system for water that is more generalist and displays less precision in its supervision. Also, the issue of water quality was dominated by the Ministry of Health during the 1980s, as it controlled the granting of permits to discharge waste water, and had considerably more staff to do this than its rival ministries of industry or environment.[51] However, the most significant factor that has limited the Greek capacity to adapt to Europeanization lies with the responsibility for inspection. Greece has neither a unified national inspectorate, nor what the Germans, Dutch, and Spanish all have: targeted, local, and dedicated water agencies. Instead, inspectors are scattered across the ministerial and prefectural levels.

Although the quality of fresh water in Greece is considered to be generally very good, pollution, stemming from the discharge of untreated domestic sewage and industrial wastes, has been found. Concern exists in some areas about pollutants in run-offs from agricultural operations. No extensive pollution has been detected in surface water, and the water of rivers and lakes is suitable for irrigation and fish farming. Inland water pollution has been observed, in particular, in seasonal increases of phosphates and nitrates.[52] An interesting feature appears to be the extent to which Greece is on the receiving end of water pollution from rivers originating outside her borders, and indeed outside the EU—in particular, Turkey and Bulgaria.

Greek compliance with the bathing water directive seems to be adequate in view of the overall quality of coastal water.[53] None the less, serious pollution does exist along some of the coast, stemming from the concentration of the population and lack of investment in sewage treatment plant. Indeed, in Greece only an estimated 10 per cent of the population is currently served by waste water treatment plants. Nevertheless, directive 91/271 and the availability of EU funds have speeded up the construction of such facilities. The Greater Athens sewage plant currently under construction is considered to be the largest of its kind in the Mediterranean. Athens, then, remains the focus of Greek pollution trends, and the gulf of Saronikos is a receptacle for all the municipal waste water produced by Greater Athens. Additionally, some 50 per cent of Greek industry is located in the area.

Notwithstanding these problems for bathing waters, an estimated 97 per cent of the areas sampled satisfied requirements. Yet evaluations of results over several bathing seasons show that pollution continues to occur at the same places. The completion in the next few years of treatment plants financed by the EU Structural Funds is expected to ease the problems faced by those areas that are now permanently polluted.

Italy

From the perspective of the Europeanization trend we identify here, it is noteworthy that recent Italian clean water legislation emerged at the same time as the EU approach was developing. The so-called 'Merli law', Law 319, passed in 1976 after ten years of domestic debate and delay, obviously prompted by EU developments. This 1976 water pollution law lays down a single set of regulations for the entire country, including technical criteria for the evaluation and control of water pollution. Yet it is important to note that at least some of the detail of this law was influenced by legislation introduced by the Lombardy region in 1974, while Tuscany and Triente provinces had begun around the same time to produce their own water legislation.[54] Therefore the Italian experience suggests an important feature of the multi-level governance is that subnational innovation can be vitally important, with the result, as Lewanski and Liberatore describe it, that the national Italian government found itself 'somewhat caught in the middle between regional initiatives on one side, and the first EU directives on water quality issued in 1976 on the other'.[55]

Europeanization thus appears as a more subtle phenomenon in Italy. Alongside a reception of EU clean water policy, the Italian central state has undertaken a domestic programme of institutional modernization which could copy ideas from other states, such as Spain. The Framework Law 183/1989 is a good example of this, as it identifies river basins as the geographic basis for coordinating land use and water management issues—a very Spanish theme. The 'Galli law' (Law 36/1994) completes this picture of a late modernization project by the Italian state in water policy, providing for a consolidation of water services (both water supply and waste water) into larger and more unified management units. Again, this mimics developments in Spain and the Netherlands towards unified regional water authorities, which do not directly owe their origins to specific EU legislation. For example, one Italian innovation that this law provides for is that the authority can set user charges and raise finances from water consumption. However, as we would expect from a generally laggardly state, these charges had still not been introduced by 1990.[56] As a result, the cost of drinking water in Italy is much lower than in other European countries, and charges for the use of water for agricultural purposes are also very low. Another example of distinctive Italian innovation lies in the field of nitrates. The region of Emilia Romagna, for example, experimented during the 1970s with voluntary agreements on the clean-up of detergents.

However, even where member states show such signs of innovation, we need not assume that it is more important or effective in securing policy goals than EU approaches; for nitrate emissions from non-point agricultural sources in this region continued unchecked and eradicated any potential reductions from the programme. Thus, domestic subnational innovation had to wait until the EU turned its attention substantively to nitrates with a directive in 1991.

The importance of tourism and its demand for clean bathing waters is manifest in the Italian case through a higher degree of apparent state mobilization to address the issue. As a result, Italy ostensibly monitors the suitability of coastal bathing waters more than any other EU country (4,288 sites).[57] Additionally, the Ministry of Health publishes annually a report about the quality of bathing water in Italy. Although this seems impressive, there are some concerns from Italian environmental NGOs that the constant switching of monitored sites may be a sign of a certain institutional shopping around for the best water quality to advertise. While bathing water standards are generally good, microbiological water quality parameters remain the biggest problem at non-complying sites. As a result, figures for 1991 suggest that 8 per cent of the Italian coast was not suitable for bathing.[58]

Implementation of the EU clean water policy in Italy is of course hampered by the familiar problem of institutional fragmentation. At the national level the environmental ministry still has to share power with the minister of public works, which retains powers in the water sphere. To confuse matters even more, regional governments are responsible for planning the means of pollution control within their territories and coordinating local plans, whereas provinces are charged with monitoring water quality and sewage discharges. Municipalities are then left to provide public services which affect water resources. It is with this profusion of actors and tiers of governance that the Italian river basin authorities must attempt to draw up plans aimed at guiding territorial authorities in land use planning and setting ambient water quality objectives. These river basin management agencies were opposed from the outset by the newly formed regions, who saw them as a challenge to the growth of their fledgling competences. The result was that proper river basin authorities like those in Spanish example were actually prevented from emerging.[59]

As for the urban waste water directive, it is clear that this has led to a substantial concentration of domestic resources: almost 43 per cent of the funding made available through the first Three-Year Programme for the environment of the regions was allocated for waste water treatment.[60] However, the Italian implementation of such investment programmes has been deeply problematic. As a result, many hundreds of sewage treatment plants, estimated at about 25 per cent of the total built, do not actually function owing to a lack of electricity or shoddy construction.[61]

With regard to drinking water, there has certainly been legal transposition, for example presidential decree 515/1982 incorporating EU directive 75/440. This is significant in terms of Europeanization, in that this decree was the first Italian legislation to deal specifically with drinking water. However, a very lax regime of enforcement and implementation can then undermine such EU standards. Lewanski and Liberatore for instance provide an example of what happened when administrators found out that drinking water levels exceeded EU pesticide levels: they simply introduced a decree that raised national limits.[62] Equally, because groundwater is the source of 90 per cent of the water supply in Italy, this may have led to a certain complacency about surface water quality. Indeed, an overall study of water quality in Italy indicates that the country's major rivers all have serious water quality problems.[63] The OECD indicates that heavy metal contaminant levels are of the same range as those of other European rivers.[64]

The Netherlands

Although the Dutch water pollution regime goes back a long way, with a Surface Water Pollution Act introduced in 1970 and a Pollution of Sea Water Act in 1975,[65] there appears to be intriguing evidence that the national policy style has been importantly modified by the EU multi-level experience. Hanf in particular makes the point that EU water policy has led to a substantial change in the orientation of domestic Dutch policy, especially with regard to the setting of water quality standards in terms of the distinctive EU approach of the late 1970s, based on the functional use of water. Prior to this, and much like the older British concept of 'wholesomeness of water', the Dutch had always adopted a generalist approach, striving for 'basic water quality' that could meet all uses.[66]

Yet patterns of interaction in multi-level environmental governance are two-way. Member states not only are the passive recipients of policy outputs, but actively try to export their domestic concerns to the Brussels level. The Dutch, suffering from downstream Rhine pollution, were the most motivated of the six states studied here to engage in such behaviour and pushed hard for international agreements on the management of the Rhine, eventually secured in the mid-1970s. However, such 'national policy export' strategies have not always been successful. For instance, their distinctive concerns during the negotiations over directive 80/778 on drinking water failed to get a supporting coalition for the setting of very high standards for chlorine and sodium. Thus, in certain cases leader states will not succeed outright in selling leader policies to their partners. This failure may have also been in part because the higher standards the Dutch were arguing for could be seen as being targeted at other states. In this context, it appears these member states feared that the Dutch were simply hoping that Brussels would impose on them the type of water regime that would clean up Dutch waters as well.

Two important domestic sub-themes of Dutch approaches to water pollution raise challenges for the multi-level EU approach.[67] Firstly, eutrophication, which is mainly from agricultural sources, is a sensitive area which the legislation of the 1970s touched upon only lightly, but one that the Dutch themselves have had to confront. Thus, whereas the EU directive 80/778 merely set out that member states should not exceed the relevant WHO values, for the Dutch the problem was more pressing and demanded serious detailed domestic innovation.[68] Indeed, it featured as one of the five core themes in the National Environmental Policy Plan.[69] This distinctive focus caused problems when the EU finally turned its attention towards nitrates and eutrophication in a more serious way with a directive in 1991. In the negotiations that ensued over this directive, the Dutch did not adopt a 'leader' position, fearful that it would upset their own delicate domestic compromises which had evolved after protracted negotiations with the powerful farmers' lobby. The latter had won concessions on issues of compensation and self-regulation, which the EU directive on nitrates potentially threatened to upset.[70]

The second challenging trend has been the reliance on bilateral and multilateral institutions other than the EU for securing water policy objectives. This is perhaps understandable, with the Netherlands being the recipient of major pollution flows from Germany (Rhine), France, and Belgium (Meuse and Schelde). Yet, while substantial political capital has been invested in the Rhine's particular scheme of multi-level water governance, the project has had limited success in achieving its targets. It now seems that there is a political acceptance by the Dutch authorities that the demanded 50 per cent reduction in the emissions of nutrients by the Rhine is simply impossible to achieve. As a result, the second National Environment Policy Plan merely expresses the general desirability of reducing emissions to a lower level.[71] While member states may invest in alternative structures of governance to the EU, therefore, these may actually prove more problematic and potentially embarrassing. Hence there may be a tendency to spread risks and political capital by relying on such multi-level structures as essentially complementary to the predominant EU process.

As regards fiscal instruments, there has been a comparative protraction in EU moves to innovate in clean water policy which is not mirrored by the Dutch approach. Water charges that were introduced under the Surface Waters Pollution Act have proved particularly effective against the more basic forms of water pollution and have led to knock-on effects such as major investment in extra sewage capacity. Following the Dutch imposition of water charges, discharges from large emitters in the manufacturing industry have decreased by 80 per cent in the period 1975–91.[72] According to Bressers, the domestic clean-up policy of water undertaken during 1975–9 was largely successful, owing to the unexpected effect these charges had on changing firms' behaviour. In contrast to the German experience, where funds from such charges were merged into general budgets (see below), the Dutch waste water charges regime has provided regional water quality managers with a substantial fund from which to finance investment in water quality. The Dutch charging system appears also to be more extensive in factoring externalities into the tax rate, as it includes the cost of investment in waste water treatment plant, etc.[73] Equally, the Dutch have innovated not just by introducing fiscal instruments such as charges; some water abstraction companies are drawing cheap loans available from a national green fund provided they carry out conservation work.[74]

Thus, the Dutch continue to exhibit their domestic distinctiveness in the face of Europeanization by using fiscal instruments which the EU directives on water examined here do not do. Indeed, this is one conspicuous example where the member states have been much more innovative in experimenting with fiscal instruments than the EU.

Institutionally, of course, the Dutch case is interesting as it is an example of a sophisticated policy emerging, even though the institutional system for water administration is somewhat fragmented.[75] In Chapter 8 we presented institutional fragmentation as a limit on the extent to which EU laws could be implemented fully. In the Dutch case, however, it is noteworthy that the extraordinary complexity of the various relations between competent bodies on Dutch water policy has not led to a more serious problem with implementation. In particular, the VROM (Ministry for Housing, Physical Planning, and Environment) has had to coordinate with the Ministry of Transport and Waterworks. While this has usually been successful, there has also been some evidence that backlogs exist in the granting of permits owing to administrative complexity.[76]

The United Kingdom

From the earliest directives in the 1970s, UK governments and policy-makers have been sceptical of the EU's approach. For example, when the Commission first published proposals for a directive on bathing waters in 1975, the debate in the European Parliament revolved entirely around amendments from UK MEPs. The relevant House of Lords select committee thought the proposed standards so ill-defined as to be virtually unenforceable. And wider expert opinion in the UK supported this view.[77]

Perhaps in part as a result of this scepticism, the British track record on the implementation of EU water directives, whether on bathing water or drinking water, is poor. A number of reasons can be cited to account for this implementation failure.

Firstly, transposition was attempted through purely administrative means, departmental circulars and the like, which of course failed to create specific legal rights or to have the transparency of a legal instrument. A classic example of this was directive 80/778, which had to wait until the 1989 Water Act before it found a legal 'parent'.[78] In fairness, however, it should be noted that this administrative approach was not just the preserve of the UK, as by 1982 only Denmark had actually implemented this directive by means of legislation.[79]

Related to this was a second trend: the lack of a sophisticated corpus of modern domestic law to act as an adequate platform for legally transposing the directives. Indeed, it was not until 1996 that proper legal regulations were introduced which finally transposed directives 75/440 and 79/869, the former of which should have come into force by 1977 and the latter by 1981.[80] Britain eventually achieved the type of modern water pollution legislation that most countries had had by the mid-1980s only in 1989. Prior to this there was actually no means for setting statutory water quality standards![81] Even after this legislation was enacted, delays continued to hamper British performance. For example, the regulations enacting the urban waste water directive were over a year late.[82]

Thirdly, even where directives did demand more concrete action, as with the bathing water directive's demand that bathing beaches be designated and monitored, British foot-dragging and regulatory minimalism were evident. As a result, famous English beaches at Blackpool and Brighton were left conspicuously undesignated, while Scotland was deemed to have no bathing beaches worthy of designation at all![83]

A distinctive British trend affecting the UK–EU water policy relationship was undoubtedly the privatization of the water industry by the Conservative government. These plans at one stage even included an attempt to create private regulatory agencies. On the one hand, the dynamics of privatization meant that politically the British government of the late 1980s did not want to agree to any legislation that would increase environmental standards and demand costly investment for these new private companies. On the other hand, industry and financial interests disliked uncertainty and preferred that several outstanding disputes with the Commission should be resolved.[84]

We see here in particular the unique power of the European Court of Justice in the integration process, as the threat that future court verdicts would make private companies implement European water quality norms at vast expense had a powerful concentrating effect on the minds of shareholders and management. In such a context it was perhaps felt better to attempt to negotiate with an assertive Commission over the poor implementation record, particularly with regard to directive 80/778. Therefore towards the end of the 1980s British approaches to EU water directives became distinctly conciliatory, and the early period of foot-dragging and open conflict was replaced by a period of direct negotiation with the Commission.[85] For example, in 1987 the British dramatically conceded that they had massively under-designated bathing waters and promptly identified some 362 more.[86] As an example of a political strategy, however, this national special pleading proved largely fruitless, as the Commission pushed ahead with legal action and in 1993 scored a victory in the first successful action against Britain over non-implementation of an environmental directive (80/778).[87]

Thus, despite the undoubted power of the nation states in the process, the rule of law and the Community working style are political realities which impinge on national autonomy and are not merely legal fictions. Moreover, despite a profound whole-scale national policy change (water privatization), it would seem that the EU's clean water laws were none the less able to persevere and influence this domestic British water policy agenda.

The implementation of the urban waste water treatment directive provides another example of suffusion as well as an illustration of the way in which economic considerations have weighed in the decision calculus of UK policy-makers.

Under the directive, member states were allowed to designate certain coastal waters as 'less sensitive' and therefore in need of only primary, rather than secondary, treatment. Having designated fewer areas as sensitive than recommended by its own Implementation Group, the Department of the Environment sought to have the Humber and Severn estuaries designated less sensitive because they supposedly had high natural dispersion (an unsubtle echo of traditional principles).[88] The local authorities challenged the decision in each case, and in early 1996 the High Court decided that the designation had been legally faulty because it had not been based on objective criteria.[89] In this sense, the EU directive provided the framework of a move towards a more formal system in the UK.

An important part of the background to the government's original decision were concerns in the UK government about the costs of the directive. Here we need to understand the distinctive regulatory framework created by privatization.[90] Privatized utilities in the UK are subject to regulation in respect of both price controls and the environment. Administratively, the two forms of regulation are distinct. The price regulator for water is OFWAT. Until April 1996 the National Rivers Authority was responsible for waste water quality. Ever since privatization there have been disputes between OFWAT and the National Rivers Authority (as well as concerns in the UK Treasury) about the costs of water pollution control measures. In particular, OFWAT has objected to the costs of implementing European environmental standards.[91]

It is an interesting question whether these institutional arrangements have exacerbated the tension between economic costs and environmental improvement in the UK or whether, for reasons to do with broader political culture, UK governments have been particularly sensitive to the cost dimensions of policy. Certainly, the experience over air pollution in the 1980s (see next chapter), in which the cost implications for a *nationalized* industry were paramount, would suggest that privatization, through its creation of a dual regulatory structure, has facilitated, rather than caused, a clearer articulation of economic values. Conversely, it would be reasonable to agree with Ward that the urban waste water treatment directive has been instrumental in raising UK coastal water quality.[92] More generally, the conclusion must surely be that, of all the states studied here, Britain has had the most overtly difficult relationship with the EU clean water policy. In this sector, the 'laggard' side of the British split personality seems to have asserted itself.

CONCLUSIONS

On the basis of the above descriptions of various national regimes, what can we conclude regarding the impact of the EU clean water policy on the national systems—predominance, co-evolution and suffusion? This is not an easy question to answer, as there are clearly elements of all three trends in evidence. Yet we argue that in the majority of cases a co-evolution of EU clean water policy appears evident. Thus, as the Commission expanded its brief in clean water policy from the late 1970s onwards, this coincided and coexisted remarkably peacefully with the maturation of national policy styles. The main exception to this peaceful co-existence has been the UK, which for a variety of reasons has ended up consistently at odds with the Commission on the water directives. That is not to say that in other states EU clean water policy has not suffered from implementation failures: even a brief glance at the case law of the Court of Justice will suggest that it has. But the EU approach, particularly the 'water use' approach of 1976, however unusual and different for national administrations, has in the main been accepted for better or for worse and worked with pragmatically.

None of this of course has precluded substantial national innovation, or even, in the case of Italy and Spain, subnational innovation. In that regard, most of the innovation has been focused on the use of fiscal instruments such that the EU legislation of the 1970s and 1980s now appears rather dated in its comparative neglect of such instruments. The belated endorsement of such approaches in the proposed framework water quality directive of 1997, which demands a mandatory regime of total cost recovery pricing, further suggests that the member states have been comparatively slow and less successful in exporting their domestic innovations upwards to Brussels. In this regard, EU clean water policy appears a little less dynamic than air policy, which has seen more overt national strategies for the European level adopted.

There is no simple north–south dichotomy in water policy. While the southern states have clearly embarked on a modernization of their water infrastructure in tandem with EU support, in many cases this has involved their actually beginning to build their first substantial sewage plant and water treatment infrastructure under EU tutelage. None the less, they share some problems and even institutional features with the northern states. For example, Spain and the Netherlands appear to have developed water institutions that share a unified regional water management structure, independently of the EU influence. In contrast, Germany's institutional setup has slowed down its capacity to transpose and implement EU directives, while domestic UK policy orientations and actors have responded in ways that are more consistently like a 'laggard' than a leader state. Perhaps the crucial element that makes the southern states more accepting of the EU's water law is precisely that it is tied up with a substantial programme of transfers and domestic modernization, particularly with regard to the urban waste water directive.

What can we say about factors that either advance a process of Europeanization or make it less likely? A number of factors appear to have limited the extent to which states exhibit signs of Europeanization. Interestingly, outright political hostility of and in itself does not seem to limit the scope of EU water law. As the UK found out, a bitter attritional Europeanization can be forced by the Commission through the European Court of Justice. Institutional factors do seem to contribute, but it does not seem that important whether a given state has a particularly developed institutional water structure in place. States that have had this, such as the

Netherlands for hundreds of years, none the less exhibit signs of adopting common European approaches previously quite foreign to them. Equally, states where it might be supposed that national institutions are less developed, and thus that there would be more 'space' for European norms to take up a dominant position, can none the less show signs of considerable innovation in distinct directions, Italy and Spain both illustrating this. However, where there are very many actors involved in the transposition of EU directives, this does add complexity and bottlenecks in what should be theoretically an otherwise smooth 'top-down' transposition process.

In conclusion, we suggest it is through uneven and sometimes poor implementation processes that a Europeanization of clean water policy has been most delayed or hindered. In fairness, this problem may show signs of improvement with the introduction of the special implementation directive 91/692, which states that since 1993 specific annual reports from each state should have been lodged with the Commission on their implementation of directive 80/778.[93] Of course, implementation is not just a question of legal transposition. It is also about practical enforcement and field agency work. In that regard, one consistent failure of all the water directives, particularly for example in the bathing waters directive, has been a failure to specify how monitoring should be carried out, as there is at present considerable scope for cheating and error. Indeed, this is such a serious cause for concern that one authoritative source has even suggested that various reports issued by the member states and the Commission may not be that reliable.[94]

It is also clear that as a multi-level scheme of governance the water policy regime of the EU has been massively influenced by parallel non-EU intergovernmental developments which leader member states have been deeply involved in. Foremost among these have been the Rhine Action Plan and the North Sea Action Plan, the former of which since 1987 has committed members to a 50 per cent reduction of priority substances by 1995. Similar demands were made that same year when the North Sea Ministerial Conference committed all the North Sea states to a 50 per cent reduction of toxic, persistent, and bio-accumulative substances reaching the North Sea.[95] However, in the cases where such developments were assessed here, we did not find evidence to suggest that such regimes were as important as EU law. Indeed, many appear to be in at least as serious a state of crisis as EU policy norms, owing to non-implementation.

In contrast with the reliance on periodic interactions with international water politics described above, a local politicization of water issues has been engendered by the EU directives. This is perhaps best illustrated in the case study of sewage pollution of the east Devon coast in the South-West of England region, presented by Ward *et al.*[96] However, the authors add, this has not been a result of the effectiveness of the European directives *per se*, but rather because the public was demanding that commitments made by the government were fully implemented and observed.[97]

To conclude, we might add that the trends identified in European water quality are not that hopeful. Almost twenty years after the application of EU legislation on the protection of surface and coastal waters, the general opinion is that water quality is lower than might have been expected. Nevertheless, some improvements have been seen. These include a better effluent control at source, and the extension of sewage systems and improvement to treatment procedures. EU legislation and national environment policies operating together have stimulated much of this action. Yet clearly, a number of problems remain, and in several parts of the EU levels of water pollution have risen. The primary reason for this is the lack of monitoring and lack of structures to control implementation and enforcement, resulting from inherent inefficiencies in the local administration. As an example of this, one could point to the Italian regions which, after demanding a key role in environmental protection, were subsequently slow to act.

As we currently stand on the threshold of a major new review of existing clean water policy in the proposed framework directive, it is perhaps safe to say that any evaluation of the EU water directives would clearly opt for the trite 'could do better' type of characterization. Yet that alone would surely miss the rapid growth of the EU's role in water quality. For the European institutions have together developed a policy that demands detailed local coordination, complicated interactions with specific water institutions, and recently even massive financial transfers. As a policy, it has survived direct legal conflict with member states such as Britain and the challenge from those wishing to roll back the EU's environmental competences. Judged from this perspective, perhaps what is most surprising is the extent to which EU involvement has been so readily accepted.

NOTES TO CHAPTER 10

1. N. Haigh, *Manual of Environmental Policy: The EC and Britain* (London: Cartermill International, 1992 and subsequent revisions), p. 4.2–1.
2. P. Sands, *Principles of International Environmental Law*, I (Manchester: Manchester United Press, 1995), p. 560.
3. House of Commons Environment Committee, *Fourth Report: Pollution of Beaches*, ii (London: HMSO, 1990), evidence from National Rivers Authority at p. 42, para. 159.
4. See Commission Press Release: IP/96/607, 07.09.96. 'Infringement Procedure: Commission takes Germany to Court for Non-Implementation of Directive on Dangerous Substances into Water'.
5. W. Grant, 'Large Firms, SMEs, and Deregulation' in U. Collier (ed.), *Deregulation in the European Union: Environmental Perspectives* (London: Routledge, 1998), pp. 147–64 at 156.
6. Haigh, *Manual*, p. 4.4–3.
7. See 'Water Management 46: EEC Argues over Pesticides in Drinking Water', *ENDS Report*, 161 (1988), pp. 13–15.
8. See the following Commission press releases: MEMO/94/48, 06.07.94, 'Pesticide Legislation Ensures Maintenance of High Standards for Water Quality'; Speech/ 96/179, 28.06.96, 'Speech by Mrs Ritt Bjerregaard: The View of the European

Commission on Environment and Pesticides at the Second Weed Control Congress-Copenhagen, 28 June 1996'. In particular see 'Uniform Principles Setback to Stall Approval of Pesticides', *ENDS Report*, 261 (1996), pp. 45–6.

9. COM(97)47.

10. Commission of the European Communities, 'Proposal for Council Directive establishing a Framework for Community Action in the Field of Water Policy', COM(97)49 97/00067 (SYN) Brussels 26.02.97, pp. 5–7.

11. See esp. A. Jordan, 'European Community Water Policy Standards: Locked In or Watered Down?' *Journal of Common Market Studies*, 37:1 (1999), pp. 13–37, esp. at 26–34.

12. House of Commons Environment Committee, *Fourth Report: Pollution of Beaches*, evidence from National River Authority, p. 32.

13. J. Richardson, 'EU Water Policy: Uncertain Agendas, Shifting Networks and Complex Coalitions', *Environmental Politics*, 3:4 (1994), pp. 139–67 at 146.

14. O. Brouwer, Y. Comtois, M. van Empel, D. Kirkpatrick, and P. Larouche, *Environment and Europe: European Union Environment Law and Policy and its Impact on Industry* (Deventer: Stibbe Simont Monahan Duhot, 1994), p. 124.

15. See e.g. OECD, *Environmental Indicators, 1991* (Paris: OECD, 1991), pp. 57–9. However, in Greece only an estimated 10% of the population is currently served by waste water treatment plants (interview with officials in the Prefecture of Lasithiou, Agios Nikolaos, Crete, October 1994). These OECD figures indicate that the percentage of the population served by waste water treatment has increased from 33% in 1970 to 60% in the late 1980s.

16. A. K. Brown, 'Impact of European Legislation: Urban Wastewater Directive', *Proceeding of the Institute of Civil Engineers-Municipal Engineer*, 93 (1992), pp. 205–9.

17. House of Commons Environment Committee, *Fourth Report: Pollution of Beaches*, evidence from Water Services Association, p. 124, para. 390.

18. 'Cleaning Up the Sewage Business', *ENDS Report*, 182 (1990), pp. 12–16.

19. E. Thairs, 'Business Lobbying on the Environment: The Perspective of the Water Sector', in P. Lowe and S. Ward (eds.), *British Environmental Policy and Europe* (London: Routledge, 1998), pp. 153–70 at 161–2.

20. 'Billions at Stake as Brussels Launches Sewage Treatment Dumping Proposals', *ENDS Report*, 178 (1989), pp. 29–30. See also 'Ministers Agree Directives on Wastewater, Diesel Emissions and Chemical Testing', *ENDS Report*, 194 (1991), pp. 34–6.

21. See Commission press release: IP/98/750, Brussels, 3.08.98, 'Greece to Get ECU 60 million from the Cohesion Fund'.

22. See Commission press release: IP/89/673, 12.09.89, 'Spain and Portugal Work Together to Submit the First Transnational Regional Development Programme'. See also Commission press releases: IP/90/1023, 17.12.90, 'Regional Policies: the Commission Adopts a Series of Regional Programmes and Major Projects in Spain'; IP/90/830, 15.10.90, 'Regional Policies: Regional Programmes for Greece'; and IP/90/1074, 21.12.90, 'Regional Policies: Commission Adopts a Series of Regional Programmes for Italy'.

23. See Commission press release IP/89/78, 29.11.89, 'Development Policy and Environment Policy: ENVIREG Initiative and Medspa Programme'. The ENVIREG programme was a complement to an earlier 1988 scheme for the development of

Mediterranean regions, called Medspa, which had a smaller budget, but broadly the same objectives.

24. See Commission press release: IP/91/274, 27.03.91, 'Regional Policies: Commission Adopts First Operational Programmes for the New German *Länder*'.

25. Haigh, *Manual*, p. 4.6–4.

26. Ministry Housing, Physical Planning and Environment [VROM]/Environmental Resources Ltd, *Comparison of Environmental Policy Planning in Industrial Countries in the Context of the National Environmental Policy Plan* (London: ERL, 1990), pp. 58, 69, 90.

27. R. A. Krämer, 'An East–West Tug of Water: Water Services in United Germany', in H. Bressers and L. J. O'Toole Jr (eds.), *International Comparative Policy Research* (Enschede: University of Twente Press, 1992), pp. 102–26 at 104.

28. H. Pehle, 'Germany: Domestic Obstacles to an International Forerunner', in M. S. Andersen and D. Liefferink (eds.), *European Environmental Policy: The Pioneers* (Manchester and New York: Manchester University Press, 1997), pp. 161–209. For evidence of the limited impact that the German water legislation of the 1970s has had, see W. Rüdig and R. A. Krämer, 'Networks of Cooperation: Water Policy in Germany', *Environmental Politics*, 3:4 (1994), pp. 52–79 at 65.

29. Pehle, 'Germany', p. 175. Because such administrative regulations are binding only on German civil servants, they do not confer general legal rights on citizens and thus do not allow German/EU citizens the right to rely on the provisions of a directive before domestic courts (direct effect).

30. Pehle, 'Germany', p. 191.

31. Ibid. 191, 197.

32. Rüdig and Krämer, 'Networks of Cooperation', p. 68.

33. For a conventional account of the importance of the *Länder* in German water policy see, Rüdig and Krämer, 'Networks of Cooperation'.

34. Pehle, 'Germany', pp. 162, 169.

35. Krämer, 'An East–West Tug of Water', pp. 103–6.

36. Ibid. 114.

37. Ministry of Housing, Physical Planning and Environment [VROM]/Environmental Resources Ltd, *The Structure and Functions of Environmental Enforcement Organizations in EC Member States* (The Hague: VROM, 1991), p. 24.

38. Ministry of Housing, Physical Planning and Environment [VROM]/Environmental Resources Ltd, *Comparison of Environmental Policy Planning in Industrial Countries* (The Hague: VROM, 1990), p. 55.

39. J. Vera Bermejo, *Constitución y Planificación Hidrológica'* (Madrid: Civitas, 1995), p. 21.

40. Scientific advice is provided by the National Water Council and CEDEX (Centre for Experiments and Studies of Public Works) of the Ministry of Public Works, Transport and the Environment, the CDTI (Centre for Technical Development for Industry) of the Ministry of Industry, and the Institute for Health Carlos III of the Ministry of Health and Consumer Affairs. See Ministerio de Obras Públicas, Transportes y Medio Ambiente, *Guía de la Organización Administrativa en Medio Ambiente* (Madrid: Ministerio de Obras Públicas, 1993).

41. Ministry of Housing, Physical Planning and Environment [VROM]/Environmental Resources Ltd, *Comparison of Environmental Policy Planning*, p. 69.

42. Ministerio de Obras Públicas and Urbanismo, *The Shores Act* (Madrid: Ministerio de Obras Publicas and Urbanismo, 1989), p. 14.

43. M. Estevan, *Implicaciones Económicas de la Protección Ambiental de la CEE: Repercusiones en España* (Madrid: Ministerio de Economia, 1991), p. 186.

44. Ministerio de Obras Públicas, *Medio Ambiente en España 1992* (Madrid: Ministerio de Obras Públicas, 1993), pp. 138–44.

45. Estevan, *Implicaciones Económicas*, pp. 185–6.

46. Ministerio de Obras Públicas, *Medio Ambiente en España 1992*, p. 69.

47. Commission of the European Community, *Quality of Bathing Water, 1993* (Luxembourg: Commission of the European Community, 1994), p. 47.

48. Ministerio de Obras Públicas, *Medio Ambiente en España 1992*, p. 153.

49. 'Agua Cara', *El País*, 31 July 1994, p. 8.

50. *El País*, 24 July 1994, p. 5.

51. Ministry of Housing, Physical Planning and Environment [VROM]/Environmental Resources Ltd, *The Structure and Functions of Environmental Enforcement Organizations*, pp. 27–28.

52. Ministry of Environment (YPEHODE), *National Report of Greece, UN Conference on Environment and Development, Brazil, June 1992* (Athens: Ministry of the Environment, 1991), p. 72.

53. *To Vima*, 4 June 1995, pp. A54–5.

54. See fn. 30 in R. Lewanski and A. Liberatore, 'Environment Protection in Italy: Analyzing the Local, National and European Community Levels of Policy Making', in U. Desai (ed.), *Comparative Environmental Policy and Politics* (Albany, NY: SUNY Press, 1997).

55. Lewanski and Liberatore, 'Environment Protection in Italy'.

56. OECD, *Environmental Performance Review: Italy* (Paris: OECD, 1994), p. 79.

57. Commission of the European Community, *Quality of Bathing Water, 1993*, p. 11. The other member states covered by the research project had the following number of sampling points for sea water: Germany 436, Greece 1,250, Spain 1,405, Netherlands 45, and the UK 457.

58. See fn. 7 in Lewanski and Liberatore, 'Environment Protection in Italy'.

59. See ibid.

60. OECD, *Environmental Performance Review: Italy*, pp. 79–80.

61. See *c*. fn. 52 in Lewanski and Liberatore, 'Environment Protection in Italy'.

62. Ibid.

63. Ministero Dell' Ambiente, *Relazione sullo Stato dell' Ambiente*, (Rome: Ministero dell' Ambiente, 1992), pp. 186–7.

64. OECD, *Environmental Performance Review: Italy*, p. 77.

65. D. Liefferink, 'The Netherlands: A Net Exporter of Environmental Policy Concepts', in M. S. Andersen and D. Liefferink (eds.), *European Environmental Policy: The Pioneers* (Manchester and New York: Manchester University Press, 1997), pp. 210–50 at 214 and 220. See also H. Bressers, D. Huitema, and S. M. M. Kuks, 'Policy Networks in Dutch Water Policy', *Environmental Politics*, 3:4 (1994), pp. 24–51 at 25.

66. K. Hanf, 'European Community Policy', in H. Bressers, and L. J. O'Toole Jr (eds.), *International Comparative Policy Research* (Enschede: University of Twente Press, 1992), pp. 85–98 at 97. On the old British 'common sense' approach to water quality, see Haigh, *Manual*, p. 4.1.

67. Perhaps a possible third candidate for a distinctive Dutch approach to water policy has been the ideal of integrated water management that first received serious expression in the 1985 document, *Living with Water*. For useful discussion, see Bressers, Huitema, and Kuks, 'Policy Networks', p. 25.

68. Bressers, Huitema, and Kuks, 'Policy Networks', p. 31, suggest that more than 50% of Dutch groundwater is likely to become unsuitable as a drinking water source in the near future.

69. Liefferink, 'The Netherlands', p. 217.

70. Ibid. 237. On Dutch nitrates policy and farmers, see Bressers, Huitema, and Kuks, 'Policy Networks', p. 31.

71. Liefferink, 'The Netherlands', pp. 236–7.

72. European Environment Agency, *Environmental Taxes: Implementation and Effectiveness* (Copenhagen: European Environment Agency, 1996), pp. 59–60; OECD, *Evaluating Economic Instruments for Environmental Policy* (Paris: OECD, 1997), pp. 37–9.

73. H. T. A. Bressers, 'The Cleaning Up Period', in H. T. A. Bressers and L.J.O'Toole Jr (eds.), *International Comparative Policy Research* (Enschede: University of Twente Press, 1992), pp. 155–74 at 164, 172.

74. 'Green Water on Tap', *Environmental News from the Netherlands*, 1 (1997), p. 9.

75. For an explanation of this institutional structure in detail see Bressers, Huitema, and Kuks, 'Policy Networks', p. 36. Basically, regional waters are the responsibility of the provinces, but in most cases these have delegated their responsibility to semi-democratic water quality boards which manage treatment plants. Municipalities look after domestic sewage.

76. Ministry of Housing, Physical Planning and Environment [VROM]/Environmental Resources Ltd, *The Structure and Functions of Environmental Enforcement Organizations*, p. 49.

77. For the references, see A. Jordan and J. Greenaway, 'Shifting Agendas, Changing Regulatory Structures and the "New" Politics of Environmental Pollution: British Coastal Waters Policy, 1955–1995', *Public Administration*, 76:4 (1998), pp. 669–94 at 677–8.

78. Haigh, *Manual*, p. 4.4–4.

79. Ibid.

80. Ibid. 4.3–1, 4.3–3, 4.3–2.

81. Ibid. 4.6–7.

82. Ibid. 4.5–7.

83. Ibid.

84. Ibid. 4.4–6, and see 4.5–5 for the way in which the bathing water directive worked in the same way.

85. Ibid. 4.4–9.

86. Ibid. 4.5–6.

87. Ibid. 4.4–7.

88. N. Ward, 'Water Quality', in P. Lowe and S. Ward (eds.), *British Environmental Policy and Europe* (London: Routledge, 1998), pp. 244–64 at 252.

89. 'Court Quashes Gummer's Decisions on Urban Waste Water Directive', *ENDS Report*, 253 (1996), pp. 46–7.

90. For a discussion of the implications of this administrative separation, see A. Weale, 'Environmental Regulation' in P. Vass (ed.), *Regulatory Review 1997* (London: Centre

for the Study of Regulated Industries, 1997), pp. 201–16 and the references cited therein. See also our discussion of the UK policy style in Ch. 5.

91. I. Byatt, 'The Impact of EC Directives on Water Customers in England and Wales', *Journal of European Public Policy*, 3:4 (1996), pp. 665–74. It should also be noted, however, that there has also been concern that the *environmental* consequences of the urban waste water treatment directive have not been thought through, and that the alternatives to long sea outfall might not be environmentally sound. This was of concern, for example, to the environment sub-committee of the House of Lords Select Committee on the European Communities. See House of Lords Select Committee on the European Communities *10th Report 1990–91: Municipal Waste Water Treatment* (London: HMSO, 1991).

92. Ward, 'Water Quality', p. 255.

93. Haigh, *Manual*, p. 4.4–3.

94. Ibid. 4.5–3.

95. Ministry of Housing, Physical Planning and Environment [VROM]/Environmental Resources Ltd, *Comparison of Environmental Policy Planning in Industrial Countries*, p. 58.

96. N. Ward, H. Buller, and P. Lowe, 'The Europeanisation of Local Environmental Politics: Bathing Water Pollution in the South West of England', *Local Environment*, 1:1 (1996), pp. 21–32.

97. Ibid. 31.

11

Air Pollution Control and Multi-Level Governance

Control of air pollution has been a long-standing objective of governments. Traditional air pollution, in the form of smoke and particulates, is highly visible, typically local, and usually severely damaging or at least costly. Pigou caught these elements of traditional air pollution well in writing about the economic effects of the smoking chimney in *The Economics of Welfare*: 'for this smoke in large towns inflicts a heavy uncharged loss on the community, in injury to buildings and vegetables, expenses for washing clothes and cleaning rooms, expenses for the provision of extra artificial light, and in many other ways'.[1] Experience and analysis of the London smog of 1952 was able to show that the uncharged loss of traditional forms of air pollution also included premature death from respiratory diseases.[2]

Although a source of economic and human loss, the smoking chimney has always been an ambiguous symbol. In the Ruhr after the First World War, the phrase 'the chimneys are smoking again' came to express the satisfaction with the return of productive industry and the beginning of the end of wartime privations. Precisely because it is so visible, the traditional smoking chimney carries connotations of prosperity as well as damage.

Much of this complex symbolism is carried over into modern air pollution problems. In Europe air pollution of the traditional kind is now a thing of the past. London no longer has its 'pea-soup' fogs that were once so characteristic. National policies and changes in technology have now largely remedied the problems of smoke and particulate matter in towns from fixed production points.

This is not to say, however, that the problems of air pollution are a thing of the past. Today a major effect of fixed production points concerns not local urban environments but national and international environments. Smoke from chimneys, while still important, is only one item of policy concern. Sulphur dioxide and nitrogen oxides are now seen as contributors to the problem of acidification on a large scale, causing damage to buildings, vegetation, soil quality, and human health. The pollutants involved can often travel long distances in pathways that are complex and often poorly understood. A good example of this complexity is provided by the emissions from UK power stations. For a long time they have been thought to contribute to acid precipitation in Scandinavian countries, but the problem was not a purely transboundary one. Travelling through complex pathways, emissions also contributed to increased acidification in the UK, including sites of special scientific interest.[3]

If the problem of acidification illustrates the increased scale of air pollution problems, issues of urban air pollution illustrate the changes in the sources of pollution. When Pigou was writing the main contributors to urban air pollution were stationary sources, whether factories or domestic coal fires. Today the main culprit is car and vehicle use in towns, as increased affluence has enabled people to rely more and more on their own transport. Thus, while it is true that much of the air pollution problem of Athens is due to its climatic and geographical conditions, its photochemical smog (*nefos*) stems from vehicle emissions, in a situation in which random checks showed more than 50 per cent of cars were exceeding prescribed emission limit values.[4] Moreover, in many ways the new urban pollution illustrates the extent to which the problems are multi-level. Cars are traded internationally. Monitoring is local, as are the effects.

The effects are not only local, however, since photochemical smog can affect large areas. Thus, new sources like increases in traffic can contribute to problems such as increased levels of tropospheric ozone, which is not purely an urban phenomenon and which can give rise to health problems, particularly for those suffering from respiratory diseases. Moreover, photochemical smog can produce novel forms of environmental degradation, including visual intrusion, as any visitor to the Alps can experience on a hot summer's day when the clear view becomes hazy.

In this chapter we examine the policy processes associated with two of the main sets of directives aimed at these modern forms of air pollution: the large combustion plant directive, agreed in 1988, and a series of vehicle emissions directives controlling car emissions. In many ways these two sets of directives have many features in common. In both cases, the surge of interest in environmental standards, which had much of its origin in Germany, the Netherlands, and Denmark in the first half of the 1980s, and which came to be characteristic of Europe more widely in the late 1980s, was an influential turning-point. Both sets of developments have been highly controversial, particularly in the balance they have struck between economic costs on the one hand and environmental quality on the other. Both have involved 'technical fixes' that were themselves contested in terms of effectiveness and efficiency. And both issues pitted the UK government against the German government in the Council of Ministers in the 1980s in ways that some observers took to symbolize a more general conflict between Rhineland capitalism and Anglo-Saxon capitalism, played out in the development of the single market and the process of European integration. In these respects, the directives concerning air pollution in the 1980s were typical of a phase of European environmental policy, characterized by the attempt to impose higher engineering standards to combustion processes in ways that were novel and challenging to a number of member states.

Despite these similarities, there were also significant differences between the two sets of directives. The most notable, from our point of view, is found in the legislative processes under which the issues were taken. The large combustion plant directive was an environmental measure, pure and simple. Of course, its adoption implied economic costs, showing up most clearly for industry in the form of higher electricity costs. It is also true that energy is traded across national borders. But, unlike products, no one could plausibly claim that, if one country imposed increased costs through higher environmental standards on its electricity producers, those measures implicitly created a barrier to international trade. The international aspect of the problem arose from the fact that it was the pollution that moved across borders, not the product or process from which it originated.

Control of car exhaust emissions is a different matter, however. As early as 1970, it was recognized that the environmental standards imposed on vehicles in one country had implications for cross-border trade within Europe. Just as important by the early 1980s was the recognition by many European policy elites that vehicle emission standards were increasingly a global concern, so that policy decisions taken in Washington or Tokyo were likely to be as important as the thinking in European capitals.

Between 1987 and 1993 this difference of issue characterstic was reflected in the European legislative process. Under the Single European Act, single market matters required only qualified majority voting in the Council of Ministers, and involved the cooperation procedure with respect to the agreement of the European Parliament. The cooperation procedure in particular meant that, if the Parliament could agree an amendment to the original Council proposal, there would have to be unanimity in the Council to overturn that amendment. By contrast, measures that were regarded as being purely environmental required unanimity in the Council and involved only the consultation procedure with the Parliament. This difference, as we shall see, had significant implications for the political dynamics of the legislative process. In what follows, we seek to trace out these similarities and differences in the way in which these air pollution measures were treated.

THE LARGE COMBUSTION PLANT DIRECTIVE

The large combustion plant directive (88/609/EEC), agreed in 1988, aims at the control of sulphur dioxide, nitrogen oxides, and particulate matter from fossil fuel power stations and other large combustion furnances (defined for the most part as those being over 50 MW).

Power plants are capital-intensive pieces of equipment with a long pay-back period for the resources invested. A notable feature of the directive was its attempt to limit the emissions of sulphur dioxide and nitrogen oxides from existing plants as well as new installations. 'Existing plants' were defined for the purposes of the directive as those where there was an operating or construction licence in place before 1 July 1987. Its principal tool for such plant was the requirement for member states to introduce by 1990 national plans for reductions in total emissions of the relevant gases over a specified period of time. The targets for percentage reductions are specified in five yearly intervals from 1988 for 1993, 1998, and 2003. In many cases the percentage reductions in total emissions required under the directive are substantial. For example, Belgium, Germany, France, and the Netherlands have been assigned the target of a 70 per cent reduction in sulphur dioxide emissions between 1980 and 2003; Denmark, Italy, Luxembourg, and the UK each have reduction targets that are at least 60 per cent over the same period. Three countries (Greece, Ireland, and Portugal) are allowed some increases.

New plants are governed, by this directive, by emission limits specified according to the principle of best available technology not entailing excessive costs. Most of the emission limits that are applicable cover a variety of fuel types, but an exception is made for solid fuel burning plants in the range 50–100 MW, where the limit, applicable under an amendment of 1994 (94/66/EC), has been set at 2000 mg of sulphur dioxide per cubic metre.[5] There are also requirements under the directive for monitoring the performance of operating plants, as well as obligations on member states to report on their programmes for total emissions reductions.

The origins of the directive were quite clearly located in Germany in the early 1980s, although planning for the measure had gone back to 1978.[6] By 1982 the coalition of Social Democrats and Free Democrats, which had been in office since 1969, was showing signs of strain. The Chancellor Helmut Schmidt faced opposition within his own ranks for his stance on nuclear defence policy and his style of leadership. The Greens had been doing well in *Land* elections, often picking up the support of younger voters, and the Free Democrats began to lose support, threatening their eclipse under Germany's 5 per cent threshold rule for securing seats in *Land* and national parliaments. In June 1982 the German government announced at the Stockholm Conference on the Acidification of the Environment that they would change their position and move in favour of strong international action to deal with the problem of acid rain. At the same time, Germany submitted a memorandum to the EU's Environment Council advocating effective policies against air pollution in the Union.[7] In September 1982 the government proposed a new domestic air pollution control ordinance under legislation first introduced in 1974, the Grossfeuerungsanlagen-Verordnung (Large Combustion Plant Ordinance, GFAV). The Social–Liberal coalition fell on a constructive vote of no confidence in October 1982, to be replaced with a Christian–Liberal coalition headed by Helmut Kohl. Seeking electoral legitimacy, the new government called an election for March 1983, and this gave the Christian–Liberal coalition a safe majority of 278 and for the first time allowed the Greens into the Bundestag with 27 seats.

The new Christian–Liberal coalition government was able to reaffirm the policy position of stringent control measures in the GFAV, which imposed a 60 per cent across-the-board reduction in sulphur dioxide for all large furnaces, to be achieved within five years. Although the controls were specified in terms of emission limit values, the standards were so stringent that it would have been impossible for plant to meet them without the use of expensive flue-gas desulphurization technology. The most significant aspect of the policy was that the standards were to apply to existing as well as new plant. Hence, the standards required the retrofitting of flue-gas desulphurization technology to existing electricity stations and other large furnaces.

The policy change is sometimes characterized almost as though it were a simple electoral response to the emergence of the Greens as a party represented in the Bundestag by a government under the influence of the sometimes apocalyptic public mood created by the press reports of *Waldsterben* (forest death). Careful studies of the policy process, however, have shown it to involve a complex series of elements. Public opinion was certainly important, as was the emergence of the Greens in the Bundestag. However, it is also important to consider the role of more traditional political rivalries in Germany. The Christian parties, particularly the CSU in Bavaria, could portray environmental damage as being due to coal-fired power stations operated in Social Democratic *Länder*, especially in the North Rhine –Westphalia region where Rheinisch Westfalische Elektrizitätswerke (RWE) operated plant was responsible for over 40 per cent of electricity generated by major producers in Germany.[8] There were also plans to continue the development of nuclear power in Bavaria, and an attack on coal-fired electricity generation could have been thought a useful political weapon in that context.

Once the policy was adopted in 1983, there was considerable concern on the part of German industry, which, knowing that it would be faced with higher electricity prices, sought to persuade the German government to put forward proposals for similar measures at the European level, to ensure that German industry was not placed at a competitive disadvantage. However, it would be wrong to infer from this pressure the existence of a 'politico-industrial complex' that could adjust to domestic popular pressures by displacing costs more widely. German industry originally fought the proposed ordinance in the German administrative courts, arguing that the costs involved were disproportionate in relation to the benefits that were likely (the requirement of proportionality being a general principle of German administrative law). In this context, Europeanization looks distinctly like a second-best strategy for industry.

Nor does it follow that the sole reason for the German government seeking to Europeanize the issue is to be found in pressure from German industry. Acidification was already an international issue in the early 1980s. The Nordic countries had put it on to the international agenda in various ways but particularly through the offices of the UN Economic Commission for Europe (UNECE) and via a proposal for a convention on Long Range Trans-Boundary Air Pollution (LTRAP), established in 1979. So there was already a precedent for thinking about the issue in international terms and for seeking to impose controls at the international level in order to prevent transboundary pollution. Later in the decade the German government also sought to secure stronger international control of the North Sea, where the domestic industrial pressures were absent. So, while it would be wrong to ignore pressure from industry, it would be equally wrong to see the move purely as seeking to equalize the economic burdens of pollution control.

What happened when the issue came on to the EU agenda? In order to understand the response of other EU countries, we need to appreciate the diverse circumstances in which the different member states were placed. The sulphur dioxide and nitrogen oxide emissions between 1980 and 1990 are shown in Figures 11.1 and 11.2. It is clear that, although most countries were on a downward trend in respect of sulphur dioxide emissions during the early 1980s, their absolute positions varied enormously. Since these are figures for total national emissions, we would expect the larger countries, notably Germany, Italy, and the UK, to be the principal contributors to total emissions across all countries, as indeed they were. There is a similar divergence in respect of the figures for nitrogen oxide emissions, but in that case there is not the general downward trend that we see in the case of sulphur dioxide. What is more, with a smaller population than the other large countries, Spain had a relatively high level of sulphur dioxide emissions.

The underlying logic of the situation is clear, therefore. Unless a large emitter underwent a significant change of mind, it would have been implausible in, say, 1980 to expect much policy impetus from it to tighten standards on an international level. For large countries the problem would have been a signficant one for them to tackle, and they could always argue that emissions were on a downward trend anyway, as new investment produced cleaner and more efficient plant, so that there was no need to adopt precipitate measures. Until 1982 this expectation was borne out. Not only was there little development in the European Union, but Germany joined the UK in opposing the development of the LTRAP convention

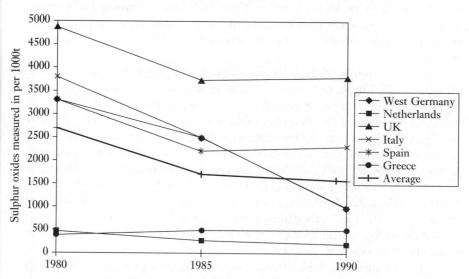

Fig. 11.1 Total emissions of sulphur oxides in member states, 1980–1990

Note: No data are available for Italy for 1990.

Source: *Europe's Environment: The Statistical Compendium to the Dobris Assessment* (Paris: Eurostat), p. 38

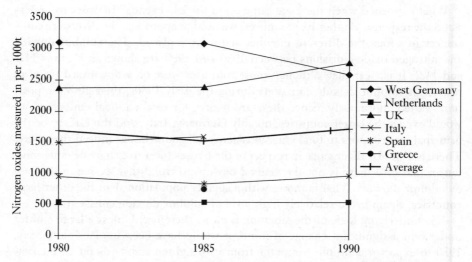

FIG. 11.2 Total emissions of nitrogen oxides in member states, 1980–1990

Note: No data was available for Italy for the year 1990. Data was available for Greece for the year 1985 only.

Source: *Europe's Environment: The Statistical Compendium to the Dobris Assessment* (Paris: Eurostat), p. 38

that the Nordic states were proposing. Conversely, once Germany had undergone its conversion, we might have expected to see opposition from the large emitters, such as the UK and Spain, after its accession in 1986, which is exactly what happened.

Within six months of the adoption of the German Large Combustion Plant Ordinance, the European Commission had produced its own draft large combustion plant directive, largely modelled on the German legislation.[9] The proposal was greeted with resistance by a number of member states, especially the UK. Within the Council a process of intergovernmental bargaining began as the government of each member state aligned behind the interest of its own industries. As the negotiations dragged on, the Commission lost considerable authority and the initiative passed to the member state holding the Council presidency at any one time, particularly in the latter stages of the negotiation, when the presidency moved in turn through the UK, the Netherlands, Denmark, and Germany. Indeed, it was the German presidency, with Klaus Töpfer in the chair, that used its authority to draw negotiations to a close in June 1988.

In order to understand the character of the bargaining process, we need to consider both the positions of the individual member states and the institutional rules under which the negotiations occurred. Nigel Haigh points out that the member states were aligned in four fairly stable groups. The first consisted of the enthusiatic countries: Germany, the Netherlands, and Denmark, the countries that comprised the core leader coalition in the 1980s. Their preference was for something like the original proposals. The second group comprised France and Belgium; both had large nuclear programmes enabling them to meet any targets quite easily, and therefore they too could accept something like the original proposals. The third group involved the UK and Italy, both of which were large emitters and so were hostile to large reductions. The fourth group included Spain and the smaller countries, most of which were relatively poor, developing quickly, and anxious to secure *increases*, if anything, in the ceilings on emissions.[10]

An important element in the disagreement among the countries concerned the scientific status of the assumptions underlying the proposal, in particular the assumption that large cuts in sulphur dioxide emissions would make a contribution to a reduction in the problems associated with acidification. Boehmer-Christiansen and Skea have described how the German government came quickly to adopt the rhetoric that linked sulphur dioxide emissions with forest death, even though there were many competing hypotheses at the time and the causal processes involved are complex and still not fully understood. Conversely, the UK government not only could see the economic disadvantages associated with the expensive retrofitting of flue-gas desulphurization equipment, but also was sensitive to the argument stemming from its own scientific advisory system that the effectiveness and efficiency of the measure were doubtful.[11]

Given the economic interests involved, particularly after the accession of Spain and Portugal in 1986, there were only five countries that were ever likely to come anywhere near supporting the original German proposal: Germany itself, Belgium, Denmark, France, and the Netherlands. Even under qualified majority voting, therefore, the measure could not have passed in its original form if member countries were at all motivated by the concern about protecting their economic self-interest. Nor, given the weakness of the consultation procedure with the Parliament, could the Parliament itself play the role, which it was to play over car exhaust emissions, of shifting the decision of the Council in a more stringent direction with respect to environmental protection. The decision process therefore consisted essentially of intergovernmental bargaining to see whether it was possible to find a revised package of measures that all countries felt that they could support.

Although the overall aim of the proposal was to secure reductions in emissions, there were a number of distinct dimensions to the draft directive that were the subject of bargaining and dispute. The first was the stringency of the overall target to be achieved. In the original draft proposal, the target for sulphur dioxide reduction was for a 60 per cent reduction in total between 1983 and 1995, but based on 1980 levels. Some member states sought to challenge that figure on the grounds that it was unrelated to any plausible hypothesis about the environmental benefits that would follow in its wake, and that it certainly would not yield environmental benefits proportionate to the costs that were involved. (These were of course the same grounds on which the ordinance had been challenged by industry in the German courts.) Second, there was the issue of the share-out of the burden of reduction among the member states. This was a matter of considerable concern to the industrially less developed countries like Ireland and Greece, as well as Spain and Portugal after their accession in 1986.

The third issue was the timetable within which the percentage reduction had to be achieved. The original proposal was for a period of twelve years. In order to make the package politically acceptable to the more sceptical or recalcitrant member states, it was always possible to adjust the period over which the reductions were called for. Fourthly, there was the stringency of the limit values as measured by the volume of pollutant per cubic metre of air emitted. Fifthly, and finally, there was the issue of the minimum size of plant to which any measures that were adopted might be applied. All these different dimensions of the proposal were brought into play at some time during the negotiations in an attempt to secure the requisite consensus. The bargaining process thus consisted of successive presidencies seeking to come up with policy proposals under each of these headings that would form a package that was acceptable to all.[12]

The opposition to the original proposal was led most forcibly by the UK. Its stance stemmed from a number of sources. As we have seen, it was a high emitter, and was heavily dependent upon coal. Moreover, of its total emissions of sulphur dioxide, a relatively high proportion (over 80 per cent in 1980) was made up of emissions from large combustion plants. Germany and the Netherlands, by contrast, produced less than 70 per cent of their sulphur dioxide emissions from large combustion plants. Thus, any strategy that sought to solve the issue of sulphur dioxide emissions by focusing on large combustion plants would have a disproportionate influence on the UK. Moreover, the implication of the measure for the UK was that flue-gas desulphurization technology would have to be fitted to existing plants, as was happening in Germany under its domestic legislation. Not only is retrofitting of equipment expensive in itself, but it would have been due to occur midway through the then investment cycle, when pay-back periods were short. Since electricity generation in the UK was owned and managed by a nationalized industry, the Central Electricity Generating Board (CEGB), whose investment showed up as expenditure in the public accounts, there was little incentive for a cost-conscious government anxious to turn public expenditure savings into income tax cuts to undertake any measures.

The above account characterizes the rationale of the UK's position solely in terms of economic self-interest, and undoubtedly there is a large measure of truth in looking at things in this way. However, there was another facet of the acidification problem that was important in the UK's position: namely, the issue of scientific uncertainty. Of course, governments may use scientific uncertainty as a fig-leaf, a way of avoiding commitments that they would prefer not to undertake for other reasons anyway.[13] However, it is striking that doubts about the soundness of the putative cause–effect relationship underlying the directive were expressed by a number of individuals and organizations in the UK environmental policy community, including the House of Lords Select Committee on the European Communities'

Environment Sub-Committee, a group not noted for being a government poodle. It is also striking that the CEGB changed its own mind about the acidification problem, leading to the retrofitting of flue-gas desulphurization equipment at Drax power station, as a result of joint research it conducted with Swedish scientists under the surface waters acidification programme, the results from which showed that sulphur from acid deposition built up in soils with serious environmental consequences.[14]

The UK's resistance to the Commission's proposal meant that no agreement had been reached by the end of 1985, even though the Commission had sought to isolate the UK by granting derogation to Greece, Ireland, and Luxembourg.[15] At this point the initiative passed to the member states chairing the Council. Firstly, the Dutch sought to modify the initial proposal in the light of 'objective criteria', which related target reductions by country to the pattern of damage that was caused. This approach abandoned the principle of uniform reductions for all countries by differentiating the targets that each had to achieve. The Dutch also introduced the idea of a two-stage reduction timetable, proposing a 45 per cent reduction by 1995 and the original 60 per cent reduction by 2005 in the overall targets.

In the latter half of 1986 the UK took these principles further, differentiating the targets still further and specifying variable percentage reductions for each country for 2005. They also suggested a 100 MW threshold for plant to which the measures should apply and a sliding scale of emission limits for plants between 100 and 300 MW. Then the Belgians, in the early part of 1987, went back to uniform emission limits, though modified in various ways, and most importantly introduced the idea of three target stages: 1993, 1998, and 2005. Denmark in late 1987 made further concessions to the smaller states, but also introduced a target for 2010 in place of the 2005 target. In early 1988 the Germans, anxious to wrap the issue up, modified the 2010 target back to 2005, and proposed leaving open for future decision some technical matters, such as the permissible sulphur dioxide limits for plants between 50 and 100 MW. It is generally agreed by observers that the UK had an incentive to agree to a directive in the light of the impending privatization of electricity and the consequent need to remove uncertaintly for investors. An amendment to the directive, originally proposed in 1992 and agreed in 1994, tidied up the outstanding technical issues left over from the 1988 directive.

The 1988 agreement is noteworthy in a number of respects for what it tells us about the policy and political process. Firstly, in terms of the international politics of the environment in the 1980s, it captured one major theme, namely the contrast between two overall approaches to environmental policy, symbolized by the opposition between the UK and Germany. In part, this was a difference in the willingness of the two respective governments to see costly measures put in place, a difference that in turn related to the perception by some German policymakers that Germany's traditional industrial strength in engineering could be put to good advantage in a world in which the demand for pollution control opened up new markets on an international scale. In this sense, Germany, along with other countries like the Netherlands,[16] could be viewed as proponents of ecological modernization, whereas the UK could be viewed as enmeshed in the old paradigm of environment versus economic growth.

The dispute about the directive also encapsulated a difference of conflicting national regulatory styles, symbolized as well by the contrast between Germany and the UK. The German style in respect of air pollution control was to favour the application of uniform emission limits to particular processes. Although not technology-forcing in the strict sense of requiring particular items of equipment, it is an approach that can, if the limits are sufficiently tight, foreclose on all but a few technological options. Ironically, the traditional UK approach in the field of air control had the potential to be explicitly technology-forcing, since under the legislation that prevailed in the 1980s regulators had to apply the test of 'best practicable means' to the setting of standards. In practice, however, this technology-forcing aspect of the regulatory approach was never a serious element, since it was offset by the discretion the inspectorates had to vary emission requirements by locality.

We thus see in the traditional German and UK approaches two poles of the contrast between forms of regulation in which standards are applied uniformly and those in which they are applied with maximum discretion. In terms of the content of the directive, this contrast shows up in the way that new plant is distinguished from old. With respect to standards for new plant, the German approach was dominant. Although emission values were allowed to vary by size of plant, with smaller plants being allowed higher levels of emissions of sulphur dioxide, all plants of a given size had to operate with the same emission values wherever they were located. The situation is different for larger plant, however, and this is of course by far and away the larger category. Here the constraint is specified in terms of plans for overall national targets; and in the development of the plans member states are free to vary the stringency of emissions standards applied to any particular plant as much as they wish. The fact that there is a national plan means that discretion will be constrained by the need to conform to targets that apply to the sum of individual plant emissions, so that in this sense the national plan targets function as a 'bubble'. But within the bubble, there is a great deal of freedom of manoeuvre.

The national plans also highlight another feature of the process, namely the extent to which the EU's system of multi-level governance can reinforce, rather than erode, the power and standing of the nation state. The indispensable and privileged space of the member states was seen in the process of bargaining that led to the 1988 directive, and interestingly, the Commission did not gain strength from a situation in which the member states were deeply divided. However, the position of the member states was also reinforced by the content of the directive itself. National reduction plans place the governments of the member states in the centre of the process. Those governments are forced to confront the problems to which the international targets give rise. But at the same time, this may well involve consolidating and strengthening their own institutions of policy, as happened in the UK for example with the passing of the 1990 Environmental Protection Act, a result in large part of the need to deal with EU air pollution directives. Thus, the internationalization of pollution control in the EU does not of itself imply a diminishing role for the member states.

However, the effect on the member states is likely to be positive in this way only when there is a well developed institutionalization of policy. For instance, in Greece all commercial air polluting activities, from a small bakery to a large industrial plant, are obliged to undertake environmental impact studies and to apply for a licence at the prefectural office of the Environment and Public Works Ministry. But this has led to a chronic overload of work, and because of a shortage of staff authorizations can take a long time and inspections only rarely take place. Where administrative capacity is underdeveloped in this way, the effects of complex regulatory instruments like the large combustion plant directive may not work to strengthen the state.

Even if we say, however, that the internationalization of pollution control brings the EU to the fore, this is not to say that the EU is the only important international body, as the 1979 Convention on Long-Range Transboundary Air Pollution (LTRAP) goes to show. In 1984 a protocol was agreed under this convention establishing the European Monitoring and Evaluation Programme (EMEP) to cover the costs of international centres taking part in research and the exchange of information on transboundary pollutants, in particular sulphur dioxide and nitrogen oxides. LTRAP also became important in the EU policy developments that followed the 1988 directive. In order to appreciate this importance, we need to consider the conceptual basis on which the problem of air pollution control is built.

So far we have largely presented the issue of sulphur dioxide and nitrogen oxides control as an air pollution issue, in which the main policy goal is to prevent harmful emissions into the atmosphere. However, as noted at the beginning of the chapter, although excessive atmospheric concentrations of sulphur dioxide and nitrogen oxides have harmful effects, particularly on human health, the pollution arising from emissions is not restricted solely to the atmosphere. Acid deposition damages freshwater, soils, and buildings. The control of sulphur dioxide and nitrogen oxides, therefore, should really be thought of in the context of acidification 'in the round'. The task of a control policy can be viewed as the reduction or elimination of a problem that produces a range of different forms of damage.

The institutional framework of the LTRAP convention provided the context in which the intellectual move of reconceptualizing sulphur and nitrogen oxide emissions as the origin of a problem for all three environmental media (air, water, soil) could take place. Much also appears to have been borrowed from the development of thinking in Dutch policy discourse, through the involvement of the Dutch public health and environmental research institute, RIVM, in the work of LTRAP. The LTRAP work also developed the idea of 'critical loads' into the international policy discourse. A critical load is defined as the 'highest level of pollution which will not cause permanent harm to the environment'.[17] In the context of acidification, the approach via the notion of critical loads suggests that it is important to measure the extent to which the deposition of acidifying substances exceeds some particular figure.

The influence of this line of thinking can be seen directly in the Fifth Action Programme.[18] There the objective is set out as to prevent exceeding the critical load for acidifying substances, and this objective is taken to imply more stringent standards beyond those already agreed to date. This line of thinking was reinforced in December 1995, when the Swedish government was the initiator in asking the Commission to develop a strategy to deal with acidification. First presented in January 1997, the draft strategy showed the influence of the large combustion plant directive and also revealed the extent to which the nature and form of the policy discussion are transformed by being placed in the broader context of acidification and the continuing work under LTRAP.[19]

In terms of the use of instruments developed in the context of the large combustion plant directive, the clearest influence is seen in the way in which the strategy makes use of the tool of setting national reduction plans. Each member state is assumed to have responsibility for ensuring that critical loads are not exceeded.[20] In 1994 the signatories to LTRAP had adopted the Oslo protocol, which obliged ratifying states to reduce sulphur dioxide emissions even further than they had already done in order to ensure that acid deposition was closer to the estimated critical load. This was the so-called 'gap closure' approach. In the context of the EU, national plans have become the device by which the Commission proposes to member states that the gap be closed between existing performance and desired performance.

The complication that arises from this transformation of the policy approach, however, is that the development of policy necessarily moves from an independent consideration of the merits of a particular policy measure to a consideration of the interrelationship of the various sources that contribute to the incidence of critical loads being exceeded. In other words, not only do policy-makers have to consider emission limits for one source, say stationary combustion plants, but they also have to consider any such limit in the light of other measures, say the permissible levels of sulphur in liquid fuel oil. (We shall see how this becomes an issue in connection with the regulation of car exhaust emissions.) Indeed, the extent of interrelationship goes even further; in March 1997 the Commission was not able to present the Council with nitrogen oxide targets under the acidification programme, since those targets depended on work also being done on low-level ozone.[21]

However, on top of all these complications, the chief effect of introducing the critical loads approach has been significantly to increase the pressure for even more stringent targets on acidifying emissions beyond 2003. In March 1997, on the basis of critical loads analysis, the Commission presented the Council with targets that were even tighter than those that had previously been suggested. In discussions on Commission proposals for revising the 1988 directive, all member states thought the targets infeasible, and even Sweden was led to question that aspect of the strategy that involved setting sectoral targets.[22] The 1997 targets also proposed moving the base year for comparison from 1980 to 1990, leading many of the greener states, in an unconscious and ironic echo of the UK in the 1980s, to say that they were being penalized for having met earlier reduction goals. The chief difficulty is that there is no obvious technological fix, no matter how expensive, that will deliver the requisite targets in the way that flue-gas desulphurization did in the 1980s.

How are we to evaluate the development of EU air pollution policy in the wake of the large combustion plant directive? A number of preliminary points are worth making. Firstly, it is clear that, as policy development has taken place, so a reconceptualization of the problem has occurred. In place of the end-of-pipe policy implied by the imposition of flue-gas desulphurization technology, policy-makers now think in terms of the effects of pollution and the various sources of those effects. Neither the Commission nor the EU's broader policy system was responsible for the intellectual innovation that made this approach practicable, namely the concept of critical loads. Instead, that innovation had to come from policy-makers outside the EU's system of environmental governance. It is also clear, however, that the reconceptualization was part of a broader stream of thinking among European environmental policy elites, particularly exemplified in the approach of the Dutch National Environmental Policy Plan.

None of this means that a supranational policy system has supplanted national governments. Policy development at the EU level still needs national champions, whether it be the German government in 1983 or the Swedish government in 1995. Champions also need allies within the Council of Ministers. And the implementation of something as ambitious as national reduction plans requires considerable administrative and technical capacity. This is not quite the European rescue of the nation state, but it is a reminder that multi-level governance is an enduring feature of the EU. Moreover, as policy has developed, so the old tension between environmental protection on the one hand and economic/technical feasibility on the other has reasserted itself. We shall see a similar dynamic at work in the case of car exhaust emissions.

DIRECTIVES ON CAR EXHAUST EMISSIONS

Transport now contributes significantly to air pollution and to the problems associated with acidification more generally. The importance of its contribution to environmental problems can be seen, for example, in the contrasting patterns of sulphur dioxide and nitrogen oxides emissions (Figures 11.1 and 11.2). The former are largely the product of stationary sources, and fell significantly in the 1980s and 1990s as a result of measures like the large combustion plant directive and similar measures adopted at national level. By contrast, nitrogen oxide emissions, many of which are generated by transport, have remained stable or risen as more cars and an increasing number of journeys make their effects felt. Moreover, oxides of nitrogen are not the only form of pollution that transport is responsible for—significant other pollutants include carbon monoxide, hydrocarbons, volatile organics compounds, particulates, and carbon dioxide. The effects of these pollutants are felt at a number of levels. Transport emissions contribute to poor air quality in many cities in Europe. They also contribute to the formation of tropospheric ozone, which is not only a health hazard but also adversely affects visibility on warm sunny days. And emissions of carbon dioxide also contribute to the volume of greenhouse gases.

Although passenger cars are not the only form of transport causing pollution, we shall concentrate in this section on the development of measures solely in relation to passenger vehicles. This is partly on grounds of economy. There are many directives covering light and heavy goods vehicles, public transport vehicles, farm vehicles and the like, and we lack the space to cover them all. However, the development of measures seeking to control passenger vehicles has been interesting in itself and is illustrative of some broader developments in the multi-level policy-making process of the European Union. Moreover, there is an argument for saying that the very familiarity of the car provides a good test case for examining how pollution can be dealt with (or not) from the paradigmatic symbol of modern affluence.

In principle, there are two ways of controlling pollution from cars, leaving aside measures to modify behaviour such as persuading people to use their cars less or drive more slowly on motorways.[23] The first is to control the content of the fuel that is used; the second is to specify maximum emission levels, with the implication that there has to be some redesign of the combustion or exhaust system. EU environmental policy has traditionally acted on both. Since 1975 there has been a directive, sometimes strengthened, that has limited the sulphur content of car fuel oil (though not the heavier fuel used in power stations and other large plant). Since 1970 there have also been directives that have limited the emissions of various pollutants from vehicles. These two approaches are not entirely distinct, even conceptually. The type of emission limits it is sensible to impose depends in part upon the type of fuel that is being burnt; for example, different limits in the various directives on emissions apply to petrol and to diesel. However, the two approaches, via control of fuel imputs or via restrictions on outputs, can be distinguished, and for much of the period of EU environmental policy have been dealt with separately. As we shall see, it is an important feature of the politics of the policy-making process that these two approaches to pollution control came together in the 1990s.

The evolution of policy and the development of policy approaches shows many continuities over time, and any attempt to impose a sense of periodization is arbitrary. Nevertheless, it is useful to divide the history of vehicle pollution control into three phases:

1. the period up to 1983, when policy towards car emissions was seen primarily as a problem of harmonization according to the principles of a single market;

2. the period 1983–9, during which there was a 'ecologization' of emissions legislation in Europe;
3. the period 1989–98, when there was a working out of the ecological perspective.

Simplifying greatly, we can say that the three stages mark an increasing commitment towards controlling the adverse environmental effects of cars. During the
last period came the point at which the logic of the conventional approach was finally
inverted, and policy-makers began their analysis with the effects and started to work
back to the causes, just as happened in the case of emissions from stationary sources.
This last stage raises intriguing and as yet unanswerable questions about the future
direction of policy, but may yet prove to be the most significant.

1. The period up to 1983

Control of car emissions can be regarded as an early example of EU environmental
policy, with the first measure being adopted in 1970 (70/220/EEC) in a directive
that imposed limits on emissions of carbon monoxide and hydrocarbons from a
wide range of petrol vehicles. However, the thinking behind the directive was as
much to do with the single market as it was to do with the environment.[24] The
objective of the directive was to prevent the standards imposed by member states
becoming barriers to trade, and it was adopted only after France and Germany
had themselves adopted standards likely to hinder EU trade.[25] Accordingly, the
operative principle of the directive was mutual recognition within the framework
of modest uniform emission standards, and any vehicle that met the minimum standards had 'type approval' and could not be excluded from any national market.[26]

Although a permissive regime, this early phase of policy did exhibit two features that were to become important elements of the institutional process later.
The first was that the standards at issue were defined within the framework of
UNECE, a body that included not only east and west Europe, but also Canada
and the United States. The EU's own decision-making process was therefore nested
in that of a wider international regime, the original purpose of which was the economic reconstruction of Europe after the war. The second aspect of the early policy
developments that was to have long-term significance was to be found precisely
in the fact that the measures did have a single market rationale. This implied that
the issue of car exhaust emissions would be seen after the passing of the Single
European Act as one of those environmental policies that none the less had a clear
relationship to the single market, with all that would imply about the decision-
making process.

2. The 1983–9 period

As with a number of other significant environmental policy developments in the
1980s, the impetus to strengthen controls on car exhaust emissions began with
Germany. The background was the same popular concern about air pollution and

forest damage that had led to pressure for the passing of the large combustion plant directive. In 1983 the minister responsible for environmental affairs, the interior minister Dr Zimmermann, announced, apparently on his own initiative, that all cars marketed in Germany by 1 January 1989 would meet the standards on emissions that prevailed in the United States, the so-called US 83 standards.[27]

The significance of this announcement needs to be understood in the context of the three main technical engineering possibilities of the time.[28] The first was a change in engine design, to produce the so-called 'lean burn' engine, using fuel more efficiently and reducing emissions of carbon monoxide, nitrogen oxides, and hydrocarbons. The objection to this option was that the lean burn engine was only at the developmental stage at the time, so that there would be a delay in tightening emission standards. The second possibility was to fit an oxydization catalyst to models in order to capture some of the polluting gases before emission. The objection to this alternative was that it was not especially effective and did nothing to reduce nitrogen dioxide emissions. The third possibility was the three-way catalytic converter. This reduced emissions of carbon dioxide, hydrocarbons, and nitrogen oxides and was available as a workable technical option. It was therefore the only alternative capable of enabling cars to meet US 83 standards in anything like the period of time envisaged in Zimmermann's announcement.

The logic of the situation has been well explained by Henning Arp.[29] Once a powerful actor wanted more stringent standards, the context of the single market made it inevitably an issue for the EU. Just as the permissive regime of mutual recognition had arisen in the early 1970s in order to forestall the erection of barriers to trade after the first postwar upsurge in environmental concern, so there was a need to deal with the single market implications of the German desire for stricter emissions. Moreover, within Germany officials were conscious of another, related, problem. Cars fitted with three-way catalytic converters had to run on unleaded petrol, and German tourists in southern Europe would be stranded unless there was a European element to this emission reduction method.[30]

Within a matter of months of the German announcement, in June 1984, the Commission had put forward a proposal (COM(84) 226 OJ) aimed at establishing common EU-wide rules. Moreover, in a logic reminiscent of that in the USA in the late 1960s, when individual states began to contemplate rules on emissions, it became clear to manufacturers that, if there was going to be a tightening of rules, it would have to be Europe-wide.[31]

In order to understand the politics of the subsequent decision process, it is important to see the implications of adopting three-way catalyst technology. Not only are catalysts important in themselves, they also require electronic fuel injection in place of the conventional carburettor, thus leading to extra costs associated with the redesign of models. These costs fall disproportionately on different types of vehicle manufacturers, with makers of the larger and more expensive cars finding it easier to absorb or pass on the costs than makers of smaller vehicles.[32] Smaller vehicle manufacturers could therefore argue that environmental benefits were being bought at a relatively high cost, and they could also point to the adverse environmental consequences of the three-way catalyst, including the need to dispose, at the end of their life, of the heavy metals (nickel and chromium) they contained.

However, the uneven impact on manufacturers of different sizes of car was not the whole story. The manufacturers themselves were unevenly distributed among the member states. Makers of the larger and more prestigious vehicles (for example Mercedes or BMW) were concentrated in Germany, whereas makers of the small cars were disproportionately to be found in France, Italy, and the UK. Super-imposed on the conflict between different types of manufacturer, therefore, was a conflict of national identities, with some firms being regarded as national 'champions'. These differences fed through to the negotiating positions of member states within the Council of Ministers. The Commission's proposals had in effect phased in the introduction of US 83 standards in two stages by 1995. In the Council meeting in 1985, these proposals were modified by the introduction of a distinc-tion between vehicles falling into three categories: those with a capacity of less than 1.4 litres; those with between 1.4 and 2 litres; and those vehicles with over 2 litres' capacity. The supposed basis of this distinction was the argument that the meas-ures needed to accord with the equivalent effect that different sizes of car had on the environment.

However, although this amendment was acceptable to many members of the Council, it was not acceptable to either Denmark, which thought that the proposed standards were too lax, or Greece, which wished to use its veto to bargain for more funds for development. The line-up of states, therefore, ran from the least enthu-siastic for the swift introduction of stringent standards (the UK, Italy, and France), all of which had domestic manufacturers of small cars to consider, through Ger-many and the Netherlands, which could live with the compromise as a way of improving on the status quo, to Denmark and Greece, which, with no domestic manufacturers to consider, were prepared to hold out for the most stringent stand-ards, even at the risk of jeopardizing any advance at all.

This deadlock was broken by the coming into force of the Single European Act in 1987, which allowed the Council of Ministers to make decisions on items of single market legislation according to the principle of qualified majority voting. In December 1987 the Council agreed a directive (88/76/EEC), which in effect applied the Commission's first-stage emission limits, but distinguished according to the three categories of capacity. That still left, however, the determination of the second-stage limits. In February 1988 the Commission introduced its proposals. In its first reading in September the European Parliament thought that these pro-posals did not go far enough for small cars and voted for US 83 standards instead. The Commission rejected these amendments and in December 1988 the Council adopted the Commission's position by a qualified majority. It was this measure that went to the European Parliament in April 1989 for its second reading.

It was at this stage that the other important institutional reform introduced by the Single European Act came into its own. Under the Single European Act, the cooperation procedure was introduced between the Council and the Parliament. Under this procedure the Parliament was entitled to amend a draft item of legislation adopted by the Council, and if it was against certain measures contained therein the Council could reject the amendment only by a unanimous decision. The logic of the game played under these rules was therefore complex. In the event, the Parliament decided at its second reading to require US 83 standards for all vehicles, irrespective of capacity, by 1992. Sending the measure back to the Council in this revised form, the Council then came down on the side of the Parliament's proposal.

How did it come about that a 'weak' parliament could exercise such strong powers? In part, the answer to this question depends, as Tsebelis has explained, on the logic of the decision rules.[33] According to the cooperation procedure, if the Council wished to reaffirm its original decision, then it had to do so by unanimity, even if the original decision had been taken by qualified majority vote. So, with a majority in the Council in favour of a move from the status quo, the Parliament could pull the whole Council further in the direction of stronger environmental measures than the Council on its own would go by presenting amendments to the Council's agreed position. It did this, in effect, by presenting the majority in the Council with a stark alternative: either some movement would be accepted in the direction the Parliament wished, or the status quo would prevail. Faced with such a choice, the majority on the Council preferred a change to a reversion to the status quo, thus conceding to the Parliament.

The logic of this explanation has been questioned, however.[34] The argument is that we cannot understand why the policy outcome should have been as it was unless we assume either a preference change on the part of one of the Council members, or a preference change on the part of the Commission, or a change in the character of the status quo, the so-called 'reversionary point'. Hubschmid and Moser themselves argue that the third possibility was the one that pertained, and in particular that the ECJ's decision in the Danish bottles case meant that the potential status quo would revert to one in which member states could impose unilateral restrictions on vehicle emissions.[35] Such a possibility cannot be entirely discounted, but it does require that a great deal of significance had been attached by the actors to a particular decision, the exact implications of which were unclear. To be sure, the underlying logic as set out by Tsebelis is unlikely to be the whole story; none the less, it makes a great deal of sense of what would otherwise be obscure. In effect, he offers the theoretical explanation of what seasoned observers like Nigel Haigh have inferred from experience: following the Single European Act, 'the Commission and the Parliament acting together can put considerable pressure on the Council, since it can only change a revised proposal by unanimity'.[36]

There were other points of complexity as well. There was a great deal of negotiation with the Commission before a text emerged that the Council could agree to.[37] It has also been argued that in practice the European Parliament's amendments were not so serious.[38] Some point to the fact that French manufacturers, who had opposed the stringent standards, were adapting their production processes anyway, so that the need to defend the interests of French makers of small vehicles was correspondingly reduced.[39] However, if true, perhaps a further lesson can be drawn. Legislative systems that rest upon a strong version of the principle of the separation of powers are often slow to make decisions. It can be argued that the measure went through in the form that it did because the slowness of the legislative procedure gave interested parties time to adjust their behaviour and expectations.

3. The 1989–98 period

The upshot of these developments was that by 1989 the development of policy on car exhaust emissions had reached the point where single market concerns had been transcended by environmental concerns. A small, but significant, range of pollutants were subject to control, including carbon monoxide, hydrocarbons, and nitrogen oxides, with the permissible limits of the last two being stated jointly. Manufacturers had wanted common standards, but the only way to account for the stringency of the standards finally adopted was to place them in the context of the incentives to parliamentarians to pass strong measures combined with the opportunities they possessed under the institutional changes introduced by the Single European Act.

Despite these developments, the form and nature of the regulation was in many ways conventional. The precedent had already been set in 1970, albeit for a very limited range of pollutants. Moreover, the stringency of the standards was not especially marked. After all, Europe was legislating in 1989 for standards to come into effect for 1992 based on US standards that were formulated under powers originally determined in 1970 and updated in 1977.[40]

The following nine years can be viewed in some ways as the continuation of this pattern and style. However, the period contained two new and significant elements. The first was an innovative strategy for the setting of standards known as the Auto/Oil Project. The second was a reconceptualization of the problem of car emissions within the context of a more general approach to the problem of acidification, as had also taken place with emissions from stationary sources. Approaching the problem of car emissions within the context of a plan for acidification inverted the logic of the traditional policy-making. Instead of focusing on the regulation of the causes of pollution, and on what was a feasible technical improvement from that point of view, the focus was first on the effects and on what alterations to the causes were necessary to improve the situation. Although the logic of this inversion still has to work itself out, it promises to be significant. However, before examining the changes, we need first to look at the continuities.

In 1989 the Commission started on the follow-up work to 89/458. In December 1991 the Council accepted the Commission's proposals from that follow-up, which required all new model cars to meet US 83 standards by 31 July 1992 and all new cars to do so by the end of 1992. The European Parliament had threatened to repeat its uncompromising stand of 1989 and press for even tougher standards, but in the end it backed down in the face of industry lobbying.

A tussle between the Council and the Parliament was to take place in 1994, however, by which time the rules of the game had once again been changed by the Maastricht Treaty, which came into force in 1993. Under Article 130s of the treaty, decisions on general objectives, such as the setting of emissions standards, were to be taken according to the co-decision procedure. Under this procedure, a measure goes in the first instance to both the Council and the Parliament. The Council adopts a position taking into account any modifications suggested by the Parliament that it deems fit. The measure adopted by the Council then goes to the full European Parliament. If the measure is rejected by a simple majority of the Parliament, the matter is referred to a Conciliation Committee, comprising twelve representatives each of the Council and the Parliament. It should be borne in mind that the default position in case of non-agreement at this stage is reversion to the status quo.

The draft directive that had come before the Council was to implement stricter 'second-stage' limits from 1996, as required by 91/441. It also required the Commission to come forward before the end of 1994 with proposals for controls applying after 2000. In the first reading the European Parliament had suggested a number of amendments, but none were incorporated into the common position of the Council. On 16 February 1994 the Environment Committee of the Parliament decided that it wanted all the amendments reinstated. These included separate standards for hydrocarbons and nitrogen oxides, specific limits on carbon dioxide emissions, and an extended testing period for the life of the vehicle.[41] However, under intensive lobbying from industry and a warning from the Commission that the measure might be lost entirely, the full Parliament on 9 March rejected the recommendations of the Environment Committee.[42]

Although the process of attempting to strengthen emissions standards between 1989 and 1994 was an extension of the existing approach to the problem of car emissions, the car industry in particular began to feel that developments were moving too fast from its point of view. As the manufacturers saw it, achieving emissions limits was too costly and was disproportionate to the environmental benefits that it would bring. Behind this thinking lay a number of different elements. One was the obvious trend in Europe towards the rapid strengthening of emissions standards, particularly as seen against the background of the 1990 US Clean Air Act. Another was the recognition that newly promulgated WHO air quality targets would require a cut in emissions, and that this would need to be achieved in the most cost-effective way.

The concrete outcome of this thinking was the establishment of the Auto/Oil Project. This was a tripartite research project between the car and oil industries on the one hand and the Commission on the other. It thus involved Europia, as the representative body for the European oil industry, and ACEA, the Association of European Car Manufacturers. From the Commission's point of view, the advantage of the Auto/Oil Project was that it reflected the dominant mood of interest in a 'soft law' approach to regulation and experiments with the use of instruments. From the oil and car industries' point of view, the initiative made sense, in part because of the two ways in which air pollution from vehicles can be regulated—via fuel standards or via emissions standards. There was an incentive on each to ensure that the costs of regulation did not bear down too heavily on either. The project itself consisted of an £8 million joint research programme between the oil and car industries to look at the most effective way of regulating emissions, with complementary research conducted by the Commission on the maintenance of air quality in Athens, Cologne, The Hague, London, Lyons, Madrid, and Milan.[43]

The consultation involved in the Auto/Oil Project took some four years, but the reception of the legislative proposals issued does not suggest that it was a success. On 19 June 1996 the Commission put forward proposals for reductions in emissions by the year 2000 of between 20 and 40 per cent for major pollutants; by 2005 it envisaged indicative reductions of 50–70 per cent, provided that the necessary technology could be developed in time. Proposals for reductions in the pollutant content of fuel oil, by contrast, were relatively modest and had significantly lower cost implications for the refineries than for the car manufacturers. Whereas the estimated costs in respect of passenger cars was envisaged to be 4.1 billion ECU, the costs to the refining industry were expected to be only 766 million ECU.[44]

Not surprisingly, the motor industry was strongly opposed to the proposals, though its position was somewhat undermined by the fact that they had emerged from the Auto/Oil Project itself, where the argument was that the most cost-effective way of securing improvements in air quality was by a reduction in emissions rather than by improvements in fuel quality. The Commission's proposal also contained important provisions about on-board diagnostic devices to ensure that the catalytic equipment was working satisfactorily.

The draft directive came under the co-decision procedure and so went on first reading to both the Parliament and the Council. The Parliament not only confirmed in its first reading important elements of the Commission's plan, but in some respects strengthened them, in particular insisting on tougher standards for the sulphur content of fuel oil, and making mandatory the indicative 2005 standards for both emissions and fuel oil content.

The position of the Council was affected by the views of various member states. The Dutch government, which held the presidency, took a strong line on the sulphur content of fuel oils, proposing a limit of 50 p.p.m. for both petrol and diesel. (This at least suggests that its oil refining industry, which traditionally has a great deal of influence with Dutch governments on these matters, did not see such limits as a threat.) In this tough stance it was supported by the Nordic countries, some of which were used to a regime in which the sulphur content of fuel oils was much lower. (In Sweden for example 90 per cent of petrol sold has a sulphur content of only 10 p.p.m.)[45] The new UK Labour government also supported tougher

TABLE 11.1 *Positions taken on the setting of emission and fuel oil limits*
(a) *Fuel oil content*

	Comm. proposal	Leader states	Council agreed		EP		Final	
			2000	2005	2000	2005	2000	2005
Petrol sulphur	200	50	150	50	50	30	150	50
Diesel sulphur	350	50	350	50[a]	100	50	350	50

(b) *Emission Limits*

	Existing	Proposed, 2000	Indicative, 2005
Petrol cars			
CO	2.7	2.3	1.00
HC	0.341	0.20	1.00
NO_x	0.252	0.15	0.08
Diesel			
CO	1.06	0.64	0.50
$HC+NO_x$	0.71	0.56	0.30
NO_x	0.566	0.5	0.25
Particulates	0.08	0.05	0.025

[a] Indicative limits only.
Source: *ENDS Reports*, no. 257, p. 42; no. 269, pp. 43–4; no. 277, p. 44; no. 281, p. 48.

standards than those implied by the Commission's proposals, although whether it was explicitly taking its cue from a report by the Royal Commission on Environmental Pollution, which had also suggested lowering the limit, is not clear. When it came to making a decision in June 1997, the Council toughened the standards on the sulphur content of fuel oil, but not to such a high standard as the Parliament. It squared the cohesion countries who were worried about the costs of the measures by agreeing a provision for derogations to be allowed in particular cases. The main positions of the various parties are summarized in Table 11.1.

In April 1998 the European Parliament voted in plenary session to uphold its tougher standards against the position of the Council, and, by contrast with 1994, the matter had to go to the conciliation procedure. In that process the Parliament conceded on the stringency of standards, but the Council conceded on the question of their status after 2005, agreeing to make them mandatory. It also conceded to the Parliament on the issue of on-board diagnostics. Once again, the Parliament had pushed the European legislative process to the limit. An important element in the decision-making process appears to have been the lobbying, particularly of the Parliament, undertaken by the car industry, unhappy at having to bear what it saw as a disproportionte share of the costs of reducing air pollution. The new process of standard-setting that had been implied in the Auto/Oil Project ended in a form of legislative standard-setting in which a representative body takes it upon itself to legislate for high technical standards of pollution control—behaviour that is not dissimilar to that of the US Congress.

CONCLUSIONS

What features of the EU's evolving system of multi-level environmental governance do the cases of these air pollution directives illustrate?

It should be clear from our story that, though air pollution control is now well institutionalized in the EU, member states are still important and in many ways occupy a privileged place in the system of decision-making. This is not to say that member states are always decisive, as the conflicts between the Council and the Parliament in 1989 and 1998 over vehicle emissions go to show. However, it is impossible to understand the policy-making process without recognizing the prominent role that the member states play, both in the determination of policy and in the protection of what are taken to be important national economic interests. The role of the leader countries remains important, both in putting issues on the policy agenda and in insisting that high standards are legislated. Conversely, when proposed standards seem too high, as appeared in the Commission's proposals for controlling acidifying emissions from stationary sources, the member states in Council can effectively prevent the measures from being implemented.

However, though distinctively important, member states are not solely important. Much depends upon the institutional opportunities that are given to the Parliament in particular. The relationship between Parliament and Council is one of the separation of powers, albeit on an unequal basis. In this context, it is interesting to see MEPs functioning like legislators in the USA, insisting on tangible technical fixes for pollution problems according to timetables that they wish to specify. MEPs have not had an opportunity to debate emissions from stationary sources in a legislative context. In the USA, however, Congress has behaved in similar ways in respect of stationary sources as it has done over mobile sources, requiring serious emissions reductions according to legislated timetables. Perhaps there is a set of incentives established in separation-of-power systems that provides a motive for this behaviour.

It is also clear that the origins of air pollution are to be found in single market concerns rather than in transboundary flows of pollutants. Acidification is a problem on a continental scale, but the development of the 'critical loads' approach, though latterly imported into the conceptualization of EU policy-making, took place in the context of a quite distinct international regime. Both the problem of large combustion plants and that of the control of vehicle emissions have been transformed by being placed in the context of the critical loads approach, which suggests that the optimism about the complementarity of economic growth and environmental protection in the 1980s may have been overstated. The very stringent emissions limits that the critical loads analysis suggests imply costly measures for all EU countries. The EU is not the regime in which the major policy thinking and analysis have been conducted, even if it has provided the forum in which important binding decisions are made.

NOTES TO CHAPTER 11

1. A. C. Pigou, *The Economics of Welfare* (London: Macmillan, 1952, 4th edn), p. 184.
2. See P. Hall *et al.*, *Change, Choice and Conflict in Social Policy* (London: Heinemann, 1975), pp. 375–6.
3. In June 1982 a group from the Institute for Terrestial Ecology published a report in *Nature* claiming that acidity levels in Britain were comparable to those causing fish death in Scandinavia. See M. Hajer, *The Politics of Environmental Discourse* (Oxford: Clarendon Press, 1995), p. 108. Reports continued in subsequent years; see e.g. 'Acid Rain Damage to SSSIs', *ENDS Report*, 213 (1992), pp. 7–8.
4. Country report: Greece, *European Environmental Law Review*, October 1994, p. 286.
5. N. Haigh, *Manual of Environmental Policy: The EC and Britain* (London: Cartermill International, 1992 and subs. rev.), p. 6.10–3.
6. E. Müller, *Innenwelt der Umweltpolitik* (Opladen: Westdeutscher Verlag, 1986), p. 295.
7. D. Liefferink, *Environment and the Nation State: The Netherlands, The EU and Acid Rain* (Manchester: Manchester University Press, 1996), p. 117.
8. Calculated from S. Boehmer-Christiansen, *The Politics of Environment and Acid Rain in the Federal Republic of Germany*, SPRU Occasional Paper Series no. 29 (Brighton: Science Policy Research Unit, 1989), table 8, p. 57.
9. See S. A. Boehmer-Christiansen and J. Skea, *Acid Politics* (London: Belhaven Press, 1991), p. 234.
10. Haigh, *Manual*, p. 6.10–4.
11. See Boehmer-Christiansen and Skea, *Acid Politics*, pp. 206–10, and, in particular, Hajer, *Politics of Environmental Discourse*, pp. 112–17, on what he terms the 'traditional–pragmatist story line'.
12. Boehmer-Christiansen and Skea, *Acid Politics*, pp. 239–42.
13. S. Boehmer-Christiansen, 'Black Mist and Acid Rain: Science as a Fig Leaf of Policy', *Political Quarterly*, 59: 2 (1988), pp. 145–60.
14. A. Weale, T. O'Riordan, and L. Kramme, *Controlling Pollution in the Round* (London: Anglo-German Foundation, 1991), citing evidence from the CEGB to the House of Commons Select Committee on the Environment.
15. Boehmer-Christiansen and Skea, *Acid Politics*, p. 239.
16. See Hajer, *Politics of Environmental Discourse*; A. Weale, *The New Politics of Pollution* (Manchester and New York: Manchester University Press, 1992), ch. 3.
17. *Dictionary of Ecology and the Environment* (Teddington: Peter Collins, 1988), *sub* 'critical'.
18. Commission of the European Communities, *Towards Sustainability: A European Community Programme of Policy and Action in Relation to the Environment and Sustainable*

Development, COM (92) 23 final (Luxembourg: Commission of the European Communities, 1992), pp. 42–6.

19. 'EC Move on Acidification Leaves UK Strategy Adrift', *ENDS Report*, 264 (1997), pp. 37–8.
20. Haigh, *Manual*, p. 6.2–2.
21. 'Acidification Plan Spells End for High-Sulphur Fuel Oil', *ENDS Report*, 266 (1997), pp. 40–1.
22. See 'Row over Combustion Plant Spells Trouble for Acidification Plan', *ENDS Report*, 268 (1997), pp. 40–1 and 'Ministers Hold Fire on Climate, Reach Compromise on Landfills', *ENDS Report*, 275 (1997), pp. 41–2 at 42.
23. Haigh, *Manual*, p. 6.8–2.
24. Ibid. 6.8–2.
25. H. Arp, 'Technical Regulation and Politics: The Interplay between Economic Interests and Environmental Policy Goals in EC Car Emission Legislation', in J. D. Liefferink, P. D. Lowe, and A. P. J. Mol (eds.), *European Integration and Environmental Policy* (London and New York: Belhaven Press, 1993) pp. 150–71 at 152.
26. Haigh, *Manual*, p. 6.8–2.
27. Boehmer-Christiansen, *Politics of Environment and Acid Rain*, p. 2.
28. Arp, 'Technical Regulation and Politics', pp. 157–60.
29. Ibid. 153.
30. Interview evidence, Ministry of the Environment, Bonn.
31. For the US situation, see C. J. Bailey, *Congress and Air Pollution* (Manchester and New York: Manchester University Press, 1998).
32. Arp, 'Technical Regulation and Politics', p. 159.
33. G. Tsebelis, 'The Power of the European Parliament as a Conditional Agenda Setter', *American Political Science Review*, 88:1 (1994), pp. 128–42.
34. C. Hubschmid and P. Moser, 'The Co-operation Procedure in the EU: Why Was the European Parliament Influential in the Decision on Car Emissions?' *Journal of Common Market Studies*, 35:2 (1997), pp. 225–42.
35. Ibid. 238–40.
36. Haigh, *Manual*, p. 6.8–7.
37. D. Judge, ' "Predestined to Save the Earth": The Environment Committee of the European Parliament', *Environmental Politics*, 1:4 (1992), pp. 186–212, at 202.
38. Arp, 'Technical Regulation and Politics', p. 167.
39. D. Vogel, *Trading Up* (Cambridge, Mass., and London: Harvard University Press, 1995), p. 74.
40. Bailey, *Congress and Air Pollution*, chs. 5 and 6.
41. 'Car Emissions Set to Test New EC Legislative Procedure', *ENDS Report*, 229 (1994), pp. 35–6.
42. 'European Parliament Backs Down over Vehicle Emissions', *ENDS Report*, 230 (1994), p. 41.
43. *Financial Times*, 26 June 1996, p. 20.
44. 'Car Industry Lashes Out at Auto/Oil Proposals', *ENDS Report*, 257 (1996), pp. 41–3.
45. Ibid.

12

Packaging and Packaging Waste

This chapter explores the issue dynamic associated with the 1994 packaging and packaging waste directive (94/62). It offers a case study that focuses primarily on the processes of rule enactment rather than on the concern with implementation and impact in the case of water or the co-evolution of primary and secondary rules in the case of vehicle emissions. It seeks to provide answers to the two central questions: to what extent does the case show that there are routine and well developed ways for dealing with environmental problems that rest upon participation of a set of actors at EU level; and how do such processes relate to the national level of decision-making?

Despite this focus, it is none the less important to note that concerns over secondary rules were involved at the same time. In fact, the deliberations over the proposed directive started some three years after the Single European Act came into effect but came to a head just over a year after the Treaty on European Union had done so. The effect of this was that the new co-decision process was applied for the second reading of the European Parliament and the directive became the first major piece of EU legislation to be submitted to the conciliation procedure between the Parliament and the Council of Ministers. This directive therefore provides an interesting vehicle with which to examine the impact of rule-shaping developments on the rule enactment process, even though one should excercise some caution in interpreting the outcome in these terms, given that a significant amount of the decision-making had run its course by the time the Treaty on European Union changes came into effect.

In more specific terms, the consideration of the packaging and packaging waste directive allows us to explore one of the most contested areas in the single market/ environmental policy issue dynamic, namely waste management. As discussed in Chapter 1, this involves the tension between, on the one hand, the application of the 'proximity principle' which limits the movement of waste, and, on the other, market pressures which are tending to expand the distances travelled by wastes. Two dichotomies are relevant to this tension: that between 'waste' and 'goods' and that between 'product' and 'process'. Environmental policy dealing with 'processes' rather than 'products' is becoming more common,[1] but it is just this distinction that is causing problems in international trade where liberalization has focused not on process but on product standards.[2] Not surprisingly, these are problems that must be approached in the EU context, too, and which reveal themselves in discussions over the packaging and packaging waste directive, especially in the arguments over the status of 'waste' that has positive market value (thus becoming a tradable product) and the 'waste management hierarchy'.

But this directive also takes us to the heart of a wider question: to what extent should uniform standards be designed to achieve a single market where environmental diversity might dictate that the optimal specificity of policies be at regional, national, or even more local levels? There is a strong case to consider a non-uniform approach to many environmental problems in the EU because of the diversity of environments, administrative competences, public awareness, economic viability, and so on, that exist, and which have been described in Part II. However, as part of the logic of ecological modernization, there are also strong arguments in favour of a uniform approach so as to minimize barriers to trade within the single market while encouraging a high level of environmental protection as stipulated by the Single European Act. These are reinforced by those economic interests from member states with high environmental standards seeking to attain what they see as a level playing field with their competitors. The difficulty is that the imposition of uniformly strict environmental standards across the EU may fail to take sufficiently into account exactly the diversity that may demand a variegated approach to the environmental problem at issue. As the case of packaging and packaging waste illustrates, this is far from being a simple north–south problem but may involve differences between many member states.

What becomes apparent from this case is that basic economic, political, and environmental diversity among the member states of the EU informs not just different 'policy styles' but also widely differing perceptions of policy problems. Thus, an important 'environmental' problem to some countries may be considered in others to be at best a less important issue, at worst an irrelevance or even a problem for an entirely 'non-environmental' reason. When the environmental problems of a minority of member states begin to be addressed at the EU level, and where they are not uniformly shared by the others, there is a very stong likelihood that the 'issue' will become one in which a variety of political and policy concerns come to the fore. In the context of the single market, trade implications may feature just as much, particularly where the solutions to the national environmental problems of some member states affect trade with others.

The framing of the issue dealt with by the packaging and packaging waste directive illustrates just such a process where the environment/single market issue dynamic developed and the balance between the two policy objectives altered. The dynamic reflects essentially the different and evolving concerns of the EU member states, but its processing reflects the unique EU institutional and policy context in which it occurred.

THE PACKAGING AND PACKAGING WASTE DIRECTIVE

The 1994 packaging and packaging waste directive seeks to achieve a balance between the twin objectives of a single market and the EU's environmental policy. As stated in the directive, its objectives are both:

(a) the harmonization of national measures dealing with packaging and packaging waste in order to avoid distortions of competition and barriers to trade within the EU's Internal Market; and

(b) the minimization of the impact of packaging and packaging waste on the environment.

The key provisions of the directive from an environmental point of view concern targets for recovery (50–65 per cent) and the recycling (25–45 per cent) of packaging waste after five years, the requirement for all member states to establish systems to achieve these, and the setting up of databases to keep track of developments in each country on a comparable basis. Packaging placed on the EU market after 1998 should have to comply with certain 'essential requirements', some of which are designed primarily to protect the environment, such as limits on heavy metals.

From a single market point of view, the directive makes it more difficult for countries to develop national initiatives concerning packaging waste which hinder intra-EU trade, and it avoids specific reuse and minimization targets. It also imposes a requirement on countries seeking to exceed the recovery and recycling limits to submit their plans for Commission approval in order to ensure that there is sufficient capacity in place to deal with the waste rather than export it to other countries. It also holds out the prospect of a 'Euro-package', which conforms to minimum 'essential requirements' and is able to circulate without hindrance throughout the EU.

Although gaining sufficient support in the EU institutions to be passed, the fine balance struck by the directive had its critics, most notably the governments of Germany, the Netherlands, and Denmark, which claimed that it placed insufficient emphasis on environmental objectives and too much on those of the single market. These three member states had voted against it in the final Council negotiations but were unable to prevent its passage because of the use of qualified majority voting. This was possible because the directive had been proposed as a single market measure under Article 100a rather than as an environmental measure under Article 130s, where unanimity was still usual. However, it was interesting that in the Conciliation meetings observers commented on the fact that, despite the temptations for the three outvoted countries to pursue their own objectives, the Council maintained an outwardly unaminous approach *vis-à-vis* the Parliament, suggesting that institutional power-play between the two was more important than the considerations concerning the directive's provisions.

Given that the choice of Article 100a implied that the primary objective of the directive was market harmonization rather than environmental protection,[3] one might wonder why the European Parliament and in particular its environment committee, which has a reputation for being actively 'green',[4] supported this choice of legal base. The answer is three-fold and further demonstrates the complex institutional dynamic that underpins the EU's definition and processing of any issue. The additional leverage that the Parliament gained under measures introduced using this article is certainly one reason. There was also the precedent set by the ruling of the ECJ in the titanium dioxide case, which suggested that, where there was a choice between Articles 100a and 130s, the former should be chosen because of the greater democratic input it provides through increased parliamentary scrutiny. Lastly, however, there were key MEPs, notably the chairman of the environment committee, who considered that agreement would not be reached in the Council if unanimity were applicable and that a directive was imperative in order to prevent damage to recycling industries in member states from the impact of Germany's packaging laws. This reasoning of the Parliament on the choice of legal base illustrates both the impact of the EU's institutional setup and the importance of the actions of member states, in the definition and processing of the issue being addressed at the EU level.

The Background

The twin considerations of the EU's particular policy context and the influence of national initiatives are key factors in understanding the historical background to the dynamics surrounding the packaging and packaging waste directive. The EU began to consider the issue of packaging waste in its own right only in May 1990, following a resolution from the Council of Ministers[5] which endorsed the waste management strategy that the Commission had outlined the previous year.[6] Although there was no explicit mention of packaging waste in the first document, the Council called on the Commission to draw up a proposal on this subject as soon as practicable. Previously, the EU had addressed only certain types of packaging waste (e.g. drinks containers) or materials (e.g. plastics). What is striking is that, while the environmental issues have become increasingly bound up with considerations concerning the single market, they are rarely predominant in EU policy. In fact, as the runup to the consideration of this directive confirms, the EU generally considers such waste issues when prompted by national actions that threaten adverse impacts on the single market, not because of overriding evidence of common environmental problems throughout all EU countries.

As we might expect from our analysis in Part I, from the beginnings of the EU's waste management strategy in 1975 up to the ECJ ruling in the Danish bottles case in 1988, the balance of concerns regarding packaging waste suggests that the EU's preoccupation was more with the functioning of the single market than with environmental protection; as a result, policy regarding the latter tended to be relatively ineffective. In fact, the pressures for the development of the earliest EU waste legislation stemmed from national waste management measures which prompted consideration by the Commission of their effects on the 'common market', and as such they bear remarkable similarity to those that influenced the development of the packaging and packaging waste proposal. Several member states (notably the UK, France, and Germany) were beginning to transfer responsibility for waste management from a local or regional level to a national one while the Commission was drawing up its proposal. The outcome was the framework waste directive, which sought to lay out a uniform set of measures throughout the EU.[7] This in fact bears much similarity to the 1974 British Control of Pollution Act.[8]

It is within the framework of the 1975 waste legislation that more detailed 'daughter' directives on a variety of classes of waste, such as toxic waste and polychlorobiphenyls (PCBs), have been agreed, as well as legislation relating to packaging waste. The first of these was a 1981 Council recommendation on the reuse and recycling of waste paper, whose impact was limited.[9] A more significant piece of legislation was the 1985 'beverage cans' directive.[10] Like the framework waste directive, national initiatives determined the timing of Commission action and influenced the form and content of the legislation. In this case it was the Danish government's proposal to introduce a law that would make standardized returnable containers for beer and soft drinks obligatory that was the spur, although another influence was apparently the 'Bottle Bill' introduced by the American state of Oregon in 1972.[11] While the ostensible purpose of the directive was to reduce the impact on the environment of the disposal of beverage containers and to encourage a reduction in the consumption of energy and raw materials, there was clearly, once again, an impetus provided by single market considerations.

The institutional discussion of the proposal took over four years, illustrating not only the complexity of packaging issues but also the difficulties of reconciling different national and institutional interests. Following drawn-out discussions in effect between the Parliament and the Commission, an amended Commission proposal was presented to the Council,[12] largely following the amendments suggested by the Parliament.[13] The final negotiations in the Council then led to the dropping of the binding objectives and, at the UK's insistence, to the requirement that national measures be notified to the Commission in advance of implementation to ensure that no discrimination occurred between the different types of container and the different types of packaging. These two key changes not only give an indication of the extent to which Council bargaining can crucially influence the content of the final legislation, but even mirror some of the most important changes made to the packaging waste proposal at the Council stage.

In this context it is also interesting to note that the lobbying by industrial interests to water down the proposal, considered successful by them at the time, merely gained them a 'pyrrhic victory', according to a Commission official speaking in 1989, because the weak provisions of the directive caused problems with the single market.[14]

At this point it is important to recall the general atmosphere of the mid-1980s, which was dominated by considerations of the relaunch of the single market project. Following the publication of the Commission's White Paper on this,[15] a considerable impetus was given to the goal when it was included as a formal goal of the Single European Act, and although the inclusion of the new chapter on the environment rightly represented a qualitative shift in EU priorities, the impact of this was certainly not felt immediately. The neglect of environmental considerations in the single market plan itself has already been highlighted in general terms; and, as regards packaging, the 1988 Cecchini report mentions the Danish drinks packaging legislation only in so far as it represented a problem for manufacturers and exporters of drinks to Denmark.[16] It is revealing that the first major example of the way in which the Single European Act's environmental provisions could impact upon the EU's objective of achieving the single market came in the ECJ's judgment on just this issue in the 1988 Danish Bottles case.[17]

This case was of central importance both to the general single market and to the environment debate and the specific issues concerning packaging waste, warranting a brief explanation. In 1981 Denmark had introduced a drinks packaging law which required beer, soft drinks, mineral waters, and lemonade to be marketed only in returnable bottles. Following a 1984 amendment (prompted by protests from drinks and container manufacturers, other member states, and the Commission over the anti-competitive nature of the legislation), drinks sold in non-approved containers could be marketed up to a maximum of 30,000 hectolitres per annum per producer, although metal cans were banned, which was one of the features that provoked criticism in the Cecchini report. A preliminary opinion given by the ECJ's advocate general had appeared to support the Commission's view, but to some surprise, the ECJ ruled in favour of Denmark, invoking the Single European Act's environment provisions, which provided 'good grounds for finding that protection of the environment constitutes an imperative requirement which may limit the application of' free trade rules.

The ECJ thus held that individual member states may act unilaterally provided that the primary aim of the action is to protect the environment, that this does not discriminate against products or producers from other member states, and that the measures employed are proportional to the objective set. However, the ECJ did find that the limits on the quantity of drinks that could be sold in non-approved packages were illegal, given that they too are returned and do not damage the environment.

The implications of the precedent set by this decision were enormous, because it was the first time the SEM objective had been compromised in order to protect the environment. The decision, not surprisingly, delighted environmentalists, but gave great cause for concern in industry circles. The political ramifications were also felt within the Commission: the decision to take the case to the ECJ was the subject of considerable dispute between DG XI and DG III in the first place, and it was reckoned to have strengthened the hand of the former considerably.[18] The German government took the decision as a green light to introduce plans for mandatory deposits on plastic bottles. None the less, the ECJ ruling did not wholly clarify the situation, leaving uncertain where the appropriate balance might lie between the needs of trade and those of the national environmental protection, especially because the test of proportionality is a difficult and contentious one.[19]

The Danish bottles ruling also influenced the implementation of the beverage cans directive with which there had been considerable difficulties. By the end of 1990 the Commission had been obliged to initiate legal proceedings against five countries (Belgium, Spain, France, Luxembourg, and Portugal) for the improper application of the directive.[20] The variety of national implementing measures (including voluntary agreements, compulsory recycling schemes, mandatory deposit systems, and taxes) was inevitable, given the flexibility inherent in the directive, which failed to define the level of environmental protection to be achieved and gave a large scope to member states in defining the legal base of their measures, the rates of recovery, and the means by which to achieve this.[21] Not only were environmental objectives not being achieved, but concerns were being voiced by a variety of groups criticizing many of the national measures as anti-competitive and incompatible with the aims of the single market.[22] This was certainly a key factor in the Commission's decision to propose a new packaging waste directive.

In a vain attempt to remedy the situation from both an environmental and a single market point of view, in 1989 the Commission proposed a new plastics directive and amendments to the beverage cans directive. The latter included ambitious material recovery and recycling targets, which by early 1990 had risen to 70 per cent by weight.[23] However, both proposals were abandoned later that year when it became clear that both were partial in their coverage of the 'priority waste stream' of packaging. As part 1 of the Appendix to this chapter indicates, one of the merits of a comprehensive approach to packaging waste was that it might prevent new barriers to trade developing by pre-empting conflicting national schemes. Although national packaging legislation was being discussed by Germany and the Netherlands, at that stage no legislation had reached the statute books, and other national measures either were non-existent or took a one-sided approach to the issue.

FROM NATIONAL DIVERSITY IN APPROACHING THE 'PACKAGING WASTE' PROBLEM . . .

Even approaching the issue for single market reasons required pan-EU environmental data on packaging waste; however, as DG XI was to discover, not only were these inadequate, but they revealed considerable national diversity in the actuality and perception of the issue to be addressed. Such diversity was to sit very uneasily with the objective of achieving a single market with uniformly high standards of environmental protection. By the middle of 1990, DG XI had compiled the statistics shown in Table 12.1.

TABLE 12.1 *DG XI estimates of quantities of packaging waste, the quantity of recycled packaging waste, and the percentage recycled, 1990 (millions of tonnes)*

Waste stream	Total	Non-recycled	Recycled
Domestic waste	25.0	22.5 (90%)	2.5 (10%)
Office/shop/service	15.0	12.5 (83%)	2.5 (17%)
Industrial waste	10.5	6.0 (57%)	4.5 (43%)
Total	50.5	41.0 (81%)	9.5 (19%)

Source: DG XI, Draft Proposal for a Commission Communication on Packaging Waste, 17 December 1990 (not officially published).

While these figures appear to be comprehensive, no national or sectoral break-down is given and it is evident that in both areas comprehensive, reliable data were hard to come by. Furthermore, such data that there were tended to be of dubious reliability or difficult to compare cross-nationally. Within-country data from trade and industry groups were not consistent with governmental estimates, while between member states differing methodologies or an absence of data prevented reliable comparisions. Such problems led the OECD to conclude that 'a strong argument can be made that policy-makers do not have adequate data on waste generation and recycling' to make sensible policy.[24]

One implication of there being only partial information was that there was a bias in favour of those member states from which data had been gathered: France, Germany, Italy, Belgium, Denmark, the UK, and the Netherlands. The figures on which DG XI's work was based relied heavily on these northern European countries; in particular, 'the most complete facts and figures were found in the brief informative document from the Dutch Ministry for Environmental Affairs. . . . It has to be noted that the estimated quantities which are dealt with in this chapter often are an extrapolation of the above-mentioned facts and figures.'[25] Even the so-called 'independent experts', upon which DG XI relied for its initial data and policy proposals, were either Belgian or Dutch consultancies (with input also from a British academic at University College London via one of these). The sources of the data meant that a northern European bias was inevitable, although there turned out to be considerable variation just among these countries. It also pro-vided opportunities for those groups with access to data on packaging and pack-aging waste to contribute much to the proposal's development, and, as is shown later, these were predominantly trade and industry groups.

In addition to problems relating to a lack of comprehensive, reliable data on pack-aging waste, another problem that beset the EU was whether the issue was prim-arily one of packaging waste or should more properly be treated as also dealing with packaging prior to its becoming waste. As the title of the final directive sug-gests, the dilemma was resolved by tackling both packaging and packaging waste at the same time. However, while obviously closely related, they can be seen as distinct problems requiring distinct solutions. One problem relates to packaging waste disposal and management, while the other relates to the overall resource consumption involved in the production, use, and disposal of packaging. Among the twelve member states of the EU, there were distinct national and sectoral variations in where the most pressing policy 'problem' lay, and this inhibited the formation of a uniform EU definition of the issue.

While the rise in waste production and the shortage of landfill capacity are genuine environmental problems on a European scale,[26] there were several difficulties with the decision to focus on packaging waste as the solution to them. Firstly, the impact on these problems of action centred on packaging waste is disputed, notably by trade and industry groups. Although packaging is an extremely visible manifestation of the amount of waste that a 'throw-away' society produces, its part in the overall waste problem is less certain. The British group Incpen, for example, estimated that in the UK and other EU countries packaging constituted approximately one-third of municipal solid waste by weight, the latter itself comprising only 4 per cent of the total waste generated.[27] Packaging waste would on these figures account for a mere 1 or 2 per cent of total waste generated. Such statistics certainly suggest that the public's perception of the significance of action to reduce packaging waste is somewhat exaggerated[28] and that, if the issues of waste avoidance and diversion from landfill are to be prioritized, packaging would not warrant the degree of attention it has received: as even environmentalists have argued, other waste streams, in particular that from industry, would be a more logical target.[29]

However, consumers are confronted with packaging on a daily basis, and, because of effective campaigns by environmental pressure groups designed to highlight the unsustainable character of the throw-away society, packaging is generally perceived by EU consumers as excessive, wasteful, and bad for the environment.[30] Consequently, those governments in EU member countries where this feeling was most accentuated started to take action on the issue, in particular by encouraging recycling. In this context, it is noteworthy that those countries where such measures were first proposed are those with particular problems of landfill and waste disposal—Germany, the Netherlands, and Denmark; countries with more abundant landfill availability or a lower generation of packaging waste were under less pressure to develop measures to deal with the problem and tended not to take such active measures. Measures introduced to minimize the generation and encourage the recycling of packaging waste in Germany, for example, have resulted especially from public concern about the need to reduce landfill and worries about incineration. The availability of landfill is an especially urgent problem in the Netherlands, where, because half of the country is below sea level, there is a minimal capacity.

However, although waste disposal is arguably a common EU problem, it is not a uniform one. Variation in national political and environmental circumstances means that a variety of national perceptions of the policy problem has lead to an equally diverse range of policy solutions being proposed and adopted (see part 2 of the Appendix to this chapter). Thus, unlike the Netherlands, landfill availability is not a particularly severe problem for the UK, although it is becoming so; although public awareness of packaging waste and recycling had been frequently highlighted in campaigns by Friends of the Earth, there are no statutory provisions affecting packaging waste. Ireland, a country with a relatively low overall consumption of packaging, had no incinerators and a mainly rural, dispersed population, making easily available landfill an attractive option in many instances. Portugal has a low per capita consumption of packaging resources, and does not therefore perceive the packaging waste issue to be an urgent one; in common with other Mediterranean countries like Spain, it was also able to compost more waste because of favourable climatic conditions. Greece, like Portugal, has a relatively dispersed population, and numerous small islands with specific waste disposal problems.

Even between the 'greenest' member states there are differences in policy responses: the Danes tend to have a high public acceptance of incineration with energy recovery because many homes are heated in this way; the German public, on the other hand, is more concerned with the potential for such incinerators to emit pollution and according greater opposition to incinerators has been encountered. Not surprisingly, the recovery and recycling rates, and the use of incineration and landfill, vary not just for different materials but considerably among the member states of the EU.

. . . TO THE IMPACT OF THE GERMAN PACKAGING ORDINANCE

One scheme in particular, the German packaging ordinance, had a considerable impact on the way in which the EU (and other member states) considered the 'problem' of packaging waste. The packaging ordinance was developed as a specific measure under German waste management law. Originally devised by German officials out of their reflection on the failure of earlier bottle recycling schemes in the 1980s, it also fitted the vision of the then German environment minister, Professor Klaus Töpfer, of the 'circular economy', in which the central idea is to prevent the run-off of materials from the activities of the economy.

This ambitious system, which came into operation during 1991, was focused on an environmental issue but had impacts that, ironically, meant that the discussions at the EU level centred on single market concerns rather than environmental ones. Although the intention was to reduce the amount of packaging waste being generated in Germany, the ordinance also fundamentally affected packaging prior to its becoming waste. Companies wishing to market their goods in Germany either had to take back their own packaging waste or to join the Duales System Deutschland organization (DSD), which had been set up by German companies to meet the requirements of the ordinance: for a fee, this membership gave them the right to use the 'green dot' on their packaging which would indicate to consumers that it would be collected and recycled in line with the ordinance.

From 1991 onwards, the Commission received complaints from trade and industry over the allegedly anti-competitive nature of this system, which was not only costly but was perceived as favouring domestic German companies, discriminating against imported goods, and therefore infringing EU-free movement and competition rules.[31] Although this was disputed by the German government, from 1992 onwards DG IV was considering taking action in the ECJ over this but was wary, both because of legal uncertainties and because of the politically unpopular nature of such a move. Although the decision to do so was taken in principle during 1994, it was not until the end of 1995, one year after the agreement on the directive, that the Commission in fact initiated this legal action.

However, at the same time as the complaints over the anti-competitive nature of DSD were being registered, there were additional problems generated by the fact that the system was proving 'too successful' and had led to the collection of such huge amounts of packaging waste that it was impossible to recycle all of it in Germany. The result was some illegal dumping, shipments of waste to eastern Europe, and even as far afield as Indonesia,[32] and vastly increased exports to member states with spare recycling capacity. However, such was the volume of this waste that German waste management companies were not selling it as a secondary raw material: they were giving it away or even paying recycling firms to take it off their hands, although the German government always insisted that there was no direct subsidy to the recyclate itself in the system, merely a cost recovery scheme to cover administration.

Whatever the cause, the result was that the price for recyclate in the UK, France, Italy, and Spain dropped dramatically, causing severe problems for the domestic recycling industries there.[33] For example, representatives of the British Paper and Board Industry Federation explained the situation, rather intemperately, to a House of Commons select committe thus:

In terms of the Single Market, the Germans for their own reasons (basically based on their Green Movement rather than based on the paper industry) have come out with a certain series of laws which are absolutely and totally distorting our business and are very, very damaging to the business here in the United Kingdom.[34]

The UK, France, and Spain submitted a formal complaint at an Industry Council meeting in May 1993 urging the Commission to take action over this.[35] At one point France even threatened to ban the imports of waste because of this.[36] These problems therefore raised additional single market concerns relating to the free trade in waste goods and ensured that several countries viewed the issue of packaging waste as an economic rather than an environmental issue in the first instance.

The German experience with its own packaging legislation had other lessons for the EU. One lay in the problems it had experienced in trying to finance the scheme: DSD had very nearly been bankrupted during 1992 because of the problem of free-riders using the green dot without paying the fee to the organization. This meant that whatever environmental benefits the system offered were balanced by the difficulties involved in running it, thereby making an extension of the system to the EU level somewhat less likely. A second lesson was that in an integrated EU market a preferred national solution to a problem could have negative environmental as well as negative economic effects elsewhere. It was even suggested that, had an environmental impact assessment been carried out from an EU perspective, it would have found that the packaging ordinance was less than the advance claimed by its creators and would not have been agreed to.[37] Indeed, were the test of proportionality to be applied to the German scheme, some of its detractors allege that it would not pass.

Indeed, a third lesson from the German experience was that environmentally negative side-effects should be fully considered and that unrealistically high targets for recycling might be unachievable. Although the legislation was leading to a reduction in the amount of waste generated and landfilled according to the German government, it was argued that a repeat of the experience on an EU level would only lead to exports of waste to non-EU countries, especially eastern Europe, in contravention of the EU international obligations under the Basel Convention. It also indicated that there were problems with such an emphasis on recycling, without allowing incineration. Indeed, by the middle of 1993 the German government was known to be reconsidering the restrictions on incineration[38] and also to be considering a slight relaxation of the recycling and incineration targets it had set. Not only did these considerations influence national policy-makers, prompting more of them to establish their own packaging schemes, which differed from the German one and therefore would have to be considered by EU decision-makers in their own right, but it also contributed to the intense debate surrounding the waste hierarchy.

THE WASTE MANAGEMENT HIERARCHY
AND THE SINGLE MARKET

Once the issue of packaging waste had arrived on the agenda, it became apparent that wider single market issues were becoming increasingly important. The German legislation also provided clear evidence that, as the OECD, the House of Lords, many industrialists, and environmentalists argued, the danger of a focus on recycling alone is that it might mask other environmental impacts.[39] Although the purpose of the German legislation was to prevent waste generation, in some cases it was claimed that use of packaging could actually contribute to this objective. While the desirability of reducing packaging waste could be agreed upon by scientists, academics, industry, and governments from all the member states, the objective of reducing the amount of packaging *per se*, as suggested in early drafts of the proposal, was not unanimously accepted. More than this, the recycling solution was increasingly questioned as always being the best environmental option.

Rather than merely avoid landfill, if the intention is to reduce the impact that packaging has on the environment over the course of its entire life-cycle (i.e. from its production and use through to its final disposal), as suggested by the Fifth Action Programme, then a slightly different set of questions is raised. Such packaging life-cycle analysis (LCA) promised to provide a more realistic impression of environmental impact, if not all the answers.[40] The type of questions asked in such analyses no longer assumes that recycling is the best option but concentrates on overall resource use. For example, is the amount of energy involved in converting plastic packaging waste into new plastic greater than the amount of energy used in transporting waste plastic packaging to a recycling centre? Is the energy recovered by the incineration of packaging materials greater than the energy needed to incinerate them, and can the emissions released from the process be disposed of without causing pollution? The problem was that, although the waste management hierarchy outlined in the Commission's 1989 waste strategy was 'indicative' or 'flexible', the one outlined in DG XI's initial proposals and the targets derived therefrom (90 per cent recovery; 60 per cent recycling; maximum 30 per cent incineration, and a 10 per cent reduction in the amount of packaging waste sent to landfill) suggested a stricter interpretation of it. Debate on this issue centred on LCAs and especially on whether these justified a preference for reuse over recycling.

However, LCAs, though promising, were problematic: few had been carried out, and those that had had worked on differing methodologies such that a variety of conclusions could be drawn.[41] Conclusions were contested, and even commonly accepted LCAs did not remove the need for difficult political decisions. The role of distribution and distance was particularly important, given that the growth of packaging and packaging waste has paralleled the shift from local markets and local diversity to national and international markets preparing standardized products,[42] and the single market exemplified this process. Fairlie even contended that many LCAs ignored the role of distance as a variable, because 'any attempt to define or regulate the distance that a commodity or its packaging travelled would be an interference with free trade'.[43] This therefore raised the whole issue of the compatibility of the single market (which encourages greater distances to be travelled) with national and local regulation concerning packaging and packaging waste (which may have the effect of limiting it). In particular, there was an intense argument over whether reuse (which limits distance) was preferable to recycling (which does not necessarily) in which LCAs supporting both sides of the argument were produced.

The issue of a waste management hierarchy thus became a central issue in the discussions because of its potential to limit the operation the single market if applied rigidly. However, although DG XI had commissioned such packaging LCAs,[44] an insufficient number of such analyses had been carried out before agreement on the directive had been reached and there was no proof that reuse was environmentally superior in all instances. While the waste management hierarchy was supported in an indicative sense by most member states, there were some LCAs that showed the potential for it to provide environmentally sub-optimal solutions if applied very rigidly.[45] Although the environmental merits suggested that a flexible approach be applied, in a situation where free movement in a single market was prioritized, the balance favoured single market considerations in the absence of a comprehensive set of LCAs precisely because of the assumption that free trade should be a preferred solution where evidence is inconclusive.

The argument over the ability of national schemes to favour reuse over recycling went to the heart of the question of whether the measure was fundamentally designed to address an environmental problem or gave more priority to achieving a uniform EU approach. This argument was central to the choice of legal base, and during the period of negotiations over the packaging and packaging waste directive there were two ECJ rulings that affected this choice of legal base. The first was the ruling in the case that the Commission had brought against the Belgian region of Wallonia, which had banned imports of hazardous waste.[46] Although somewhat ambiguous, the ruling strengthened the proximity principle, but also emphasized that in principle waste should be treated as a good in the single market. Because this made it less likely that the ECJ would support bans on the movement of raw materials (goods) within the EU, it increased the incentive for setting up an EU-wide solution to the problems of packaging waste exports and hence preventing the situation occurring in the first place. This strengthened the argument for a quick resolution of the single market dimension to the issue.

The second ruling, delivered in 1993, concerned the framework waste directive.[47] Encouraged by its success in the ECJ's 1991 ruling in the titanium dioxide case supporting the use of Article 100a where the aims of a piece of legislation were both harmonization and protection of the environment, the Commission took the Council to the ECJ over the legal basis for the framework waste directive. The Council had proposed Article 130s but the Commission had argued for 100a, saying that the legal basis of the original directive (Articles 100 and 235) had been replaced by this in the Single European Act.[48] However, this time the ECJ supported the Council's contention, although again somewhat ambiguously. Despite stressing that waste was a good and therefore legally entitled to free movement in the single market, the ECJ ruled that, because the primary aim of the directive was to protect the environment and in particular to underline the ideal of disposing of waste as close as possible to its source (the proximity principle), the single market implications were ancillary and Article 130s was appropriate.[49] Ironically, this ruling actually made it more likely that the stated objectives of the packaging and packaging directive would be made more overtly harmonization rather than environmental protection so as to strengthen the case for use of Article 100a if the legal basis of the directive were challenged by one of the member states most opposed to it.

INSTITUTIONAL DISCUSSIONS

Given the background of national diversity in the severity of the environmental problems to be addressed and the EU policy context which tended to favour a solution based on Article 100a, and which addressed single market issues as a priority, the final directive should be considered a compromise designed to achieve agreement among very different interests. The targets are little more than the lower end of the pre-existing objectives of member states, and where they are not there are derogations. (Portugal, Greece, and Ireland have exemptions because of their 'special status'—low amounts of packaging waste generation or dispersed populations.) On the other hand, the possibilities for more ambitious schemes to exceed the targets are circumscribed by single market considerations. Such an outcome suggests that the member states in the Council of Ministers play a crucial role in the way in which the EU defines a 'high level of environmental protection'. The diversity of national approaches to the environmental problem itself suggests that the policy styles approach has much to commend it in understanding the member states' actions.

However, as the instutional discussions reveal, this provides only some of the explanation for the policy outcome. The EU policy context clearly shapes the issue definition as well as the final outcome, and the fact that three member states have had to implement policy that they voted against illustrates the limits of national manoeuvre. While the Council of Ministers may remain the most powerful EU institution, the individual member states now clearly operate in an environment where many other political actors have an impact, the most obvious being the other EU institutions.

Between the first proposal from DG XI in 1990 and the final agreement on the directive in 1994, several important changes were introduced to the directive other than in the Council. Some of the most important changes were introduced relatively early on between DG XI's proposal and the first proposal from the Commission as a whole. These included the removal of the so-called 'standstill' provision on per capita packaging waste output, the dropping of the binding five-year targets, the inclusion of a per material target of 60 per cent recycling, the weakening of the strict emphasis on a hierarchy of waste management options, the upgrading of the objective of harmonization, and the specification of Article 100a as the appropriate legal basis for the directive. The amendments suggested by both the Environment Committee and the plenary session of the Parliament were relatively limited, the key ones being the advocacy of a stricter hierarchy and tighter limits on heavy metals. The Commission subsequently rejected the waste management hierarchy amendment while accepting that on heavy metals and several more minor ones. Key changes to the directive really occurred only at the Council stage: the new recovery and recycling targets and provisions concerning the restrictions of waste packaging within the single market. Thereafter, despite the process of conciliation between Council and Parliament, there were no major changes whatsoever introduced the final directive retaining all of the key features of the common position agreed in December 1994.

In terms of the relative impact of the various institutions on the evolution of the directive, therefore, the bargaining in the Council of Ministers in the second half of 1993 had the most effect. However, the Commission's role in setting the agenda was, in formal terms at least, very important, because it provided the context for the arguments that were to follow, circumscribing certain policy options and opening up others.

It is also noteworthy that, in respect of other changes concerning per material targets, the possibility for very limited exemptions, and stricter limits on heavy metals, most of the Commission's proposal remained unaltered between its first and amended proposals, indicating the relative lack of parliamentary impact on the directive. In particular, the Commission's targets remained the same up to the Council consideration of the proposal. However, the initial objectives of DG XI in terms of highlighting packaging waste as an environmental issue were compromised, and the Commission's subsequent objectives of balancing the single market and the environment were realized only in very general terms by the common position, which was criticized by several parties for shifting too much towards the former objective. To the extent that a shift in balance towards the single market did occur, however, it could mean that the Commission's own initially preferred solution was itself too focused on a uniform EU solution than on an optimum environmental solution. As such, one should exercise a degree of caution in criticizing the ultimate proposal in this respect.

Once the Commission's first proposal was issued, the influence of the Commission and the Parliament was evident but not great. The number of amendments that were adopted by the Parliament, incorporated by the Commission in its amended proposal, and subsequently included in the common position suggests that the views of these two institutions does play some part in the Council negotiations. However, the fact that the targets were made more flexible suggests that the influence of the member states was most crucial in this regard. The main changes introduced by the Parliament were not adopted by the common position. On this evidence, the key player in institutional terms is the Council of Ministers, and the member states that compose it were evidently crucial in the outcome of these negotiations.

Only in terms of the number of amendments achieved does the influence of the Commission and Parliament on the final directive appear more impressive: there were 52 changes (additions, modifications, or deletions) in the common position compared with the Commission's amended proposal, a number that indicates the degree of change needed in order to reach a compromise between the member states; there were 27 amendments that the Parliament had suggested, the Commission had included, and which also remained in the common position; there were 22 amendments that had been suggested by the Parliament which had been included in the Commission's amended proposal but were not incorporated in the common position; finally, there were nine elements in the common position incorporating amendments suggested by the Parliament which had not been incorporated by the Commission's amended proposal.[50] However, as the preceding discussion suggests, the substance of the changes suggested by the Commission and the Parliament and incorporated by the Council was less impressive than their number indicates.

EU POLICY STYLE

The EU's own policy style thus warrants investigation in order fully to understand its rule-enacting dynamic. The changes that were made to the directive between 1990 and 1994 suggest that other actors have considerable influence over the course of events and should not be neglected from an analysis of EU decision-making.

Behind the changes introduced by these institutional actors, one witnesses a hotbed of activity from interest groups, especially those representing trade and industry. As the first independent experts' report for DG XI suggested,[51] there was a wide range of organizations with a potential interest in the proposal: industry (producers of raw materials and semi-finished products); producers of packaging materials; packaging industries (users); wholesalers; retailers; collectors/recycling industries; waste processors; government (environment, and economic ministries as well as regional authorities with environmental competence); and non-governmental organizations (consumer and environmental groups). Consequently, during the course of 1991, in the words of DG XI's director general, 'the widest consultation ever organised inside and outside the Commission was arranged for this very complex issue',[52] with all the main interests being consulted on three occasions prior to the formal publication of the proposal in July 1992. In addition, DG XI convened meetings of national experts representing the member states' environment and economics ministries and ensured that a range of other Commission services were consulted in advance of the proposal being presented to the cabinets of the Commissioners. For such interservice meetings there were up to fifteen sections of the Commission (in addition to DG XI) that were involved, a figure indicating the wide range of interests that this issue touched.[53]

Given this range of interested actors, trade and industry groups had identified this problem and in early 1993 formed a new organization, SPOLD, to develop a methodology for packaging LCAs.[54]

The sections of the Commission involved in the packaging and packaging waste proposal discussions were: the Secretariat General; the Legal Service; the Consumer Protection Service; DG III (Internal Market and Industrial Affairs); DG IV (Competition); DG VI (Agriculture); DG VII (Transport); DG IX (Personnel and Administration); DG XI (Environment, Nuclear Safety, and Civil Protection); DG XII (Science, Research and Development); DG XVII (Financial Institutions and Company Law); DG XIX (Budgets); DG XX (Financial Control); DG XXI (Customs Union and Indirect Taxation); and DG XXIII (Enterprises Policy, Distributive Trades, Tourism, and Social Economy).

CONCLUSIONS

The experience of the packaging directive contains a number of important points that are worth bringing out in conclusion.

Firstly, there is a clear issue linkage between this department of environment policy and single market concerns. Worries about an implicit, if unintended, eco-protectionism of the original German packaging ordinance and also about the export of German paper materials while recycling capacity was being extended had major political consequences. Spillover in policy terms can take many forms.

Secondly, the diversity of national situations means that waste management problems are perceived differently in the member states. In part, this is simply a consequence of the different geographical and population features of different countries; but it also reflects different and incompatible waste managment practices, the range of associated policies (for example policies on the cost of disposing to landfill), and differing patterns of relationship between government and industry.

Thirdly, these differences of practice are compounded by a lack of information. The original definition of the scale of the problem by DG XI suffered from the difficulties of obtaining relevant statistics on a comparable basis for member states. Information deficits become even more serious when waste management policy comes to be considered in the light of evidence about life-cycle analysis. There are large questions about whether the legal imposition of one version of the waste management hierarchy, in no matter how attenuated a form, really does represent the best practicable environmental option.

Fourthly, the experience of the packaging directive does not provide much evidence in favour on the view that it is possible to base EU environmental policy on the principles of ecological modernization. No new technologies are being promoted so that environmental leaders gain a first-mover advantage in emerging markets for pollution control technology. Nor are relatively under-industrialized countries like Ireland, Spain, and Greece being prevented from committing the same mistakes as the more developed by the imposition of higher standards.

APPENDIX

1. Member States' Packaging Legislation in the EU, Early 1990

BELGIUM

Free market.

DENMARK

Re-fillable bottles were mandatory for domestically produced beers and soft drinks; for imports, a deposit, return and recycling system had to be set up with equivalent effects.

Non-approved bottles were permitted for a maximum of 30,000 hectolitres per year per producer. There was a ban on metal cans for beers and soft drinks.

EIRE

Free market. A proposal was made for legislation involving bans on metal cans and plastic containers for beer, metal cans for cider and wine, and cans for soft drinks with detachable ring-pulls. It was dropped following Commission complaints, but nothing else was proposed in its place.

FRANCE

Free market.

GERMANY

Glass recycling targets for July 1991 were set at 90 per cent for beer and mineral waters, 80 per cent for soft drinks, 50 per cent for still wines. By July 1991 glass recycling generally should be 24 per cent higher than in 1986; packaging taxes would be imposed on plastics and metal packaging.

GREECE

Free market.

ITALY

Glass and metal cans were to have separate collection systems as of January 1990 with a 50 per cent recycling target to be met by end-1992. Taxes on this packaging would be imposed if the targets were not met. On plastic drinks containers, a 40 per cent recycling target by end-1992 was set, of which half could be by incineration with energy recovery. From March 1989, a L100 tax was imposed on non-biodegradable shopping bags.

LUXEMBOURG

An enabling law was introduced in January 1990 imposing mandatory deposits on all refillable/recyclable drinks containers.

NETHERLANDS

Free market in glass and metal cans. PET was to be allowed only if a return and packaging system was set up.

PORTUGAL

Free market.

SPAIN

Free market.

UNITED KINGDOM

Free market.

Source: David Perchards Associates.

2. Member States' Packaging Legislation, 1994

BELGIUM

Voluntary agreements on the recovery of packaging waste in three Belgian regions were signed in 1992. A law introducing eco-tax on beverage containers and other disposable products was adopted in July 1993. *Scope*: beverage containers, paper products, industrial packaging for hazardous products, razors, cameras, batteries, and pesticides. By 1998 reuse targets set at 60 per cent for soft drinks and 95 per cent for beers; recycling rates for remaining containers set at 80 per cent for glass and metal, and 70 per cent for plastics. An organization called FOST-Plus was proposed by trade and industry to organize, coordinate, and support financially the recovery of packaging waste using a green dot system like the Germans.

DENMARK

Under the Environmental Protection Act and several subsidiary regulations, manufacturers and importers had to ensure that packaging was either reusable or could be recovered to the greatest extent without adverse environmental effects. A total ban was imposed on metal beverage cans, and refill bottles for beers and soft drinks were made compulsory. By the year 2000, targets include: 15 per cent reduction in the total volume of packaging waste; 80 per cent recovery of packaging waste; 50 per cent reuse of packaging; 75 per cent of all beverage containers containing recycled materials; 85 per cent reduction of plastic packaging produced with PVC. Municipalities control the funding of recovery of all packaging waste except of soft drinks and beers, which is arranged by industry. There is a differentiated unit tax on all beverage packaging. Government proposals have been made for 'green' taxes on plastic and paper carrier bags and possibly other one-way materials and packaging. A draft voluntary agreement on the recovery of transport packaging could be made compulsory and extended to all industrial companies.

EIRE

No legislation as such was passed. The country was still trying to implement beverage cans directive; there were no targets. The DoE was preparing legislation designed to oblige local authorities to establish recycling plans. Several voluntary initiatives were in operation.

FRANCE

In January 1992, a household packaging waste decree was issued which set a recovery target of 75 per cent by 1 January 1997, two-thirds of which should be recycled and one-third incinerated with energy recovery; a long-term aim was to close 6,700 public tips. In addition to a landfill tax, packaging producers, importers, and distributors were made responsible for taking back and 'valorizing' waste, either by establishing a deposit system for their packaging, organizing an autonomous collection network, or joining the recognized state organization 'eco-emballages' which would seek to do this (which most companies chose to join). While the use of a 'green dot' by 'eco-emballages' resembles the German scheme, it does runs not in parallel with municipal authorities but in conjunction with them; furthermore, incineration is considered a valid means of valorization. This came into operation on 1 January 1993. An agreement with the DSD meant that the green dot could be used by eco-emballages. An additional decree covering transport packaging waste was also under consideration by the government.

GERMANY

In June 1991 the *Verpackungsverordnung* (Packaging Ordinance) imposed an obligation on manufacturers and/or distributors to take back packaging for reuse or recycling. The intention was to keep the packaging waste separate from the municipal waste stream, and avoid landfill and incineration. Targets varied by material, but by 1 July 1995 the objective for all materials was for 80 per cent collection, 90 per cent sorting, and either 72 or 64 per cent recycling rates. All packaging was included in the scope of the ordinance. Six hundred German companies set up the Duale System Deutschland (DSD) to achieve these objectives. Participating companies paid a fee to DSD in order to be able use a 'green dot' on their packaging which meant that it would be collected and recycled separately from the municipal waste stream. DSD was increasingly seen as a 'victim of its own success', able to collect more packaging waste than it could recycle, especially of plastics and owing to 'free-riders'; it only narrowly avoided bankruptcy (DM900 shortfall). This led to problems with exports of packaging waste to EU and non-EU countries. The government was known to be considering a slight re-evaluation of the targets and a less restrictive attitude towards incineration.

GREECE

No legislation was passed or targets set, but legislation had been promised by the end of 1993. The Hellenic Recovery and Recycling Association was in consultation with the authorities and was running a pilot project in the greater Athens area. Local authorities had also started pilot recycling schemes for glass, paper, and aluminium.

ITALY

The government was considering a comprehensive re-write of the various legal provisions covering packaging waste which had been in effect since 1988. Consortia involving packaging manufacturers, users, and importers had been set up for each packaging material and had worked with local authorities/municipalities to operate recycling schemes. Industry had requested a two-year extension of the target to recover 50 per cent of glass and metal packaging and 40 per cent of plastic packaging waste (with 50 per cent recycling/50 per cent incineration with energy recovery) by mid-1993. The government was also considering a tax on liquid containers if recycling targets were not met.

LUXEMBOURG

An enabling law was introduced in January 1990 which would impose mandatory deposits on all refillable/recyclable drinks containers.

NETHERLANDS

In 1991 a 'packaging covenant' was signed between the packaging industry and the government which laid out the objective of a total ban on landfilling and a material recycling rate of 60 per cent by 2000 for all packaging. By 2000 the annual production of packaging waste had to be 10 per cent less than the 1986 figure of 2 million tonnes. It called on the packaging chain to set up recycling facilities, use recycled materials, and offer domestic collection of 'dry packaging'. Immediate objectives were a ban on gift packaging for spirit bottles, weight reductions in drinks cartons, a ban on free carrier bags, encouragement of refill systems for detergents, and the investigation of substitutes for PVC and blister packs. A new environmental policy plan was under consideration during 1993 which might alter the targets and the set-up of the system.

PORTUGAL

No legislation or targets had been established.

SPAIN

No legislation as such was passed in 1994. Spain was still trying to implement the beverage cans directive; no targets had been set. Spanish industry wanted to set up a voluntary collection system along the lines of the French 'eco-emballages', while the government intended to issue packaging waste legislation that could allow for this based on a take-back obligation through mandatory deposits. Catalonia had issue a packaging waste law imposing an obligation for cities of more than 5,000 inhabitants to collect and recycle packaging waste.

UNITED KINGDOM

A government announcement in July 1993 challenged UK packaging chain members to produce a plan by the end of the year for the recovery of between 50 and 75 per cent of packaging waste by 2000. The industry association COPAC (Consortium of the Packaging Chain) had responded by proposing a voluntary scheme which was designed to 'valorize' 60 per cent of packaging waste by 2005 but which was still subject to discussions with the government.

Sources: AIM, 'Update on National Situations with Regard to Packaging and Packaging Waste Legislation', 4 November 1993; *EC Packaging Report Monthly*, October 1993, issue no. 10.

NOTES TO CHAPTER 12

1. B. Verhoeve, and G. Bennett, 'Products and the Environment: An International Overview of Recent Developments', *European Environmental Law Review*, 31:3 (1994), pp. 74–9.
2. D. Brack, 'Balancing Trade and the Environment', *International Affairs*, 71:3 (1995), pp. 497–514.

3. This legal opinion is shared by the special advisory committee to the House of Lords Select Committee on the European Communities, which produced a report on the directive. See House of Lords Select Committee on the European Communities, *Packaging and Packaging Waste*, Session 1992–93, 26th Report, HL Paper 118-I (London: HMSO, 1993).

4. D. Judge, ' "Predestined to Save the Earth": The Environment Committee of the European Parliament', *Environmental Politics*, 1:4 (1992), pp. 186–212.

5. Council Resolution of 7 May 1989.

6. SEC (89) 934 final, September 1989.

7. Directive 75/442/EEC in OJ L194 of 25.7.75.

8. N. Haigh, *Manual of Environmental Policy: The EC and Britain* (London: Cartermill International, 1992 and subs. revs.), p. 5.3–4.

9. OJ L335, 10.12.81.

10. Directive 85/339/EEC; OJ L 176, 6.7.85.

11. N. Haigh, *EEC Environmental Policy and Britain* (London: Longman, 1989, 2nd edn), pp. 165–6.

12. COM(83), 638 final.

13. Haigh, *EEC Environmental Policy*, p. 166.

14. 'Recycling Waste Plastics: A New Agenda Emerges', *ENDS Report*, 172 (1989), pp. 11–14 at 11.

15. Commission of the European Communities, *Completing the Internal Market*, COM(85) 310 final (Luxembourg: Commission of the European Communities, 1985).

16. Commission of the European Communities, *Research on 'The Costs of Non-Europe' Executive Summaries: Groupe MAC, Technical Barriers in the EC* (Luxembourg: Commission of the European Communities, 1988), p. 22.

17. *Commission* v. *Denmark*, Case 302/86.

18. 'Landmark EEC Court Case on Returnable Bottles Gives Boost to Environment', *ENDS Report*, 164 (1988), pp. 3–4.

19. I. J. Koppen, 'The Role of the European Court of Justice', in J. D. Liefferink, P. D. Lowe, and A. P. J. Mol, *European Integration and Environmental Policy* (London and New York: Belhaven Press, 1993), pp. 126–49 at 141.

20. Commission 1990 Annual Report on Monitoring and Application of EC Law, COM (91) 321, p. 216.

21. G. H. Williamson, 'Review of Environmental Legislation in the European Community', in G. Levy (ed.), *Packaging and the Environment* (London and New York: Blackie Academic and Professional, 1992), pp. 53–71.

22. One of the cases cited by the British group Incpen in evidence to the House of Lords Report on the EU's Fourth Environmental Action Programme, given in March 1987, was an Irish government proposal to ban metal cans and plastic containers for beer, metal cans for cider and wine, and cans for soft drinks that had detachable ring-pulls, for example. See House of Lords Select Committee on the European Communities, *Fourth Environmental Action Programme*, 1986–87 Sessions, HL 135, (London: HMSO, 1987), p. 116.

23. 'Tough Recovery Targets Expected in Proposal on Beverage Containers', *ENDS Report*, 187 (1990), pp. 21–2.

24. OECD, *Reduction and Recycling of Packaging Waste* (Paris: OECD, 1992), p. 83.

25. DG XI discussion document on Packaging Waste, undated, AEH/3/91, p. 12.

26. As recognized in the EU's waste management strategy document and the Fifth Environmental Action Programme.

27. Incpen, *Factsheet on Waste Management* (London: Incpen, 1992).

28. J. Hitchens, *Recyclopaedia: Recycling Domestic Waste—Meeting the Challenge: The Views of Leading Experts* (London: SCRIB, 1992); G. M. Levy (ed.), *Packaging and the Environment* (London: Blackie Academic and Professional, 1992).

29. S. Fairlie, 'Long Distance, Short Life: Why Business Favours Recycling', *The Ecologist*, 22 (1992).

30. A. Biod, J. Probert, and C. Jones, 'The Packaging Industry is Not Carried Away by Public Opinion', *Business Strategy and the Environment*, 3:1 (1994), pp. 31–5.

31. 'Recycling Plan Draws Protests', *Financial Times*, 9 August 1991.

32. Greenpeace International, *Critique of the Proposal for a Council Directive on Packaging and Packaging Waste* (Brussels: Greenpeace, 1992).

33. 'Recycling Has Neighbours Crying Foul', *Financial Times*, 25 January 1993.

34. House of Commons Trade and Industry Committee, *Trade with Europe* Minutes of Evidence, HC 216-iv (London: HMSO, 1993), p. 46. Later in the testimony, one representative volunteered the following thought: 'the French government sits down and finds a loophole in the law and does not have to rely on having legislation; they have put it under *eco-emballage*, the French waste paper industry, so that there industry does not lose out to the Germans'. In the light of this comment, it may seem more than a little ironic that the eventual British implementation of the packaging directive resembled closely the *eco-emballage* scheme (see below).

35. 'Export of Waste is Burying Neighbours', *Financial Times*, 5 May 1993.

36. 'France Threatens Waste Import Ban: EC Engulfed by Row over Flood of German Packaging for Recycling', *Fiancial Times*, 30 June 1993; 'Stop the EC Waste War', *Financial Times*, editorial, 1 July 1993.

37. 'Green behind the Ears', *The Economist*, 3 July 1993; 'Clean Europe Sinks under Piles of Cash', *The European*, 1–4 July 1993.

38. 'France Threatens Waste Import Ban', *Financial Times*, 30 June 1993, p. 2.

39. OECD, *Reduction and Recycling of Packaging Waste*; House of Lords, *Packaging and Packaging Waste*; Levy, *Packaging in the Environment*; and Fairlie, 'Long Distance, Short Life'.

40. P. White, P. Hindle, and K. Dräger, 'Life Cycle Assessment of Packaging', in G. M. Levy (ed.), *Packaging in the Environment* (London: Blackie Academic, 1993), pp. 118–47.

41. C. Charlton and B. Howell, 'Life Cycle Assessment: A Tool for Solving Environmental Problems?' *European Environment*, 12:2 (1992), pp. 2–5; Fairlie, 'Long Distance, Short Life'.

42. OECD, *Reduction and Recycling of Packaging Waste*.

43. Fairlie, 'Long Distance, Short Life', p. 279.

44. 'Commission Life Cycle Analysis', *EC Packaging Report Monthly*, 11 (November 1993).

45. See e.g. 'Advantages for Plastic', *EC Packaging Report Monthly*, 8 (July 1993); 'Life Cycle Assessment', Special Report, *EC Packaging Report Monthly*, 9 (September 1993); 'Life Cycle Assessment: *Carton* v. *Glass*', *EC Packaging Report Monthly*, 11 (November 1993).

46. *Commission* v. *Belgium*, Case C-2/90.

47. *Commission* v. *Council*, Case 155/91.

48. 'Brussels in New Legal Challenge on Framework Directive on Waste', *ENDS Report*, 199 (1991), pp. 34–5.
49. 'Legal Basis for EC Environmental Laws', *ENDS Report*, 221 (1993), pp. 44–5.
50. M. Porter, *Interest Groups, Advocacy Coalitions and the EC Environment Policy Process: A Policy Network Analysis of the Packaging and Packaging Waste Directive*, Ph.D. thesis (University of Bath, 1995).
51. DG XI Consultants (DHV) Preparatory Programme: EC Project Packaging Materials, 11 July 1990/Discussion paper for the preparation of a preliminary draft directive on waste packaging, Doc. XI/429/90—EN, 25 July 1990.
52. Proposal for a Council Directive on Packaging and Packaging Waste, COM(92), 278 final–SYN 436, Brussels, 15 July 1992
53. Porter, *Interest Groups*.
54. 'Life Cycle Analysis Association Formed', *EC Packaging Report Monthly*, 3 (February 1993).

Part IV

Models of Environmental Governance

Introduction to Part IV

Our central contention in this book is that over the last thirty years the European Union has created a system of environmental governance that is multi-level, complex, incomplete, and evolving. There is thus an international system of decision-making with sufficient authority to make rules for the protection of the environment, yet one the full character of which is still to be fully determined. We can say that we have a system of governance not only because there are primary rules that control and constrain polluting activity (ineffective though some of these rules might be for certain times and places), but also because there is a system of secondary rules—including associated conventions, norms, and practices—for the making of these primary environmental rules. The primary rules that define policy in any one area are thus housed within a developing body of secondary rules.

We have argued that the system is multi-level, because important decisions are made at different tiers of authority—the EU, the national, and the subnational—so that we cannot understand what happens at any one level without also understanding what happens at these other levels. It is also multi-level in the sense that it is likely to retain these features. Multi-level governance should not be seen as a stage through which European environmental policy will pass; rather, it should be seen as an ineradicable and permanent feature of environmental policy-making within the EU.

The system is complex because there are many actors involved in the making of decisions at any one level and, at the European level, we need to take into account both the wide range of actors and the institutional balance of power and authority among them. It is incomplete because, although it has developed strong and effective policies in some areas, it shows considerable signs of weakness in others. It is evolving because not only has policy developed, but it has developed in ways that often raise fundamental questions about the balance of authority within the EU, giving rise to regular disputes not only about the rules to be decided about environmental policy, but also about the rules for making rules. Subject to considerable change and fluctuation in its operating rules, conventions, norms, and practices, this system of governance has developed the capacity to make significant choices for the European environment, but it also prompts significant questions about its political significance.

So far we have sought to document the EU's system of environmental governance. We have seen how it emerged during the course of the 1970s and was given impetus by the single market programme and the associated political decision-making embodied in the Single European Act. We have seen how the institution-alization of decision-making powers contained in the Single European Act was itself subject to rapid evolution consolidated in the Maastricht Treaty on European Union. Moreover, even during the period of economic recession in the 1990s, and in a period when there was both a downturn in the environmental issue attention cycle and a waning of enthusiasm for European integration, significant developments took place in environmental policy, developments that were often at odds with the rhetoric of an adoption of 'soft' policy instruments.

In addition to these processes at the European level, we have explored the diversity of its underlying national systems, including not only their institutional differences but also their divergent policy paradigms. These continuing differences are one of the reasons why we identify the EU system of environmental governance as being multi-level. Our case studies in Part III were intended to illustrate both this feature of the system and the extent to which it has become horizontally complex.

But how is this system of governance to be understood, and what is its political significance? Answering these questions is the task we seek to accomplish in this Part. To that end, we return to the issues we began with in Part I. There we argued that the emergence of environmental policy within the EU took us to the heart of contemporary debates about European integration. Those debates are standardly cast in terms of the controversy between neo-functionalists and neo-realists. For neo-functionalists, European integration grows out of functional interdependence that is increasingly transcending the boundaries of the nation state. By virtue of the logic of spillover, we should expect that integration in one sector of European public policy will have implications for other sectors. Caught in a web of unintended consequences and facing complex problems and pressures, it is not surprising from this point of view to find transnational structures of governance emerging.

For neo-realists, by contrast, sovereignty is lent, not transferred. There are spillovers to be dealt with, but they arise as a consequence of economic interdependence and characteristically take the form of transnational flows of pollutants that require international action for their solution. From this point of view European environmental governance should be seen as the product of an international bargain in which states agree to enter into systems of mutual constraint to achieve benefits that they could not obtain on their own. National interests, including national interests in the definition of pollution control policy, remain domestically defined.

From these two contrasting sets of assumptions flow a whole series of implications. But in dealing with these contrasting theories we suggested that their comparative evaluation was not straightforward. Neither is as easily tested empirically as one might like. The propositions to which they gave rise are therefore better regarded as heuristic tools of analysis than as hypotheses to be rigorously tested, although this does not imply that we should shirk the task of theoretical evaluation.

What then of the putative third view, that we should study the EU in an institutionalist fashion? As we pointed out in the beginning of this study, the notion that 'institutions matter' is a way of saying that some insight is to be gained about the way in which environmental policy is made by considering the character of the rules that define the making of policy. So in our view we should not take institutionalism as an alternative theoretical paradigm to neo-functionalism or neo-realism, but rather should treat the claim that institutions matter as a working hypothesis and attempt examine empirically how they matter.

Taking this conclusion as our starting-point, we suggest that four questions need examining in the light of the evidence that we have sought to document in the first three parts of this book.

The first of these is motivated primarily by the need to understand the origins of the system and concerns the extent to which those origins can be understood according to the logic of spillover. To what extent should we see institutionalized environment governance in a neo-functionalist way as the consequence of the spillover of integration processes from one policy sector to another? How far did the process have its own logic of development in which member states were caught up, perhaps despite themselves? Conversely, to what extent were the spillovers simply examples of international externalities that member states found it convenient to deal with through international action in which policy outcomes represented a compromise among domestically defined national preferences?

The second question concerns the functioning of the multi-level system. A system of decision-making can be multi-level in some sense and yet still conform to neo-realist assumptions about the nature and character of the international process. So long as the primary direction of influence is from the domestic definition and aggregation of interests to international bargains among political elites, we can think of multi-level governance as consistent with the neo-realist account of integration. How far does the evidence suggest that this is the character of the process? Or does multi-level governance mean that there is a more continuous process of two-way interaction between the international and the national levels, such that interests in the domestic settings are to be understood, partially at least, as the product of transnational forces?

The third question also concerns the functioning of the system but focuses on one of its levels, namely the extent to which Hoffmann's 'logic of diversity' still prevails at the nation state level in the comparative politics of environmental policy in Europe. Here the evidence that we presented in Part II of our study is of particular relevance.

Fourthly, and arguably most importantly, we need to consider the extent to which there has been a transfer of authority from the national to the international level in the EU, and in particular how far we should regard the EU as coming to play the same function in the formulation and implementation of environmental policy that was once performed by the nation state. This is the ultimate question of the political significance of the EU's system of environmental governance.

We seek to address these questions in this part of the book. We offer our own evaluation of each of the questions in the next chapter. We then go on to consider one special question that we think offers special insights into the dynamic of environmental policy integration, namely: to what extent can we meaningfully speak of a north–south divide in environmental policy, a sharp and special case of the logic of diversity? In the final chapter we ask the question: how might the EU's system of environmental governance be reformed so as better to approximate to the public interest of the citizens of Europe?

In the next chapter we analyse the Europeanization of environmental policy in the light of the theoretical expectations that inform our work. We then consider in the subsequent chapter the significance of the north–south dichotomy, before going on in the final chapter to look at possible principles of reform.

13

Understanding European
Environmental Governance

To say that institutions matter—whether we are speaking of domestic institutions, international regimes, or a unique set of institutions like those of the EU—is to treat them as variables that mediate between the preferences and interests of powerful actors and the policy choices that are made. Institutions matters because, so it is assumed, the same pattern of preferences and interests will give rise to different policy decisions in different institutional contexts. Clearly, the claim that there is a system of EU environmental governance implies that, in the making of EU environmental rules and policies, the process through which policy preferences pass is important. However, in order for it to matter, institutions have first to be created. In the case of the EU, this means showing how environmental policy and rule-making grew out of institutions and processes that were established prior to 1972.

If we accept the claim that creating a set of rules is distinct from taking decisions under a set of rules, then it would seem natural to say that theories drawn from the field of International Relations are most likely to have a purchase in explaining rule creation—the 'super-systemic' level of activity.[1] Accordingly, in the first section of this chapter we look at the extent to which the rise of EU environmental governance is best explained in neo-functional or neo-realist terms. Accepting that both traditions appeal to a notion of 'spillover', though the notion is understood in different ways, we ask: how far can the emergence of environmental governance be accounted for by a logic of spillover?

In the second section we look at the functioning of the system in terms of its multi-level features, and in the subsequent section at the horizontal complexity of the system. We seek to ascertain how far the workings of the system correspond to the patterns that we would expect, given the complex institutional process that has been created.

THE ORIGINS OF EU ENVIRONMENTAL GOVERNANCE

Since its earliest development in the 1970s, EU environmental policy has been linked to single market concerns. As we saw in Chapter 1, this was true even before the first explicit recognition of environmental policy in 1972, in directives on chemicals labelling or permissible sound emissions from motor vehicles. During the 1970s and 1980s the relationship between the free movement of goods in a market without barriers to trade and national rules for protecting the environment were raised on a number of occasions, most importantly in the Danish bottles case that went before the European Court of Justice. Moreover, single market concerns are a continuing feature of environmental policy development in the EU. As our case study of the packaging and packaging waste directive in Chapter 12 showed, important measures in the 1990s were also driven by similar concerns and taken under procedures that were formally related to market harmonization, not environmental protection in and of itself.

In seeking to understand the pattern of this issue dynamic, it is useful to look at three factors. Firstly, there are often strong political pressures in a single market to harmonize standards. Consumers find it easier to make choices between products that conform to a common set of standards, and manufacturers can achieve longer production runs if they are not having to tailor their products to national markets. Car manufacturers may want laxer emission standards than do environmentalists. However, they do not want stricter standards in some countries and not in others, when all are supposed to be operating in an integrated market: if there are going to be emissions standards, they should be common across the whole of Europe. Such a view has an obvious structural logic in economic interest, as witnessed by the fact that it is found as much among car makers in the USA as it is in Europe[2]—indeed, there is every reason to think that, in industries such as car manufacturing, the pressure is for common global standards.

Secondly, there is the fear of eco-protectionism, the worry on the part of economic and political actors that environmental standards will operate as barriers to trade. Policy-makers will therefore be under pressure to guard their country's economic interests and will want to examine the compatibility of environmental measures with the free trade regime established under the 1992 programme. This was an important element in the political pressure to develop an EU packaging directive, and, as our discussion showed, the spillover effects of legislation in one country could also have important implications for industries in other countries. Another example of a related phenomenon is provided by the new entrants in 1995. Within a short time, some were already highlighting environmental regulations as a barrier to trade.[3]

Thirdly, important economic interests will be anxious to ensure that the imposition of high domestic environmental standards does not put them at a competitive disadvantage within the single market. Stationary sources like large combustion plants provide the clearest example of how important this has been in the past. Genetic modification and standards in the biotechnology industry may well prove important examples in the future.

In terms of the origins of the system of environmental governance, therefore, we can identify the influence of spillover, as neo-functionalist logic would suggest.

However, this is not to say that the logic operates in impersonal or automatic terms. Rather, it is to say that, given the balance of political forces in different countries, there will be strong political pressures for rule-making arising from the creation of the single market to spill over into rule-making for the environment.

How far is this logic one of 'inherently expansive' tasks, to use the phrase of Haas?[4] There is a clear sense in which the creation of the internal market was an inherently expansive task, since it could always be argued that the completion of the single market entailed a whole series of other changes apart from the removal of physical, technical, and financial barriers to trade. The rule changes needed to bring it about are complex in themselves, have wide repercussions, and their full implications are not always apparent. However, in the case of environmental policy, the logic of policy spillover was somewhat distinctive. The creation of a single market can be presented in purely negative terms in the sense that it involves removing barriers to trade. However, environmental policy does not entail simply the removal of barriers to trade: it also entails the imposition of rules at a European level that were not there before. For this reason, the adoption of environmental rules and rule-making marks a shift from negative integration to positive integration—from measures, that is to say, that create a common market to processes that involve measures to define the conditions under which markets operate.[5]

As Rehbinder and Stewart have pointed out, the transition from negative to positive integration has always been implicit in environmental policy and indeed involves straddling the two logics of European integration built into the treaties.[6] Those two logics can be defined in terms of the removal to barriers to trade in a common market and the demarcation of sectors of public policy, for example agriculture, where market logic is suspended. Environmental policy straddles this divide because, in so far as the removal of trade barriers involves restricting the freedom of member states to impose their own environmental rules, it requires a positive imposition of rules at the European level to provide a substitute.

None of this is to say that the logic of spillover explains fully the emergence of the EU's system of environmental governance. A fuller explanation needs to look beyond simple neo-functionalist logic. Neo-functionalists makes a large, but appropriate, concession to neo-realists when they argue that there is no automaticity in the development of European integration.[7] Once we start to recognize that EU developments may grow out of the interacting strategies of national agents, we begin to see how national preferences may play a role in shaping the character of the environmental governance system. This in turn means that we have to look to that character of the intergovernmental bargains that were struck in the various stages of the development of environmental governance.

Here it is possible to detect the influence of various political pressures, both in the form of public opinion and in the form of international negotiation. Thus, as we saw, the beginning of European environmental policy as a distinct sector of policy is normally traced back to the European Council meeting in Paris in 1972, which reflected the surge of public concern about environmental protection that had swept through the developed world in the late 1960s and early 1970s.[8] Although the early developments were closely related to the development of the single market, they were also related to growing popular concern about the effects of economic growth on environmental amenity and the quality of life, concerns from which politicians, whether they were sitting in national cabinets or in the European Council, were not immune. This political tension between a Europe made conformable to the business and economic interests in favour of an expanded market and a Europe that established its political legitimacy in the eyes of its citizens by its action on those matters that people cared deeply about is one that found renewed expression in the developments of the 1980s and early 1990s, when environmental activism was again revived.

We argued in Chapter 1 that, given the underlying balance of national interests, the condition that made possible the crucial development of EU environmental policy in the Single European Act was a political log-roll, in which the northern leader countries pressed for high environmental standards within the single market and the southern countries pressed for access to structural funds in order to meet the economic demands that those standards implied. This is not to say that there would not have had to have been some formal recognition in the SEA of what the Union had been doing already, but it is to say that the treaty reform would have been unlikely to have taken the form it did, in particular with its insistence on a high standard of environmental protection, unless there had been member state pressure.

We also need to understand the importance of Germany in this process. Until its 'conversion' to environmental protection in 1982, it was often laggardly about international environmental developments. Indeed, for some time it took a narrow and cautious interpretation of the agricultural and transport provisions of the Treaty of Rome in relation to their possible significance for providing a legal basis for environmental policy.[9] European environmental governance received a big impetus from the change of mind of such an important member state. Moreover, the role of Germany can be seen to illustrate an important theme in the neo–realist approach to European integration. States can use their international commitments to strengthen, or at least buttress, their domestic interests. Having made a domestic decision about air pollution policy in 1983, Germany was anxious that other countries did not gain a competitive advantage over it in terms of their energy costs. Although it has played less of a leader role in the 1990s, its place has to some extent been taken by a coalition of environmental leader Nordic states, which have their own domestic pressures to respond to.

Neo–realists argue for their own version of the logic of spillover. However, instead of being defined in terms of inherently expansive tasks, spillover for the neo–realist arises when nation states find they have to deal with transboundary issues, including the transboundary movement of pollutants.[10] 'Pollution knows no borders', as the popular saying has it. Confronted with such a situation, nation states may find it advantageous to establish international regimes to define and enforce public goods at an international level. It might therefore be argued that behind the process of EU task expansion there was an international aspect to the EU issue dynamic.

Confirmation of this view might be sought in the origins of the environmental policy activism of the 1980s, with the German government's acceptance of the seriousness of the problem of acidification and its belief that more should be done to control cross-boundary flows of sulphur dioxide. This dimension of environmental policy received a further impetus with the nuclear reactor accident at Chernobyl, which did much to convince both members of the public and policy-makers in Europe that it was difficult for one country to insulate itself from the harmful effects of its neighbours' behaviour. Similarly, the economic implications on other countries of the implementation of the German packaging ordinance could be thought to have created an incentive to international regulation.

These arguments about the international character of environmental protection could also be intertwined with arguments about the development of the single European market. With products moving more freely across national boundaries, the pressure to harmonize standards of national protection become stronger, as is clearly illustrated in the case of vehicle emissions. Moreover, the argument might even be linked with the claim that the development of global markets requires Europe to mandate the same high standards in its products as the USA and Japan.

However, although the EU has been one forum within which issues of cross-boundary pollution have been internationalized, there is a case for saying that other international bodies have been at least as important in Europe. The Rhine Commission, the United Nations Economic Commission for Europe, and the Conference of North Sea Ministers either came into existence or became more active during the same period as EU environmental policy activism. Moreover, as we saw particularly in the case of acidification policy, the United Nations Economic Commission for Europe has been especially important, not only in providing the legal framework within which international agreements have been struck, but even more importantly in providing an institutional context for the development of research and the application to policy for the notion of 'critical loads', which now promises to drive EU air pollution policy itself.

We can point to an inherent logic of expansion in the international field with environmental policy, but its effects have not been as significant as at first sight they might appear. The explanation for this is presumably to be found in the fact that the boundaries of the EU are not drawn in a functionally specific way, but are fixed for all the policy sectors in which it has competence. For many environmental problems, of which acidification is a good example, these boundaries are insufficiently wide to internalize the relevant externality. This is not to say that the EU is an unimportant forum for international agreements over cross-boundary flows of pollutants. It is to say, however, that there is not a simple one-to-one relationship between the interests of member states in reducing environmental risks and the development of environmental rule-making within the EU.

The emergence of the system of environmental governance therefore needs to be understood both in terms of neo-functionalist logic and in terms of neo-realist logic—the Monnet method overlaid with an intergovernmentalist bargain, if one likes to put it that way. There is a simple reason for this. Unification by stealth, the essence of the Monnet method, has been historically the only way of achieving European integration that is acceptable to the member states. For the same reason that we see the need to combine neo-functionalist with neo-realist logic, we do not wish to separate too sharply the logic of theories for constitutional change and the logic of theories for routine decision-making. Given the logic of integration by stealth, we might expect significant 'constitutional' changes to be the accumulation of everyday decisions, and this is certainly illustrated in the early years of environmental policy. What is more, the origin of the system of environmental governance will have implications for its functioning. We seek to show these influences in the way we look at its character.

THE FUNCTIONING OF ENVIRONMENTAL
GOVERNANCE: MULTI-LEVEL FEATURES

If it is this combination of logics that has given rise to EU environmental policy, what characteristics in its operation does the system of governance display? From our discussion so far, we can identify the following features: the extent and limits of supranationalism, the persistence of national norm-setting, the tendency of countries to go it alone, and the underlying variety in the environmental problems that member states face.

The Extent and Limits of Supranationalism

Within the neo-functionalist interpretation of EU integration, supranational bodies are central. Independent supranational authority is intrinsic to the Monnet method, and its role is reinforced by various features of the formal, legal, and institutional arrangements of the EU. The Commissioners themselves, though nominated by the member states, undertake to be independent of national affiliation and loyalty. Their appointment and term of office was protected during the relevant period by their being in effect immune to parliamentary censure and removal. The Commission is also given the sole formal right to initiate measures, though in practice this has been qualified by the growth of various conventions which allow the Council and the Parliament to bring to the attention of the Commission items that they want on the agenda.

Against this background, it is striking that, in the development of proposals for environmental measures, the Commission is highly dependent upon the member states. How is it that the formal independence of the Commission coexists with *de facto* dependence? Such *de facto* dependence is built into the policy process by the form that integration has taken. Monnet's own predilections, both when developing French economic planning and in the original staffing of the ECSC, was for a small-scale bureaucracy. In his view this both encouraged *esprit de corps* and, in the development of French planning, prevented other ministries from being envious of resources.

This approach was transferred to the EU. As he rather nicely put it in his memoirs, Monnet's principle was that a few hundred European civil servants would be enough to set thousands of national experts to work.[11] In addition, as Peters has noted, the Commission is highly fragmented for a bureaucracy of its size, so that the staff of any one directorate-general is likely to be small in relation to the tasks at hand.[12]

Moreover, as Scharpf has noted, the EU lacks those attributes that confer a high degree of policy-making autonomy on federal states: a relatively homogeneous political culture, a party system operative at the federal level, and a high degree of economic and cultural homogeneity.[13] The lack of these characteristics would make for a weak centre in any system of governance, so it is hardly surprising that their effect is most keenly felt by the Commission, as the body responsible for initiating and overseeing the implementation of European legislation. In the case of environmental policy, there is some offsetting pressure to these centrifugal trends from the strong commitment that a number of observers have noted among staff in Directorate-General XI to the cause of the environment.[14] However, a shared conviction of the importance of the issue you are dealing with does not of itself make for an autonomous policy-making capacity. In a system of multi-level governance like that of the EU, with an intrinsically heterogeneous issue like that of the environment, a small Commission staff becomes vulnerable to whatever parallelogram of forces is most active at the time, and it is made more vulnerable by the absence of the common 'formation' to which all civil servants would be subject if they were staffing national bureaucracies.

Héritier and her colleagues have set out some of the central features of this dependence of the EU upon its member states.[15] They show that EU policy results from tension or competition between leading member states. The capacity of a member state to lead on a particular issue will depend on the extent to which relevant regulation already exists in that state and upon the extent to which its proposed regulatory changes fit into the overall policy objectives of the Commission. It will also depend on the coalitions that can be formed at EU level. Thus, tension arises when member states attempt to retain their traditional regulatory cultures and problem-solving mechanisms by getting them translated to the European level. Germany was successful in the 1980s with its *Stand der Technik* approach, but later things seemed to move towards the more informal approach favoured by the British, in particular on the principles of integrated pollution control.

This interpretation would help explain the heterogeneous nature of EU legislation, especially as the policy relationship between member states and the EU is recognized as a two-way street. The argument here, then, is that the European system of environmental governance provides a stage on to which various national concerns are displaced. Although statehood is being transformed, it still remains central to our understanding of European environmental policy.

National pressures in the making of EU environmental policy may even become stronger rather than weaker as that policy develops. In part, the motive for member states to push their own priorities and approaches stems from the fact that implementation is made easier if EU legislation borrows from the pattern of one's own national system. Fewer changes in standard operating procedures need to be made, and measures are likely to be less costly to implement, if they are incremental changes from a national status quo. So, a relatively small Commission faces states with strong incentives to advance their own conceptions of environmental policy.

As we saw in Part II, there is a marked lack of convergence among member states in their environmental policy stances. They differ in terms of their administrative structures and policy principles. Their patterns of party competition, interest group representation, and associated policy networks vary considerably, and such change as occurs is often more a product of national developments than responses or adaptations to a pattern of European environmental policy-making. The result is that the system of European environmental governance can coexist alongside persisting patterns of policy-making showing considerable national divergence.

In addition, environmental policy has become a policy area in which rival conceptions of European integration and competing national priorities are played out. Thus, Germany, the Netherlands, and Denmark have been anxious since the early 1980s to legislate for high environmental standards, and they were keen to see the Community take the initiative in pushing through more stringent pollution control measures. The UK has often resisted these measures, partly on grounds of cost and partly on the grounds that it disputed their scientific basis. Behind these conflicts of priority lie differences in public sentiment in the different countries, differences in the political priority to be given to environmental policy over competing political goals, differences over the priority to be given to different forms of environmental policy, differences of national understandings of policy problems, differences of economic capacity, and different traditions of thinking about economic development and government intervention. In short, environmental policy appears to display some of the elements of the two-stage logic to which liberal intergovernmentalists in the neo-realist tradition, like Moravcsik, have drawn attention.[16] Governments first define interest domestically and then bargain internationally. Indeed, we can go further and say that we witness not simply differences of interest, but also differences of institutionalization and policy paradigm.

During the 1980s, the most significant point at which these differences were revealed at the EU level was in relation to the negotiations over what eventually became the large combustion plant directive of 1988, as we saw in Chapter 11. The story of vehicle emissions control shows a similar pattern of national differences, both in relation to the priority to be accorded to environmental protection and in the capacity and willingness to take on the economic costs associated with reducing vehicle emissions. National differences in public opinion about the importance of clean air policy and the differing structures of national car industries meant that ministers negotiating in the Council were under contradictory pressures to favour some outcomes at the expense of others. In the 1990s a similar pattern was observed in the packaging directive. Domestic processes define a policy strategy for Germany which then has negative external consequences for other countries that are dealt with through negotiated policy coordination.

As the examples of environmental regulation for both large combustion plants and vehicle emissions go to show, the conflicting national positions on the priority to be given to environmental measures in part reflect the differences of economic capacity of the member states. But they also reflect more general differences of economic philosophy. In particular, there is a much greater emphasis in some continental European countries on the 'steering' of the market by the government, by contrast with the strong anti-interventionist views of the Thatcher and successor governments. Within an interventionist mode of policy market, arguments for publicly supported developments in cleaner technology were more likely to get a hearing than was possible in a more *laissez faire* ideological context. Just as the ideology of ecological modernization has been attractive to parts of the Commission seeking the development of environmental policy, so similar arguments have been particularly influential in some EU countries.

These differences of economic paradigm also extend to questions of compliance and implementation, as the battles over the various directives on the quality of drinking water, bathing water, and standards of waste water treatment plants go to show. Given the complex domestic background, as we saw in Chapter 10, it is perhaps not surprising that the British government was anxious to achieve greater control over the implementation of clean water policy so that its electoral popularity was not damaged by the imposition of steeply rising water charges. In the wake of the Danish referendum, when the Commission was on the defensive, the British government launched its attempt to repatriate various Community competences, including those related to water quality.

However, it would be wrong to portray the European level of decision-making as simply the playing field on which different national policy priorities, approaches to pollution control, and differences of economic paradigm are played out. Institutional processes have an autonomy that means that, once inside the process of decision-making, any issue is subject to capture by other actors, so that what eventually emerges at the other end may contain elements uncongenial to its original proponents. Again, given the impact of apparently small 'technical' features of rules on costs and compliance, there is a great deal of scope for a transformation of proposals during the course of their passage: timetables for implementation can be changed, emission limit values altered, new processes brought under control, administrative requirements changed, and so on. Moreover, the need to secure a concurrent majority in the process of decision-making means that there is little incentive for policy participants to point out the full implications of measures to member states even if they know them. It is much more attractive to secure agreement in principle and then argue later about the extent to which member states are implementing what they have signed up to.

A good example of the complexities at work is provided in the example of the development of the directive on integrated pollution prevention and control. Integrated pollution control has been a cause close to the heart of UK environmental policy-makers and advisers for a number of years.[17] Although it originally sought to put the issue on to the EU agenda, the UK found that its scope and significance was expanded in the course of the directive's passage through the process of decision-making, in particular to include a wider range of industries, especially intensive livestock rearing and food and drink plants. In other words, the development of the directive took a more stringent direction than had originally been intended by the UK and the original initiative was thereby transformed.

European environmental standards, then, are neither a reflection of a dominant coalition of countries pushing their own national style of regulation nor a merry-go-round in which different countries have a go at imposing their own national style in a sector that is of particular importance to them (as might be implied by a simple neo-realist analysis). Instead, they are the aggregated and transformed standards of their original champions, modified under the need to secure political accommodation from powerful veto players in a horizontally complex system.

The Persistence of National Norm Setting

Another important aspect of the functioning of multi-level governance is the continuing persistence of national norm-setting. The amount, scope, and stringency of EU environmental regulation has certainly grown since the early 1980s, but this is consistent with a great deal of important norm and standard-setting going on at national level.

One clear indication of this is to be found in the fields of product norms and packaging. As developments were stalled at the European level, so individual member states went ahead, developing their own schemes. In the case of eco-labelling, for example, national organizations set different standards for products and, just as importantly, identified different products as priorities. Moreover, even in sectors that are regulated at the European level such as air and water pollution, there are many pollutants that are left to individual member states to set standards.

In addition to the forms of environmental protection that are not covered by European standards, there is a great difference from country to country in the way the attainment of standards is embedded within the different national policy-making styles. Consider for example the contrast between Dutch and UK policy-making styles. As we saw in Chapter 6, as environmental policy developed in the Netherlands in the 1970s, it became the practice to construct medium-term plans (the IMPs) setting out explicit reduction aims for specified pollutants negotiated with target groups. This approach was generalized in 1989 in the National Environmental Policy Plan, which sought to set more comprehensive plans for a wider range of pollutants but still in the context of negotiation with target groups.

The British policy style, by contrast, has been conducted within a less explicit public framework of consultation and on the assumption that policy networks were relatively small and closed. Privatization and the 1990 legislation changed much in respect of the formal situation, particularly in the water industry, but there is evidence that the culture of negotiated compliance that was so characteristic of the former Alkali Inspectorate persisted in some parts of its successors for some time.

It is also worth noting that there is an open question about the extent to which there is a genuine convergence of interpretation around measures that have been formally agreed at an international level. Consider, for example, the principle of 'best available technology not entailing excessive cost', which is to be found in the 1984 air pollution framework directive. This provision is also found in the national legislation that followed in the implementation of the measure; but, as Michael Faure and Marieke Ruegg have pointed out, there can be considerable differences of national interpretation as to what the principle means in particular cases.[18]

This is not to say that we cannot identify clear instances in which the environmental policy of the EU has altered the policy position, institutions, or practices of member states. The UK provides the most obvious source of examples. As the reluctant or 'awkward' partner in Europe, one might expect the most resistance to environmental policy developments from the UK. Hence, if we observe clear influences on policy, this ought to be a sign that something significant is happening. The 1984 air pollution framework directive provides evidence that touches on this question. Much of the UK's 1990 Environmental Protection Act was necessary in order to implement the requirements of the directive, and it was this directive that led to the creation of air quality standards in the UK for the first time. Similarly, the retrofitting of flue-gas desulphurization equipment to power stations was necessary in order to conform with the 1988 large combustion plant directive. By the end of the 1980s the UK's environmental policy had been driven from Brussels for most of the decade.

The UK is not alone in this regard, however. It is possible to point to instances in all member states where practices have had to be changed in order to conform to EU legislation. Perhaps the most striking example among the new member states of the 1980s is provided by Spain. Its dependence upon Brussels has been notably marked in the environmental field, where, as we have seen, it chose to adopt the whole corpus of EU legislation after its entry in 1986. This decision was taken in the atmosphere of high politics in which entry to the EU was seen as confirming Spain's transition to democracy. However, there is also a clear sense in which the example of Spain confirms the 'persistence of national norm-setting' thesis. Although it adopted the corpus of EU environmental legislation, it has taken the most cautious view of EU environmental policy of all the cohesion countries, stressing the priority of economic development over environmental protection within the Council of Ministers. Here again, domestic policy processes play a big part in determining international policy positions.

The Tendency of Countries to Go It Alone

It could be argued that there is a fallacy in inferring the Europeanization of environmental policy from observations of the policy-making process in Brussels. Such a basis of evidence is bound to distort our perceptions since we are looking only at the cases that countries think are worth arguing about at an international level. What about the times when they are happy to pursue their own priorities or simply are not bothered about kicking up a fuss because their own standards are higher than the Commission is proposing anyway?

Liefferink provides an interesting example in this context in connection with the development of policy on the 1980 directive on air quality limit values and guide values for sulphur dioxide and suspended particulates.[19] Dutch policy had already developed on this issue, and there was little interest in seeking to influence the Commission in its drafting process since it was clear that any standard that was set at the European level would be less strict than had already been agreed in the Netherlands. For this reason there was no lobbying by Dutch industry at European level. Similar considerations apply, Liefferink argues, in connection with the air quality standards on lead and nitrogen oxides.

This tendency to go it alone acquires special significance in the context of the accession of Austria and the Nordic countries in 1995.[20] With a relatively strong institutionalization of environmental policy and marked pro-attitudes to international control, one might have thought that the Nordic countries in particular would favour further Europeanization; however, as Andersen points out, the potential for the dilution of environmental standards in a Europe in which most decisions are made by qualified majority voting might lead them instead to favour a Danish position, in which the stress is laid upon the continuing ability of a country to set higher standards than the EU if it so chooses.

Varying Conditions

Behind the persistence of distinctive member state positions lies the fact of uneven development, which is also a source of conflict and an impediment to the achievement and implementation of an EU environmental policy. There are four countries in a less advanced development stage: Spain, Portugal, Ireland, and Greece. Their less developed economic status is the source of their position on a number of issues ranging from climate change through the time-scale for the implementation of clean-up measures to their energy policies. It is not, of course, a simple matter to escape the consequences of such uneven development.

Economically advanced northern states, initially Denmark, the Netherlands, and Germany and more latterly the UK, have tried to set an agenda dealing with environmental issues of ozone depletion, global warming, and biodiversity. By contrast, the southern member states have insisted on the linkage between environmental protection and development, identifying the northern member states as most implicated in the consumption of natural resources and demanding that financial resources and technology be transferred in various ways to enable the southern member states to cope with the environmental problems arising from inadequate infrastructure and underdevelopment.[21] It is for that reason that, as we saw in Chapter 10, the Cohesion Fund played an important role in securing the acceptance of an important directive like that on urban waste water treatment. Because of varying conditions, the politics of regulation cannot be separated from the politics of redistribution.

However, without being geographically determinist, it is possible to argue that the national differences in policy-making style and priorities are not simply a lagged response by countries at different levels economic development to a common set of environmental problems, but reflect the fact that national environments differ so that their policy needs differ. The most marked contrast here, of course, is between the relatively undeveloped countries of the south (Portugal, Spain, and Greece, as well as the Mezzogiorno) and the industrialized, densely populated countries of the north (notably Germany and the Netherlands). Here the argument is that there simply are objective differences in the nature of the problems faced by these different countries, and some of these differences will not be eroded over time. Germany, post-unification, is not going to acquire a longer coastline, and Spain is not going to acquire a river Rhine. Hence, so the argument goes, it is unrealistic to expect a high degree of policy convergence, and we should not be surprised if the issue dealt with at the European level did not reveal the priorities of different countries.

The important role of the member states means that the neo-functionalist logic of supranational authority is constantly being qualified in the field of environmental policy. EU environmental policy can certainly have an important effect on member states, but conversely it is constrained and shaped in its functioning by those member states. Moreover, the privileged position of the member states, as given by their bureaucratic and political strengths, is only partially offset by other institutions and transnational interests in the horizontally complex elements of the EU's system of environmental governance.

THE FUNCTIONING OF ENVIRONMENTAL GOVERNANCE: HORIZONTAL COMPLEXITY

The period between 1972 and 1997 involved several phases in which the pace of institutional change was significant. In particular, between agreement on the Single European Act in 1986 and the ratification of the Maastricht Treaty in 1993, formal institutional rules for the making of environmental policy changed, altering the balance of power among EU institutions. Lodge characterizes the general shape of institutional arrangements after Maastricht in terms of imperfect bicameralism, imperfect parliamentary supervision of ministers, imperfect cooperation among the institutions, different interpretations of the decision rules, and inadequate information sharing among the institutions.[22] In order to evaluate this characterization, it is useful to look at the role of the European Parliament and the European Court of Justice, as well as the influence of policy networks.

The European Parliament: The Power of the Parvenu

From the point of view of parliamentary systems in Europe, the powers of the European Parliament appear few. It is not the formal source of legislation; it does not appoint or overthrow governments; its party alignments are not well established; it is less attractive than national parliaments to those for whom politics is a career rather than a form of early retirement; it does not have the last say on legislative matters. In short, it still has to make the transition fully from a consultative body to a legislative body holding the executive to account (although no doubt the increase in its powers in the Treaty of Amsterdam will strengthen its hand). Moreover, by comparison with the Council of Ministers, its formal powers are few.

There is much truth in this view. However, the more we accept it, the more we are presented with a paradox. The environmental rule-making and standard-setting process in *national* political systems is not one in which parliaments play a strong role once the legislative powers under which governments can set standards are in place. It is possible to find examples where there is a strong parliamentary influence in matters of environmental policy—for example the collapse the Christian Democrat–Liberal coalition in the Netherlands in 1989, or the rejection by the UK Parliament of the proposals for VAT on domestic fuel at the standard rate—and in Germany the *Länder* are able to have their say on proposed measures in the Bundesrat. However, by and large, the initiative for the changing of standards comes from the government, and typically involves bureaucratic, rather than parliamentary, activity.

As we saw in Chapter 11, in the case of car emissions, the reason why a 'weak' parliament can exercise such strong powers is due in large part to the logic of the institutional rules under which it operates. Located in what is, in effect, a system built on the principle of the separation of powers, the Parliament has been able to present a majority in the Council sizeable enough to be a winning faction with amendments leading that majority to accept tougher standards than they would have done on their own. Moreover, the Parliament was also important in placing the issue of poor implementation on the European political agenda, extending the powers of the European Environment Agency,[23] and sending back to the Council the draft directives on landfill.[24] In each case, the Parliament has taken a tougher pro-environment position than the common, or agreed, position of the Council. The power of the Parliament is, of course, by no means uniform, and certainly does not mean that it is as powerful an actor in the process as the Council, whose predominance we saw illustrated in the example of amendments to the packaging directive as it was reshaped during the course of its passage into legislation. However, in some respects the Parliament has exercised stronger powers than its counterparts at national level.

In noting that the European Parliament does not control a government in the way national parliaments do, we are simply committing a category mistake if we then infer that the Parliament's influence on environmental policy is weak. The correct comparison is not with the powers of national parliaments in Europe, but with a system like that in the USA in which there is a separation of powers between the executive and the legislature. To be sure, the European Parliament does not have the powers of the US Congress, but it would be surprising if it did after so short a period in its history. Even so, the adoption of the cooperation and co-decision procedures under Maastricht gave the Parliament important powers, and with ratification of the Treaty of Amsterdam it will be further strengthened in its veto power under the extension of the co-decision procedure. We should also note that the Parliament in many ways behaves as we would expect unconstrained legislators to do, being prone to take strong stands on symbolic issues, like car emissions and consumer packaging, independently of the merits of the arguments of particular cases.

The Role of the Court

The formal development of policy at the European level has also been fostered by the European Court of Justice. Arguably, the ECJ is at the 'federal' end of a federalist/intergovernmentalist spectrum of EU institutions.[25] It deals directly with the citizens of Europe, and early in its life it developed the doctrine of the direct effect of European law and its precedence over domestic law in cases of conflict. In the environmental field it has passed down a series of landmark judgments that have affected the character and scope of environmental policy. Thus, it has allowed that the protection of the environment is a legitimate ground for restraint of international trade, provided the means employed are not disproportionate to the purpose in hand, and it sided with the Commission against the Council of Ministers in the titanium dioxide case, deciding that a measure should have been taken under Article 100 rather than Article 130s when the Single European Act still made a distinction between single market measures and environmental protection measures in terms of the use of qualified majority voting. Hence the ECJ has both supported strong environmental measures and made their passage easier.

It is useful to distinguish between the direct and the indirect roles of the Court in the horizontal division of powers. Its direct role relates to its decisions on primary rules, for example in its doctrine that measures of environmental protection are sometimes legally valid restrictions on trade, provided they are proportionate to the ends being sought. Its indirect role involves its adjudicating on the procedures by which decisions are taken and the legal competence of EU actors under the treaties to participate in decision-making. This indirect role is thus related to adjudicating on secondary rules. In many ways it is this indirect power that is most striking in defining the horizontal complexity of the EU's system of environmental governance. To be sure, some of its crucial judgments about the powers under which measures should be taken were a feature of the development of institutional rules of the EU at a particular stage of their development. However, to the extent to which the Court has a constitutional role, it is not impossible to imagine its having to decide in cases where the Council was at odds with the Commission or the Parliament about where the correct balance of authority lay. Such a role in shaping decision processes is inseparable from the horizontal complexity of the system.

European Policy Networks

But the complexity of the story does not stop here. In addition to the formal involvement of various actors in the decision-making process, the Commission has also been called a 'promiscuous bureaucracy',[26] because of its tendency to involve interest groups in the making of policy.

Our case studies revealed several ways in which the EU's system of environmental governance relates to the practice and behaviour of interest and lobby groups. Its rule-making powers obviously provide a focal point of attraction for groups from all sides to influence the way in which rules are framed. Given diminishing marginal returns in the imposition of environmental standards, many of what appear to be a small 'technical' changes in the rules can turn out to have major cost or environmental implications, providing business groups in particular with an incentive to participate actively in the rule-making process. Sometimes, as was evident both in the case of the urban waste water directive and the packaging directive, the importance of the rules being made was such that new groups from the affected industry were actually created in order to lobby subsequently on future policy developments.

For environmental groups, the EU, and the Commission in particular, can be a target of influence and a source of support, including financial support. Within the multi-level system, this support is manifest as much at the national as at the European level. Precisely because there is European legislation in cases where it otherwise might not exist, environmental groups are provided with increased sources of power and bargaining, as they point to implementation failure or use national courts to secure action that would otherwise not take place. Moreover, certain European directives, for example the directive on freedom of environmental information, provide a resource for environmental groups that would otherwise not exist. The involvement of interest groups in the processes of standard-setting and rule-making should not be regarded as trivial or simply as a matter of decision-making courtesy. Instead, we should think of it as involving the concurrence of functional groups, in which sectional interests often can have something close to veto power.

AN INCOMPLETE SYSTEM

It is one thing to claim, as we have done, that there is an institutional autonomy manifested in EU environmental policy-making, even when EU policy processes are subject to the pressure and influence of member states. It is another thing to show that there is a fullness of institutional development, such that we can see in the EU's system of environmental governance a complete and integrated system of decision-making. We can see the incompleteness in the lack of environmental integration in other EU policy sectors, the limited range of policy instruments used by the EU, and the mismatch between the scale of policy problems and the patterns of institutional task assignment.

Why So Little Environmental Policy Integration?

The development of environmental policy involved an issue dynamic in which environmental control intersected with policies for the creation of a single market. From one point of view, this is not surprising. The creation of the single market is an 'inherently expansive' task, to use Haas's formulation. The rule changes needed to bring it about were significant in themselves, had wide ramifications in terms of their effects on the balance of decision-making authority within the EU, and had implications that were not always apparent at the time at which they were adopted.

However, the logic of task expansion applies with special force in the case of environmental policy, but in the reverse direction. Pollution problems typically arise as by-products of otherwise legitimate activities in society, including industry, agriculture, and transport.[27] In so far as governments seek to deal with these questions, they are required to use some technique of regulation. In one sense, therefore, we can say that there is not just the logic of spillover from the single market to environmental policy, but also a logic of spillover from environmental policy to the single market. Indeed, there is a need to integrate environmental considerations into a wide range of policy sectors if there is to be policy success.

Although the need for policy integration has been formally recognized in the Action Programmes since the earliest days of environmental policy, the implementation of the principle has been at best partial. Andrea Lenschow has shown that implementation has been more successful in some policy sectors than in others.[28] In respect of the regional funds, policy moved effectively between 1988 and 1993 from being a reminder of the importance of environmental concerns in the granting of funds to institutionalizing environmental assessment as an obligatory part of the decision process. Even so, implementation was sometimes deficient. In the case of the Cohesion Funds, there was also formal recognition of the importance of environmental concerns, but this was often accompanied by a failure to achieve practical integration, at least until administrative reorganization under the Santer Commission. The most conspicuous example of a failure of integration was agricultural policy, however, where it has been known for some time that pollution was a by-product of the system of agricultural subsidies that were aimed at promoting production. Even when subsidies after the MacSharry reforms in 1992 began the process of decoupling subsidies from production and linking them more to income support, the scale was not large and the funds available for more extensive forms of production were limited.[29]

The failure of environmental considerations to penetrate other policy sectors such as agriculture at the European level is accounted for in part by the organizational structure of the Commission itself, in which strong vertical divisions favour highly sectorized policy-making, according to the institutionalized policy belief systems of different DGs, and in part by the central political place of agricultural policies in the Treaty of Rome. In these respects, then, the development of environmental policy is inhibited by the logic of the institutions created in the process of European integration. These disjointed patterns have been reinforced by the multi-level logic of the Structural and Cohesion Funds, where project development occurs at the level of the member states whose practices are difficult to monitor by the Commission. We can thus summarize the role of spillover by saying that its direction has been more usually from the single market to environmental policy than from environmental policy to the single market.

Illiberal Instruments and Liberal Foundations

The basis upon which European political unification developed was economically liberal: the creation of a common market without barriers to trade in goods and services and allowing the free movement of capital and people. This approach goes back to Monnet himself, who, with his own career background in international business, was hostile to the traditional French policy of protectionism.

Of course, economic liberalism is not the whole story, as the existence of the interventionist Common Agricultural Policy testifies. Nevertheless, the liberal elements were of crucial importance. Moreover, such a view of European integration must represent more than a personal vision on the part of Monnet himself. That Jacques Delors was able to revive the pace of European integration in the 1980s by stressing the importance of the completion of the single market and the added impetus that the 1992 programme gave to integration are both likely to reflect important features of the underlying dynamic of the process. Enough member states could see enough advantages over a suitably defined range of issues to give the completion of the single market priority. It is not evidence against this conclusion to note that the implementation of the programme has not been perfect and that protectionist sentiments have not been eliminated.

Within this context, Majone has identified the case for saying that there is a liberal argument in favour of the EU developing a strong environmental policy, in order to correct for market failure.[30] The essence of the argument rests upon the claim that regulation by a political authority is sometimes necessary in order to promote economic efficiency. In fact, as we saw in Chapter 2, the EU Commission and Council have long accepted the logic of the argument that an effective approach to pollution control requires the need to internalize the external costs arising from pollution by the use of economic instruments.

Despite these commitments of principle, it is striking that little opportunity has been taken for using economic instruments in the attainment of environmental objectives. For example, policies aimed at the reduction of sulphur dioxide emissions have not used the sort of permit trading that has been developed in the United States in order to achieve least-cost reductions. This is so despite the structural similarity of the problem on both sides of the Atlantic, with sulphur deposition in both Europe and the USA arising in large measure from spatially concentrated electricity-generating sources, often operating with old plant, with regions suffering the pollution being asymmetrically situated with respect to those causing it.

Similarly, the Commission has not attempted to extend and make mandatory in all member states the successful use of emissions for water pollution that exist in some. Most strikingly, perhaps, is the failure at European level to develop economic instruments for the control of greenhouse gases, of which the failed carbon-energy tax is the clearest example.

Indeed, the failure to develop instruments is even more striking than these examples suggest, since the resistance of economic instruments can go as far as the Commission wishing to prevent member states from using such instruments to meet their own pollution control objectives. The clearest example here is probably provided by the Commission's opposition to the Dutch attempt in the 1980s to encourage cleaner cars. In the wake of the Council decision of 1985, which established the framework within which subsequent measures on emissions controls for cars were negotiated, the Dutch government introduced a subsidy to encourage the purchase of cleaner vehicles.[31] This stimulated opposition from other member states, most notably France, which protested to the Commission about the measure. In 1989 there was even the threat of a European Court of Justice reference by the Commission, though it was not acted on in the end. Thus, not only do we find little use of economic instruments, but we even find instances where there is opposition to their use at member state level.

In large measure, these restrictions stem from the legal constraints imposed by EU treaties. The effect of these treaty agreements is to give member states veto powers over the development of taxed-based instruments for environmental protection at the European level. Under the Maastricht Treaty, the use of fiscal instruments for environmental policy objectives was subject to unanimous voting in the Council of Ministers, rather than qualified majority voting, thus giving veto power to any one member state. A clear example of the use of such veto powers was seen in the opposition of the UK to the proposed carbon-energy tax. To be sure, there were doubts about the wisdom of the tax in the UK environmental policy community,[32] but the UK government opposed the measure on the principled grounds that the EU should not acquire more tax-raising capacity.

We have in this case, therefore, an indication of the inherent limits of functional integration and a symptom of the influence of member states in the intergovernmental logic of environmental governance. In order to avoid raising the large constitutional questions about sovereignty, the Monnet method adopts the approach of focusing on the low-politics issues of technical standards and market integration. However, if there is a need to use fiscal instruments in order to raise standards, it is impossible to avoid intruding on one of the responsibilities that on any definition is at the heart of the modern state: tax policy. If we then embed the Monnet method in a system of decision-making that gives the member states a privileged, if not all-powerful, place in the making of policy, the limits of functional integration are reinforced by the desire of member states to preserve their own resources.

Supranational Authority and Subnational Public Goods

The EU is clearly more than an international regime, even though it may be constrained in its development and freedom of manoeuvre by its constituent national states. The legal doctrine of the direct effect of Community law, its powers of implementation, and the extensive scope of the issues with which it deals all mark it out as a supranational authority of a distinct kind. However, this fact alone highlights a third form of incompleteness: how does it come about that a supranational body, which might be thought best tailored to the protection of international public goods, has spent a great deal of time and effort on matters concerned with local public goods, including urban air quality, bathing water, and drinking water? In other words, how has it come about that task assignment in EU environmental policy has taken the form of highly developed strategies on local public goods and relatively underdeveloped strategies on international public goods?

Task assignment involves the specification of functions and competences to different levels with a multi-level system of governance. If we were looking for a coherent rationalization of task assignment, one obvious source would be within welfare economics and the utilitarian tradition more generally. According to this approach, policy competence and political authority should be placed at the level at which it will be most effective and efficient. In particular, jurisdictional competence for the protection of public goods should be set at the level at which the public authorities are large enough to internalize the relevant externalities.[33] A contrast with this approach would be the principle of subsidiarity, according to which (in its most natural interpretation at least), there should be a bias to the local in the assignment of functions, and a distrust of centralization. Logically speaking, a proponent of the principle of subsidiarity ought to be prepared to countenance forgoing some of the benefits of centralization in order to preserve the advantages of local control. Whichever of these two views we take, however, neither would suggest that an international organization like the EU should be regulating the supply of subnational public goods.

Once again, in answering this question, we need to look at the specific features of the Monnet method. Integration through functional interaction is bound to the logic of spillover. The solution to one set of problems leads on to other problems. Just as the customs union led to the single market, which in turn led to economic and monetary union, so we cannot say in advance where the resolution of policy problems will lead. The efficient secret, to use Bagehot's useful term,[34] of this approach is the *acquis communautaire*. Roughly speaking this means that, having acquired a competence, the EU will not give it up. There is therefore no role in the constitutional politics of the EU for an equivalent to the tenth amendment of the US constitution, which states that powers not expressly granted by the states to the federal government remain reserved to the states' governments. The *acquis* is central to the Monnet method of European integration, since it imparts a bias against the ability of member states to reclaim their historic rights against the supra-national authority of the EU.

Moreover, this distinctive feature of the constitution of the EU is reinforced by the form in which functions are assigned. In this respect, to the extent that the EU is federal in form, it follows the logic of German rather than US federalism. Scharpf has argued that the EU is one of a class of political systems in which decision-making authority is not allocated in a zero-sum fashion between differ-ent levels of government but is instead shared.[35] Thus, the German federal gov-ernment shares authority with the *Länder* through the need to secure a majority in the Bundesrat, and in many matters the division is not one of responsibility for policy sector but for stages of the policy process, with *Länder* governments hav-ing the responsibility for the implementation of policies agreed at the federal level. This pattern applies in environmental policy within the EU, since the typical mode of carrying out environmental measures is for the member states to implement, according to their own procedures and laws, the measures that are contained in environmental directives.[36] So, rather than having a neat division of sectors of pol-icy between Europe and the member states, we have the less clear-cut distinction of responsibility for different phases of the policy process.

Following the first Danish referendum on the Maastricht Treaty in June 1992, the British government secured an EU review of environmental legislation in an attempt to see whether some responsibilities could be repatriated. The argument was that the principle of subsidiarity, according to which functions should be carried out at the lowest feasible level, implied that the regulation of bathing water quality, for example, should be a matter for the member states and not for the EU. However, the review did not issue in a change of responsibility. In practice, the application of the principle of subsidiarity was not used to reassign compet-ences for particular issues of policy, but interpreted as an opportunity to assert the importance of 'soft law' approaches to environmental regulation.[37] In place of the formal directives and regulations that had characterized environmental policy during the 1980s, greater stress would be placed on voluntary agreements, nego-tiated rule-making, and other non-legal forms of environmental policy control.

Significantly, not a single piece of legislation has been repealed, and reform of the drinking and bathing waters directives is taking a great deal of time.

CONCLUSIONS

It is tempting to draw an analogy between the Europeanization of environmental policy and the nationalization of environmental policy that took place in the early 1970s in many countries. The nationalization process involved harmonizing environmental standards and aspirations across subnational governmental authorities, reassigning policy responsibilities in a number of fields from local to national authorities, creating or enhancing national administrative capacity, and placing new legislative policy instruments on the statute book. It also involved significant changes and developments in the political practices of various states, ranging from the incorporation of environmental policy goals into party programmes, through the expansion of relevant interest groups and environmental policy organizations to the establishment of new political parties.[38]

With this background in mind, can we say that the Europeanization of environmental policy involved similar changes but this time with a shift of authority from the national to the European level? Just as the nationalization of policy involved taking environmental issues up into the processes of democratic competition at the national level, so the Europeanization of environmental policy should involve a similar process in the context of European democratic competition.

If there were these close parallels between the two processes, then this would be evidence for a strong version of the neo-functionalist interpretation of European integration. Consider the famous account by Haas:

Political integration is the process whereby political actors in several distinct national settings are persuaded to shift their loyalties, expectations and political activities toward a new centre, whose institutions possess or demand jurisdiction over the pre-existing national states. The end result of the process of political integration is a new political community, superimposed on the existing ones.[39]

However, the simple analogy between the nationalization of environmental policy in the 1970s and its Europeanization in the 1980s and 1990s is more complex than the process that Haas suggests. Superimposition is more than a simple replacement.

One respect in which there is a significant difference is that it is not possible for environmental issues to be taken up in a process of democratic competition at the European level as it was at the national level. There simply is no effectively functioning process of democratic competition at the European level. Not only is the EU heavily conditioned, in constitutional terms, by its origins as a union of member states, but the infrastructure of democratic competition (European-wide political parties, European political leaders, and a European system of communications) is simply lacking. Thus, if we set out to look for indicators at the European level similar to those that we can identify at the national level, we simply shall not find them.

At this point, some will say that the absence of the conditions for democratic competition at the European level means that policy is not Europeanized. But this would simply be a category mistake. To say that a policy field has become Europeanized is not to say that it has been democratized. The two features are logically independent of one another. Europeanization with the democratic deficit is clearly an option—indeed, the only option—that we can meaningfully speak about under the present institutional arrangements.

It is worth stressing this latter point. The fact that we could not observe the Europeanization of environmental policy in the same form in which we can observe the nationalization of environmental policy in the 1970s is a consequence of the Monnet method of European integration. The aim of abolishing barriers to the internal market was incorporated into the Treaty of Rome, and has led to the predominance of negative over positive integration. That is to say, it has been easier (though not of course easy) to secure the reduction in barriers to trade than to achieve the pre-eminence of European over national policy-making. Some significant elements of the European legal order and the practices of policy-making have helped to create a situation in which policy-making authority is shared, including the fact of bureaucratic opportunism and the doctrine of the *acquis communautaire*; however, except in the fields of international trade negotiations and large parts of agriculture and fishing, the development of European policy competence has been in conjunction with national systems.

What, then, might be the implications of this institutional and functional sharing of rule-making authority? The first consequence is that, in a system in which the agreement of so many actors is necessary in order to have any chance of policy change, policy-makers within the Commission have a strong incentive to be opportunistic in their agenda-setting, taking proposals from member states, safe in the knowledge that there is at least some support at the beginning for a measure. Add to this incentive the organizational disadvantage of having little by way of resources to conduct policy analysis and development, and the stage is set for opportunistic decision-making relying upon the initiative of member states.

However, even the supranational elements of the decision-making system are often heavily dependent upon the capacity of the member states, with the Commission reflecting in its own priorities the items that powerful member states wish to bring on to the agenda. In this respect at least, the logic of diversity prevails. The capacity of the Commission to develop its own distinctive intellectual paradigm is limited, and even where there are articulated principles it is often difficult to put them into effect. There is a lack of a genuinely transnational European 'public space' within which issues of environmental policy can be debated or discussed. Although the European Parliament has been an agent of supranational standard-setting, its influence is intermittent and it is subject to the checks and balances of a decision-making system in which the member states have a privileged position, and which operates in any case according to the principle of concurrent decision-making. The two-level game of European policy-making still operates in a context in which not only the actors differ at the two levels, but the rules and practices do too.[40]

However, the principle of shared authority applies not simply to the relations between the EU and the member states, but also to the relations between different elements of the EU decision-making process itself: the Commission, the Court, the Parliament, and the Council of Ministers. The involvement of all these actors in the decision-making process increases the number of 'veto players', that is, actors whose agreement is required for a change in policy.[41] The principle of concurrent majorities thus operates both vertically, in respect of the EU and the member states, and horizontally, in respect of policy actors at the European level itself.

Despite the persistence of these intergovernmentalist features, there *was* environmental spillover from the single market. It was *not* anticipated in the creation of the internal market. Even before the single market was created, there was a trend towards task expansion in the creation and development of environmental policy. Environmental standard-setting is often a technical process, and member states have found themselves involved in a web of unanticipated consequences. All of these features are in line with the theoretical predictions we would derive from neo-functionalism.

We can also speak of an institutionalization of environmental policy, and we can study the system of decision-making as we would study any institution, provided we bear in mind that the shape and character of the institutional arrangements are a consequence of the complex functional and intergovernmental processes by which they arose. It is an interesting question how the European system of environmental governance might be reformed in order to overcome some of the decision-making pathologies to which political systems built on the principle of concurrent majorities are prone. This is a question we shall take up in the final chapter. However, before we do so we consider the extent to which the divisions between northern and southern Europe present a unique problem with which European environmental policy needs to cope.

NOTES TO CHAPTER 13

1. J. Peterson, 'Decision-Making in the European Union: Towards a Framework for Analysis', *Journal of European Public Policy*, 2:1 (1995), pp. 69–93.
2. C. J. Bailey, *Congress and Air Pollution* (Manchester and New York: Manchester University Press, 1998), p. 145; cf. the views of those responsible for emissions from stationary sources at 149.
3. The following gives a good example of the complaint: 'The consequences of over-enthusiatic regulation are most acute on environmental issues, where member states

are free to set higher standards than those specified by Brussels: "This is actually posing a risk to the single market," says Mr Kari Jalas, who represents Finnish industry and employers in Brussels. He says he has received hundreds of complaints from Finnish exporters who cannot operate effectively in Germany because of German laws requiring packaging materials to be recycled.' E. Tucker, 'No Appetite to Change the Mix', *Financial Times*, 31 October 1996, p. 15.

4. E. Haas, 'International Integration: The European and Universal Process', *International Organization*, 15 (1960), pp. 366–92, at 376.

5. For this definition, see F. W. Scharpf, 'Negative and Positive Integration in the Political Economy of European Welfare States', in G. Marks, F. W. Scharpf, P. C. Schmitter, and W. Streeck, *Governance in the European Union* (London: Sage, 1996), pp. 15–39, at 15.

6. E. Rehbinder and R. Stewart, *Environmental Protection Policy* (Berlin and New York: Walter de Gruyter, 1985), p. 22.

7. See P. C. Schmitter, 'Examining the Present Euro-Polity with the Help of Past Theories', in G. Marks, F. W. Scharpf, P. C. Schmitter, and W. Streeck, *Governance in the European Union* (London: Sage, 1996), pp. 1–14, at 7.

8. See N. Haigh, *EEC Environmental Policy and Britain: An Essay and a Handbook* (London: Longman, 1989, 2nd edn), p. 9; Rehbinder and Stewart, *Environmental Protection Policy*, p. 17; and R. Wurzel, 'Environmental Policy' in J. Lodge (ed.), *The European Community and the Challenge of the Future* (London: Pinter, 1993, 2nd edn), pp.178–99.

9. Rehbinder and Stewart, *Environmental Protection Policy*, pp. 19–20.

10. A. Moravcsik, 'Preferences and Power in the European Community: A Liberal Intergovernmentalist Approach', *Journal of Common Market Studies*, 31:4 (1993), pp. 473–524, at 474.

11. J. Monnet, *Memoirs*, trans. by R. Mayne, with a forward by Roy Jenkins (London: Collins, 1978), p. 373.

12. B. G. Peters, 'Escaping the Joint-Decision Trap: Repetition and Sectoral Politics in the European Union', *West European Politics*, 20:2 (1997), pp. 22–36, at 28.

13. F. W. Scharpf, 'Community and Autonomy: Multi-Level Policy-Making in the European Union', *Journal of European Public Policy*, 1:2 (1994), pp. 219–42, at 222; also cited in A. Hurrell and A. Menon, 'Politics like Any Other? Comparative Politics, International Relations and the Study of the EU', *West European Politics*, 19:2 (1996), pp. 386–402, at 39.

14. J. Peterson, 'Playing the Transparency Game: Consultation and Policy-Making in the European Commission', *Public Administration*, 73:3 (1995), pp.473–92, at 482.

15. A. Héretier, S. Mingers, C. Knill, and M. Becka, *Die Veränderung von Staatlichkeit in Europa* (Opladen: Leske & Budrich, 1994).

16. Moravcsik, 'Preferences and Power', p. 481.

17. A. Weale, T. O'Riordan, and L. Kramme, *Controlling Pollution in the Round* (London: Anglo-German Foundation, 1991).

18. M. Faure and M. Ruegg, 'Environmental Standard Setting through General Environmental Law', in M. Faure, J. Vervaele, and A. Weale (eds.), *Environmental Standards in the European Union in as Interdisciplinary Framework* (Antwerpen and Apeldoorn: MAKLU, 1994), pp. 39–60.

19. D. Liefferink, *Environment and the Nation State: The Netherlands, the EU and Acid Rain* (Manchester and New York: Manchester University Press, 1996), ch. 5.

20. M. S. Andersen, 'From Narvik to Naples: Environmental Policy in an Enlarged European Union', paper presented at the conference 'Governing Our Environment', Copenhagen, 17–18 November 1994.

21. This process is not unlike the relationship between developed and underdeveloped countries more generally. Compare the remark of Klaus Töpfer to the effect that when he was German environment minister he came to see that for the north it was the 'United Nations Conference on Environment and Development', but for the South the 'United Nations Conference on Development and the Environment'. K. Töpfer, 'Sustainable Development im Spannungsfeld von internationaler Herausforderung und nationalen Handlungsmöglichkeiten', in H. Steinmann, and G. R. Wagner (eds.), *Umwelt und Wirtschaftsethik* (Stuttgart: Schäffer-Poeschel Verlag, 1998), pp. 93–103, at 99.

22. J. Lodge, 'The European Parliament', in S. S. Andersen and K. A. Eliassen (eds.), *The European Union: How Democratic Is It?* (London: Sage Publications, 1996), pp. 187–214, at 197–8.

23. D. Judge, ' "Predestined to Save the Earth": The Environment Committee of the European Parliament', *Environmental Politics*, 1:4 (1992), pp. 186–212.

24. See 'EC Waste Policy up in the Air as MEPS Reject Landfill Directive', *ENDS Report*, 256 (1996), pp. 38–9.

25. M. Shapiro, 'The European Court of Justice', in A. M. Sbragia (ed.), *Euro-Politics: Institutions and Policy-making in the 'New' European Community* (Washington: Brookings Institution, 1992), pp. 123–56.

26. S. Mazey and J. J. Richardson (eds.), *Lobbying in the European Community* (Oxford and New York: Oxford University Press, 1993).

27. A. Underdal, 'Integrated Marine Policy. What? Why? How?' *Marine Policy*, 4:3 (1980), pp. 159–69.

28. A. Lenschow, 'The Greening of the EU: The Common Agricultural Policy and the Structural Funds', *Environment and Planning* C, 17:1 (1999), pp. 91–108.

29. For details of these evaluations, see Lenschow, 'The Greening of the EU', pp. 94–103.

30. G. Majone, *Regulating Europe* (London and New York: Routledge, 1996), pp. 28–31.

31. G. J. I. Schrama and P-J. Klok, 'The Swift Introduction of "Clean Cars" in the Netherlands, 1986–1992: The Origin and Effect of Incentive Measures', in M. Jänicke and H. Weidner (eds.), *Successful Environmental Policy: A Critical Evaluation of 24 Cases* (Berlin: Edition Sigma, 1995), pp. 203–22.

32. House of Lords Select Committee on the European Communities, *Carbon-Energy Tax*, HL 52 (London: HMSO, 1992).

33. See e.g. S. Peltzman and T. N. Tideman, 'Local versus National Pollution Control: Note', *American Economic Review*, 62:5 (1972), pp. 959–63; J. Rothenberg, 'Local Decentralization and the Theory of Optimal Government', in J. Margolis (ed.), *The Analysis of Public Output* (New York and London: Columbia University Press, 1970), pp. 31–64. Most of the relevant arguments were anticipated by H. Sidgwick, *The Elements of Politics* (London: Macmillan, 1891), pp. 496–500.

34. W. Bagehot, *The English Constitution*, ed. with an introduction by R. H. S. Crossman (London: Fontana/Collins, 1867; 1963 edn) at 65.

35. F. W. Scharpf, 'The Joint-Decision Trap: Lessons from German Federalism and European Institutions', *Public Administration*, 66:3 (1988), pp. 239–78, at 242.

36. A. Jordan, 'The Implementation of EU Environmental Policy: A Policy Problem without a Political Solution?' *Environment and Planning* C, 17:1 (1999), pp. 69–90.

37. B. Flynn, *Subsidiarity and the Rise of Soft Law*, Occasional Paper no. 40 (Colchester: University of Essex Human Capital and Mobility Network, 1997).
38. See A. Weale, *The New Politics of Pollution* (Manchester and New York: Manchester University Press, 1992), ch. 1.
39. E. B. Haas, *The Uniting of Europe: Political, Social and Economic Forces, 1950–1957*, Stanford, Calif.: Stanford University Press, 1968, 2nd edn), p. 16.
40. R. D. Putnam, 'Diplomacy and Domestic Politics: The Logic of Two-Level Games', *International Organization*, 42:3 (1988), pp. 427–60.
41. G. Tsebelis, 'Decision Making in Political Systems: Veto Players in Presidentialism, Parliamentarianism, Multicameralism and Multipartyism', *British Journal of Political Science*, 25:3 (1995), pp. 289–325, at 301.

14

North and South in the European Union:
From Diffusion to Learning?

It is clear that there are considerable differences among member states in the EU with regard to the position they take on environmental policy, and the strategies they have developed, or failed to develop, in order to deal with problems of pollution. In this respect, Hoffman's 'logic of diversity' prevails. Indeed, it is precisely this variation that our selection of countries has been chosen to bring out in order to test the possibilities of, and the problems associated with, European integration in this field.

The six countries we have examined in detail span different levels of economic development, have been members of the European Union for varying lengths of time, and frequently maintain different stances on environmental policy in forums like the Council of Ministers. Domestically, they contain political and policy processes that are often sharply distinct from one another, with strong legacies from history that shape both policy style and substance. On the other hand, as we have discovered in our analysis of national systems and their functioning in Part II, in addition to common, secular influences, a range of Europeanizing pressures have gradually begun to modify national diversity. The EU has undoubtedly had significant effects in the environmental area.

Yet, despite this diversity and emerging patterns of Europeanization, one major cleavage among these countries has impressed many observers: that between the northern group of countries on the one hand, and the southern group on the other. This is a view fairly widely held within both policy circles and the media. It is also held, in some incohate form, at the public level, although more informed members of policy and media networks are aware of its complexities. It is an assumption possibly coloured by a more general perception of north–south differences and conflicts over the environment. Northern countries have a reputation for post-materialist environmental sensitivity, while the southern countries, still struggling with developmental problems and motivated by the urge for economic modernization and higher productivity, place a much lower priority on environmental concerns.

There are, admittedly, contextual factors that encourage debate about a north–south dichotomy. Firstly, the majority of southern member states are relative newcomers to the EU: Greece joined in 1981 and Portugal and Spain in 1986. Since the EU was a largely northern organization in the first decade of its environmental policy development, and as the activist countries were precisely the 'verdant' member states, it is self-evident for historical reasons that this policy originated very much in the north. To describe the southern countries as 'laggards' can be misleading, however. Precisely because of their late arrival in the EU, they have been under considerable pressure to adapt environmentally, not to mention developmentally.

Secondly, there is some justification for seeing the southern countries as having different environmental problems from those in the north stemming both from nationally specific problems and from common regional problems. A number of the common problems relate to the Mediterranean sea, which has been described as 'the world's biggest liquid dustbin'; other problems derive from an extremely arid climate. There is furthermore a shared emphasis on the importance of natural habitats, for the Mediterranean environment is characterized by a profusion of rare flora and fauna. At the same time, certain common northern problems such as acid rain are not issues, just as the southern countries generally do not suffer from the overall population density of countries like Britain and the Netherlands (apart from the coastal strips and a few metropolitan areas).

The EU has recognized that certain socioeconomic characteristics differentiate the southern countries (and Ireland) and warrant special treatment. For instance, it has attempted to develop a strategy for the protection of the Mediterranean environment, on the grounds that this is subject to distinctive problems such as coastal overpopulation, recent industrialization, and mass tourism. These were seen as not just local problems, but also European ones, requiring coordinated international action where different EU instruments and policies were relevant.[1] This has resulted since the later 1980s in a series of special programmes to that effect, including ENVIREG, MEDSPA, LIFE, and also the Cohesion Fund. While limited, they respond to southern appeals for special assistance with environmental adaptation. Significantly, they involve official recognition that the south *is* different from the north in terms of developmental stage.

Thirdly, there are said to be cultural factors that demarcate perceptions of the environment in the southern countries from those in the north. The most brazen interpretation of this is the thesis of a 'Mediterranean syndrome', whereby

the production of the 'environment as a collective good' becomes highly problematic, not only because individuals 'stubbornly' free-ride, but also because the democratic Leviathan, with its regulatory and enforcement functions, is neither able nor willing to overcome the impasse.[2]

This thesis refers also to a civic culture which sanctions non-cooperative and non-compliant behaviour, along with a 'syndrome' which marks the functioning of administrative and political structures, and thus impacts directly on the policy process. Significantly, the outcome is a non-existent or even negative form of social learning.[3]

If true, such a syndrome makes for considerable value conflict if not cognitive dissonance when it comes to adopting 'northern' policies and procedures demanded by Brussels. However, lumping together the southern states is risky as it rides roughshod over cross-national variation within the region. As we have seen above in Part II, there are enough differences between our three southern countries on grounds of administrative structures, policy patterns, and record as well as cultural patterns to make generalizations of this nature about the 'south' somewhat questionable. There is clearly a strong oversimplification in any assertion of a simple north–south dichotomy in the EU over the environment. It involves forcing national histories into a particular regional mould, and thus suppressing cross-national differences within both parts of Europe, if not significant subnational differences within individual member states of the EU wherever they are located. Furthermore, cross-national differences may also vary over time, although probably to a limited degree.

In this chapter, therefore, we seek to explore the perceptions as well as reality of north–south differences among our six countries, using evidence from our elite interviews. In particular, we assess how far this matters with respect to environmental policy and whether or not the common experience of EU membership can actually affect these differences. In examining push and pull factors, conclusions are drawn about the possibilities for moving beyond the diffusion of policy strategies and ideas to international learning.

IS THERE A NORTH–SOUTH DICHOTOMY?

Since policy-makers are often aware of basic differences between north and south, it may be assumed this outlook influences policy presentation and even substance. A tendency to generalize and to group member states is evident both in policy statements and in informed media commentary. For example, a European Commission overview of environmental policy in the EU in 1990 referred to north–south differences in the following terms:

There is friction between those who demand strict Community norms to control pollution and those who believe in the setting of less severe quality objectives. And especially since the enlargement of the Mediterranean bloc in the Community in the mid-1980s, there has been a fundamental split between those who stress the legislative, standard setting approach of Community policy, and those who seek more concrete but costly actions to help member states and their regions remedy problems like soil erosion, forest fires and coastal pollution.[4]

Similarly, a report of 1989 on the 'greening' of Europe in *The Economist* categorized the then twelve member states in a threefold way: (*a*) the 'most verdant' (well developed national policies, combined with seeing the EU as a threat to their 'greenery')—the Netherlands, Germany, and Denmark; (*b*) the 'least verdant' (in the earlier stages of developing environmental policies, where European legislation has become 'the framework and the spur')—Greece, Portugal, Spain, Ireland, and to some extent Italy; and (*c*) countries in between, where environmental policy has existed for years but where the EU had tended to force its pace—Britain, France, and Belgium.[5] As we saw in Chapter 1, one way of interpreting the bargain that was struck by the Single European Act was as a log-roll in which the north obtained high environmental standards and the single market and the south obtained access to the Structural Funds along with the environmental obligations of achieving those high standards.

From their point of view, policy-makers in southern countries also recognize this difference of perspective and interests. We conducted interviews with political and bureaucratic elites in environmental policy-making circles as well as with prominent leaders of environmental organizations. These included general questions on the possible existence of a north–south dichotomy. Our interviews establish the significance in respondents' minds of differences between north and south, but also throw light on how far the perception of a north–south dichotomy might affect policy.

In *Greece*, the first of the new Mediterranean entrants to the EU, it is possible to find this attitude clearly stated. But there is often an ambivalent view taken of Brussels' role in environmental affairs. On the one hand, Brussels is a welcome source for funds to assist environmental modernization; on the other hand, it is also much criticized for its particular sectoral priorities in the area, ones that are commonly seen as not in accord with Greek interests. Greece is, of course, the one member state that lacks a border with the rest of the EU. Therefore, the sense of common transnational problems, at least within the EU, is less pronounced, although this does not apply to pollution of the Mediterranean sea.

In *Italy*, reaction to a hypothetical dichotomy and the influence of northern countries on EU environmental policy was distinctly less polemical or aggressive than in Greece or Spain. This might simply reflect Italy's much longer membership of the EU and the fact it has not had to adapt too suddenly to accommodating much past European legislation. But it is also likely to exemplify the lack of 'nationalist' outlook among Italian elites, an attitude often coloured by an expressed or implicit desire for the Italian system to be buttressed by Brussels.

Our interviews in Rome revealed strong support for Mediterranean cooperation in the environmental field. Its various intergovernmental forums were accorded detailed and positive mention by a high-ranking official (deputy head of the *cabinet* of the minister of the environment), who commented on 'the growing attention we are giving the problems of the environment, not only *vis-à-vis* the EU, but also all the other neighbouring countries that in one way or another have habitats comparable to Italy's'.[6] A strong awareness of the transnational nature of many environmental problems reinforced Italy's sense of dependence on the EU and other international bodies: 'therefore, we are firmly convinced that a serious and

productive environmental policy is only possible by means of a network, the tex-
ture of agreements and international activity'.[7]

However, it became clear that this Mediterranean cooperation was not particularly replicated among the southern European states within the EU. According
to the head of the international office of the same ministry, there was little coordination with other countries in the region aside from cooperation over environmental research programmes, such as with Spain.[8] The lack of any pronounced
sense of a north–south dichotomy in Rome probably related to this. The most common feature of responses there on this general question, not only among political
circles but also among economic leaders and environmental organizations, was to
differentiate between the ways in which one could or could not speak about a
north–south distinction. Thus, a director of Confindustria responsible for environmental matters acknowledged such a dichotomy as 'an incontestable fact', which
it was important to attenuate. But it could not be eliminated, simply because such
differences existed within Italy itself—'between Piedmont and Sicily, one imagines
between Sicily and the region of Uppsala or Finland'.[9]

An official in the national office of the major environmental organization, Lega
per l'Ambiente, differentiated in other respects. He agreed there was a dichotomy
between north and south when it came to the functioning of institutional structures ('the environmental policy of the Italian government is, without doubt, not
at the same level as that of the government in Germany, in Denmark, or the
Netherlands'). However, he also pointed out that the environmental organizations
in Italy were not inferior to those in the same northern countries, and this marked
Italy off from Spain and Greece[10]—a self-interested but accurate remark. The same
respondent also criticized these other two southern countries, which 'cause me fear',
as, in order to reach the levels of the economically strongest states, they put the
environmental concerns in the background.[11]

In the case of *Spain*, there was some similarity with Greece but one noteworthy difference. Political circles in Madrid also showed a fairly strong sense of
EU environmental policy being 'northern' in its priorities and approach, all the
more so as Spain was seen to be a latecomer as a member state. As in Greece,
respondents expressed concern and also resentment about this. At the same time,
Madrid sought to try and make changes in European policy. No doubt, an awareness of being a larger member state and one desirous of influence in Brussels encouraged such an intention. There was also less fatalism felt in Spanish governmental
circles compared with those in Greece. This was reflected in the remarks of a Spanish
MEP and former head of the cabinet of Prime Minister Suarez. She agreed that
for 'historical reasons' EU policy was very northern-oriented, and that sectoral concerns were somewhat divergent between north and south, but she voiced a belief
that matters could change: 'The North Sea is a *communautaire* sea, but the Mediterranean is also a *communautaire* sea—and that, it should be made understood.'[12]

From the evidence of our interviews, it is clear therefore that there is a perceived difference between north and south, although it is nuanced in various ways.

As the *Economist* classification makes clear, what we are dealing with here is not just a simple dichotomy—we need at least to recognize the intermediate position of the UK. Nor can Italy be regarded as simply southern: not only do we have to recognize the familiar split between its own north and south, but we also have to acknowledge that it will distinguish itself from other southern member states, not least because of its founder status within the EU. Also, Italy has been somewhat more open to policy innovation, while environmental awareness developed earlier these than elsewhere in the south.

Moreover, when it comes to the European level of decision-making, the line-up of countries on environmental issues is not always easily predictable in north–south terms; for example, Greece sided with Denmark in holding that proposed car emission standards were not stringent enough. Yet, despite its obvious oversimplification, the contrast between north and south does raise an important issue within the system of European environmental governance: to what the extent can the ambitions of those who favour more sustainable development within the European Union be realized?

In many ways, as we have seen in our case studies, differences in policy priorities do present problems. Conflicting policy preferences of member states at the European level are one of the principal sources of political disagreements in the legislative process. And the privileged position of member states within the decision-making process means that these differences are often the ones that dominate the policy process taken as a whole. However, such differences can also be viewed another way. Instead of a problem of political coordination, they can be seen as an opportunity for policy learning. After all, policy learning presupposes differences among those who might learn from one another. Although countries may do things differently, if understood in the right light, these differences can be powerful intellectual sources of improved policy understanding. Precisely because no two countries are the same, there is an opportunity to observe how problems may be dealt with successfully by political systems other than one's own.

In the case of environmental policy, there is an important twist to this argument. According to at least some proponents of stronger environmental measures, countries that are less developed economically need not repeat the environmental mistakes of the more developed. The World Commission on Environment and Development, for example, noted at several points in its report that attempts to maintain social and ecological stability through old approaches to development and environmental protection would increase instability. And it pointed out that experience in the industrialized countries was that anti-pollution control technology had been cost-effective in terms of health, property, and avoiding environmental damage.[13] Implicit in these claims is the view that new forms of economic growth that pay greater attention to environmental and ecological constraints are likely to be sustainable in the long run in the way that conventional economic growth is not.

Within the EU this argument has received expression in many places, but it was clearly stated in the 1989 report of the Task Force on the Environment and the Single Market. Noting that there was no automatic association between economic growth and improvements in environmental quality, the Task Force asserted that the failure to promote the demand for clean technologies would mean that the most likely course of economic development within the internal market would predominantly be ' "dirty growth" with some "end-of-pipe" pollution control systems only where required'.[14] They foresaw a role for environmental regulation, therefore, in creating the market in Europe within which pollution control technologies could be stimulated and developed, helping less economically developed EU countries to avoid the pollution burdens of the more developed. From this perspective, differences of economic circumstance become the opportunity to learn internationally from the experience of other countries and to implement alternative forms of economic development.

In many ways, it may be thought that the EU provides a highly favourable institutional arrangement for learning compared with existing environmental international regimes. By contrast with other contexts within which international learning is said to have taken place—for example the Mediterranean Action Plan, where epistemic communities of scientists have been ascribed an important role[15] —there is much greater opportunity for exchange of information and understanding as well as continuing policy interaction within the EU deriving from its status of being more than a regime, as well as much greater ability to transfer economic resources between participants. Moreover, although the disparities of income and wealth in the EU are significant, they are not as great as those between countries on the north of the Mediterranean and those (African countries) on its southern rim. Hence we should expect even greater international learning in the case of the EU than we find elsewhere.

The north–south difference exists, therefore, but its implications for the EU system of environmental governance and the extent to which it can be transformed into a mechanism of international learning is a matter for debate. In examining the possibilities inherent in the present system, we shall distinguish between the *diffusion* of policy strategies and ideas and international *learning*. Diffusion exists when policy principles and strategies are transferred from one country to another. We conceive it as a one-way process in which principles and practices from one political system are transferred to another. Learning, by contrast, involves discovering how to operate with principles and strategies and applying them to one's own context in a creative way. Moreover, we shall be concerned with the extent to which there is emerging a two-way flow of policy information and ideas between north and south. This is an aspect of the system of governance that we would take as indicating that an international network of policy learning was being created in Europe.

We shall argue that the international diffusion of policy strategies has taken place. Various factors—including the search for competitive advantage by leading countries, the legal requirements of the EU expressed in the *acquis communautaire*, and evolving institutional change within the EU—have led to international diffusion.

On the other hand, there are also restraining factors that pull the EU system of environmental governance back from the diffusion of ideas and approaches from north to south, including the importance of different environmental problems, the barriers created by the economic costs of effective pollution control, and (more contentiously) the place of cultural inhibitions. How these forces of push and pull have worked themselves out to create a specific pattern for the diffusion of environmental policy strategies from north to south is the subject of the next section. Subsequently, we consider how far this diffusion ought to be thought of as learning.

PUSH AND PULL IN INTERNATIONAL DIFFUSION

As we noted in the previous chapter, one of the principal causes for the diffusion of high pollution control standards is the attempt by northern countries to ensure that their industries are not put at a competitive disadvantage by having to incur higher costs than industries within other EU countries. This demand for higher emission control standards across Europe has been provided with an intellectual rationale: the need to create a market in pollution control technologies that is large enough to rival the market in Japan and the USA. This theme is found, for example, in the Task Force Report on Environment and the Single Market, which pointed out that the standards embodied in the 1983 German legislation on air pollution required the use of catalytic reduction processes that could be purchased only from Japan.[16] The argument of the Task Force was that the single market would not develop the capacity to produce world-class pollution control technology without some pressure from high standards of environmental regulation; and therefore the claim is made that the EU needs to adopt high standards. It is significant in this context, as the report points out, that Spain, Portugal, and Greece have only one firm each ranked among leading engineering exporters worldwide.[17]

Similar arguments were advanced in the case of car exhaust emissions, but in this case they were given a further twist by the argument from tourism. The German minister Dr Zimmermann, responsible for the environment between 1983 and 1986, announced that Germany would require the use of catalytic converters on cars by 1989 (see Chapter 11). This immediately raised issues about the availability of lead-free petrol, since catalytic converters cannot function on leaded petrol. But this in turn led to a further problem. As an official in the German environment ministry explained to us, Germans like to holiday in the south, but in countries like Spain unleaded petrol was sparse in the 1980s. There was therefore a need to seek to ensure that *all* European countries would adopt higher standards of car emissions, in order to foster an infrastructure of supply that would overcome this latent problem.

If a key northern member state like Germany was politically important in the diffusion of higher environmental standards throughout Europe, the institutional and legal framework of the EU itself was also crucial, particularly the principle of the *acquis communautaire*. According to this, new member states are obliged to accept the entirety of existing EU legislation. Temporary derogations are allowed only in specific circumstances. Because the distinction over membership between new and old overlaps so much with the distinction between north and south, inevitably there has been a diffusion of policies from north to south, particularly for those states that joined after the renewed surge of environmental activism in the early 1980s. This was notably the case of Spain's accession in 1986, for example, when that country simply adopted—lock, stock and barrel—the EU's environmental legislation as part of its domestic law. Lacking much history of its own legislation, it was left with little choice.

The pressures as we have described them have emerged largely through the political priorities of member states, typically Germany, or through the structural pressure of the *acquis*. By contrast, we can find little evidence of the role of epistemic communities in fostering EU policy developments.[18] Such epistemic communities are said to consist of institutionally affiliated scientists and other experts, who have come to share a common understanding of a policy problem and to favour a particular set of solutions. There are few epistemic communities in this strict sense. For example, during the 1980s and the 1990s the German Council of Environmental Experts published a number of significant reports on matters of environmental policy, but we cannot trace any evidence of their influence outside Germany, unless mediated through the international pressure of the German government. Indeed, in the case of the UK, which, with the Royal Commission on Environmental Pollution, has one of the most highly developed and sophisticated expert bodies in Europe, there is evidence of formal contact, but little evidence of intellectual exchange.

There is, however, some evidence that administrative and scientific exchanges have been useful as a way of building mutual understanding. This showed up in interviews with senior figures in the Istituto Superiore di Sanita, a large research organization attached to the Italian Ministry of Health, who were interviewed in 1995. One recognized the strong influence of northern countries at this level. But implicit in his comments was a positive view of fruitful exchanges with scientists elsewhere, especially those from EU and other international programmes which facilitated and funded such exchanges. Drawing on his experience here, he saw various differences among the northern countries in professional terms (for example different ways of modelling carcinogenic risk assessment), and was particularly flattering about Dutch contacts for the extent of their expertise and initiative as well as the efficiency of their research teams.[19] By comparison, experience with Greek contacts was more variable and was affected by some different concerns. One other respondent noted, for instance, that Italian research circles were far more numerous and better structured than those in Greece—and, for that matter, much better equipped than those in Spain.[20]

If there was one northern country praised in the southern countries for its assistance and lessons offered, that was the Netherlands. The then director-general of environmental policy in the Spanish Ministry of Public Works, Transport, and the Environment, Señor Beltran, mentioned the fruitful and regular contacts between Madrid and The Hague, in particular concerning the use of strategic plans where Holland is 'one of the pioneer countries'.[21] Interviews in Athens revealed a similar pattern of beneficial collaboration with the Dutch. There has been bilateral cooperation between the two countries on environmental matters since 1983. This commenced in the early years of the Greek Ministry of the Environment, since the then minister Tritsis 'thought that it would be a good thing to gain some experience from a more experienced country on environmental issues'[22] Cooperation since has focused on such matters as training personnel (with a continuous flow of technical personnel between the two countries), problems of organizing environmental inspectorates, and exchanges of information and advice.[23] Italian respondents, by comparison, revealed a less intimate relationship with any northern country at the policy level, although, as we have already noted, those interviewed in the Ministry of Health's Istituto Superiore di Sanita were positive about north–south links in official scientific circles. Again, the Netherlands was selected for particular mention. The Dutch National Environment Plan of 1989 was a source of admiration among Italian environmental groups.[24]

So far we have focused on elite-level factors that have played a role in the diffusion of policies and ideas from north to south. What of the influence of movements in civil society? There is in fact little evidence, as distinct from opinion, that pressures arising from civil society have played a role in the diffusion of environmental policy strategies between north and south, or indeed between countries within each region. However, large environmental groups in some southern countries indicated that their participation in multilateral projects and conferences (for example on Mediterranean pollution) was fruitful for scientific learning and strengthening contacts. These were often funded by the EU, which was welcome, given scarce resources in the south.[25] Such activity related to the pattern of transnational networking by larger environmental groups, discussed in Chapter 7 on national political environments.

If these are the push factors, leading to the diffusion of certain ideas, what are the pull factors, holding back the development of environmental policy and the transfer of strategies and measures from the north to the south? One important reality is simply the difference between the environmental situations and problems of the northern and southern countries. These differences are well understood by participants in the policy processes, and were expressed clearly during our interviews. The southern countries face several different environmental problems from those in the north. Some of these problems are specific to particular countries, but there are also common regional problems, notably those associated with the Mediterranean sea and with an arid climate. On the other side, there are certain common northern problems, such as acid rain, population density, and traffic intensity.

These differences emerged very clearly in the Spanish experience when acceding to existing EU legislation and priorities. A section head in the environmental structure of the Ministry of Works recalled his own observations when Spain first joined:

And when we entered, because we entered late, there is a price. There are structures and habits very difficult to break. In the environment area, we arrived late, the Community already had an environmental philosophy. The themes of Spain like the drought . . . I remember having gone to Brussels, to speak about the drought, and they looked at me as if I were extra-terrestrial. I was negotiating the entry of Spain at this very point . . . They looked amazed at me when I spoke about deserts and desertification and drought, which mean that the *quality* of water is not important to one, that what one wants is *quantity*, what one wants is water even though it is dirty . . . Spain will not reach the levels of central Africa, but in Spain too we lack water. Our problem is the lack of water; and, after that, the quality. And these problems the Community does never [appreciate, as with] forests fires.[26]

There was some tendency to highlight north–south differences among senior officials in the Ministry in Madrid. The head of the air pollution section selected acid rain as an example:

The problems that we countries of the south have are not the problems of the countries of the north. For the problems of acid rain, that have been one of the central issues of the Community in its environmental legislation, affect us very little. Here, we practically have no problems of acid rain, among other things because our soil is alkaline, it has a large component of limestone and, therefore, certain acid rains favour us because they have a neutralizing effect on the soil. Our problem has nothing in common with the problem that Germany can have with the deterioration of the Black Forest. It is totally different. And this is not always contemplated at the moment of planning a Community directive or Community legislation on environmental matters.[27]

The same sense of a north–south dichotomy could be felt at the regional level. The head of an environmental section in the government of Catalonia, that region closest to the European core, described EU environmental policy as expressing 'a mentality of the north, of the north of Europe, compared with that of the Mediterranean'.[28]

If differences of environmental problems are important in delaying or slowing the diffusion of northern environmental policies and ideas, so are differences of priority arising from the cost implications of environmental measures. Again Spain provides a relevant example, particularly in its bargaining position concerning the large combustion plant directive. Within the Council of Ministers, attention was often focused on the conflicts between the UK and other member states, including Germany and the Netherlands, which supported the proposed directive. But, in fact, Spain was as much an opponent of it as the UK. With its orientation towards development, Madrid feared that high electricity prices would make its relatively unproductive economy uncompetitive.

Given the greater productivity of the northern countries, southern countries like Spain can compete only on factor costs such as lower wages and environmental standards, an aspect of their economic development that is particularly important in the case of process regulation—like the large combustion plant directive.[29] Moreover, high environmental standards are likely to prevent southern countries using what some of their policy elites would regard as an allowable margin of deterioration in environmental quality in order to achieve higher economic growth. There is thus a common concern in the south about environmental costs, a concern more pronounced in Spain and Greece than in Italy. There are also similar sectoral concerns (most notably, coastal water quality and its implications for tourism), as well as a high priority placed on economic development (again, more marked in the two entrants of the 1980s), with a tendency to view environmental standards as an obstacle to a high rate of growth.

These differential concerns about costs and benefits in the adoption of stringent pollution control measures by and large worked themselves out in predictable ways among northern and southern members. It is of course the persistent UK concern with issues to do with the costs of environmental regulation that has made London an ally to some southern countries, for example Spain on the large combustion plant directive and Greece on a number of issues. However, the political consequences that emerge from the typical pattern of costs and benefit do not always follow the simple lines of north versus south. Greece was able to take a tough stand along with Denmark on the control of emissions from car exhausts, in part because of its concern over damage to its historical architecture and in part because it does not have its own car industry, so that Athens was not subject to the same pressures on the topic as, for instance, the Italian government.

Moreover, we should be careful not to interpret this argument about costs and benefits in terms of a simple thesis that greater prosperity in a country leads to higher levels of awareness about environmental problems. After all, Germany was prosperous in relative terms well before its government became a strong proponent of environmental policy in Europe; so there is no straightforward association between high levels of income and environmental awareness in a population. Conversely, within the southern states, there may be higher levels of public awareness about the environment than there were in more developed societies at comparable periods of development. In other words, southern countries have the combined task of fostering economic development and at the same time dealing with higher environmental expectations among their populations.

One problem restraining the diffusion of ideas is the notion that what is involved is a form of 'policy imperialism'. This attitude was particularly marked in interviews with policy circles in Greece. The strength of feeling about a north–south dichotomy in the EU was revealed in an interview in 1992 with the Minister of the Environment, Physical Planning, and Public Works, Achilleas Karamanlis, in the then New Democracy government. The tone was defensive about Greek policy, but also highly critical of northern countries for their own 'neglect' of environmental protection. It is worth quoting at length:

many times we are subject to an unjustified criticism, if you don't mind [my saying so], from all those that are criticizing us for not taking measures for the protection of the environment, when they themselves ignored the environment . . . It is an issue between north and south, between developed and developing countries . . . More or less, it happens this way. We the southerners, that follow the issues because we have to protect the environment, feel that we have some pressure from the northern countries on what to do and not to do. There is, no doubt, there is this different appreciation, you see, and different responsibilities, you see! The truth is that there is pressure. On the other side, nevertheless, we have intense problems of growth . . . of course, today development in order to take place under environmental considerations costs very much . . . Anyway, always, within the framework within which the Community decides regarding the environment, we harmonize and we care to act in conjunction with economic development and the protection of the environment.[30]

The only acknowledged departure from a north–south confrontation was that 'in particular with Great Britain, we agree on many environmental issues; therefore, it is not absolute that a north–south interest exists'.[31] This is likely to refer to a common sensitivity to environmental demands from Brussels than to a range of common sectoral preferences on environmental policy. The interview was typical in expressing a Greek sense of identity with developing countries in general.

The feeling of resentment, evident here at the top, was present too in bureaucratic circles across ministries in Athens. Particular Greek environmental interests were cited. A round-table discussion with environmental officials in the Ministry of Agriculture explored why:

I believe the EU is not helping very much in certain things. That is, the Community policy is selective—it gives more weight to ENVIREG. It helped the infrastructure, because it was related to the technology of waste treatment, etc., but for the protection of wild life, fauna and flora, we struggled for a year in order to convince them to give some money for the protection of the wolf, and they were not so eager to help. This means that we accept the directives, [but] we have difficulties in complying with them. We do not have training, personnel, money, but also we do not have the assistance that we wished to have, a balanced help. It [the Community] helps where it wants; when it does not want to it does not help. But criticism is very easy that Greece does not implement. How to implement is not easy, how to perform monitoring in Greece where a large percentage of [the] habitats of Europe are in Greece; [whereas] in Spain [there are just] two or three places.[32]

An official in a government research institute with long experience of Greek environmental policy confirmed this view: 'we strongly reject even general ideas coming from northern Europe under this kind of superstition; you could say that, whatever comes from there, finally it will be at the cost of the poor Mediterranean countries'. At the same time, she stressed that, were Greece 'not connected to all those things' (referring to northern countries with 'their better knowledge, better technology, better managerial abilities'), then 'things would be much, much worse' for the Greek environment.[33] While it was expected that suspicion of Brussels was for populist reasons more likely to be present under a PASOK government, in reality attitudes were not always as straightforward as categories or impressions would like.

An interview in 1995 with the adviser (a young professional scientist) to the deputy minister of the environment in the PASOK government produced a more differentiated response on the question of a north–south dichotomy than is usual in the rhetoric of government circles. He identified a difference of sectoral concern between countries in both regions, again focusing on the natural environment: 'if you look at the claims by the Danish government, it is not for a nature protection programme but for a nature restoration environmental programme; whereas in the southern countries they talk about a nature protection environmental programme; and that reflects the different level of existing positions'.[34] On certain particular environmental matters, Greek authorities encountered difficulties with European legislation especially where this touched on cultural differences from the north, reflecting on the lack of collective consciousness.

Transplanting northern techniques or experiences sometimes proved positive, but in other instances was unsuccessful in the south 'because it lacks acceptability from local people; practically, it is incompatible with the cultural and ethical characteristics of the country'.[35] One example given was waste treatment, a major problem in Greece on organizational and financial grounds. Greek municipalities were averse to installing incineration plants, despite arguments on grounds of efficiency and pressure from northern European companies marketing their facilities. The reason for continuing to prefer landfilling was a mixture of doubt about the environmental effects of incineration and sheer superstition about this method.[36] Other respondents viewed planning processes in the EU as distinctly 'northern' and rather alien to the Greek outlook: 'it is too rational for the south'.[37]

This sense of 'policy imperialism' was somewhat particular to Greece. As the least developed of the six countries being examined, that was not very surprising; although certain attitudes linked to Greek identity also played a part. As we have seen, resentment of 'the north' was to some degree present in Spanish policy circles, though not relating to national identity; while in Italy there was much less feeling of this kind.

FROM DIFFUSION TO LEARNING?

Diffusion, with all the problems associated with the pull factors, has certainly taken place. But how far has this led to genuine learning? That is to say, how far has it led not simply to the adoption of a policy strategy but to its incorporation into policy thinking and action such that local issues can be dealt with and new creative advances made? In particular, how far has it led to a reconceptualization of the relationship between environment and economy and the new possibilities of sustainable development? Has there been a transformation such that we could even expect ideas and practices to flow from the south to the north?

The principal obstacle to policy learning in the southern countries is likely to lie with the functioning of the state. As we have stressed in the general discussion of national policy styles, these count for much in the performance of member states. The UK's pollution control system has had difficulty adapting to the more formal demands of environmental regulation in the EU. If such a northern country has had adaptation problems, it is hardly surprising that Italy, Spain, and Greece have also had difficulties. Some of these have shown up most clearly on the issue of implementation. In the past there has been a marked difference in formal trans-position of EU into national laws among the southern countries. However, in recent years the Italian record has improved considerably, so cross-national differences are less between the southern countries and, for that matter, across the EU. The greatest similarity between the southern countries occurs over problems of prac-tical application. Although Italy has improved its monitoring procedures, there is nevertheless a general problem in the south of administrative accountability and control. Furthermore, competing policy priorities, especially economic develop-ment, as well as anxiety about environmental costs raise doubts in the minds of new entrants.

Thus, these countries have acquired a persistent reputation for being the worst defaulters over environmental legislation. But reputations can persist despite evid-ence of improvement. They also tend to make for simplistic interpretations, some-times being coloured by, say, northern images about the way of political life in the south (for example British accusations that other member states are much less assidu-ous about implementation), often directed implicitly if not explicitly towards south-ern partners. In fact, the different forms of official EU complaints about deficient practical application show some differentiation between both parts of Europe, hence do not support any stark north–south polarity. At the same time, it should be remem-bered that reliable and complete information on practical application is hard to unearth.

In our view, despite these problems, there has been some learning in certain policy circles in the south, such as in Spain. This came out most clearly in the interview with Señor Beltran, when he was still director-general of environmental policy in the Spanish Ministry of Public Works, Transport, and the Environ-ment. Beltran elaborated on the need for Spain to press for some redirection of EU policy. Recognizing that this owed much to the 'weight and initiatives' of north-ern member states, he saw a leadership role for Spain in trying to 'dynamicize the position of the countries of the south so far as taking initiatives and balancing out Community policy is concerned'. A major item in bringing this about would be to plan the preservation of what is 'Europe's natural heritage' in the countries of the south, where 'forty per cent of nature reserves in Europe are in Spain'—thus, neatly linking national interests with European policy options.[38] Since Spain and other southern countries had contributed such 'natural capital' to the EU, it was therefore incorrect to typologize southern countries as representing an 'obstacle for the environment' and northern countries as being environmentally cleaner and more environmentalist.[39] In bringing about such a redirection of policy, Señor Beltran saw the establishment of the Cohesion Fund as significant in its recognition that this was not so; for this Fund is 'not an effort to impose laws on the countries of the south, rather an effort to make sure that the countries of the south respect the environment'. Directives like the one on habitats were seen as evidence that the EU was beginning to change its priorities.[40]

This kind of thinking reflected Spain's more activist approach compared with Greece and, to some degree, Italy. It also illustrated Spain's greater ambitions, as a large and new member state, to play an influential role in the EU. Beltran also spoke of Spanish intentions to coordinate and promote a greater or more active 'presence' of the southern countries in EU environmental policy-making.

However, the evidence from interviews in all three southern countries is that there has been an almost complete lack of cooperation, let alone coordination, between the southern member states over the environment. It seems that experience of cooperation over Mediterranean problems in other international bodies (for example over the Mediterranean Action Plan under UNEP) has not produced any combined effort by some of the same southern countries in their capacity as EU member states. Any effort to change this on Spain's part will not be easy, despite some common national interests and other compelling arguments, because it would involve challenging ingrained habits and rooted governmental practices.

Even where a consciousness of a north–south dichotomy was high in policy circles and viewed polemically, there was an appreciation of the possibilities for north–south collaboration, not necessarily via Brussels but more often bilaterally between member states. This was evident on the part of the Greek minister of the environment, interviewed in 1992. While attacking northern countries for their criticism of the south because they themselves 'massacred the environment', he also agreed that 'we want their assistance and their agreement' on both developing and protecting the environment.[41]

When asked to specify lessons learned from the north, the use of clean technology was mentioned by the adviser to the Greek deputy minister. According to him, 'there is a transfer of expertise mostly from the north to the south rather than from the south to the north in the European Union'. But there are also 'cases where the north listens to the south more in environmental issues', referring to the creation of marine sea parks and also the question of coastal management.[42] Innovative ideas about coastal management have been developed in Spain, for instance, following the important Law of the Coasts (Ley de Costas) of 1988 and its programmes of investment.

The key to this interest lies in the great economic importance of tourism in these southern countries. For example, the Greek EU presidency took the initiative in May 1994 to call a special informal Council on tourism and the environment at

Santorini. This discussed, among other things, the development of local environment management plans, such as with respect to networks of islands.[43]

One important innovation of the mid-1990s has been the establishment of the European Environment Agency, which clearly has the potential to become a channel of communication and a conduit for experience between countries. Señor Beltran became its first director-general and spoke fairly optimistically of the south's chances in an interview given in 1994 after his appointment. In his view, the EU now recognized the importance of such southern concerns as bio-diversity and reforestation but also the need to integrate environmental with economic policy. This was 'most important for the countries of the south, in order not to fall into the same mistakes as the countries of the north'[44] Here, then, we have a clear example at a high level of the potential for reconceptualizing the relationship between the economy and the environment.

How far, however, has this reconceptualization been carried into practice? One way of assessing the answer to this question is to look at the record on environmental taxes. This is a good example to take, since their primary rationale is to help internalize the environmental costs of economic activity by the parties responsible for those costs. In other words, they have a rationale in terms of greater economic efficiency. In this context, a review of environmental taxes published by the European Environment Agency suggests that the reconceptualization of economy and environment has not developed very far in the south.[45] The proportion of total tax revenue that was taken in the form of environmental taxes remained largely flat in the southern countries; and there were virtually no examples of environmental tax reform in the south. The major exception to this generalization was in Italy, with the introduction of a polyethylene levy as a primary input to plastic bags in 1994, although the innovations in Portugal with threshold water pollution charges are also mentioned.

The one area in which there did appear to be an expansion of environmentally related taxation was in the energy sector, where in all three southern countries there was a significant increase in the percentage of total taxes accounted for by energy taxes between 1980 and 1993. Thus, in Greece the percentage rose from just over 4 per cent to over 10 per cent; in Italy from around 5 to nearly 7 per cent; and in Spain from 0 to over 4 per cent. However, the natural way in which to interpret these trends is as revenue-raising measures, motivated by the need to balance strained budgets in a fiscally squeezed decade.

The lack of development in the south is highlighted by contrast with the UK. In some respects in the context of this chapter, the UK is the odd one out. For some purposes it can be grouped with northern countries, but it has not developed the green reputation that is associated with the Netherlands and Germany. However, in the 1990s even the UK began moving towards environmentally motivated taxes, with a policy of above-inflation increases on road fuel and the introduction of the landfill disposal levy. So in this regard, whatever may be the perception of policy actors about the need to integrate environmental considerations into economic development, the old paradigm still seems strong in the south. More generally, there is no 'big idea' to have yet emerged from the southern countries, in the way that technology-forcing environmental regulation emerged in Germany in the 1980s or environmental taxation has been pursued in the Scandinavian countries and the Netherlands in the 1990s.

As a measure of the scale of transformation that is involved, let us imagine that the EU provided a framework of environmental governance in Europe within which extensive international learning occurred, and in which the paradigm of ecological modernization and sustainable development was incorporated. On this hypothesis, the south could learn the lessons of the dirty growth of the north, and could adapt its own processes of economic development accordingly. In return, it would offer the north a model of how to preserve natural resources and how to adapt old lifestyles to new demands, lessons that the north could use in its attempts to restore its own environment. What patterns might we expect to see in the outcomes and processes of environmental policy?

In terms of outcomes, we should expect to see the transfer of technology and expertise to the south that would enable sustainable patterns of economic development to take place. Urban transport in the south would follow the highest standards of cities in the north, with extensive and high-quality public transport systems that avoided problems of pollution. Over longer distances, high-speed rail links would provide the south with access to the core economic areas of the north. Low-intensity agriculture providing high-quality foods would be geared to preventing soil and groundwater pollution. Low-waste technologies would limit as far as possible emissions to air and water, and the principle of proximity would be adopted in the disposal of solid wastes. High levels of protection from tourist development and market agriculture would be given to landscapes of special scenic or cultural significance.

Within the north there would have to be parallel development: a rediscovery of the taste in food, and a willingness to see competitive technological advantage eroded in the interests of a wider Europe. Tourist preferences would have to change so that visitors were more respectful of the distinctive environments and heritage that the south has to offer. The south would be less of a playground and more a part of a common European heritage. More long-distance journeys would be made by train than by road.

To suppose these changes is to provide a measure of how much alteration to existing patterns of policy and practice is necessary to achieve sustainable development. It is also to indicate how far both north and south are from implementing the paradigm to which they both formally subscribe.

NOTES TO CHAPTER 14

1. Commission of the European Communities, *Protection of the Environment in the Mediterranean*, 392 (Brussels, 1988), pp. 3, 5, and 11.

2. A. La Spina and G. Sciortino, 'Common Agenda, Southern Rules: European Integration and Environmental Change in the Mediterranean States', in J. D. Liefferink, P. D. Lowe, and A. P. J. Mol (eds.), *European Integration and Environmental Policy* (London: Belhaven, 1993), pp. 217–36, at 220.
3. Ibid. 225.
4. Commission of the European Communities, *Environmental Policy in the European Community* (Luxembourg, 1990), p. 17.
5. *The Economist*, 14 October 1989, pp. 27–34.
6. Interview with Oliviero Montanaro, Ministry of the Environment, Rome, May 1992.
7. Interview with Montanaro.
8. Interview with Anna Maria Villa, Ministry of the Environment, Rome, May 1992.
9. Interview with Lucio Scialpi, Confidustria, Rome, April 1995.
10. Interview with Mauro Albrizio, Lega per l'Ambiente, Rome, April 1995.
11. Interview with Albrizio.
12. Interview with Carmen Diez de Rivera, Madrid, October 1992.
13. See e.g. World Commission on Environment and Development, *Our Common Future* (Oxford and New York: Oxford University Press, 1987), pp. 16 and 309.
14. Task Force on the Environment and the Single Market, '1992: The Environmental Dimension', mimeo (1989), p. 9.11.
15. See P. M. Haas, *Saving the Mediterranean* (New York and Oxford: Columbia University Press, 1990), esp. pp. 214–34.
16. Task Force, '1992', p. 9.12.
17. Ibid. 9.11.
18. For the notion of 'epistemic communities', see P. M. Haas, *Saving the Mediterranean* (New York and Oxford: Columbia University Press, 1990).
19. Interview with Giovanni Zapponi, Istituto Superiore di Sanita, Rome, April 1995.
20. Interview with Angelo Carere, Istituto Superiore di Sanita, Rome, April 1995.
21. Interview with Domingo Jimenez Beltran, Ministry of Public Works, Madrid, April 1994.
22. Interview with Constantinos Cartalis, adviser to the Deputy Minister for the Environment, Ministry of the Environment, Athens, March 1995.
23. Interview with Cartalis.
24. Interview with Albrizio.
25. Interview with Albrizio.
26. Interview with Joaquin Ros Vicent, Ministry of Public Works, Madrid, October 1992.
27. Interview with Luis Mas, Ministry of Public Works, Madrid, October 1992.
28. Interview with Joan Puigdollers, environmental policy directorate, Generalitat, Barcelona, October 1992.
29. F. W. Scharpf, 'Negative and Positive Integration in the Political Economy of European Welfare States', in G. Marks, F. W. Scharpf, P. C. Schmitter, and W. Streeck, *Governance in the European Union* (London: Sage, 1996), pp. 15–39, esp. 19–25.
30. Interview with Achilleas Karamanlis, Minister of the Environment, Physical Planning and Public Works, Athens, November 1992.
31. Interview with Karamanlis.
32. Interviews with Charalambos Tsafaras, with Dimitrios Koumas, and with Tzortzis Georgios, Ministry of Agriculture, Athens, November 1992.
33. Interview with Dimitra Katohianou, Centre of Planning and Economic Research (KEPE), Athens, March 1995.

34. Interview with Cartalis.
35. Interview with Cartalis.
36. Interview with Cartalis.
37. Interview with Michalis Modinos, 'Nea Oikologia' and Ministry of National Economy, Athens, March 1995.
38. Interview with Domingo Jimenez Beltran, Ministry of Public Works, Madrid, April 1994.
39. Interview with Beltran.
40. Interview with Beltran.
41. Interview with Karamanlis.
42. Interview with Cartalis.
43. See G. Pridham, *Tourism Policy in Mediterranean Europe: Towards Sustainable Development?* Occasional Paper no. 15 (Bristol: Centre for Mediterranean Studies, University of Bristol, May 1996).
44. *Pais Internacional*, 9 May 1994.
45. European Environment Agency, *Environmental Taxes: Implementation and Environmental Effectiveness*, Environmental Issues Series no. 1 (Copenhagen: European Environment Agency, 1996).

15

Competing Models of European Environmental Governance

The European system of environmental governance is, to paraphrase Hayek, the product of political action but not of political design.[1] It borrows much from the Monnet method of European integration, as we saw in Chapter 13. This method is one of integration by stealth. Instead of confronting the major questions of constitutional principle involved in the integration of European societies, the Monnet method involves policy-makers focusing on apparently technical matters of low politics in order to promote greater political cooperation among member states. Indeed, in some ways environmental policy can be regarded as a textbook illustration of the Monnet method at work. With its background in the low politics of the harmonization of technical standards within the single market, it spilled over into an institutionalized domain of policy in its own right. Completely unanticipated in 1957, it moved from silence to salience within thirty years. This is not to say that conscious, intergovernmental choice was unimportant, but what governments negotiated in the treaty amendments were modifications of an existing status quo shaped by a functionalist logic.

One important aspect of spillover is that it is no respecter of the distinction between primary and secondary rules. In the Introduction we defined the distinction between these two sets of rules in terms of their scope. Primary rules concerned the regulation of a sphere of activity; secondary rules were rules for the making of rules. One feature of spillover, well illustrated in the case of environmental policy, is that it may easily take the form of a move from primary rules to secondary rules. This may happen either because there is dispute about whether the EU should be regulating in a particular area or regulating in a particular way, or because the practice of dealing with environmental problems creates a precedent in decision-making. It is not generally possible to say when an apparently routine matter of decision-making will turn into a constitutional issue.

The collapsing of this distinction between primary and secondary rules is one of the ways in which the member states are locked into the integration process. In the case of international environmental regimes outside the EU, for example the Convention on the Long Range Transport of Pollution, the institutional framework is one that a country can decide either to join or to leave alone. Within the EU, by contrast, countries are already locked into a shared system of authority, so that the emergence of unforeseen constitutional issues out of routine matters of decision-making is not one that is likely to have an easy answer. Moreover, this dynamism of rule development is part of the process. As the familiarly used bicycle metaphor is intended to underline, European integration depends upon a certain political momentum being maintained.

This form of political integration has left its mark on the decision-making style of the EU system of environmental governance. We saw in Chapter 13 that the Monnet method had led to one of a class of systems in which decision-making authority is not allocated in a zero-sum fashion between different levels of government but instead is shared.[2] In such systems decision-making takes the form of requiring concurrent majorities of actors. Some implications of this decision-making structure were also spelt out in Chapter 13. National actors can block certain measures, and there is a constant tendency for member states to seek to displace their own agendas on to the European level. We also saw that horizontal complexity increases the number of 'veto players', that is actors whose agreement is required for a change in policy.[3] The principle of concurrent majorities thus operates both vertically, in respect of the EU and the member states, and horizontally, in respect of policy actors at the European level itself.

The Monnet method has been highly successful. Perhaps no other way of securing European integration could have succeeded as well. This does not mean, however, that it marks out the path for the future. The Monnet method may have played an important part in the creation of the European system of environmental governance, but how far can it be expected to continue to play this role in the future? Certainly there are those who are sceptical of the view that the Monnet method is the most credible and plausible way to continue the general process of European integration. They argue that the revival of the impetus for European integration requires mass mobilization of a sort that Monnet himself shunned, along with a strong emphasis inside the EU on the need for greater economic security for Europe's citizens. Without this transformation in the logic of European integration, it is argued, it will be impossible to generate the political conditions that are necessary to sustain the European project.[4]

Can this line of reasoning be applied to EU environmental policy? Are we at a turning-point in the evolution of European environmental governance, and will the system need to be reshaped according to different principles from those on which it has been constructed so far? It is this question we seek to discuss in the final chapter.

To pose the question about the future of the Monnet method is not to ignore intergovernmental factors. The Monnet method is overlaid with an intergovernmental bargain—or rather, a series of intergovernmental bargains. Indeed, one of the reasons why the Monnet method has successfully shaped EU governance is that it did not confront the large constitutional questions that European integration could be said to raise. In that sense, it sought not to overcome the authority of the nation state, but to persuade national governments to share their authority in the common interest. There is a sense in which the functional approach pre-supposes the central position of the state that is such an important assumption of the realist tradition. Were state sovereignty not so important, the Monnet method would not have to take such an indirect route to integration. When we reflect upon the inadequacies of the Monnet method, therefore, we are implicitly acknowledging the continuing importance of the nation state.

PATHOLOGIES OF THE STATUS QUO

In a system like that of the European Union, where not only are the rules being made quickly but the rules for making rules are also changing rapidly, there are plenty of opportunities for policy and procedural wrangling, as we have already documented in a number of instances. Super-majoritarian systems are well known to have high transaction costs attached to them, most notably as the decision rule tends to unanimity.[5] Procedural wrangling adds to such transaction costs by creating disputes not just about the substance of the measure, but also about the terms and conditions under which the measure is to be taken.

The theory of social choice suggests that, as actors with diverse policy positions obtain a share of decision-making power, so the chances of policy change go down.[6] One typical example of such delay, in addition to the cases we have already discussed, is the development of a proposed landfill directive. In that case the crucial issue was a provision that would have enabled member states with a low density of inhabitants to exempt smaller landfills (favoured by Portugal and Ireland), an exemption to which the European Parliament was opposed. Thus, requiring simultaneous agreement between the Council and the Parliament resulted in a situation in which it is difficult to move from the status quo.

When we turn to the functional component of the concurrent majority, one feature in particular is evident: namely that environmental policy involves coordination with other policy sectors, most notably industry, transport, and agriculture. Thus, an environmental policy taken on its own may secure the reduction in harmful emissions from individual vehicles, but if transport policy is leading to more vehicles being put on the road, then the gain at the individual level is offset by the increase in total emissions arising from the volume increase, a phenomenon that has been observed in respect of nitrous oxide emissions from cars, for example. Since, at the European level, DGs are the guardians of their sectoral interests, it is hardly surprising that sectoral complexity makes for difficult decision-making in institutional terms.

By contrast, environmental policy-makers will also want to be seen to be supporting their own functional constituency, a trend reinforced in the case of

DG XI by the fact that a number of the officials clearly have a commitment to environmental protection that is personal as well as professional. Similarly, there are officials in DG XI who will volunteer the thought that no one in agriculture is willing to talk to anyone about the environmental problems that the CAP causes.

Can we characterize the decision-making style that emerges from this institutional process? One important feature of it is that is it difficult for policy actors to adopt what Scharpf terms a 'problem-solving' mentality as distinct from a 'bargaining' mentality. In this sense, the attempt to create a discourse of ecological modernization around which policy could be organized and discussed has failed. There is simply too much heterogeneity of interest (especially arising from different stages of economic development) for there to be a consensus on the priority to be given to environmental measures. Moreover, even if it is true in the aggregate that environmental protection and economic development pull in the same direction, there is too much conflict in the particular case for the tension to be easily eliminated.

One consequence is that over time the development of environmental policy tends to follow the pattern of *immobilisme* punctuated by activism. Between 1982 and 1992 there was an upsurge of activism in which many environmental measures were passed, partly as a consequence of the need to harmonize environmental measures in the context of the internal market, and partly because of the high salience that the environment had as an issue among European publics and governments. Despite some consolidation and advance since 1992, the scale and pace of development has slowed down considerably, and some high-profile measures have been stalled.

Moreover, there are still strong formal constraints at the European level limiting the range of measures that can be adopted. The EU is limited in the amount of taxation that it can collect, and its principal source of revenue is from VAT proceeds. This means that it cannot impose pollution taxes as an instrument of policy, and under the Treaty on European Union any environmental measures that involve fiscal considerations have to be agreed by all member states before they can be passed. If we contrast this restriction of powers with those that obtain in federal political systems like Germany or the USA, it is clear that there is a significant limitation built into the development of environmental policy at the European level. Hence, although we can properly talk of an increase in the size, scope, and stringency of European environmental legislation, there are still important issues that remain outside the sphere of European control.

Suppose that this characterization of the decision-making pattern as it has historically developed is accepted. Are there any other principles on which we could imagine the European system of environmental governance being constructed? One possible way of identifying such principles is to hypothesize what would happen to environmental policy in a European constitutional convention. It is to this hypothesis that we now turn.

A CONSTITUTIONAL CONVENTION ON
ENVIRONMENTAL GOVERNANCE

Suppose that the process of European integration has reached the point at which the Monnet method is exhausted. Integration by stealth is no longer a possibility, and any further integration depends upon agreement among political representatives of the peoples of Europe who are to decide in a constitutional convention among themselves the principles and rules that will govern the basic terms of their association.[7] What agreement might we expect to emerge from such a process?

In coming to any such agreement, let us suppose that the delegates are free from the constraints of history. That is to say, they need not assume that a rule or practice should be respected simply because it exists. In other words, the whole purpose of a constitutional convention would be to sift arguments and establish the principled basis for European environmental governance in terms that all could accept as impartial and in the general interest. Burkean appeals to inherited prescriptive rights or integrationist appeals to the *acquis* would not of themselves count as an argument in such an assembly.[8]

In this sort of situation, what principles of environmental governance would be acceptable? The first point at issue would concern the legitimacy of intervention in the single market for the purposes of environmental protection. As we have seen, there are not only complementarities but also conflicts between the rules needed for a single market. From one point of view, it is not surprising that there is a potential conflict between a liberalizing economic policy that lays stress upon the deregulation of markets on the one hand and the requirement of environmental policy on the other. One standard justification for having a public policy on the environment is that regulatory measures are needed in order to cope with market failures. From this point of view, environmental pollution is an economic externality in which the costs of production or consumption are not fully internalized to the transactions of vountarily contracting parties.

In these circumstances, a case for public intervention exists on grounds of economic efficiency alone. Correcting for externalities by forcing producers to internalize the costs will lead to a better use of resources. On such liberal grounds, the case is especially strong for the regulation of international environmental pollution by the EU, since its boundaries are extensive enough to ensure that externalities are internalized across the full extent of its authority, whatever national boundaries are involved.

In principle, there are a number of ways in which the internalization of externalities might take place: through a clearer specification of property rights enforceable at law, through voluntary agreements among affected parties, or through public intervention in the form of administrative regulation or economic instruments. Cutting a very long story very short, a constitutional convention is likely to arrive at a justification for public intervention by noting that the property rights solution is either incomplete (relevant property rights cannot be fully specified) or infeasible (no one can plausibly own the European air shed or the Mediterranean sea), whereas the use of voluntary measures is subject to the problem of free-riders and the danger that scrupulous firms will be exploited by the unscrupulous. In practice, then, environmental protection legitimates some form of public intervention to close the gap between internal and external costs.

What form would the intervention take? It is common, though by no means universal, in neo-classical treatments of the externality problem to underline the extent to which regulation by means of economic instruments is superior, by the test of economic efficiency, to regulation by means of administrative rules. Such economic instruments include: taxes on emissions, usually by volume emitted; refund schemes for returnable items, ranging from cars to bottles; taxes on polluting substances, for example fuel oil or pesticides; and so on. The arguments favouring such measures are many and varied, depending on the case at hand. Such measures allow greater freedom to producers to find least-cost solutions to their pollution problems than do uniform emission limits. Economic instruments such as taxes on pesticides are likely to be more effective at dealing with dispersed, non-point sources of pollution. And where pollution arises from consumption rather than production externalities, economic instruments are often the only effective instrument. In this context, the important point is not that one would accept in every case the arguments for the superiority of economic instruments over direct regulation: rather, it is that there would be no reason of principle to rule out the admissibility of such instruments at the European level. The suitablility of economic instruments compared with direct regulation is something that should be decided on the technical merits of the argument when applied to a particular problem.

Moreover, if international conflict is to be constrained by the liberal policy of free trade within the boundaries defined by the treaty parties, as was the idea of the original Monnet method, then it would seem that a liberal approach to pollution control would be a natural corollary, and perhaps a way in which a constitutional convention would want to develop the argument. At present the restriction on the use of tax instruments by the EU is one that can only be explained by the history of European integration rather than justified by appeal to principles that could gain consent in a European constitutional convention.

However, if this is the way that members of a constitutional convention would think about environmental policy, we need to note that a number of conditions must be met if public intervention is to be successful. In outline, these conditions are that public intervention needs to be at the right level (i.e. that the standard-setting or regulatory authority needs to operate on a scale such that major externalities can be internalized), and to the right degree (levels of regulation need to be adjusted with respect to competing values).

One principle of task allocation within a multi-level system of governance is that of subsidiarity. This principle already finds a place within existing EU legislation within the Treaty on European Union:

In areas which do not fall within its exclusive competence, the Community shall take action, in accordance with the principle of subsidiarity, only if and in so far as the objectives of the proposed action cannot be sufficiently achieved by the Member States and can therefore, by reason of the scale or effects of the proposed action, be better achieved by the Community.[9]

As stated in the Treaty, this principle involves at least two separate elements: the notion that member states cannot sufficiently achieve the objectives of a given environmental policy on their own, and the notion that the objectives can be better achieved by action at the European level. The first element gives the principle a bias to the local, for if the objectives can be achieved 'sufficiently' then there is no case for European action, even if European action would achieve the objectives more completely or satisfactorily.

It is not clear that a constitutional convention would accept this bias to the local. To be sure, within an ongoing process of integration of the sort implied by the Monnet method, there is no point in disturbing the activities of the nation state provided that goals are being adequately achieved by action at the national level. However, if the provision of environmental benefits can be better achieved by assigning standard-setting responsibility to a higher level, then there would appear to be an argument for doing that. In other words, the constitutional convention might accept not the principle of subsidiarity, but rather what we might term a principle of functional effectiveness, namely that the appropriate level at which to set standards is one at which the externalities are internalized to the boundaries of the administering authority.

Set against the principle of subsidiarity in this way, the principle of functional effectiveness would seem to be a centralizing principle. It removes the bias to the local implied by the sufficiency clause of the principle of subsidiarity. However, set against the principle of the *acquis communautaire*, it might seem to be a decentralizing principle, since it would not license European levels of standard-setting in cases where only local public goods were at issue.

In concrete terms, then, application of the principle of functional effectiveness would imply much stronger competence in those fields of policy (acidification, global climate change, and ozone depletion) in which there are problems of collective action at a European level combined with less authority in relation to those issues that are essentially concerned with local public goods, including bathing water and drinking water quality. Moreover, to say that policy competence should be lodged more firmly at the European level for certain matters would not of itself imply a distinction among instruments. So the principle of functional effectiveness would reinforce our conclusion when discussing the basic logic of public intervention.

Setting regulation appropriately relative to other values raises more problems. The principal question here is whether the stringency of an environmental standard is justified in terms of its cost, particularly in the light of scientific and other evidence about effectiveness. Given the diversity of economic circumstance and the stage of development of member states, the most probable principle at a constitutional convention would be a prohibition (*a*) against poorer states simply displacing some of their development costs on to richer states in the form of cross-boundary pollution, and (*b*) against richer states imposing higher standards in local public goods than poorer states would choose for themselves. For those matters in which *European* collective action was required, most importantly issues of global climate change, it is difficult not to imagine that the price for agreeing to European powers would be more equitable cost-sharing arrangements.

So far we have considered the hypothetical deliberations of our constitutional convention on environmental governance purely in terms of a theory of the efficient functioning of markets. However, in the course of its development, EU environmental policy has gone way beyond what would be strictly necessary in order to ensure that markets function efficiently. It has developed regulations to conserve natural environments for aesthetic reasons (for example, the protection of countryside from large project developments through environmental impact assessments) as well as to protect some species from human predation (for example, the birds directive). These developments reflect the important political functions that environmental policy performs, in particular the legitimation of EU institutions *vis à vis* the citizens of Europe by providing some protection for values that are not purely economic.

In this context, some of the simpler prescriptions that emerge from the economic analysis of environmental policy functions may need revision. Although it is possible to argue within the economic framework that bathing waters or drinking waters are essentially local public goods, there will be some who maintain at a constitutional convention that the ability of children to swim in clean seas or drink wholesome water should be regarded as a right of European citizenship, and not an accidental by-product of the country in which one lives. This is in effect a political argument about the constitutional status of principles for the assignment of functions, and in particular about whether considerations deriving from a wider European conception of citizenship should be a reason for requiring at least some sharing of authority within a system of multi-level governance between member states and the EU.

It is impossible to say how such a dispute might be resolved at a constitutional convention. The opportunistic policy-making of the Commission in the 1970s which led to the directives on water quality might be regarded as a breach of justifiable constitutional principle, in line with the economic conception; or they might be regarded as a happy accident for European citizenship. Just as importantly, it may be that pragmatic considerations enter the picture, not least the thought that it is stretching the attention span of the European authorities too much to give them powers over local public goods when important issues of global and continental concern need addressing.

The issue does, however, highlight one question that would be bound to emerge at a constitutional convention, namely that of how political disputes would be solved within the system of shared authority. Here there are the well known problems of the democratic deficit. As we saw in Chapter 13, one of the differences between the Europeanization of policy and the earlier nationalization was that environmental policy was not located within conventional systems of democratic competition. The EU lacks the apparatus of party competition, a European-wide party system, and an encompassing political culture that are some of the preconditions of democratic decision-making within the nation state.

However, this does not mean that democratic accountability has been entirely absent from EU environmental policy. Indeed, there is a good argument for saying that the European Parliament has played a more interventionist role in the setting of environmental standards than the majority of national parliaments. Within national systems the setting of standards is essentially a bureaucratic matter, and where it involves parliaments is normally within the system of party discipline under which national parliaments operate. Because there is a separation of powers horizontally within the EU, a separation that the Treaty of Amsterdam has strengthened by making the co-decision procedure the norm for European legislation, the European Parliament has played an active role, as the examples of car emissions and the difficulties of securing a landfill directive go to show.

The problem to which this gives rise, as we have seen, is that it is just this separation of powers that creates the conditions for policy stagnation, with there being no alternative that is mutually acceptable to all the decision-making bodies. However, it is difficult to see a solution to this problem even if we look at it in the context of reasoning at a constitutional convention. It is difficult to conceive of any European-level policy process that did not institutionalize the member states' interests as well as give a role to directly elected members and maintain the separation of powers between the democratically chosen politicians and the appointed commissioners. In so far as the separation of powers is part of the problem rather than part of the solution, the convention would have to face the implications of this built-in conflict.

One way of approaching the issue is to stress the need to strengthen the conditions under which policies can be debated and criticized. Thus, in the setting of standards, a constitutional convention would be likely to wish to uphold and improve transparency and accountability in the process. At a minimum, this would mean that the grounds on which the position is being taken by each body should be made clear, and that there should be adequate opportunities for critical discussion and debate. It would also almost certainly mean ensuring that the the European Environment Agency had sufficient resources to gather information and evidence relating to the environmental policy performance of member states. The European public interest can be served only by having reliable sources of information by reference to which policies and proposals can be tested.

Putting these points together, we might expect a European constitutional convention on the environment to agree on a number of principles that had not emerged through the Monnet method, including the strengthening of the regulatory powers of the EU to protect the environment, a shift of some powers from the national level to the European level, and greater transparency and accountability in the making of decisions. It is also possible that there would be a *quid pro quo* for the nation states in the form of a constitutional guarantee that the regulation of certain local public goods would not be subject to European authority.

We have said that the deliberations of our hypothetical constitutional convention would be independent of the constraints of history. But how free are we to assume this? The Monnet method, for all its faults, did solve a problem that other constitutional designs could not tackle. Europe could not live with its sovereign nation states, and it could not live without them: bypass the problem by stealth, and it may eventually go away. The legacy of history, including its pathological effects on the making of environmental rules, is the price we may have to pay for the success of the European Union in bringing integration to previously war-torn societies.

In any case, the question of the relationship between history and principle may not matter. In a way, the most striking thing about the arguments of principle is that they issue in conclusions many of which are already implicit in the evolution of European environmental governance under the Monnet method. To be sure, there are some significant divergences. The Monnet method has almost certainly given more power to the nation states, particularly in the field of environmental taxation, than a constitutional convention would have allowed, and the progress towards greater transparency and accountability has been more hesitant than democratic principle would suggest. However, the thought-experiment suggests not a radical break with the past, but a summons to the European system of environmental governance to achieve ideals that are implicit in its current practices, so that it can become an open and transparent system of decision-making, performing the task of protecting a priceless environmental heritage for all of Europe's citizens.

NOTES TO CHAPTER 15

1. Cf. F. A. Hayek, *Law, Legislation and Liberty* (London: Routledge, 1982), ch. 2.
2. F. W. Scharpf, 'The Joint-Decision Trap: Lessons from German Federalism and European Institutions', *Public Administration*, 66:3 (1988), pp. 239–78, at 242.
3. G. Tsebelis, 'Decision Making in Political Systems: Veto Players in Presidentialism, Parliamentarianism, Multicameralism and Multipartyism', *British Journal of Political Science*, 25:3 (1995), pp. 289–325, at 301
4. J. Hayward, 'Has European Unification by Stealth a Future?' in J. Hayward (ed.), *Élitism, Populism, and European Politics* (Oxford: Clarendon Press, 1996), pp. 252–7.
5. B. Barry, *Political Argument* (London: Routledge and Kegan Paul, 1965), chs. 14 and 15.
6. Tsebelis, 'Decision Making in Political Systems', pp. 308–13.
7. For contrasting uses of this general contractarian approach to the EU, see A. Føllesdal, 'Democracy, Legitimacy and Majority Rule in the European Union', in A. Weale and

M. Nentwich (eds.), *Political Theory and the European Union* (London and New York: Routledge, 1998), pp. 34–48; and H. Abromeit, 'How to Democratise a Multi-Level, Multi-Dimensional Polity', in A. Weale and M. Nentwich (eds.), *Political Theory and the European Union* (London and New York: Routledge, 1998), pp. 112–24.

8. Compare B. Barry, *Justice as Impartiality* (Oxford: Clarendon Press, 1995), p. 6.
9. Treaty on European Union, Article 3b.

Bibliography

This bibliography contains the details of major works referred to in the text. It does not contain details of newspaper articles, reports and press releases.

Books and articles

Abromeit, H., 'How to Democratise a Multi-Level, Multi-Dimensional Polity', in A. Weale and M. Nentwich (eds.), *Political Theory and the European Union* (London and New York: Routledge, 1998), pp. 112–24.

Adonis, A. and Jones, S., *Subsidiarity and the Community's Constitutional Future*, Discussion Paper no. 2 (London: Centre for European Studies, 1992).

—— and Tyrie, A., *Subsidiarity as History and Policy* (London: Institute of Economic Affairs, 1990).

Aguilar-Fernandez, S., 'Spanish Pollution Control Policy and the Challenge of the European Union', *Regional Politics and Policy*, 4:1 (1994), pp. 102–17.

Albert, M., *Capitalism against Capitalism*, trans. P. Haviland (London: Whurr, 1993).

Alexander, D., 'Pollution, Policies and Politics: The Italian Environment', in F. Sabetti and R. Catanzaro (eds.), *Italian Politics: A Review* (London: Pinter, 1991), pp. 90–111.

Allison, G. T., *Essence of Decision* (Boston: Little, Brown, 1971).

Almond, G. A., *The American People and Foreign Policy* (New York: Fredick A. Praeger, 1960).

Andersen, M. S., 'From Narvik to Naples: Environmental Policy in an Enlarged European Union', paper presented at the conference 'Governing our Environment', Copenhagen, 17–18 November 1994.

—— *Governance by Green Taxes: Making Pollution Prevention Pay* (Manchester and New York: Manchester University Press, 1994).

Anderweg, R., 'The Reshaping of National Party Systems', in J. Hayward (ed.), *The Crisis of Representation in Europe* (London: Frank Cass, 1995), pp. 58–78.

Arp, H., 'Technical Regulation and Politics: The Interplay between Economic Interests and Environmental Policy Goals in EC Car Emission Legislation', in J. D. Liefferink, P. D. Lowe, and A. P. J. Mol (eds.), *European Integration and Environmental Policy* (London and New York: Belhaven Press, 1993), pp. 150–71.

Ashby, E., and Anderson, M., *The Politics of Clean Air* (Oxford: Clarendon Press, 1981).

Bagehot, W., *The English Constitution*, ed. with an introduction by R. H. S. Crossman (London: Fontana/Collins, 1867; 1963 edn).

Bailey, C. J., *Congress and Air Pollution* (Manchester and New York: Manchester University Press, 1998).

Bainbridge, T., and Teasdale, A., *The Penguin Companion to the European Union* (Harmondsworth: Penguin, 1995).

Baldock, D., and Long, T., *The Mediterranean Environment under Pressure: The Influence of the CAP on Spain and Portugal and the IMPs in France, Greece and Italy* (London: Institute for European Environmental Policy, 1987).

Banfield, E. C., *The Moral Basis of a Backward Society* (Chicago: Free Press, 1958).

Barry, B., *Political Argument* (London: Routledge & Kegan Paul, 1965).

—— *Justice as Impartiality* (Oxford: Clarendon Press, 1995).

Bätcher, K., 'Reduction of the Calculated Use of Cadmium in German Industry', in M. Jänicke and H. Weidner (eds.), *Successful Environmental Policy: A Critical Evaluation of 24 Cases* (Berlin: Edition Sigma, 1995), pp. 325–41.

Beckerman, W., *Small is Stupid* (London: Duckworth, 1995).

Bennett, C. J., 'What is Policy Convergence and What Causes It?' *British Journal of Political Science*, 21:2 (1991), pp. 215–33.

Bennett, G., *Air Pollution Control in the European Community: Implementation of the EC Directives in the Twelve Member States* (London: Graham & Trotman, 1991).

—— and von Moltke, K., 'Integrated Permitting in the Netherlands and the Federal Republic of Germany', in N. Haigh and F. Irwin (eds.), *Integrated Pollution Control in Europe and North America* (Washington: Conservation Foundation, 1990), pp. 105–45.

Bermejo, J. Vera. *Constitución y Planificación Hidrológica'* (Madrid: Civitas, 1995).

Bernauer, T. and Moser, P., 'Reducing Pollution of the River Rhine: The Influence of International Co-operation', *Journal of Environment and Development*, 5:4 (1996), pp. 389–415.

Bianchi, A., 'Environmental Policy', in F. Francioni (ed.), *Italy and EC Membership Evaluated* (London: Pinter, 1992), pp. 71–105.

Biod, A., Probert, J., and Jones, C., 'The Packaging Industry is not Carried Away by Public Opinion', *Business Strategy and the Environment*, 3:1 (1994), pp. 31–5.

Blyth, M. M., 'Any More Bright Ideas? The Ideational Turn of Comparative Political Economy', *Comparative Politics*, 29:2 (1997), pp. 229–50.

Boehmer-Christiansen, S., 'Black Mist and Acid Rain: Science as a Fig Leaf of Policy', *Political Quarterly*, 59:2 (1988), pp. 145–60.

—— *The Politics of Environment and Acid Rain in the Federal Republic of Germany*, SPRU Occasional Paper Series no. 29 (Brighton: Science Policy Research Unit, 1989).

—— 'The Precautionary Principle in Germany: Enabling Government', in T. O'Riordan and J. Cameron (eds.), *Interpreting the Precautionary Principle* (London: Earthscan, 1994).

—— and Skea, J., *Acid Politics* (London and New York: Belhaven, 1991).

Bomberg, E., *Green Parties and Politics in the European Union* (London and New York: Routledge, 1998).

Brack, D., 'Balancing Trade and the Environment', *International Affairs*, 71:3 (1995), pp. 497–514.

Brand, K.-W., 'Dialectics of Institutionalisation: The Transformation of the Environmental Movement in Germany', in C. Rootes (ed.), *Environmental Movements: Local, National and Global* (London and Portland: Frank Cass, 1999), pp. 35–58.

Bressers, H. T. A., 'The Cleaning Up Period' in H. T. A. Bressers and L. J. O'Toole Jr (eds.), *International Comparative Policy Research* (Enschede: University of Twente Press, 1992), pp. 155–74.

—— 'The Impact of Effluent Charges: A Dutch Success Story', in M. Jänicke and H. Weidner (eds.), *Successful Environmental Policy: A Critical Evaluation of 24 Cases* (Berlin: Edition Sigma, 1995), pp. 27–42.

—— Huitema, D., and Kuks, S. M. M., 'Policy Networks in Dutch Water Policy', *Environmental Politics*, 3:4 (1994), pp. 24–51.

—— and Plettenburg, L. A., 'The Netherlands', in M. Jänicke and H. Weidner (eds.), *National Environmental Policies: A Comparative Study of Capacity-Building* (Berlin: Springer Verlag, 1997), pp. 109–31.

Brittan, S., *A Restatement of Economic Liberalism* (Basingstoke: Macmillan, 1988).

Brouwer, O., Comtois, Y., van Empel, M., Kirkpatrick, D., and Larouche, P., *Environment and Europe: European Union Environment Law and Policy and its Impact on Industry* (Deventer: Stibbe Simont Monahan Duhot, 1994).

Brown, A. K., 'Impact of European Legislation: Urban Wastewater Directive', *Proceeding of the Institute of Civil Engineers-Municipal Engineer*, 93 (1992), pp. 205–09.

Brown, G. M. Jr and Johnson, R. W., 'Pollution Control by Effluent Charges: It Works in the Federal Republic of Germany, Why Not in the United States?' *Natural Resources Journal*, 24:4 (1984), pp. 929–66.

Budge, I., Robertson, D., and Hearl, D. J. (eds.), *Ideology, Strategy and Party Change in 19 Democracies* (Cambridge: Cambridge University Press, 1987).

Buitendijk, G. J., and van Schendelen, M. P. C. M., 'Brussels Advisory Committees: A Channel for Influence?' *European Law Review*, 20:1 (1995), pp. 37–56.

Buller, H., 'Supra-national Policy Making and Local Implementation Practice: Perspectives of an Anglo-French Comparison of Environmental Management', paper for Anglo-French conference, University of Bristol, December 1991.

Bulmer, S., 'Domestic Politics and European Community Policy-Making', *Journal of Common Market Studies*, 21:4 (1983), pp. 349–63.

—— 'The Governance of the European Union: A New Institutionalist Approach', *Journal of Public Policy*, 13:4 (1994), pp. 351–80.

Burrows, P., 'Pricing versus Regulation for Environmental Protection', in A. J. Culyer (ed.), *Economic Policies and Social Goals* (Oxford: Martin Robertson, 1974), pp. 273–83.

Butler, D., Adonis, A., and Travers, T., *Failure in British Government* (Oxford: Oxford University Press, 1994).

Byatt, I., 'The Impact of EC Directives on Water Customers in England and Wales', *Journal of European Public Policy*, 3:4 (1996), pp. 665–74.

Cameron, D. R., 'The 1992 Initiative: Causes and Consequences', in A. M. Sbragia (ed.), *Euro-Politics: Institutions and Policymaking in the 'New' European Community* (Washington: Brookings Institution, 1992), pp. 23–74.

Capria, A., 'Formulation and Implementation of Environmental Policy in Italy', paper for 12th International Congress on Social Policy, Paris 1991.

Carter, N., and Lowe, P., 'Britain: Coming to Terms with Sustainable Development?' in K. Hanf and A.-I. Jansen (eds.), *Governance and Environment in Western Europe: Politics, Policy and Administration* (Harlow: Addison Wesley Longman, 1998), pp. 17–39.

Charlton, C., and Howell, B., 'Life Cycle Assessment: A Tool for Solving Environmental Problems?' *European Environment*, 12:2 (1992), pp. 2–5.

Christofilopoulou, P., 'Professionalism and Public Policy Making in Greece: The Influence of Engineers in the Local Government Reforms', *Public Administration*, 70:1 (1992), pp. 99–118.

Collins, K., and Earnshaw, D., 'The Implementation and Enforcement of European Community Environment Legislation', *Environmental Politics*, 1:4 (1992), pp. 213–49.

Copius Peereboom, J. W., and Bouwer, K., 'Environmental Science "Milieukunde" in the Netherlands: A Review', *The Science of the Total Environment*, 129 (1993), pp. 157–70.

Corbett, R., 'The 1985 Intergovernmental Conference and the Single European Act', in R. Pryce (ed.), *The Dynamics of European Union* (London: Croom Helm, 1987), pp. 238–72.

Cowan, S., 'Regulation of Several Market Failures: The Water Industry in England and Wales', *Oxford Review of Economic Policy*, 9:4 (1993), pp. 14–23.

Cram, L., 'Integration Theory and the Study of the European Policy Process', in J. J. Richardson (ed.), *European Union: Power and Policy-Making* (London and New York: Routledge, 1996), pp. 40–58.

—— *Policy-Making in the EU: Conceptual Lenses and the Integration Process* (London: Routledge, 1997).

Crewe, I., 'Values: The Crusade that Failed', in D. Kavanagh and A. Seldon (eds.), *The Thatcher Effect* (Oxford: Clarendon Press, 1989), pp. 239–50.

Croci, E., Frey, M., and Molocchi, A., *Agenzie e Governo dell'Ambiente* (Milan: Franco Angeli, 1994).

Dalton, R. J., *The Green Rainbow* (New Haven and London: Yale University Press, 1994).

de Esteban Alonso, A. and Lopez Lopez, A., 'Environmental Policy', in A. Almarcha Barbado (eds.), *Spain and EC Membership Evaluated* (London: Pinter, 1993), pp. 60–8.

Delbeke, J., 'The Prospects for the Use of Economic Instruments in EC Environmental Policy', in *Economic Instruments in EC Environmental Policy*, Report on the LMO/EEB Conference in The Hague, September 1991.

Del Carmen, M., 'Spain's Accession to the EC: Repercussions on Environmental Policy', *European Environment Review*, 1:1 (1986), pp. 13–17.

Demmke, C., 'National Officials and their Role in the Executive Process: "Comitology" and European Environmental Policy', in C. Demmke (ed.), *Managing European Environmental Policy: The Role of the Member States in the Policy Process* (Maastricht: European Institute of Public Administration, 1997), pp. 23–39.

Dente, B., and Lewanski, R., 'Administrative Networks and Implementation Effectiveness: Industrial Air Pollution Control Policy in Italy', *Policy Studies Journal*, 11:1 (1982), pp. 116–29.

Dictionary of Ecology and the Environment (Teddington: Peter Collins, 1988).

Diekmann, A., 'Moral oder Ökonomie? Zum Umweltverhalten in Niedrigkostensituationen', in H. Steinmann and G. R. Wagner (eds.), *Umwelt und Wirtschaftsethik* (Stuttgart: Schäffer-Poeschel Verlag, 1998), pp. 233–47.

Dolan, E. G., 'Controlling Acid Rain', in W. Block (ed.), *Economics and the Environment: A Reconciliation* (Vancouver: Fraser Institute, 1990), pp. 215–32.

Donnelly, M., 'The Structure of the European Commission and the Policy Formulation Process', in S. Mazey and J. J. Richardson (eds.), *Lobbying in the European Community* (Oxofrd: Oxford University Press, 1993), pp. 74–92.

Eberg, J., *Waste Policy and Learning: Policy Dynamics of Waste Management and Waste Incineration in the Netherlands and Bavaria* (Utrecht: Uitgeverij Eburon, 1997).

Elleniki Etairia, *The State of the Greek Environment* (Athens, Elleniki Etairia, 1991).

Enloe, C. H., *The Politics of Pollution in Comparative Perspective* (New York and London: Longman, 1975).

Ensor, R. C. K., *England 1870–1914* (Oxford: Clarendon Press, 1936).

Estevan, M., *Implicaciones Economicas de la Proteccion Ambiental de la CEE: Repercusiones en España* (Madrid: Ministerio de Economia, 1991).

European Environment Bureau, *Review of the Fifth Action Programme* (European Environment Bureau: Brussels: 1996).

—— *Review of the Fifth Action Programme* (European Environment Bureau: Brussels: 1996).

Evans, G., 'Hard Times for the British Green Party', *Environmental Politics*, 2:2 (1993), pp. 327–33.

Evans, P., Rueschemeyer, D., and Skocpol, T., (eds.), *Bringing the State Back In* (New York: Cambridge University Press, 1985).

Faure, M., and Ruegg, M., 'Environmental Standard Setting through General Environmental Law', in M. Faure, J. Vervaele, and A. Weale (eds.), *Environmental Standards in the European Union in an Interdisciplinary Framework* (Antwerp and Apeldoorn: MAKLU, 1994), pp. 39–60.

Federici, P., and Galeotti, A. G., 'Environmental Regulation in Italy', in T. Handler (ed.), *Regulating the European Environment* (London: Wiley, 1997, 2nd edn), pp. 125–33.

Flynn, B., *Subsidiarity and the Rise of Soft Law*, Occasional Paper no. 40 (Colchester: University of Essex Human Capital and Mobility Network, 1997).

Føllesdal, A., 'Democracy, Legitimacy and Majority Rule in the European Union', in A. Weale and M. Nentwich (eds.), *Political Theory and the European Union* (London and New York: Routledge, 1998), pp. 34–48.

Fondazione Agnelli, *Manuale per la Difesa del Mare e della Costa* (Turin: Fondazione Agnelli, 1990).

Fousekis, P., and Lekakis, J., 'Greece's Institutional Response to Sustainable Development', *Environmental Politics*, 6:1 (1997), pp. 131–52.

Franklin, M. N., van der Eijk, C., and Marsh, M., 'Referendum Outcomes and Trust in Government: Public Support for Europe in the Wake of Maastricht', in J. Hayward, *The Crisis of Representation in Europe* (London: Frank Cass, 1995), pp. 101–17.

Freeman, G. P., 'National Styles and Policy Sectors: Explaining Structured Variation', *Journal of Public Policy*, 5:4 (1985), pp. 467–96.

Galbraith, J. K., *The Affluent Society* (Harmondsworth: Penguin, 1970, 2nd edn), p. 212.

Garcia-Ferrando, M. *et al.* (eds.), *Ecologia, Relaciones Industriales y Empresa* (Bilbao: Fundacion BBV, 1994).

Garrett, G., 'International Cooperation and Institutional Choice: The European Community's Internal Market', *International Organization*, 46:2 (1992), pp. 533–60.

—— and Weingast, B., 'Ideas, Interests and Institutions: Constructing the European Community's Internal Market', in J. Goldstein and R. Keohane (eds.), *Ideas and Foreign Policy: Beliefs, Institutions and Political Change* (London: Cornell University Press, 1993), pp. 173–206.

George, S., 'The European Union: Approaches from International Relations', in H. Kassim and A. Menon (eds.), *The European Union and Industrial Policy* (London: Routledge, 1996), pp. 11–25.

Goldsmith, J., and Keohane, R. (eds.), *Ideas and Foreign Policy: Beliefs, Institutions and Political Change* (Ithaca, NY: Cornell University Press, 1993).

Golub, J., *British Integration into the EEC: A Case Study of European Environmental Policy*, D.Phil. thesis (Oxford University, 1994).

—— 'British Sovereignty and the Development of EC Environmental Policy', *Environmental Politics*, 5:4 (1996), pp. 700–28.

—— 'Sovereignty and Subsidiarity in EU Environmental Policy', *Political Studies*, 44:4 (1996), pp. 686–703.

—— 'State Power and Institutional Influence in European Integration: Lessons from the Packaging Waste Directive', *Journal of Common Market Studies*, 34:3 (1996), pp. 313–39.

Grant, C., *Delors: Inside the House that Jacques Built* (London: Nicholas Brealey, 1994).

Grant, W., 'Large Firms, SMEs, and Deregulation', in U. Collier (ed.), *Deregulation in the European Union: Environmental Perspectives* (London: Routledge, 1998), pp. 147–64.

—— *Pressure Groups, Politics and Democracy in Britain* (Oxford: Philip Allan, 1989).

Greenpeace International, *Critique of the Proposal for a Council Directive on Packaging and Packaging Waste* (Brussels: Greenpeace, 1992).

Griffiths, R. T., 'The European Integration Experience', in K. Middlemas, *Orchestrating Europe: The Informal Politics of the European Union 1973–95* (London: Fontana Press, 1995), pp. 1–70.

Haas, E., 'International Integration: The European and Universal Process', *International Organization*, 15 (1960), pp. 366–92.

—— *The Uniting of Europe: Political, Social and Economic Forces, 1950–1957* (Stanford, Calif.: Stanford University Press, 1968, 2nd edn).

Haas, P. M., *Saving the Mediterranean* (New York and Oxford: Columbia University Press, 1990).

Haigh, N., *EEC Environmental Policy and Britain: An Essay and a Handbook* (London: Longman, 1989, 2nd edn).

—— *Manual of Environmental Policy: The EC and Britain* (London: Cartermill International, 1992 and subsequent revisions).

—— 'The Introduction of the Precautionary Principle in the UK', in T. O'Riordan and J. Cameron (eds.), *Interpreting the Precautionary Principle* (London: Earthscan, 1994), pp. 229–51.

—— 'A Green Agenda', paper for UACES Conference, 'A Green Agenda for the Intergovernmental Conference: The Future of EU Environmental Policy', London 29 March 1996.

—— and Baldock, D., *Environmental Policy and 1992* (London: Institute for European Environmental Policy, 1989).

—— with Bennett, G., Kromarek, P., and Lavoux, T., *Comparative Report. Water and Waste in Four Countries: A Study of the Implementation of the EEC Directives in France, Germany, Netherlands and Unitied Kingdom* (London: Graham and Trotman, 1986).

—— and Irwin, F. (eds.), *Integrated Pollution Control in Europe and North America* (Washington: Conservation Foundation, 1990).

Hajer, M. A., *The Politics of Environmental Discourse: Ecological Modernization and the Policy Process* (Oxford: Clarendon Press, 1995).

Hall, P. A. (ed.), *The Political Power of Economic Ideas* (Princeton: Princeton University Press, 1980).

—— *Governing the Economy* (Cambridge: Polity Press, 1986).

—— 'Policy Paradigms, Social Learning, and the State', *Comparative Politics*, 25:2 (1993), pp. 275–96.

—— and Taylor, R. C. R., 'Political Science and the Three New Institutionalisms', *Political Studies*, 44:5 (1996), pp. 936–57.

—— *et al.*, *Change, Choice and Conflict in Social Policy* (London: Heinemann, 1975).

Hanf, K., 'The Impact of European Policies on Domestic Institutions and Politics: Observations on the Implementation of Community Environmental Directives', ECPR paper, 1991.

—— 'European Community Policy', in H. Bressers and L. J. O'Toole Jr (eds.), *International Comparative Policy Research* (Enschede: University of Twente Press, 1992), pp. 85–98.

—— and Gronden, E. van de, 'The Netherlands: Joint Regulation and Sustainable Development', in K. Hanf and A.-I. Jansen (eds.), *Governance and Environment in Western Europe* (Harlow: Addison Wesley Longman, 1998), pp. 152–80.

Hanley, N., Hallett, S., and Moffatt, I., 'Why Is More Notice Not Taken of Economists' Prescriptions for the Control of Pollution?' *Environment and Planning* A, 22 (1990), pp. 1421–39.

Hart, H. L. A., *The Concept of Law* (Oxford: Clarendon Press, 1961).

Hartkopf, G., and Bohne, E., *Umweltpolitik* (Opladen: Westdeutscher Verlag, 1983).

Hartley, T. C., *The Foundations of European Community Law* (Oxford: Clarendon Press, 1988).

Hatch, M. T., 'The Politics of Global Warming in Germany', *Environmental Politics*, 4:3 (1995), pp. 415–40.

Hawkins, K., *Environment and Enforcement* (Oxford: Clarendon Press, 1984).

Hayek, F. A., *Law, Legislation and Liberty* (London: Routledge, 1982).

Hayes-Renshaw, F., 'The Role of the Council', in S. S. Andersen and K. A. Eliassen (eds.), *The European Union: How Democratic Is It?* (London: Sage, 1996), pp. 143–63.

—— and Wallace, H., 'Executive Power in the European Union: The Functions and Limits of the Council of Ministers', *Journal of European Public Policy*, 2:4 (1995), pp. 559–82.

—— and —— *The Council of Ministers* (London: Macmillan, 1997).

Hayward, J., 'Has European Unification by Stealth a Future?' in J. Hayward (ed.), *Élitism, Populism, and European Politics* (Oxford: Clarendon Press, 1996), pp. 252–57.

Heclo, H., *Modern Social Politics in Britain and Sweden* (New Haven and London: Yale University Press, 1974).

Heinze, R. G., and Voelzkow, H., 'Der Deutsche Bauernverband und das "Gemeinwohl"', in R. Mayntz (ed.), *Verbände zwischen Mitgliederinteressen und Gemeinwohl* (Gütersloh: Verlag Bertelsmann Stiftung, 1992), pp. 122–61.

Hellenic Society for the Protection of the Environment and the Cultural Heritage, *The State of the Greek Environment* (Athens, 1991).

Heller, T., and Pelkmans, J., 'The Federal Economy: Law and Economic Integration and the Positive State—the USA and Europe Compared in an Economic Perspective', in M. Cappelletti, M. Seccomble, and J. Weiler (eds.), *Integration through Law* (Berlin: De Gruyter, 1986).

Héritier, A., Mingers, S., Knill, C., and Becka, M., *Die Veränderung von Staatlichkeit in Europa* (Opladen: Leske & Budrich, 1994).

Hildebrand, P. M., 'The European Community's Environmental Policy, 1957 to "1992": From Incidental Measures to an International Regime?' *Environmental Politics*, 1:4 (1992), pp. 13–44.

Hill, J., 'The Precautionary Principle and the Release of Genetically Modified Organisms (GMOs) to the Environment', in T. O'Riordan and J. Cameron (eds.), *Interpreting the Precautionary Principle* (London: Earthscan, 1994), pp. 172–82.

Hine, D., *Governing Italy: The Politics of Bargained Pluralism* (Oxford: Clarendon Press, 1993).

Hirsch, F., *The Social Limits to Growth* (London: Routledge, 1977).

Hirschman, A., *The Rhetoric of Reaction* (Cambridge, Mass.: Belknap Press, 1991).

Hitchens, J., *Recyclopaedia. Recycling Domestic Waste—Meeting the Challenge: The Views of Leading Experts* (London: SCRIB, 1992).

Hix, S., 'Approaches to the Study of the EC', *West European Politics*, 17:1 (1994), pp. 1–30.
—— 'CP, IR and the EU! A Rejoinder to Hurrell and Menon', *West European Politics*, 19:4 (1996), pp. 802–4.
Hoffmann, S., 'Obstinate or Obsolete? The Fate of the Nation-State and the Case of Western Europe', *Daedalus* 95:3 (1966), pp. 862–916.
Hubschmid, C., and Moser, P., 'The Co-operation Procedure in the EU: Why Was the European Parliament Influential in the Decision on Car Emissions?' *Journal of Common Market Studies*, 35:2 (1997), pp. 225–42.
Huelsdorff, M. G., and Pfeiffer, T., 'Environment Policy in the EC: Neo-functionalist Sovereignty Transfer or Neo-realist Gate-Keeping?' *International Journal*, 47:1 (1991–2), pp. 136–58.
Hukkinen, J., 'Corporatism as an Impediment to Eclogical Sustenance: The Case of Finnish Waste Management', *Ecological Economics*, 15 (1995), pp. 59–75.
Hull, R., 'Lobbying Brussels: A View from Within', in S. Mazey and J. Richardson (eds.), *Lobbying in the European Community* (Oxford: Oxford University Press, 1993), pp. 82–92.
Hurrell, A., and Menon, A., 'Politics like any Other? Comparative Politics, International Relations and the Study of the EU', *West European Politics*, 19:2 (1996), pp. 386–402.
Hurst, P., 'Pesticide Reduction Programs in Denmark, the Netherlands, and Sweden', *International Environmental Affairs*, 4:3 (1992), pp. 234–53.
Immergut, E. M., *Health Politics: Interests and Institutions in Western Europe* (Cambridge: Cambridge University Press, 1993).
Incpen, *Factsheet on Waste Management* (London: Incpen, 1992).
Inglehart, R., *The Silent Revolution: Changing Values and Political Styles among Western Publics* (Princeton: Princeton University Press, 1977).
—— *Culture Shift in Advanced industrial Societies* (Princeton: Princeton University Press, 1990).
—— and Abrahamson, P. R., 'Economic Security and Value Change', *American Political Science Review*, 88:2 (1994), pp. 336–54.
Institute for Environmental Studies/Milan, *European Environmental Yearbook* (London: DocTer International UK, 1990).
Jacobs, F., Corbett, R., and Shackleton, M., *The European Parliament* (Harlow: Longman, 1992, 2nd edn).
Jahn, D., 'Environmental Performance and Policy Regimes: Explaining Variations in 18 OECD-Countries', *Policy Sciences*, 31 (1998), pp. 107–31.
Jamison, A., *et al.*, *The Making of the New Environmental Consciousness* (Edinburgh: Edinburgh University Press, 1990).
Jänicke, M., 'Erfolgungsbedingungen von Umweltpolitik im Internationalen Vergleich', *Zeitschrift für Umweltpolitik*, 3 (1990), pp. 213–32.
—— and Weidner, H., 'Germany', in M. Jänicke and H. Weidner (eds.), *National Environmental Policies: A Comparative Study of Capacity-Building* (Berlin: Springer, 1997), pp. 133–55.
—— and —— *National Environmental Policies: A Comparative Study of Capacity Building* (Berlin: Springer, 1997).
Jenkins-Smith, H. C., and Sabatier, P., 'Evaluating the Advocacy Coalition Framework', *Journal of Public Policy*, 14:2 (1994), pp. 175–203.
Johnson, S. P., and Corcelle, G., *The Environmental Policy of the European Communities* (London: Graham & Trotman, 1989).

Jordan, A., 'Integrated Pollution Control and the Evolving Style and Structure of Environmental Regulation in the UK', *Environmental Politics*, 2:3 (1993), pp. 405–27.

—— 'Implementation Failure or Policy Making? How Do We Theorise the Implementation of European Union Legislation? ECPR paper, 1995.

—— *Post-Decisional Politics in the EC: The Implementation of EC Environmental Policy in the UK*, Ph.D. thesis (University of East Anglia, 1997).

—— ' "Overcoming the Divide" between Comparative Politics and International Relations Approaches to the EC: What Role for "Post-Decisional Politics"?' *West European Politics*, 20:4 (1997), pp. 43–70.

—— 'European Community Water Policy Standards: Locked In or Watered Down?' *Journal of Common Market Studies*, 37:1 (1999), pp. 13–37.

—— 'The Construction of a Multi-Level Environmental Governance Structure: EU Environmental Policy at 25', *Environment and Planning* C, 17:1 (1999), pp. 1–17.

—— 'The Implementation of EU Environmental Policy: A Policy Problem without a Political Solution?' *Environment and Planning* C, 17:1 (1999), pp. 69–90.

—— and Greenaway, J., 'Shifting Agendas, Changing Regulatory Structures and the "New" Politics of Environmental Pollution: British Coastal Waters Policy, 1955–1995', *Public Administration*, 76:4 (1998), pp. 669–94.

Jordan, G. and Maloney, W., *The Protest Business? Mobilizing Campaign Groups* (Manchester and New York: Manchester University Press, 1997).

Judge, D., ' "Predestined to Save the Earth": The Environment Committee of the European Parliament', *Environmental Politics*, 1:4 (1992), pp. 186–212.

—— Earnshaw, D., and Cowan, N., 'Ripples or Waves: The European Parliament in the European Community Policy Process', *Journal of European Public Policy*, 1:1 (1994), pp. 27–52.

Junquera, X. and Pujol, E., 'Environmental Regulation in Spain', in T. Handler (ed.), *Regulating the European Environment* (London: John Wiley, 1997, 2nd edn), pp. 177–200.

Kato, J., 'Institutional Rationality in Politics: Three Varieties of Neo-institutionalists', *British Journal of Political Science*, 26:4 (1996), pp. 553–82.

King, A., 'Ideas, Institutions, and the Policies of Governments: A Comparative Analysis, Parts I and II', *British Journal of Political Science*, 3:3 (1973), pp. 291–313.

—— 'Ideas, Institutions, and the Policies of Governments: A Comparative Analysis, Part III', *British Journal of Political Science*, 3:4 (1973), pp. 409–23.

Keohane, R. O., and Nye, J. S., *Power and Interdependence* (London: Harper-Collins, 1989).

Kinnersley, D., *Coming Clean: The Politics of Water and the Environment* (Harmondsworth: Penguin, 1994).

Kirchner, E. J., *Decision-Making in the European Community* (Manchester and New York: Manchester University Press, 1992).

Klingemann, H.-D., Hofferbert, R. I., Budge, I., *et al.*, *Parties, Policies and Democracy* (Boulder, Colo.: Westview Press, 1994).

Knoepful, P., and Weidner, H., 'Implementing Air Quality Programs in Europe', *Policy Studies Journal*, 11 (1990), pp. 103–15.

Kohler-Koch, B., 'Changing Patterns of Interest Intermediation in the European Union', *Government and Opposition*, 29:2 (1993), pp. 166–80.

Koppen, I. J., 'The Role of the European Court of Justice', in J. D. Liefferink, P. D. Lowe, and A. P. J. Mol, *European Integration and Environmental Policy* (London and New York: Belhaven Press, 1993), pp. 126–49.

Krämer, L., *EC Treaty and Environmental Law* (London: Sweet & Maxwell, 1995).
—— *Focus on European Environmental Law* (London: Sweet & Maxwell, 1992).
Krämer, R. A. 'An East–West Tug of Water: Water Services in United Germany', in H. Bressers and L. J. O'Toole Jr (eds.), *International Comparative Policy Research* (Enschede: University of Twente Press, 1992), pp. 102–26.
Kreps, D. M., *A Course in Microeconomic Theory* (New York: Harvester Wheatsheaf, 1990).
La Spina, A., and Sciortino, G., 'Common Agenda, Southern Rules: European Integration and Environmental Change in the Mediterranean States', in J. D. Liefferink, P. D. Lowe, and A. P. J. Mol (eds.), *European Integration and Environmental Policy* (London: Belhaven, 1993), pp. 217–36.
Laffan, B., 'Policy Implementation in the European Community: The European Social Fund as a Case Study', *Journal of Common Market Studies*, 21:4 (1983), pp. 389–408.
Laursen, F., 'The Role of the Commission', in S. S. Andersen and K. A. Eliassen (eds.), *The European Union: How Democratic Is It?* (London: Sage, 1996), pp. 119–41.
Laver, M., and Budge, I., *Party Policy and Government Coalitions* (London: Macmillan, 1992).
Lean, G., 'The Role of the Media', in L. Roberts and A. Weale (eds.), *Innovation and Environmental Risk* (London and New York: Belhaven, 1991).
Lees, C., *'Red–Green' Coalitions in the Federal Republic of Germany: Models of Formation and Maintenance*, Ph.D. thesis (University of Birmingham, 1998).
Lega per l'Ambiente, *Ambiente Italia 1990* (Milan: Arnaldo Mondadori, 1990).
Lenschow, A., 'The Greening of the EU: The Common Agricultural Policy and the Structural Funds', *Environment and Planning* C, 17:1 (1999), pp. 91–108.
Levitt, R., *Implementing Public Policy* (London: Croom Helm, 1980).
Levy, G. M. (ed.), *Packaging in the Environment* (London: Blackie Academic, 1993).
Lewanski, R., 'Environmental Policy in Italy: From the Regions to the EEC, A Multiple Tier Policy Game', ECPR paper, 1993.
—— *Governare L'Ambiente: attori e processi della political ambientale* (Bologna: Il Mulino, 1997).
—— 'Italy: Environmental Policy in a Fragmented State', in K. Hanf and A.-I. Jansen (eds.), *Governance and Environment in Western Europe* (Harlow: Addison Wesley Longman, 1998), pp. 131–51.
—— and Liberatore, A., 'Environment Protection in Italy: Analyzing the Local, National and European Community Levels of Policy Making', in U. Desai (ed.), *Comparative Environmental Policy and Politics* (Albany, NY: SUNY Press, 1997).
Liberatore, A., 'Problems of Transnational Policymaking: Environmental Policy in the European Community', *European Journal of Political Research*, 19 (1991), pp. 281–305.
Liefferink, J.D., *The Making of European Environmental Policy* (Manchester, Manchester University Press, 1996).
——, *Environment and the Nation State: The Netherlands, the EU and Acid Rain* (Manchester and New York: Manchester University Press, 1996).
—— 'The Netherlands: A Net Exporter of Environmental Policy Concepts', in M. S. Andersen and D. Liefferink (eds.), *European Environmental Policy: The Pioneers* (Manchester and New York: Manchester University Press, 1997), pp. 210–50.
—— and Andersen, M. S., 'Strategies of the "Green" Member States in EU Environmental Policy-Making', *Journal of European Public Policy*, 5:2 (1998), pp. 254–70.

Lindberg, L. N., *The Political Dynamics of European Economic Integration* (London: Oxford University Press, 1963).

Little, R., and Smith, S. (eds.), *Belief Systems and International Relations* (Oxford: Basil Blackwell, 1988).

Lodge, J., 'Environment: Towards a Clean Blue–Green EC', in J. Lodge (ed.), *The European Community and the Challenge of the Future* (London: Pinter, 1989), pp. 319–26.

—— 'The European Parliament', in S. S. Andersen and K. A. Eliassen (eds.), *The European Union: How Democratic Is It?* (London: Sage, 1996), pp. 187–214.

Lopez Bustos, F. L., *La Organizacion Administrativa del Medio Ambiente* (Madrid: Editorial Civitas, 1992).

Lowe, P. D., 'The Royal Commission on Environmental Pollution', *Political Quarterly*, 46 (1975), pp. 87–94.

—— and Goyder, J., *Environmental Groups in Politics* (London: George Allen & Unwin, 1983).

—— and Ward, S., 'Domestic Winners and Losers', in P. Lowe and S. Ward (eds.), *British Environmental Policy and Europe* (London and New York: Routledge, 1998), pp. 87–104.

Lowi, T. J., 'American Business, Public Policy, Case Studies and Political Theory', *World Politics*, 6 (1964), pp. 677–715.

Macridis, R. C. (ed.), *Modern Political Systems* (Hemel Hempstead: Prentice-Hall, 1990, 7th edn).

Macrory, R., 'The Enforcement of Community Environmental Laws: Some Critical Issues', *Common Market Law Review*, 29 (1992), pp. 347–69.

Majone, G., *Evidence, Argument and Persuasion in the Policy Process* (New Haven and London: Yale University Press, 1989).

—— 'Cross-National Sources of Regulatory Policymaking in Europe and the United States', *Journal of Public Policy*, 11:1 (1991), pp. 79–106.

—— 'Market Integration and Regulation: Europe after 1992', *Metroeconomica*, 43:1–2 (1992), pp. 131–56.

—— 'The European Community between Social Policy and Social Regulation', *Journal of Common Market Studies*, 31:2 (1993), pp. 153–70.

—— *Independence vs Accountability? Non-Majoritiarian Institutions and Democratic Government in Europe*, EUI Working Papers in Political and Social Sciences, SPS no. 94/3 (1994).

—— 'Public Policy and Administration: Ideas, Interests and Institutions', in R. E. Goodin and H.-D. Klingemann, *New Handbook of Political Science* (Oxford: Oxford University Press, 1996), pp. 610–27.

—— *Regulating Europe* (London and New York: Routledge, 1996).

Malnes, R., *Valuing the Environment* (Manchester and New York: Manchester University Press, 1995).

Maloney, W. A. and Richardson, J., *Managing Policy Change in Britain: The Politics of Water* (Edinburgh: Edinburgh University Press, 1995).

Marks, G., Scharpf, F. W., Schmitter, P. C. and Streeck, W., *Governance in the European Union* (London: Sage, 1996).

Marmor, T. R., and Klein, R., 'Cost vs Care: American's Health Care Dilemma Wrongly Considered', *Quarterly Journal of Health Services Management*, 4:1 (1986), pp. 19–24; reprinted in part as ch. 6 of T. R. Marmor, *Understanding Health Care Reform* (New Haven and London: Yale University Press, 1994).

Marquand, D., *The Unprincipled Society* (London: Jonathan Cape, 1988).

510   *Bibliography*

Marsh, D., and Rhodes, R. A. W. (eds.), *Policy Networks in British Government* (Oxford: Oxford University Press, 1992).

Mazey, S., 'The Development of the European Idea: From Sectoral Integration to Political Union', in J. J. Richardson (ed.), *European Union: Power and Policy-Making* (London and New York: Routledge, 1996), pp. 24–39.

—— and Richardson, J. J., 'Introduction: Transference of Power, Decision Rules and Rules of the Game' in S. Mazey and J. J. Richardson (eds.), *Lobbying in the European Community* (Oxford and New York: Oxford University Press, 1993), pp. 3–26.

—— and —— (eds.), *Lobbying in the European Community* (Oxford and New York: Oxford University Press, 1993).

—— and —— 'Policy Co-ordination in Brussels: Environmental and Regional Policy', *Regional Politics and Policy*, 4:1 (1994), pp. 22–44.

McGowan, F., and Seabright, P., 'Regulation and Subsidiarity: Finding the Balance', in D. G. Mayes (ed.), *Aspects of European Integration* (London: National Institute of Economic and Social Research, 1993), pp. 45–53.

Metz, L., 'Reduction of Exhaust Gases at Large Combustion Plants in the Federal Republic of Germany', in M. Jänicke and H. Weidner (eds.), *Successful Environmental Policy: A Critical Evaluation of 24 Cases* (Berlin: Edition Sigma, 1995), pp. 171–86.

Middlemas, K., *Orchestrating Europe* (London: Fontana Press, 1995).

Milward, A., *et al.*, *The European Rescue of the Nation State* (London: Routledge, 1992).

Mitrany, D., *The Functional Theory of Politics* (London: Martin Robertson, 1975).

Mol, A. P. J., *The Refinement of Production* (Utrecht: Van Arkel, 1995).

Moltke, K. von, 'The *Vorsorgeprinzip* in West German Environmental Policy', Royal Commission on Environmental Pollution, Twelfth Report, *Best Practicable Environmental Option* (London: HMSO, 1988), Cm. 310, app. 3, pp. 57–70.

Monnet, J., *Memoirs*, trans. R. Mayne, with a forward by Roy Jenkins (London: Collins, 1978).

Moravcsik, A., 'Negotiating the Single European Act', in R. O. Keohane and S. Hoffmann (eds.), *The New European Community* (Boulder, Colo., San Francisco, and Oxford: Westview Press, 1991), pp. 41–84.

—— 'Preferences and Power in the European Community: A Liberal Intergovernmentalist Approach', *Journal of Common Market Studies*, 31:4 (1993), pp. 473–524.

Morris, A., 'A Sea Change in Spanish Conservation: With Illustrations from Gerona Province', *Journal of the Association for Contemporary Iberian Studies*, 5:2 (1992), pp. 23–30.

Müller, E., *Innenwelt der Umweltpolitik* (Opladen: Westdeutscher Verlag, 1986).

Nas, M., 'Green, Greener, Greenest', in J. W. van Deth and E. Scarbrough (eds.), *The Impact of Values: Beliefs in Government*, iv (Oxford: Oxford University Press, 1995), pp. 275–300.

Noam, E., 'The Choice of Government Level in Regulation', *Kyklos*, 35:2 (1982), pp. 278–91.

Nordlinger, E. A., *On the Autonomy of the Democratic State* (Cambridge, Mass.: Harvard University Press, 1981).

North, D. C., *Institutions, Institutional Change and Ecnomic Performance* (Cambridge: Cambridge University Press, 1990).

Nugent, N., *The Government and Politics of the European Community* (London: Macmillan, 1991, 2nd edn).

Ogus, A., 'Standard Setting for Environmental Protection: Principles and Processes', in M. Faure, J. Vervaele, and A. Weale (eds.), *Environmental Standards in the European Union in an Interdisciplinary Framework* (Antwerp: MAKLU, 1994), pp. 25–37.

O'Riordan, T., 'Stability and Transformation in Environmental Government', *Political Quarterly*, 62:2 (1991), pp. 167–85.

—— and Cameron, J. (eds.), *Interpreting the Precautionary Principle* (London: Earthscan, 1994).

—— and Weale, A., 'Administrative Reorganisation and Policy Change: The Case of Her Majesty's Inspectorate of Pollution', *Public Administration*, 67:3 (1989), pp. 277–94.

Pehle, H., 'Germany: Domestic Obstacles to an International Forerunner', in M. S. Andersen and D. Liefferink (eds.), *European Environmental Policy: The Pioneers* (Manchester and New York: Manchester University Press, 1997), pp. 161–209.

—— and Jansen, A.-I., 'Germany: The Engine in European Environmental Policy?' in K. Hanf and A.-I. Jansen (eds.), *Governance and Environment in Western Europe* (Harlow: Addison Wesley Longman, 1998), pp. 82–109.

Pelekasi, K., and Skourtos, M., *Atmospheric Pollution in Greece* (in Greek) (Athens: Papazisi, 1992).

Pelkmans, J., 'The Assignment of Public Functions in Economic Integration', *Journal of Common Market Studies*, 21 (1982), pp. 97–121.

Peltzman, S., and Tideman, T. N., 'Local versus National Pollution Control: Note', *American Economic Review*, 62:5 (1972), pp. 959–63.

Peters, B. G., 'Escaping the Joint-Decision Trap: Repetition and Sectoral Politics in the European Union', *West European Politics*, 20:2 (1997), pp. 22–36.

Peterson, J., 'Decision-Making in the European Union: Towards a Framework for Analysis', *Journal of European Public Policy*, 2:1 (1995), pp. 69–93.

—— 'Playing the Transparency Game: Consultation and Policy-Making in the European Commission', *Public Administration*, 73:3 (1995), pp. 473–92.

Pierson, P., 'The Path to European Integration: An Historical Institutionalist Account', *Comparative Political Studies*, 29:2 (1996), pp. 123–63.

Pigou, A. C., *The Economics of Welfare* (London: Macmillan, 1952, 4th edn).

Poguntke, T., 'Between Ideology and Empirical Research', *European Journal of Political Research*, 21:4 (1992), pp. 337–56.

Pollack, M., 'The New Institutionalism and EC Governance', *Governance*, 9:4 (1996), pp. 429–58.

Pollitt, C., *Manipulating the Machine* (London: Allen & Unwin, 1987).

Porter, M., *Interest Groups, Advocacy Coalitions and the EC Environment Policy Process: A Policy Network Analysis of the Packaging and Packaging Waste Directive*, Ph.D. thesis (University of Bath, 1995).

Postiglione, A., *Manuale dell'Ambiente: Guida alla Legislazione Ambientale* (Rome: La Nuova Italia Scientifica, 1984).

Pridham, G., 'National Environmental Policy-Making in the European Framework: Spain, Greece and Italy in Comparison', *Regional Politics and Policy*, 4:1 (1994), pp. 80–101.

—— *Tourism Policy in Mediterranean Europe: Towards Sustainable Development?* Occasional Paper no. 15 (Centre for Mediterranean Studies, University of Bristol, May 1996).

—— and Cini, M., 'Enforcing Environmental Standards', in M. Faure, J. Vervaele, and A. Weale (eds.), *Environmental Standards in the European Union: An Interdisciplinary Perspective* (Antwerp: MAKLU, 1994), pp. 251–77.

—— Verney, S., and Konstadakopulos, D., 'Environmental Policy in Greece: Evolution, Structures and Process', *Environmental Politics*, 4:2 (1995), pp. 244–70.

Putnam, R. D., 'Diplomacy and Domestic Politics: The Logic of Two-Level Games', *International Organization*, 42:3 (1988), pp. 427–60.

Radaelli, C., 'The Role of Knowledge in the Policy Process', *Journal of European Public Policy*, 2:2 (1995), pp. 159–83.

Rawcliffe, P., *Environmental Pressure Groups in Transition* (Manchester and New York: Manchester University Press, 1998).

Rehbinder, E., 'Vorsorgeprinzip im Umweltrecht und präventive Umweltpolitik', in U. E. Simonis (ed.), *Präventive Umweltpolitik* (Frankfurt/New York: Campus Verlag, 1988), pp. 129–41.

—— and Stewart, R., *Environmental Protection Policy* (Berlin and New York: Walter de Gruyter, 1985).

Rhodes, R. A. W., *Beyond Westminster and Whitehall* (London: Unwin Hyman, 1988).

Richardson, J. J. (ed.), *Policy Styles in Western Europe* (London: George Allen & Unwin, 1982).

—— 'EU Water Policy: Uncertain Agendas, Shifting Networks and Complex Coalitions', *Environmental Politics*, 3:4 (1994), pp. 139–67.

—— and Watts, N. S. J., *National Policy Styles and the Environment*, Discussion Paper 85–16 (Berlin: International Institute for Environment and Society: Wissenschaftszentrum Berlin, 1985).

Ridley, N., *Policies against Pollution: The Conservative Record—and Principles*, Policy Study no. 117 (London: Centre for Policy Studies, 1989).

Rose-Ackerman, S., *Controlling Environmental Policy* (New Haven and London: Yale University Press, 1995).

Ross, G., *Jacques Delors and European Integration* (Cambridge: Polity Press, 1995).

Rothenberg, J., 'Local Decentralization and the Theory of Optimal Government', in J. Margolis (ed.), *The Analysis of Public Output* (New York and London: Columbia University Press, 1970), pp. 31–64.

Rothstein, B., 'Political Institutions: An Overview', in R. E. Goodin and H.-D. Klingemann (eds.), *A New Handbook of Political Science* (Oxford: Oxford University Press, 1996), pp. 133–66.

Rucht, D., and Roose, J., 'The German Environmental Movement as a Crossroads?' in C. Rootes (ed.), *Environmental Movements: Local, National and Global* (London and Portland: Frank Cass, 1999), pp. 59–80.

Rüdig, W., and Krämer, R. A., 'Networks of Cooperation: Water Policy in Germany', *Environmental Politics*, 3:4 (1994), pp. 52–79.

Sabatier, P. A., 'Knowledge, Policy-Oriented Learning and Policy Change: An Advocacy Coalition Framework', *Knowledge: Creation, Diffusion, Utilization*, 8:4 (1987), pp. 64–92.

—— and Jenkins-Smith, H. C. (eds.), *Policy Change and Learning: An Advocacy Coalition Approach* (Oxford: Westview Press, 1993).

Sandholtz, W., and Stone Sweet, A. (eds.), *European Integration and Supranational Governance* (Oxford: Oxford University Press, 1998).

Sandholtz, W., and Zysman, J., '1992: Recasting the European Bargain', *World Politics*, 42:1 (1989), pp. 95–128.

Sands, P., *Principles of International Environmental Law*, I (Manchester: Manchester United Press, 1995).

Sbragia, A., 'Environmental Policy: The "Push-Pull" of Policy-Making', in H. Wallace and W. Wallace (eds.), *Policy-Making in the European Union* (Oxford: Oxford University Press, 1996), pp. 235–55.

—— and Damro, C., 'The Changing Role of the European Union in International Environmental Politics: Institution Building and the Politics of Climate Change', *Environment and Planning C*, 17:1 (1999), pp. 53–68.

Scarrow, H. A., 'The Impact of British Air Pollution Legislation', *British Journal of Political Science*, 2:3 (1972), pp. 261–82.

Schaltz, R., *EU Environmental Policy Process: A Role for the European Parliament?* MA dissertation (University of Essex, 1998).

Scharpf, F. W., 'Does Organization Matter? Task Structure and Interaction in the Ministerial Bureaucracy', in E. H. Burack and A. R. Negandhi (eds.), *Organization Design: Theoretical Perspectives and Empirical Findings* (Kent, Ohio: Kent State University Press, 1977).

—— 'The Joint-Decision Trap: Lessons from German Federalism and European Institutions', *Public Administration*, 66:3 (1988), pp. 239–78.

—— 'Community and Autonomy: Multi-Level Policy-Making in the European Union', *Journal of European Public Policy*, 1:2 (1994), pp. 219–42.

—— 'Negative and Positive Integration in the Political Economy of European Welfare States', in G. Marks, F. W. Scharpf, P. C. Schmitter, and W. Streeck, *Governance in the European Union* (London: Sage, 1996), pp. 15–39.

Schmitter, P. C., 'Examining the Present Euro-Polity with the Help of Past Theories', in G. Marks, F. W. Scharpf, P. C. Schmitter and W. Streeck, *Governance in the European Union* (London: Sage, 1996), pp. 1–14.

Schrama, G. J. I. and Klok, P.-J., 'The Swift Introduction of "Clean Cars" in the Netherlands, 1986–1992: The Origin and Effect of Incentive Measures', in M. Jänicke and H. Weidner (eds.), *Successful Environmental Policy: A Critical Evaluation of 24 Cases* (Berlin: Edition Sigma, 1995), pp. 203–22.

Scott, J., *Development Dilemmas in the European Community: Rethinking Regional Development Policy* (Buckingham: Open University Press, 1995).

Scruggs, L., 'Institutions and Environmental Performance in Seventeen Western Democracies', *British Journal of Political Science*, 21:1 (1999), pp. 1–31.

Shapiro, M., 'The European Court of Justice', in A. M. Sbragia (ed.), *Euro-Politics: Institutions and Policymaking in the "New" European Community* (Washington: Brookings Institution, 1992), pp. 123–56.

Sidgwick, H., *The Elements of Politics* (London: Macmillan, 1891).

Sidjanski, D., 'Transition to Democracy and European Integration: The Role of Interest Groups in Southern Europe', in G. Pridham (ed.), *Encouraging Democracy: The International Context of Regime Transition in Southern Europe* (Leicester: Leicester University Press, 1991), pp. 195–211.

Siedentopf, H., and Ziller, J. (eds.), *Making European Policies Work: the Implementation of Community Legislation in the Member States*, i, *Comparative Syntheses* (London: Sage, 1988).

Simon, H., *Reason in Human Affairs* (Oxford: Basil Blackwell, 1983).

Sinnott, R., 'Policy, Subsidiarity and Legitimacy', in O. Niedermayer and R. Sinnott, *Public Opinion and Internationalized Governance* (Oxford: Oxford University Press, 1995), pp. 246–76.

Skjaerseth, J. B., 'The Climate Policy of the EC: Too Hot to Handle', *Journal of Common Market Studies*, 32:1 (1994), pp. 25–45.

Smith, M. J., *Pressure, Power and Policy: State Autonomy and Policy Networks in Britain and the United States* (New York: Harvester Wheatsheaf, 1993).

Snyder, F., 'The Effectiveness of European Community Law: Institutions, Processes, Tools and Techniques', *Modern Law Review*, 56:1 (1993), pp. 19–54.

Spanou, C., 'Greece: Administrative Symbols and Policy Realities', in K. Hanf and A.-I. Jansen (eds.), *Governance and Environment in Western Europe* (Harlow: Addison Wesley Longman, 1998), pp. 110–30.

Spelsberg, G., *Rauchplage* (Aachen: Alano Verlag, 1984).

Steger, U., 'Umwelt-Auditing', in M. Junkernheinrich, P. Klemmer, and G. R. Wagner (eds.), *Handbuch zur Umweltökonomie* (Berlin: Analytica, 1995), pp. 245–50.

Steiner, J., 'Subsidiarity under the Maastricht Treaty', in D. O'Keefe and P. Twomey (eds.), *Legal Issues of the Maastricht Treaty* (London: Chancery, 1994), pp. 49–64.

Steinmo, S., *Taxation and Democracy: Swedish, British and American Approaches to Fiancing the Modern State* (New Haven: Yale University Press, 1993).

—— Thelen, K. and Longstreth, F. (eds.), *Structuring Politics: Historical Institutionalism in Comparative Analysis* (New York: Cambridge University Press, 1992).

Stgliani, W. M., Jaffé, P. R., and Anderberg, S., 'Heavy Metal Pollution in the Rhine Basin', *Environmental Science and Technology*, 27:5 (1993), pp. 786–93.

Stokke, O. S., 'Environmental Performance Review: Concept and Design', in E. Lykke (ed.), *Achieving Environmental Goals* (London: Belhaven Press, 1992), pp. 3–24.

Stone Sweet, A., and Sandholtz, W., 'European Integration and Supranational Governance', *Journal of European Public Policy*, 4:2 (1997), pp. 297–317.

Szanton, P. (ed.), *Federal Reorganization: What Have We Learned?* (Chatham NJ: Chatham House, 1981).

Taylor, B., 'Green in Word . . .', in R. Jowell *et al.*, *British Social Attitudes: The 14th Report* (Aldershot: Ashgate, 1997), pp. 111–36.

Taylor, D., Diprose, G., and Duffy, M., 'EC Environmental Policy and the Control of Water Pollution: The Implementation of Directive 76/464 in Perspective', *Journal of Common Market Studies*, 33:3 (1986), pp. 225–46.

Taylor, P., *Limits of European Integration* (London and Canberra: Croom Helm, 1983).

Taylor, S., *Making Bureaucracies Think* (Stanford, Calif.: Stanford University Press, 1984).

Thairs, E., 'Business Lobbying on the Environment: The Perspective of the Water Sector', in P. Lowe and S. Ward (eds.), *British Environmental Policy and Europe* (London: Routledge, 1998), pp. 153–70.

Tietenberg, T. H., *Emissions Trading: An Exercise in Reforming Pollution Policy* (Washington: Resources for the Future, 1985).

Timagenis, G., and Pavlopoulos, P., *The Law and Practice relating to Pollution Control in Greece* (London: Graham & Trotman, 1982).

Tinbergen, J., 'The Theory of the Optimum Regime', in L. H. Klassen, L. M. Koyck, and H. J. Witteveen (eds.), *Jan Tinbergen: Selected Papers* (Amsterdam: North-Holland, 1959), pp. 264–304.

Töpfer, K., 'Sustainable Development im Spannungsfeld von internationaler Herausforderung und nationalen Handlungsmöglichkeiten', in H. Steinmann and G. R. Wagner (eds.), *Umwelt und Wirtschaftsethik* (Stuttgart: Schäffer-Poeschel Verlag, 1998), pp. 93–103.

Tsebelis, G., *Nested Games* (Berkeley: University of California Press, 1990).

—— 'The Power of the European Parliament as a Conditional Agenda Setter', *American Political Science Review*, 88:1 (1994), pp. 128–42.

—— 'Decision Making in Political Systems: Veto Players in Presidentialism, Parliamentarianism, Multicameralism and Multipartyism', *British Journal of Political Science*, 25:3 (1995), pp. 289–325.

Tukey, E., *Exploratory Data Analysis* (Reading, Mass.: Addison-Wesley, 1977).

Underdal, A., 'Integrated Marine Policy: What? Why? How?' *Marine Policy*, 4:3 (1980), pp. 159–69.

Usher, J., 'The Commission and the Law', in G. Edwards and D. Spence (eds.), *The European Commission* (Harlow: Longman, 1994), pp. 146–68.

Vandermeersch, D., 'The Single European Act and the Environmental Policy of the European Economic Community', *European Law Review*, 12:6 (1987), pp. 407–29.

Verhoeve, B., and Bennett, G., 'Products and the Environment: An International Overview of Recent Developments', *European Environmental Law Review*, 31:3 (1994), pp. 74–9.

Vlassopoulou, C. A., *La Politique de l'Environnement: Le Cas de la Pollution Atmospherique à Athenes*, Ph.D. thesis (University of Picardy, 1991).

Vogel, D., *National Styles of Regulation* (Ithaca, NY, and London: Cornell University Press, 1986).

—— 'The Making of EC Environmental Policy', in S. S. Andersen, and K. A. Eliassen (eds.), *Making Policy in Europe: The Europeification of National Policy-Making* (London: Sage, 1993), pp. 115–31.

—— *Trading Up* (Cambridge, Mass., and London: Harvard University Press, 1995).

Wagner, G. R., *Betriebswirtschaftliche Umweltökonomie* (Stuttgart: Lucius & Lucius, 1997).

Wallace, H., 'Implementation across National Boundaries', in D. Lewis and H. Wallace (eds.), *Policies into Practice: National and International Case Studies in Implementation* (London: Heinemann, 1984), pp. 129–43.

—— *Regional Integration: The West European Experience* (Washington: Brookings Institution, 1994).

—— 'Government without Statehood', in H. Wallace and W. Wallace (eds.), *Policy-Making in the European Union* (Oxford: Oxford University Press, 1996), pp. 439–60.

—— 'Has Government by Committee Lost the Public's Confidence?' in J. Hayward (ed.), *Elitism, Populism, and European Politics* (Oxford: Clarendon Press, 1996), pp. 238–51.

Ward, N., 'Water Quality', in P. Lowe and S. Ward (eds.), *British Environmental Policy and Europe* (London: Routledge, 1998), pp. 244–64.

—— Buller, H., and Lowe, P., 'The Europeanization of Local Environmental Politics: Bathing Water Pollution in the South West of England', *Local Environment*, 1:1 (1996), pp. 21–32.

Weale, A., *The New Politics of Pollution* (Manchester and New York: Manchester University Press, 1992).

—— 'Ecological Modernisation and the Integration of European Environmental Policy', in J. D. Liefferink, P. D. Lowe, and A. P. J. Mol, *European Integration and Environmental Policy* (London and New York: Belhaven Press, 1993), pp. 196–216.

—— 'The Kaleidoscopic Competition of European Environmental Regulation', *European Business Journal*, 7:4 (1995), pp. 19–25.

—— 'Environmental Regulation and Administrative Reform in Britain', in G. Majone, *Regulating Europe* (London and New York: Routledge, 1996), pp. 106–30.

—— 'Environmental Rules and Rule-Making in the European Union', *Journal of European Public Policy*, 3:4 (1996), pp. 594–611.

—— 'Grinding Slow and Grinding Sure? The Making of the Environment Agency', *Environmental Management and Health*, 7:2 (1996), pp. 40–3.

—— 'Environmental Regulation', in P. Vass (ed.), *Regulatory Review 1997* (London: Centre for the Study of Regulated Industries, 1997), pp. 201–16.

—— 'The Single Market, European Integration and Political Legitimacy', in D. G. Mayes (ed.), *The Evolution of the Single European Market* (Cheltenham, Glos: Edward Elgar, 1997), pp. 199–225.

—— O'Riordan, T., and Kramme, L., *Controlling Pollution in the Round* (London: Anglo-German Foundation, 1991).

—— Pridham, G., Williams, A., and Porter, M., 'Environmental Administration in Six European States: Secular Convergence or National Distinctiveness?' *Public Administration*, 74:2 (1996), pp. 255–74.

—— and Williams, A., 'Between Economy and Ecology? The Single Market and the Integration of Environmental Policy', *Environmental Politics*, 1:4 (1992), pp. 45–64.

Weaver, R. K., and Rockman, B. A., 'Assessing the Effects of Institutions', in R. K. Weaver and B. A. Rockman (eds.), *Do Institutions Matter? Government Capabilities in the United States and Abroad* (Washington: Brookings Institution, 1993), pp. 1–41.

Webster, C., *The Health Services since the War* (London: HMSO, 1988).

Webster, R., 'Environmental Collective Action: Stable Patterns of Cooperation and Issue Alliances at the European Level', in J. Greenwood and M. Aspinwell (eds.), *Collective Action in the European Union* (London: Routledge, 1998), pp. 176–95.

Weidner, H., *25 Years of Modern Environmental Policy in Germany: Treading a Well-Worn Path to the Top of the International Field* (Berlin: Wissenschaftszentrum Berlin für Sozialforschung gGmbH, 1995).

Weinberg, A., 'Science and Trans-Science', *Minerva*, 10:2 (1972), pp. 209–22.

Wey, K.-G., *Umweltpolitik in Deutschland* (Opladen: Westdeutscher Verlag, 1982).

White, P., Hindle, P., and Dräger, K., 'Life Cycle Assessment of Packaging', in G. M. Levy (ed.), *Packaging in the Environment* (London: Blackie Academic, 1993), pp. 118–47.

Williams, R., 'Innovation and the Political Context of Technical Advice', in L. Roberts and A. Weale (eds.), *Innovation and Environmental Risk* (London and New York: Belhaven, 1991), pp. 124–37.

Williamson, G. H., 'Review of Environmental Legislation in the European Community', in G. Levy (ed.), *Packaging and the Environment* (London and New York: Blackie Academic and Professional, 1992), pp. 53–71.

Winch, D., *Economics and Policy* (London: Fontana, 1972).

Wise, M., and Gibb, R., *Single Market to Social Europe* (Harlow: Longman, 1993).

Witherspoon, S., 'Democracy, the Environment and Public Opinion in Western Europe', in W. M. Lafferty and J. Meadowcroft (eds.), *Democracy and the Environment* (Cheltenham, Glos.: Edward Elgar, 1996), pp. 39–70.

Wiweriks, K., and Schulte-Wülwer-Leidg, A., 'Integrated Water Management for the Rhine Basin, from Polluted Prevention to Ecosystem Improvement', *Natural Resources Forum*, 21:2 (1997), pp. 147–56.

Woodcock, S., 'Competition among the Rules in the European Union', in D. G. Mayes (ed.), *The Evolution of the Single European Market* (Cheltenham, Glos: Edward Elgar, 1997), pp. 66–86.

Wurzel, R., 'Environmental Policy', in J. Lodge (ed.), *The European Community and the Challenge of the Future* (London: Pinter, 1993, 2nd edn), pp. 178–99.

—— 'The Role of the EU Presidency in the Environmental Field: Does it Make a Difference which Member State Runs the Presidency?' *Journal of European Public Policy*, 3:2 (1996), pp. 272–91.

Young, O. R., *International Cooperation: Building Regimes for Natural Resources and the Environment* (Ithaca, NY: Cornell University Press, 1989).

—— *International Governance: Protecting the Earth in a Stateless Society* (Ithaca, NY, and London: Cornell University Press, 1994).

Young, S. C., *The Politics of the Environment* (Manchester: Baseline Books, 1993).

Zito, A. R., 'Task Expansion: A Theoretical Overview', *Environment and Planning* C, 17:1 (1999), pp. 19–35.

Official publications

Bundesumweltministerium, *Umweltschutz in Deutschland* (Bonn: Economica Verlag, 1992), trans. as Federal Ministry for the Environment, *Environmental Protection in Germany* (Bonn: Economica Verlag, 1992).

Commission of the European Communities, 'Memorandum: The "Polluter Pays" Principle', in House of Lords Select Committee on the European Communities, *The Polluter Pays Principle*, Session 1982–83, 10th Report (London: HMSO, 1983), pp. 102–3.

—— *Completing the Internal Market*, COM(85), 310 final (Luxembourg: Commission of the European Communities, 1985).

—— *Fourth Environmental Action Programme 1987–92*, COM (86) 328 final (Luxembourg: Commission of the European Communities, 1986).

—— 'Directive on the Limitation of Certain Pollutants into the Air from Large Combustion Plants' (88/609/EEC), *Official Journal of the European Communities*, L336/1 (1988).

—— *Research on 'The Costs of Non-Europe' Executive Summaries: Groupe MAC, Technical Barriers in the EC* (Luxembourg: Commission of the European Communities, 1988).

—— *The Greenhouse Effect and the Community/Commission Work Programme Concerning the Evaluation of Options to Deal with the 'Greenhouse Effect'*, COM (88), 656 final (Luxembourg. Commission of the European Communities, 1988).

—— *Protection of the Environment in the Mediterranean*, 392 (Brussels, 1988).

—— *Environmental Policy in the European Community* (Luxembourg, 1990).

—— *Towards Sustainability: A European Community Programme of Policy and Action in Relation to the Environment and Sustainable Development*, COM (92) 23 final (Luxembourg: Commission of the European Communities, 1992).

—— DG XI, *Administrative Structures for Environmental Management in the European Community* (Brussels, 1993).

—— *Growth, Competitiveness, Employment: The Challenges and Ways Forward into the 21st Century*, 2 vols. (Luxembourg: Commission of the European Communities, 1993).

Commission of the European Communities, *The 10th Annual Report to the European Parliament on Commission Monitoring of the Application and Monitoring of Community Law* COM (93) 329 final, *Official Journal of the EC*, C233, pp. 1–214.

—— *Economic Growth and the Environment: Some Implications for Policy Making*, Communication from the Commission to the European Parliament and Council, COM(94) 465 final (Luxembourg: Commission of the European Communities, 1994).

—— *XXIIIrd Competition Report*, COM(94), 161 final (Luxembourg: Commission of the European Communities, 1994).

—— *Quality of Bathing Water, 1993* (Luxembourg: Commission of the European Communities, 1994).

—— *Report of the Group of Independent Experts on Legislative and Administrative Simplification: Summary and Proposals*, COM (95) 288 final (Luxembourg: Commission of the European Communities, 1995).

Committee of the Regions, 'Opinion of the Committee of the Regions on the Proposal for a Council Ditrective amending Directive 85/337/EEC on the Assessment of the Effects of Certain Public and Private Projects on the Environment, COM(93) 575, final', CDR 245/94, *Official Journal of the European Communities*, C210/95/12, vol. 38 (1995), pp. 78–80.

Commission of the European Communities, *The 12th Annual Report on the Monitoring and Application of Community Law* COM (95) 500, *Official Journal of the European Communities* C254, pp. 1–167.

—— *Two Years of Consultative Work 1994–1995: The Contributions of the Committee of the Regions to the Construction of Europe* (Luxembourg: Office for Official Publications of the EC, 1996).

Department of the Environment, *A Guide to Risk Assessment and Risk Management for Environmental Protection* (London: HMSO, 1995).

Economic and Social Committee of the EC, 'Opinion on the Proposal for a Council Directive Introducing a Tax on Carbon Dioxide Emissions and Energy, COM(92) 226, final', *Official Journal of the European Communities*, C108/93/06, vol. 36 (1993), pp. 20–24.

European Environment Agency, *Environmental Taxes: Implementation and Effectiveness* (Copenhagen: European Environment Agency, 1996).

House of Commons Environment Committee, *Fourth Report: Pollution of Beaches*, ii (London: HMSO, 1990).

House of Commons Trade and Industry Committee, *Trade with Europe*, Minutes of Evidence, HC 216-iv (London: HMSO, 1993).

House of Lords Select Committee on the European Communities, *Fourth Environmental Action Programme*, 1986–87 Sessions, HL 135 (London: HMSO, 1987).

—— *10th Report 1990–91: Municipal Waste Water Treatment* (London: HMSO, 1991).

—— *Carbon–Energy Tax*, HL 52. (London: HMSO, 1992).

—— *Implementation and Enforcement of Environmental Legislation*, Session 1991–92, Ninth Report, HL Paper 53-I and II. (London: HMSO, 1992).

—— *Packaging and Packaging Waste*, Session 1992–93, 26th Report, HL Paper 118-I (London: HMSO, 1993).

Kloepfer, M., and Messerschmidt, K., *Innere Harmonisierung des Umweltrechts* (Berlin: Erich Schmidt Verlag, 1986).

—— *et al.*, *Umweltgesetzbuch* (Berlin: Erich Schmidt Verlag, 1990).

Mayntz, R., *et al.*, *Vollzugsprobleme der Umweltpolitik* (Wiesbaden: Rat von Sachverständigen für Umweltfragen, 1978).

Ministerio de Obras Publicas, *Medio Ambiente en España 1988* (Madrid: Ministerio de Obras Publicas, 1989).

—— *Medio Ambiente en España 1989* (Madrid: Ministerio de Obras Publicas, 1990).

—— *Medio Ambiente en España 1990* (Madrid: Ministerio de Obras Publicas, 1991).

—— *Medio Ambiente en España 1992* (Madrid: Ministerio de Obras Publicas, 1993).

—— Transportes y Medio Ambiente, *Guía de la Organización Administrativa en Medio Ambiente* (Madrid: Ministerio de Obras Publicas, 1993).

—— *Informacion de Medio Ambiente*, November 1993.

Ministero dell'Ambiente, *Rapporto sullo Stato dell'Ambiente* (Rome: Ministero dell'Ambiente, 1989).

—— *Nota Aggiunta del Ministro Giorgio Ruffolo* (Rome: Ministero dell'Ambiente, 1989).

—— *Rapporto al Ministro sulle Linee di Politica Ambientale a Medio e Lungo Termine* (Rome: Ministero dell'Ambiente, 1989).

—— *Rapporto sullo Stato dell'Ambiente* (Rome: Ministero dell'Ambiente, 1989).

—— *Bilancio di un Quinquennio di Politiche Ambientali* (Rome: Ministero dell'Ambiente, 1992).

—— *Relazione sullo Stato dell'Ambiente* (Rome: Ministero dell'Ambiente, 1992).

Ministry of the Environment (YPEHODE), *National Report of Greece, UN Conference on Environment and Development, Brazil, June 1992* (Athens: Ministry of the Environment, 1991).

Ministry of Housing, Physical Planning and Environment (VROM)/ Environmental Resources Limited, *The Structure and Functions of Environmental Enforcement Organizations in EC Member States* (The Hague: VROM, 1991).

OECD, *Environmental Policies in Greece* (Paris: OECD, 1983).

—— *Environmental Indicators, 1991* (Paris: OECD, 1991).

—— *Environmental Performance Review, Italy* (Paris: OECD, 1994).

—— *Evaluating Economic Instruments for Environmental Policy* (Paris: OECD, 1997).

—— *OECD Environment Performance Reviews: Germany* (Paris: OECD, 1993).

—— *Reduction and Recycling of Packaging Waste* (Paris: OECD, 1992).

Rijksinstitut voor Volksgezondheid en Milieuhygiene, *Zorgen voor Morgen: Nationale Milieuverkenning 1985–2021* (Alphen aan den Rijn: Samson H. D. Tjeenk Willink, 1989).

Royal Commission on Environmental Pollution, *First Report*, Cmnd. 4585 (London: HMSO, 1971).

—— *Fifth Report: Air Pollution Control: An Integrated Approach*, Cmnd. 6371 (London: HMSO, 1976).

—— *Twelth Report: Best Practicable Environmental Option*, Cm. 310 (London: HMSO, 1988).

—— *Twenty-First Report: Setting Environmental Standards*, Cm. 4053 (London: The Stationery Office, 1998).

Second Chamber of the States General, *National Environmental Policy Plan: To Choose or Lose* ('s-Gravenhage: SDU uitgeverij, 1989).

Task Force on the Environment and the Internal Market, '1992: The Environmental Dimension', (mimeo, 1989).

UK Government, *This Common Inheritance: Britain's Environmental Strategy* (London: HMSO, 1990).

—— *Sustainable Development: The UK Strategy* (London: HMSO, 1994).

Umweltbericht '76 (Stuttgart: W. Kohlhammer, 1976).

World Commission on Environment and Development, *Our Common Future* (Oxford: Oxford University Press, 1987).

Name Index

Albert, M. 36
Alders, H. 276
Anderson, M. 181
Arp, H. 400
Ashby, Lord 176–7, 181

Bagehot, W. 461
Baker, K. 225
Baldock, D. 37
Beltran, D. J. 477, 482, 483, 484
Bennett, C. J. 138
Bjerregaard, R. 88
Bouwer, K. 227
Brack, D. 30
Brand, K.-W. 259, 271
Bressers, H. T. A. 372
Brinkhorst, L.-J. 77, 89
Bulmer, S. 138, 146
Burke, T. 264

Caithness, Earl of 179
Carter, N. 180
Christofilopoulou, P. 198
Clinton-Davis, S. 362
Cockfield, Lord 79
Collins, K. 323
Cram, L. 24
Crosland, A. 226

Dalton, R. 256, 258, 263
Delors, J. 36, 40, 88, 115, 122–3, 458

Earnshaw, D. 323

Faure, M. 451

Gaulle, General de 21
Genscher, H. D. 203

Haigh, N. 1, 37, 67, 72, 328, 357, 390, 402
Hallstein, W. 20
Hauff, V. 204
Hayek, F. A. 488
Heath, E. 224
Héritier, A. 447
Heseltine, M. 225, 264, 320

Hirschman, A. 77
Hoffman, S. 468

Jacobs, Advocate-General 39
Jänicke, M. 140
Jordan, A. 297, 331, 359

Karamanlis, A. 479
Kohl, H. 101, 203, 387

Laffan, B. 322
Lenschow, A. 457
Lodge, J. 453
Lowe, P. 180, 265
Lowi, T. J. 139

Macrory, R. 330
Majone, G. 7, 79, 104, 141, 458
Major, J. 101
Manos, S. 211
Mansholt, S. L. 76
Matteoli, A. 169–70, 262
Merkl, A. 206
Mitrany, D. 16
Mol, A. P. J. 275
Moltke, K. von 67
Monnet, J. 16, 20, 115, 446–7, 458
Moravcsik, A. 17, 19, 21

Nijpels, E. 254, 276, 285, 348

Paleokrassas, Y. 88
Patten, C. 225, 348, 361
Pehle, H. 259
Pentreath, J. 324
Pereboom, J. W. C. 222
Peterson, J. 22
Pierson, P. 21
Pigou, A. C. 37, 384
Pollack, M. 21

Ridley, N. 225
Ripa di Meana, C. 87–8, 121–3, 266, 267
Rockman, B. A. 23
Rose-Ackerman, S. 160

Ruegg, M. 451
Ruffolo, G. 168–9, 170, 218, 262, 274, 285, 313, 347, 348

Sandholtz, W. 21
Santer, J. 457
Scharpf, F. W. 447, 461, 491
Schmidt, H. 387
Siedentopf, H. 326, 328
Simon, Sir John 202
Sinnott, R. 241
Smith, Angus 181
Spierenburg, D. 20
Steger, U. 270
Stone Sweet, A. 21

Thatcher, M. 224, 225
Töpfer, K. 204, 206, 270, 285, 348, 390, 419, 446

Tritsis, A. 211, 272, 348, 477
Tsebelis, G. 402

Van Miert, K. 88

Wagner, G. 270
Waldegrave, W. 225
Wallace, H. 323
Wallmann, W. 204
Ward, N. 375, 377
Ward, S. 265
Weaver, R. K. 23
Weber, M. 204
Winsemius, P. 173, 254, 276, 285, 348

Young, S. 263

Ziller, J. 326, 328
Zimmermann, F. 203, 400, 475

Subject Index

acquis communautaire 23, 359–60, 461, 463, 474, 476, 494
administration (member states) 192–229
  EU influence 211–12, 215–16, 219
administrative discretion 159, 181–2, 394
amoral familism 242–6, 282
  see also 'Mediterranean syndrome'
Auto/Oil project 404–5

barriers to trade and environmental policy 32–3
bathing waters directive 356–7
BATNEEC (best available technology/technique not entailing excessive cost) 176, 178, 387, 451
bounded rationality 23
BPEO (best practicable environmental option) 176, 178–9, 266
Brent Spar 264, 266
Brundtland report, *see* World Commission on Environment and Development

cabinets 88–9
car exhaust emissions directives 397–407
Cassis de Dijon 34
Cecchini report 33, 415
CEGB (Central Electricity Generating Board, UK) 393
Chernobyl 197, 203, 229, 241, 245
citizenship in EU 495–7
co-decision procedure 5, 124–5, 404–7, 410, 496
comitology in EU 116
Committee of the Regions 105–6
compliance, *see* implementation
concurrent majorities, principle of 489
constitutional convention 492–7
convergence-divergence 295, 338–49, 323–31, 416–21, 438, 453
  administrative 194–9, 200–2
  policy 138–48, 186, 193
  in problems 477–8
cooperation procedure 5, 124, 402
corporatism 269–71, 274–6, 277, 280–1, 282, 283

costs of environmental protection 368, 374–5, 385–6, 393–4, 400–1, 475, 478–9, 494–5
Council of Environmental Experts (Germany) 206–7, 476
Council of Ministers 21
covenants (Netherlands), *see* voluntary agreements
critical loads 395–7, 407–8

dangerous substances to water directive 357–60
Danish bottles law 33, 402, 413–16
democratic deficit in EU 496
DG XI 4, 89–91
DG XVI 105–6
diversity, logic of 491
  see also neo-realism
drinking water directives 356–60
Duales System Deutschland 419–20

ecological modernization 37, 56, 59–60, 76–8, 138, 144, 158–9, 183–6, 183–6, 236, 268–71, 277, 280–1, 282, 283, 286, 342–3, 345, 393–4, 411, 427, 484–5, 491
Economic and Social Committee 106
economic competitiveness 34–7, 77–9
economic demand for environmental protection 143
economic efficiency 492–3
economic growth and environment, *see* ecological modernization and sustainable development
ENVIREG 362
Environment Committee 4, 92
Environment Council (EU) 3, 93–100
Environment Institute, Ispra 122
Environment Policy Review Group 107
environmental action programmes 56–62
environmental governance 1–11, 15
  evolving 6, 437, 488–97
  horizontal complexity 6, 10, 437, 453–6
  incomplete 6, 437, 457–62
  multi-level 6, 10, 68, 437, 439, 446–53

environmental management, principles of
64–6
environmental organizations 256–67
and EU 266–7
environmental quality standards 64–5
environmental taxation 9, 169, 259, 364,
372, 376, 458–60, 484–5, 493
epistemic communities 476
Eurobarometer 238–40
European Coal and Steel Community 20
European Commission 16, 21, 21, 87–92,
115–17
European Council 100–2
European Court of Auditors 105
European Court of Justice 4, 16, 102–4
European Environment Agency 104, 484,
496
European Environmental Bureau 101–2, 106
European integration, theories of 15–25,
438–9, 441–6
European Parliament 4, 91–3, 117
European Union, agenda-setting 114–17
policy formation 117–23
standard setting 117–23
expansion, logic of, *see* neo-functionalism
expert advice 205–7, 212, 214–15, 216, 218,
221–2, 226–7
externalities 492–4

Federal Environment Office (Germany)
UBA 205–6, 208
Fifth Action Programme 396
formal compliance, rates of 299–303
functional effectiveness, principle of 494

General Consultative Forum (EU) 106–7

implementation 62, 102–3, 295–331, 377, 482
and subnational government 364–5,
365–6, 366–7, 373
costs 308–9, 311–12, 316, 317–18, 328–9
genetic factors 324
national administrative practice 304–6,
307–8, 312–22, 364–5, 373–4
political system 306, 313–14, 320, 327
public attitudes 306, 309, 312, 315, 329
public pressure 316
sub-national government 303–6, 310–11,
313, 326–7
institutional actors (EU) 87–107
institutionalism 21–5
institutionalization, process of 1, 7–9, 53,
86, 192–229

Instituto Superiore di Sanito (Italy) 476, 477
integrated pollution control 65
inter-governmental processes 40–8
inter-institutional relations 123–30
internalization 173, 276
issue characteristics 139–40, 193
issue linkage, *see* spillover

large combustion plant directive 478–9
large combustion plant ordinance 387, 390
leader–laggard hypothesis 94–8, 100, 376
legitimacy 492–7
lobbying 116
log-roll and SEA 45
LTRAP (Long-Range Transboundary Air
Pollution Convention) 388, 389, 395–7,
488
Luxembourg compromise 21

Manifesto Group 247
market failure 37–8, 78–9
'Mediterranean syndrome' 469–70
see also amoral familism
MOLITOR Group 101–2
Monnet method 9, 11, 16, 19–20, 29–30,
80, 445–7, 460, 461, 463, 488–97
multi-level governance and nation state
394–7
mutual recognition 34, 138, 359, 400

National Environmental Policy Plan
(Netherlands) 172–3, 174, 276, 477
national policy principles 150–86
national policy styles 141–3, 150–86, 193,
266
negative and positive integration 443
neo-functionalism 16–25, 257, 438, 441–6
neo-liberalism 284–5
neo-realism 16–25, 438, 441–6
nested games 19
nested regimes 399
new social movements 256–7
non-economic values 495–6
north–south differences 106, 198, 228,
245–6, 280, 286, 302, 329–30, 362–3,
376, 411, 468–85
Dutch cooperation 476–7
policy diffusion 474–5
policy imperialism 479–81
policy learning 474–5

OECD (Organization for Economic
Cooperation and Development) 145

OFWAT (Office of Water Services, UK)
182, 278, 375

packaging and packaging waste directive
410–34
packaging ordinace (Germany) 419–21
Paris summit 1972 56–7
party competition and the environment 235,
246–56
path-dependency 23
policy coordination 192, 204–5, 209–11,
214, 221, 228
policy discourse 55–6, 62–80
policy integration 70–3, 119–21
policy networks 235–6, 456
policy paradigms 55–80, 150–86, 411, 438,
449
policy principles, *see* policy paradigms
policy styles 150–86, 411, 424, 426
polluter-pays principle 58, 72–3
post-materialism 144, 237, 245, 282–3
precaution, principle of 156–8, 179–80, 358,
361
privatization 374, 393
proportionality, principle of 415–16, 421
proximity principle 39, 410–11, 423
public opinion and the environment 235,
237–46

qualified majority voting 5, 94, 98–9, 401,
412
quality of life concerns 57, 71

regimes 29–30
RIVM Rijks Instituut voor Volksgezondheid
en Milieuhygiëne (Dutch Government
Research Institute and Advisory Body)
395
Royal Commission on Environmental
Pollution (UK) 226, 476
rules, primary and secondary 4–5, 8–9, 22,
124–30, 296, 437, 488–9

scientific evidence 392–3
separation of powers 407, 454–5, 496
see also inter-institutional relations;
horizontal complexity

Seveso 168, 241, 274, 297
Single European Act 5, 9, 17, 33, 43–6, 60
single market 7, 25, 29–40, 79, 268, 297,
410–27, 441–3
spillover, logic of 10, 17, 19, 29–40, 427,
438–9, 441–6, 457–8, 461, 488
standard-setting, principles of 66–8
national processes 450–2
subnational/national relations 199–202,
207–8, 216, 219–20, 227
subsidiarity, principle of 69, 359, 460–2,
493–4
supranationalism 446–50
sustainable development 5, 61–2, 71–5,
165–6, 169, 180, 182–3, 253, 342–3,
347, 473, 482, 484–5

task-assignment, principles of 68–9
Task Force on Single Market and
Environment 38, 72–3, 119, 280,
473–4, 475
technocratic rationality 114–15
territorial identification 244–5, 311
titanium dioxide, directive 125–6, 413, 423
tourism 483–4
Treaty of Rome 2, 5, 32–3
Treaty on European Union 5, 9, 47–8
Twyford Down 266

unanimity, principle of in Council 59, 459
UNECE (United Nations Economic
Commission for Europe) 30, 388, 399
uniform emission limits 64–5
United Nations Conference on the Human
Environment, 1972 3, 76, 152, 154
urban waste water directive 360–3

vehicle emissions, *see* car exhaust emissions
verinnerlijking, *see* internalization
veto powers 456, 459, 464
voluntary agreements 174–5, 184, 220–1,
223, 274, 276–7, 369–70

Wallonian Waste Decree 39, 64, 423
waste management 38–40
World Commission on Environment and
Development, 145, 175, 473